Revision Checklist

Considering Your Whole Essay—Chapter 3

Using the <u>FACT</u> acronym, ask yourself these questions:

- ❑ Does my essay <u>F</u>IT together, presenting a central point for a specific audience? Does my thesis statement accurately reflect the content of my essay, or have I included material that has no bearing on the main point?
- ❑ Have I included all the material my reader will need to grasp my meaning, or do I need to <u>A</u>DD information or examples?
- ❑ Have I included material that fits the thesis but needs to be <u>C</u>UT because it is uninteresting, uninformative, or repetitious?
- ❑ Does a <u>T</u>EST of my organization show that the writing flows smoothly, with clear transitions between the various ideas?

Strengthening Paragraph Structure and Development—Chapter 14

- ❑ Does each paragraph have only one central idea?
- ❑ Is the idea stated in a topic sentence or clearly implied?
- ❑ Does the topic sentence help develop the thesis statement?
- ❑ Does each paragraph contain enough supporting detail?
- ❑ Is each paragraph appropriately organized?
- ❑ Is the relationship between successive sentences clear?
- ❑ Is each paragraph clearly and smoothly related to those that precede and follow it?
- ❑ Does the introduction arouse interest and set the appropriate tone?
- ❑ Does the conclusion reflect the content of the essay and provide a sense of completeness?

Sharpening Sentences and Words—Chapters 15 and 16

- ❑ Are my sentences clearly and effectively constructed?
- ❑ Have I varied the pattern and length of my sentences?
- ❑ Do I know the meanings of the words I use?
- ❑ Do I explain meanings my reader may not know?
- ❑ Have I used the appropriate tone and level of diction?
- ❑ Does/would figurative language enhance my style?
- ❑ Have I avoided wordiness, euphemisms, clichés, mixed metaphors, and sexist language?

Editing the Draft—Handbook

- ❑ Have I inspected my writing for the types of errors listed in the editing symbols on the last page of the book?

Strategies for Successful Writing

A Rhetoric, Research Guide, Reader, and Handbook

Second Canadian Edition

James A. Reinking
Ferris State University

Andrew W. Hart
Ferris State University

Robert von der Osten
Ferris State University

Sue Ann Cairns
Kwantlen University College

Robert Fleming
Kwantlen University College

PEARSON
Prentice
Hall

Toronto

National Library of Canada Cataloguing in Publication

Strategies for successful writing : a rhetoric, research guide, reader, and handbook /
James A. Reinking ... [et al.]. — 2nd Canadian ed.

Includes bibliographical references and index.
ISBN 0-13-112318-1

1. Report writing. 2. English language—Rhetoric. 3. College readers. I. Reinking,
James A.

PE1408.S77 2004   808'.0427   C2002-906074-5

ISBN 0-13-112318-1

Vice President, Editorial Director: Michael J. Young
Acquisitions Editor: Marianne Minaker
Sponsoring Editor: Andrew Winton
Marketing Manager: Toivo Pajo
Supervising Developmental Editor: Suzanne Schaan
Editorial Coordinator: Söğüt Y. Güleç
Copy Editor: Nancy Carroll
Proofreader: Susan James
Production Coordinator: Peggy Brown
Art Director: Julia Hall
Cover Design and Page Layout: Monica Kompter/Silver Birch Graphics
Cover Image: Image Bank/S. V. & B. Productions

3 4 5   08 07 06 05 04

Printed and bound in Canada.

Contents

■ Reader   377

Strategies for Successful Reading 379

Rhetorical Table of Contents

Narration 386

Description 397

Process Analysis 413

Illustration 425

Classification 442

Comparison 462

Cause and Effect 474

Definition 488

Argument 501

Mixing the Writing Strategies 536

Thematic Table of Contents

Life's Changes

Identity

Family Relationships

Humanity and Nature

Diversity in Society

Health

Contemporary Issues

Gender Issues

Technology

Cultural Identity

Ethics

■ Handbook 549

Sentence Elements 551

Editing to Correct Sentence Errors 581

Editing to Correct Faulty Punctuation and Mechanics 608

Spelling 635

Glossary of Word Usage 641

The Second Canadian Edition of *Strategies for Successful Writing: A Rhetoric, Research Guide, Reader, and Handbook* is a versatile, comprehensive textbook that offers ample material for a full-year composition course. Instructors teaching a one-term course can make selections from Chapters 1–16, from whatever types of specialized writing suit the needs of their students, and from appropriate essays in the Reader.

Because we strongly believe that an effective composition textbook should address the student directly, we have aimed for a style that is conversational, clear, and concise. We believe that our accessible style invites students into the book, lessens their apprehensions about writing, and provides a model for their own prose.

■ Changes in the Second Canadian Edition

This edition retains the many strengths of the previous Canadian edition and the six U.S. editions while incorporating a number of changes that should enhance the usefulness of the text for a Canadian audience. We have retained the book's reader-friendly layout and tone, but have provided new examples, essays, and exercises with a Canadian emphasis. Among these changes the following are noteworthy.

- Fourteen of the essays in the Reader, more than half of the total, are new. The variety of choice essays will engage a Canadian audience of diverse ages, backgrounds, and interests. We have included more academic, documented essays such as the essay on civil liberties by Patricia Baird, and an essay that analyzes shopping by Candace Fertile. The large range of possible selections—serious or humorous, longer or shorter, personal or social—will lead to stimulating discussion that will prompt ideas for writing.

- Discussion of writing and ethics begins in the first chapter and is threaded throughout the chapters on writing strategies.

- The section on developing a thesis statement is expanded in Chapter 2.

- The library research chapters now include guidelines for evaluating Internet material along with expanded and updated guidelines for online documentation. There is also additional advice on avoiding plagiarism, whether intentional or unintentional.

- There are more writing suggestions, some of which refer students to relevant Web sites.

- The argument section of the Reader contains two pairs of contrasting essays on topical issues, along with an essay by Neil Bissoondath that could easily be paired with another essay in the reader, or with an online government document on multiculturalism mentioned in the book. We also give suggestions for oral argument.

- Assorted updates and additional examples throughout should help make the text even more effective.

The Rhetoric

The text offers many other noteworthy features. The Rhetoric consists of eighteen chapters, grouped into four parts. The first part includes three chapters. Chapter 1 introduces students to the purposes of writing, the need for audience awareness, and the qualities of good writing. Chapter 2 looks at the planning and drafting stages. Chapter 3 takes students through the various revision stages, starting with a systematic procedure for revising the whole essay and then moving to pointers for revising its component parts. Sets of checklists pose key questions for students to consider. Chapters 2 and 3 are unified by an unfolding case history that includes the first draft of a student paper, the initial revision marked with changes, and the final version. Notes in the margin highlight key features of the finished paper. Students can relate the sequence of events to their own projects as they work through the various stages. Chapter 3 explains and demonstrates peer evaluation of drafts and collaborative writing.

The ten chapters in the second part (Chapters 4–13) feature the various strategies, or modes, used to develop papers. These strategies, which follow a general progression from less to more complex, are presented as natural ways of thinking, as problem-solving strategies, and therefore as effective ways of organizing writing. A separate chapter is devoted to each strategy. Chapter 12 provides a framework for structuring classroom debates, along with suggestions for oral argument. This part concludes with a chapter on mixing the writing strategies, which explains and shows that writers frequently use these patterns in assorted combinations for various purposes. Planning and writing guidelines are presented for problem/solution and evaluation reports, two common types that rely on a combination of strategies.

Except for Chapter 13, the discussion in each chapter follows a similar approach, first explaining the key elements of the strategy; next pointing out typical classroom and on-the-job applications to show students its practicality; and then providing specific planning, drafting, and revising guidelines. Practical heuristic questions are also posed. A complete student essay, accompanied by questions, follows the discussion section. These essays represent realistic, achievable goals and spur student confidence, while the questions reinforce the general principles of good writing and underscore the points we make in our discussions. Carefully chosen writing suggestions follow the questions. All chapters conclude with a section entitled "The Critical Edge." These sections, intended for above-average students, explain and illustrate how they can advance their writing purpose by synthesizing material from various sources. Synthesis, of course, helps students develop and hone their critical reading and thinking skills.

In the third part, we shift from full-length essays to the elements that make them up. Chapter 14 first discusses paragraph unity; it then takes up the topic sentence, adequate development, organization, coherence, and finally introductory, transitional, and concluding paragraphs. Throughout this chapter, as elsewhere, carefully selected examples and exercises form an integral part of the instruction.

Chapter 15 focuses on various strategies for creating effective sentences. Such strategies as coordinating and subordinating ideas and using parallelism help students increase the versatility of their writing. The concluding section offers practical advice on crafting and arranging sentences so that they work together harmoniously. Some instructors may wish to discuss the chapters on paragraphs and sentences in connection with revision.

Chapter 16, designed to help students improve their writing style, deals with words and their effects. We distinguish between abstract and concrete words as well as between specific and general terms, and we also discuss the dictionary and thesaurus. Levels of diction—formal, informal, and technical—and how to use them are explained, as are tone, various types of figurative language, and irony. The chapter concludes by pointing out how to recognize and avoid wordiness, euphemisms, clichés, mixed metaphors, and non-inclusive language.

The fourth and final part of the Rhetoric concentrates on two specialized types of writing. Chapter 17 offers practical advice on studying for exams, assessing test questions, and writing essay answers. To facilitate student comprehension, we analyze both good and poor answers to the same exam question and provide an exercise that requires students to perform similar analyses.

Chapter 18 uses Alice Munro's "An Ounce of Cure" as a springboard for its discussion. The chapter focuses on plot, point of view, character, setting, symbols, irony, and theme—the elements students will most likely be asked to write about. For each element, we first present basic features and then offer writing guidelines. Diverse examples illustrate these elements. The chapter ends with sections that detail the development of a student paper and explain how to include the views of others when writing about literature.

■ The Research Guide

The Research Guide consists of three chapters. Chapter 19 is a thorough and practical guide to writing library research papers. A sample pacing schedule not only encourages students to plan their work and meet their deadlines but also enables them to track their progress. As in Chapters 2 and 3, a progressive case history gradually evolves into an annotated student paper, which includes the results of a personal interview, thus demonstrating that primary research can reinforce secondary research.

Chapter 20 details and illustrates the correct formats for bibliographical references and in-text citations for both the MLA and APA systems of documentation. The chapter also explains how to handle the various types of quotations and how to avoid plagiarism. Instructors and students who wish more in-depth coverage of academic honesty are referred to relevant Web sites.

Chapter 21 offers a discussion of interview, questionnaire, and direct-observation reports. We point out the nature, usefulness, and requirements of primary research, explain how to plan and write each report, and conclude with an annotated student model that illustrates the guidelines.

The Reader

The Reader, sequenced to follow the order of the strategies as presented in the Rhetoric, expands the utility of the text by providing a collection of forty-four carefully selected professional models that illustrate the various writing strategies and display a wide variety of styles, tones, and subject matter. These essays, together with the nine student models that accompany the various strategy chapters, should make a separate reader unnecessary.

The Reader section opens with a unit entitled "Strategies for Successful Reading." In it, we discuss how to read for different purposes—for information/evaluation, to critique—and explain how students can use their reading to improve their writing as well as how they can synthesize information from various sources. Several of the guidelines are applied to a professional essay.

Each of the essays clearly illustrates the designated pattern, each has been thoroughly class-tested for student interest, and each provides a springboard for a stimulating discussion. We have aimed for balance and variety in our selections, choosing essays from a variety of sources.

The first essay in each strategy section is annotated in the margin in order to highlight features of the rhetorical strategy under discussion and other stylistic or structural elements. These annotations facilitate student understanding and help link the Rhetoric and Reader into an organic whole. A brief biographical note about the author precedes each selection, and stimulating questions designed to enhance student understanding of structure and strategy follow it. In addition, a segment entitled "Toward Key Insights" poses broadbased questions prompted by the essay's content. Answering these questions, either in discussion or writing, should help students gain a deeper understanding of important issues. Finally, we include a writing assignment suggested by the essay's topic.

The Handbook

The comprehensive Handbook, which features tab indexing on each page for easy access to all material, consists of five parts: "Sentence Elements," "Editing to Correct Sentence Errors," "Editing to Correct Faulty Punctuation and Mechanics," "Spelling," and "Glossary of Word Usage." Explanations skirt unneeded grammatical terminology and are reinforced by sets of sentence exercises in the first three sections. The section on "Sentence Elements" explains how students can use these elements to improve their writing skills. We also include connected-discourse exercises—unfolding narratives that engage and retain student interest and therefore facilitate learning—in the "Sentence Errors" and "Punctuation and Mechanics" sections. Extra sets of twenty-item exercises that parallel those in the Handbook are available upon request to instructors who adopt the book. The "Spelling" unit presents four useful spelling rules and an extensive list of commonly misspelled words. The "Glossary of Word Usage" offers similarly comprehensive coverage of troublesome usages. Instructors can use the Handbook either as a reference guide or as a basis for class discussion.

■ Acknowledgments

Many thanks to our reviewers for their insightful comments and helpful suggestions:

Christine Liotta, British Columbia Institute of Technology
Trudy MacCormack, St. Francis Xavier University
Jane Magrath, University of Prince Edward Island
Karen Overbye, Mt. Royal College
Lisa Richardson, Lakehead University
Melanie Rubens, Seneca College
Steven Scott, Brock University
Ritva Seppanen, Concordia University
Jane Shen, Kwantlen University College
Anne Simpson, University of New Brunswick (Fredericton)

We are indebted to our colleagues: Jane Shen for reviewing this text and offering suggestions to include more intercultural writing topics; to Maureen Shaw for suggesting useful Web sites; and to others who offered their ideas.

We would also like to thank the outstanding team at Pearson Education, whose editorial expertise and good humour supported us in our task. Special thanks go to Marta Tomins and Andrew Winton.

R.F.
S.A.C.

Rhetoric

Writing: A First Look

Why write? Hasn't the tempest of technology swept all of us into a brave new electronic world? Aren't e-mail, voice mail, cellular phones—all the magical devices of our new electronic estate—fast dooming ordinary writing? Not long ago, some people thought and said so, but events haven't supported those predictions. Although electronic devices have made some writing unnecessary, the written word flourishes both on campus and in the world of work. Furthermore, there's every evidence that writing will become even more important in the future.

Writing offers very real advantages to both writers and readers:

1. It gives writers time to reflect on and research what they want to communicate and then lets them shape and reshape the material to their satisfaction.
2. It makes communication more precise and effective.
3. It provides a permanent record of thoughts, actions, and decisions.
4. It saves the reader time; we absorb information more swiftly when we read it than when we hear it.

Many people will expect you to write for them. Instructors ask you to write reports, research papers, and essay exams. Job hunting usually requires you to write application letters. And once you're hired, writing will probably figure in your duties. You might be asked to discuss the capabilities of new computer equipment, report on a conference you attended, or explain the advantages of new safety procedures to supervisors or staff. Perhaps you'll propose that your organization install a new security system, conduct a market survey, or develop an alternative traffic flow pattern. The ability to write will help you earn better grades, land the job you want, and advance afterwards in your career.

Furthermore, writing ability yields personal benefits. You might need to defend a reimbursement claim that you filed with your dental insurer, request clarification of an inadequate or ambiguous set of directions, or document a demand for replacement of a faulty product. Skill in writing will help you handle these matters.

As you can see, we usually write in response to a situation. This situation often determines the purpose and audience of our paper as well as its content, style, and organization. We don't, then, write in isolation but rather to communicate with others who have an interest in our message. To do an effective job, you will need to understand the different situations that can prompt a piece of writing and respond accordingly.

■ The Purposes of Writing

Whenever you write, some clear purpose should guide your efforts. If you don't know why you're writing, neither will your reader. Fulfilling an assignment doesn't qualify as a real writing purpose, although it may well be what sends you to your desk. Faced with a close deadline for a research paper or report, you may tell yourself, "I'm doing this because I have to." An authentic purpose, however, requires you to answer this question: What do I want this piece of writing to do for both my reader and me? Purpose, as you might expect, grows out of the writing situation.

Here are four common *general writing purposes,* two or more of which often join forces in a single piece:

To Inform Presenting information is one of the most common writing purposes. The boating enthusiast who tells landlubber classmates how to handle a skiff plays the role of teacher, as does the researcher who summarizes the results of an investigation for co-workers. Instructors often ask you to write exams and papers so that they can gauge how well you have mastered the course material.

To Persuade You probably have strong views on many issues, and these feelings may sometimes impel you to try swaying your reader. In a letter to the editor, you might attack a proposal to establish a nearby chemical waste dump. Or, alarmed by a sharp jump in provincial unemployment, you might write to your MLA and argue for a youth employment program.

To Express Yourself Creative writing includes personal essays, fiction, plays, and poetry, as well as journals and diaries. But self-expression has a place in other kinds of writing too. Almost everything you write offers you a chance to display your mastery of words and to enliven your prose with vivid images and fresh turns of phrase.

To Entertain   Some writing merely entertains; some writing couples entertainment with a more serious purpose. A lighthearted approach can help your reader absorb dull or difficult material. Satire lets you expose the shortcomings of individuals, ideas, and institutions by poking fun at them. An intention to entertain can add savour to many kinds of writing.

Besides having one or more *general purposes,* each writing project has its own *specific purpose.* Consider the difference in the papers you could write about herbal medicines. You might explain why readers should take herbal medicines, or argue that these medicines should be federally regulated.

Having a specific purpose assists you at every stage of the writing process. It helps you define your audience; select the details, language, and approach that best suit their needs; and avoid going off in directions that won't interest them. The following example from Celia Milne's essay, "Pressures to Conform," has a clear and specific purpose.

> Unhappiness with body image seems to be a national preoccupation. According to statistics compiled by the National Eating Disorder Information Centre in Toronto, 90 per cent of Canadian women are dissatisfied with some aspect of their bodies. One of the main battlegrounds in the fight for improvement, of course, is eating. According to *Maclean's* year-end poll published in late December, 43 per cent of Canadian women—compared with 33 per cent of men—believe they are overweight. The eating disorder centre says that its surveys show that fully 70 per cent of Canadian women are preoccupied with their weight, and 40 per cent are yo-yo dieting. "For most women, when they get together in a group a common topic is trying to lose weight," says Dr. Christine Davies, a family physician in Saint John, N.B., who is concerned about how that may rub off on their daughters. Margaret Beck, acting director of the eating disorder centre, affirms that danger. "The research," she says, "does seem to suggest that mothers who are food- and weight-preoccupied tend to have daughters who are the same."

The topic sentence that begins Milne's paragraph clearly focuses on her claim that dissatisfaction with "body image" is a widespread concern in Canada. The subsequent four sentences provide statistical evidence from the National Eating Disorder Information Centre in Toronto and a *Maclean's* poll reinforcing her specific argument that the majority of women are unhappy with their weight or how they look. The final three sentences further corroborate Milne's argument by introducing statements from medical experts who confirm that weight and body image concerns among Canadian women are prevalent and likely to continue.

Now examine the next paragraph, which does *not* have a firmly fixed specific purpose:

> Community is a sea in which people swim unconsciously, like fish. We fail to recognize our neighbours as fellow humans, and they show the same lack of fellow feeling for us. A complete lack of concern for one another is evident in today's complex society. What is community? Is it a plant? A building? A place? A state of being? Knowing what it is, we can see if such a place exists. To know community, one must realize who he or she is. Identity of a person is the first step in establishing a community.

This student writer can't decide what aspect of community to tackle. The opening sentence attempts a definition, but the next two veer onto the shortcomings of the modern community. Notice how aimlessly the thoughts drift. The vague leadoff sentence asserts "Community is a sea. . .," but the later question "What is community?" contradicts this opening. Also, if community is a plant, a building, or a place, why must we realize who we are in order to know it? This contradictory and illogical paragraph reveals a writer groping for a purpose.

The paragraph, however, isn't a wasted effort. These musings offer several possibilities. By developing the first sentence, the writer might show some interesting similarities between community and a sea, so that instead of taking community for granted, readers can see it in a new light. By pursuing the idea in the second and third sentences, the writer might show the callous nature of modern society to encourage readers to act more humanely. The last two sentences might lead to a statement on the relationship between individual and community in order to overcome the common view that the two are in conflict. A specific purpose can sometimes emerge from preliminary jottings.

■ The Audience for Your Writing

Everything you write is aimed at some audience—a person or group you want to reach. The ultimate purpose of all writing is to have an effect on a reader (even if that reader is you), and therefore purpose and audience are closely linked. Our discussion on pages 4–5 makes this point clear by noting that your purpose can be to inform *someone* of something, to persuade *someone* to believe or do something, to express feelings or insights to *someone,* or to entertain *someone.* All of these objectives require that you *know* that someone, the audience for your writing.

Writing operates on a delayed-action fuse, detonating its ideas in readers' minds at a later time and place. Sometimes problems follow. In face-to-face conversations, you can observe your listeners' reactions, and whenever you note signs of hostility, boredom, or puzzlement, you can alter your tone, offer some examples, or ask a question. You can also use gestures and facial expressions to emphasize what you're saying. When you write, however, the words on the page carry your message. Once written work has left your hands, it's on its own. You can't call it back to clear up a misunderstanding or satisfy a disgruntled reader.

Establishing rapport with your audience is easy when you're writing for your friends or someone else you know a great deal about. You can then judge the likely response to what you say. Often, though, you'll be writing for people you know only casually or not at all: employers, customers, fellow townsfolk, and the like. In such situations, you'll need to assess your audience before starting to write and/or later in the writing process.

A good way to size up your readers is to develop an audience profile. This profile will emerge gradually as you answer the following questions:

1. What are the educational level, age, and economic status of the audience I want to reach?

2. Why will this audience read my writing? to gain information? learn my views on a controversial issue? enjoy my creative flair? be entertained?

3. What attitudes, needs, and expectations do they have?

4. How are they likely to respond to what I say? Can I expect them to be neutral? opposed? friendly?

5. How much do they know about my topic? (Your answer here will help you gauge whether you're saying too little or too much.)

6. What kind of language will communicate with them most effectively? (See the "Level of Diction" section in Chapter 16.)

Writing assignments sometimes ask you to envision a reader who is intelligent but lacking specialized knowledge, receptive but unwilling to put up with boring or trite material. Or perhaps you'll be assigned, or choose, to write for a certain age group or one with particular interests. At other times, you'll be asked to write for a specialized audience—one with some expertise in your topic. This difference will affect what you say to each audience and how you say it.

The Effect of Audience on Your Writing

Let's see how audience can shape a paper. Suppose you are explaining how to take a certain type of X-ray. If your audience is a group of lay readers who have never had an X-ray, you might note at the outset that taking one is much like taking an ordinary photograph. Then you might explain the basic process, including the positioning of the patient and the equipment; comment on the safety and reliability of the procedure; and note how much time it takes. You probably would use few technical terms. If, however, you were writing for radiology students, you might emphasize exposure factors, film size, and required views. This audience would understand technical terms and want a detailed explanation of the procedure. You could speak to these readers as colleagues who appreciate precise information.

Audience shapes all types of writing in similar fashion, even your personal writing. Assume you've recently become engaged, and to share your news you write two letters: one to your minister, the other to your best friend back home. You can imagine the differences in details, language, and general tone of each letter. Further, think how inappropriate it would be if you accidentally sent the letter intended for one to the other. Without doubt, different readers call for different approaches.

Discourse Communities

Professionals often write as members of specific communities. For example, biologists with similar interests often exchange information about their research. The members of a community share goals, values, concerns, background information, and expectations, and this fact in turn affects how they write. Because such writing is closely tied to the interests of the community, professional articles often start with a section linking their content to previous research projects and articles. Often, too, custom dictates what information must be included, the pattern of organization, and the style the paper should follow. Throughout your studies, you will discover that part of learning to write is becoming familiar with the values and customs of different discourse communities. To do this, you'll need to read carefully in your major field, acquainting yourself with its current issues and concerns and learning how to write about them. Ask yourself these questions as you start reading in any professional area:

1. What are the major concerns and questions in this field?
2. What seems to be common knowledge?
3. To what works do writers regularly refer?
4. How do those in the field go about answering questions?
5. What methods do they follow?
6. Which kinds of knowledge are acceptable? Which are not?
7. What values seem to guide the field?
8. What kinds of information must writers include in papers?
9. How are different writing projects organized?
10. What conventions do writers follow?

We all, of course, belong to many different communities. Furthermore, a community can involve competing groups, conflicting values, differing kinds of writing projects, and varying approaches to writing. Writing a quick e-mail to a friend, you follow different conventions than if you were submitting a formal research paper at school. Again, if you are writing a research paper for sociology, you will be using slightly different kinds of vocabulary, and following slightly different conventions, than if you are writing a research paper for your English class. As part of your growth as a writer and professional, you'll need to understand the goals and rules of any community you enter.

EXERCISE   *The three excerpts below deal with the same subject—antigens—but each explanation is geared to a different audience. Read the passages carefully; then answer the following questions:*

1. Identify ways in which each author address? How do you know?
2. Identify ways in which each author appeals to a specific audience.

1. The human body is quick to recognize foreign chemicals that enter it. "Foes" must be attacked or otherwise got rid of. The most common of these foes are chemical materials from viruses, bacteria, and other microscopic organisms. Such chemicals, when recognized by the body, are called *antigens*. To combat them, the body produces its own chemicals, protein molecules called *antibodies*. Each kind of antigen causes the production of a specific kind of antibody. Antibodies appear in the body fluids such as blood and lymph and in the body's cells.
    L. D. Hamilton, "Antibodies and Antigens," *The New Book of Knowledge*

2. [An] *antigen* [is a] foreign substance that, when introduced into the body, is capable of inducing the formation of antibodies and of reacting specifically in a detectable manner with the induced antibodies. For each antigen there is a specific antibody, the physical and chemical structure of which is produced in response to the physical and chemical structure of the antigen. Antigens comprise virtually all proteins that are foreign to the host, including those contained in bacteria, viruses, protozoa, helminths, foods, snake venoms, egg white, serum components, red blood cells, and

other cells and tissues of various species, including man. Polysaccharides and lipids may also act as antigens when coupled to proteins.

"Antigen," Encyclopaedia Britannica

3. The substance which stimulates the body to produce antibodies is designated antigen (antibody stimulator). . . .

    Most complete antigens are protein molecules containing aromatic amino acids, and are large in molecular weight and size. However, it has been demonstrated that other macromolecules, such as pure polysaccharides, polynucleotides, and lipids, may serve as complete antigens.

    However, certain other materials, incapable of stimulating antibody formation by themselves can, in association with a protein or other carrier, stimulate antibody formation and are the antigenic determinants. These determinants are referred to as *incomplete antigens* or *haptens* and they are able to react with antibodies which were produced by the determinant-protein complex.

    However, before an antigen can stimulate the production of antibodies, it must be soluble in the body fluids, must reach certain tissues in an unaltered form, and must be, in general, foreign to the body tissues. Protein taken by mouth loses its specific foreign-protein characteristics when digested in the alimentary tract. It reaches the tissues of the body as amino acids or other altered digested products of protein. Consequently, it no longer meets the requirements for antigenic behavior.

Orville Wyss and Curtis Eklund, Microorganisms and Man

Just as you would not dial a telephone number at random and then expect to carry on a meaningful conversation, so you should not expect to communicate effectively without a specific audience in mind.

One other note: as you shape your paper, it is important that the writing please you as well as your audience—that it satisfy your sense of what good writing is and what the writing task requires. You are, after all, your own first reader.

■ The Qualities of Good Writing

Three qualities—fresh thinking, a sense of style, and effective organization—help to ensure that a piece of prose will meet your reader's expectations.

Fresh Thinking You don't have to astound your readers with something never before discussed in print. Genuinely unique ideas and information are scarce commodities. You can, however, freshen your writing by exploring personal insights and perceptions. Using your own special slant, you might show a connection between seemingly unrelated items, as does a writer who likens office "paper pushers" to different kinds of animals. Do not strain too desperately for originality, as farfetched notions spawn skepticism.

Sense of Style Readers don't expect you to display the stylistic flair of Margaret Atwood or Rohinton Mistry. Indeed, such writing would impair the neutral tone needed in certain kinds of writing, such as technical reports and legal documents. Readers *do,* however, expect you to write in a clear style. And if you strengthen it with vivid, forceful words, readers will absorb your points with even greater interest.

The chapters ahead show you how to use language in ways that project your own views and personality. Chapters 15 and 16, in particular, will help you develop a sense of style, as will the many readings throughout the book.

Effective Organization A paper should have a beginning, a middle, and an end, that is, an introduction, a body, and a conclusion. The introduction sparks interest and acquaints the reader with what is to come. The body delivers the main message and exhibits a clear connection between ideas so that the reader can easily follow your thoughts. The conclusion ends the discussion so the reader feels satisfied rather than suddenly cut off. Overall, your paper should follow a pattern that is suited to its content. Organizational patterns, or strategies of development, are the subject of Chapters 4–13. Pages 199–205 discuss introductions and conclusions.

Freshness, style, and organization are weighted differently in different kinds of writing. A writer who drafts a proposal to pave a city's streets will probably attach less importance to fresh thinking than to clear writing and careful organization. On the other hand, fresh thinking can be very important in a description of an autumn forest scene. You will learn more about these qualities throughout this book.

■ Writing and Ethics

Think for a minute about how you would react to the following situation. You decide to vacation at a Canadian country resort after reading a brochure that stressed its white-sand beach, scenic trails, fine dining, and peaceful atmosphere. When you arrive, you find the beach overgrown with weeds, the trails littered, and the view unappealing. The gourmet restaurant is a greasy-spoon cafeteria. Worse, whenever you go outside, swarms of vicious black flies attack you. Wouldn't you feel cheated? Closer to home, think how you'd feel if you decided to attend a college because of its distinguished faculty members only to discover upon arrival that they rarely teach on campus. The college counts on their reputations to attract students even though they are usually unavailable. Hasn't the college done something unethical?

As these examples show, good writing is also ethical writing. Like you, readers expect that what they read will be dependable information. Few if any would bother with a piece of information that they realized was intended to deceive. A good test of the ethics of your writing is whether you would read your own work and act on the basis of it. Would you feel comfortable with it, or would you feel cheated, manipulated, belittled, or deceived? By learning and practising the principles of ethical writing, you show respect to your readers and to yourself.

The Principles of Ethical Writing

Accuracy Writing perceived as truthful should *be* truthful. Granted, a writer may use humorous exaggeration to make us laugh, and some sales pitches may stretch the truth a bit in order to entice buyers ("Try Nu-Glo toothpaste and add sparkle to your life.") Most readers recognize and discount such embellishments which harm nobody. Deliberate distortions and falsehoods, however, may hurt not only the reader but the writer as well. If you were angered by misrepresentations in the vacation brochure, you would likely warn your friends against the resort; you might even take legal action against it.

No Deliberate Omissions Writing meant to be perceived as truthful should tell the whole truth, omitting nothing the reader needs to know in order to make informed decisions. The text should not be deliberately incomplete so as to mislead. Suppose a university's recruitment brochures stress that 97 percent of its students get jobs upon graduation, but omit the fact that only 55 percent of these jobs are in the graduates' chosen field of study. Certainly these brochures are deceptive, perhaps attracting students who would otherwise choose schools with better placement records.

Clarity Writing should be clear to the reader. All of us know the frustration of trying to read a crucial regulation that is impossible to comprehend. A person who writes instructions so unclear that they result in costly or harmful mistakes is partially responsible for the consequences. An annual report that deliberately obscures information about its yearly losses is not fair to potential investors.

Honest Representation Writing should not present itself as something different from what it is. It would be unethical for a drug company's advertising department to prepare an advertisement in the form of an impartial news story.

No Intentional Harm Writing should not be intended to harm the reader. Certainly it is fair to point out the advantages of a product or service that readers might not need. But think how unethical it would be for a writer to encourage readers to follow a diet that the writer knew was not only ineffective but harmful. Think of the harm a writer might cause by attempting, deliberately, to persuade readers to try crack cocaine.

chapter

2

Planning and Drafting Your Paper

Many students believe that good essays are dashed off in a burst of inspiration by born writers. Students themselves often boast that they cranked out their top-notch papers in an hour or so of spare time. Perhaps. But for most of us, writing is a process that takes time and work. Better writers are not born with their gift but learn through informed practice how to incorporate their ideas into a paper.

Although successful writers can often describe how they go about their work, writing is a flexible process. No one order guarantees success, and no one approach works for every writer. Some writers establish their purpose and draft a plan for carrying it out at the start of every project. Others begin with a tentative purpose or plan and discover their final direction as they write. As a project proceeds, the writer is likely to leapfrog backward and forward one or more times rather than to proceed in an orderly, straightforward sequence.

Regardless of how it unfolds, the writing process consists of the following stages. Advancing through each stage will guide you if you have no plan or if you've run into snags with your approach. Once you're familiar with these stages, you can combine or rearrange them as needed.

Understanding the assignment
Zeroing in on a topic
Gathering information
Organizing the information

Developing a thesis statement
Writing the first draft

■ Understanding the Assignment

Instructors differ in making writing assignments. Some specify the topic; some give you several topics to choose from; and still others offer you a free choice. Likewise, some instructors dictate the length and format of the essay, whereas others don't. Whatever the case, be sure you understand the assignment before you go any further.

Think of it this way: If your boss asked you to report on ways of improving the working conditions in your office and you turned in a report on improving worker benefits, would you expect the boss's approval? Following directions is crucial, so if you have any questions about the assignment, ask your instructor to clear them up right then. Make sure also that you understand your instructor's expectations and emphasis for a particular assignment: for example, some assignments ask for more formal academic writing, while others may ask for a more informal and personal style. An essay for a sociology class may follow somewhat different conventions than an essay for a first-year university English class. Don't be timid; it's much better to ask for clarity than to receive a low grade for failing to follow directions.

Once you understand the assignment, consider the project *yours*. Whether you are writing about your favourite vacation spot for a local newspaper, for a friend, or for your instructor and classmates in an English class, here is your chance to inform others about a place that's special to you. By asking yourself whom you are writing for, and what the assignment allows you to accomplish, you can find your purpose.

■ Zeroing In on a Topic

A subject is a broad discussion area: sports, academic life, Canadian culture, and the like. A topic is one small segment of a subject, for example, testing athletes for drug use, changes in health care, the websurfing phenomenon. If you choose your own topic, pick one narrow enough that you can develop it properly within any length limitation. Avoid sprawling, slippery issues that lead to a string of trite generalities.

In addition, choose a familiar topic or one you can learn enough about in the time available. Avoid overworked topics such as arguments about abortion or the legal drinking age, which generally repeat the same old points. Instead, select a topic that lets you draw upon your unique experiences and insights and offer a fresh perspective to your reader.

Strategies for Finding a Topic

Students sometimes prefer having a larger, more general area to write about than a more focused topic, but writing is usually easier—and more interesting for you and your reader—if you take on something more specific and manageable. Would you rather read an essay entitled "My Life in Canada" or an essay with a more focused title such as "Why Hockey Is No Longer Canadian"? Whenever your instructor assigns a general subject, you'll need to stake out a limited topic suitable for your paper. If you're lucky, the right one will come to mind immediately. More often, though, you'll need to resort to some special strategy. Here are six proven strategies that many writers use. Not all of them will work for everyone, so experiment to find those that produce a topic for you.

Tapping Your Personal Resources Personal experience furnishes a rich storehouse of writing material. Over the years, you've packed your mind with memories of family gatherings, school activities, movies, concerts, plays, parties, jobs, books you've read, TV programs, dates, discussions, arguments, and so on. All these experiences can provide suitable topics. Suppose you've been asked to write about some aspect of education. Recalling the difficulties you had last term at registration, you might argue for better registration procedures. Or if you're a hopeless TV addict who must write on some advertising topic, why not analyze video advertising techniques?

Anything you've read in magazines or journals, newspapers, novels, short stories, or textbooks can also trigger a topic. Alice Munro's short story "Boys and Girls," in which a girl growing up in rural Canada comes to accept the gender role she is assigned, might suggest a paper on gender socialization, or on farm work. An article reviewing the career of a well-known politician might stir thoughts of a friend's experience in running for the student council. Possibilities crowd our lives, waiting for us to recognize and seize them.

> **EXERCISE**   *Select five of the subjects listed below. Tapping your personal resources,*
> *name one topic suggested by each. For each topic, list three questions that*
> *you might answer in a paper.*
>
> | | |
> |---|---|
> | City life | Some aspect of nature |
> | A particular field of work | Contemporary forms of dancing |
> | Drugs | Youth gangs |
> | Concern for some aspect of the environment | Fashions in clothing |
> | Saving money | Trendiness |
> | Home ownership | Human rights |

Keeping a Journal Many writers record their experiences in a journal—a private gathering of entries accumulated over a period of time. In addition to helping writers remember and reflect on their experiences, journal keeping provides an abundance of possible writing topics as well as valuable writing practice.

The hallmark of the journal entry is the freedom to explore thoughts, feelings, responses, attitudes, and beliefs. In your own private domain you can express your views without reservation, without concern for "doing it right." *You* control the content and length of the entry without being held to a specified topic or number of words. Journal writing does not represent a finished product but rather an exploration.

A few simple guidelines ensure effective journal entries:

1. Write in any kind of notebook that appeals to you; the content, not the package, is the important thing.
2. Write on a regular basis—at least five times a week if possible. In any event don't write by fits and starts, cramming two weeks' entries into one sitting.
3. Write for ten to twenty minutes, longer if you have more to say. Don't aim for uniform entry length, for example, three paragraphs or a page and a half. Simply explore your reactions to the happenings in your life or to what you have read, heard in class, or seen on television. The length will take care of itself.

Let's examine a typical journal entry by Sam, a first-year composition student. This journal entry could spawn several essays. Sam might explore the causes of residential deterioration, define sportsmanship, explain how Mrs. Wynick made learning a game, or argue for stricter pollution control laws.

Last week went back to my hometown for the first time since my family moved away and while there dropped by the street where I spent my first twelve years. Visit left me feeling very depressed. Family home still there, but its paint peeling and front porch sagging. Sign next to the porch said house now occupied by Acme Realtors. While we lived there, front yard lush green and bordered by beds of irises. Now an oil-spattered parking lot. All the other houses on our side of the street gone, replaced by a row of dumpy buildings housing dry cleaner, bowling alley, hamburger joint, shoe repair shop, laundromat. All of them dingy and rundown looking, even though only a few years old.

 Other side of the street in no better shape. Directly across from our house a used-car dealership with rows of junky looking cars. No trace left of the park that used to be there. Had lots of fun playing baseball and learned meaning of sportsmanship. To left of the dealership my old grade school, now boarded and abandoned. Wonder about my fifth-grade teacher Mrs. Wynick. Is she still teaching? Still able to make learning a game, not a chore? Other side of dealership the worst sight of all. Grimy looking plant of some sort pouring foul smelling smoke into the air from a discoloured stack. Smoke made me cough.

 Don't think I'll revisit my old street again.

EXERCISE   *Write journal entries over the next week or two for some of the following items that interest you. If you have trouble finding a suitable topic for a paper, review the entries for possibilities.*

Pleasant or unpleasant conversations	Cultural or sporting events
Developing relationships	Academic life: myth vs. reality
Single or married life	Public figures—politicians; movie,
Parents	rock, or sports stars

Sorting Out a Subject All of us sort things. We do it whenever we tackle the laundry, clear away a sinkful of dishes, or tidy up a basement or garage. Let's see how we might handle a cluttered basement. To start off, we'd probably sort the contents according to type: books in one spot, clothing in a second, toys in a third. That done, chances are we'd do still more sorting, separating children's books from adults' and stuffed animals from games. As we looked over and handled the different items, long-buried, bittersweet memories might start flooding from our subconscious: memories of an uncle, now dead, who sent this old adventure novel . . . of our parents' pride when they saw their child had learned to ride that now battered bicycle . . . of the dance that marked the debut of the evening gown over there.

Sorting out a subject follows a similar scenario. First, we break our broad subject into categories and subcategories, and then we allow our minds to roam over the different items and see what topics we can turn up. The chart on page 17 shows what one student found when she explored the general subject of public transportation.

As you'll discover for yourself, some subjects yield more topics than others; some, no topics at all.

EXERCISE   *Select two of the following subjects, and then subdivide those two into five topics each.*

Advertising	Movies	Transportation
Computers	Occupations	Sports
Fashions	Popular music	Television programs

Asking Questions Often, asking questions such as those below will lead you to a manageable topic:

How can this subject be described?

How is this subject accomplished or performed?

What is an example of my subject?

Does the subject break into categories?

If so, what comparisons can I make among these categories?

If my subject is divided into parts, how do they work together?

Does my subject have uses? What are they?

What are the causes of my subject?

What is the impact of my subject?

How can my subject be defined?

What case could be made for or against my subject?

Results of Sorting Out the Subject Public Transportation

	Land			Water		Air	
Buses	Taxis	Trains	Seagoing	Lake, River	Airplanes	Helicopters
Local bus services for the handicapped	Rights of passengers	The Orient Express, the Twentieth Century Limited	The Titanic	Barge cruises	Airline strikes	Air taxis
Bus tours	Preventing crimes against drivers		Luxury liners		Overbooking flights	Cargo
City buses		Subways	Theme cruises		Making air travel safer	
Improving bus terminals		Via Rail	Modern sea pirates		Coping with hijacking	
Designing buses to accommodate the handicapped		Japan's high-speed trains	Travelling by freighter		Causes and prevention of jet lag	
		Deterioration of railroad track beds	The impact of overseas flights on ship travel		Noise pollution around airports	

Let's convert these general questions into specific questions about telescopes, a broad general subject:

Description:	How can a telescope be described?
Process:	How does one use a telescope?
Illustration:	What are some well-known telescopes?
Classification:	What are the different kinds of telescopes?
Comparison:	How are they alike? How are they different?
Analysis:	What are the parts of the telescope, and how do they work together?
Functional analysis:	How is a telescope useful?
Causal analysis:	Why did the telescope come about?
Analysis of effects:	What effects have telescopes had on human life and knowledge?
Definition:	What is a telescope?
Argument:	Why should people learn to use telescopes?

Each of these questions offers a starting point for a suitably focused essay. Question 3 might be answered in a paper about the Hubble Space Telescope and the problems experienced with it; Question 5 might launch a paper that compares reflecting and refracting telescopes.

EXERCISE   *Convert two of the general subjects below into more manageable topics; then, drawing from the list of questions suggested above, ask specific questions about the topics. Finally, come up with two essay topics for each of your two subjects.*

Example: Take a general subject such as Music, and then narrow it to a more manageable topic such as "Downloading Music from the Computer." After running through the list of questions above, you might choose two essay topics such as "How to Download Music from the Internet" and "The Advantages of Downloading Music."

Tourism	Games	Health
Sports	Free Trade	Business Schools
Languages	Television	

Freewriting   The freewriting strategy snares thoughts as they race through your mind, yielding a set of sentences that you then look over for writing ideas. To begin, turn your pen loose and write for about five minutes on your general subject. Put down everything that comes into your head, without worrying about grammar, spelling, or punctuation. What you produce is for your eyes alone. If the thought flow becomes blocked, write "I'm stuck, I'm stuck . . . " until you break the mental logjam. When your writing time is up, go through your sentences one by one and extract potential topic material. If you draw a blank, write for another five minutes and look again.

The following example shows the product of one freewriting session. Jim's instructor had assigned a two- or three-page paper on some sports-related topic;

and since Jim had been a member of his high school tennis team, his thoughts naturally turned toward this sport.

> Sports. If that's my subject, I'd better do something on tennis. I've played enough of it. But what can I say that would be interesting? It's very popular, lots of people watch it on TV. Maybe I could write about the major tennis tournaments. I'm stuck. I'm stuck. Maybe court surfaces. That sounds dull. I'm stuck. Well, what about tennis equipment, clothing, scoring? Maybe my reader is thinking about taking up the game. What do I like about tennis? The strategy, playing the net, when to use a topspin or a backspin stroke, different serves. I'm stuck. I'm stuck. Maybe I could suggest how to play a better game of singles. I used to be number one. I can still remember Coach harping on those three C's, conditioning, concentration, consistency. I'm stuck. I'm stuck. Then there's the matter of special shots like lobs, volleys, and overheads. But that stuff is for the pros.

This example suggests at least three papers. For the beginning player, Jim could focus on equipment and scoring. For the intermediate player, he might write on conditioning, concentration, and consistency; for the advanced player, on special shots.

Brainstorming Brainstorming, a close cousin of freewriting, captures fleeting ideas in words, fragments, and sometimes sentences, rather than in a series of sentences. Brainstorming garners ideas faster than the other strategies do. But unless you move immediately to the next stage of writing, you may lose track of what some of your fragmentary jottings mean.

To compare the results of freewriting and brainstorming a topic, we've converted our freewriting example into this list, which typifies the results of brainstorming:

Popularity of tennis	Equipment
Major tournaments	Clothing
Court surfaces	Scoring
Doubles strategy	Conditioning
Singles strategy	Concentration
Playing the net	Consistency
Topspin	Special shots—lobs, drop volleys,
Backspin	overheads
Different serves	

EXERCISE   *Return to one set of five topics you selected for the exercise on page 16. Freewrite or brainstorm for five minutes on each one; then choose a topic suitable for a two- or three-page essay. State your topic, intended audience, and purpose.*

Narrowing a familiar subject may yield not only a topic but also the main divisions for a paper on it. Jim's freewriting session uncovered several possible tennis topics as well as a way of approaching each: by focusing on lobs, drop volleys, and overheads when writing about special shots, for example. Ordinarily, though, the main divisions will emerge only after you have gathered material to develop your topic.

Identifying Your Audience and Purpose

You can identify your purpose and audience at several different stages in the writing process. Sometimes both are set by the assignment and guide your selection of a topic. For example, you might be asked to write to your university or college president to recommend improvements in the school's registration system. At other times, you may have to write a draft before you can determine either. Usually, though, the selection of audience and purpose goes hand in hand with determining a topic. Think of the different types of information Jim would gather if he wrote for (1) beginning players to offer advice on improving their game, (2) tennis buffs to point out refinements of the game, (3) a physics professor to show the physical forces controlling the behaviour of tennis balls in flight.

Case History

Now that you're familiar with some narrowing strategies, let's examine the first segment of a case history that shows how one student handles a writing assignment. This segment illustrates the use of a narrowing strategy to find a topic. Later segments focus on the remaining stages of the writing process. Trudy's class has been talking and reading about memories from childhood, and about how these memories change their meaning over time. Trudy's instructor assigns a three- or four-page paper describing or narrating a childhood experience that led to an insight of some kind. Trudy begins by sorting out possible experiences to write about and comes up with two major categories: memories from elementary school and memories from secondary school. Under the first category, she includes memories of teachers who made an impression on her, a soccer game in which she scored the winning goal, and an autistic boy she knew who had trouble fitting in. In the second category, she includes memories of struggling with French and her experience of losing her boyfriend. Because the secondary school experiences still seem too close to her to write about, she decides to write about one of the memories from elementary school. After weighing the possibilities, she decides that she will be able to write the most interesting narrative about the autistic boy she once knew.

This case history continues on page 23.

■ Gathering Information

Once you have a topic, you'll need things to say about it. This supporting material can include facts, ideas, examples, observations, sensory impressions, memories, and the like. Without the proper backup, papers lack force, vividness, and interest and may confuse or mislead readers. The more support you can gather, the easier it will be for you to write a draft. Time spent gathering information is never wasted.

Strategies for Gathering Information

If you are writing on a familiar topic, much of your supporting material may come from your own head. Brainstorming is the best way to retrieve it. With unfamiliar topics, brainstorming won't work. Instead, you'll have to do some background reading. Whatever the topic, familiar or unfamiliar, talking with friends, parents, neighbours, or people knowledgeable about the topic can also produce useful ideas.

Brainstorming Brainstorming a topic, like brainstorming a subject, yields a set of words, fragments, and occasionally sentences that will furnish ideas for the paper. Assume that Jim, the student who explored the subject of tennis, wants to show how conditioning, concentration, and consistent play can improve one's game. His brainstorming list might look like this:

keeping ball in play	courtside distractions
don't try foolish shots	temper distractions
placing ball so opponent	don't continually drive ball
runs	with power
staying in good condition	two-on-one drill
yourself	lobbing ball over opponent's head
running	returning a down-the-line passing
jogging	shot
skipping rope	don't try spectacular overheads
keeps you on your toes	chance for opponent to make
keeping your mind only on	mistake
the game	game of percentages
personal distractions	games are lost, not won

You can see how some thoughts have led to others. For example, the first jotting, "keeping ball in play," leads naturally to the next one, "don't try foolish shots." "Placing ball so opponent runs" leads to "staying in good condition yourself," which in turn leads to ways of staying in condition and so forth.

Branching is a helpful and convenient extension of brainstorming that allows you to add details to any item in your list. Here's how you might use this technique to approach "courtside distractions":

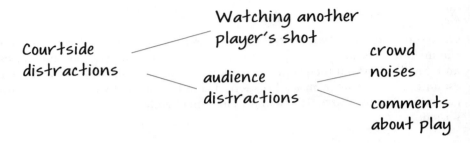

Don't worry if your brainstorming notes look chaotic and if some seem irrelevant. Sometimes the most unlikely material turns out to be the freshest and most interesting. As you organize and write your paper, you'll probably combine, modify, and omit some of the notes, as well as add others.

| **EXERCISE**   *Prepare a brainstorming sheet of supporting details for one of the topics you developed for the exercise on page 19.*

Reading   When you have to grapple with an unfamiliar topic, look in the library for material to develop it. Before going there, however, turn to Chapter 19, "The Library Research Paper," and review the guidelines under the headings "Computerized Card Catalogue" and "Periodical Indexes." (If your library uses a conventional card catalogue, review the guidelines in that part of the chapter.) These sections tell you how to unearth promising references to investigate. Once you have a list of references, start searching for the books or articles. Look through each one you find and jot down any information that looks useful, either as direct quotations or in your own words.

Whenever you use a direct quotation or rephrased material in your paper, you must give proper credit to the source. If you don't, you are guilty of plagiarism, a serious offence that can result in a failing grade for the course or even expulsion. See "Handling Quotations" and "Avoiding Plagiarism," in Chapter 20.

Talking with Others   You can expand the pool of ideas gained through brainstorming or reading by talking with some of the people around you. Imagine you're writing a paper about a taxpayers' revolt in your province. After checking the leading provincial newspapers at the library, you find that most of the discontent centres on property taxes. You then decide to supplement what you've read by asking questions about the tax situation in your town.

Your parents and neighbours tell you that property taxes have jumped 50 percent in the last two years. The local tax assessor tells you that assessed valuations have risen sharply and that the law requires property taxes to keep pace. She also notes that this situation is causing some people on fixed incomes to lose their homes. A city council member explains that part of the added revenue is being used to repair city streets, build a new library wing, and buy more fire-fighting equipment. The rest is going to the schools. School officials tell you they're using their extra funds to offer more vocational courses and to expand the program for learning-disabled students. As you can see, asking questions can broaden your perspective and provide information that will help you to write a more worthwhile paper.

Case History *(Continued from page 20)*

After choosing to write about a student in elementary school, Trudy brainstorms to generate ideas. The result is a 15-item list. After checking her items over, Trudy decides that since she is focusing on a narrative about a boy named Steven, she will eliminate items on learning disorders and treatment of autism as not directly relevant to her purpose. She also decides not to deal with information on Steven's family, on where Steven is now, or on other bullies today. The remaining items are as follows:

teasing of Steven   why people bully
Steven's appearance   my mother's response
Steven at lunch time   confronting the bullies
Steven's loneliness   effects of bullying
incident in park   taking time to listen

This case history continues on page 25.

■ Organizing the Information

If you have ever listened to a rambling speaker spill out ideas in no particular order, you probably found it hard to pay attention to the speech, let alone make sense of it. So, too, with disorganized writing. A garbled listing of ideas serves no one; an orderly presentation highlights your ideas and helps communication succeed.

Your topic determines the approach you take. In narrating a personal experience, such as a mishap-riddled vacation, you'd probably trace the events in the order they occurred. In describing a process, say caulking a bathtub, you'd take the reader step by step through the procedure. To describe a hillside view near your home, you might work from left to right. Or you could first paint a word picture of some striking central feature and then fan out in either direction. Other topics dictate other patterns, such as comparison and contrast, cause and effect, and illustration. Chapters 4–12 describe the basic patterns in detail.

You can best organize long pieces of writing, such as library research papers, by following a formal outline. (See Chapter 19, "Organizing and Outlining.") For shorter papers, however, a simple, informal system of *flexible notes* will do nicely.

The Flexible Notes System

To create a set of flexible notes, write each of your key points at the top of a separate sheet of paper. If you have a thesis statement (see page 26), refer to it for your key points. Next, list under each heading the supporting details that go with that heading. Drop any details that don't fit and expand any points that need more support. When your sheets are finished, arrange them in the order you expect to follow in your essay. The notes for the tennis paper might look like this:

Conditioning

staying in good condition   two-on-one drill
    yourself   lobbing ball over opponent's head
running   returning a down-the-line
jogging   passing shot
skipping rope keeps you on
    your toes

Concentration

keeping your mind only on the game
overcome distractions: personal, courtside, temper

Consistency

keeping ball in play
don't try foolish shots
placing ball so opponent runs
don't continually drive ball with power
don't try spectacular overheads
chance for opponent to make mistake
game of percentages
games are lost, not won

Since conditioning, concentration, and consistency are simultaneous concerns, this listing arranges them according to their probable importance—starting with the least important.

Now you're ready to draft a plan showing how many paragraphs you'll have in each part of the essay and what each paragraph will cover. Sometimes the number of details will suggest one paragraph; other times you'll need a paragraph block—two or more paragraphs. Here's a plan for the tennis essay:

Conditioning

staying in good condition yourself   ⎫
running   ⎪   Off-the-court
jogging   ⎬   conditioning
skipping rope keeps you on your toes   ⎪
two-on-one drill   ⎭
lobbing ball over opponent's head   ⎫ On-the-court
returning a down-the-line passing shot   ⎭   conditioning

Concentration

keeping your mind only on the game
overcome distractions: personal, courtside,
temper

Consistency

keeping ball in play
don't try foolish shots
placing ball so opponent runs   Placing shots
don't continually drive ball with power
don't try spectacular overheads

chance for opponent to make mistake
game of percentages   Playing percentages
games are lost, not won

These groupings suggest two paragraphs about conditioning, one about concentration, and two about consistency.

EXERCISE   *Organize into flexible notes the supporting details that you prepared for the exercise on page 22. Arrange your note pages in a logical sequence and draft a plan showing the number and content of the paragraphs in each section.*

Case History *(Continued from page 23)*

A careful look at her brainstorming list suggests how Trudy can arrange her items in a logical order. Since she is writing a narrative, she will follow a chronological order, or time sequence. She will begin with a description of Steven in the schoolyard, proceed to the story of the bullies teasing Steven in the park, then to her mother's confrontation with the bullies, and will end with the insight about taking time to listen. She draws up the following plan.

Background—Steven at Lunch Time

Searching for stick
Waving his stick
Others whisper and giggle

Steven's Appearance

Faded and second-hand clothing
Strawberry stains on mouth

Incident at Park

Bullies taunt Steven
I fail to stop them

Going Home for Help

Explaining to my mother
Heading for the park

Arriving at the Park

Steven is crying
Bullies fail to see us

My Mother's Confrontation

Mother yells
Bullies leave

We Walk Steven Home

Mother asks Steven where
    home is
Mother seems angry

Steven Questions Why People Are Mean	My Thoughts Today
Steven's question No real answer	How Steven made a difference Listening to someone can help

This case history continues on page 29.

■ Developing a Thesis Statement

A thesis statement—one or two sentences that express the main idea in your essay—can help you stay on track. If you do not have a thesis, or point you are heading toward when you write, your reader will probably feel frustrated. Whether or not it is spelled out explicitly, the thesis statement governs and unifies the entire essay. The thesis statement points you, and your reader, in a specific direction. In addition, it tells your reader what to expect.

Thesis statements can emerge at several points in the writing process. If an instructor assigns a controversial topic on which you hold strong views, the statement may pop into your head right away. Usually, though, it emerges gradually, after you have gathered and examined supporting information, or during the writing process itself.

Often a preliminary thesis may evolve into something more focused and interesting as you write. In these cases, return to your original thesis and reshape it. A thesis such as "Downloading music from the Internet has advantages" could, as you write, become more refined: "Downloading music from the Internet can help musical artists as well as their audience."

As you examine your information, search for the central point and the key points that back it up; then use these to develop your thesis statement. If you convert a topic to a question, the answer to this question may be your thesis statement. For example:

Topic:	The uncertain future of robots in Canadian industry.
Question:	What are some of the drawbacks of using robots in Canadian industry?
Thesis statement:	The expense of producing robots, the lack of qualified personnel to service them, and the moral problems of replacing workers with them—all cloud the future of robots in Canadian industry.

The thesis statement stems from the specifics the student unearthed while answering the question.

Requirements of a Good Thesis Statement

Unity Unless intended for a lengthy paper, a thesis statement *focuses on just one central point or issue.* Suppose you prepare the following thesis statement for a two- or three-page paper:

```
Centreville College should re-examine its policies on open admis-
sions, vocational programs, and aid to students.
```

This sprawling statement would commit you to grapple with three separate issues. At best, you could make only a few general remarks about each one.

To correct matters, consider each issue carefully in light of how much it interests you and how much you know about it. Then make your choice and draft a narrower statement. The following thesis statement would do nicely for a brief paper. It shows clearly that the writer will focus on *just one issue:*

```
Because of the rising demand among high school graduates for job-
related training, Centreville College should expand its vocational
offerings.
```

Tailored Scope A good thesis statement also *tailors the scope of the issue to the length of the paper.* No writer could deal adequately with "Many first-year university and college students face crucial adjustment problems" in two or three pages. The idea is too broad to yield more than a smattering of poorly supported general statements. Paring it down to "Free time is a responsibility that challenges many first-year university and college students," however, results in an idea that could probably be developed adequately.

Indication of Writer's Attitude An essay is not simply a statement of fact or a bland report, but a piece of writing that reflects a particular point of view. The thesis statement will imply purpose by suggesting the writer's attitude toward his or her subject. A thesis statement such as "Airport security has increased since 9/11" simply states a fact, but does not indicate the writer's attitude or position. Consider instead how the following thesis statements suggest the writer's point of view: "Increased airport security since 9/11 gives us the illusion of security" or "Despite the inconvenience, increased airport security is necessary for many reasons" or "Airports should tighten security measures even more than they have."

Accurate Forecasting A good thesis statement further provides *an accurate forecast of what's to come.* If you plan to discuss the effects of overeating, don't say, "Overeating stems from deep-seated psychological factors and the easy availability of convenience foods." Such a statement, incorrectly suggesting that the paper will focus on causes, would only mislead and confuse your reader. On the other hand, "Overeating leads to obesity, which can cause or complicate several serious health problems" accurately represents what's to follow.

Preview of Organization Finally, a good thesis statement is precise, often previewing the organization of the paper, indicating a strategy of development. Assertions built on fuzzy, catch-all words like fascinating, bad, meaningful, or interesting, or statements like "My paper is about . . . " tell neither writer nor reader what's going on. To illustrate:

- Montreal is a fascinating city.

- My paper is about health benefits in Canada.

These examples raise a host of questions. Why does the writer find Montreal fascinating? Because of its architecture? Its night life? Its theatres? Its restaurants? Its museums? Its shops? Its cultural diversity? And what about health benefits? Will the writer explain how to apply for health benefits, or defend the current system of benefits, trace its history, suggest ways of improving it? Without a clear road-map sentence that suggests the writer's direction, we must labour through the paper, hoping to find our way.

Now look at the rewritten versions of those vague, imprecise thesis statements:

- Montreal's ethno-cultural diversity offers visitors the chance to sample cuisine from every continent.

- Our national health-care system should be a two-tier system that allows patients the options of receiving medical treatment from private clinics and hospitals at their own expense or from public clinics or hospitals at public expense because such a system would reduce waiting lists and lower the costs of health care paid by the Canadian government.

These thesis statements tell the reader not only what points the writer will make but also suggest the order and strategy of development they will follow. The first essay will proceed by way of illustration, offering examples of different ethno-cultural dishes that a visitor might sample. The second thesis statement suggests the writer will be arguing the reasons why a two-tier health care system would be desirable. Note that the second thesis statement could easily be broken into two sentences, with the first sentence stating the writer's position, and the second sentence providing the road-map—a preview of the writer's main points.

Placement of Thesis Statement

In most academic essays, the thesis statement comes somewhere in the first paragraph. Many essays take two or three sentences to lead into the thesis, but some, such as an essay for an in-class midterm, may provide the thesis immediately in the first sentence. In arguments, the writer may hold off stating the thesis, especially if it is controversial, until close to the end. Some essays, in particular, narratives and descriptions, or those by professional writers, may have implied thesis statements. Nonetheless, a core idea underlies and controls all effective writing.

Changing Your Thesis Statement

Unlike diamonds, thesis statements aren't necessarily forever. Before your paper is in final form, you may need to change your thesis statement several times. If you draft the thesis statement during the narrowing stage, you might change it to reflect what you uncovered while gathering information. Or you might amend it after writing the first draft so that it reflects your additions and deletions.

Tentative or final, formulated early or late, the thesis statement serves as a beacon that spotlights your purpose.

Case History *(Continued from page 26)*

Her essay plan completed, Trudy now drafts a thesis statement—the larger point that her entire essay will make:

> We should listen to other people, even if they seem different from us.

This case history continues on pages 31–32.

EXERCISE

A. Write a thesis statement for the flexible notes that you developed for the exercise on page 25.

B. Reread "Requirements of a Good Thesis Statement"; then explain why each of the following does or does not qualify as an effective thesis statement for a two- or three-page essay.

1. My paper discusses the problem of employee absenteeism in Canadian industry.

2. Living on a small island offers advantages: a quiet pace of life, the opportunity to know your neighbours, and the chance to be close to nature.

3. Although I don't know much about running a college, I know that Acme College is not run well.

4. Increasing government outlays for education would have pluses and minuses.

5. It is not entirely fair for teens that getting a Canadian driver's licence is more difficult than it was a few years ago.

■ Writing the First Draft

Now on to the first draft of your essay. Some people, especially for less formal essays, write a discovery draft, which is rather like focused freewriting, and then zero in on the most promising material in order to write a more official first draft. Other people prefer to spend more time preparing a written plan to follow. In any case, the writing should go rather quickly, especially if you have a topic you're qualified to write about, a thesis statement that indicates your purpose, enough information to develop it, and perhaps even a written plan to follow.

But sometimes when you sit down to write, the words won't come; and all you can do is doodle or stare at the blank page. Perhaps the introduction is the problem. Many writers are terrified by the thought of the opening paragraph. They want to get off to a good start but can't figure out how to begin. If this happens to you, additional brainstorming or freewriting can make you more comfortable and may suggest an opening. Keep in mind that any lead-in you write now can be changed later. If these suggestions don't solve your problem, skip the introduction for the time being. Once you have drafted the body of the paper, an effective opening should come more easily.

Here are some general suggestions for writing a first draft:

1. Stack your thesis statement, flexible notes, and written plan in front of you. They will start you thinking.
2. Skip every other line (double-space) and leave wide margins. Then you'll have room to revise later.
3. Write quickly; capture the drift of your thoughts. Concentrate on content and organization. Get your main points and supporting details on paper in the right sequence. Don't spend time correcting grammatical or punctuation errors, improving your language, or making the writing flow smoothly. You might lose your train of thought and end up doodling or staring again.
4. Take breaks at logical dividing points, for example, when you finish discussing a key point. Before you start to write again, scan what you've written.

Now for some specific suggestions that will help you with the actual writing:

1. Rewrite your thesis statement at the top of your first page to break the ice and build momentum.
2. Write your first paragraph, introducing your essay and stating your thesis. If you get stuck here, move on to the rest of the paper.
3. Follow your plan as you write. Begin with your first main point and work on each section in turn. Remember that you can change the order of main points later if a different arrangement of ideas seems more effective.
4. Look over the supporting details listed under the first heading in your flexible notes. Write a topic sentence stating the central idea of the paragraph.
5. Turn the details into sentences; use one or more sentences to explain each one. Add other related details, facts, or examples if they occur to you.
6. When you move from one paragraph to the next, try to provide a transitional word or sentence that connects the two.
7. Write your last paragraph, ending your essay in an appropriate fashion. If you get stuck, set your conclusion aside and return to it later.

Writing a draft isn't always so systematic. If you are inspired, you may want to abandon your plans and simply use your first draft to explore ideas. You can always revise, so don't be overly concerned if you get off track. Because writing is an act of discovery, sometimes the best ideas come when you think you are digressing, or coming to the end of a preliminary draft.

EXERCISE   *Using the plan you prepared for the exercise on page 25, write the first draft of an essay.*

Case History *(Continued from page 29)*

Trudy now uses her thesis statement and essay plan to write the following draft. Notice that she chooses to write her thesis statement at the end rather than at the beginning of the essay, a common technique in the writing of narratives. Certainly this draft will need revision. We'll return to it in the next chapter to discuss the necessary changes.

A Memory

1   When I remember back to elementary school, I remember an autistic boy named Steven Villman. Autism is a withdrawal from reality. It's really hard to understand, and takes lots of patience. I didn't understand Steven. I used to watch him in awe during lunch times as he ran about on his tiptoes with a stick waving about in his hand like a magic wand. His sticks were his trademark. Every lunch hour, rain or shine, he would dart outside and begin his search through the woods behind the school, in search of the best stick. Steven could always be found darting in and out of the trees, gleefully shaking his stick.

2   His high-pitched screeches and nonsense babbling would never fail to catch the attention of children deep in their play. Children always found enough time to stop and stare but never to talk.

3   Steven always seemed to have a dirty film covering his clothing, which was rumoured to be bought at second-hand shops. He was a large boy with dark, messy hair who appeared to be born with strawberry stains around his mouth.

4   Some kids would actually follow him around during lunch time, watching in awe at the odd tasks he'd perform, whispering and giggling about how weird he was.

5   One afternoon I was playing in a park located close to my house. Suddenly loud screeches alerted me as a large boy came running towards the park. Two smaller boys were trailing behind him, creeping up behind him and screeching in his ear to watch Steven's terrified reaction for their own amusement.

6   I immediately recognized the terrified boy as Steven Villman. I stood up on top of the slide and stared with wide eyes and mouth open. Murmuring and tightly holding onto his stick, Steven would bolt about like a wild animal full of fear.

7   "Hey, leave him alone, you bullies," I yelled, but the bullies paid no attention. Steven looked up to where I stood, but then quickly turned back to the bullies. I pushed myself down the slide quickly and made my way home to get some help.

8   Inside my home I stood huffing and puffing and babbling out the situation I had witnessed to my mom. I went on to explain how different Steven was from other kids. My mother took a deep breath. We headed back to the park immediately.

9   By the time we arrived at the park Steven was now blubbering uncontrollably and hollering at the boys. Still fascinated as ever and untouched by Steven's distress, the bullies failed to see my mom and me hustling over to where they stood.

10   "You two should be ashamed of yourselves!" my mother lectured with both hands on her hips. The boys whipped their heads around to be greeted by my furious mother as I watched with a small smirk.

11   The bullies looked at one another and then walked away, without even attempting to explain their behaviour.

12   Steven watched them go with a look of relief. "Where do you live, Steven?" my mom asked.

13   "That way." Steven pointed with a long dirty finger decorated with an uncut nail. He was looking toward the ground as he swayed from side to side, as if he were rocking himself to sleep. He was wearing faded blue shorts that were a couple of sizes too small. He was without shoes or socks on his feet and was covered from head to toe in dirt. "C'mon, Steven, we'll walk you home," my mother stated dryly, as if she were angry. We walked down the road at a slow pace listening to Steven's bare feet slap the hot concrete with each step he made. "Those bullies tricked me," Steven whined. Steven went on talking to himself rather than us, and it's a good thing he was, because it was clear that my mom had no answers to why the bullies were so mean.

14   As my mom and I walked back home, we walked in silence.

15   I still think about Steven Villman. I wonder if he realizes what a difference he can make in the lives of others. When I walked Steven home that day, I learned that we all need to listen to people who are different than we are.

This essay will be revised in the next chapter.

Revising and Editing Your Paper

All of us at one time or another have said something careless to a friend, date, or partner and then spent the rest of the night regretting our words. In contrast, when we write we can make sure we say exactly what we mean. Good writers don't express themselves perfectly on the first try, but they do work hard at revising their initial efforts.

Just what is revision? Don't confuse it with proofreading or editing, the final stage of the writing process, where you carefully inspect your word choice, spelling, grammar, and punctuation. Revision is much more drastic, often involving an upheaval of your draft as you change its content and organization in order to communicate more effectively.

Most of what you read, including this book, has been considerably altered and improved as the writers progressed through early drafts. This fact shouldn't surprise you. After all, a rough copy is merely a first attempt to jot down some ideas in essay form. No matter how well you gather and organize your material, you can't predict the outcome until you've prepared a draft. Sometimes only touch-up changes are required. More often though, despite your efforts, this version will be incomplete, unclear in places, possibly disorganized. You might even discover an entirely different idea, focus, or approach buried within it. During revision you keep changing things—your focus, approach to the topic, supporting material, and thesis statement—until the results satisfy you.

Inexperienced writers often mistakenly view initial drafts as nearly finished products rather than as experiments to alter, or even scrap, if need be. As a result, they often approach revision with the wrong attitude. To revise successfully, you need to control your ego and your fear and become your own first critical reader. Set aside natural feelings of accomplishment ("After all, I've put a great deal of thought into this") and dread ("Actually, I'm afraid of what I'll find if I look too closely"). Instead, recognize that revision offers an opportunity to upgrade your strong features and strengthen your weak ones.

■ Preparing to Revise

To distance yourself from your writing and sharpen your critical eye, set your first draft aside for at least half a day, longer if time permits. When you return to it, gear up for revision by jotting down your intended purpose and audience before you read your paper. These notations will help keep your changes on track. In addition, note any further ideas that have occurred to you.

The right attitude is vital to effective revision. Far too many students hastily skim their essays to reassure themselves that "Everything sounds O.K." Avoid such a quick-fix approach. If your draft appears fine on first reading, probe it again with a more critical eye. Try putting yourself in your reader's place. Will your description of a favourite getaway spot be clear to someone who has never seen it? Will your letter home asking for money really convince parents who might think they've already given you too much? Remember: If you aren't critical now, anticipating confusion and objections, your reader certainly will be later.

Read your essay at least three times, once for each of these reasons:

To improve the development of the essay as a whole
To strengthen paragraph structure and development
To sharpen sentences and words

When you finish reading your paper for content, make a final, meticulous sweep to search for errors and problems that mar your writing. Use the Personal Revision Checklist on the inside back cover of this book to note your own special weaknesses, perhaps some problem with punctuation or a failure to provide specific support. Later chapters discuss paragraphs, sentences, and words in detail. Check these chapters for more information about the points introduced here.

■ Considering the Whole Essay

If you inspect your draft only sentence by sentence, you can easily overlook how its parts work together. A better approach is to step back and view the overall essay rather than its separate parts, asking questions such as "Does the beginning mesh with the end?" "Does the essay wander?" "Has anything been left out?" In this way you can gauge how part relates to part and to the whole. Use the acronym *FACT* to guide this stage of your revision.

F. Ask yourself first whether the whole essay *FITS* together, presenting a central point for a specific audience. Have you delivered what the thesis statement promises? First drafts often include paragraphs, or even large sections, that have little bearing on the main point. Some drafts contain the kernels of several different essays. Furthermore, one section of a draft might be geared to one audience (parents, for example) and another section to an entirely different audience (students, perhaps). As you read each part, verify its connection to your purpose and audience. Don't hesitate to chop out sections that don't fit, redo stray parts so they accord with your central idea, or alter your thesis statement to reflect better your supporting material. Occasionally, you might even expand one small, fertile section of your draft into an entirely new essay.

A. Whenever we write first drafts, we unwittingly leave out essential material. As we revise, we need to identify and fill these gaps. Ask yourself: "Where will the reader need more information or examples to understand my message?" Then **ADD** the appropriate sentences, paragraphs, or even pages.

C. First drafts often contain material that fits the thesis but doesn't contribute to the essay. Writing quickly, we tend to repeat ourselves, include uninteresting or uninformative examples, and crank out whole paragraphs when one clear sentence would suffice. As you revise, **CUT** away this clutter with a free hand. Such paring can be painful, especially if you're left with a skimpy text, but your message will emerge with much greater clarity. As you've probably guessed, revising a draft often requires both adding and cutting.

T. Carefully **TEST** the organization of your essay. The text should flow smoothly from point to point with clear transitions between the various ideas. Test the organization by outlining your major and minor points, then checking the results for logic and completeness. Alternatively, read the draft and note its progression. Look for spots where you can clarify connections between words and thus help your readers.

Chapters 4–12 explain nine different writing strategies, each concluding with revision questions geared specifically to that strategy. Use these questions, together with the *FACT* of revision, to help you revise more effectively.

Case History *(Continued from page 32)*

Now let's apply the *FACT* approach to Trudy's essay on Steven Villman, which you read on pages 31–32. Like most early drafts, this draft needs work.
FIT. The thesis doesn't fit the rest of the essay very well, since the narrative doesn't really demonstrate the importance of listening. Trudy can rewrite her essay to bring out the importance of listening, or she can rewrite her thesis and conclusion so that they fit her essay better.
ADD. Trudy needs to expand her essay in a couple of places, as the reader cannot see why the bullies tricked Steven, or whether or not the mother is really angry. She will want to supply a transition between paragraphs 3 and 4,

since the reader may be confused by the jump in time and locale. She also needs to work on the conclusion, which seems rushed.

CUT. Since Trudy's purpose is more to promote compassion than to inform readers about autism, she can condense her introduction, zeroing in more immediately on her story. She can also cut some sentences that tell the reader what she has already demonstrated.

TEST. The first five paragraphs can be rearranged, combined, and condensed, as they seem rather choppy. It would be more logical to describe Steven's appearance before giving the description of his activities at lunchtime. The essay does flow well for the most part, although the paragraphs seem to be broken up arbitrarily in a few places, creating choppiness.

This case history continues below.

As you read your own essay, note on a separate sheet of paper problems to solve, ideas to add, and changes to try. When you mark the actual essay, make your job easier by using these simple techniques:

1. To delete something, cross it out lightly; you may decide to resurrect it later.
2. To add a section of text, place a letter *(A, B, C, D)* at the appropriate spot and write the new material on a separate sheet, keyed to the letter. Make changes within sections by crossing out what you don't want and writing the replacement above it or nearby.
3. To rearrange the organization, draw arrows showing where you want things to go, or cut up your draft and rearrange the sections by taping them on new sheets of paper. Use whatever method works best for you.

When you finish revising your draft, you might want to team up with one or more classmates and read one another's work critically. The fresh eye you bring to the task can uncover shortcomings that would otherwise go unnoticed. Pages 45–51 discuss peer editing in detail.

EXERCISE   *Use the FACT acronym to revise the draft you prepared for the exercise on page 30.*

Case History *(Continued from above)*

After setting her draft aside for a couple of days, Trudy revises it carefully. Compare the original draft with the revised version below. What changes has Trudy made?

A Memory

1   I remember watching Steven Villman in horrified awe
   during lunch times at my elementary school. Steven always

seemed to have a dirty film covering his faded clothing, which was rumoured to be bought at second-hand stores. He was a large boy with dark hair, who appeared to be born with strawberry jam stains around his mouth.

2   Sticks were his trademark. Every lunch hour Steven would rush outside to begin his search through the woods behind the school, in search of the best stick. Darting around the trees, he would run on his tip toes, with a stick grasped tightly in his hand, waving about like a magic wand.

3   His high-pitched screeches and nonsense babbling would never fail to catch the attention of children deep in their play. Sometimes a couple of children would follow him, giggling about how weird he was.

4   One summer afternoon I was playing alone in a park in my neighbourhood. Suddenly loud screeches alerted me as a large boy came running towards the park like a drunken ballerina. Two smaller boys trailed him with a look of mischief sparkling in their eyes. For their own amusement the boys were sneaking up behind Steven and screeching in his ear, just to watch Steven's terrified reaction. I stared with wide eyes and mouth open. Steven's stick shook uncontrollably as he bolted like a wild animal, trying to escape the bullies. I quickly pushed myself down the slide and made my way home to get some help.

5   Inside my home I stood huffing and puffing as I informed my mother about what I had witnessed. I went on to explain how Steven was different from other kids. When I finished my story my mother took a deep breath. We headed back to the park immediately.

6   When we arrived at the park Steven was blubbering like a baby and hollering at the boys. Still fascinated as ever and untouched by Steven's distress, the bullies failed to see my mother and me hustling over to where they stood, poking and laughing at Steven. With both hands on her hips my mother lectured, "You two should be ashamed of yourselves." Shocked, the bullies looked at one another and then just walked away, without even attempting to explain

their behaviour. Steven watched them with a look of relief as they walked out of sight. "Where do you live, Steven?" Steven pointed. "That way." He looked towards the ground as he swayed from side to side, as if he were rocking himself to sleep. Without shoes or socks on his feet, he was covered from head to toe in dirt.

7   "C'mon Steven, we'll walk you home," my mother said dryly, as if she was angry. Now I know different.

We walked down the road at a slow pace listening to Steven's bare feet slap against the hot concrete with every step he took.

8   "Those bullies tricked me," Steven whined. "Why would they want my shoes anyway?" He concentrated on his feet as he walked. "Why do kids like them always bug me ... and what's my mom gonna say?" Steven went on talking to himself rather than to my mother and me, and it's a good thing that he was, because it was obvious my mother had no explanations as to why people could be so mean.

After my mother and I bought Steven home we walked back in silence. It seemed so unfair that Steven had to deal not only with his disability, but also with the stupidity of those who didn't understand. By walking Steven Villman home that day I learned that we all need to take the time to understand people who are different from us.

Although this draft is not perfect, Trudy's revisions have considerably improved the paper. As Trudy continues polishing her essay, she can look for ways to cut unnecessary words. By finding more accurate word choice, she can make her essay even stronger. (The final, polished version of the essay appears on pages 42–43.) Never stop revising your essay until you are completely satisfied with the result.

This case history continues on page 42.

■ Strengthening Paragraph Structure and Development

Once you finish considering the essay as a whole, examine your paragraphs one by one, applying the *FACT* approach that you used for the whole paper. Make sure each paragraph *FITS* the paper's major focus and develops a single central idea. If a paragraph needs more support or examples, *ADD* whatever is necessary. If a paragraph contains ineffective or unhelpful material, *CUT* it. *TEST* the flow of ideas from paragraph to paragraph and clarify connections, both between and within paragraphs, as necessary. Ask the basic questions in the checklist that follows about each paragraph, and make any needed revisions.

REVISION CHECKLIST FOR PARAGRAPHS

- Does the paragraph have one, and only one, central idea?
- Does the central idea help to develop the thesis statement?
- Does each statement within the paragraph help to develop the central idea?
- Does the paragraph need additional explanations, examples, or supporting details?
- Would cutting some material make the paragraph stronger?
- Would reorganization make the ideas easier to follow?
- Can the connections between successive sentences be improved?
- Is each paragraph clearly and smoothly related to those that precede and follow it?

Don't expect to escape making any changes; some readjustments will undoubtedly be needed. Certain paragraphs may be stripped down or deleted, others beefed up, still others reorganized or repositioned. Chapter 14 contains more information on writing effective paragraphs.

EXERCISE   *Here are two sample student paragraphs. Evaluate each according to the Revision Checklist for Paragraphs and suggest any necessary changes.*

1.   I can remember so many times when my father had said that he was coming to pick me up for a day or two. I was excited as a young boy could be at the thought of seeing my father. With all the excitement and anticipation raging inside of me, I would wait on the front porch. Minutes would seem like hours as I would wait impatiently.

2.   For hours we had been waiting under the overhang of an abandoned hut. None of us had thought to bring ponchos on our short hike through the woods. Soon it would be dark. Earlier in the day it had been a perfectly clear day. We all agreed that we didn't want to stand here all night in the dark, so we decided to make a dash for it.

■ Sharpening Sentences and Words

Next, turn your attention to sentences and words. You can improve your writing considerably by finding and correcting sentences that convey the wrong meaning or are stylistically deficient in some way. Consider, for example, the following sentences:

> Just Mary was picked to write the report.
> Mary was just picked to write the report.
> Mary was picked to write just the report.

The first sentence says that no one except Mary will write the report; the second says that she was recently picked for the job; and the third says that she will write nothing else. Clearly, each of these sentences expresses a different meaning.

Now let's look at a second set of sentences:

> Personally, I am of the opinion that the results of our membership drive will prove to be pleasing to all of us.
> I believe the results of our membership drive will please all of us.

The wordiness of the first sentence slows the reader's pace and makes it harder to grasp the writer's meaning. The second sentence, by contrast, is much easier to grasp.

Like your sentences, your words should also convey your thoughts precisely and clearly. Words are, after all, your chief means of communicating with your reader. Examine the first draft and revised version of the following paragraph, which describes the early morning actions of the writer's roommate. The underlined words identify points of revision.

First Draft

Coffee cup in hand, she <u>moves</u> toward the bathroom. The coffee spills <u>noisily</u> on the tile floor as she <u>reaches</u> for the light switch and <u>turns</u> it on. After <u>looking</u> briefly at the face in the mirror, she <u>walks</u> toward the bathtub.

Revised Version

Coffee cup in hand, she <u>stumbles</u> toward the bathroom. The coffee she spills on the tile floor makes <u>a slapping sound</u> as she <u>gropes</u> for the light switch and <u>flips</u> it on. After <u>squinting</u> briefly at the face in the mirror, she <u>shuffles</u> toward the bathtub.

Note that the words in the first draft are general and imprecise. Exactly how does she move? with a limp? with a strut? with a spring in her step? And what does "noisily" mean? a thud? a roar? a sharp crack? The reader has no way of knowing. Recognizing this fact, the student revised her paragraph, substituting vivid, specific words. As a result, the reader can visualize the actions more sharply.

Don't confuse vivid, specific words with "jawbreaker words"—those that are complex and pretentious. (Most likely all of the words in the revised version are in your vocabulary.) Words should promote communication, not block it.

Reading your draft aloud will force you to slow down, and you will often hear yourself stumble over problem sections. You'll be more likely to uncover errors such as missing words, excessive repetition, clumsy sentences, and sentence fragments. Be honest in your evaluation; don't read in virtues that aren't there or that exaggerate the writing quality.

REVISION CHECKLIST FOR SENTENCES

- What sentences are not clearly expressed or logically constructed?
- What sentences seem awkward, excessively convoluted, or lacking in punch?
- What words require explanation or substitution because the reader may not know them?
- Where does my writing become wordy or use vague terms?
- Where have I carelessly omitted words or mistakenly used the wrong word?

EXERCISE   *Reread exercise paragraph 1 on page 39 and revise the sentence structure and word choice to create a more effective paragraph.*

■ Proofreading Your Draft

After revising your draft, proofread or edit it to correct errors in grammar, punctuation, and spelling. Since we often overlook our own errors simply because we know what we meant, proofreading can be difficult. Inch through your draft deliberately, moving your finger along slowly under every word. Repeat this procedure several times, looking first for errors in grammar, then for sentence errors and problems in punctuation and mechanics, and finally for mistakes in spelling. Be especially alert for problems that have plagued your writing in the past.

Effective proofreading calls for you to assume a detective role and probe for errors that weaken your writing. If you accept the challenge, you will certainly improve the quality of your finished work.

■ Writing the Introduction and Conclusion

If you've put off writing your introduction, do it now. Generally, short papers begin with a single paragraph that includes the previously drafted thesis statement, which sometimes needs to be rephrased so that it meshes smoothly with the rest of the paragraph. The introduction acquaints the reader with your topic; it should clearly signal your intention as well as spark the reader's interest. Pages 199–202 discuss and illustrate effective introductions.

The conclusion wraps up your discussion. Generally a single paragraph in short papers, a good ending summarizes or supports the paper's main idea. Pages 202–05 discuss and illustrate effective conclusions.

■ Selecting a Title

All essays require titles. Unless a good title unexpectedly surfaces while you are writing, wait until you finish the paper before choosing one. Since the reader must see the connection between what the title promises and what the essay delivers, a good title must be both accurate and specific.

Titling the essay about Steven Villman "Autism" would mislead the reader, since the essay does not focus on autism, but on human interaction with a person who happens to be autistic. A specific title suggests the essay's focus rather than just its topic. For example, "A Cruel Joke" is clearer and more precise than "A Memory."

A Cruel Joke

General title made more specific

I remember watching Steven Villman in horrified awe during lunch times at my elementary school. Steven always seemed to have a dirty film covering his faded clothing, rumoured to be bought at second-hand stores. He was a large boy with dark hair, rough and choppy across his forehead, who appeared to have been born with strawberry jam stains around his mouth.

Second sentence slightly condensed. Third sentence made more vivid, with more appropriate verb tense "to have been born."

Sticks were his trademark. Every lunch hour Steven would rush outside to begin his search through the woods behind the school, in search of the best stick. Darting around the trees, he would run on his tip toes, with a stick grasped tightly in his hand, waving it about like a magic wand. His high-pitched screeches and nonsense babbling would never fail to catch the attention of children deep in their play. Sometimes a couple of children would follow him, giggling, as he performed his usual ritual. Children always found enough time to stop and stare, but never dared to invite him to join them in their play.

Second and third paragraphs combined to improve coherence. Last sentence made more precise.

I remember one summer afternoon as I played alone in a park in my neighbourhood. Loud screeches alerted me as a large boy, whom I immediately recognized as Steven Villman, came running towards the park like a drunken ballerina. Two smaller boys trailed him with a look of mischief sparkling in their eyes. For their own amusement the boys were sneaking up behind Steven and screeching in his ear, just to watch Steven's terrified reaction. I stared with wide eyes and mouth open. Steven's stick shook uncontrollably as he bolted like a startled deer, trying to escape the bullies. I quickly pushed myself down the slide and made my way home to get some help.

Transition improved in the first sentence by the cue "I remember one summer afternoon" and the mention of Steven's name right away. "Wild animal" replaced with a more vivid image of "startled deer."

Inside my home I stood huffing and puffing as I informed my mother about what I had witnessed. When I finished my story, my mother put down the dishes she was washing and took a deep breath as she dried her hands on a towel. We headed back to the park immediately.

When we arrived at the park Steven was crying wildly and hollering at the boys. Still fascinated as ever and untouched by Steven's distress, the bullies failed to see my mother and me hustling over to where they stood, poking and laughing at Steven. With both hands on her hips my mother scolded, "You two should be ashamed of yourselves." Shocked, the bullies looked at one another and then just walked away, without even attempting to explain their behaviour. Steven watched them with a look of relief as they walked out of sight.

"Where do you live, Steven?" my mother asked. "That way." Steven pointed. He looked towards the ground as he swayed from side to side, as if he were rocking himself to sleep. Without shoes or socks on his feet, he was covered from head to toe in dirt.

"C'mon Steven, we'll walk you home," my mother said dryly. At the time I thought she was angry with Steven for the trouble he brought to our neighbourhood, or maybe at me for interrupting her dishwashing, but now I know she was angry about the cruelty of the bullies.

We walked down the road at a slow pace listening to Steven's bare feet slap against the hot concrete with every step he took.

"Those bullies tricked me," Steven whined. "Why would they want my shoes anyway?" He concentrated on his feet as he walked. "Why do kids like them always bug me? And what's my mom gonna say?" Steven went on talking to himself rather than to my mother and me, and it's a good thing he did, because it was obvious my mother had no explanation for why people could be so mean.

After my mother and I brought Steven home we walked back in silence. Steven's words burned in our minds. Why was it that Steven had to deal not only with his disability, but also with the stupidity of those who didn't understand? By walking Steven Villman home that day, I learned that sometimes the kindest thing is just to take the time to understand.

Unnecessary sentence deleted.
More explanation of what mother was doing.

Tone improved by replacing "blubbering" with "crying," the word "lectured" with "scolded"

New speaker identified with new paragraph

Better development as possibilities for mother's anger are suggested

---

Point of essay made clearer. Question is left in reader's mind as well as the writer's.

It is crucial that you view revision not as a hasty touch-up job or as a quick sweep through your draft just prior to handing it in. Instead, revision should be an ongoing process that often involves an upheaval of major sections as you see your draft through your reader's eyes and strive to write as well as you can. Only when you reach that summit have you finished revising.

■ Revising on the Computer

Computer programs such as *Word* or *Word Perfect* allow you to write over unwanted sections of your draft, add new information, cut useless material, and move parts of the text around. Learn all the commands of your particular program and experiment to see exactly what your options are. The following practical tips will improve your efficiency:

1. Always keep a backup copy of everything. Accidentally erasing a file or losing your work to an electrical power surge is not uncommon. In addition, save copies of your earlier drafts, either as hard copies or on disk; selected parts may prove useful later, and new papers sometimes sprout from old drafts.

2. Jot down helpful ideas or comments in your text as you revise. Enclose them with a special symbol, such as < >, and either save them in a separate file or delete them later if they serve no purpose.

3. If you struggle with a section of the text, write two or three versions and then pick your favourite. You might even open a new file, experiment freely, and then use the best version in your draft.

4. Don't allow the program to control how you revise. The easy-to-use, gentle-touch keyboards can lull you into a lapse of judgment and cause you to forget whether your words are worth writing. Pages of worthless material could pile up. Furthermore, don't be tempted to do what the commands make easiest: fiddle endlessly with sentences and words, never develop the essay as a whole, and move blocks of writing around indiscriminately.

5. Always revise using a hard copy. If you use just the computer, you are limited to only one screen at a time. A printed page has a different look. In addition, a hard copy allows you to compare several pages at once.

6. When you finish revising, check the coherence of your draft. The writing must flow smoothly at the points where you have added, deleted, or moved sections of text. In addition, altered sentences must be clearly written and logically constructed.

7. Proofreading with tools such as Spell Check can pose certain problems. For example, a spelling check function can't judge whether you used the wrong word (*form* instead of *from*) or confused identical sounding but differently spelled words (*their, there, they're*). *You* are still the ultimate proofreader.

■ Peer Evaluation of Drafts

At various points in the writing process, your instructor may ask you and your classmates to read and respond to one another's papers. Peer response often proves useful because even the best writers cannot always predict how their readers will react to their writing. For example, magazine articles designed to reduce the fear of AIDS have, in some cases, increased anxiety about the disease. Furthermore, we often have difficulty seeing the problems with our own drafts because so much hard work has gone into them. What seems clear and effective to us can be confusing or boring to our readers. Comments from our peers can frequently launch a more effective essay.

Just as the responses of others help you, so will your responses help them. You don't have the close, involved relationship with your peers' writing that you do with your own. Therefore, you can gauge their drafts objectively. This type of critical evaluation will eventually heighten your awareness of your own writing strengths and weaknesses. And knowing how to read your own work critically is one of the most important writing skills you can develop.

Responding to Your Peers' Drafts

Responding to someone else's writing is easier than you might imagine. It's not your job to spell out how to make the draft more effective, how to organize it, what to include, and what language to use. The writer must make these decisions. Your job is to *identify* problems, *not solve* them. You can do that best by responding honestly to the draft.

Some responses are more helpful than others. You don't help the writer by casually observing that the draft "looks O.K." Such a response doesn't point to problem areas; rather it suggests that you didn't read the paper carefully and critically. Wouldn't you inform a friend who was wearing clothes that looked terrible *why* they looked terrible? The same attitude should prevail about the writing of others, something that makes a statement just as clothes do. Nor is a vague comment such as "The introduction is uninteresting" helpful. Point out *why* it is uninteresting. For instance, you might note: "The introduction doesn't interest me in the paper because it is very technical, and I get lost. I ask myself why I should read on." Below is another example of an ineffective response and a more effective counterpart.

Ineffective

The paper was confusing.

Effective

Paragraphs 2, 3, and 4 confused me. You jumped around too much. First you wrote about your experience on the first day of college, then you went on to how much you enjoyed junior high school, and finally you wrote about what you want to do for a career. I don't see how these ideas relate or why they are in the order that they are.

Here are some steps to follow when responding to someone else's draft. First, read the essay from beginning to end without interruption. On a separate sheet of paper, indicate what you consider the main idea. The writer can then see whether the intended message has come through. Next, identify the biggest strength and the biggest problem. Writers need both positive and negative comments. Finally, reread the paper and write either specific responses to each paragraph or your responses to general questions such as the ones that follow. In either case, don't comment on spelling or grammar unless it really inhibits your reading.

PEER RESPONSE CHECKLIST

- What is the main point of this essay?
- What is the biggest strength? What is the biggest problem?
- What material doesn't seem to fit the main point or the audience?
- What questions has the author not answered?
- Where should more details or examples be added? Why?
- At what point does the paper fail to hold my interest? Why?
- Where is the organization confusing?
- Where is the writing unclear or vague?

As you learn the various strategies for successful writing, new concerns will arise. Questions geared to these concerns appear in the revision section that concludes the discussion of each strategy.

An Example of Peer Response

The following is the first draft of a student essay and a partial peer response to it. The response features three of the nine general questions and also comments on one paragraph. Before you read the response, try evaluating this essay yourself and then compare your reactions to those of the other student.

Captive Breeding in Zoos

1   This paper is about captive breeding. Today, humans hinder

nature's species' right to survive. We are making it hard for over one hundred species of animals to continue to exist. But captive breeding in the world's zoos may be just what the doctor ordered. This rescue attempt is a complex and difficult undertaking. Captive breeding of endangered species is complicated by the special social and physical requirements of individual species.

2   There are many social problems that have to be solved for the successful reproduction of endangered species in zoos. Mating is one of the most important of these problems. One propagation "must" for many felines, pandas, and pygmy hippopotamuses is the complete separation of sexes until they're "ready." Leland Stowe says that cheetahs almost never get together unless they can't see or smell each other ahead of time. When females exhibit a certain behaviour, they bring on the male.

3   Male-female compatibility is a social problem. Great apes seem to be as particular as people in choosing mates. Stowe tells about an orangutan that turned a cold shoulder on the females in the U.S. National Zoo located in Washington, D.C. Then they shipped him to the zoo in Toronto. There, he took up with one of the females. The curator of the zoo, William Zanten, says he's "been siring offspring ever since."

4   Social factors hurt care of infant primates. Sheldon Campbell talks about this in *Smithsonian* magazine. He writes about the problems of breeding golden marmosets. These are monkeys that live in Brazil. The scientists found that captive-born parents neglected their young. Sometimes they even killed them. The problem was due to the fact that the marmosets had no experience living in a family situation. They didn't know what to do. Emily Hahn writes about gorillas in *The New Yorker.* She says that those raised by humans make poor mothers. Those raised by dutiful mothers make good parents.

5   The second important stumbling block to successful captive breeding is physical problems. Ignorance of dietary needs can be bad. Stowe talks about the captive breeding of gorillas and says that when this breeding was first getting started, infants exhibited a very high mortality rate. Then the babies were given iron and meat protein, the latter rich in vitamin B-12. They were sprinkled on bananas, and the bananas were fed to the babies. The survival rate markedly improved.

6   Animals can be bred more easily if they are in an environment that duplicates that animal's natural habitat. Hooved and horned animals are an easy job because of the similarity in terrain and climate of their natural habitats to zoo habitats. Polar bears are a lot tougher. Mothers want to be left alone until their cubs are up and about. Because of this fact, the bears often kill their babies. Stowe says they solved this problem by building replicas of arctic ice caves. The mothers and cubs are left alone until they emerge from the cave. John Perry, Director of the U.S. National Zoo, said this:

> The world is our zoo--a zoo that must be well managed, its resources carefully husbanded, for these are the only resources it can ever have. We have appointed ourselves the keepers of this zoo, but we cannot live outside its gates. We are of it. Our lives are inextricably intertwined with the lives of all that live within. Their fate will be ours.

Our endangered species can survive only by nature's implacable test—sustained births by second and third generations. It will take decades to reach such a verdict of success. Thus we can see that captive breeding is beset by many problems.

What is the main point of this essay?

I think this paper is saying that the only chance for endangered species is that they reproduce in zoos but that it is hard to get them to breed in captivity.

What is the biggest strength?

I hadn't thought much about this question, so it was something new for me. I liked the examples about specific animals and the problems that they have in captivity. I especially liked the fact that the writer gave me several problems that occur when animals are bred in captivity. The writer didn't oversimplify.

What is the biggest problem?

I can't see how the paragraphs connect to the main part of the paper or to each other. They seem disconnected. What does Male-female compatibility is a social problem have to do with the problem of reproduction or with the previous paragraph on mating? Also, there are a number of very unclear statements that leave me with many questions. How are we making it hard for over a hundred species to exist? What do you mean when you say Almost never get together, bring on the male, took up with, and an easy job?

Response to paragraph 4

Do social factors always hurt the care of infant primates? Your statement seems too general. Shouldn't you combine some of your sentences? The first six sentences seem to abruptly jump from one point to the next; the writing is not smooth. How did you get from marmosets to gorillas? The jump confuses me. Also, were the dutiful mothers humans or gorillas?

Acting upon Your Peers' Responses

Sometimes you need strong nerves to act upon a peer response. You can easily become defensive or discount your reader's comments as foolish. Remember, however, that as a writer you are trying to communicate with your readers, and that means taking seriously the problems they identify. Of course, you decide which responses are appropriate, but even an inappropriate criticism sometimes sets off a train of thought that leads to good ideas for revision.

Examine the revised version of the captive breeding essay that follows and note how some of the peer responses have been taken into account. Clear transition sentences link paragraphs to the thesis statement and to each other. Vague statements identified in the earlier draft have been clarified. In paragraph 4 the writer connects the discussion of the marmosets to that of the gorillas by changing the order of the two sentences that precede the final one and combining them, thereby identifying poor parenting as the key problem with both kinds of primates. Finally, she indicates what she means by "dutiful mother."

As you read this version, carefully examine the margin notes, which highlight key features of the revision.

Captive Breeding: Difficult but Necessary

Title: specific and accurate

Introduction: arresting
statement

Thesis statement and
statement of organization

Topic sentence with link to
thesis statement

Specific details:
problems with cheetahs

Mention of other species
with mating problems

Topic sentence with link to
preceding paragraph;
linking device

Specific example: problem
with particular orangutan

Topic sentence with link to
preceding paragraph

Specific details:
problems with marmosets

Mention of other species
with rearing problems

Linking device

1   Today, as in the past, humans encroach upon the basic right of nature's species to survive. Through ignorance, oversight, and technological developments, we are threatening the survival of over one hundred animal species. Until their environments can be safeguarded against harmful human intrusion, the last chance for the threatened species may be captive breeding in zoos. But this rescue attempt is a complex and difficult undertaking. <u>In particular, each species presents social and physical problems that must be solved if breeding is to succeed</u>.

2   <u>Among the social problems that complicate successful reproduction, mating problems loom especially large</u>. For instance, the male and female of many feline species must be kept completely separated until both animals are ready to mate. Leland Stowe, writing in *National Wildlife* magazine, notes that cheetahs almost never mate unless kept where the one cannot see or smell the other. Once the female shows signs of receptivity, a male is placed in her cage, and mating then occurs. Pandas and pygmy hippopotamuses show the same behaviour.

3   <u>A related social problem with certain species is male-female compatibility</u>. Great apes, <u>for instance</u>, seem to be as particular as human beings in choosing mates. Stowe relates an amusing case of a male orangutan that totally spurned the females in the Washington, D.C., National Zoo. Shipped to a zoo in Toronto, he succumbed to the charms of a new face and has, according to curator William Zanten, "been siring offspring ever since."

4   <u>Social factors can also imperil proper care of infant primates</u>. In a *Smithsonian* magazine article, Sheldon Campbell talks about the problems scientists encountered in trying to breed golden marmosets, a species of Brazilian monkey. Early attempts failed because the captive-born parents neglected and sometimes accidentally killed their babies. Observation showed that the problem occurred because the marmosets had no experience living in a family situation—they simply didn't know how to handle their offspring. Gorillas reared by humans may also make poor mothers, reports Emily Hahn in *The New Yorker*. <u>On the other hand</u>, those reared by dutiful mothers, whether human or gorilla, are usually good parents themselves.

5   <u>Physical problems rival social problems as stumbling blocks to successful captive breeding. Ignorance of a species' dietary needs, for instance, can have disastrous consequences.</u> Early in the captive breeding of gorillas, infants exhibited a very high mortality rate, Stowe notes. Then meat protein and iron, the former rich in vitamin B-12, were sprinkled on bananas and fed to the babies. <u>As a result</u>, the survival rate markedly improved.

6   <u>An environment that duplicates a species' natural habitat favours easy propagation</u>. Hooved and horned animals present few breeding problems because the zoo habitats are similar in terrain and climate to their natural habitats. Polar bears, <u>on the other hand,</u> present difficult problems. Unless the mothers have complete privacy until the cubs can get around, they often kill the babies. To prevent this from happening, Stowe says, zoos now construct replicas of arctic ice caves and leave mothers and cubs completely alone until the new family emerges from the cave.

7   In his book *The World's a Zoo* John Perry, director of the U.S. National Zoo, has spoken of the need to save our endangered species:

> The world is our zoo--a zoo that must be well managed, its resources carefully husbanded, for these are the only resources it can ever have. We have appointed ourselves the keepers of this zoo, but we cannot live outside its gates. We are of it. Our lives are inextricably intertwined with the lives of all that live within. Their fate will be ours.

The difficulty, unfortunately, is as great as the urgency of this problem. Only sustained births by second- and third-generation captive animals can ensure the survival of our endangered species. And it will take decades to achieve the necessary success.

Sidenotes:

- Transition sentence: signals switch to discussing physical problems.
- Topic sentence with link to transition sentence
- Specific details: problems with gorillas
- Linking device
- Topic sentence
- Linking device
- Conclusion: quotation plus statement reinforcing idea that captive breeding presents difficulties

■ Collaborative Writing

In many careers you'll have to work as part of a group to produce a single document. Recognizing this fact, many instructors assign collaborative writing projects. Writing as part of a group offers some advantages and poses some challenges. You can draw on many different perspectives and areas of expertise, split up the work, and enjoy the feedback of a built-in peer group. On the other hand, you must also coordinate several efforts, resolve conflicts over the direction of the project, deal with people who may not do their fair share, and integrate different styles of writing.

Even though you write as part of a group, the final product should read as though it were written by one person. Therefore, take great pains to ensure that the paper doesn't resemble a patchwork quilt. You can help achieve this goal by following the principles of good writing discussed throughout this book. Here are some suggestions for successful collaborative work:

1. Select a leader with strong organizational skills.
2. Make sure each person has every other group member's phone number.
3. Analyze the project and develop a work plan with clearly stated deadlines for each step of the project.
4. Assign tasks on the basis of people's interests and expertise.
5. Schedule regular meetings to gauge each person's progress.
6. Encourage ideas and feedback from all members at each meeting.
7. If each member will develop a part of the paper, submit each one's contribution to the other members of the group for peer evaluation.
8. To ensure that the finished product is written in one style and fits together as a whole, give each member's draft to one person and ask him or her to write a complete draft.
9. Allow plenty of time to review the draft so necessary changes can be made.

Collaborative writing provides an opportunity to learn a great deal from other students. Problems can arise, however, if one or more group members don't do their work or skip meetings entirely. This irresponsibility compromises everyone's grade. The group should insist that all members participate, and the leader should immediately contact anyone who misses a meeting. If a serious problem develops despite these efforts, contact your instructor.

Collaboration Using E-Mail

Increasing numbers of college students are using e-mail to collaborate on writing projects. E-mail allows you to exchange material and comment at every stage of the writing process. To illustrate, you can share

Brainstorming ideas developed during the search for a writing topic
Brainstorming ideas developed during the search for supporting information
Tentative thesis statements or any general statements that will shape the document
Individual sections of the writing project
Copies of the entire original draft

Whenever you use e-mail for collaborative writing, it's a good idea to designate a project leader who will ensure that all members participate and who will receive and distribute all materials. Your instructor may request copies of the e-mail exchanges in order to follow your work.

■ Maintaining and Reviewing a Portfolio

A portfolio is an organized collection of your writing, usually kept in a three-ring binder or folder. It's a good idea to retain all your work for each class, including the assignment sheet, your prewriting, and all your drafts. Organize this material either in the order the papers were completed or by type of assignment.

Why assemble a portfolio? Not only can a portfolio be a source of ideas for future writing, but it also allows you to review the progress of your current papers. In addition, should any confusion arise about a grade or an assignment, the contents of your portfolio can quickly clarify matters.

Some instructors will require you to maintain a portfolio. They will probably specify both what is to be included and how it is to be organized. They may use the portfolio to help you gain a better understanding of your strengths and weaknesses as measured by the series of papers. Furthermore, portfolios give your instructor a complete picture of all your work. Some departments collect student portfolios to assess their writing program; by reviewing student progress, instructors can determine what adjustments will make the program even more effective.

You can review your own portfolio to gain a better understanding of your writing capabilities. Answer these questions as you look over your materials:

1. With what assignments or topics was I most successful? Why?
2. What assignments or topics gave me the most problems? Why?
3. How has my prewriting changed? How can I make it more effective?
4. How has my planning changed? How can I make it more effective?
5. What makes my best writing good? How does this writing differ from my other work?
6. What are the problem areas in my weakest writing? How does this writing differ from my other work?
7. Did I use the checklists in the front of this text to revise my papers? Do I make significant changes on my own, in response to peer evaluation, or in response to my instructor's comments? If not, why not? What kinds of changes do I make? What changes would improve the quality of my work?
8. What organizational patterns have I used? Which ones have been effective? Why? Which ones have given me trouble? Why?
9. What kinds of introductions have I used? What other options do I have?
10. What kinds of grammar or spelling errors mar my writing? (Focus on these errors in future proofreading.)

chapter
4

....

Narration:
Relating Events

Clicking off the evening news and padding toward bed, Heloise suddenly glimpsed, out of the corner of her eye, a shadow stretching across the living room floor from under the drawn curtains.

"Wh—who's there?"

No response.

Edging backward toward the phone, her eyes riveted on the shadow, she stammered, "I—I don't have any money."

Still no answer.

Reaching the phone, she gripped the receiver and started to lift it from its cradle. Just then . . .

Just now you've glimpsed the start of a *narrative*. A narrative relates a series of events. The events may be real—as in histories, biographies, or news stories—or imaginary, as in short stories and novels. The narrative urge stirs in all of us, and like everyone else, you have responded almost from the time you began to talk. As a child, you probably swapped many stories with your friends, recounting an exciting visit to a circus or amusement park or an unusually funny experience with your pet. Today you may tell a friend about the odd happening in your biology laboratory or on the job.

Many classroom and on-the-job writing occasions call for narratives. Your English instructor might want you to trace the development of some literary character. Your history instructor might have you recap the events leading to a major war or your sociology instructor have you relate your unfolding relations with a stepparent or someone else. At work, a police officer may record the events leading to an arrest, a scientist recount the development of a research project, and a department manager prepare a brief history of an employee's work problems.

Purpose

A narrative, like any other kind of writing, makes a point or has a purpose. The point can either be stated or left unstated, but it always shapes the writing. Some narratives simply tell what happened or establish an interesting or useful fact. The reporter who writes about a heated city council meeting or a lively cabinet committee hearing usually wants only to set facts before the public.

Most narratives, however, go beyond merely reciting events. Writers of history and biography delve into the motives underlying the events and lives they portray, while narratives of personal experience offer lessons and insights. In the following conclusion to a narrative about an encounter with a would-be mugger, the writer offers an observation on self-respect.

> I kept my self-respect, even at the cost of dirtying my fists with violence, and I feel that I understand the Irish and the Cypriots, the Israelis and the Palestinians, all those who seem to us to fight senseless wars for senseless reasons, better than before. For what respect does one keep for oneself if one isn't in the last resort ready to fight and say, "You punk!"?

> Harry Fairlie, "A Victim Fights Back"

Action

Action plays a central role in any narrative. Other writing often only suggests action, leaving readers to imagine it for themselves:

> A hundred thousand people were killed by the atomic bomb, and these six were among the survivors. They still wonder why they lived when so many others died. Each of them counts many small items of chance or volition—a step taken in time, a decision to go indoors, catching one streetcar instead of the next—that spared him. And now each knows that in the act of survival he lived a dozen lives and saw more death than he ever thought he would see. At the time, none of them knew anything.

> John Hersey, *Hiroshima*

This passage suggests a great deal of action—the flash of an exploding bomb, the collapse of buildings, screaming people fleeing the scorching devastation—but *it does not present the action.* Narration, however, re-creates action:

> When I pulled the trigger I did not hear the bang or feel the kick—one never does when a shot goes home—but I heard the devilish roar of glee that went up from the crowd. In that instant, in too short a time, one would have thought, even for the bullet to get there, a mysterious, terrible change had come over the

elephant. He neither stirred nor fell, but every line of his body had altered. He looked suddenly stricken, shrunken, immensely old, as though the frightful impact of the bullet had paralyzed him without knocking him down. At last, after what seemed a long time—it might have been five seconds, I dare say—he sagged flabbily to his knees. His mouth slobbered. An enormous senility seemed to have settled upon him. One could have imagined him thousands of years old. I fired again into the same spot. At the second shot he did not collapse but climbed with desperate slowness to his feet and stood weakly upright, with legs sagging and head drooping. I fired a third time. That was the shot that did it for him. You could see the agony of it jolt his whole body and knock the last remnant of strength from his legs. But in falling he seemed for a moment to rise, for as his hind legs collapsed beneath him he seemed to tower upward like a huge rock toppling, his trunk reaching skywards like a tree. He trumpeted, for the first and only time. And then down he came, his belly towards me, with a crash that seemed to shake the ground even where I lay.

George Orwell, "Shooting an Elephant"

Orwell's account offers a stark, vivid replay of the slaying, leaving nothing significant for the reader to infer.

A few words of caution are in order here. Action entails not only exotic events such as the theft of mass-destruction weapons, then the ransom demand, then the recovery of the weapons and the pursuit of the villains. A wide variety of more normal events also qualify as action: a long, patient wait that comes to nothing, an unexpected kiss after some friendly assistance, a disappointing gift that signals a failed relationship. Furthermore, the narrative action must all relate to the main point—not merely chronicle a series of events.

■ Conflict

The events in our lives and our world are often shaped by conflicts that need to be resolved. It should not be surprising then that conflict and its resolution, if any, are crucial to a narrative since they motivate and often structure the action. Some conflicts pit one individual against another or against a group, such as a union, company, or religious body. In other cases, the conflict may involve either an individual and nature or two clashing impulses in one person's head. Read the following student paragraph and note how common sense and fear struggle within the writer, who has experienced a sharp, stabbing pain in his side:

> Common sense and fear waged war in my mind. The first argued that a pain so intense was nothing to fool with, that it might indicate a serious or even life-threatening condition. Dr. Montz would be able to identify the problem and deal with it before it worsened. But what if it was already serious? What if I needed emergency surgery? I didn't want anyone cutting into me. "Now wait a minute," I said. "It's probably nothing serious. Most aches and pains aren't. I'll see the doctor, maybe get some pills, and the problem will clear up overnight. But what if he finds something

major, and I have to spend the night in the hospital getting ready
for surgery or recovering from it? I think I'll just ignore the
pain."

Luis Rodriguez

■ Point of View

Narrative writers may adopt either a first-person or third-person point of view. In first-person narratives, one of the participants tells what happened, whereas with third-person narration the storyteller stays completely out of the tale. Narratives you write about yourself use the first person, as do autobiographies. Biographies and histories use the third person, and fiction embraces both points of view.

In first-person narration, pronouns such as *I, me, mine, we,* and *ours* identify the storyteller. With the third person, the narrator remains unmentioned, and the characters are identified by nouns and such pronouns as *he, she, him,* and *her.* These two paragraphs illustrate the difference:

First-Person Narration

After that I took the beer to the front verandah, and some bread and cheese for our supper to have with it, and I sat out there with Nancy and Jamie Walsh while the sun declined, and it became too dark to sew. It was a lovely and windless evening, and the birds were twittering, and the trees in the orchard near the road were golden in the late sunlight, and the purple milkweed flowers that grew beside the drive smelled very sweetly; and also the last few peonies beside the verandah, and the climbing roses; and the coolness came down out of the air, while Jamie sat and played on his flute, so plaintively it did your heart good. After a while McDermott came skulking around the side of the house like a tamed wolf, and leant against the side of the house, and listened also. And there we were, in a kind of harmony; and the evening was so beautiful, that it made a pain in my heart, as when you cannot tell whether you are happy or sad; and I thought that if I could have a wish, it would be that nothing would ever change, and we could stay that way forever.

Margaret Atwood, *Alias Grace*

As this example shows, first-person narrators may refer to other characters in the narrative by using nouns and third-person pronouns.

Third-Person Narration

People driving by don't notice Spit Delaney. His old gas station is nearly hidden now behind the firs he's let grow up along the road, and he doesn't bother to white-wash the scalloped row of half-tires someone planted once instead of fence. And rushing by on the Island highway today, heading north or south, there's little chance that anyone will notice Spit Delaney seated on the big rock at the side of his road-end, scratching at his narrow chest, or hear him muttering to the flat grey highway and to the scrubby firs and to the useless old ears of his neighbour's dog that he'll be damned if he can figure out what it is that is happening to him.

Jack Hodgins, "Separating"

▪ Key Events

Any narrative includes many separate events, enough to swamp your narrative boat if you try to pack them all in. Suppose you wish to write about your recent attack of appendicitis in order to make a point about heeding early warnings of an oncoming illness. Your list of events might look like this:

Awakened	Greeted fellow employees	Ate lunch
Showered		Returned to work
Experienced acute but passing pain in abdomen	Began morning's work	Began afternoon's work
Dressed	Felt nauseated	Collapsed at work station
Ate breakfast	Met with boss	Was rushed to hospital
Opened garage door	Took coffee break	
Started car	Visited bathroom	Underwent diagnostic tests
Drove to work	Experienced more prolonged pain in abdomen	Had emergency operation
Parked in employee lot	Walked to cafeteria	
Entered building		

A narrative that included all, or even most, of these events would be bloated and ineffective. To avoid this outcome, identify and build your narrative around its key events—those that bear directly on your purpose. Include just enough secondary events to keep the narrative flowing smoothly, but treat them in sketchy fashion. The pain and nausea certainly qualify as key events. Here's how you might present the first attack of pain:

> My first sign of trouble came shortly after I stepped out of the shower. I had just finished towelling when a sharp pain in my lower right side sent me staggering into the bedroom, where I collapsed onto an easy chair in the corner. Biting my lip to hide my groans, I sat twisting in agony as the pain gradually ebbed, leaving me grey faced, sweat drenched, and shaken. What, I asked myself, had been the trouble? Was it ulcers? Was it a gallbladder attack? Did I have stomach cancer?

This passage convinces, not just tells, the reader that an attack has occurred. Its details vividly convey the nature of the attack as well as the reactions of the victim. As in any good narrative, the reader shares the experience of the writer, and the two communicate.

■ Dialogue

Dialogue, or conversation, animates many narratives, livening the action and help-ing draw the reader into the story. Written conversation, however, doesn't dupli-cate real talk. In speaking with friends, we repeat ourselves, throw in irrelevant comments, use slang, lose our train of thought, and overuse expressions like *you know, uh,* and *well.* Dialogue that reproduced real talk would weaken any narrative.

Good dialogue resembles real conversation without copying it. It features sim-ple words and short sentences while avoiding the over-repetition of phrases like *she said* and *he replied.* If the conversation unfolds smoothly, the speaker's identity will be clear. To heighten the sense of reality, the writer may use an occasional sen-tence fragment, slang expression, pause, and the like, as in this passage:

Mom was waiting for me when I entered the house.

"Your friends. They've been talking to you again. Trying to per-suade you to change your mind about not going into baseball. Honey, I wish you'd listen to them. You're a terrific ballplayer. Just look at all the trophies and awards you've . . ." She paused. "Joe's mother called me this morning and asked if you were playing in the game on Saturday. Davey, I wish you would. You haven't played for two weeks. Please. I want you to. For me. It would be so good for you to go and—and do what you've always . . ."

"O.K., Mom, I'll play," I said. "But remember, it's just for you."

                                                        Diane Pickett

Note the mother's use of the slang expression "terrific" and of sentence frag-ments like "your friends" and "for me" as well as the shift in her train of thought and the repetition of "and." These strategies lend an air of realism to the mother's words.

Besides making your dialogue realistic, be sure that you also punctuate it cor-rectly. Here are some key guidelines: Each shift from one speaker to another re-quires a new paragraph. When an expression like *he said* interrupts a single quoted sentence, set it off with commas. When such an expression comes between two complete quoted sentences, put a period after the expression and capitalize the first word of the second sentence. Position commas and periods that come at the end of direct quotations inside the quotation marks. Our example illustrates most of these guidelines.

■ Ethical Issues

Think how you'd react to a supervisor who wrote a narrative about the development of a new product that exaggerated his role and minimized your crucial contribu-tion to the result. The report might cost you the opportunity for promotion. As you mull over any narrative you write, you'll want to think about several ethical issues.

- Have I provided a truthful account that participants will recognize and accept? Deliberate falsification of someone's behaviour that tarnishes that person's reputation is libel and could result in legal action.

- Would the narrative expose any participants to possible danger if it became public? Do I need to change any names in order to protect people from potential harm? Say your narrative includes someone who cooperates behind the scenes with authorities to help solve a case of cybervandalism. You should probably give that person a fictitious name.

- Does the narrative encourage unethical behaviour? For example, extolling the delights of using the drug Ecstasy for a teenage audience is clearly unethical.

These guidelines don't rule out exaggerated, humorous, or partially truthful narratives, but as with any kind of writing, you should consider the possible effects of your writing on others.

■ Writing a Narrative

Planning and Drafting the Narrative

Most of the narratives you write for your composition class will relate a personal experience and therefore use the first person. On occasion, though, you may write about someone else and therefore use the third person. In either case make sure the experience you pick illustrates some point. A paper that indicates only how you violated a friend's confidence may meander along to little purpose. But if that paper is shaped by some point you wish to make—for instance, that you gained insight into the obligations of friendship—the topic can be worthwhile. To get started, do some guided brainstorming, asking yourself these questions:

What experience in my life or that of someone I know would be worth narrating?
What point does this experience illustrate? (Try to state the point in one or two sentences.)
What people were involved and what parts did they play?

When you have pinpointed a topic, use further brainstorming to garner supporting material. Here are some helpful questions:

What background information is needed to understand the events?
What action should I include?
What is the nature of the conflict? Was it resolved? If so, how?
Which events play key roles, which are secondary, and which should go unmentioned?
Is any dialogue necessary?

Before you start to write, develop a plot outline showing the significant events in your narrative. For each one, jot down what you saw, heard, or did, and what you thought or felt.

Use the opening of your paper to set the stage for what follows. You might tell when and where the action occurred, provide helpful background information, note the incident that activated the chain of events, or identify the problem from which the action grew. If you state your main point directly, do it here or in the conclusion.

The body of the narrative should move the action forward until a turning point is about to be reached. Build the body around your key events. To avoid stranding your reader, use time signals whenever the development of the action might be unclear. Words, phrases, and clauses like *now, next, finally, after an hour,* and *when I returned* help the reader understand the sequence of events. Don't get carried away, though; a paper loaded with time signals makes the sequence seem more important than the events themselves. Finally, think about how you can best use conflict and dialogue to heighten narrative interest.

The conclusion should tie up any loose ends, settle any unresolved conflicts, and lend an air of completion to the narrative. Effective strategies to think about include introducing a surprise twist, offering a reflective summary of the events, noting your reaction to them, or discussing the aftermath of the affair.

Revising the Narrative

As you revise, follow the guidelines in Chapter 3, and in addition ask yourself these questions:

Have I made the point, stated or unstated, that I intended?

Does all of the action relate to the main point?

Is the conflict handled appropriately?

Have I included all of the key events that relate to my purpose? given each the right emphasis? used time indicators where needed?

Is my point of view appropriate?

Does my dialogue ring true?

Example Student Essay of Narration

Christmas Surprise

Rita White

1   A week before this last Christmas, the nurses who were due to work in our unit on Christmas day planned to have a pot-luck as our Christmas lunch. My husband was visiting his relatives in Ontario, and I had time--too much time--to think about what to make. My favourite colleagues, Janet, Aurora, Sally, and Brenda were working that day, and I wanted to impress them.

2   I decided I would make Wonton soup.

3   At home I searched through my collection of recipes which were piled up in the corner of my living room. This corner is always messy. All my course books, cookbooks, and my husband's joke books are jumbled together. I promised myself many times to keep that corner better organized, but then I forget all my promises and get busy with something else--in this case, working on my recipe. I was pleasantly surprised to find it waiting for me right on top of the pile.

4   Even though I was alone on Christmas Eve, I was surprised I did not feel lonely at all. I guess it was because I was busy with all my shopping and preparation for the Wonton. I chose to wrap the Wonton in the Chinese imperial style which makes each Wonton look like a flower. I wanted the soup to be outstanding.

5   On Christmas day, early in the morning, I grabbed everything I needed--my rice cooker, a big bowl, and of course, the Wontons, and drove to work feeling both happy and a bit nervous. At the hospital parking lot I met Brenda who carried a big box of food. I was anxious to know what kind of food she was going to make because she was famous for her desserts, especially her Dutch apple pie and angel food cake. I must admit that I was worried about how my Wonton would compare.

6   The morning seemed to drag along. Dr. Glazos, as usual, made his ward round slowly. By the time the ward round team was at my patient's bedside, it was already eleven o'clock. I was a bit worried that I might not have enough time to prepare my soup. I presented my case as quickly as possible and hoped that the round would be uncomplicated. Surprisingly, it took only ten minutes to finish the presentation. Suddenly Dr. Glazos stretched out his hand and shook hands with me. He wished me Merry Christmas and gave me a complimentary card for a Latte at the Second Cup coffee shop. I was happily surprised, particularly as Dr. Glazos, who is always serious at work and never smiles when he is working, actually smiled. I was tempted to invite him to try my Wonton soup but I was afraid the other nurses would be annoyed.

7   I suddenly realized it was already fifteen minutes past eleven. I had only fifteen minutes to get my soup ready. I asked Aurora, who was in my cubicle, to keep an eye on my patient while I sneaked out to the pantry to start cooking. The water in the rice cooker

always takes a long time to boil but it seemed to take even longer this time. At half past eleven, all these hungry nurses started coming in to the nurses' lounge, hoping to taste someone else's food. Finally at twenty to twelve my soup was ready to serve. It was really very presentable with white Wonton floating in the hot chicken broth which was decorated with green onions and cherry blossom shaped carrots. As I looked at it, I was reminded of water lilies floating on a pond in the early morning mist. The comforting aroma wafted through the lounge. I compared my soup to the other dishes on the table, and felt proud.

8   Suddenly I started to worry again. The first round nurses were not too enthusiastic about my soup. Sally ate only two Wontons instead of the three that everybody usually takes. Brenda and the two other nurses did not even touch the soup because they did not eat pork which was the main ingredient of the Wonton. Disappointed, I worried that the whole bowl of Wonton would be wasted. I decided the only way to hide this embarrassment was to eat more myself so that there would not be too much left behind. I was so full afterwards that I did not have enough room to sample the dishes the other nurses brought in. When the first group of nurses finished their lunches, the second group had their turn. I went back to the unit and waited anxiously for their response. I felt like I was waiting for the results of an examination.

9   To my surprise again, this group of nurses nearly cleaned out the Wonton soup. They complimented me on how delicious it was, saying that they had never tasted such good Wonton before. Thrilled, I promised to copy down my recipe for them. My recipe became a hot topic around the unit.

10   I was surprised that making a bowl of soup kept me from being lonely when my husband was away and helped to me to socialize with my co-workers. In fact the whole experience was full of surprises. I think next year I will put a spring of holly in the soup and call it Christmas Surprise.

DISCUSSION QUESTIONS

1. Identify the point of view of the narrative.
2. List the words, phrases, and clauses that serve as time signals. What has the writer accomplished by using them?

3. This narrative spans about a week. At what points has the writer omitted events? Why?

4. What larger point does the narrative make? Is it stated or implied?

SUGGESTIONS FOR WRITING

1. **Write a personal narrative about an experience that**

   a. altered either your opinion of a friend or acquaintance or your views about some important matter;

   b. taught you a lesson or something about human nature;

   c. caused you great sorrow or joy; or

   d. exposed you to the danger of serious injury or death.

Keep in mind all the key narrative elements: purpose, action, conflict, point of view, key events, and dialogue.

2. **A *maxim* is a concise statement of a generally recognized truth. Noting the key elements above, write a personal narrative that illustrates one of the following maxims or another that your instructor approves:**

   a. A little learning is a dangerous thing.

   b. The more things change, the more they stay the same.

   c. It's an ill wind that blows no good.

   d. Don't judge a book by its cover.

Sometimes writers create narratives by weaving together information from different sources. When developing a narrative about some childhood experience, you might supplement your own recollections by asking relatives and friends to supply details that you've forgotten or clear up points that have become hazy. A police officer investigating an accident questions witnesses, examines physical evidence, and uses the findings to draft an accurate report.

Integrating material from several sources into a coherent piece of writing is called *synthesis*. When you synthesize, you reflect on ideas you have found in various sources, establish on your own the connections among those ideas, and then determine how the ideas and connections can advance the purpose of your writing. Thus, synthesis features independent thinking in which *you* evaluate, select, and use the material of others—which, of course, must be properly documented—to further your own purpose. Although synthesis can be challenging and does call for judgment on your part, following an effective procedure can help ensure success. Start by jotting down the main points of information from your sources and identifying where those points agree. Sometimes accounts of the same event differ. A friend's memory of your childhood experience may differ markedly from your own. A police officer may find that two witnesses disagree about how an accident happened. When you encounter this type of contradiction, you'll need to weigh each position carefully in order to determine the most believable account. Then, as in developing any narrative, arrange your material in a pattern that helps make your point.

Let's say, for example, that you're narrating the history of a suburban housing development for low-income families built on land that was formerly owned by a nearby chemical plant and later was found to be contaminated by toxic chemicals. Company officials admit that wastes were buried there but insist that the chemicals were properly contained and posed absolutely no health threat. After stating the company's position, you present the findings of government investigators who analyzed soil samples from the site. These findings revealed that the containers were corroded and leaking and that the wastes included chemicals that attack the nervous system, as well as highly toxic herbicides designed for chemical warfare operations. You conclude that the company is responsible for the serious health problems that now plague the people living in the housing development. Note how the strategy of presenting the company's position early in the narrative lends added force to the point that shapes your writing—company accountability for the health of the housing development's residents.[*]

SUGGESTIONS FOR WRITING

1. Read "Lend Me Your Light" (page 399) and "I Have a Dream" (page 516) and then write a narrative that relates an experience of a particular ethnic group and incorporates material from either of the two essays.

2. Take notes from several different newspaper accounts of an important or controversial event and write an account of the event that includes your notes.

---

[*]Because synthesis involves using several sources, including information from published ones, it is important to read the sections on card catalogues and periodical indexes in Chapter 19 and those on handling quotations and avoiding plagiarism in Chapter 20. As always, follow your instructor's guidelines for documenting sources.

Description: Presenting Impressions

> The sound of hot dogs sizzling on a grease-spattered grill gave way
> to the whirling buzz of a cotton-candy machine. Fascinated, we
> watched as the white cardboard cone was slowly transformed into a
> pink, fluffy cloud. Despite their fiberglass appearance, the sticky
> puffs dissolved on my tongue into a sugar-like sweetness. Soon our
> faces and hands were gummed with a sticky mess.

You are there. Seeing, hearing, touching, tasting. This is one student writer's *description* of a small segment of a county fair. Effective description creates sharply etched word pictures of objects, persons, scenes, events, or situations. Sensory impressions—reflecting sight, sound, taste, smell, and touch—form the backbone of descriptive writing. Often, they build toward one dominant impression that the writer wants to evoke.

The human mind is not merely a logical thinking machine. Because of our emotional makeup, we react with shock to a photo of a battered victim of child abuse. We feel stirrings of nostalgia upon hearing a song from our past. We smile with satisfaction when quenching our summer thirst with tart sips from a tall, frosted drink. Responses like these, as much as the ability to think rationally, help define who we are.

Many occasions call for description. Your chemistry instructor might ask you to characterize the appearance and odour of a series of substances prepared in the laboratory; your art instructor might want you to describe a painting; your hospitality management instructor might have you portray an appealing banquet room. On the job, a realtor might write a glowing advertisement to sell a house; a nurse might describe the postoperative status of a surgical incision; and a journalist might describe the eruption of a volcano. All are attempts to capture the world through description.

■ Purpose

Sometimes description stands alone; sometimes it enriches other writing. It appears in histories and biographies, fiction and poetry, journalism and advertising, and occasionally even in technical writing. Some descriptions merely create images and mood, as when a writer paints a word picture of a boggy, fog-shrouded moor. But description can also stimulate understanding or lead to action. A historian may juxtapose the splendour of French court life with the wretchedness of a Paris slum to help explain the French Revolution.

Description will provide effective backup for the writing you do in your composition classes, helping you to drive home your points vividly.

■ Sensory Impressions

Precise sensory impressions begin with close physical or mental observation. If you can re-examine your subject, do it. If not, recall it to mind; then capture its features with appropriate words. When you can't find the right words, try a comparison. Ask yourself what your subject (or part of it) might be likened to. Does it smell like a rotten egg? A ripe cantaloupe? Burning rubber? Does it sound like a high sigh? A soft rustle? To come across, the comparison must be accurate and familiar. If the reader has never smelled a rotten egg, the point is lost.

Most descriptions blend several sense impressions rather than focusing on just one. In the following excerpt, Mark Twain, reminiscing about his uncle's farm, includes all five. As you read it, note which impressions are most effective.

> As I have said, I spent some part of every year at the farm until I was twelve or thirteen years old. The life which I led there with my cousins was full of charm, and so is the memory of it yet. I can call back the solemn twilight and mystery of the deep woods, the earthy smells, the faint odors of the wild flowers, the sheen of rain-washed foliage, the rattling clatter of drops when the wind shook the trees, the far-off hammering of woodpeckers and the muffled drumming of wood pheasants in the remoteness of the forest, the snapshot glimpses of disturbed wild creatures scurrying through the grass—I can call it all back and make it as real as it ever was, and as blessed. I can call back the prairie, and its loneliness and peace, and a vast hawk hanging motionless in the sky, with his wings spread wide and the blue of the vault showing through the fringe of their end feathers. I can see the woods in their autumn dress, the oaks purple, the hickories washed with gold, the maples and the sumachs luminous with crimson fires, and I can hear the rustle made by the fallen

leaves as we plowed through them. I can see the blue clusters of wild grapes hanging among the foliage of the saplings, and I remember the taste of them and the smell. I know how the wild blackberries looked, and how they tasted, and the same with the pawpaws, the hazelnuts, and the persimmons; and I can feel the thumping rain, upon my head, of hickory nuts and walnuts when we were out in the frosty dawn to scramble for them with the pigs, and the gusts of wind loosed them and sent them down. I know the stain of blackberries, and how pretty it is, and I know the stain of walnut hulls, and how little it minds soap and water, also what grudged experience it had of either of them. I know the taste of maple sap, and when to gather it, and how to arrange the troughs and the delivery tubes, and how to boil down the juice, and how to hook the sugar after it is made, also how much better hooked sugar tastes than any that is honestly come by, let bigots say what they will.

Mark Twain, *Autobiography*

EXERCISE   *Spend some time in an environment such as one of the following. Concentrate on one sense at a time. Begin by observing what you see; then jot down the precise impressions you receive. Now do the same for impressions of touch, taste, smell, and sound.*

1. The woods in the early morning
2. A city intersection
3. A restaurant or cafeteria
4. A scenic spot under a full moon
5. A holiday gathering

■ Dominant Impression

Skillful writers select and express sensory perceptions in order to create a *dominant impression*—an overall mood or feeling such as joy, anger, terror, or distaste. This impression may be identified or left unnamed for the reader to deduce. Whatever the choice, a verbal picture of a storm about to strike, for example, might be crafted to evoke feelings of fear by describing sinister masses of slaty clouds, cannon salvos of thunder, blinding lightning flashes, and viciously swirling wind-caught dust.

The following paragraph establishes a sense of security as the dominant impression:

A marvelous stillness pervaded the world, and the stars together with the serenity of their rays seemed to shed upon the earth the assurance of everlasting security. The young moon recurved, and shining low in the west, was like a slender shaving thrown up from a bar of gold, and the Arabian Sea, smooth and cool to the eye like a sheet of ice, extended its perfect level to the perfect circle of a dark horizon. The propeller turned without a check, as though its beat had been part of the scheme of a safe universe; and on each side of the *Patna* two folds of water, permanent and sombre on the unwrinkled shimmer, enclosed within their straight and diverging ridges a few white swirls of foam bursting in a low hiss, a few wavelets, a few ripples, a few undulations that, left behind, agitated the surface of the sea for an instant after the passage of the ship, subsided splashing gently, calmed down at last into the circular stillness of water and sky with the black speck of the moving hull remaining everlastingly in its centre.

Joseph Conrad, Lord Jim

The first sentence directly identifies the impression, "security," to which the "stillness" and the "serenity" contribute. Other details also do their part: the "smooth" sea, the "perfect circle" of the horizon, the "safe universe," the quick calming of the water, and the moving hull "everlastingly" in the centre of water and sky.

> **EXERCISE**   *Select one of the following topics and write a paragraph that evokes a particular dominant impression. Omit any details that run counter to your aim.*
>
> 1. A multi-alarm fire
> 2. A repair facility (automobile, appliance, and so on)
> 3. A laboratory
> 4. Some aspect of summer in a particular place
> 5. Some landmark on your university or college campus

■ Vantage Point

You may write a description from either a fixed or a moving vantage point. A fixed observer remains in one place and reports only what can be perceived from there. Here is how Emily Carr describes a native carving she encounters in a remote coastal village.

> Her head and trunk were carved out of, or rather into, the bole of a great red cedar. She seemed to be part of the tree itself, as if she had grown there at its heart, and the carver had only chipped away the outer wood so that you could see her. Her arms were spliced and socketed to the trunk, and were flung wide in a circling, compelling movement. Her breasts were two eagleheads, fiercely carved. That much, and the column of her great neck, and her strong chin, I had seen when I slithered to the ground beneath her. Now I saw her face.
>
> The eyes were two rounds of black, set in wider rounds of white, and placed in deep sockets under wide, black eyebrows. Their fixed stare bored into me as if the very life of the old cedar looked out, and it seemed that the voice of the tree itself might have burst from that great round cavity, with projecting lips, that was her mouth. Her ears were round, and stuck out to catch all sounds. The salt air had not dimmed the heavy red of her trunk and arms and thighs. Her hands were black, with blunt fingertips painted a dazzling white. I stood looking at her for a long, long time.

Emily Carr, "D'Sonoqua"

A moving observer views things from a number of positions, signalling changes in location with phrases such as "moving through the turnstile" and "as I walked around the corner." Below, Michael Ondaatje takes us along with a young boy as he goes out of his home in winter.

One winter night when he was eleven years old, Patrick walked out from the long kitchen. A blue moth had pulsed on the screen, bathed briefly in light, and then disappeared into darkness. He did not think it would go far. He picked up the kerosene lamp and went out. A rare winter moth. It was scuffing along the snow as if injured and he could follow it easily. In the back garden he lost it, the turquoise moth arcing up into the sky beyond the radius of the kerosene light. What was a moth doing at this time of year? He hadn't seen any for months. It may have been bred in the chicken coop. He put the hurricane lamp onto a rock and looked over the fields. Among the trees in the distance he saw what looked like more bugs. Lightning bugs within the trees by the river. But this was winter! He moved forward with the lamp.

The distance was further than he thought. Snow above the ankles of his untied boots. One hand in a pocket, the other holding a lamp. And a moon lost in the thickness of clouds so it did not shine a path for him towards the trees. All that gave direction was a blink of amber. Already he knew it could not be lightning bugs.

Michael Ondaatje, *In the Skin of a Lion*

The phrase "walked out" tells the reader that Patrick will be a moving observer. The lamp which Patrick carries reveals a progressively widening picture—first the moth, then the fields and trees, and what look like lightning bugs. The reader, like Patrick, has no idea what the lightning bugs are until later in the story, when Patrick gets to the bank of the frozen river, and sees skaters on the river holding flaming cattails.

Whatever your vantage point, fixed or moving, report only what would be apparent to someone on the scene. If you describe how a distant mountain looks from a balcony, don't suddenly leap to a description of a mountain flower; you couldn't see it from your vantage point.

EXERCISE

1. **Writing as a fixed observer, describe in a paragraph your impressions of one of the following. Be sure to indicate your vantage point.**

   a. A hotel lobby two weeks before Christmas

   b. The scene following a traffic accident

   c. A classroom when the bell rings

   d. A campus lounge

   e. An office

2. **Writing as a moving observer, describe in a paragraph or two your impressions as you do one of the following things. Clearly signal your movements to the reader.**

   a. Walk from one class to another

   b. Shop in a grocery store

   c. Walk from your home to the corner

   d. Cross a long bridge

   e. Go through a ticket line and enter a theatre, auditorium, or sports arena

Selection of Details

Effective description depends as much on exclusion as on inclusion. Don't try to pack every possible detail into your paper by providing an inventory of, for example, a room's contents or a natural setting's elements. Such an approach shows only that you can see, not write. Instead, select details that deliberately point toward the mood or feeling you intend to create. Read the following student description of nighttime skiing:

> The glowing orb of the moon, shedding its pale, silvery radiance on the ski slope, seemed to cast a spell. Crystal iridescence of powdered snow twinkled in the night. Shadows cast by the skiers appeared as mysterious silhouettes darting in and out among snow-covered trees. The gentle breeze combing through the branches created a lulling musical chant that drifted into my head, taking control. Delicate snowflakes danced by, kissed me on the face, and seemed to beckon me up the hill.
>
> Sue Mutch

This writer evokes a sense of enchantment by noting the "pale, silvery radiance" of the moon, the "crystal iridescence" of the snow, the "mysterious silhouettes" of the skiers, and the "lulling musical chant" of the wind. She ignores such details as the boisterous snatches of conversation among the skiers, the crunch of ski poles digging into the snow, and the creaking towline moving to the top of the slope. Mentioning these things would detract from the desired mood.

Arrangement of Details

Description, like any other writing, must have a clear pattern of organization to guide the reader and help you fulfill your purpose. Often some spatial arrangement works nicely. You might, for example, move systematically from top to bottom, left to right, front to back, nearby to far away, or the reverse of these patterns. To describe Saturday night at the hockey game, you might start with the crowded parking lot; move into the bustling arena; and finally zoom in on the sights and sounds of the rink. Or if you wanted to highlight the surroundings rather than the central event, the order could be reversed. Going another route, you might start with some striking central feature and then branch out to the things around it. To capture the centre of a mall, you might first describe its ornate fountain illuminated with flashing, multicoloured lights, shift to the reflection of the lights on the skylight above, and end by portraying the surrounding store fronts.

Sometimes a description follows a time sequence. A writer might, for example, portray the changes in a woodland setting as winter gives way to spring and spring, in turn, yields to summer.

◼ Ethical Issues

Imagine a police description of an auto accident that misstated the length of a car's skid marks or failed to note the icy patches of road at the scene. It might cost a blameless driver a heavy fine and a steep increase in auto insurance premiums. Imagine your disappointment and anger if you booked a weekend at a distant resort only to find it situated on an algae-covered pond instead of the beautiful lake described in the brochure. Imagine your irritation if a going-out-of-business sale described as "fabulous" turned out to offer only 10 percent price reductions. Clearly inaccurate descriptions create a wide range of undesirable consequences. Ask yourself these questions about your description:

- Would readers find my writing credible if they were at the scene?

- Have I given readers adequate clues so that they will recognize any deliberate exaggeration?

- Will the description deceive readers in a harmful way?

- You have an ethical obligation to present a reasonably accurate portrayal of your topic.

◼ Writing a Description

Planning and Drafting the Description

If you're choosing your own topic, always select one that is familiar. Don't describe a ski run at Jasper National Park or the bridge from Prince Edward Island if you've never seen either one. Instead, opt for some place where you've actually worked or a locale you've recently visited. If you keep a journal, thumb through it for possible leads.

For each potential topic that surfaces, ask yourself the following questions. They will direct your attention to matters you'll need to address.

What do I want to accomplish by writing this description? create one or more impressions? help the reader understand something? persuade the reader to act?

Who is my audience and why would this topic interest them?

What dominant impression will I develop?

To help gather and organize support for your topic, pose these additional questions:

What details should I include?

What sensory impressions are associated with each detail? (Jot down any words that you feel will best convey the impressions.)

How does each detail contribute to the dominant impression?

What sequence should I follow in presenting my impressions? (Map out the sequence, setting up a 1-2-3 listing or possibly a paragraph-by-paragraph plan.)

After brainstorming a list of potential details, you might use branching (see pages 21–22), to start accumulating sensory impressions. Here's how Kim Swiger, who wrote the passage below, used this technique:

Begin your paper with an introduction that eases the reader into your topic. You might, for example, provide a historical overview, ask a provocative question, or snare the reader's attention with an arresting statement.

Develop each major feature in one or more paragraphs. Present each feature in the order you've mapped out. To ensure that the reader follows your thoughts, clearly signal any shifts in vantage point or time. As you write, aim for vivid, original language. We've all encountered writers who tell us that raindrops "pitter-patter," clouds are "fleecy white," and the sun is "a ball of fire." Such stale, worn-out language does nothing to sharpen our vision of the rain, the clouds, or the sun. In contrast, read how one student describes the sounds in her kitchen at breakfast time:

Sure signs of a new day are the sounds in the kitchen as breakfast is prepared. The high sigh of the gas just before it whooshes into flame and settles into a whispering hum blends with the gurgling of the water for the morning coffee. Soon the gloop, gloop, gloop of the coffee sets up a perky beat. Then in mingles the crackle of creamy butter on a hot skillet and the shush of an egg added to the pan. Ribbons of bacon start to sizzle in the spitting grease. The soft rustle of plastic as bread is removed from its wrapper contributes to the medley. The can opener whirs, and the orange juice concentrate drops with a splat into the blender, which whizzes together the orange cylinder and splashed-in water. For minutes after the blender stops, bubbles of various sizes fizz.

Kim Burson Swiger

You are there in the kitchen, hearing the carefully selected and freshly described sounds.

A word of caution about going overboard—stringing together a chain of adjectives without considering the effect on a reader. Think how you'd react if told that

> A dented, cylindrical, silver-grey, foul-smelling, overloaded garbage can sat in the alley.

As you can see, more than the garbage can is overloaded here. Resist the temptation to inject similar sentences into your description. Carefully examine your adjectives and eliminate those that don't advance your purpose.

End your paper by pulling your material together in some way. If you've created an impression or mood, you might offer your reaction to it. If you want your reader to understand something, you might spell your message out. If you wish to persuade, you might urge some action.

Revising the Description

As you revise, apply the guidelines in Chapter 3 and ask the following questions:

Have I written with a clear sense of purpose and audience in mind?

Have I conveyed how my topic looks, sounds, feels, tastes, or smells? Would comparisons or more precise descriptive terms help convey my perceptions?

Have I evoked one dominant impression? Can I strengthen this impression by adding certain selected details? by eliminating details that detract from the impression?

Have I used an appropriate vantage point? If the observer is moving, have I signalled changes in location? Have I included only details that would be visible to the observer?

Have I arranged my details in an order appropriate to the topic?

Example Student Essay of Description

The Big One

Rebecca Mutch

1   With a final crack of a bat and a lofting fly ball, baseball ended for the year. The last swirl of water gurgling down the drain of the community pool marked the end of its season. These closings marked the beginning of another event, the county fair. This season I was elected to take my little brother on a ride—"the big one," in his words.

2   Once again I found myself in the familiar grass lot bordering the fairground. The fair itself was completely surrounded by a fence. No one could see what was inside. The only clues were carried in the wind. Muffled echoes of carnies hawking their games, excited squeals of children, and blaring carnival tunes, frequently punctuated by sharp, crackling static, blended with the tantalizing fragrance of popcorn, the spicy aroma of pizza, and the sweet molasses smell of caramel corn.

3   As we entered the main gate and handed our tickets to the men whose baskets already overflowed with torn stubs, my eyes immediately confirmed what my ears and nose had already reported. In one step we had gone from a semiquiet and relaxed world into an ever-revolving one. Dazzling lights, blinking out of control, seemed to flirt with anyone and everyone. Children, their white T-shirts covered with splotches of chocolate and mustard, dashed ahead of their parents and returned shortly, screaming about the giant bear that waited ahead. The distant, shuffling crowds appeared as moving shadows, their features blurred.

4   The little tug on my sleeve reminded me of that big ride that waited ahead. The path up the midway, packed with a cushion of sawdust, was strewn with empty popcorn boxes, scraps of papers, and crumpled cigarette packages.

5   Game booths and food huts, their pennants whipping and snapping in the wind, dotted the path on both sides and formed two long serpent-like strings of pleasure. BB's clinked against tin objects in the shooting gallery. Hawkers with greased hands and pudgy fingers tried to lure suckers toward their gaudy booths. A backboard thudded and a hoop clanked as still another young man tried to win the enormous purple teddy bear that smiled down mockingly from its perch above. The sound of hot dogs sizzling on a grease-spattered grill gave way to the whirling buzz of a cotton-candy machine. Fascinated, we watched as the white cardboard cone was slowly transformed into a pink, fluffy cloud. Despite their fibreglass appearance, the sticky puffs dissolved on my tongue into a sugar-like sweetness. Soon our faces and hands were gummed with a sticky mess.

6   We scuffled along with the rhythm of the crowd and before long arrived at those metallic contraptions of nuts and bolts—the rides. The sounds of metal clanging and banging filled the air. Sparks

shot out from where the metal pieces slapped together. Swirling and whirling, these pieces caught the reflection of the neon lights and, together with the sparks, produced a world of spectrum colours.

7   This was it. The Ferris wheel stood towering before us. As the seat gently swayed, we waited for the ride to begin. The motor belched and then slowly started to turn; goose bumps formed on my brother's bare arms, and his eyes grew larger as the ride picked up speed. The fairground was soon a kaleidoscope of fantastic images and colours. The wind whipped through my hair and snapped it back, stinging my face at times. Both of us were screaming uncontrollably. Suddenly, with no apparent slowdown, the ride was over, and we made our way dizzily to the car.

8   My brother talked about the big one for weeks. For me it brought back many fond memories and let me, just for an evening, be a child again.

DISCUSSION QUESTIONS

1. This description features a moving observer. Where are the writer's movements indicated?
2. Point out details that appeal to each of the five senses.
3. Reread paragraph 7. Identify perceptual observations used to describe the Ferris wheel ride.
4. How is the essay organized? Given its purpose, why is this pattern effective?

SUGGESTIONS FOR WRITING
Choose one of the following topics or another that your instructor approves for an essay of description. Create a dominant impression by using carefully chosen, well-organized details observed from an appropriate vantage point. Try to write so that the reader actually experiences your description.

1. Holiday shopping
2. A rock concert
3. An exercise class
4. A graduation audience
5. A shopping centre
6. A pet store or zoo
7. A busy city intersection
8. The view from your bedroom window
9. Getting caught in a storm
10. Your house after a party

The Critical Edge

Most of us know that any two people are likely to see and describe the same object, place, or event differently. A motorist whose car broke down in the desert would note the impossible distances, the barrenness, the absence of human life, the blazing sun. A biologist who was well-supplied with food and water would see a rich ecosystem with a wide variety of plant life and an interesting population of insects and animals. Each would produce a different description that served a different purpose. The motorist would emphasize the gruelling heat and desolation to establish the danger of the situation. The biologist would provide a detailed description of the plants, insects, and animals to advance scientific understanding of the area.

As a writer, you may occasionally need to synthesize (see pages 64–65) information supplied by others when creating your own description. Suppose that you're writing a paper about the old growth forests of Vancouver Island. You may read a naturalist's description of the ancient, rare species of trees and how the forest provides a habitat for much unique wildlife. You might also read a lumber industry study indicating that the trees are an important economic resource. You might even uncover an account by an early explorer that captures the emotions aroused by the discovery of the forest.

Armed with these and other descriptions, you could create a composite picture that captures all the different perspectives. You might start by offering the views of the Native Canadian forest inhabitants, then detail the towering majesty of the trees and the abundance of game as reported by early explorers. Next, you might turn to the accounts of early farmers, who regarded the forest as an obstacle to be cleared away, and continue by presenting the view of the forest as a lumber resource, perhaps including a description of a depleted lumbering site. To end the paper, you might note how contemporary conservationists view what remains of the forest. Collectively, this information would offer a stark portrayal of the near-total destruction of a splendid natural resource and by implication argue for preserving what is left. While this kind of writing task seems daunting, you can simplify it if you take up one perspective at a time.

Because different people are likely to see and describe the same object, place, or event differently, it's important to look critically at any description you consider for your paper. When you finish reading, ask yourself what features might have been omitted and what another slant on the material might have yielded. To illustrate, in "Lend Me Your Light," Rohinton Mistry describes the repugnant smell of his school lunchroom:

> The drillhall would be filled with a smell that is hard to forget, thick as swill, while the aromas of four hundred steaming lunches started to mingle. The smell must have soaked into the very walls and ceiling, there to age and rancify. No matter what the hour of the day, that hot and dank grotto of a drillhall smelled stale and sickly, the way a vomit-splashed room does even after it is cleaned up. (See paragraph 4, pages 399–403.)

If Mistry had found the smell appealing, he might have chosen to describe the fragrant smell of steaming rice or the refreshing sweetness of *chai* at the end of morning studies. Clearly, description demands choices. Different impressions, varying emphases can be selected. And like any other writer, you should carefully consider the details and slant of any description you write.[*]

SUGGESTIONS FOR WRITING

1. Rewrite a shortened version of an essay such as "Lend Me Your Light" by building on the original details to create a different emphasis.
2. Interview several students to learn their impressions of your campus and weave those impressions into a descriptive essay.

[*]Because this type of paper includes information from published sources, it is important to read the sections on card catalogues and periodical indexes in Chapter 19 and those on handling quotations and avoiding plagiarism in Chapter 20. As always, follow your instructor's guidelines for documenting sources.

Process Analysis: Explaining How

"Hey Bill, I'd like you to take a look at Mr. Gorgerise's car. He's really fuming. Says the engine's burning too much oil, running rough, and getting poor mileage. Check it out and see what you can find."

Bill begins by removing the spark plugs, hooking a remote-control starter to the starter in the car, and grounding the ignition to prevent the car's starting accidentally. Next, he fits a compression pressure gauge into the spark plug hole by cylinder number one, starts the engine, and reads and records the pressure; then he does the same for each of the other cylinders. Finally, he compares the readings with one another and the automaker's engine specs. The verdict? An excessively worn engine that needs rebuilding. Bill has carried out a *process*, just one among many that fill his workdays.

As we pursue our affairs, we perform processes almost constantly, ranging from such daily rituals as brewing a pot of coffee to taking a picture, preparing for a date, or replacing a light switch. Often we share our special technique for doing something—for example, making chicken cacciatore—by passing it on to a friend.

Many popular publications feature process analyses that help readers to sew zippers in garments, build canoes, live within their means, and improve their wok technique. Process analysis also frequently helps you meet the writing demands of your courses. A political science instructor may ask you to explain how your premier won an election. Another instructor may call for directions relating to some process in your field—for example, analyzing a chemical compound, taking fingerprints, or obtaining a blood sample.

On the job, a greenhouse crew leader may provide summer employees with directions for planting various kinds of shrubs and flowers. A sanitation department technician may write a brochure telling city residents how to get paper, glass, and metal garbage ready for recycling.

■ Kinds of Process Analysis Papers

Process papers fall into two categories: those intended for readers who will perform the process and those intended to explain the process for nonperformers. Papers in either category can range from highly technical and sophisticated to non-specialized and simple.

Processes for Readers Who Will Perform Them   The audience for these papers may be technical and professional personnel who need the information to carry out a work-related task or individuals who want to perform the process for themselves.

A how-to-do-it paper must include everything the reader needs to know in order to ensure a successful outcome. Its directions take the form of polite commands, often addressing readers directly as "you." This approach helps involve readers in the explanation and emphasizes that the directions must, not merely should, be followed. Here is an illustration:

> To prepare a bacterial smear for staining, first use an inoculating loop to place a drop of distilled water on a clean glass microscope slide. Next, pass the loop and the opening of the tube containing the bacterial culture to be examined through a Bunsen burner flame to sterilize them. From the tube, remove a small bit of culture with the loop, and rub the loop in the drop of water on the slide until the water covers an area one and one-half inches long and approximately the width of the slide. Next, reflame the opening of the culture tube to prevent contamination of the culture, and then plug it shut. Allow the smear to air dry, and then pass the slide, smear side up, through the flame of the burner until it is warm to the touch. The dried smear should have a cloudy, milky-white appearance.
>
> Darryl Williams

Processes for Readers Who Won't Perform Them   These kinds of papers may tell how some process is or was performed or how it occurs or occurred. A paper might, for instance, detail the stages of grief, the procedure involved in an operation, the role of speech in the development of children's thinking, or the sequence involved in shutting down a nuclear reactor. These papers serve many purposes—for example, to satisfy popular curiosity; to point out the importance, difficulty, or danger of a process; or to cast a process in a favourable or unfavourable light. Even though the writers of such papers often explain their topic in considerable detail, they do not intend to provide enough information for readers to carry out the process.

Papers of this sort present the needed information without using polite commands. Sometimes a noun, a pronoun like *I, we, he, she,* or *it,* or a noun–pronoun combination identifies the performer(s). At other times, the performer remains unidentified. Three examples follow.

Pronouns Identify Performer

Thus, when I now approach a stack of three two-inch cinder blocks to attempt a breaking feat, I do not set myself to "try hard," or to summon up all my strength. Instead I relax, sinking my awareness into my belly and legs, feeling my connection with the ground. I breathe deeply, mentally directing the breath through my torso, legs, and arms. I imagine a line of force coming up from the ground through my legs, down one arm, and out through the stone slabs, and down again into the ground, penetrating to the center of the earth. I do not focus any attention on the objects to be broken. Although when I am lifting or holding them in a normal state of consciousness the blocks seem tremendously dense, heavy, and hard, in the course of my one- or two-minute preparation their reality seems to change, as indeed the reality of the whole situation changes. . . . When I make my final approach to the bricks, if I regard them at all they seem light, airy, and friendly; they do not have the insistent inner drive in them that I do.

Don Ethan Miller, "A State of Grace: Understanding the Martial Arts"

Noun–Pronoun Combination Identifies Performers

Termites are even more extraordinary in the way they seem to accumulate intelligence as they gather together. Two or three termites in a chamber will begin to pick up pellets and move them from place to place, but nothing comes of it; nothing is built. As more join in, they seem to reach a critical mass, a quorum, and the thinking begins. They place pellets atop pellets, then throw up columns and beautiful, curving, symmetrical arches, and the crystalline architecture of vaulted chambers is created. It is not known how they communicate with each other, how the chains of termites building one column know when to turn toward the crew on the adjacent column, or how, when the time comes, they manage the flawless joining of the arches. The stimuli that set them off at the outset, building collectively instead of shifting things about, may be pheromones released when they reach committee size. They react as if alarmed. They become agitated, excited, and then they begin working, like artists.

Lewis Thomas, "Societies as Organisms"

Performer Unidentified

The analyzer was adjusted so the scale read zero and was connected to the short sampling tube, which had previously been inserted into the smokestack. The sample was taken by depressing the bulb the requisite number of times, and the results were then

read and recorded. The procedure was repeated, this time using the
long sampling tube and sampling through the fire door.

Charles Finnie

> **EXERCISE** *Examine your favourite newspaper or magazine for examples of process analysis. Bring them to class for group discussion of which kind each represents and the writer's purpose.*

■ Ethical Issues

Unclear, misleading, incomplete, or erroneous instructions written for someone
to follow can spawn a wide range of unwanted consequences. Often frustration and
lost time are the only results. Sometimes, though, the fallout is more serious, as in
the case of a lab explosion. And in extreme cases, the outcome can be potentially
catastrophic, as when an accident occurs in a nuclear power plant. As writers, we
have an ethical obligation to write clear and complete instructions. To help you do
this, ask and answer the following questions when you're writing a process that
the reader will perform.

- Have I used clear and unambiguous language so the reader will not encounter unnecessary frustration and inconvenience?

- Have I clearly indicated any requirements such as time needed or additional supplies that will have to be purchased?

- Have I clearly warned readers about any possible harm they could face?

■ Writing a Process Analysis

Planning and Drafting the Process Analysis

As always, when the choice is yours, select a familiar topic. If you're not the outdoor
type and prefer a Holiday Inn to the north woods, don't try to explain how to
plan a camp-out. Muddled, inaccurate, and inadequate information will result.
On the other hand, if you've pitched many a tent, you might want to share your
technique with your readers.

Finding a suitable topic should be easy. But if you do hit a snag, turn to the
strategies on pages 13–20. In any event, answer the following questions for each potential choice:

Will the reader find the process important, interesting, or useful?

Should I provide directions for the reader to follow, explain how the process takes
place, or explain how others perform it?

Can I explain the process adequately within any assigned length?

Processes for Readers Who Will Perform Them   If you will develop a process for readers to follow, ponder this second set of questions to help you accumulate the details you'll need:

What separate actions make up the process? (Be especially careful not to omit any action that is obvious to you but wouldn't be to your reader. Such an oversight can ruin your reader's chances of success.)

What is the reason for each action?

What warnings will the reader need in order to perform the process properly and safely?

When you have your answers, record them in a chart similar to this one:

Action	Reason for Action	Warning
First action	First reason	First warning
Second action	Second reason	Second warning

Sometimes a reason will be so obvious no mention is necessary, and many actions won't require warnings. When you've completed the chart, review it carefully and supply any missing information. If necessary, make a revised chart.

Once you've listed the actions, group related ones together to form steps, the major subdivisions of the procedure. The following actions constitute the first step—getting the fire going—of a paper explaining how to grill hamburgers:

remove grill rack   light briquets
stack charcoal briquets   spread out briquets

EXERCISE

1. **Develop a complete list of the actions involved in one of the following processes; then arrange them in an appropriate order.**

   a. Baking bread

   b. Assembling or repairing some common household device

   c. Carrying out a process related to sports

   d. Breaking a bad habit

2. **Examine your favourite newspaper or magazine for examples of process analysis. Bring them to class for group discussion of how they illustrate step-by-step directions.**

Start your paper by identifying the process and arousing your reader's interest. You might, for example, note the importance of the process, its usefulness, or the ease of carrying it out. Include a list of the items needed to do the work, and note any special conditions required for a successful outcome. The paper explaining how to grill hamburgers might begin as follows:

Grilling hamburgers on an outdoor charcoal grill is a simple process that almost anyone can master. Before starting, you will need a clean grill, charcoal briquets, charcoal lighter fluid and matches, hamburger meat, a plate, a spatula, and some water to put out any flames caused by fat drippings. The sizzling, tasty patties you will have when you finish are a treat that almost everyone will enjoy.

DISCUSSION QUESTION

1. How does the writer try to induce the reader to perform the process?

Use the body of the paper to describe the process in detail, presenting each step in one or more paragraphs so that each is distinct and easily grasped. If you've ever muttered under your breath as you struggled to assemble something that came with fuzzy or inadequate directions, you know the importance of presenting steps clearly, accurately, and fully. Therefore, think carefully and include everything the reader needs to know. Note the reason for any action unless the reason is obvious. Flag any difficult or dangerous step with a cautionary warning. If two steps must be performed simultaneously, tell the reader at the start of the first one. In some places, you may want to tell readers what to expect if they have completed the instructions properly. Feedback lets readers know they are on track or that they need to redo something.

Let's see how the first step of the hamburger-grilling paper might unfold:

The first step is to get the fire going. Remove the grill rack and stack about twenty charcoal briquets in a pyramid shape in the centre of the grill. Stacking allows the briquets to burn off one another and thus produces a hotter fire. Next, squirt charcoal lighter fluid over the briquets. Wait about five minutes so that the fluid has time to soak into the charcoal. Then toss in a lighted match. The flame will burn for a few minutes before it goes out. When this happens, allow the briquets to sit for another fifteen minutes so that the charcoal can start to burn. Once the burning starts, do not squirt on any more lighter fluid. A flame could quickly follow the stream back into the can, causing it to explode. As the briquets begin to turn from pitch black to ash white, spread them out with a stick so that they barely touch one another. Air can then circulate and produce a hot, even fire, the type that makes grilling a success.

DISCUSSION QUESTIONS

1. At what points has the writer provided reasons for doing things?
2. Where has the writer included a warning?

Some processes can unfold in *only one order*. When you shoot a free throw in basketball, for example, you step up to the line and receive the ball before lining up the shot, and you line up the shot before releasing the ball. Other processes can be carried out in an *order of choice*. When you grill hamburgers, you can make the patties either before or after you light the charcoal. If you have an option, use the order that has worked best for you.

End your paper with a few brief remarks that provide some perspective on the process. A summary of the steps often works best for longer, multistep processes. Other popular choices include evaluating the results of the process or discussing its importance. The paper on hamburger grilling notes the results.

> Once the patties are cooked the way you like them, remove them from the grill and place them on buns. Now you are ready to enjoy a mouthwatering treat that you will long remember.
>
> E. M. Pryzblyo

Processes for Readers Who Won't Perform Them Like how-to-do-it processes, those intended for non-doers require you to determine the steps, or for natural processes the stages, that are involved and the function of each before you start to write. In addition, since this type of essay will not enable readers to perform the process, think carefully about why you're presenting the information and let that purpose guide your writing. If, for instance, you're trying to persuade readers that the use of rabbits in tests of the effects of cosmetics should be discontinued, the choices you make in developing your steps should reflect that purpose.

To arouse your reader's interest, you might, among other possible options, begin with a historical overview or a brief summary of the whole process, or you could note its importance. The following introduction to an essay on the aging of stars provides a brief historical perspective:

> Peering through their still-crude telescopes, eighteenth-century astronomers discovered a new kind of object in the night sky that appeared neither as the pinprick of light from a distant star nor as the clearly defined disk of a planet but rather as a mottled, cloudy disk. They christened these objects planetary nebulas, or planetary clouds. . . . Modern astronomers recognize planetary nebulas as the fossil wreckage of dying stars ripped apart by powerful winds.

Because the reader will not perform the process, supply only enough details in the body of the paper to provide an intelligent idea of what the procedure entails. Make sure the reader knows the function of each step or stage and how it fits into the overall process. Present each in one or more paragraphs with clear transitions between the steps or stages. The following excerpt points out the changes that occur as a young star, a red giant, begins the aging process:

> As the bloated star ages, this extended outer atmosphere cools and contracts, then soaks up more energy from the star and again puffs out: with each successive cycle of expansion and contraction the atmosphere puffs out a little farther. Like a massive piston, these pulsations drive the red giant's atmosphere into space in a dense wind that blows with speeds up to 15 miles per second. In as little as 10,000 years some red giants lose an entire sun's worth of matter this way. Eventually this slow wind strips the star down close to its fusion core.

As with processes aimed at performers, end your paper with a few remarks that offer some perspective. You might, for example, evaluate the results of the process, assess its importance, or point out future consequences. The ending of the essay on star aging illustrates the last option:

> The cloud of unanswered questions surrounding planetaries should not obscure the real insight astronomers have recently gained into the extraordinary death of ordinary stars. In a particularly happy marriage of theory and observation, astronomers have discovered our own sun's fate. With the interacting stellar winds model, they can confidently predict the weather about 5 billion years from now; very hot, with *really* strong gusts from the east.
>
> Adam Frank, "Winds of Change"

Revising the Process Analysis

To revise, follow the guidelines in Chapter 3 and pose these questions:

Have I written consistently for someone who will perform the process or someone who will merely follow it?

If my paper is intended for performers, have I included every necessary action? Explained any purpose that is unclear? Warned about any steps that are dangerous or might be performed improperly?

Are my steps presented in an appropriate order? Developed in sufficient detail?

Example Student Essay of Process Analysis

The ABCs of CPR

Kathy Petroski

1   A heart attack, choking, or an electric shock--any of these can stop a person's breathing. The victim, however, need not always die. Many lives that would otherwise be lost can be saved simply by applying the ABCs of CPR--cardiopulmonary resuscitation. Although presence of mind is essential, CPR requires no special equipment. Here's how it is performed. When you are certain that the victim's breathing and pulse have stopped, start CPR immediately. If breathing and circulation aren't restored within five minutes, irreversible brain damage occurs.

2   <u>A</u> stands for opening the airway. Lay the victim in a supine (face up) position on a firm surface. Then tilt the head as far

back as possible by gently lifting the chin with one hand. In an unconscious person, the tongue falls to the back of the throat and blocks the air passages. Hyperextending the head in this fashion pulls the tongue from that position, thus allowing air to pass. At the same time tilt the forehead back with the other hand until the chin points straight upward. The relaxed jaw muscles will then tighten, opening the air passage to the lungs. Remove your hand from the forehead and, using your first two fingers, check the mouth for food, dentures, vomitus, or a foreign object. Remove any obstruction with a sweeping motion. These measures may cause the patient to start breathing spontaneously. If they do not, mouth-to-mouth resuscitation must be started.

3   B stands for breathing. Position one hand on the forehead and pinch the victim's nostrils shut with the index finger and thumb of your other hand. Open your mouth, and place it over the victim's mouth so that a tight seal is formed. Such contact allows air to reach and expand the lungs. If the seal is incomplete, you will hear your own breath escaping. Deliver two quick, full breaths without allowing the victim's lungs to deflate completely between breaths; then remove your mouth and allow him or her to exhale passively. At this point, check the carotid pulse to determine whether the heart is beating. To do so, place the tips of your index and middle fingers laterally into the groove between the trachea (windpipe) and the muscles at the side of the neck. If no pulse is evident, artificial circulation must be started.

4   C means circulation. Locate the lower end of the sternum (breastbone), and move upward approximately the width of two fingers. At this point, firmly apply the heel of one hand, positioning the fingers at right angles to the length of the body and keeping them slanted upward. If the hand is positioned any higher or lower on the sternum, serious internal injuries in the abdomen or chest are possible. Now place the heel of your second hand on top of your first. The fingers may be interlaced or interlocked, but they must not touch the chest, or the force of your compressions may fracture ribs.

5   Keeping your elbows straight and pushing down from the shoulders, apply firm, heavy pressure until the sternum is depressed approximately one and one-half to two inches. Rock

forward and backward in a rhythmic fashion, exerting pressure with the weight of your body. This action squeezes the heart against the immobile spine with enough pressure to pump blood from the left ventricle of the heart into general circulation. Compress the chest, and then immediately release the pressure, fifteen times. Do not, at any point in the cycle, remove your hands from the chest wall. Counting the compressions aloud will help develop a systematic cycle, which is essential for success. When the fifteen have been completed, pinch the nose as described above, seal the victim's mouth with your own, and deliver two quick breaths of air. Then compress the chest an additional fifteen times. Alternate respiration and compression steps, timing yourself so as to deliver approximately eighty compressions per minute.

6   At various intervals, quickly check the effectiveness of your CPR technique. Lift the eyelids and notice if the pupils are constricted—a key sign that the brain is receiving enough oxygen. In addition, if the bluish colour of the victim is decreasing and spontaneous breathing and movement are increasing, the victim has responded favourably.

7   To maximize the chances for survival, do not interrupt this technique for more than five or ten seconds. Continue the ABCs of CPR until competent medical help or life-support equipment arrives.

DISCUSSION QUESTIONS

1. How does the writer use the letters *A*, *B*, and *C* from the CPR technique in this paper?
2. How does the opening paragraph prepare the reader for what follows?
3. Where does the essay indicate the purposes of actions?
4. What order has the writer used? Explain why this order is a good choice.
5. Is the writer merely explaining how the process is carried out, or does she intend for the reader to follow the directions? Defend your answer.

SUGGESTIONS FOR WRITING
Write a process analysis on one of the topics below or one approved by your instructor. The paper may provide instructions for the reader to follow, tell how a process is performed, or describe how a process develops. Prepare a complete list of steps, arrange them in an appropriate order, and follow them as you write the body of your essay.

1. A natural process, such as erosion, that you observe or research
2. The stages of a developing relationship

3. The stages in a technical process such as paper production

4. The stages in a student's adjustment to college

5. Dealing with the bite of a poisonous snake

6. Training a dog or other pet

7. Using a particular computer program

8. The stages in the development of an argument

9. Carrying out a process related to your hobby

10. Preparing your favourite meal

Is there only one way to study effectively, develop a marketing campaign, or cope with a demanding supervisor? No, of course not. As you've already learned, not all processes unfold in a single, predetermined order. The writing process itself illustrates this point.

If you were to think about how you write and talk with other students about their writing processes, you would learn that different writing occasions call for different approaches. When you write a letter to a good friend, you probably spend little or no time on preliminaries but start putting your thoughts on paper as they occur to you. By contrast, other kinds of correspondence, such as inquiry and claim letters, require careful planning, drafting, and perhaps rewriting.

Sometimes the same writing occasion may allow for differing procedures. If you're writing an essay for your English class, you might brainstorm for ideas, develop a detailed outline, rough out a bare-bones draft, and add details as you revise. In talking to other students with the same assignment, you might find that they prefer to write a much longer draft and then whittle it down. Still other students might do very little brainstorming or outlining but a great deal of revising, often making major changes in several drafts. Research papers present a more complex challenge, requiring that the student find and read source material, take notes, and document sources properly. Here again variations are possible: One student might prepare the list of works cited before writing the final draft, while another might perform this task last.

If you decided to synthesize (see pages 64–65) your findings about student writing practices, you would, of course, need to organize your material in some fashion. Perhaps you might focus on the differences that distinguish one writing occasion from another. You could develop each occasion in a separate section by presenting the practices followed by most students while ignoring any variations. A second possibility would be to report different practices used for the same writing occasion, first considering the most common practice and then describing the variations. The result might be likened to a cookbook that gives different recipes for the same dish.

Some important processes have been disputed in print, and if you wanted to investigate them you would need to consult written sources rather than talk to others. Informed disagreements exist about how the human species originated, how language developed, and how children mature. Police officers debate the best way to handle drunks, management experts the best way to motivate employees. When you investigate such controversies, determine which view is supported by the best evidence and seems most reasonable. Then, as a writer, you can present the accounts in an appropriate order and perhaps indicate which one you think merits acceptance.[*]

SUGGESTIONS FOR WRITING

1. Interview several students about the stages they experienced in a developing friendship and write a paper that discusses these stages. Note any discrepancies in the accounts provided by different students.

2. Research a controversial process, such as the extinction of the dinosaurs. After presenting different theories about the process, explain which one seems most plausible and why.

---

[*]If you'll rely on information obtained through interviews, read pages 359–362 in Chapter 21. If you'll rely on published sources, read the sections on card catalogues and periodical indexes in Chapter 19 and those on handling quotations and avoiding plagiarism in Chapter 20. As always, follow your instructor's guidelines for documenting sources.

Illustration: Making Yourself Clear

"It doesn't pay to fight City Hall. For example, my friend Josie . . ."
"Many intelligent people lack common sense. Take Dr. Brandon . . ."
"Top-notch women tennis players are among the biggest moneymakers in sports.
    Last year, for instance, Martina Hingis . . ."

Have you ever noticed how often people use *illustrations* (examples) to clarify general statements?

Ordinary conversations teem with "for example . . ." and "for instance . . .," often in response to a furrowed brow or puzzled look. Sarah McLachlan serves as an excellent example of a singer with broad appeal, and West Edmonton Mall illustrates a multipurpose mall. But illustration is not limited to concrete items. Teachers, researchers, and writers often present an abstract principle or natural law, then supply concrete examples that bring it down to earth. An economics instructor might illustrate compound interest by an example showing how much $100 earning 5 percent interest would appreciate in ten years. Examples can also persuade, as when advertisers trot out typical satisfied users of their products to induce us to buy.

Many classroom writing assignments can benefit from the use of illustration. A paper defining democracy for a political science course will be more effective if it offers examples of several democratic governments. An explanation of irony for a literature course will gain force and clarity through examples taken from stories and poems. Illustration plays a similarly important role in work-related writing. A teacher wanting a bigger student-counselling staff might cite students who need help but can't get it. A union steward wanting a better company safety program might call attention to several recent accidents.

The old saying that a picture is worth a thousand words best explains the popularity of illustration. The concrete is always easier to grasp than the abstract, and examples add flavour to what might otherwise be flat and vague.

■ Selecting Appropriate Examples

Make sure that your examples stay on target, that is, actually support your general statement and do not veer off into an intriguing side issue. For instance, if you're making the point that the lyrics in a rock group's latest CD are not in good taste, don't inject comments on the decadent lifestyle of one of its members. Instead, provide a variety of examples of lyrics that support your claim in order to head off objections that your examples aren't representative.

Furthermore, see that your examples display all the chief features of whatever you're illustrating. Don't offer Sarah McLachlan as an example of a singer with broad appeal unless you know she has many different kinds of fans. Alternatively, consider this example of a hacker, a compulsive computer programmer:

> Bob Shaw, a 15-year-old high-school student, is a case in point. Bob was temporarily pulled off the computers at school when he began failing his other courses. But instead of hitting the books, he continues to sulk outside the computer center, peering longingly through the glass door at the consoles within.
>
> Pale and drawn, his brown hair unkempt, Bob speaks only in monosyllables, avoiding eye contact. In answer to questions about friends, hobbies, school, he merely shrugs or mumbles a few words aimed at his sneakered feet. But when the conversation turns to the subject of computers, he brightens—and blurts out a few full sentences about the computer he's building and the projects he plans.
>
> Dina Ingber, "Computer Addicts"

Clearly, Shaw fits Ingber's description of hackers as programmers who have "a drive so consuming it overshadows nearly every other part of their lives and forms the focal point of their existence."

■ Number of Examples

How many examples will you need? One long one, several fairly brief ones, or a large number of very short ones? Look to your topic for the answer. To illustrate the point that a good nurse must be compassionate, conscientious, and competent, your best bet would probably be one example, since one person must possess all these traits.

When dealing with trends, however, you'll need several examples. To show that parents have been raising children more and more permissively over the last half century, at least three examples are called for: one family from around 1950, a second from about 1975, and a third from the present time. Sometimes topics that do not involve trends require more than one example, as when you demonstrate the sharp differences between Canadian and American attitudes toward handgun registration.

Finally, some topics require a whole series of examples. If you were contending that many everyday expressions have their origins in the world of gambling, you'd need many examples to demonstrate your point.

EXERCISE

1. **Choose one of the following topic sentences. Select an appropriate example and write the rest of the paragraph.**

    a. Sometimes a minor incident drastically changes a person's life.

    b. _____'s name exactly suits (her/his) personality.

    c. I still get embarrassed when I remember _____.

    d. Not all education goes on in the classroom.

2. **Explain why you would use one extended illustration, several shorter ones, or a whole series of examples to develop each of the following statements. Suggest appropriate illustrations.**

    a. Many parents I know think for their children.

    b. The hamburger isn't what it used to be.

    c. The ideal pet is small, quiet, and affectionate.

    d. Different college students view their responsibilities differently.

■ Organizing the Examples

A single extended example often assumes the narrative form, presenting a series of events in time sequence. One person's unfolding experience might show that "doing your thing" doesn't always work out for the best. Sets of examples that trace trends also rely on time sequence, moving either forward or backward. This arrangement would work well for the paper on the growing permissiveness in child rearing.

On the other hand, a paper showing that different individuals exhibit some characteristic to different extents would logically be organized by order of climax (from the least to the greatest extent) or perhaps the reverse order. To demonstrate how salesclerks differ in their attitudes toward customers, you might first describe a hostile clerk, then a pleasant one, and finally an outstandingly courteous and helpful one.

Sometimes any arrangement will work equally well. Suppose you're showing that Canadians are taking various precautions to ward off heart attacks. Although you might move from a person who exercises to one who diets and finally to one who practises relaxation techniques, no special order is preferable.

Large numbers of examples might first be grouped into categories and the categories then arranged in a suitable order. For example, the expressions from the world of gambling could be grouped according to types of gambling: cards, dice, horse racing, and the like. Depending upon the specific categories, one arrangement may or may not be preferable to another.

■ Ethical Issues

In writing an illustration, we try to show readers something truthful about our understanding of the world. They wouldn't read what we have written if they suspected we were unusually careless in our thinking or knew we were trying to deceive them. Deception may stem from prejudice, which causes people to distort examples. For instance, parents trying to talk their teenager out of a career in acting will probably cite only examples of failed or struggling performers. Such a distortion isn't fair to the acting profession or the teenager. Some distortions can be outright lies. In past debates about welfare, some commentators wrote about people who lived like millionaires while on welfare. It turned out that the examples were falsified, and no real instances of such massive abuse could be found. To help avoid ethical pitfalls, ask and answer the following questions.

- Have I given adequate thought to the point I'll make and the examples I'll use?

- Are the examples supporting my point truthful, or are they slanted to deceive the reader?

- Could my illustrations have harmful consequences? Do they stereotype an individual or group? harm someone's reputation unjustly?

- Will my examples promote desirable or undesirable behaviour?

■ Writing an Illustration

Planning and Drafting the Illustration

Assertions, unfamiliar topics, abstract principles, natural laws—as we've seen, all of these can form the foundation for your paper. If you have a choice, you should experience little difficulty finding something suitable. After all, you've observed and experienced many things—for example, how people can be TV junkies and the ways students manage the stresses of academic life. As always, the strategies on pages 13–20 can help generate some possibilities, which you can then evaluate by asking these questions:

Exactly what point am I trying to make? (Write it down in precise terms.)

Why do I want to make this point? to show how bad something is? to encourage something? to scare people into or away from something?

Who is my prospective audience?

Should I use one extended example, or will I need more? Why?

Once you've picked your topic, ask yourself, "What example(s) will work best with my audience?" Then brainstorm each one for supporting details. Use a chart patterned after the one below to help you.

Example 1	**Example 2**	**Example 3**
First supporting detail	First supporting detail	First supporting detail
Second supporting detail	Second supporting detail	Second supporting detail

Review your details carefully and add any new ones you think of; then make a new chart and re-enter the details into it, arranged in the order in which you intend to present them.

Your introduction should identify your topic and draw your reader into the paper. If you're illustrating a personal belief, you might indicate how you developed it. If you're trying to scare the reader into or away from something, you might open with an arresting statement.

Present your examples in the body of your paper, keeping your purpose firmly in mind as you plan your organization. If you have many brief examples, perhaps group them into related categories for discussion. The paper on expressions from gambling, for instance, might devote one paragraph each to terms from the worlds of cards, dice, and horse racing. If you're dealing with a few relatively brief examples—say to show a trend—put each in its own paragraph. For a single extended example, use the entire body of the paper, suitably paragraphed. Thus, an extended example of someone with an eccentric lifestyle might include paragraphs on mode of dress, living accommodations, and public behaviour.

Conclude in whatever way seems most appropriate. You might express a hope or recommendation that the reader implement or avoid something, or you might issue a personal challenge that grows out of the point you've illustrated.

Revising the Illustration

Think about the following questions and the general guidelines in Chapter 3 as you revise your paper:

Exactly what idea am I trying to put across? Have I used the examples that best typify it?

Do my examples illuminate my idea without introducing irrelevant material?

Are my examples interesting?

Have I used an appropriate number of examples?

Have I organized my paper effectively?

Example Student Essay of Illustration

A Lesson from Nature

Mike Braendle

1   As I was growing up, my parents often passed along little maxim-like sayings to me. Most of these have since slipped my mind, but I still remember the exact words of my father's favourite: "The door to success is labelled Push." Although for a while these were just words to me, I came to understand their true meaning as I observed the struggles of a crayfish while I was fishing one day.

2   There it lay, trapped in the small plastic compartment of my steel tackle box, which was sitting on the bank of the river. The sun had been shining for some time, and the plastic of the compartment surrounding the crayfish intensified the heat. In fact, the heat had become so great that the skin covering the small hard-shelled body was beginning to wrinkle. Nevertheless, the pinching claws continually groped about, trying to find something to grasp, some means of escape. The hard and heavy shell, acting like an anchor, burdened the crayfish greatly. The two small eyes, always moving, searched wildly for some way out, but found none. The segmented tail, as large as the rest of the body, was constantly pushing, trying to hoist the heavy body over the edge of the compartment.

3   The eyes at last fell upon a possibility for escape: the back wall of the compartment was slightly lower than the other three walls. Sensing an advantage, the crayfish seemed to labour more deliberately. The tail, pushing vigorously, tried to lift the heavy shell out of the plastic compartment. As the tail struggled, the claws slashed savagely back and forth, searching for something to grab.

4   Finally, after some time and struggle, the crayfish grasped the back wall. As it pulled, with every muscle straining, the hard shell edged up and over the wall of the compartment. Stopping abruptly and gazing at its surroundings, the crayfish tried to orient itself. Off to one side in another compartment lay a strange-

looking creature, unmoving. The crayfish did not recognize this odd-shaped thing as a fishing lure, but it did sense that the creature, with its bright metallic tint and protruding hooks, was not alive.

5   It took only a moment for the determined crustacean to figure out which way to go. It moved, as if driven by instinct, across this compartment and then others, occasionally getting caught on a protruding hook. These hooks slowed its progress, scratching grooves and gouges in the hard shell.

6   As the crayfish moved steadily toward the edge of the box, the thought of cold water seemed to excite it. It moved faster, more deliberately now. When reaching the edge of the box, it stopped for a moment, as if pondering what to do next. Then, defiantly, it flopped over the edge, landing on its hard shell. It stayed on its back for some time but then turned over and dragged itself to the water.

7   The crayfish lay there for a long time, soaking in the cool and refreshing river. Then with a powerful flap of its tail, it disappeared into the depths. Here, where there was no threat of drying out, it could and probably would recuperate from this tiring experience.

DISCUSSION QUESTIONS

1. What general statement does this essay illustrate?
2. Why is one extended illustration effective here?
3. Explain the organization of the essay and why it is appropriate.
4. In paragraph 2, the writer says the crayfish "continually groped" and "searched wildly" with its tail "constantly pushing." How do these descriptions relate to the writer's purpose?
5. Point out specific sentences in paragraphs 3 and 4 that seem particularly effective in engaging the reader's interest.

SUGGESTIONS FOR WRITING   *Use one of the ideas below or another that your instructor approves for your illustration essay. Select appropriate examples, determine how many you will use, and decide how you will organize them.*

1. Canadians are a wasteful people.
2. Brand names are becoming increasingly important to young people's sense of identity.
3. Americans have strange myths about Canadians.

4. Women are becoming increasingly prominent (in politics, business, sports, or some other area).

5. Dedication is the secret of success for many hockey players (or use any other area or occupation).

6. People have many strange remedies for hangovers.

7. Movies (or some other form of media) are getting more and more disturbing.

8. A good nurse must be compassionate, conscientious, and competent (or use another occupation with appropriate characteristics).

9. Ideas about what is considered healthy (or attractive) keep changing.

10. Using the Internet does (or does not) make life simpler.

When we write an illustration paper, we don't always draw our examples from personal experience. As we reflect on a topic, we may talk with other people and read various source materials to broaden our understanding. We explore differing perspectives and determine the connections between them en route to arriving at our own views and insights. Take, for instance, the topic of eating disorders. "An Insatiable Emptiness" (page 404) and "Pressures to Conform" (page 525) offer poignant illustrations of how eating disorders affect people's personal lives. Reading these essays, drawing upon your own observations, and perhaps questioning fellow students could lead you to an important insight: for example, that eating disorders are subtly encouraged by society. You might then synthesize (see pages 64–65) others' illustrations and your own to produce a paper that presents this insight.

Sometimes illustrations don't reflect reality. An author trying to make the point that many students are irresponsible might offer examples of students who skip classes, fail to hand in assignments, and party constantly. These examples, however, overlook the many students who hold part-time jobs while taking a full load of classes, participate in professional organizations, and function successfully as spouses, and even parents, while earning good grades. Because published material can paint an inaccurate picture, develop the habit of judging the examples you read in the light of what your knowledge, further investigation, and other sources reveal. Critical thinking is one of the most important skills a writer can cultivate.[*]

SUGGESTIONS FOR WRITING

1. Examine the Reader essays on eating disorders cited above. Then, drawing upon examples from the essays and perhaps the observations of students you know, write a paper that illustrates the physical, psychological, and emotional damage that may result from obsession with weight or body image.

---

[*]Because this type of paper draws upon published information, it is important to read the sections on card catalogues and periodical indexes in Chapter 19 and those on handling quotations and avoiding plagiarism in Chapter 20. As always, follow your instructor's guidelines for documenting sources.

2. Read several issues of a magazine such as *Saturday Night* or *Canadian Living* and determine what the articles suggest about Canadian life. Then write an essay that illustrates your conclusions and incorporates relevant material from the articles.

3. In his article "Security's Serpentine Coils," Alan Borovoy states: "It is believed that a climate of compulsory informing would erode social harmony." Write an essay supporting this proposition by drawing from literary examples (*1984*, *Handmaid's Tale*) or from history (China's Cultural Revolution, or the McCarthyist era in the United States).

chapter

Classification: Grouping into Categories

*H*elp Wanted, Situations Wanted, Real Estate, Personal. Do these terms look familiar? They do if you've ever scanned the classified ads of the newspaper. Ads are
grouped into categories, and each category is then subdivided. The people who assemble this layout are *classifying*. Figure 8.1 (see page 101) shows the main divisions
of a typical classified ad section and a further breakdown of one of them.

As this figure indicates, grouping allows the people who handle ads to divide
entries according to a logical scheme and helps readers find what they are looking
for. Imagine the difficulty of checking the real estate ads if all the entries were
run in the order in which the ads were placed. Classification helps writers and
readers come to grips with large or complex topics. It breaks a broad topic into categories according to some specific principle, presents the distinctive features of each
category, and shows how the features vary among categories. Segmenting the
topic simplifies the discussion by presenting the information in small, neatly sorted
piles rather than in one jumbled and confusing heap.

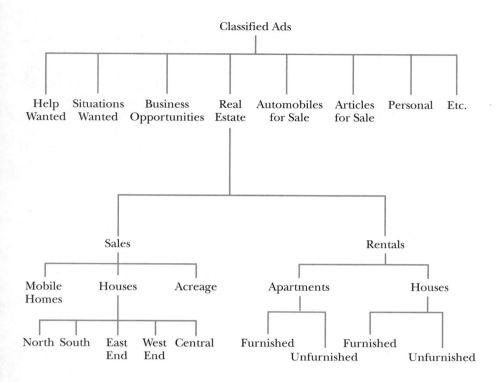

Figure 8.1 A Typical Classified Ad Section

Furthermore, classification helps people make choices. Identifying which groups of consumers—students, accountants, small-business owners—are most likely to buy some new product allows the manufacturer to advertise in appropriate media. Knowing the engine size, manoeuvrability, seating capacity, and gas mileage of typical subcompact, compact, and intermediate-size cars helps customers decide which one to buy.

Because classification plays such an important part in our lives, it is a useful writing tool in many situations. Your accounting instructor may ask you to categorize accounting procedures for retail businesses. In a computer class, you may classify computer languages and then specify appropriate applications for each grouping. For an industrial hygiene class, you might categorize different types of respiratory protective equipment and indicate when each type is used.

■ Selecting Categories

People classify in different ways for different purposes, which generally reflect their interests. A clothing designer might classify people according to their fashion sense, an advertising executive according to their age, and a politician according to their party affiliations.

When you write a classification paper, choose a principle of classification that suits not only your purpose but also your audience. If you're writing for students, don't classify instructors according to their manner of dress, body build, or cars they drive. These breakdowns probably wouldn't interest most students and certainly wouldn't serve their needs. Instead, develop a more useful principle of classification—perhaps by teaching styles, concern for students, or grading policies.

Sometimes it's helpful or necessary to divide one or more categories into subcategories. If you do, use just one principle of classification for each level. Both levels in Figure 8.2 meet this test because each reflects a single principle: place of origin for the first, number of cylinders for the second.

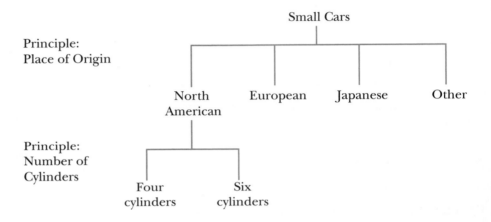

Figure 8.2   Proper Classification of Small Cars

Now examine Figure 8.3. This classification is *improper* because it groups cars in two ways—by place of origin and by kind—making it possible for one car to end up in two different categories. For example, the German Porsche is both a European car and a sports car. When categories overlap in this way, confusion reigns and nothing is clarified.

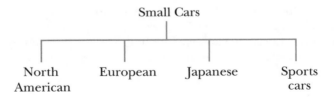

Figure 8.3   Improper Classification of Small Cars

EXERCISE

1. **How would each of the following people be most likely to classify the families in a Canadian town?**

   a. The Member of Parliament who represents the city

   b. A social worker

   c. The director of the local credit bureau

2. **The following lists contain overlapping categories. Identify the inconsistent item in each list and explain why it is faulty.**

Nurses	Pictures	Voters in Saskatoon
Surgical nurses	Oil paintings	Liberals
Psychiatric nurses	Magazine illustrations	Progressive Conservatives
Emergency room nurses	Lithographs	Reformers
Terminal care nurses	Watercolours	New Democrats
Night nurses	Etchings	Nonvoters

Number of Categories

Some classification papers discuss every category included within the topic. Others discuss only selected categories. Circumstances and purpose dictate the scope of the discussion. Suppose you work for the finance department of your province and are asked to write a report that classifies the major nonservice industries in a certain city and assesses their strengths and weaknesses. Your investigation shows that food processing, furniture making, and the production of auto parts account for over 95 percent of all nonservice jobs. Two minor industries, printing and toy making, provide the rest of the jobs. Given these circumstances, you'd probably focus on the first three industries, mentioning the others only in passing. But if printing and toy making were significant industries, they too would require detailed discussion.

Developing Categories

Develop every category you include with specific, informative details that provide a clear picture of each one and help the reader grasp the distinctions and relationships among them. The following excerpt from a student paper classifying public restrooms for women discusses two of the writer's three categories:

> Luxurious washrooms are found in upscale department stores, chic boutiques, and the better restaurants. This aristocrat of public facilities usually disdains the term <u>washroom</u>, masquerading instead under the alias of <u>ladies' room</u>. Upon entering its plush environs, the user is captivated by its elegance. Thick carpet reaches up to cushion tired feet, wood panelled or brocade velvet walls shut the outside world away, and softly glowing wall sconces soothe the

eyes. Inviting armchairs and gold-and-velvet tables add to the restful, welcoming atmosphere, and the latest issues of upscale magazines such as *Vogue* and *Elle* entice customers to sit and read. Mirrors in carved frames, designer basins with gleaming gold faucets, and creamy scented soap suggest a spa-like luxury. Soft music, piped in through invisible speakers, may take patrons back in time, as if no one is waiting for them outside the door.

The adequate washroom offers utility without the swankiness of its lavish cousin. Typically located in a large shopping mall or mass-market department store, it is a stark world of hard, unadorned surfaces--tile floors, tile walls, and harshly glaring fluorescent lights recessed in the ceiling. For those who wish to rest, there is a garishly coloured Naugahyde couch and next to it a battered metal or wood table holding a few tattered copies of *Homemakers*, *People*, *Canadian Living*, and similar publications. The mirrors have steel frames, the sinks, set in a formica counter, have plain chrome faucets, and the soap dispenser emits a thin stream of unscented liquid. There is no soothing music--just the relentless whining of someone's tired child.

Student Unknown

The concrete details in these paragraphs effectively characterize each category and clearly distinguish between them. Imagine how vague and indistinct the categories would be without these details.

■ Ethical Issues

Classification can seem quite innocent, and yet it can cause great harm. In India, an entire group numbering millions of people was once classified as "untouchables" and so was denied the jobs and rights of other citizens. In Canada during World War II, innocent people of Japanese descent were classified as a threat and were stripped of property and moved away from their homes. In many high schools, students are often lumped into categories with labels such as "geeks," "druggies," "jocks," etc. Clearly you'll have to evaluate the appropriateness and consequences of your classification scheme. To avoid problems, ask and answer these questions:

- Is my classification called for by the situation? It may be appropriate to classify students in a school environment according to their reading skills, but classifying factory workers in this fashion may well be inappropriate and unfair to the people involved.

- Have I avoided the use of damaging classifications? We resent stereotyping because it unjustly reduces us to some distorted general idea. No one is simply a "hillbilly" or a "jock."

- Have I applied my classification without resorting to overgeneralization? In a paper classifying student drinkers, it would be a mistake, and even harmful, to imply that all college students drink excessively.

- Could my classification promote harmful behaviour? When classifying the behaviour patterns of young urban dwellers, it would be unethical to present favourably the lifestyle of a group that uses hard drugs and engages in criminal activities.

We are ethically responsible for the classification systems that we use in our writing. Always examine the one you use for suitability, fairness, and potential harm.

Writing a Classification

Planning and Drafting the Classification

Many topics that interest you are potential candidates for classification. If you're selecting your own topic, you might explain the different kinds of rock music to novices, take a humorous look at different types of teachers, or, in a more serious vein, identify different types of discrimination. As always, use one or more of the narrowing strategies on pages 13–20 to help stimulate your thinking. As possibilities come to mind, examine each one in light of these questions:

What purpose will this classification serve?
Who is my audience and what will interest them?
What are the categories of this topic?
What features distinguish my categories from one another?

Next, determine whether you'll discuss every category or only selected ones, and then set up a classification chart similar to the one following.

Category 1	**Category 2**	**Category 3**
First distinguishing feature	First distinguishing feature	First distinguishing feature
Second distinguishing feature	Second distinguishing feature	Second distinguishing feature

Such a chart helps you see the relationships among categories and provides a starting point for developing your specific details. Proceed by jotting down the details that come to mind for each distinguishing feature of every category. Then prepare a second chart with the distinguishing features and details arranged in the order in which you want to present them.

Begin your paper by identifying your topic and capturing your reader's attention in some way. A paper classifying hair dyes might point out their growing popularity among both men and women. Or you could cite a personal experience that relates to your topic. As always, circumstances dictate your choice.

In the body discuss your categories in whatever order best suits your purpose. Order of climax—least important, more important, most important—often works well. Or perhaps your topic will suggest arranging the categories by behaviour, income, education, or physical characteristics. Whatever your arrangement, signal it clearly to your reader. Don't merely start the discussions of your categories by saying first . . . , second . . . , another . . . , next . . . , and the like. These words offer no hint of the rationale behind your order.

In addition, make sure the arrangement of material within the categories follows a consistent pattern. Recall the two categories of washrooms discussed on pages 103–04. In each case, after noting where the washroom can be found, the writer discusses its floor, walls, and lighting, moves to the furniture, and ends by discussing the sinks, soap, and sound.

The strategies for ending a classification paper are as varied as those for starting it. A paper on hair dyes might conclude by predicting their continued popularity. In other cases, you might express a hope of some kind or advise your reader to do something.

Revising the Classification

Revise your paper by following the guidelines in Chapter 3 as well as by pondering these questions:

Does my classification have a clear sense of purpose and audience?

Does my principle of classification accord with my purpose?

Do any of my categories overlap?

Have I chosen an appropriate number of categories?

Are these categories developed with sufficient details?

Are the categories and details arranged in an effective order?

Example Student Essay of Classification

Undesirable Produce Market Customers

Clarence DeLong

1   You will find almost as large a variety of customers at a produce market as you will find fruits and vegetables. Undesirable produce market customers fall into three main categories--those who squeeze the fruit, those who complain constantly, and those who try to cheat the market--and when you meet them all in one day, you

have one big headache. Perhaps you will recognize these people as I describe them.

2   "Sammy Squeezer" is the least annoying of these undesirables. He wants to make sure that everything he buys is "just right." He pokes his thumbs into the top of a cantaloupe. If they penetrate very deeply, he won't buy this particular specimen, considering it to be overripe. He squeezes the peaches, plums, nectarines, and any other fruit he can get his hands on. After ten of these people squeeze one piece of fruit, it will surely be soft, even if it wasn't originally. Moving on to the corn, Sammy carefully peels back the husk to examine the kernels inside. If they don't suit him, he doesn't bother to fold the husk back to protect the kernels; he simply tosses the ear back into the basket. The problems he creates for the employees are primarily physical--removing the damaged items after he leaves.

3   A more annoying customer is "Betty Bitcher." She is never satisfied with the quality of the produce: the bananas are too green, the lettuce has brown spots, the berries are too ripe, and the potatoes have green spots. Sometimes you wonder if Betty would have been satisfied with the fruit grown in the Garden of Eden.

4   The produce has no monopoly on her complaints, however. Betty also finds fault with the service she receives from the employees. Talking to other customers or directly to the clerks, she can be heard saying such things as "Why is this the only place I ever have to wait in line? They must have trouble getting good help here." Even as she leaves the market, which is none too soon, she must make one last complaint: "You mean I have to carry my own potatoes to the car?" The problems she creates for the employees are primarily mental--she can make your nerves quite active.

5   Perhaps the most annoying customer of all is "Charlie Cheater." You have to keep your eye on him constantly because he knows all the tricks of cheating. He will add berries to an already full basket. He will take 6/79¢ oranges and tell you they're the 6/59¢ ones. He will put expensive grapes in the bottom of a sack and add cheaper ones on top. Then he'll tell you that they are all the cheaper variety. Likewise, he will put expensive nectarines in a sack, place a few cheaper peaches on top, and try to pass them all off as peaches. If he is caught, he usually says, "I don't know how

that happened. My little girl (or boy) must have put them in there." The child usually looks dumbfounded.

6   The problem Charlie creates for the market is twofold: financial and legal. If you don't catch him, your profits suffer. If you do catch him, you almost have to prosecute, usually for amounts of only a dollar or two, or you'll have every Charlie in town at your door.

7   Did you recognize any of these customers? If you didn't and would like to see some of them in action, stop in at Steve's Produce Market. That's where I work, and that's where I meet them.

DISCUSSION QUESTIONS

1. What is the writer's purpose in developing this classification? Where does he state it?
2. In what order has he arranged his categories? Refer to the essay when answering.
3. Demonstrate that the writer has avoided overlapping categories.
4. How do you know he hasn't discussed every category of undesirable customers?

SUGGESTIONS FOR WRITING   *Write a classification paper on one of the topics below or one approved by your instructor. Determine your purpose and audience, select appropriate categories, decide how many you'll discuss, develop them with specific details, and arrange them in an effective order.*

1. College teachers (or college pressures)
2. Pet owners (or types of pets)
3. Kinds of extreme sports
4. Alternative medicines
5. Web sites
6. Computer games
7. Party-goers
8. Car advertisements
9. Canadian TV shows
10. Easy to make recipes
11. Music for driving
12. Attitudes toward death
13. Lies
14. Ways to break off a relationship
15. Bores

The Critical Edge

Classification provides an effective tool for organizing material into categories. But you won't always rely exclusively on your own knowledge or experience to determine or develop categories. At times you'll supplement what you bring to a writing assignment with information gained through outside reading.

Suppose that for an introductory business course, you're asked to prepare a paper that explores major types of investments. You realize that some research will be necessary. After consulting a number of books and magazines, you conclude that stocks, bonds, and real estate represent the three main categories of investments and that each category can be divided into several subcategories. Bonds, for example, can be grouped according to issuer: corporate, municipal, and federal.

At this point, you recognize that the strategy of classification would work well for this assignment. Reading further, you learn about the financial risks, rewards, and tax consequences associated with ownership. For example, Canada Savings Bonds offer the greatest safety, while corporate bonds, as well as stocks and real estate, entail varying degrees of risk depending on the financial condition of the issuer and the state of the economy. Similarly, the income from the different categories and subcategories of investments is subject to different kinds and levels of taxation.

After assimilating the information you've gathered, you could synthesize (see pages 64–65) the views expressed in your sources as well as your own ideas about investments. You might organize your categories and subcategories according to probable degree of risk, starting with the least risky investment and ending with the most risky. For your conclusion you might offer purchase recommendations for different groups of investors such as young workers, wealthy older investors, and retirees.

Before using the material of others in your writing, examine its merits. Do some sources seem more convincing than others? Why? Do any recommendations stem from self-interest? Are any sources overloaded with material irrelevant to your purpose? Which sources offer the most detail? Asking and answering questions such as these will help you write a more informed paper.[*]

SUGGESTIONS FOR WRITING

1. Examine the Reader essays on gender issues or technology and then write a paper that draws upon these sources and classifies their content.

2. Reflect on the Reader essays that you've studied and then write a paper that presents an appropriate classification system for them, perhaps based on the writers' levels of diction, tone, or reliance on authorities.

---

[*]Because you'll rely on published sources, it is important to read the sections on card catalogues and periodical indexes in Chapter 19 and those on handling quotations and avoiding plagiarism in Chapter 20 before you start to write. As always, follow your instructor's guidelines for documenting sources.

Comparison: Showing Relationships

Which candidate for mayor should get my vote, Ken Conwell or Jerry Mander?
Let me know whether this new shipment of nylon thread meets specs.
Doesn't this tune remind you of a Diana Krall song?
How does high school in Australia stack up against high school in this country?

Everyone makes *comparisons,* not just once in a while but day after day. When we compare, we examine two or more items for likenesses, differences, or both. Comparison has a purpose. Sometimes it helps us see through superficial similarities to significant differences that we might easily overlook. When the similarities between two things are obvious, we may choose to emphasize how two things which appear at first glance to be similar are actually quite different. On the other hand, when the differences are obvious, we may choose to demonstrate how two things which impress us with their differences actually share underlying similarities. Comparison often serves an evaluative purpose, showing why one person, thing, or plan of action is superior to another. It may also help us choose between alternatives as we decide on matters small and large. At a restaurant, we may compare the appeal and value of ordering a pasta dinner with the appeal and value of ordering a sub sandwich. Comparison also influences our more important decisions. We weigh majoring in chemistry against majoring in physics, buying against renting, working for Macintosh against working for IBM. An instructor may ask us to write a paper comparing the features of two behavioural organization models. An employer may have us weigh two proposals for decreasing employee absenteeism and write a report recommending one of them.

Comparison also acquaints us with unfamiliar things. To help Canadian readers understand the English sport of rugby, a sportswriter might compare its field, team, rules, and scoring system with those for football. To teach students about France's government, a political science textbook might discuss the makeup and election of its parliament and the method of picking its president and premier, using our own government as a backdrop.

Both your classes and your job will call for comparison writing. Academic assignments commonly call for comparative analysis. Your humanities instructor may ask you to compare baroque and classical music and their contributions to later musical developments. Your psychology instructor may want you to compare two different types of psychosis and assess the legal and medical ramifications of each. Your biology instructor may have you consider how the features of two different kinds of body cells enable them to perform their functions. A criminology instructor might ask you how a restorative justice model compares with a model of adversarial justice in a specific context. In the workplace, comparisons are also common because they help people make decisions. An office manager may compare several phone systems to determine which one would be more useful for the company, a nurse may assess the condition of a patient before and after a new medicine is given, an insurance agent may point out the features of two insurance policies to highlight the advantages of one.

■ Selecting Items for Comparison

Any items you compare must share some common ground. For example, you could compare two golfers on driving ability, putting ability, and sand play, or two cars on appearance, gas mileage, and warranty; but you can't meaningfully compare a golfer with a car, any more than you could compare guacamole with Guadalajara or chicken with charcoal. There's simply no basis for comparison.

Any valid comparison, on the other hand, presents many possibilities. Suppose you head the music department of a large store and have two excellent salespeople working for you. The manager of the store asks you to prepare a one- or two-page report that compares their qualifications for managing the music department in a new branch store. Assessing and evaluating their abilities becomes the guiding purpose that motivates and controls the writing. You can immediately rule out points such as eye colour, hairstyle, and religion, which have no bearing on job performance. Instead, you must decide what managerial traits the job will require and the extent to which each candidate possesses them. Your thinking might result in a list like this.

Points of Similarity or Difference	Pat	Mike
1. Ability to deal with customers, sales skills	Excellent	Excellent
2. Effort: regular attendance, hard work on the job	Excellent	Excellent
3. Leadership qualities	Excellent	Good

4. Knowledge of ordering and accounting procedures   Good   Fair
5. Musical knowledge   Excellent   Good

This list tells you which points to emphasize and suggests Pat as the candidate to recommend. You might briefly mention similarities (points 1 and 2) in an introductory paragraph, but the report would focus on differences (points 3, 4, and 5), since you're distinguishing between two employees.

EXERCISE   *Say you want to compare two good restaurants in order to recommend one of them. List the points of similarity and difference that you might discuss. Differences should predominate because you will base your decision on them.*

■ Developing a Comparison

Successful comparisons rest upon ample, well-chosen details that show just how the items under consideration are alike and different. Such support helps the reader grasp your meaning. Read the following two student paragraphs and note how the concrete details convey the striking differences between south and north 14th Street:

On 14th Street running south from P Street are opulent luxury stores such as Birks and Holt Renfrew, and small but expensive clothing stores with richly dressed mannequins in the windows. Modern skyscraping office buildings hold banks and travel bureaus on the ground floors and insurance companies and corporation headquarters in the upper stories. Dotting the concretescape are high-priced movie theatres, gourmet restaurants, multilevel parking garages, bookstores, and candy-novelty-gift shops, all catering to the prosperous population of the city. This section of 14th Street is relatively clean: the city maintenance crews must clean up after only a nine-to-five populace and the Saturday crowds of shoppers. The pervading mood of the area is one of bustling wealth during the day and, in the night, calm.

Crossing P Street toward the north, one notes a gradual but disturbing change in the scenery of 14th Street. A pan-handler sits nodding on the sidewalk in front of a rundown hotel, too tired, or too drugged, to bother asking for money. A liquidation store promises bargains, but the window display shows an unattractive tangle of chains, watches, knives, and dusty tools. Outside a tavern with opaque windows, a homeless person is

curled up, sleeping beneath a tattered blanket. On the opposite
side of the street, a restaurant advertising curry competes for
customers with the house of noodles and pizza-to-go restaurant.
Sometimes, even when the air is chill, one sees young women in
short skirts, low-cut tops, and high boots standing near the
curb, or leaning into the windows of cars momentarily stopped,
talking to the drivers.

Student Unknown

Vivid details depict with stark clarity the economic differences between the
north and south ends of the street. These differences contribute to the writer's implied thesis: *The contrast between wealth and poverty on opposite ends of the same street is
horrifying.*

■ Organizing a Comparison

Comparison papers can be organized by two basic patterns: *block pattern*, also called
comparison of wholes; *alternating pattern*, also called comparison by parts. Typically
a comparison paper will use some combination of these two patterns.

The Block Pattern   The block pattern first presents all of the points of comparison for one item and then all of the points of comparison for the other. Here is the
comparison of the two salespeople, Pat and Mike, outlined according to the block
pattern:

   I. Introduction: mentions similarities in sales skills and effort but recom-
       mends Pat for promotion.
  II. Specific points about Mike
       A. Leadership qualities
       B. Knowledge of ordering and accounting procedures
       C. Musical knowledge
 III. Specific points about Pat
       A. Leadership qualities
       B. Knowledge of ordering and accounting procedures
       C. Musical knowledge
  IV. Conclusion: reasserts that Pat should be promoted.

For a shorter paper or one that includes only a few points of comparison, the
block pattern can work well, since the reader can remember all the points from the
first block while reading the second. Be careful, however, that you do not dwell too
long on one half of the comparison without mentioning the other, or your essay
might seem to break in two. Often the reader may find it easier to follow a modified block pattern, in which you refer back to the first item of comparison as you
get to the second.

The Alternating Pattern   The alternating pattern presents a point about one item, then follows immediately with a corresponding point about the other. Organized in this way, the Pat-and-Mike paper would look like this:

I. Introduction: mentions similarities in sales skills and effort but recommends Pat for promotion.
II. Leadership qualities
    A. Mike's qualities
    B. Pat's qualities
III. Knowledge of ordering and accounting procedures
    A. Mike's knowledge
    B. Pat's knowledge
IV. Musical knowledge
    A. Mike's knowledge
    B. Pat's knowledge
V. Conclusion: reasserts that Pat should be promoted.

If there are many points of comparison, the alternating method, which deals with each point in turn, can help your reader grasp similarities and differences. Be aware, however, that moving back and forth between, for example, two different poems, or two different historical periods, may become rather dizzying. To ground your reader you may blend the block approach and the alternating approach. In comparing heroines from two books, for example, you might give an overview of the two books' similarities in the block approach, and then use the alternating approach to focus on salient points of difference.

Once you select your pattern, arrange your points of comparison in an appropriate order. Take up closely related points one after the other. Depending on your purpose, you might work from similarities to differences or the reverse. Often, a good writing strategy is to move from the least significant to the most significant point so that you conclude with punch.

EXERCISE   *Using the points of comparison you selected for the exercise on page 112, prepare outlines for a paper organized according to the block and then the alternating pattern.*

■ Using Analogy

An *analogy,* a special type of comparison, calls attention to one or more similarities underlying two different kinds of items that seem to have nothing in common. While some analogies stand alone, most clarify concepts in other kinds of writing. Whatever their role, they follow the same organizational pattern as ordinary comparisons.

An analogy often explains something unfamiliar by likening it to something familiar. Here is an example:

The atmosphere of Earth acts like any window in serving two very important functions. It lets light in, and it permits us to look out. It also serves as a shield to keep out dangerous or uncomfortable things. A normal glazed window lets us keep our houses warm by keeping out cold air, and it prevents rain, dirt, and unwelcome insects and animals from coming in. . . . Earth's atmospheric window also helps to keep our planet at a comfortable temperature by holding back radiated heat and protecting us from dangerous levels of ultraviolet light.

Lester del Ray, The Mysterious Sky

Conversely, an analogy sometimes highlights the unfamiliar in order to help illuminate the familiar. The following paragraph discusses the qualities and obligations of an unfamiliar person, the mountain guide, to shed light on a familiar practice—teaching:

The mountain guide, like the true teacher, has a quiet authority. He or she engenders trust and confidence so that one is willing to join the endeavor. The guide accepts his leadership role, yet recognizes that success (measured by the heights that are scaled) depends upon the close cooperation and active participation of each member of the group. He has crossed the terrain before and is familiar with the landmarks, but each trip is new and generates its own anxiety and excitement. Essential skills must be mastered; if they are lacking, disaster looms. The situation demands keen focus and rapt attention: slackness, misjudgment, or laziness can abort the venture.

Nancy K. Hill, "Scaling the Heights: The Teacher as Mountaineer"

When you develop an analogy, keep these points in mind:

1. Your readers must be well acquainted with the familiar item. If they aren't, the point is lost.
2. The items must indeed have significant similarities. You could develop a meaningful analogy between a kidney and a filter or between cancer and anarchy but not between a fiddle and a flapjack or a laser and Limburger cheese.
3. The analogy must truly illuminate. Overly obvious analogies, such as one comparing a battle to an argument, offer few or no revealing insights.
4. Overextended analogies can tax the reader's endurance. A multipage analogy between a heart and a pump would likely overwhelm the reader with all its talk of valves, hoses, pressures, and pumping.

■ Ethical Issues

Although an old adage declares that "comparisons are odious," most people embrace comparisons except when they are unfair. Unfortunately, this situation occurs all too often. For example, advertisers commonly magnify trivial drawbacks in competitive products while exaggerating the benefits of their own merchandise. Politicians run attack ads that distort their opponents' views and demean the opponents' character. And when scientific theories clash, supporters of one view have been known to alter their findings in order to undermine the other position.

Your readers expect any comparison to meet certain ethical standards. Ask and answer these questions to help ensure that those you write measure up.

- Have I avoided skewing one or both of my items in order to ensure a particular outcome?

- Are the items I'm comparing properly matched? It would be unethical to compare a student essay to a professional one in order to demonstrate the inadequacy of the former.

- If I'm using an analogy, is it appropriate? Comparing immigration officials to Nazi storm troopers is ethically odious: It trivializes the suffering and deaths of millions of Nazi victims and taints the officials with a terrible label.

■ Writing a Comparison

Planning and Drafting the Comparison

Don't write merely to fulfill an assignment; if you do, your paper will likely ramble aimlessly and fail to deliver a specific message. Instead, build your paper around a clear sense of purpose. Do you want to show the superiority of one product or method over another? Do you want to show how sitcoms today differ from those twenty years ago? Purpose governs the details you choose and the organization you follow. Whether you select your own topic or write on an assigned one, answer these questions:

What purpose will my comparison serve?
Who will be my audience and why will they want to read the essay?
What points of similarity or difference will I discuss?

To develop the comparison, draw up a chart similar to this one.

Item A	Item B
First point of comparison	First point of comparison
Second point of comparison	Second point of comparison

Next, brainstorm each point in turn, recording appropriate supporting details. When you finish, stand back and ask these questions:

Do all the details relate to my purpose?
Do any new details come to mind?
In what order should I organize the details?

When you decide upon an order, copy the points of comparison and the details, arranged in the order you will follow, into a chart like the one below.

Item A
First point of comparison
    First detail
    Second detail
Second point of comparison

Item B
First point of comparison
    First detail
    Second detail
Second point of comparison

Use the introduction to identify your topic and arouse the reader's interest. If you intend to establish the superiority of one item over the other, you might call attention to your position. If you're comparing something unfamiliar with something familiar, you might explain the importance of understanding the unfamiliar item.

Organize the body of your paper according to whichever pattern—block or alternating—suits its length and the number of points you're planning to take up. If you explain something familiar by comparing it with something unfamiliar, start with the familiar item. If you try to show the superiority of one item over another, proceed from the less to the more desirable one. Note that both of the Pat-and-Mike outlines (page 113) put Mike ahead of Pat, the superior candidate.

Write whatever kind of conclusion will round off your discussion effectively. Many comparison papers end with a recommendation or a prediction. A paper comparing two brands of stereo receivers might recommend purchasing one of them. A paper comparing a familiar sport, such as football, with an unfamiliar one, such as rugby, might predict the future popularity of the latter. Unless you've written a lengthy paper, don't summarize the likenesses and differences you've presented. If you've done a proper writing job, your reader already has them clearly in mind.

Revising the Comparison

Revise your paper in light of the general guidelines in Chapter 3 and the questions that follow:

> Have I accomplished my purpose, whether to choose between alternatives or acquaint the reader with something unfamiliar?
>
> For something unfamiliar, have I shown clearly just how it is like and unlike the familiar item?
>
> Have I consistently written with my audience in mind?
>
> Have I considered all points of similarity and difference that relate to my purpose?
>
> Have I included appropriate supporting details?
>
> Are my comparisons arranged effectively?

Example Student Essay of Comparison

Different Shifts, Different Actions

Claire Mutter

1   The nursing team in a small hospital meets the routine and special daily needs of patients. A registered professional nurse usually leads the team, and members often include registered and practical nurses, nurse's aides, and attendants. Although all nurses care for patients, the duties and working conditions of team members on the first and second shifts differ considerably.

2   The first shift begins at 7:00 A.M., when nurses awaken patients and prepare them for laboratory tests, X-rays, or medications. Additional nursing duties include taking temperatures, pulses, and respirations and giving enemas or preoperative injections. Team members also serve breakfast and then administer medications such as pain pills.

3   By this time doctors have arrived to visit their patients. The nursing station swirls with activity. Doctors write new orders at desks cluttered with their patients' charts. Laboratory and X-ray technicians explain test results. The pharmacist brings medications and inquires about any new orders for drugs. Inhalation and physical therapists check charts for their new orders. The dietitian asks why Mr. Bowers is not eating his prescribed foods. Telephones ring and patients' signal lights flash continually. The members of the nursing team, all with their own duties, try desperately to keep up with these frenzied activities, which leaves little time to spend with their patients. This pace continues through most of the first shift.

4   Second shift team members, starting work at 3:00 P.M., usually can devote more attention to their patients' personal needs. To prepare for supper, nurses clear flowers and cards from tables, wash faces and hands where necessary, and position patients for eating comfort. After supper, when visitors have departed, team members inform patients about their conditions and teach them how

to care for themselves after discharge. For example, they show dia-
betic patients how to administer insulin injections and to care for
their skin, and tell them what foods to eat.

   To prepare patients for the night, nurses straighten and change
beds and give last medications. By 10:00 most patients are asleep.
Calmness and quiet prevail at the nursing station, with only two or
three nurses doing their charting—recording how patients have tolerated treatment and medication. Except for an occasional signal
light from a patient, activities cease for the night.

5   Although both shifts have the same responsibilities, the care
and welfare of the patient, the second shift usually works in a
much more relaxed atmosphere. Fewer staff people and a slower pace
result in more personalized treatment.

DISCUSSION QUESTIONS

1. Comment on the significance of the phrase "the duties and working conditions"
   in paragraph 1.
2. Point out effective supporting details in the essay. What do they accomplish?
3. What pattern of organization does the writer use?
4. Explain why the writer ends the third sentence of paragraph 5 as follows:
   "recording how patients have tolerated treatment and medication." What can
   you learn from this explanation?

SUGGESTIONS FOR WRITING

1. **Write a comparison essay on one of the topics below or another that your instructor
   approves. Determine the points you will discuss and how you will develop and
   arrange them. Emphasize similarities, differences, or both.**
   a. A liberal arts education versus a technical education
   b. The physical or mental demands of two jobs
   c. Two advertisements for similar things
   d. An online course and a face-to face course
   e. Two popular trends among people your age
   f. A day-to-day relationship and a virtual one
   g. Two different forms of exercise
   h. Two cultural customs (weddings, funerals, dating) with which you are familiar

2. **Develop an analogy based on one of the following sets of items or another set that
   your instructor approves. Proceed as you would for any other comparison.**
   a. Ending a relationship and leaving a job

   b. Drug addiction and shopping addiction

   c. Trouble shooting a computer and writing an essay

   d. Learning to drive and learning a new language

   e. The structure of an atom and that of the solar system

   f. A parent and a farmer

   g. A workaholic and an alcoholic

   h. A cluttered garage and a disorderly mind

Although you rely on your own knowledge or findings to develop many comparisons, in some cases you'll synthesize (see pages 64–65) material from other sources.

Let's say that your business management instructor has asked you to prepare a report on the management styles of two high-profile chief executive officers (CEOs) at successful companies that manufacture the same kinds of products. You realize that you'll need to do some reading in business periodicals like *Canadian Business, The Economist,* and *Fortune* in order to complete this assignment. Your sources reveal that the first CEO favours a highly centralized managerial structure with strict limits on what can be done by all employees except top executives. The company has pursued foreign markets by establishing factories overseas and has aggressively attempted to merge with or acquire its domestic competitors. The second CEO has established a decentralized managerial structure that allows managers at various levels of the company to make key decisions. The company has also established a strong foreign presence, but it has done so primarily by entering into joint ventures with foreign firms. Most of its domestic expansion has resulted from the construction of new plants rather than from mergers or takeovers. Both CEOs have borrowed heavily to finance their companies' expansion. These three differences and one similarity are your points of comparison, which you can organize using either the block or alternating pattern. You might conclude by indicating why you prefer one of the two management styles.

After you've read the views expressed by your sources, examine them critically. Does any of the information about the two CEOs seem slanted so that it appears to misrepresent their management styles? For example, do any of the writers seem to exaggerate the positive or negative features of centralized or decentralized management? Do appropriate examples support the writers' contentions? Does any relevant information appear to be missing? Does any source contain material that isn't related to your purpose? Judging the works of others in this fashion will help you write a better report.[*]

---

[*]Because you'll rely on published sources, it is important to read the sections on card catalogues and periodical indexes in Chapter 19 and those on handling quotations and avoiding plagiarism in Chapter 20 before you start to write. As always, follow your instructor's guidelines for documenting sources.

SUGGESTIONS FOR WRITING

1. Read any two essays in this book on a similar issue (for example, the two articles on cloning in the Argument section) and then compare the views of these two writers. In your comparison, make an argument for which essay or article is more persuasive.

2. Read several reviews of the same movie and then compare what the critics have written in order to demonstrate that film critics bring different values to their viewing.

Cause and Effect: Explaining Why

Cause and effect, like the two sides of a coin, are inseparably linked and together make up *causation*. Cause probes the reasons why actions, events, attitudes, and conditions exist. Effect examines their consequences. Causation is important to us because it can explain historical events, natural happenings, and the actions and attitudes of individuals and groups. It can help us anticipate the consequences of personal actions, natural phenomena, or government policies.

Everyone asks and answers questions of causation. Scott wonders why Sue *really* broke off their relationship, and Jennifer speculates on the consequences of changing her major. People wonder why child abuse and homelessness are on the rise, and millions worry about the effects of corporate cost cutting and rising crime rates.

Inevitably, therefore, you will need to write papers and reports that employ causation. Your instructors might ask you to write on topics such as the causes of the Quebec separatist movement, the psychological consequences of workplace violence, the reasons why so many couples are divorcing, or the effects of different fertilizers on plant growth. An employer may want a report on why a certain product malfunctions, what might happen if a community redesigns its traffic pattern, or how increased security costs might affect business.

■ Patterns in Causal Analysis

Several organizational patterns are possible for a causal analysis. Sometimes, a single cause produces several effects. For instance, poor language skills prevent students from keeping up with required reading, taking adequate notes, and writing competent papers and essay exams. To explore such a single cause–multiple effect relationship, construct outlines similar to the following two:

I.   Introduction: identifies cause
II. Body
   A. Effect number 1
   B. Effect number 2
   C. Effect number 3
III. Conclusion

I.   Poor language skills
II. Body
   A. Can't keep up with required reading
   B. Can't take adequate notes
   C. Can't write competent papers or exams
III. Conclusion

Alternatively, you might discuss the cause after the effects are presented.

On the other hand, several causes may join forces to produce one effect. Lumber production in British Columbia, for example, has decreased over the last few years because stumpage fees are higher, international demand is lower, and foreign competition is stronger. Here's how you might organize a typical multiple cause–single effect paper:

I.   Introduction: identifies effect
II. Body
   A. Cause number 1
   B. Cause number 2
   C. Cause number 3
III. Conclusion

I.   Decrease in B.C. lumber
II. Body
   A. Higher stumpage fees
   B. Lower international demand
   C. Stronger foreign competition
III. Conclusion

Sometimes discussion of the effect follows the presentation of causes.

At times a set of events forms a causal chain, with each event the effect of the preceding one and the cause of the following one. For example, a student sleeps late and so misses breakfast and ends up hungry and distracted, which in turn results in a poor performance on an exam. Interrupting the chain at any point halts the sequence. Such chains can be likened to a row of upright dominoes that fall one after the other when the first one is pushed. Belief in a domino theory, which held that if one nation in Southeast Asia fell to the communists all would, one after the other, helped bring about U.S. entry into the Vietnam War. Causal chains can also help explain how devices function and some social changes proceed. The following outlines typify the arrangement of a paper explaining a causal chain:

I.   Introduction
II. Body
   A. Cause
   B. Effect

I.   Introduction
II. Body
   A. Sleep late
   B. Miss breakfast

C. Cause
D. Effect
III. Conclusion

C. Become hungry and distracted
D. Perform poorly on exam
III. Conclusion

Papers of this kind resemble process analyses, but process is concerned with *how* the events occur, cause and effect with *why*.

In many situations the sequence of causes and effects is too complex to fit the image of a chain. Suppose you are driving to a movie on a rainy night. You approach an intersection screened by bushes and, because you have the right-of-way, start across. Suddenly a car with unlit headlights looms directly in your path. You hit the brakes but skid on the slippery pavement and crash into the other car, crumpling its left fender and damaging your own bumper. Later, as you think about the episode, you begin to sense its complexities.

Obviously, the *immediate cause* of the accident was the other driver's failure to heed the stop sign. But other causes also played roles: the bushes and unlit headlights that kept you from seeing the other car sooner; the starts and stops, speedups and slowdowns that brought the two cars to the intersection at the same time; the wet pavement you skidded on; and the movie that brought you out in the first place.

You also realize that the effects of the accident go beyond the fender and bumper damage. After the accident, a police officer ticketed the other driver. As a result of the delay, you missed the movie. Further, the accident unnerved you so badly that you couldn't attend classes the next day and therefore missed an important writing assignment. Because of a bad driving record, the other driver lost his licence for sixty days. Clearly, the effects of this accident rival the causes in complexity.

Here's how you might organize a multiple cause–multiple effect essay:

I. Introduction
II. Body
    A. Cause number 1
    B. Cause number 2
    C. Cause number 3
    D. Effect number 1
    E. Effect number 2
    F. Effect number 3
III. Conclusion

I. The accident
II. Body
    A. Driver ran stop sign
    B. Bushes and unlit headlights impaired
    C. Wet pavement caused skidding
    D. Missed the movie
    E. Unnerved so missed classes next day
    F. Other driver lost licence
III. Conclusion

In some situations, however, you might first present the effects, then turn to the causes.

EXERCISE

1. Read the following selection and then arrange the events in a causal chain:

At a key moment, labour, business, and government leaders abandoned ideological differences and constructed a shared socio-economic strategy. These factors, in concert with strategic investment in education and a focused effort to attract new foreign direct investment, produced over 500,000 new jobs in the 1990s. Ireland's recent economic success has been achieved, in part, through a social or strategic partnership. Armed with a consensus on the problem, they took a long-term, strategic approach to economic and social change. The steps they took established a positive labour relations climate and stabilized the macro-economic and fiscal situation in Ireland.

> "Strategic Partnership," The Strategic Partnership Study Group, Province of Newfoundland and Labrador, June 2002

2. Trace the possible effects of the following occurrences:

   a. You pick out a salad at the cafeteria and sit down to eat. Suddenly you notice a large green worm on one of the lettuce leaves.

   b. As you leave your composition classroom, you trip and break your arm.

■ Reasoning Errors in Causal Analysis

Ignoring Multiple Causes

An effect rarely stems from a single cause. The person who believes that permissive parents have caused the present upsurge of sexually transmitted diseases or the one who blames television violence for the climbing numbers of emotionally disturbed children oversimplifies the situation. Permissiveness and violence perhaps did contribute to these conditions. Without much doubt, however, numerous other factors also played important parts.

Mistaking Chronology for Causation

Don't assume that just because one event followed another, the first necessarily caused the second. This kind of faulty thinking feeds many popular superstitions. Horace walks under a ladder, later stubs his toe, and thinks that his path caused his pain. Sue breaks a mirror just before Al breaks their engagement; then she blames the cracked mirror. Today some people believe that the testing of atomic weapons has altered our weather patterns. Don't misunderstand: One event *may* cause the next, but before you go on record with your conclusion, make sure that you're not dealing with mere chronology.

Confusing Causes with Effects

Young children sometimes declare that the moving trees make the wind blow. Similarly, some adults may think that Lee and Paul married because they fell in love, when in reality economic necessity mandated the vows, and love came later. Scan your evidence carefully in order to avoid such faulty assertions.

EXERCISE

1. Which of the following statements point toward papers that will focus on causes? Which point toward papers focusing on effects? Explain your answers.

    a. There are many reasons why more boys than girls are dropping out of school.

    b. While offshore oil exploration will produce new jobs, it may also damage the marine environment in a number of ways.

    c. Children who live in poverty are twice as likely as other children to have poor health, to score low on school readiness exams, and to require remedial education.

■ Ethical Issues

Causation is not immune from abuse, either accidental or deliberate. Imagine the consequences of an article that touts a new herbal remedy but fails to mention several serious side effects that could harm many users. Think about the possible strain on your relationship with a friend if she unjustly suspected you of starting a vicious rumour about her. Writing cause-and-effect papers creates an ethical responsibility. Asking and answering these questions will help you meet that obligation.

- Have I tried to uncover all of the causes that might result in a particular outcome? A report blaming poor instruction alone for a high school failure rate in a certain town's public schools almost certainly overlooks such factors as oversized classes, inadequate facilities, and poor home environments.

- Have I carefully weighed the importance of the causes I've uncovered? If a few, but not most, of the classes in the school system with problems are oversized, then the report should not stress their significance.

- Have I tried to uncover and discuss every important effect, even one that might damage a case I'm trying to make? A report emphasizing the beneficial effects of jogging would be negligent if it failed to note the potential for injury.

- What would be the consequences if people acted on my advice?

Careful evaluation of causes and effects fulfills not only your writing obligation but also your ethical one.

■ Writing a Causal Analysis

Planning and Drafting the Causal Analysis

Because you have probably speculated about the causes and effects of several campus, local, provincial, or national problems, writing this type of paper should pose no great difficulty. If you choose your own topic, perhaps your personal experience will suggest something promising. Topics such as "Why I Dislike (or Like) Sports Cars" and "How My Father's (or Someone Else's) Death Has Changed My Life" might work well. Nonpersonal topics also offer writing possibilities. For instance, "What's Behind Teenage Suicides?" and "The Impact of Global Markets on Canadian Corporations" would allow you to draw on library resources.

The strategies on pages 13–20 can also help you find several topics. Answer these questions about each potential candidate:

What purpose will guide this writing?

Who is my audience? Will the topic interest them? Why or why not?

Shall I focus on causes, effects, or both?

Brainstorming your topic for supporting details should be easy. If you're dealing with causes, pose these questions about each one:

How significant is this cause?

Could it have brought about the effect by itself?

Does it form part of a chain?

Precisely how does it contribute to the effect?

For papers dealing with effects, substitute the following questions for the ones above:

How important is this effect?

What evidence will establish its importance?

Charting your results can help you prepare for writing the paper. To tabulate causes, use an arrangement like this one:

Cause	Contribution to Effect
First cause	Specific contribution
Second cause	Specific contribution

For effects, use this chart:

Effect	Importance
First effect	Why important
Second effect	Why important

Once your items are tabulated, examine them carefully for completeness. Perhaps you've overlooked a cause or effect or have slighted the significance of one you've already mentioned. Think about the order in which you'd like to discuss your items and prepare a revised chart that reflects your decision.

Use the opening of your paper to identify your topic and indicate whether you plan to discuss causes, effects, or both. You can signal your intention in a number of ways. To prepare for a focus on causes, you might use the words *cause, reason,* or *stem from,* or you might ask why something has occurred. To signal a paper on effects, you might use *effect, fallout,* or *result,* or you might ask what has happened since something took place. Read these examples:

Signals causes: Sudbury's recent decrease in street crime stems primarily from its expanded educational program, growing job opportunities for young people, and falling rate of drug addiction.

Signals effects: Since my marriage to Rita, how has my social life changed?

At times you may choose some dramatic attention-getter. For a paper on the effects of radon, a toxic radioactive gas present in many homes, you might note, "Although almost everyone now knows about the hazards associated with smoking, eating high-cholesterol foods, and drinking excessively, few people are aware that just going home could be hazardous to one's health." If you use an arresting statement, be sure the content of your paper warrants it.

How you organize the body of the paper depends on your topic. Close scrutiny may reveal that one cause was indispensable; the rest merely played supporting roles. If so, discuss the main cause first. In analyzing your automobile mishap, which fits this situation, start with the failure of the other driver to yield the right-of-way; then fan out to any other causes that merit mentioning. Sometimes you'll find that no single cause was essential but that all of them helped matters along. Combinations of this kind lie at the heart of many social and economic concerns: inflation, depression, and urban crime rates, to name just a few. Weigh each cause carefully and rank them in importance. If your topic and purpose will profit from building suspense, work from the least important cause to the most important. Otherwise, reverse the order. For analyzing causal chains, chronological order works effectively.

If space won't permit you to deal adequately with every cause, pick out the two or three you consider most important and limit your discussion to them. To avoid giving your reader an oversimplified impression, acknowledge that other causes exist. Even if length poses no problem, don't attempt to trace every cause to some more remote cause and then to a still more remote one. Instead, determine some sensible cutoff point that accords with your purpose, and don't go beyond it.

Treat effects as carefully as you do causes. Keep in mind that effects often travel in packs, and try to arrange them in some logical order. If they occur together, consider order of climax. If one follows the other in a chainlike sequence, present them in that fashion. If space considerations dictate, limit your discussion to the most interesting or significant effects. Whatever order you choose for your paper, don't jump helter-skelter from cause to effect to cause in a way that leaves your reader bewildered.

As you write, don't restrict yourself to a bare-bones discussion of causes and effects. If, for instance, you're exploring the student parking problem on your campus, you might describe the jammed lots or point out that students often miss class because they have to drive around and look for spots. Similarly, don't simply assert that the administration's insensitivity contributes to the problem. Instead, cite examples of their refusal to answer letters about the situation or to discuss it. To provide statistical evidence of the problem's seriousness, you might note the small number of lots, the limited spaces in each, and the approximate number of student cars on campus.

It's important to remember, however, that you're not just listing causes and effects; you're showing the reader their connection in order to serve a larger purpose.

Let's see how one student handled this connection. After you've read "Why Students Drop Out of University" the student essay that follows in this chapter, carefully re-examine paragraph 3. Note how the sentence beginning "In many schools" and the two following it show precisely how poor study habits develop. Note further how the sentence beginning "This laxity produces" and the three following it show precisely how such poor habits result in "a flood of low grades and failure." University students who read this causal analysis are better armed to avoid poor study habits and their consequences.

Causal analyses can end in several ways. A paper discussing the effects of acid rain on Canada's lakes and streams might specify the grave consequences of failing to deal with the problem or express the hope that something will be done. Frequently, writers use their conclusions to evaluate the relative importance of their causes or effects.

Revising the Causal Analysis

Follow the guidelines in Chapter 3 and answer these questions as you revise your causal analysis:

Have I made the right decision in electing to focus on causes, effects, or both?

Have I ferreted out all important causes and effects? mistakenly labelled something as an effect merely because it follows something else? confused causes with effects?

Am I dealing with a causal chain? An immediate cause and several supporting causes? multiple causes and effects?

Have I presented my causes and effects in an appropriate order?

Have I supported my discussion with sufficient details?

Example Student Essay of Cause and Effect

Why Students Drop Out of University

Diann Fisher

1   Each fall a new crop of first-year university students, wavering between high hopes for the future and intense anxiety about their new status, scan campus maps searching for their classrooms. They have been told repeatedly that university is the key to a well-paying job, and they certainly don't want to support themselves by flipping hamburgers or working at some other dead-end job. So, notebooks at the ready, they await what university has in store.

Unfortunately many of them--indeed, over 30 percent--will not return after the first year. Why do so many students leave? There are several reasons. Some find the academic program too hard, some lack the proper study habits or motivation, others fall victim to the temptations of the environment, and a large group leave for personal reasons.

2   Not surprisingly, the academic shortcomings of university students have strong links to high school. In the past, a high school student who lacked the ability or desire to take a preparatory course could settle for a diploma in general studies and afterward find a job with decent pay. Now that possibility scarcely exists, so many poorly prepared students feel compelled to try university. Getting accepted by some schools isn't difficult. Once in, though, the student who has taken nothing beyond general mathematics, English, and science faces serious trouble when confronted with advanced algebra, first-year composition, and biological or physical science. Most universities do offer remedial courses and other assistance that may help some weaker students to survive. In spite of everything, however, many others find themselves facing ever-worsening grade-point averages and either fail or just give up.

3   Like academic shortcomings, poor study habits have their roots in high school, where even average students can often breeze through with a minimum of effort. In many schools, outside assignments are rare and so easy that they require little time or thought to complete. To accommodate slower students, teachers frequently repeat material so many times that slightly better students can grasp it without opening their books. And when papers are late, teachers often don't mark them down. This laxity produces students who can't or don't want to study, students totally unprepared for the rigorous demands of university. There, courses may require several hours of study each week in order to be passed with even a C. In many programs, outside assignments are commonplace and demanding. Instructors expect students to grasp material after one explanation, and many won't accept late papers at all. Students who don't quickly develop disciplined study habits face a flood of low grades and failure.

4   Poor student motivation aggravates faulty study habits. Students who thought high school was boring find even less allure in the

more challenging university offerings. Lacking any commitment to do well, they shrug off assigned papers, skip classes, and avoid doing required reading. Over time, classes gradually shrink as more and more students stay away. With final exams upon them, some return in a last-ditch effort to salvage a passing grade, but by then it is too late. Eventually, repetition of this scenario forces the students out.

5   The wide range of freedoms offered by the university environment can overwhelm even well-prepared newcomers. While students are in high school, parents are on hand to make them study, push them off to class, and send them to bed at a reasonable hour. Once away from home and parents, however, far too many students become caught up in a constant round of parties, dates, bull sessions, and other distractions that seem more fascinating than school work. Again, if such behaviour persists poor grades and failure result.

6   Personal reasons also take a heavy toll on students who might otherwise complete their programs successfully. Often, money problems are at fault. For example, a student may lose a scholarship or grant, fail to obtain needed work, or find that the family can no longer afford to help out. Some students succumb to homesickness; some are forced out by an illness, injury, or death in the family; and yet others become ill or injure themselves and leave to recuperate. Finally, a considerable number become disillusioned with their programs or the size, location, or atmosphere of their schools and decide not to return.

7   What happens to the students who drop out? Some re-enroll later, often in less demanding schools that offer a better chance of academic success. Of the remainder, the great bulk find jobs. Most, whatever their choice, go on to lead productive, useful lives. In the meantime, campus newcomers need to know about the dangers that tripped up so many of their predecessors and make every effort to avoid them.

DISCUSSION QUESTIONS

1. Identify the thesis statement in this essay. Who is the audience and what is the larger purpose for this essay?
2. Trace the causal chain that makes up paragraph 2.
3. In which paragraphs does the writer discuss causes? Effects?

SUGGESTIONS FOR WRITING *Use one of the topics below, or another that your instructor approves, to develop a causal analysis. Determine which causes and/or effects to consider. Scrutinize your analysis for errors in reasoning, settle on an organization, and write the essay.*

1. Effects of the Internet or e-mail on your family life, social life, or work life
2. Causes and/or effects of a particular kind of stress on your life
3. Causes and/or effects of bullying at school or elsewhere
4. Effects of an unwise choice that you have made
5. Reasons for the popularity of a particular trend among teenagers (street racing, real-time Internet communication, gang culture) or another group of people
6. Effects of a recent change in policy regarding health care, education, law, or other public policy
7. Effects of media coverage of a recent incident of violence that has occurred in Canada or elsewhere
8. Effects (or mixture of causes and effects) of a particular obsession or minor addiction (worry, gossip, video games, cell phones, etc.)
9. Reasons for (or effects of) your choice to go to college or university
10. Benefits of participating in a particular healthful practice or sport

The Critical Edge

Although nearly everyone recognizes the role of causation in human affairs, differences of opinion often surface about the causes and effects of important matters. What lies behind the widespread incivility in society today? Why are women more likely than men to leave management jobs? How do video games affect children? What impact does the high divorce rate have on society? Obviously such questions lack simple answers; as a result, investigators, even when they agree on the causes and effects involved, often debate their relative importance.

Suppose your women's studies instructor has asked you to investigate the departure of women from managerial positions. A library search reveals several articles on this topic as well as a number of reasons for resigning. Some women leave because they find it harder to advance than men do, and as a result they seldom attain senior positions. Others leave because they receive lower salaries than their male counterparts. Still others leave because of the stifling effects of corporate rigidity, unrealistic expectations, the demands of raising a family, or possibly diminished chances of marriage. Although most articles cite these causes, their relative importance is debatable. One writer, for example, emphasizes family concerns by discussing them last and at greatest length. Another puts the chief blame on obstacles to upward mobility—the existence of a "glass ceiling" that blocks women from upper-level positions along with an "old-boys network" of entrenched executives that parcels out jobs among its members.

Once you've finished your research, you're ready to synthesize (see pages 64–65) the views of your sources as well as your own views. Before you start to write, though, take some time to consider carefully each cause and effect you've uncovered. Obviously you should ground your paper on well-supported and widely acknowledged causes and effects, but you might also include more speculative ones as long as you clearly indicate their secondary nature. To illustrate, one writer, while mentioning corporate rigidity as a reason that women leave management jobs, clearly labels this explanation as a theory and backs it with a single example. As you examine your material, ask yourself these critical questions as well as any others that occur to you: Does any writer exhibit obvious bias? Do the studies cited include a sufficient number of examples to be meaningful? Do the statistics appear reliable, or are some out of date, irrelevant, or skimpy? Have the writers avoided the reasoning errors discussed on page 125? Whenever you find a flaw, note where the problem lies so that you can discuss it in your writing if you choose. Such discussions often clear up common misconceptions. There are various possibilities for organizing your paper. If your sources substantially agree on the most important cause, you might begin with that one and then take up the others. A second possibility, the order-of-climax arrangement, reverses the procedure by starting with secondary causes and ending with the most significant one. You can use the same options for organizing effects. When no clear consensus exists about the relative importance of the different causes and effects, there is no best arrangement of the material.*

SUGGESTIONS FOR WRITING

1. Read three articles on the causes of a major social controversy such as one related to First Nations land claims, immigration policies, or drug policies, and incorporate those causes and your own views in a paper.

2. Write an essay that corrects a common misconception about the causes or effects of a matter about which you feel strongly. Possibilities might include the causes of homelessness in your region or the effects of longer jail terms on young offenders.

---

*Because this type of paper draws upon published information, it is important to read the sections on card catalogues and periodical indexes in Chapter 19 and those on handling quotations and avoiding plagiarism in Chapter 20 before you start to write. As always, follow your instructor's guidelines for documenting sources.

chapter 11

· ·

Definition: Establishing Boundaries

That movie was egregious.
Once the bandage is off the wound, swab the proud flesh with the disinfectant.
Speaking on *Hockey Night in Canada,* Don Cherry called the player a floater.

Do you have questions? You're not alone. Many people would question the sentences above: "What does *egregious* mean?" "How can flesh be *proud?*" "What does Don Cherry mean by *floater?*" To avoid puzzling and provoking your own readers, you'll often need to explain the meaning of some term. The term may be unfamiliar *(egregious),* used in an unfamiliar sense *(proud flesh),* or mean different things to different people *(floater).* Whenever you clarify the meaning of some term, you are *defining.*

Humans are instinctively curious. We start asking about meanings as soon as we can talk, and we continue to seek, as well as supply, definitions all through life. In school, instructors expect us to explain all sorts of literary, historical, scientific, technical, and social terms. On the job, a member of a company's human resources department might prepare a brochure that explains the meaning of such terms as *corporate responsibility* and *product stewardship* for new employees. An accountant might define *statistical sampling inventory* in a report calling for a change in the inventory system. A special education teacher might write a memo explaining *learning disabled* to the rest of the staff.

When you define, you identify the features that distinguish a term, thereby putting a fence around it, establishing its boundaries, and separating it from all others. Knowing these features enables both you and your reader to use the term appropriately.

Sometimes a word, phrase, or sentence will settle a definition question. To clear up the mystery of "proud flesh," all you'd need to do is insert the parenthetical phrase (excessively swollen and grainy) after the word *proud*. But when you're dealing with new terms—*chronic fatigue* and *virtual reality* are examples—brief definitions won't provide the reader with enough information for proper understanding.

Abstract terms—those standing for things we can't see, touch, or otherwise detect with our five senses—often require extended definitions, too. It's impossible to capture the essence of *democracy* or *hatred* or *bravery* in a single sentence: the terms are too complex, and people have too many differing ideas about what they mean. The same holds true for some concrete terms—those standing for actions and things we can perceive with our five senses. Some people, for instance, limit the term *drug pusher* to full-time sellers of hard drugs like cocaine and heroin. Others, at the opposite extreme, extend the term to full- and part-time sellers of any illegal drug. Writing an argument recommending life sentences for convicted drug pushers would require you to tell just what you mean by the term so that the reader would have solid grounds for judging your position.

■ Types of Definitions

Three types of definitions—synonyms, essential definitions, and extended definitions—serve writers' needs. Although the first two seldom require more than a word or a sentence, an extended definition can run to several pages. The three types, however, are related. Synonyms and essential definitions share space between the covers of dictionaries, and both furnish starting points for extended definitions.

Synonyms

Synonyms are words with very nearly the same meanings. *Lissome* is synonymous with *lithe* or *nimble,* and *condign* is a synonym of *worthy* and *suitable.* Synonyms let writers clarify meanings of unfamiliar words without using cumbersome explanations. To clarify the term *expostulation* in a quoted passage, all you'd have to do is add the word *objection,* in brackets, after it. Because synonyms are not identical twins, using them puts a slightly different shade of meaning on a message. For example, to "protest" and to "object" are certainly similar in many ways. Yet the claim that we "object" to the establishment of a nuclear waste site in our area fails to capture the active and sustained commitment implied in our willingness to "protest" against such a site. Still, synonyms provide a convenient means of breaking communications logjams.

Essential Definitions

An essential definition does three things: (1) names the item being defined, (2) places it in a broad category, and (3) distinguishes it from other items in that category. Here are three examples:

Item Being Defined	Broad Category	Distinguishing Features
A howdah	is a covered seat	for riding on the back of an elephant or camel.
A voiceprint	is a graphical record	of a person's voice characteristics.
To parboil	is to boil meat, vegetables, or fruits	until they are partially cooked.

Writing a good essential definition requires careful thought. Suppose your instructor has asked you to write an essential definition of one of the terms listed in an exercise, and you choose vacuum cleaner. Coming up with a broad category presents no problem: a vacuum cleaner is a household appliance. The hard part is pinpointing the distinguishing features. The purpose of a vacuum cleaner is to clean floors, carpets, and upholstery. You soon realize, however, that these features alone do not separate vacuum cleaners from other appliances. After all, carpet sweepers also clean floors, and whisk brooms clean upholstery. What then does distinguish vacuum cleaners? After a little thought, you realize that, unlike the other items, a vacuum cleaner works by suction. You then write the following definition:

> A vacuum cleaner is a household appliance that uses suction to clean floors, carpets, and upholstery.

The same careful attention is necessary to establish the distinguishing features of any essential definition.

Limitations of Essential Definitions Essential definitions have certain built-in limitations. Because of their brevity, they often can't do full justice to abstract terms such as *cowardice, love, jealousy, power.* Problems also arise with terms that have several settled meanings. To explain *jam* adequately, you'd need at least three essential definitions: (1) a closely packed crowd, (2) preserves, and (3) a difficult situation. But despite these limitations, an essential definition can be useful by itself or as part of a longer definition. Writers often build an extended definition around an essential definition.

Pitfalls in Preparing Essential Definitions When you prepare an essential definition, guard against these flaws:

> *Circular definition.* Don't define a term by repeating it or changing its form slightly. Saying that a psychiatrist is "a physician who practises psychiatry" will only frustrate someone who's never heard of psychiatry. Repress circularity and provide

the proper insight by choosing terms the reader can relate to, for example, "A psychiatrist is a physician who diagnoses and treats mental disorders."

Overly broad definition. Shy away from definitions that embrace too much territory. If you define a skunk as "an animal that has a bushy tail and black fur with white markings," your definition is not precise. Many cats and dogs also fit this description. But if you add "and that ejects a foul-smelling secretion when threatened," you will clear the air, of any misconceptions at least.

Overly narrow definition. Don't hem in your definition too closely, either. "A kitchen blender is a bladed electrical appliance used to chop foods" illustrates this error. Blenders perform other operations, too. To correct the error, add the missing information: "A kitchen blender is a bladed electrical appliance used to chop, mix, whip, liquefy, or otherwise process foods."

Omission of main category. Avoid using "is where" or "is when" instead of naming the main category. Here are examples of this error: "A bistro is where food and wine are served" and "An ordination is when a person is formally recognized as a minister, priest, or rabbi." The reader will not know exactly what sort of thing (a bar? a party?) a *bistro* is and may think that *ordination* means a time. Note the improvement when the broad categories are named: "A bistro is a small restaurant where both food and wine are served" and "An ordination is a ceremony at which a person is formally recognized as a minister, priest, or rabbi."

EXERCISE

1. **Identify the broad category and the distinguishing traits in each of these essential definitions:**

   a. Gangue is useless rock accompanying valuable minerals in a deposit.

   b. A catbird is a small songbird with a slate-coloured body, a black cap, and a catlike cry.

   c. A soldier is a man or woman serving in an army.

   d. A magnum is a wine bottle that holds about one-and-a-half litres.

2. **Indicate which of the following statements are acceptable essential definitions. Explain what is wrong with those that are not. Correct them.**

   a. A scalpel is a small knife that has a sharp blade used for surgery and anatomical dissections.

   b. A puritan is a person with puritanical beliefs.

   c. A kraal is where South African tribes keep large domestic animals.

   d. A rifle is a firearm that has a grooved barrel and is used for hunting large game.

3. **Write an essential definition for each of the following terms:**

   a. spam   **c.** hit man

   b. happy hour   **d.** jock

Extended Definitions

Sometimes it's necessary to go beyond an essential definition and write a paragraph or whole paper explaining a term. New technical, social, and economic terms often require extended definitions. To illustrate, a computer scientist might need to define *data integrity* so that computer operators understand the importance of maintaining it. Terms with differing meanings also frequently require extended definitions. Furthermore, extended definition is crucial to interpretation of the law, as we see when courts clarify the meaning of concepts such as obscenity.

Extended definitions are not merely academic exercises; they are fundamental to your career and your life. A police officer needs to have a clear understanding of what counts as *reasonable grounds for search and seizure;* an engineer must comprehend the meaning of *stress;* a nuclear medical technologist had better have a solid grasp of *radiation.* And all of us are concerned with the definition of our basic rights as citizens.

Extended definitions are montages of other methods of development—narration, description, process analysis, illustration, classification, comparison, and cause and effect. Often, they also define by negation: explaining what a term *does not* mean. The following paragraphs show how one writer handled an extended definition of *sudden infant death syndrome.* The student began by presenting a case history (illustration), which also incorporated an essential definition and two synonyms.

> Jane and Dick Smith were proud new parents of an eight-pound, ten-ounce baby girl named Jenny. One summer night, Jane put Jenny to bed at 8:00. When she went to check on her at 3:00 A.M., Jane found Jenny dead. The baby had given no cry of pain, shown no sign of trouble. Even the doctor did not know why she had died, for she was healthy and strong. The autopsy report confirmed the doctor's suspicion--the infant was a victim of the "sudden infant death syndrome," also known as SIDS or crib death. SIDS is the sudden and unexplainable death of an apparently healthy, sleeping infant. It is the number-one cause of death in infants after the first week of life and as a result has been the subject of numerous research studies.

DISCUSSION QUESTIONS

1. What synonyms does the writer use?
2. Which sentence presents an essential definition?

In the next paragraph, the writer turned to negation, pointing out some of the things that researchers have ruled out about SIDS.

> Although researchers do not know what SIDS is, they do know what it is not. They know it cannot be predicted; it strikes like a thief in the night. Crib deaths occur in seconds, with no sound of pain, and they always happen when the child is sleeping. Suffocation is not the cause, nor is aspiration or regurgitation.

Researchers have found no correlation between the incidence of SIDS and the mother's use of birth control pills or the presence of fluoride in water. Since it is not hereditary or contagious, only a slim chance exists that SIDS will strike twice in the same family.

Finally, the student explored several proposed causes of SIDS as well as how parents may react to the loss of their child.

As might be expected, researchers have offered many theories concerning the cause of crib death. Dr. R. C. Reisinger, a National Cancer Institute scientist, has linked crib deaths to the growth of a common bacterium, E. coli, in the intestines of newborn babies. The organisms multiply in the intestines, manufacturing a toxin that is absorbed by the intestinal wall and passes into the bloodstream. Breast milk stops the growth of the organism, whereas cow's milk permits it. Therefore, Dr. Reisinger believes, bottle-fed babies run a higher risk of crib death than other babies. . . .

The loss of a child through crib death is an especially traumatic experience. Parents often develop feelings of guilt and depression, thinking they somehow caused the child's death. To alleviate such feelings, organizations have been established to help parents accept the fact that they did not cause the death.

Trudy Stelter

■ Ethical Issues

How we define can have devastating consequences. For centuries, the practice of defining Africans as "subhuman" helped justify the slave trade and slavery. During the 1930s and early 1940s, labelling Jews as "vermin" was used to fuel the attempt to exterminate them both in Nazi Germany and much of the rest of Western Europe. Even in the absence of malice, definitions can have far-reaching effects, both good and bad. Definitions of certain learning disabilities will affect whether or not a student in the public school system is eligible for extra assistance. Recently, the definition of "terrorist," which has political, legal, and military implications, has come under intense scrutiny. Answering the following questions will help you think about possible ethical implications of your definitions.

- Have I carefully evaluated all the features of my definition? In clarifying what constitutes "excessive force" by the police, it would be unfair to include the reasonable means necessary to subdue a highly dangerous suspect.

- Have I slanted my definition to reflect some prejudice? Let's say a writer opposed to casino gambling is defining "gambling addicts." The paper should focus on those who spend an excessive amount of time in casinos, bet and often lose large sums of money, and in so doing neglect family, financial, and personal obligations. It would be unfair to include those who visit casinos occasionally and strictly limit their losses.

- Have I avoided unnecessary connotations that might be harmful? A definition of teenagers that overemphasized their swift changes in mood might be unfair, perhaps even harmful, since it may influence the reactions of readers.

Writing an Extended Definition

Planning and Drafting the Extended Definition

If you choose your own topic, pick an abstract term or one that is concrete but unfamiliar to your reader. Why, for instance, define *table* when the discussion would likely ease the reader into the Land of Nod? On the other hand, a paper explaining *computer virus* might well prove interesting and informative. Use one of the strategies on pages 13–20 to unearth promising topics. Then answer these questions about them:

> Which topic holds the most promise? Why?
>
> What purpose will guide my writing? to clarify a technical or specialized concept? to show what the term means to me? to persuade the reader to adopt my attitude toward it? to discuss some neglected facet of it?
>
> For what audience should I write?

Here's a helpful process to follow as you think your definition through. First, select a clear example that illustrates what you wish to define: the United States could exemplify *democracy*. Then brainstorm to uncover major identifying characteristics. For democracy your list might include majority rule, free elections, a separately elected chief executive, and basic human rights. Next, test these characteristics against other legitimate examples and retain only the characteristics that apply. Canada is clearly a democracy but doesn't have a separately elected chief executive. Finally, test the unfolding definition against a clear counter example, perhaps the People's Republic of China. If the definition fits the example, something is wrong.

Now evaluate what methods you might use to develop your definition. Each method has its own set of special strengths, as the following list shows:

Narration.	Tracing the history of a new development or the changing meaning of a term
Description.	Pointing out interesting or important features of a device, an event, or an individual
Process.	Explaining what a device does or how it is used, how a procedure is carried out, or how a natural event takes place

Illustration.	Tracing changes in meaning and defining abstract terms
Classification.	Pointing out the different categories into which an item or an event can be grouped
Comparison.	Distinguishing between an unfamiliar and a familiar item
Cause and effect.	Explaining the origins and consequences of events, conditions, problems, and attitudes
Negation.	Placing limitations on conditions and events and correcting popular misconceptions

Examine your topic in light of this listing and select the methods of development that seem most promising. Don't hesitate to use a method for some purpose not mentioned here. If you think that a comparison will help your reader understand some abstract term, use it.

Chart the methods of development you'll use, and then brainstorm each method in turn to gather the details that will inform the reader. When you've finished, look everything over, rearrange the details as necessary, add any new ones you think of, and prepare a revised chart. The example that follows is for a paper utilizing four methods of development.

Narration	**Classification**	**Process**	**Negation**
First supporting detail	First supporting detail	First supporting detail	First supporting detail
Second supporting detail	Second supporting detail	Second supporting detail	Second supporting detail

Definition papers can begin in various ways. If you're defining a term with no agreed-upon meaning (for example, *conservatism*), you might note some differing views of it and then state your own. If the term reflects some new social, political, economic, or technological development (such as the *wireless Internet* or *nanotechnology*), you might mention the events that brought it into being. A colloquial or slang term often lends itself nicely to an attention-getting opener. A paper defining *chutzpah* might begin by illustrating the brash behaviour of someone with this trait. Often an introduction includes a short definition, perhaps taken from a dictionary. If you do include a dictionary definition, use the full name of the dictionary (*The Canadian Oxford Dictionary* says . . .). Draw on a dictionary definition, however, only as a last resort.

In writing the body of the paper, present the methods of development in whatever order seems most appropriate. A paper defining *drag racing* might first describe the hectic scene as the cars line up for a race, then classify the different categories of vehicles, and finally explain the steps in a race. One defining *intellectual* might start by showing the differences between intellectuals and scholars, then name several prominent intellectuals and note how their insights have altered our thinking, and conclude by trying to explain why many people hold intellectuals in low regard.

Definition papers can end in a number of ways. If you're defining some undesirable condition or event (such as the *sudden infant death syndrome*), you might express hope for a speedy solution. If you're reporting on some new development (like the *wireless Internet*), you might predict its economic or social impact. Choose whichever type of ending best supports your main idea.

Revising the Extended Definition

Use the general guidelines in Chapter 3 and these specific questions as you revise your extended definition:

Are my purpose and audience clear and appropriate?

If I've used an essential definition, does it do what it should and avoid the common pitfalls?

Are the methods of development suitable for the topic?

Is the paper organized effectively?

Are there other factors or examples I need to consider?

Have I considered appropriate ethical issues?

Example Student Essay of Definition

The Food Chain

Michael Galayda

1   It is a truism that we must eat to stay alive and that all the plants and animals we dine on must do the same. How many of us, though, ever stop to consider whether or not any pattern underlies all the cross-dining that goes on? There is a pattern, and to understand it we must first familiarize ourselves with the concept of a food chain. Such a chain can be defined as a hierarchy of organisms in a biological community, or ecosystem, with each member of the chain feeding on the one below it and in turn being fed upon by the one above it. To put the matter more simply, a food chain starts with a great quantity of plant stuffs which are eaten by a large number of very hungry diners. These diners are then eaten by a lesser number of other animals, which in turn fall prey to an even smaller number of creatures. With the passage of time, the

uneaten organisms die and become part of the soil for the plant to grow in.

2   To illustrate, let's look for a moment at one particular biological community, a marshy ecosystem, and a few events that might take place there. First, there are the marsh grasses, with millions of grasshoppers busily feeding upon them. When one grasshopper isn't looking, a shrew sneaks up and eats it. This process is repeated many times as the day wears on. Later, toward sunset, as the stuffed and inattentive shrew is crossing an open stretch of ground, a hawk swoops out of the sky and eats the rodent. The food chain is completed when the marsh hawk dies and its corpse fertilizes the marsh grasses.

3   This illustration is not meant to suggest that hawks eat only shrews or shrews eat only grasshoppers; the cycle is much more complicated than that, involving what biologists call trophic levels-- the different feeding groups in an ecosystem. For example, some creatures eat green plants and some eat meat. There are five major trophic levels. The beginning point for any food chain is green plants, known as producers, which absorb sunlight and through the process of photosynthesis turn carbon dioxide, water, and soil nutrients into food, especially carbohydrates, that animals can assimilate.

4   All of the other life forms subsist either directly or indirectly on the producers. Animals that feed directly on green plants are the herbivores, called primary consumers. This group includes, among other creatures, most insects, most rodents, and hooved animals. The secondary consumers are the carnivores and omnivores. The term carnivore, meaning an animal that eats only flesh, is more familiar than the term omnivore, which designates an animal that eats both green plants and flesh. Carnivores include such animals as lions, leopards, eagles, and hawks; whereas omnivores are represented by foxes, bears, humans, and so on.

5   The last feeding group in the food chain consists of the decomposers: bacteria and fungi. These microorganisms recycle the waste products of living animals and the remains of all dead things-- plants, herbivores, omnivores, and carnivores alike--into fertilizers that plants, the producers, can use.

6   Obviously each trophic level must produce more energy than it transfers to the next higher level. With animals, a considerable part of this energy is lost through body heat. The muscles that pump the lungs, continually pushing air out of the body and sucking it back in, consume energy. The muscles in the arms and legs sweat out energy. All of the life-supporting systems of the organism use energy to keep it going. Everything from worms to people lives in accordance with this law of energy loss. As long as life's fires burn, energy is lost, never to be regained.

7   Throughout history we humans have tried to manipulate the food chain so as to provide ever-greater outputs of energy. On the one hand, we have tried, by whatever means we could employ, to rid our fields of harmful birds, insects, and rodents, and our animals of diseases and parasites. On the other, we have constantly striven to produce healthier and more productive strains of plants and animals. Often these attempts have been spectacularly successful. Sometimes, though, the results have proved disastrous, as with the insecticide DDT.

8   Farmers first began using DDT on a large scale in 1946, right after it had proved its effectiveness in tropical military operations in World War II. As expected, the product proved equally effective as an agricultural pesticide, but there were some unexpected and disastrous side effects. The difficulties were caused by excessive DDT washing off crops, entering irrigation canals, and from there flowing to streams, rivers, and lakes. All living creatures in the path of the chemical were contaminated--worms, fish, ducks, indeed all forms of aquatic life. Contaminated worms poisoned songbirds, causing massive die-offs of birds, and many humans developed serious health problems from eating contaminated aquatic animals. Although the government has severely restricted the use of DDT in this country, the whole episode stands as a warning of what can happen when humans manipulate the food chain.

9   As time continues and the population grows, efforts will be made to further increase the food supply. Let us hope that in doing so we won't act in haste and create catastrophes of even greater magnitude.

DISCUSSION QUESTIONS

1. Identify the essay's essential definition and explain how it functions.
2. What is accomplished by the last three sentences in paragraph 1?
3. What method of development does the writer use in paragraph 2?
4. What methods of development are combined in paragraphs 3–5?
5. Cite three places in the essay where the writer uses brief definitions.

SUGGESTIONS FOR WRITING   *Write an extended definition using one of the following suggestions or one approved by your instructor. The term you define may be new, misused, or misunderstood or may have a disputed meaning. Develop the essay by any combination of writing strategies.*

1. Literacy
2. Globalism
3. Multiculturalism
4. Stress
5. Cybervandals

6. Greed
7. Computer virus
8. Biodiversity
9. Organic food
10. Rap music

Definitions are always social creations. The way various people and communities understand and use any word determines its definition. As a result, writers who use complex words such as *justice, love,* or *charisma* to convey a message may need to consult a number of sources to determine how others have used the words. With their findings of this research in mind, the writers can stake out their own meanings of those words.

If you were writing an extended definition of the word *dance* for a humanities class, you would probably find several conflicting meanings of the term. Frank Thiess, writing in *The Dance as an Artwork*, defines dance as the use of the body for expressive gesture. But as you mull over that definition, you realize that it is both too broad and too narrow. While some forms of dance, such as ballet, feature expressive gesture, so does pantomime or even a shaken fist; and neither of these qualifies as dance. A square dance clearly qualifies, but does it represent expressive gesture? Susanne Langer, in *Philosophy in a New Key*, defines dance as "a play of Powers made visible," pointing to the way dancers seem to be moved by forces beyond themselves. You recognize that this definition may apply to religious dance forms, that dancers sometimes appear swept away by the music, and that you yourself have experienced a feeling of power when dancing. Nevertheless, upon reflection you decide that often it's the dancer's skill that attracts us, and rarely do we dance to reveal invisible powers. Finally, you discover that Francis Sparshott, in *The Theory of the Arts*, defines dance as a rhythmical, patterned motion that transforms people's sense of their own existence according to the dance they do. As you evaluate Sparshott's contention, you decide that it has considerable merit, although you aren't convinced that every dance transforms our sense of existence. When you think about the kinds of dance you know and the various definitions you have uncovered, you conclude that these writers, like the blind men who felt different parts of an elephant and tried to describe it, are each only partly correct. For your humanities paper, you decide to synthesize (see pages 64–65) the different definitions. You might explain that all dance involves a rhythmical, patterned movement of the body for its own sake. Sometimes such movement can transform our sense of existence, as in trance dances or even waltzes. Other dances, such as story ballets, use rhythmical movements as expressive gestures that tell stories or convey emotions. Still other dances may suggest the manifestation of powers beyond the dances themselves. You proceed to explain each of these features with details drawn both from your sources and from personal experience.

Carrying out this type of project requires you to look critically at the definitions of others. Do they accurately reflect the examples you know about? Do they describe examples that do not fit the definition? Are any parts of the definition questionable? Once you've answered these questions, you can then draw on the appropriate elements of the definitions to formulate your own. You might organize such a paper by developing each definition in a separate section, first presenting it in detail and then pointing out its strengths and weaknesses. In the final section, you could offer your own definition and support it with your reasoning and suitable examples.[*]

SUGGESTIONS FOR WRITING

1. Read "The Sweet Smell of Success . . ." (pages 488–490), and "The Company Man" (pages 439–441).Then write your own definition of success, taking into account the views expressed in these essays.

2. Do some reading about an abstract term like *pornography, democracy, marriage,* or *terrorism* in at least three sources. Use the sources to develop your own definition of the term.

3. If you are familiar with a particular type of jargon from an area you know well (sports, computers, music, etc.), define this language for a reader uninitiated to this specialized language. This essay might blend different strategies of development such as illustration, for you will need to provide examples and definitions along the way. Alternatively, you might choose to organize your essay mainly around one extended definition of a significant word or phrase.

---

*Because you'll draw upon published sources, it is important to read the sections on card catalogues and periodical indexes in Chapter 19 and those on handling quotations and avoiding plagiarism in Chapter 20 before you start to write. As always, follow your instructor's guidelines for documenting sources.

Argument: Convincing Others

"What did you think of that movie?"

"Great!"

"What do you mean, great? I thought the acting was wooden and the story completely unbelievable."

"That's about what I'd expect from you. You wouldn't know a good movie if it walked up and bit you."

"Oh yeah? What makes you think you're such a great . . . ?"

Argument or quarrel? Many people would ask, "What's the difference?" To them, the two terms convey the same meaning, both calling to mind two angry people, shouting, trading insults, and sometimes slugging it out. In writing, however, argument stands for something quite different: a paper, grounded on logical, structured evidence, that attempts to convince the reader to accept an opinion, take some action, or do both.

The ability to argue effectively will help you succeed both in class and on the job. A business instructor may ask students to defend a particular management style. A political science instructor may want you to support or oppose limiting the number of terms that members of Parliament can serve. A special education instructor may have students make a written case for increased funding for exceptional students. In the workplace, a computer programmer may argue that the company should change its account-keeping program, an automotive service manager call for new diagnostic equipment, and a union president make a case that a company's employees merit raises.

Arguments don't always involve conflicts. Some simply support a previously established decision or course of action, as when a department manager sends her boss a memo justifying some new procedure that she implemented. Others try to establish some common ground, just as you might do when you and your date weigh the pros and cons of two films and pick one to see.

When preparing to write an argument, you need to be aware that certain kinds of topics just aren't arguable. There's no point, for instance, in trying to tackle questions of personal preference or taste (Is red prettier than blue?). Such contests quickly turn into "it is," "it isn't" exchanges that establish nothing except the silliness of the contenders. Questions of simple fact (Was Pierre Trudeau Prime Minister in 1972?) don't qualify either; one side has all the ammunition. Bickering will never settle these issues; reference books quickly will. We turn to argument when there is room for disagreement.

When you write an argument, you don't simply sit down and dash off your views as though they came prefabricated. Instead, argument represents an opportunity to think things through, to gradually, and often tentatively, come to some conclusions, and then, in stages, begin to draft your position with the support you have discovered. You should try to keep an open mind as you formulate and then express your views.

The most successful arguments rest on a firm foundation of solid, logical support. In addition, many arguments include emotion because it can play an important part in swaying reader opinion. Furthermore, writers often make ethical appeals by projecting favourable images of themselves since readers form conclusions based on their judgments of the writer.

■ The Rational Appeal

Among family, friends, and your community, and certainly in professional circles, you are usually expected to reach your conclusions on the basis of good reasons and appropriate evidence. Reasons are the key points you'll use to defend your conclusions. If, for instance, you support safe injection sites for intravenous drug users, one reason might be the considerable reduction in AIDS-related deaths that could result. If you oppose the program, one reason may be the drug dependency that will continue.

To convince readers, your reasons must be substantiated by evidence. If you favour safe injection sites, you could cite figures that project the number of deaths that will be prevented. If you're against the program, you might quote a respected authority who verifies that dependency will become entrenched.

When you appeal to reason in an argument, then, you present your reasons and evidence in such a way that if your readers are also reasonable they will likely agree with you, or at least see your position as plausible. That assumes, of course, that you and your readers start from some common ground about the principles you share and what you count as evidence. Evidence falls into several categories:

established truths, opinions of authorities, primary source information, statistical findings, and personal experience. The strongest arguments usually combine several kinds of evidence.

Established Truths

These are facts that no one can seriously dispute. Here are some examples:

Historical fact:	The Canadian Charter of Rights and Freedoms prohibits racial discrimination.
Scientific fact:	The layer of ozone in the earth's upper atmosphere protects us from the sun's harmful ultraviolet radiation.
Geographical fact:	Alberta has the largest oil reserves in Canada.

Established truths aren't arguable themselves but do provide strong backup for argumentative propositions. For example, citing the abundant oil supply in the western regions could support an argument that Canada should promote the increased use of oil to supply its energy needs.

Some established truths, the result of careful observations and thinking over many years, basically amount to enlightened common sense. The notion that everyone possesses a unique combination of interests, abilities, and personality characteristics illustrates this kind of truth. Few people would seriously question it.

Opinions of Authorities

An authority is a recognized expert in some field. Authoritative opinions—the only kind to use—play a powerful role in winning readers over to your side. The views of metropolitan police chiefs and criminologists could support your position on ways to control urban crime. Researchers who have investigated the effects of air pollution could help you argue for stricter smog-control laws. Whatever your argument, don't settle for less than heavyweight authorities, and, when possible, indicate their credentials to your reader. This information makes their statements more persuasive. For example, "Ann Marie Forsythe, a certified public accountant and vice-president of North American operations for Touche Ross Accounting, believes that the finance minister's tax cut proposal will actually result in a tax increase for most Canadians." You should, of course, also cite the source of your information. Follow your instructor's guidelines.

The following paragraph, from an article arguing that youth crime is becoming more violent, illustrates the use of authority:

> According to Roy O'Shaughnessy, clinical director of British Columbia's Youth Court Services, Youth Forensic Psychiatric Services, the perception that a segment of young people is becoming more brutally violent is well-founded. "The type of crime we're seeing now is different from what we saw 10 years ago," says O'Shaughnessy, whose unit does psychiatric assessments of delinquents between the ages of 12 and 17. "We're seeing more use of weapons, more gang-related activity, more violent behaviour.
>
> Brian Bergman, "When Children Are Vicious"

Beware of biased opinions. The agribusiness executive who favours farm price supports or the labour leader who opposes any restrictions on picketing may be writing merely to guard old privileges or garner new ones. Unless the opinion can stand close scrutiny, don't put it in your paper; it will just weaken your case. Be especially careful with using Internet sources. If you are using a general search engine, what will often come up under your key word search will be those sites that have paid for priority placement on the list. If you are writing a formal academic argument, you might want to search scholarly databases such as Academic Search Premier, Canadian NewsDisc, or Canadian Periodical Index for articles that have been juried by specialists in the field.

Because authorities don't always see eye to eye, their views lack the finality of established truths. Furthermore, their opinions will sway readers only if the audience accepts the authority as authoritative. Although advertisers successfully present hockey players as authorities on shaving cream and credit cards, most people would not accept their views on the safety of nuclear energy.

Primary Source Information

You'll need to support certain types of arguments with primary source information—documents or other materials produced by individuals directly involved with the issue or conclusions you reached by carrying out an investigation yourself. To argue whether or not Newfoundland should have joined Confederation, for example, you would want to examine the autobiographies of those involved in making the decision and perhaps even the documents that prompted it. To take a position on the violence mentioned in some gangster rap, you would want to analyze the actual lyrics in a number of songs. To make a claim about media coverage of the Persian Gulf War, you would want to read the newspaper and magazine accounts of correspondents who were on the scene. To convince readers to adopt your solution for the homeless problem, you might want to visit a homeless shelter or interview (in a safe place) some homeless people. This type of information can help you reach sound conclusions and build strong support for your position. Most university and college libraries contain a significant amount of primary source materials that you can draw on for an argument. Document the sources you use according to your instructor's guidelines.

Statistical Findings

Statistics—data showing how much, how many, or how often—can also buttress your argument. Most statistics come from books, magazines, newspapers, handbooks, encyclopedias, and reports, but you can use data from your own investigations as well. Statistics Canada is a good source of authoritative statistics on many different topics.

Because statistics are often misused, many people distrust them, so any you offer must be reliable. First, make sure your sample isn't too small. Don't use a one-day traffic count to argue for a traffic light at a certain intersection. City Hall might counter by contending that the results are atypical. To make your case, you'd need to count traffic for perhaps two or three weeks. Take care not to push statistical claims too far. You may know that two-thirds of Tarrytown's factories pollute the air excessively, but don't argue that the same figures probably apply to your town. There's simply no carryover. Keep alert for biased statistics; they can cause as serious a credibility gap as biased opinions. Generally, recent data are better than old data, but either must come from a reliable source. Older information from *The Globe and Mail* would probably be more accurate than current data from some publication that trades on sensationalism. Note how the following writer uses statistics to support the argument that "the news media plays an important role in feeding the public view that we're in the middle of a crime wave":

> And, the news media plays an important role in feeding the public view that we're in the middle of a crime wave. In 1995, the Fraser Institute studied media coverage of violent crime. In 1989, the murder rate in Canada was 2.4 per 100 000 people, and the two national networks (CBC and CTV) spent 10% of their airtime covering murder stories. By 1995, the murder rate had dropped to 2.04 per 100 000 people. However, national television news coverage of murder had more than doubled on both networks to fill 25% of airtime.
>
> "Distorted Picture"

Again, follow your instructor's guidelines when documenting your sources.

Personal Experience

Sometimes personal experience can deliver an argumentative message more forcefully than any other kind of evidence. Suppose that two years ago a speeder ran into your car and almost killed you. Today you're arguing for stiffer laws against speeding. Chances are you'll rely mainly on expert opinions and on statistics showing the number of people killed and injured each year in speeding accidents. However, describing the crash, the slow, pain-filled weeks in the hospital, and the months spent hobbling around on crutches may well provide the persuasive nudge that wins your reader over.

Often the experiences and observations of others, gathered from books, magazines, or interviews, can support your position. If you argue against chemical waste dumps, the personal stories of people who lived near them and suffered the consequences—filthy ooze in the basement, children with birth defects, family members who developed a rare form of cancer—can help sway your reader.

Despite its usefulness, personal experience generally reinforces but does not replace other kinds of evidence. Unless it has other support, readers may reject it as atypical or trivial.

An argument, then, consists of a conclusion you want to support, your reasons for that conclusion, and the evidence that supports your reasons. But how are reasons and evidence fitted together? Rational appeals include three reasoning strategies: induction, deduction, and analogy.

Induction

Induction moves from separate bits of evidence to a general observation. Suppose that on a hot, humid summer day you go to the kitchen to eat some potato chips from a bag opened the day before. As you start to munch, you make these observations:

Chip 1: limp and stale
Chip 2: limp and stale
Chip 3: limp and stale
Chip 4: limp and stale
Chip 5: limp and stale

At this point, you decide that the rest of the chips are probably stale too, and you stop eating. Inductive reasoning has led you, stale chip by stale chip, to a conclusion about the whole bag.

But probability is not proof. To prove something by induction, we must check every bit of evidence, and often that's just not practical or possible. Nonetheless, induction has great value for the conduct of human affairs. Say a food company has test marketed a new spaghetti sauce and now wants to decide whether it should start selling the product nationwide. A poll of 1200 users, representing a cross-section of the market, indicates that 78 percent rate the sauce "excellent." As a result, the company decides to go ahead. Induction has led it to conclude that future customers will favour the sauce as much as past customers did. Polls that sample political preferences and other public attitudes also operate inductively.

You have several options for organizing an inductive argument. You might begin by posing some direct or indirect question in order to snare your reader's interest, or you might simply state the position you will argue. The body of the paper provides the supporting evidence. In the conclusion you could reaffirm your position or suggest the consequences of that position. The following short example illustrates inductive argument:

Bologna is perhaps the most popular of all luncheon meats. Each day, thousands of individuals consume bologna sandwiches at noontime without ever considering the health consequences. Perhaps they should.

The sodium content of bologna is excessively high. On the average, three ounces contain over 850 milligrams, three times as much as a person needs in a single day. In addition, bologna's characteristic flavour and reddish colour are caused by sodium nitrite, which is used to prevent the growth of botulism-causing organisms. Unfortunately, sodium nitrite combines with amines, natural compounds already in most foods, to form nitrosamines, which have been proved to cause cancer in laboratory animals. Finally, from a nutrition standpoint, bologna is terrible. The fat content is around 28 percent, the water content ranges upward from 50 percent, and the meat includes very little protein.

```
    Health-conscious people, then, will choose better fare
for lunch.

                                           Alison Russell
```

Deduction

Deduction is the reverse of induction. Instead of formulating a conclusion after considering pieces of evidence, you start with an observation that most people accept as true and then show how certain conclusions follow from that observation. For example, to convince a friend to study harder, you begin with the assumption that a profitable career requires a good education; proceed to argue that for a good education students must study diligently; and conclude that, as a result, your friend should spend more time with the books. Politicians who assert that we all want to act in ways beneficial to future generations, then point out how the policies they favour will ensure that outcome, argue deductively.

As with induction, you have several options when organizing a deductive argument. You might begin with the position you intend to prove, with a question that will be answered by the argument, or with a synopsis of the argument. The body of the paper works out the implications of your assumption. In the conclusion you could directly state (or restate, in different words) your position, suggest the consequences of adopting or not adopting that position, or pose a question that is easily answered after reading the argument. Here is a short example of deductive argument:

```
    The sex object stereotype is extremely damaging to women in par-
ticular and society as a whole. The ideal of physical beauty por-
trayed by the stereotype is unattainable and unrealistic. Most
women do not have this idealized body shape: full breasts, tiny
waist, and narrow hips. To attain these features, most women would
have to resort to surgical alterations or starvation diets. Even
so, all women must ultimately fail this beauty test in time, for
the sex object is, above all else, young. Mere mortals cannot com-
pare with these perpetually young, airbrushed, and anorexic visions
of so-called beauty. Given the impossible and limiting expectations
of the sex object stereotype, no wonder so many women feel physi-
cally inadequate and are driven to unhealthy, and, ultimately, un-
successful extremes in pursuit of an unnatural body image. A
society that instills an impossible expectation of beauty for women
is complicit in eroding the self-esteem of many women. So, in order
to maintain and develop positive self-esteem in women, we, as a so-
ciety, should resist the perpetuation of the sex object stereotype
that is so prevalent in advertising and other forms of media.
```

A common and powerful form of deduction called *reductio ad absurdum* ("to reduce to absurdity") is used to attack an opponent's position by showing that its consequences are absurd if carried to their logical end. To counter the position that the government should impose no restrictions on parents' rights to discipline their children, you might point out that, carried to its logical extreme, such a policy would allow individuals to beat their children. This absurd result makes it clear that certain restrictions should apply. The question then becomes where we should draw the line.

Often, a deductive argument is built around a categorical syllogism, a set of three statements that follow a fixed pattern to ensure sound reasoning. The first statement, called the major premise, names a category of things and says that all or none of them share a certain characteristic. The minor premise notes that a thing or group of things belong to that category. The conclusion states that the thing or group shares the characteristics of the category. Here are two examples:

Major premise:	All persons are mortal.
Minor premise:	Sue Davis is a person.
Conclusion:	Therefore, Sue Davis is mortal.

Major premise:	No dogs have feathers.
Minor premise:	Spot is a dog.
Conclusion:	Therefore, Spot does not have feathers.

Note that in each case both major and minor premises are true and the conclusion follows logically.

Syllogisms frequently appear in stripped-down form, with one of the premises or the conclusion omitted. The following example omits the major premise: "Because Wilma is a civil engineer, she has a strong background in mathematics." Obviously the missing major premise is as follows: "All civil engineers have a strong background in mathematics."

Syllogistic Argument at Work A syllogism can occur anywhere in an essay: in the introduction to set the stage for the evidence, at various places in the body, even in the conclusion in order to pull the argument together. Here is an example that uses a syllogism in the introduction:

In 1966, when the Astrodome was completed in Houston, Texas, the managers concluded that it would be impossible to grow grass indoors. To solve their problem, they decided to install a ruglike synthetic playing surface that was fittingly called Astroturf. In the ensuing years, many other sports facilities have installed synthetic turf. Unfortunately, this development has been accompanied by a sharp rise in the number and severity of injuries suffered by athletes--a rise clearly linked to the surface they play upon. Obviously, anything that poses a threat to player safety is

<u>undesirable. Because synthetic turf does this, it is undesirable</u>
<u>and should be replaced by grass.</u>

Denny Witham

To support his position, the writer then notes that turf, unlike grass, often becomes excessively hot, tiring players and increasing their chances of injury; that seams can open up between sections of turf and lead to tripping and falling; that players can run faster on artificial turf and thus collide more violently; and that the extreme hardness of the turf leads to torn ligaments and tissues when players slam their toes into it.

Avoiding Misuse of Syllogisms   Two cautions are in order. *First,* make sure any syllogism you use follows the proper order. The writer of the following passage has ignored this caution:

> Furthermore, Robinson has stated openly that he supports a ban on all clear cut logging practices. For many years now, the Green Party has taken the same environmentalist stand. Robinson's position places him firmly in the Green Party camp. I strongly urge anyone supporting this man's candidacy to reconsider. . . .

Restated in syllogistic form, the writer's argument goes like this:

> Green Party members support a ban on all clear cut logging practices. Robinson supports a ban on all clear cut logging practices. Therefore, Robinson is a supporter of the Green Party.

The last two statements reverse the proper order, and as a result the syllogism proves nothing about Robinson's politics: he may or may not be "in the Green Party camp."

Second, make sure the major premise of your syllogism is in fact true. Note this example:

> All Progressive Conservatives are opposed to environmental protection. Mary is a Progressive Conservative. Therefore, Mary is opposed to environmental protection.

But is every Progressive Conservative an environmental Jack the Ripper? In some communities, political conservatives have led fights against air and water pollution, and most conservatives agree that at least some controls are worthwhile. Mary's sympathies, then, may well lie with those who want to heal, rather than hurt, the environment.

Analogy in Argument

An analogy compares two unlike situations or things. Arguers often use analogies to contend that because two items share one or more likenesses, they are also alike in other ways. Familiar analogies assume that humans respond to chemicals as rats do and that success in school predicts success on the job. You have used analogy if you ever pressed your parents for more adult privileges, such as a later curfew, by arguing that you were like an adult in many ways.

Because its conclusions about one thing rest upon observations about some different thing, analogy is the weakest form of rational appeal. Analogies never prove anything. But they often help explain and show probability and therefore are quite persuasive.

For an analogy to be useful, it must feature significant similarities that bear directly on the issue. In addition, it must account for any significant differences between the two items. It is often helpful to test an analogy by listing the similarities and differences. Here's an effective analogy, used to back an argument that a liberal education is the best kind to help us cope successfully with life:

> Suppose it were perfectly certain that the life and fortune of every one of us would, one day or other, depend upon his winning or losing a game of chess. Don't you think that we should all consider it to be a primary duty to learn at least the names and the moves of the pieces; to have a notion of a gambit, and a keen eye for all the means of giving and getting out of check? Do you not think that we should look with a disapprobation amounting to scorn, upon the father who allowed his son, or the state which allowed its members, to grow up without knowing a pawn from a knight?
>
> Yet it is a very plain and elementary truth, that the life, the fortune, and the happiness of every one of us, and, more or less, of those who are connected with us, do depend upon our knowing something of the rules of a game infinitely more difficult and complicated than chess. It is a game which has been played for untold ages, every man and woman of us being one of the two players in a game of his or her own. The chessboard is the world, the pieces are the phenomena of the universe, the rules of the game are what we call the laws of Nature. The player on the other side is hidden from us. We know that his play is always fair, just, and patient. But also we know, to our cost, that he never overlooks a mistake, or makes the smallest allowance for ignorance. To the man who plays well, the highest stakes are paid, with that sort of overflowing generosity with which the strong shows delight in strength. And one who plays ill is checkmated—without haste, but without remorse. . . .
>
> Well, what I mean by Education is learning the rules of this mighty game. In other words, education is the instruction of the intellect in the law of Nature, under which name I include not merely things and their forces, but men and their ways; and the fashioning of the affections and of the will into an earnest and loving desire to move in harmony with those laws. For me, education means neither more nor less than this. Anything which professes to call itself education must be tried by this standard, and if it fails to stand the test, I will not call it education, whatever may be the force of authority, or of numbers, upon the other side.
>
> Thomas Henry Huxley, "A Liberal Education and Where to Find It"

■ The Emotional Appeal

Although effective argument relies mainly on reason, an emotional appeal can lend powerful reinforcement. Indeed, emotion can win the hearts and the help of people who would otherwise passively accept a logical argument but take no action. Each Christmas, newspapers raise money for local charities by running stark case histories of destitute families. Organizations raise funds to fight famine by displaying brochures that feature skeletal, swollen-bellied children. Still other groups use emotion-charged stories and pictures to solicit support for environmental protection, to combat various diseases, and so on. Less benignly, advertisers use emotion to play upon our hopes, fears, and vanities in order to sell mouthwash, cars, clothes, and other products. Politicians paint themselves as God-fearing, honest toilers for the public good while lambasting their opponents as the uncaring tools of special interests. In evaluating or writing an argument, ask yourself whether the facts warrant the emotion. Is the condition of the destitute family truly cause for pity? Is any politician unwaveringly good, any other irredeemably bad?

The following passage, from a student argument favouring assisted suicide for the terminally ill, represents an appropriate use of emotion:

> When I visited Grandpa for the last time, he seemed imprinted on the hospital bed, a motionless, skeleton-like figure tethered by an array of tubes to the droning, beeping machine at his bedside. The eyes that had once sparkled with delight as he bounced grand-children on his knee now stared blankly at the ceiling, seemingly ready to burst from their sockets. His mouth, frozen in an open grimace, emitted raspy, irregular noises as he fought to breathe. Spittle leaked from one corner of his mouth and dribbled onto the sheet. A ripe stench from the diaper around his middle hung about the bedside, masking the medicinal sickroom smells. As I stood by the bedside, my mind flashed back to the irrepressible man I once knew, and tears flooded my eyes. Bending forward, I planted a soft kiss on his forehead, whispered "I love you, Gramps," and walked slowly away.
>
> Dylan Brandt Chafin

■ The Ethical Appeal

Before logic can do its work, the audience must be willing to consider the argument. If a writer's tone offends the audience, perhaps by being arrogant or mean-spirited, the reasoning will fail to penetrate. But if the writer comes across as pleasant, fair-minded, and decent, gaining reader support is much easier. The image that the writer projects is called the ethical appeal.

If you write with a genuine concern for your topic, a commitment to the truth, and a sincere respect for others, you will probably come across reasonably well. When you finish writing, check to see that an occasional snide comment or bitter remark didn't slip unnoticed onto the page. In the following excerpt from Martin Luther King's famous "I Have a Dream" speech, King does not give way to angry venting, but makes a strong ethical appeal to people's sense of justice:

> Now is the time to make real the promises of democracy; now is the time to rise from the dark and desolate valley of segregation to the sunlit path of racial

justice; now is the time to lift our nation from the quicksands of racial injustice to the solid rock of brotherhood; now is the time to make justice a reality for all of God's children.

Martin Luther King, "I Have a Dream"

◼ Ferreting Out Fallacies

Fallacies are lapses in logic that reflect upon your ability to think clearly, and therefore they weaken your argument. The fallacies described below are among the most common. Correct any you find in your own arguments, and call attention to those used by the opposition.

Hasty Generalization

Hasty generalization results when someone bases a conclusion on too little evidence. The student who tries to see an instructor during one of her office hours, finds her out, and goes away muttering, "She's never there when she should be" is guilty of hasty generalization. Perhaps the instructor was delayed by another student, attended a special department meeting, or went home ill. Even if she merely went shopping, that's not a good reason for saying she always shirks her responsibility. Several more unsuccessful office visits would be needed to make such a charge stick.

Non Sequitur

From the Latin "It does not follow," this fallacy draws unwarranted conclusions from seemingly ample evidence. Consider this example: "Bill's been out almost every night for the last two weeks. Who is she?" These evening excursions, however numerous, point to no particular conclusion. Bill may be studying in the library, participating in campus organizations, taking night classes, or walking. Of course, he could be charmed by a new date, but that conclusion requires other evidence.

Stereotyping

A person who commits this fallacy attaches one or more supposed characteristics to a group or one of its members. Typical stereotypes include "Latins make better lovers," "Blondes have more fun," and "Teenagers are lousy drivers." Stereotyping racial, religious, ethnic, or national groups can destroy an argument. The images are often malicious and are always offensive to fair-minded readers.

Card Stacking

In card stacking, the writer presents only part of the available evidence on a topic, deliberately omitting essential information that would alter the picture considerably. For instance: "College students have a very easy life; they attend classes for only twelve to sixteen hours a week." This statement ignores the many hours that students must spend studying, doing homework and/or research, writing papers, and the like.

Either/Or Fallacy

The either/or fallacy asserts that only two choices exist when, in fact, several options are possible. A salesperson who wants you to buy snow tires may claim, "Either buy these tires or plan on getting stuck a lot this winter." But are you really that boxed in? You might drive only on main roads that are plowed immediately after every snowstorm. You could use public transportation when it snows. You could buy radial tires for year-round use. If very little snow falls, you might not need special tires at all.

Not all either/or statements are fallacies. The instructor who checks a student's record and then issues a warning, "Make at least a C on your final, or you'll fail the course," is not guilty of a reasoning error. No other alternatives exist. Most situations, however, offer more than two choices.

Begging the Question

A person who begs the question asserts the truth of some unproven statement. Here is an example: "Vitamin A is harmful to your health, and all bottles should carry a warning label. If enough of us write to the Minister of Health, we can get the labelling we need." But how do we know vitamin A does harm users? No evidence is offered. People lacking principles often use this fallacy to hit opponents below the belt: "We shouldn't allow an environmental terrorist like Paul Watson to run for political office." Despite a lack of suitable evidence, voters often accept such faulty logic and vote for the other candidate.

Circular Argument

Circular argument, a first cousin to begging the question, supports a position merely by restating it. "Pauline is a good manager because she runs the company effectively" says, in effect, that "something is because something is." Repetition replaces evidence.

Arguing off the Point

The writer who commits this fallacy, which is sometimes called "ignoring the question" or "a red herring," sidetracks an issue by introducing irrelevant information. To illustrate: "Vancouver has a more moderate climate than Toronto. Besides, too many Torontonians are moving to Vancouver. They are creating congestion and driving up the price of real estate. Many Vancouverites are angry that the cost of buying a home is so high." The writer sets out to convince that Vancouver offers a more enjoyable climate than Toronto but then abruptly shifts to increasing congestion and rising house prices in Vancouver—a trend that has no bearing on the argument.

The Argument Ad Hominem

The Latin term "to the man" designates an argument that attacks an individual rather than that individual's opinions or qualifications. Note this example: "Sam Bernhard doesn't deserve promotion to personnel manager. His divorce was a disgrace, and he's always writing letters to the editor. The company should find someone more suitable." This attack completely skirts the real issue—whether Sam's job performance entitles him to the promotion. Unless his personal conduct has caused his work to suffer, it should not enter into the decision.

Appeal to the Crowd

An appeal of this sort arouses an emotional response by playing on the irrational fears and prejudices of the audience. Terms like *communists, fascists, bleeding hearts, right-wingers, welfare chisellers,* and *law and order* are tossed about freely to sway the audience for or against something. Consider the following excerpt:

> The streets of our country are in turmoil. The universities are filled with students rebelling and rioting. Communists are seeking to destroy our country. Russia is threatening us with her might, and the public is in danger. Yes, danger from within and without. We need law and order. Yes, without law and order our nation cannot survive. Elect us, and we shall by law and order be respected among the nations of the world. Without law and order our republic shall fall.

Tapping the emotions of the crowd can sway large groups and win acceptance for positions that rational thinking would reject. Think what Adolf Hitler, the author of the foregoing excerpt, brought about in Germany.

Guilt by Association

This fallacy points out some similarity or connection between one person or group and another. It tags the first with the sins, real or imagined, of the second. The following excerpt from a letter protesting a speaker at a lecture series illustrates this technique:

> The next slated speaker, Dr. Sylvester Crampton, was for years a member of the Economic Information Committee. This foundation has very strong ties with other ultraright-wing groups, some of which have been labelled fascistic. When he speaks next Thursday, whose brand of patriotism will he be selling?

Post Hoc, ergo Propter Hoc

The Latin meaning, "after this, therefore because of this," refers to the fallacy of assuming that because one event follows another, the first caused the second. Such shoddy thinking underlies many popular superstitions ("If a black cat crosses your path, you'll have bad luck") and many connections that cannot be substantiated ("I always catch cold during spring break"). Sometimes one event does cause another: a sudden thunderclap might startle a person into dropping a dish. At other times, coincidence is the only connection. Careful thinking will usually lay far-fetched causal notions to rest.

Faulty Analogy

This is the error of assuming that two circumstances or things are similar in all important respects, when in fact they are not. Here's an example: Sean McIntyre, midget hockey coach, tells his players, "Scotty Bowman has won the Stanley Cup seven times by insisting on excellent defensive positional play and requiring excellent physical conditioning. We're going to win the midget championship by following the same methods." McIntyre assumes that because he and Bowman are coaches, he can duplicate Bowman's achievements by using Bowman's methods. Several important differences, however, mark the two situations:

1.   Bowman has had very talented players, obtained through the player draft or trades; McIntyre can choose only from the children in his community.

2.   Bowman's players have been paid professionals who very likely were motivated, at least in part, by the financial rewards that come from winning the Stanley Cup; McIntyre's players are amateurs.

3.   "Excellent defensive positional play" is probably easier to attain on the professional level than on the midget level because of the players' experience.

4.   Very few of Bowman's players could resist his insistence on "excellent physical conditioning" because they were under contract. Could McIntyre expect his players, essentially volunteers, to accept the same physical demands that Bowman has expected?

EXERCISE   *Identify and explain the fallacies in the following examples. Remember that understanding the faulty reasoning is more important than merely naming the fallacy.*

1. After slicing a Golden Glow orange, Nancy discovers that it is rotten. "I'll never buy another Golden Glow product," she declares emphatically.

2. A campaigning politician states that unless the federal government appropriates funds to help people living in poverty, they will all starve.

3. A husband and wife see an X-rated movie called *Swinging Wives*. A week later the husband discovers that his wife, while supposedly attending an evening class, has been unfaithful to him. He blames the movie for her infidelity.

4. "Look at those two motorcycle riders trying to pick a fight. All those cycle bums are troublemakers."

5. "Bill really loves to eat. Some day he'll have a serious weight problem."

6. "Because no-fault divorce is responsible for today's skyrocketing divorce rate, it should be abolished."

7. "This is the best-looking picture in the exhibit; it's so much more attractive than the others."

8. "I am against the proposed ban on smoking in public places. As long as I don't inhale and I limit my habit to ten cigarettes a day, my health won't suffer."

Ethical Issues

When writing an argument we may wish to raise awareness, change attitudes, or spark some action. These objectives create an ethical responsibility for both the quality and the possible consequences of our arguments. Suppose a doctor writing a nationally syndicated advice column recommends an over-the-counter product that may cause a serious reaction in users who also take a certain prescription drug. Clearly this writer has acted irresponsibly and risks legal action if some readers suffer harm. Asking and answering the following questions will help you avoid any breach of ethics.

- Have I carefully considered the issue I'm arguing and the stance I'm taking? Since you're trying to get others to adopt your views, you'll need to make sure they are very credible or make clear that your position is tentative or dependent on certain conditions.

- Am I fair to other positions on the issue? Careless or deliberate distortion of opposing views is ethically dishonest and could raise doubts about your credibility.

- Are my reasons and evidence legitimate? It is unethical to present flawed reasons as if they were credible or falsify evidence so that it fits your thesis.

- Do I use fallacies or other types of faulty thinking to manipulate the reader unfairly?

- What consequences could follow if readers adopt my position? Say a writer strongly opposes genetically modified foods and advocates disruption of installations that help develop them. If some who are convinced by the argument then proceed to act on the writer's advice, innocent people could be injured.

Writing an Argument

Planning and Drafting the Argument

Some instructors assign argumentative topics, and some leave the choice of topic to you. If you will be choosing, many options are available. Interesting issues—

some local, some of broader importance—crowd our newspapers, magazines, and TV airways, vying for attention. Because several of them have probably piqued your interest, there's a good chance you won't have to rely on the strategies on pages 13–20 for help in choosing your topic.

Some students approach an argument with such strong attitudes that they ignore evidence that contradicts their thinking. Don't make this mistake. Instead, maintain an open mind as you research your issue, and then, after careful thought, choose the position you'll take. Often, several possible positions exist.

As you investigate the various positions, ask and answer the following questions about each:

What kinds of evidence support it?

How substantial is the evidence?

If the evidence includes statistics and authoritative opinions, are they reliable? flawed for some reason?

What are the objections to each position, and how can they be countered?

If the issue involves taking some action, what might be its consequences?

To help with this stage of the process, prepare a chart that summarizes your findings for each position; then examine it carefully to pick the position you'll argue for. The example below illustrates a three-position issue:

Position 1	Position 2	Position 3
Evidence and evaluation	Evidence and evaluation	Evidence and evaluation
Objections and how countered	Objections and how countered	Objections and how countered
Consequences	Consequences	Consequences

One effective technique for developing an argument is to first write a dialogue between two or three people that explores the various sides of an issue without trying to arrive at any conclusion. Writing such a dialogue can help start your mental juices flowing, help you see the issue from many sides, and help you develop effective material for your paper.

As you contemplate your position and evidence, consider the purpose of your argument and how that might affect the strategies you choose to employ. Arguments are written for several purposes, each requiring a different approach. Some arguments try to establish that something is a fact—nursing is hard work, residences are poor study places, bologna is an unhealthy food. This type of paper usually relies on assorted evidence, perhaps some combination of statistics, authoritative opinion, and personal experience. To prove that nursing is quite demanding, you might narrate and describe some of the strenuous activities in a typical nursing day, cite hospital nursing supervisors who verify the rigours of the job, and perhaps give statistics on nurses who quit the profession because of stress.

Other arguments defend or oppose some policy—for example, whether a company should begin drug-testing its employees—or support or oppose some action or project, such as the construction of a study lounge for students. In this type of paper, you usually discuss the need for the policy or action, how it can best be met, the cost or feasibility of your recommendation, and the benefits that will result.

Still other arguments assert the greater value of someone or something, as when a supervisor ranks one candidate for promotion ahead of another. To write this type of paper, generally you would indicate what you're trying to prove; identify the points on which the items will be evaluated; and then, using reasons along with details, examples, or statistics, demonstrate that one of the items has greater worth than the other. Often such an argument will be deductive as you show how your conclusions follow from agreed-upon values.

With an argument, as with any essay, purpose and audience are closely linked. For example, imagine that your audience is a group of readers who are neutral or opposed to your position; there's no point in preaching to the converted. Take a little time to analyze these readers so that you can tailor your arguments appropriately. Pose these questions as you proceed:

What are the readers' interests, expectations, and needs concerning this issue?
What evidence is most likely to convince them?
What objections and consequences would probably weigh most heavily with them?
How can I answer the objections?

To convince an audience of farmers that organic farming is viable, you might stress the added income they would gain from selective consumers willing to pay more for organic food, while for an audience of nutritionists, you might note the health benefits that would result. Even though you are unlikely to convince everyone, it is best to adopt the attitude that most readers are willing to be convinced if your approach is appealing and your evidence is sound.

If you're arguing an emotionally charged issue such as assisted suicide or changes in Canada's health-care system that affect people directly, you may want to use *Rogerian argument*. Named for psychologist Carl Rogers, this type of argument attempts to reduce the antagonism that people with opposing views might feel toward your position. To succeed, you must show that you understand and respect the opposing position as well as acknowledge its good points. You try to establish some common point of agreement, then present a position that addresses opposing concerns without compromising your views.

When you have a good grasp on your position, reasons, evidence, and the approach you want to take, you're ready to draft your paper. A typical introduction arouses the reader's interest and may also present the proposition—a special thesis statement that names the issue and indicates which position the writer will take. It can declare that something is a fact, support a policy, call for a certain action, or assert that something has greater value than something else. Here are examples:

1. Carron College does not provide adequate recreational facilities for its students. *(Declares something is fact.)*

2. Our company's policy of randomly testing employees for drug use has proved effective and should be continued. *(Supports policy.)*

3. Because the present building is overcrowded and unsafe, the people of Midville should vote funds for a new junior high school. *(Calls for action.)*

4. The new Ford Fire-Eater is superior to the Honda Harmony in performance and economy. *(Asserts value.)*

Any of the techniques on pages 199–202 can launch your paper. For example, in arguing for stepped-up AIDS education, you might jolt your reader by describing a dying victim. If your issue involves unfamiliar terms, you might define them up front; and if the essay will be long, you could preview its main points.

After the introduction comes the evidence, arranged in whatever order you think will work best. If one of your points is likely to arouse resistance, hold it back and begin by making points your reader can more easily accept. Argument always goes more smoothly if you first establish some common ground of agreement that recognizes the values of your reader. Where strong resistance is not a factor, you could begin or end with your most compelling piece of evidence.

The strategies discussed in earlier chapters can help you develop an argument. Some papers incorporate one strategy, while others rely on several. Let's see how you might combine several in an argument against legalized casino gambling. You might open with a brief *description* of the frantic way an all-too-typical gambling addict keeps pulling the lever of a slot machine, his eyes riveted on the spinning dials, his palms sweating, as flashing lights and wailing sirens announce winners at other machines. Next, you could offer a brief *definition* of gambling fever so that the writer and reader are on common ground, and, to show the dimensions of the problem, *classify* the groups of people who are especially addicted. Then, after detailing the negative *effects* of the addiction, you might end by *comparing* gambling addiction with drug addiction, noting that both provide a "high" and both kinds of addicts know their habits hurt them.

Whatever strategies you use, make sure that substantiating evidence is embedded within them. Strategies by themselves won't convince. To illustrate, in discussing the negative effects of gambling, you might cite statistics that show the extent and nature of the problem. An expert opinion might validate your classification of addicts. Or you might use personal experience to verify gambling's addictive effects.

Besides presenting evidence, use this part of your paper to refute, that is, to point out weaknesses or errors in the opposing position. You might try the following:

■ *Point out any evidence that undermines that position.* If one viewpoint holds that drug testing violates cherished privacy rights, you might note that employers already monitor phone calls, check employees' desks, and violate privacy in other ways.

■ *Identify faulty assumptions and indicate how they are faulty: They don't lead to the implied conclusion, they lack the effectiveness of an alternative, or they are false or unsupported.* If you oppose drug testing, you could point out problems in the assumption that such tests are necessary to protect the public. Closer supervision of work performance might be a better protection; after all, fatigue, stress, negligence, and alcohol abuse can all result in serious problems, and they are not detected by drug tests.

- *Identify problems in the logic of the argument.* Are there missing premises, faulty connections between reasons, or conclusions that don't follow from the premises? The argument against drug testing usually proceeds by asserting that privacy is a fundamental right, that drug testing violates privacy, and that therefore drug testing should not be allowed. There is a missing premise, however: that because privacy is a fundamental right it should never be violated. This premise is, in fact, at the heart of the dispute and therefore cannot be accepted as a reason to disallow drug testing.

You can place refutations throughout the body of the paper or group them together just ahead of the conclusion. Whatever you decide, don't adopt a gloating or sarcastic tone that will alienate a fair-minded reader. Resist the urge to engage in straw man tactics—calling attention to imaginary or trivial weaknesses of the opposing side so that you can demolish them. Shrewd readers easily spot such ploys. Finally, don't be afraid to concede secondary or insignificant points to the opposition. Arguments have two or more sides; you can't have all the ammunition on your side. (If you discover you must concede major points, however, consider switching sides.) Here is a sample refutation from a student paper:

> Not everyone agrees with workplace drug testing for employees in public transportation companies, electric utilities, nuclear power plants, and other industries involving public safety. Critics assert that such tests invade privacy and therefore violate one of our cherished freedoms. While the examination of one's urine does entail inspection of something private, such a test is a reasonable exception because it helps ensure public safety and calm public fears. Individuals have a right to be protected from the harm that could be caused by an employee who abuses drugs. An airline pilot's right to privacy should not supersede the security of hundreds of people who could be injured or killed in a drug-induced accident. Thus the individual's privacy should be tempered by concern for the community--a concern that benefits all of us.
>
> Annie Louise Griffith

Conclude in a manner that will sway the reader to your side. Depending on the argument, you might restate your position, summarize your main points, predict the consequences if your position does or doesn't prevail, or make an emotional appeal for support or action.

Revising the Argument

Review the guidelines in Chapter 3 and ponder these questions as you revise your argument paper:

Appropriate topic and thesis   Is my topic a clearly debatable one? Have I narrowed my topic into a clearly defined thesis that runs throughout the essay? Is my proposition clearly evident and of the appropriate type—that is, one of fact, policy, action, or value?

Focus   Do I have a clear idea of what purpose I want to achieve through my argument, and do I maintain this sense of purpose and direction throughout? Is my thesis clear and strategically positioned? Are my main points clearly related to my thesis?

Awareness of audience   Is the paper aimed at the audience I want to reach? Have I tailored my argument to appeal to that audience? Have I kept a respectful tone throughout, even when dealing with possible objections to my argument?

Thoroughness   Have I examined all of the main positions? assessed the evidence supporting each one? considered the objections to each position and either countered these objections or made concessions where necessary?

Rational appeal   Do I have enough solid evidence to support my claims? Is my evidence sound, adequate, and appropriate to the argument? Are my authorities qualified? Have I established their expertise? Are they biased? Will my audience accept them as authorities? Do my statistics adequately support my position? Have I pushed my statistical claims too far?

Emotional appeal   If I've included an emotional appeal—perhaps by including a short narrative or story that fits with my larger purpose—does it centre on those emotions most likely to sway the reader? Have I addressed possible reader resistance by adequately refuting opposing arguments? Have I avoided sentimentality and self-pity?

Ethical appeal   Have I made a conscious effort to present myself as a fair and reasonable person? Have I weighed the possible consequences if a position involves taking some action?

Logic   Have I established logical links between my claims and my evidence? Have I avoided overly broad claims and sweeping generalizations, especially ones that contain words such as "all" and "never"? If the proposition takes the form of a syllogism, is it sound? If faulty, have I started with a faulty premise, or reversed the last two statements of the syllogism? If I've used analogy, are my points of comparison pertinent to the issue? Have I noted any significant differences between the items being compared? Is my argument free of fallacies?

Organization   Does my argument follow an effective organizational plan such as the order of climax? Have I developed my position with one or more writing strategies? Are transitions smooth, from one point to the next? Do I end with an effective conclusion, rather than going on too long or stopping short?

Example Student Essay of Argument

Education ... At Any Cost?

Diane McArthur

1   Recently there has been much discussion, both in the local media and at numerous school board meetings, on the issue of allowing companies to advertise in our public schools. Proponents of allowing advertising speak often of the much-needed revenue that this practice would generate for our financially strapped school system. In fact, in the February 16, 1998 edition of the *Abbotsford News,* John Smith, British Columbia School District number thirty-four (Abbotsford) Chair, has said, "If we could raise, for example, $500 000.00 to $1 000 000.00 as a result of selectively allowing advertising, we could perhaps re-instate the music program." While I have no doubt that this statement is valid, I question whether the end result of earning revenue by allowing advertising justifies the means employed. Unfortunately, the issue is not clear-cut. Certainly, any source of extra revenue for education is much needed in these days of budget cuts, tax-hikes, and the elimination of special programs. Still, my question remains: Is allowing advertising the best means to our ultimate goal, which is to increase funding to our schools in order to allow us to educate our children in the best possible fashion? Already some advertising is present in our schools--pop machines, pizza flyers, etc.--albeit on a small scale. Who has given the okay for this? I don't recall being asked. I believe that if people were not now questioning the appropriateness of corporate advertising in schools, it would become a *fait accompli,* and the public would never have been consulted. We must carefully consider all the repercussions of our actions before we leap ahead.

2   By allowing advertising we send a message that advertising is acceptable, that it is truthful and sincere. Is it? Think of all the advertisements that assault us daily. Are they truthful and sincere? Will Virginia Slims really make people healthy and slim? Will Coors Light really make people healthy and popular? Is purchasing a 6/49 lottery ticket really an appropriate means of

achieving financial stability? I think not. Of course, those in favour of advertising in schools may claim, "We won't allow cigarette, liquor, or gambling advertisements." But I am not confident that adequate controls on advertising material can and will be maintained. Who will set policy? Who will say what is acceptable, and what is not?

3   Even though most people, even smokers, now agree that smoking is harmful to one's health, as recently as fifteen years ago, smoking was socially acceptable. There were no non-smoking areas anywhere. Few non-smokers would have dreamed of asking a smoker to butt out his or her cigarette, regardless of how much they disliked the smoke. Smokers' rights were perceived to supersede non-smokers' rights. Thankfully, the situation has changed since then. But how would our health have been affected today if tobacco advertising had been allowed in our schools when we were younger? What currently acceptable advertising might be found in the future to be harmful to our children? Do we want to take a chance?

4   Children, especially teenagers, ache to belong. They want to be one of the group. To this end they frequently dress alike, talk alike, and even act alike. More often than not the clothing and mannerisms they adopt are directly influenced by advertising. What Canadian parent has not had a child beg him or her for a particular brand of clothing or sports equipment so that the child can be just like his or her friends? Companies like Nike, Adidas, Coca-Cola, Pepsi, Calvin Klein, and Tommy Hilfiger, to name but a few, are well aware of the pack instinct of children, who are particularly vulnerable because their desire to fit in is so strong. Indeed, corporate advertising often purposefully targets impressionable children, attacking their insecurities in order to create a demand for a product. How many high school boys want to "be like Mike?" How many high school girls aspire to the emaciated "look" of Kate Moss, Calvin Klein's poster girl? Far too many, I think.

5   Certainly, one of the primary purposes of an education is to promote personal confidence and integrity--qualities that are essential to independent critical thought. We owe our children and our society the opportunity to learn in an atmosphere of trust, an atmosphere free of coercion, an atmosphere free of distractions to learning. Corporate advertisements in our schools would seriously

weaken our ability to ensure an educational environment free of undue influence from vested interests, whose underlying message is always buy, buy, buy. The question we must ask, then, is perhaps best posed by Tiffany Poirer, a high school student herself, who, in response to John Smith's claim, asks, "Are we going to prostitute our children's impressionable minds for fifty computers and a couple textbooks?"

6   If corporate advertising were allowed in our schools, presumably only the largest and most pervasive companies would be able to jump at the chance to sell to a captive and impressionable audience. For only they would have the resources readily available to provide the money that school boards seek. And in return for their contributions, these companies would certainly expect exclusive rights. Competition would not be tolerated. University and college campuses around North America already demonstrate these principles in action. At the University of British Columbia, for example, Coke is it and Pepsi is not. In 1995, the company paid in the neighbourhood of $10 000 000.00 for a ten-year deal that allows it to sell its products exclusively. So much for autonomy. So much for critical analysis. Why, we might ask, do we pay $1.00 for a Coke when a President's Choice Cola could be had for $.25? Taste alone cannot be the determining factor.

7   We must remember that companies are motivated by profit, not social conscience. The moment a company's advertisement investment fails to return a profit is the moment that its contribution to save a "music program" will cease. Realizing this truth and working under the pressure that tight budgets and tough decisions produce, school boards may very well start to make decisions based on the bottom line and not the students' best interests. Further, inequities between schools and school districts may widen, for the relative wealth of students and their parents will be a determining factor for companies when they choose to make advertising investment decisions. Very likely, a school in Kerrisdale, in the heart of the West Side of Vancouver, one of the wealthiest neighbourhoods in Canada, promises more potential return on investment for a company than does a school in Strathcona, in the heart of the Downtown East Side of Vancouver, one of the poorest neighbourhoods in Canada.

8   One of the strengths of our public school system is that it is relatively responsive to the people. We elect school boards and we elect Ministry of Education officials, and we can direct them on where, what, and how to spend our tax money in the best interests of our children. If they fall out of step with our desires, we may replace them in the next election. Such a system ensures a certain amount of accountability and equality. The education system has traditionally been managed as a whole and not on a district-by-district or school-by-school piecemeal basis. If we solicit advertising money from corporations, some districts and schools may thrive and others may not as we open up our education system to the indiscriminate opportunism of bottom line corporate economics. This mindset is not socially responsible and is certainly not reflective of the equality of opportunity that public education should provide. In addition, corporations, unlike elected officials, are not directly accountable to the people. Program funding provided by corporations could be withdrawn on a whim and without rationale. Schools that have become dependent on such funding may find themselves left without recourse, or they may find themselves compelled to attract further funding by offering incentives to corporations. Perhaps the volleyball team could wear uniforms designed by Tommy Hilfiger--logos prominently displayed, of course. Perhaps the cafeteria could sell McDonald's hamburgers. Perhaps the school science fair could feature Dow plastics and oil products . . . and so on. The slope is slippery. I hope we can maintain our footing.

9   Everywhere we go today, we are assaulted by advertisements: in movie theatres, washrooms, hospitals . . . just about everywhere. They are a byproduct of a capitalist society. However, their necessity in a market economy as a whole does not mean they should be present in all our institutions. Our educational institutions must strive to remain free of undue vested interests and to provide an environment that allows our children to develop as individuals, becoming conscious citizens, not mindless consumers.

DISCUSSION QUESTIONS

1. Identify the author's central purpose. What is her thesis, or proposition? Is it one of fact, policy, action, or value?

2. Why does the writer include a discussion of how the public's attitude toward smoking has changed in recent years? How does this observation relate to her argument?

3. What type of supporting evidence does the writer use in her argument? Identify examples.

4. What are the effects of the rhetorical questions that are used throughout the essay?

5. What type of conclusion does the writer use?

SUGGESTIONS FOR WRITING   *Write an argument on some topic you feel strongly about. Study all sides of the issue so you can argue effectively and appeal to a particular audience. Be sure to narrow and focus your argument. Support your proposition with logical evidence. Here are some possibilities to consider if your instructor gives you a free choice:*

1. Compulsory composition courses
2. Global warming
3. Saving endangered species
4. Corporate involvement in education
5. A controversial issue related to First Nations
6. Tuition fees for post-secondary education
7. Helmet laws
8. Export of water
9. Management of fisheries
10. Genetically modified foods

A successful argument, by its very nature, requires critical thinking. This chapter has given you the tools you'll need to test the logic and evaluate the evidence offered in support of argumentative positions. After all, rarely will you generate an idea on your own and then argue for it. Instead, because most important issues have already been debated in print, you'll enter a discussion that's already underway. Sometimes it's on a topic of national interest, such as the desirability of politically correct speech and writing or the need to limit the number of terms elected officials can serve. At other times, the topic may be more localized: should your province outlaw teacher strikes, your company install new equipment to control air pollution, or your university or college reduce its sports programs? On any of these issues you begin to form your own view as you read and assess the arguments of other writers.

A good way to take stock of conflicting opinions is to make a chart that summarizes key reasons and evidence on each side of the argument. Here is a segment of a chart that presents opposing viewpoints on whether industrial air pollution poses a significant threat of global warming:

Pro-threat side	No-threat side
Industrial emissions of carbon dioxide, methane, and chlorofluorocarbons let sun's rays in but keep heat from escaping.	Natural sources account for almost 50 percent of all carbon dioxide production.
Andrew C. Revkin	Dixy Lee Ray
Atmospheric levels of carbon dioxide are now 25 percent higher than in 1860. Computer models indicate continuing rise will cause temperature increase of 3–9°F.	The computer models are inaccurate, don't agree with each other, and fail to account for the warming effects of the oceans.
Revkin	H. E. Landsberg

Even though you investigate the reasons and evidence of others, deciding what position to take and how to support it—that is, establishing your place in the debate—is the real work of synthesis. (See pages 64–65.) Therefore, after evaluating your sources, outline the main points you want to make. You can then incorporate material that supports your argument. Let's say that you're considering the issue of global warming. After examining the differing viewpoints, you might conclude that although those who believe that global warming is occurring sometimes overstate their case, those who disagree tend to dismiss important scientific evidence. Because global warming is a serious possibility if not a certainty, you decide to argue for immediate environmental action. You might begin your paper by pointing out the dire consequences that will ensue if global warming becomes a reality, then offer evidence supporting this possibility, acknowledge and answer key opposing viewpoints, and finally offer your recommendations for averting a crisis.*

SUGGESTION FOR ORAL ARGUMENTATION

Oral argumentation through formal debate is an enjoyable and effective exercise that promotes research and argumentation skills, a commitment to honesty and truth, and an attitude of respect for others and their ideas. In preparing for a formal debate, the debaters must first conduct primary and/or secondary research on the proposition they will be addressing so that they may defend either a pro or con position. Because the debaters are not aware of the position they will take on the proposition while conducting their research, their priority will be to establish clear facts and specific arguments that could be offered as proofs for either side of the proposition. Once debaters are aware of the side of the proposition they will argue, they can draw from their research to develop a clear and concise argument for or against the proposition. Since the debaters will have conducted their research prior to taking a pro or con position, they should be able to advance either argument

---

*Note that papers requiring research must be documented correctly. Before starting to write this type of paper, it is important to read the sections on handling quotations and avoiding plagiarism in Chapter 20. As always, follow your instructor's guidelines for documenting sources.

with a thorough understanding of opposing views. This knowledge encourages an atmosphere of respect and tolerance.

After the debaters have completed their research on a proposition, they divide into teams representing pro and con positions. Each team then prepares opening statements outlining its arguments and compiles a set of proofs or examples that defends its positions. The actual debate can be structured in the following way:

STRUCTURING A DEBATE (ABOUT 60 MINUTES)

- Moderator asserts resolution and invites speakers from each team to direct opening statements to audience
- Each side gives opening statements outlining argument (3–5 minutes each)
- Speakers from each team give proofs
- Short break allows students to prepare statements and questions for cross-examination
- Cross-examination: Each side presents responses and rebuttals in turn (may also include questions from audience)
- Moderator asks audience to render written decision assessing debate teams according to criteria:
  – clarity of expression
  – thoroughness of research
  – effective use of rational, emotional, and/or ethical appeals
  – poise and effectiveness of oral delivery
- Moderator announces results at end of debate

PROPOSITIONS FOR DEBATE

Propositions for debate can be found after the readings classified as "argument." Alternatively, try one of the following propositions.

- Canada's policy on refugees should be stricter (or more liberal).
- Decriminalization of marijuana is (or is not) justifiable.
- Victims of crimes should be compensated by the perpetrator.
- The Internet should be subject to stricter controls.
- Animal testing should be banned.
- Grading for university English classes should be abolished.
- Seal hunting in Canada should be illegal.
- Governmental invasion of personal privacy in cyberspace is justifiable.
- Exclusive corporate advertising on college campuses is ethical.
- High schools should put stronger emphasis on trades and apprenticeships.
- Cigarette taxes should be raised.

SUGGESTIONS FOR WRITING

1. Read several sources that explore problems related to a broad topic such as free trade, or policies on drugs, health care, or the environment, and then write an argument that incorporates the views expressed in the sources and suggests the extent of the problem. Be sure to narrow your subject and define your thesis.

2. Read several articles on whether or not Canada should maintain its international peacekeeping forces, and write an argument that draws on those sources.

3. Read several sources that explore the issue of software piracy and then write an argument that incorporates the views expressed in those sources.

4. After consulting relevant articles and statistics, write an argument claiming that the drinking age should be raised, or that penalties for drunk driving should be stricter.

5. If your instructor gives you free choice of topics, you could consult a Canadian Web site such as one of the following that features articles on controversial issues for ideas to get your started:

http://www.policyalternatives.ca (Canadian Centre for Policy Alternatives)

http://www.Canadians.org (Council of Canadians—a citizens' watchdog group devoted to social and environmental concerns)

http://www.rabble.ca (progressive alternative to mainstream media)

Alternatively, you could look for topical ideas in opinion pieces, columns, or commentary available on Canadian newspaper Web sites.
Examples:

http: www.canada.com (contains daily newspapers from Canadian cities; the section called "Forums" features colloquial debate from ordinary Canadians that might trigger an idea for you if you're stuck)

http://www.nationalpost.com/commentary

http://www.globeandmail.com/columnists

http://www.canada.com/calgary/calgaryherald/columnists

chapter

13

Mixing the Writing Strategies

Writing strategies seldom occur in pure form. Writers nearly always mix them in assorted combinations for various purposes, not just in papers of definition and argument, as we've noted in Chapters 11 and 12, but also in papers of narration, description, process analysis, illustration, classification, comparison, and cause and effect. An essay that is primarily narration might contain descriptive passages or note an effect. A comparison might include illustrations or carry an implied argument. The purpose, audience, and occasion of the individual essay dictate the mixture, which can't be predetermined. Your best bet is to familiarize yourself with the individual strategies and use them as needed.

Assignments in other classes and on the job will also require you to mix the writing strategies. Your political science professor might ask for a paper that evaluates the advantages of a democratic state over a totalitarian one. You could open with contrasting *definitions* of the two forms of government and then, to make them more concrete, offer XYZ as an *illustration* of a typical democracy, ABC as a typical totalitarian state. After *describing* the key characteristics of each type, you might *compare* their social, economic, and religious effects on their citizens.

At work, a sales manager might have to write a year-end analysis that *compares* sales trends in the first and second quarters of the year, suggests the *causes* of any areas of weakness, and *classifies* the regions with superior potential in the upcoming year. And almost any employee could be asked to compose a report that *defines* and *illustrates* a problem, examines its *causes,* and *argues* for a particular solution.

When tackling a multistrategy writing assignment, break the project into separate stages. Determine first what you need to accomplish, then which strategies will serve your purpose, and finally how best to implement and organize them. It also helps to list all the strategies before you start reflecting on which ones to use. Let's apply these guidelines to the writing of a problem/solution report and then to an evaluation report, two common projects that rely on a mix of writing strategies.

■ Ethical Issues

As you might guess, when your writing includes several strategies, the ethical issues pertinent to each apply. You may, however, need to consider additional issues with problem/solution and evaluation reports.

> *Problem/Solution*   What consequences might follow if my recommendation is adopted? If a college with a grade-inflation problem implements a policy that instructors grant no more than 10 percent "A"s and 20 percent "B"s, some of the students who do excellent work may not be assigned the grades they deserve.
>
> *Evaluation*   Are my evaluation criteria fair? When evaluating the job performance of the clerks in a bookstore, it would seem unfair and discriminatory to include their ability to do heavy lifting if a number of them are older employers.

■ Problem/Solution Report

Suppose many students have experienced serious delays in getting to use the microfiche readers in your library and you want to report the situation to the administration. Your goal is to eliminate the problem. After a little thought, you realize that you must first demonstrate that a problem exists and that it warrants action.

Before you can write such a report, you need to investigate the extent of the problem (does it really need solving?), look for its causes (possibly hidden causes), and determine the possible effects. Almost always these are your first steps before you decide on any solutions. Often you can find effective solutions by addressing the causes of the problem, but you might also explore new ways of improving the situation. You'll want to consider carefully whether your solution will work. After you review your options, you decide to use illustration and description to demonstrate the problem, and then to examine the effects and their causes.

Here's how you might proceed as you write the report. Your introduction states the problem. Then you portray a typical evening with long lines of students waiting to use the microfiche readers, while others mill around, grumble, and sometimes leave in disgust. Next, you take up effects, noting a number of occasions when both you and your friends have turned in late papers due to unavailable readers and received low grades. Turning to causes, you report your findings. Perhaps the library lacks funds to buy more microfiche readers. Perhaps it needs to expand its hours, or instructors need to schedule research projects at differing times.

The solution you recommend will, of course, depend on the cause(s). If extending the library hours would solve the problem, then purchasing more readers would just waste funds. The best solution may consist of several actions: buying a few readers, extending the library hours, and persuading instructors to stagger their research assignments. In some cases, you may have to explain the process of implementing your solution and/or defend (argue) its feasibility by showing that it will not have unacceptable consequences. For instance, in our microfiche example, you would need to consider the costs of keeping the library open and staffed for longer hours.

■ Evaluation Report

Imagine that your school has been experimenting with metal whiteboards that use markers instead of chalk. The administration has asked you to assess how effectively these boards serve student and instructor needs and to present your findings in an evaluation report.

As you think the project through, you realize that you first need to determine the key criteria for evaluation, which you decide are glare, the quality of the writing left by the markers, and the effectiveness of erasing. Because these boards compete with conventional blackboards, you decide that you need a comparison of the two that includes a description of the whiteboards and illustrations supporting your observations. You also decide that a discussion of the effects the boards have on students would be in order.

After drawing your conclusions, you begin your report by indicating why it's being written, providing a definition and description of the whiteboards, and noting the criteria you will use. Following this introduction, you discuss each criterion in turn, describing with illustrative examples how well the whiteboard measures up in comparison to conventional blackboards. You also note the effects of any shortcomings on students. In your conclusion, you argue that the irregular performance of the markers, the glare of the whiteboard surfaces, and the difficulty of erasing the marking frustrate students and make classes more difficult for instructors to conduct. You recommend that the college discontinue using whiteboards except in computer classrooms where chalk dust damages the units.

EXERCISE   *Suggest what combination of writing strategies you might use in each of the situations below.*

1. The company you work for, school you attend, or club you belong to has a serious morale problem. You have been asked to evaluate its various dimensions, propose feasible solutions, and then make a recommendation to the appropriate person.

2. Your company, school, or club is about to purchase some specific type of new equipment. You have been asked to write a report examining the available brands and recommending one.

3. Your local newspaper has asked you to write about your major or occupation and how you regard it. The article will help high school students decide whether this major or occupation would be appropriate for them.

4. Your general science instructor has asked you to study and report on some industrial chemical. The report must answer typical questions a layperson would likely ask about the chemical.

The margin notes on the following essay show the interplay of several writing strategies.

Example Essay Using Several Writing Strategies

Bruce Jay Friedman

Eating Alone in Restaurants*

Bruce Jay Friedman (born 1930) is a native of New York City and a 1951 graduate of the University of Missouri, where he majored in journalism. Between 1951 and 1953, he served in the U.S. Air Force and for the next decade was editorial director of a magazine management company. He now freelances. A versatile writer, Friedman has produced novels, plays, short stories, and nonfiction, earning critical acclaim as a humorist. In our selection, taken from The Lonely Guy's Book of Life *(1979), he offers the urban male who must dine out alone witty advice on coping with the situation.*

1   Hunched over, trying to be as inconspicuous as possible, a solitary diner slips into a midtown Manhattan steakhouse. No sooner does he check his coat than the voice of the headwaiter comes booming across the restaurant.

Illustration in narrative form

2   "Alone again, eh?"

3   As all eyes are raised, the bartender, with enormous good cheer, chimes in: "That's because they all left him high and dry."

4   And then, just in case there is a customer in the restaurant who isn't yet aware of the situation, a waiter shouts out from the buffet table: "Well, we'll take care of him anyway, won't we fellas!"

5   *Haw, haw, haw,* and a lot of sly winks and pokes in the ribs.

6   Eating alone in a restaurant is one of the most terrifying experiences in America.

Definition

Description

Effect

7   Sniffed at by headwaiters, an object of scorn and amusement to couples, the solitary diner is the unwanted and unloved child of Restaurant Row. No sooner does he make his appearance than he is whisked out of sight and seated at a thin sliver of a table with barely enough room on it for an hors d'oeuvre. Wedged between busboy stations, a hair's breadth from the men's room, there he sits, feet lodged in a railing as if he were in Pilgrim stocks, wondering where he went wrong in life.

8   Rather than face this grim scenario, most Lonely Guys would prefer to nibble away at a tuna fish sandwich in the relative safety of their high-rise apartments.

9   What can be done to ease the pain of this not only starving but silent minority—to make dining alone in restaurants a rewarding experience? Absolutely nothing. But some small strategies *do* exist for making the experience bearable.

Before You Get There

Step in process

10   Once the Lonely Guy has decided to dine alone at a restaurant, a sense of terror and foreboding will begin to build throughout the day. All the more reason for him to get there as quickly as possible so that the experience can soon be forgotten and he can resume his normal life. Clothing should be light and loose-fitting, especially around the neck—on the off chance of a fainting attack during the appetizer. It is best to dress modestly, avoiding both the funeral-director-style suit as well as the bold, eye-arresting costume of the gaucho. A single cocktail should suffice; little sympathy will be given to the Lonely Guy who tumbles in, stewed to the gills. (The fellow who stoops to putting morphine in his toes for courage does not belong in this discussion.) En route to the restaurant, it is best to play down dramatics, such as swinging the arms pluckily and humming the theme from *The Bridge on the River Kwai.*

Description

Once You Arrive

Step in process

Comparison

11   The way your entrance comes off is of critical importance. Do not skulk in, slipping along the walls as if you are carrying some dirty little secret. There is no need, on the other hand, to fling your coat arrogantly at the hatcheck girl, slap the headwaiter across the cheeks with your gloves and demand to be seated immediately. Simply walk in with a brisk rubbing of the hands and approach the headwaiter. When asked how many are in your party, avoid cute responses such as "Jes lil ol' me." Tell him you are a party of one; the Lonely Guy who does not trust his voice can simply lift a finger. Do not launch into a story about how tired you are of taking out fashion models, night after night, and what a pleasure it is going to be to dine alone.

12   It is best to arrive with no reservation. Asked to set aside a table for one, the restaurant owner will suspect either a prank on the part of an ex-waiter, or a terrorist plot, in which case windows will be boarded up and the kitchen bomb-swept. An advantage of the "no reservation" approach is that you will appear to have just stepped off the plane from Des Moines, your first night in years away from Marge and the kids.

Effect

13   All eyes will be upon you when you make the promenade to your table. Stay as close as possible to the headwaiter, trying to match him step for step. This will reduce your visibility and fool some diners into thinking you are a member of the staff. If you hear a generalized snickering throughout the restaurant, do not assume automatically that you are being laughed at. The other diners may all have just recalled an amusing moment in a Feydeau farce.

14   If your table is unsatisfactory, do not demand imperiously that one for eight people be cleared immediately so that you can dine in solitary grandeur. Glance around discreetly and see if there are other possibilities. The ideal table will allow

you to keep your back to the wall so that you can see if anyone is laughing at you. Try to get one close to another couple so that if you lean over at a 45-degree angle it will appear that you are a swinging member of their group. Sitting opposite a mirror can be useful; after a drink or two, you will begin to feel that there are a few of you.

15   Once you have been seated, and it becomes clear to the staff that you are alone, there will follow The Single Most Heartbreaking Moment in Dining Out Alone—when the second setting is whisked away and yours is spread out a bit to make the table look busier. This will be done with great ceremony by the waiter—angered in advance at being tipped for only one dinner. At this point, you may be tempted to smack your forehead against the table and curse the fates that brought you to this desolate position in life. A wiser course is to grit your teeth, order a drink and use this opportunity to make contact with other Lonely Guys sprinkled around the room. A menu or a leafy stalk of celery can be used as a shield for peering out at them. Do not expect a hearty greeting or a cry of "huzzah" from these frightened and browbeaten people. Too much excitement may cause them to slump over, curtains. Smile gently and be content if you receive a pale wave of the hand in return. It is unfair to imply that you have come to help them throw off their chains.

Definition

16   When the headwaiter arrives to take your order, do not be bullied into ordering the last of the gazelle haunches unless you really want them. Thrilled to be offered anything at all, many Lonely Guys will say "Get them right out here" and wolf them down. Restaurants take unfair advantage of Lonely Guys, using them to get rid of anything from withered liver to old heels of roast beef. Order anything you like, although it is good to keep to the light and simple in case of a sudden attack of violent stomach cramps.

Effect

Some Proven Strategies

17   Once the meal is under way, a certain pressure will begin to build as couples snuggle together, the women clucking sympathetically in your direction. Warmth and conviviality will pervade the room, none of it encompassing you. At this point, many Lonely Guys will keep their eyes riveted to the restaurant paintings of early Milan or bury themselves in a paperback anthology they have no wish to read.

Step in process

Effect

18   Here are some ploys designed to confuse other diners and make them feel less sorry for you:

Classification

19   ■   After each bite of food, lift your head, smack your lips thoughtfully, swallow and make a notation in a pad. Diners will assume you are a restaurant critic.

20   ■   Between courses, pull out a walkie-talkie and whisper a message into it. This will lead everyone to believe you are part of a police stake-out team, about to bust the salad man as an international dope dealer.

21   ■   Pretend you are a foreigner. This is done by pointing to items on the menu with an alert smile and saying to the headwaiter: "Is good, no?"

22   ■   When the main course arrives, brush the restaurant silverware off the table and pull some of your own out of a breastpocket. People will think you are a wealthy eccentric.

23   ■   Keep glancing at the door, and make occasional trips to look out at the street, as if you are waiting for a beautiful woman. Half-way through the meal, shrug in a world-weary manner and begin to eat with gusto. The world is full of women! Why tolerate bad manners! Life is too short.

Step in process

Implied argument

The Right Way

24   One other course is open to the Lonely Guy, an audacious one, full of perils, but all the more satisfying if you can bring it off. That is to take off your dark glasses, sit erectly, smile broadly at anyone who looks in your direction, wave off inferior wines, and begin to eat with heartiness and enormous confidence. As outrageous as the thought may be—enjoy your own company. Suddenly, titters and sly winks will tail off, the headwaiter's disdain will fade, and friction will build among couples who will turn out to be not as tightly cemented as they appear. The heads of other Lonely Guys will lift with hope as you become the attractive center of the room.

25   If that doesn't work, you still have your fainting option.

Most writing, including writing that draws on outside sources, uses a mixture of several strategies. As you determine which strategies will help you present your ideas, you can draw upon the principles of critical thinking that you used with each individual strategy. You can, for example, evaluate the merits of different writers' opinions, look for evidence of bias, weigh the type and amount of support backing each assertion, and select the key points you'll include in your paper.

Let's say that you're taking an elementary education class and are asked to write a paper evaluating the effectiveness of computers as an educational tool in elementary schools. Obviously, this assignment would require you to synthesize (see pages 64–65) the results of your outside reading and very likely the conclusions drawn from one or more observations of computer use in classrooms. It would, in short, require both secondary (that is, library) research and direct observations (see pages 370–375), a form of primary research.

You might begin your paper by describing a typical morning's activities in a computer-equipped classroom, noting particularly the students' responses to computer instruction. Next, you might classify the different uses of computers in the classroom and provide a brief history of the movement toward this type of instruction. You could proceed by citing the positive effects of computers in the classroom, as noted by those who advocate their use, and then evaluate whether these claims are exaggerated or reflect any bias. For example, you might notice some kind of bias in a comparison of classrooms with and without computers and then suggest how to make such a comparison so as to eliminate the bias. Finally, you might also critically examine the objections of those who oppose computer instruction. After you've completed this research and analysis, you could argue for or against the use of computers as an educational tool. Even though this type of assignment may seem overwhelming, you can meet the challenge if you tackle the project one stage at a time.*

---

*Because you'll need to consult library sources, it is important to read the sections on card catalogues and periodical indexes in Chapter 19 and those on handling quotations and avoiding plagiarism in Chapter 20 before you start to write. As always, follow your instructor's guidelines for documenting sources.

SUGGESTIONS FOR WRITING

1. Using a combination of strategies, write a paper that investigates and assesses the placement of students with mental and emotional disabilities in mainstream rather than special classes. To gather information, you might interview people who work in the school system, or visit classrooms with and without students who have disabilities.

2. Examine several sources that favour or oppose the use of community tax revenues for a specific project. Then, drawing on different writing strategies you may have studied, such as illustration, causal analysis, and argument, present and assess your findings, making it clear where you stand on this issue.

3. Investigate, using outside sources, a current cultural phenomenon, such as the upsurge in reality-based television shows; the popularity of a trend such as extreme sports, street racing, or yoga; the increase in homelessness; or some other social problem. Then, drawing on different writing strategies you may have studied, such as definition, causal analysis, and argument, write a paper that presents and assesses these findings, making it clear by the end whether you see this phenomenon in a negative or positive light.

4. Identify something you consider a problem with some local or national law. Alternatively, you could identify a problem with a policy at work, at school, or in another area with which you are familiar. Perhaps you may see this law or policy as unjust, unfairly applied, outdated, too expensive to enforce, or the like. Examine several sources that discuss this law and then use a combination of strategies to write a paper that identifies the problem and proposes a reasonable solution.

5. Analyze the rhetorical strategies in a recent influential speech by a major politician. Draw on different writing strategies, such as illustration and argument, in order to show why you think the speech is or is not persuasive. If you prefer, you might choose to analyze an article from Web sites such as the Canadian Centre for Policy Alternatives (**http://www.policyalternatives.ca**), The Fraser Institute (**http://www.fraserinstitute.ca**), or the Canadian Federation of Students (**www.cfs.ca**). Remember that your purpose is not simply to say whether or not you agree with the speaker or writer, but to demonstrate how the speaker or writer does or does not use effective persuasive techniques.

14

Paragraphs

Imagine the difficulty of reading a magazine article or book if you were faced with one solid block of text. How could you sort its ideas or know the best places to pause for thought? Paragraphs help guide readers through longer pieces of writing. Some break lengthy discussions of one idea into segments of different emphasis, thus providing rest stops for readers. Others consolidate several briefly developed ideas. Yet others begin or end pieces of writing or link major segments together. Most paragraphs, though, include a number of sentences that develop and clarify one idea. Throughout a piece of writing, paragraphs relate to one another and reflect a controlling purpose. To make paragraphs fit together smoothly, you can't just sit down and dash them off. Instead, you first need to reflect on the entire essay, then channel your thoughts toward its different segments. Often you'll have to revise your paragraphs after you've written a draft.

◾ Characteristics of Effective Paragraphs

Unity

A paragraph with unity develops one, and only one, key controlling idea. To ensure unity, edit out any stray ideas that don't belong and fight the urge to take interesting but irrelevant side trips; they only create confusion about your destination.

The following paragraph *lacks unity:*

> The psychiatric nurse deals with dangerous mental patients, pathological personalities who may explode into violence at any moment. Sigmund Freud was one of the first doctors to study mental disorders. Today psychotherapy is a well-established medical discipline.

What exactly is this writer trying to say? We can't tell. Each sentence expresses a different, undeveloped idea:

1. Job of the psychiatric nurse
2. Freud's pioneering work in studying mental disorders
3. Present status of psychotherapy

In contrast, the following paragraph develops and clarifies only one central idea, the professional responsibilities of a psychiatric nurse:

> Psychiatric nurses deal with dangerous mental patients, pathological personalities who may explode into violence at any moment. For this reason, they must remain on guard at all times. When a patient displays anger or violence, they cannot respond in kind but must instead show tolerance and understanding. Furthermore, they must be able to recognize attempts at deception. Sometimes a mentally ill person, just prior to launching an attack, will act in a completely normal way in order to deceive the intended victim. The nurse must recognize this behaviour and be alert for any possible assault.

> Peggy Feltman

Because no unrelated ideas sidetrack the discussion of responsibilities, the paragraph has unity. To check your paragraphs for unity, ask yourself what each one aims to do and whether each sentence helps that aim.

EXERCISE *After reading the next two paragraphs, answer the questions that follow.*

1.   The legend--in Africa--that all elephants over a large geographical area go to a common "graveyard" when they sense death is approaching led many hunters to treat them with special cruelty. Ivory hunters, believing the myth and trying to locate such graveyards, often intentionally wounded an elephant in the hopes of following the suffering beast as it made its way to the place where it wanted to die. The idea was to wound the elephant seriously enough so that it thought it was going to die but not so seriously that it died in a very short time. All too often, the process resulted in a single elephant being shot or speared many

times and relentlessly pursued until it either fell dead or was killed when it finally turned and charged its attackers. In any case, no wounded elephant ever led its pursuers to the mythical graveyard with its hoped-for booty of ivory tusks.

Kris Hurrell

2. When I was growing up, I spent many happy hours with my brothers and sisters playing jungle games in the woodlot behind our farm home. This lot, ten acres of dense-set poplars and birches standing amidst the blackened stumps of an old pine forest, provided a perfect setting for our jungle adventures. At times we acted out African versions of cowboys and Indians; at others we sought the long-lost treasures of fabled diamond mines. Often our adventures pitted Tarzan against tomb robbers and poachers. Besides serving as a playground, our woodlot furnished most of the fuel for the iron stoves in our kitchen and living room. I can still remember the backbreaking work of chopping up stumps and fallen trees and hauling them to the house. In the winter, the woodlot offered fine small-game hunting. In the summer, it provided a cool refuge from the heat that blistered the fields and farmhouse. Today, farm and woodlot are gone, swallowed up by a sprawling suburb. I wonder whether the children who live there ever want to play jungle games or regret that there's no place for them.

Student Unknown

1. Which of these paragraphs lacks unity? Refer to the paragraphs when answering.
2. How would you improve the paragraph that lacks unity?

The Topic Sentence

The topic sentence states the main idea of the paragraph. Think of the topic sentence as a rallying point, with all supporting sentences developing the idea it expresses. A good topic sentence helps you gauge what information belongs in a paragraph, thus ensuring unity. At the same time, it informs your reader about the point you're making.

Placement of the topic sentence varies from paragraph to paragraph, as the following examples show. As you read each, note how supporting information develops the topic sentence, which is italicized.

Topic Sentence Stated First   Many paragraphs open with the topic sentence. The writer reveals the central idea immediately and then builds from a solid base.

Starting about one million years ago, the fossil record shows an accelerating growth of the human brain. It expanded at first at the rate of one cubic inch of additional gray matter every hundred thousand years; then the growth rate doubled; it doubled again; and finally it doubled once more. Five hundred thousand years ago the rate of growth hit its peak. At that time, the brain was expanding at the phenomenal rate of ten cubic inches every hundred thousand years. No other organ in the history of life is known to have grown as fast as this.

Robert Jastrow, Until the Sun Dies

Topic Sentence Stated Last   In order to emphasize the support and build gradually to a conclusion, a topic sentence can end the paragraph. This position creates suspense as the reader anticipates the summarizing remark.

An experience of my own comes handily to mind. Some years ago, when the Restaurant de la Pyramide in Vienne was without question one of the best half-dozen restaurants in the world, I visited it for the first time. After I had ordered my meal, the sommelier [wine steward] appeared to set before me a wine list of surpassing amplitude and excellence. But as I cast my eyes down this unbelievable offering of the world's most tantalizing wines, the sommelier bent over me and pointed out a wine of which I had never heard, ticketed at a price one-fifth that of its illustrious neighbors. "Monsieur," said the sommelier, "I would suggest this one. It is a local wine, a very good wine. It is not a great wine, but after all, monsieur, you are likely to pass this way only once. The great wines you will find everywhere; this wine you will find only in Vienne. I would like you to try it, while you have the opportunity." *This, to my mind, was true sophistication—on the part of M. Point for having the wine and on the part of the waiter for offering it.*

Stephen White, "The New Sophistication: Defining the Terms"

Topic Sentence Stated First and Last   Some paragraphs lead with the main idea and then restate it, usually in different words, at the end. This technique allows the writer to repeat an especially important idea.

Everything is changing. . . . This is a prediction I can make with absolute certainty. As human beings, we are constantly in a state of change. Our bodies change every day. Our attitudes are constantly evolving. Something that we swore by five years ago is now almost impossible for us to imagine ourselves believing. The clothes we wore a few years ago now look strange to us in old photographs. The things we take for granted as absolutes, impervious to change, are, in fact, constantly doing just that. Granite boulders become sand in time. Beaches erode and shape new shorelines. Our buildings become outdated and are replaced with modern structures that also will be torn down. Even those things which last thousands of years, such as the Pyramids and the Acropolis, also are changing. This simple insight is very important to grasp if you want to be a no-limit person, and are desirous of raising no-limit children. *Everything you feel, think, see, and touch is constantly changing.*

Wayne Dyer, What Do You Really Want for Your Children?

Topic Sentence Stated in the Middle   On occasion, the topic sentence falls between one set of sentences that provides background information and a follow-up set that develops the central idea. This arrangement allows the writer to shift the emphasis and at the same time preserve close ties between the two sets.

> Over the centuries, China has often been the subject of Western fantasy. In their own way, a number of scholars, journalists, and other travelers have perpetuated this tradition in recent years, rushing to rediscover the country after its long period of isolation. Some of these visitors, justifiably impressed by the Communists' achievements in eliminating the exploitative aspects of pre-1949 mandarin society, propagated the view that the revolution, after its initial successes, had continued to "serve the people," and that China was "the wave of the future"—a compelling alternative to the disorder and materialism of contemporary Western society. Human rights were not at issue, they argued, because such Western concepts were inapplicable to China. *In the past year, however, the Chinese have begun to speak for themselves, and they are conveying quite a different picture.* In the view of many of its own people, China is a backward and repressive nation. "China is Asia's Gulag Archipelago," an elderly Chinese scholar said to me shortly after I had arrived in China last spring. "I was in Germany right after the Second World War, and I saw the horrors of Buchenwald and other concentration camps. In a way—in its destruction of the human spirit these past two decades—China has been even worse."

> David Finkelstein, "When the Snow Thaws"

Topic Sentence Implied   Some paragraphs, particularly in narrative and descriptive writing, have no topic sentence. Rather, all sentences point toward a main idea that readers must grasp for themselves.

> [Captain Robert Barclay] once went out at 5 in the morning to do a little grouse shooting. He walked at least 30 miles while he potted away, and then after dinner set out on a walk of 60 miles that he accomplished in 11 hours without a halt. Barclay did not sleep after this but went through the following day as if nothing had happened until the afternoon, when he walked 16 miles to a ball. He danced all night, and then in early morning walked home and spent a day partridge shooting. Finally he did get to bed—but only after a period of two nights and nearly three days had elapsed and he had walked 130 miles.

> John Lovesey, "A Myth Is as Good as a Mile"

The details in this paragraph collectively suggest a clear central idea: that Barclay had incredible physical endurance. But writing effective paragraphs without topic sentences challenges even the best writers. Therefore, control most of your paragraphs with clearly expressed topic sentences.

EXERCISE   *Identify the topic sentences in each of the following paragraphs and explain how you arrived at your decisions. If the topic sentence is implied, state the central idea in your own words.*

1.   Unlike governments, corporations are not democratic and not charged with advancing the public good. Instead, they exist to maximize profit for shareholders— sometimes at the cost of honesty. Just last week, the giant company Worldcom imploded under allegations of a $4 billion accounting scam. Far from being a rare

occurrence, such scandals are becoming commonplace. From Enron to Dynegy to Adelphia, corporations are proving that they shouldn't be trusted, and indeed some are downright rotten to the core. Where were the government regulators and the auditors in these scandals? These were public companies and in some cases people's pensions depended on them. Yet the size and scope of the scandals indicates that regulators turned a blind eye to the problems or were prevented from taking action.

David Suzuki, "Protesters' Message Lost on the Media"

2.   What my mother never told me was how fast time passes in adult life. I remember, when I was little, thinking I would live to be at least as old as my grandmother, who was dynamic even at ninety-two, the age at which she died. Now I see those ninety-two years hurtling by me. And my mother never told me how much fun sex could be, or what a discovery it is. Of course, I'm of an age when mothers really didn't tell you much about anything. My mother never told me the facts of life.

Joyce Susskind, "Surprises in a Woman's Life"

3.   It was funny how everyone in the second half of the twentieth century suddenly started buying these large, lumpy, sculptured, multicolored shoes. It was as though people discovered overnight that their footwear didn't have to be black or brown, and didn't need to conform to what was streamlined and quietly tasteful. The traditional shoe was challenged, and it collapsed at the first skirmish. Shoes could trumpet their engineered presence, their tread, their aggressive padding; they could make all manner of wild claims, converting whole populations to athletic splendor and prodigious fitness. Larry's running shoes are red and white, with little yellow insignias located near the toe. Each of the heels has a transparent built-in bubble for additional comfort and buoyancy when running on hard pavement.

Carol Shields, *Larry's Party*

4.   That empty building on the left was once a school. Here in Cutback World we have discovered that the educational system operates far more efficiently if schools are not open. You should not conclude from this that we have closed all our schools. That would be foolish. There is a school downtown somewhere. Every city of at least 100,000 people in Cutback World is entitled to have a school. Ours has 15,000 students in it, which enables it to offer a full range of courses. When we pass it, you might notice some students hanging out the open windows. We regard this as a sign that classroom space is being fully utilized.

Charles Gordon "A Guided Tour of the Bottom Line"

EXERCISE   *Develop one of the ideas below into a topic sentence. Then write a unified paragraph that is built around it.*

1. The career (or job or profession) I want is _____.

2. The one quality most necessary in my chosen field is _____.

3. The most difficult aspect of my chosen field is _____.

4. One good example of the Canadian tendency to waste is _____.

5. The best (or worst) thing about fast-food restaurants is _____.

| **Write a topic sentence that would control a paragraph on each of the following:**

1. Preparations for travelling away from home
2. Advantages of having your own room
3. Some landmark of the community in which you live
4. The price of long-distance telephone calls
5. Registering for university or college courses

Adequate Development

Students often ask for guidelines on paragraph length: "Should I aim for fifty to sixty words? Seven to ten sentences? About one-quarter of a page?" The questions are natural, but the approach is wrong. Instead of targeting a particular length, ask yourself what the reader needs to know. Then supply enough information to make your point clearly. Developing a paragraph inadequately is like inviting guests to a party but failing to tell them when and where it will be held. Skimpy paragraphs force readers to fill in the gaps for themselves, a task that can both irritate and stump them. On the other hand, a paragraph stuffed with useless padding dilutes the main idea. In all cases, the reader, the information being presented, and the publication medium determine the proper amount of detail. A newspaper might feature short paragraphs including only key facts, whereas a scientific journal might have lengthy paragraphs that offer detailed development of facts.

The details you supply can include facts, figures, thoughts, observations, steps, lists, examples, and personal experiences. Individually, these bits of information may mean little, but added together they clearly illustrate your point. Keep in mind, however, that development isn't an end in itself but instead advances the purpose of the entire essay.

Here are two versions of a paragraph, the first inadequately developed:

Underdeveloped Paragraph

Many sports have peculiar injuries associated with them. Repetitive use of certain body parts can cause chronic injuries in athletes who play baseball, football, or basketball. All of these common sports injuries are a result of the overuse of specific body parts. However, these injuries can be greatly reduced if athletes train properly, rest fully, and respect their bodies.

Adequately Developed Paragraph

Many sports have peculiar injuries associated with them. Repetitive use of certain body parts can cause chronic injuries in athletes who play baseball, football, or basketball. *Baseball pitchers can throw up to one hundred and fifty pitches per game. This repetitive throwing action can cause pitchers' elbows to swell. Over time, tendonitis often develops. Football linemen also suffer chronic injuries in their sport. The constant jarring pressure during physical contact can cause severe back pain. Many linemen struggle with spinal disc injuries throughout their lives. Basketball players often suffer from shin splints because of the repetitive pounding on their legs when running and jumping on a hard surface.* All of these common sports injuries are a result of the overuse of specific body parts. However, these injuries can be greatly reduced if athletes train properly, rest fully, and respect their bodies.

The first paragraph lacks examples of peculiar sports injuries, whereas the second one provides the needed information.

Readability also helps set paragraph length. Within a paper, paragraphs signal natural dividing places, allowing the reader to pause and absorb the material presented up to that point. Too little paragraphing overwhelms the reader with long blocks of material. Too much creates a choppy Dick-and-Jane effect that may seem simplistic, even irritating. To counter these problems, writers sometimes use several paragraphs for an idea that needs extended development, or they combine several short paragraphs into one.

EXERCISE

1. **Indicate where the ideas in this long block of material divide logically; explain your choices.**

    During the summer following graduation from high school, I could hardly wait to get to university and "be on my own." In my first weeks at university, however, I found that independence can be tough and painful. I had expected raucous good times and a carefree collegiate life, the sort depicted in old beach movies and suggested by the selective memories of sentimental alumni. Instead, all I felt at first was the burden of increasing responsibilities and the loneliness of "a man without a country." I discovered that being independent of parents who kept at me to do my homework and expected me to accomplish certain household chores did not mean I was free to do as I pleased. On the contrary, living on my own meant that I had to perform for myself all the tasks that the family used to share. Studying became a full-time occupation rather than a nightly duty to be accomplished in an hour or two, and my instructors made it clear that they would have little sympathy for negligence or even for my inability to do an assignment. But what was more troubling about my early university life than having to do laundry, prepare meals, and complete stacks of homework was the terrifying sense of being entirely alone. I was independent, no longer a part of the world that had seemed to confine me, but I soon realized that confinement had also meant security. I never liked the feeling that people were watching over me, but I knew that my family and friends were also watching out for me--and that's a good feeling to have. At the university no one seemed particularly to be watching, though professors constantly evaluated the quality of my work. I felt estranged from people in those first weeks, desperately needing a confidant but fearful that the new and tenuous friendships I had made would be damaged if I were to confess my fears and problems. It was simply too early for me to feel a part of the university. So there I was, independent in the fullest sense, and thus "a man without a country."

2. **The following short, choppy units are inadequately developed. List some details you could use to expand one of them into a good paragraph.**

   I like living in a small town because the people are so friendly. In addition, I can always get the latest gossip from the local busybody.

   In a big city, people are afraid to get too friendly. Everything is very private, and nobody knows anything about anybody else.

3. **Scan the compositions you have written in other classes for paragraphs that are over- or underdeveloped. Revise any you find.**

Organization

An effective paragraph unfolds in a clear pattern of organization so that the reader can easily follow the flow of ideas. Usually when you write your first draft, your attempt to organize your thoughts will also organize your paragraphs. Writers do not ordinarily stop to decide on a strategy for each paragraph. But when you revise or are stuck, it's useful to understand the available choices. Here are some options:

1. The strategies discussed in Chapters 4–12
2. Order of climax

The choice you make depends upon your material and purpose in writing.

Writing Strategies   These include all of the following patterns:

Time sequence (narration)	Comparison
Space sequence (description)	Cause and effect
Process analysis	Definition
Illustration	Argument
Classification	

Four example paragraphs follow. The first, organized by *time sequence,* traces the final years of the Model T Ford, concluding with a topic sentence that sums up its impact.

In 1917 the Model T lost much of its attraction when its exterior appearance was drastically altered. The famous flat-sided brass radiator disappeared and the new style featured (in the words of the catalogue) "The stream-lined hood, large radiator and enclosed fan, crown fenders, black finish and nickel trimmings" ("crown fenders" would be described in England as domed mud-guards). Electric lighting and starting followed in 1919, and the model then continued with little alteration until 1927, when it was finally withdrawn. After a considerable pause it was replaced by the Model A, a very conventional machine with wire wheels, three-speed gearbox and four-wheel brakes (the "T" had never made this concession to progress and continued to the last with two minute brake drums on the back wheels only). While it was in preparation, others had taken the lead and the "A" never replaced the immortal "T" in the public fancy. Indeed, the "Tin Lizzy" or "Flivver" had become almost a national characteristic, and at the end of its eighteen years in production the total number sold was fifteen million.

Cecil Clutton and John Stanford, *The Vintage Motor-Car*

The next paragraph, organized by *space sequence,* describes a ceramic elf, starting from the bottom and working up to the top. Other common spatial arrangements include top to bottom, left to right, right to left, nearby to far away, far away to nearby, clockwise, and counterclockwise.

The ceramic elf in our family room is quite a character. His reddish-brown slippers, which hang over the mantel shelf, taper to a slender point. Pudgy, yellow-stockinged legs disappear into a wrinkled tunic-style, olive-green jacket, gathered at the waist with a thick, brown belt that fits snugly around his roly-poly belly. His short, meaty arms hang comfortably, one hand resting on the knapsack at his side and the other clutching the bowl of an old black pipe. An unkempt, snow-white beard, dotted by occasional snarls, trails patriarch-fashion from his lower lip to his belt line. A button nose capped with a smudge of gold dust, mischievous black eyes, and an unruly snatch of hair peeking out from under his burnt-orange stocking cap complete Bartholomew's appearance.

Maria Sanchez

Although descriptive paragraphs, like those developed by narration, often lack topic sentences, our example leads off with the central idea.

Here is a paragraph showing *process* development.

Making beer nuts is a quick, simple procedure that provides a delicious evening snack. You'll need six cups of raw peanuts, three cups of sugar, and one-and-one-half cups of water. To begin, combine the sugar and water in a two-litre saucepan and stir to dissolve the sugar. Next, add the peanuts and stir again until all of the peanuts are covered by the sugar-water solution. Leave the pan, uncovered, on a burner set at medium-high heat for ten to twelve minutes, until the sugar crystallizes and coats the peanuts thoroughly. Stay at the stove during the heating process and stir the mixture every two or three minutes to ensure even coating of the nuts. When the peanuts are thoroughly coated, pour them onto an ungreased cookie sheet and bake at 350 degrees for about thirty minutes, stirring and lightly salting at ten-minute intervals. Serve your beer nuts fresh out of the oven or eat them at room temperature.

Kimberlee Walters

Again, the topic sentence comes first.

The final example illustrates development by *comparison* and also proceeds from an opening topic sentence.

There is an essential difference between a news story, as understood by a newspaperman or a wire-service writer, and the newsmagazine story. The chief purpose of the conventional news story is to tell what happened. It starts with the most important information and continues into increasingly inconsequential details, not only because the reader may not read beyond the first paragraph but because an editor working on galley proofs a few minutes before press time likes to be able to cut freely from the end of the story. A newsmagazine is very different. It is written to be read consecutively from beginning to end, and each of its stories is designed, following the critical theories of Edgar Allan Poe, to create one emotional effect. The news, what happened that week, may be told in the beginning, the middle, or the end; for the purpose is not to throw information at the reader but to seduce him into reading the whole story, and into accepting the dramatic (and often political) point being made.

Otto Friedrich, "There Are 00 Trees in Russia"

Order of Climax Climactic order creates a crescendo pattern, starting with the least emphatic detail and progressing to the most emphatic. The topic sentence can begin or end the paragraph, or it can remain implied. This pattern holds the reader's interest by building suspense. On occasion, writers reverse the order, landing the heaviest punch first; but such paragraphs can trail off, leaving the reader dissatisfied.

Here is a paragraph illustrating climactic order:

The speaking errors I hear affect me to different degrees. I'm so conditioned to hearing "It don't make any difference" and "There's three ways to solve the problem" that I've almost accepted such usage. However, errors such as "Just between you and I, Arnold loves Edna" and "I'm going back to my room to lay down" still offend my sensibility. When hearing them, I usually just chuckle to myself and walk away. The "Twin I's"--<u>irrevelant</u> and <u>irregardless</u>-- are another matter. More than any other errors, they really grate on my ear. Whenever I hear "that may be true, but it's irrevelant" or "Irregardless of how much I study, I still get C's," I have the urge to correct the speaker. It's really surprising that more people don't clean up their language act.

Valerie Sonntag

> **EXERCISE**   *From a magazine or newspaper article, select four paragraphs that illustrate different patterns of organization. Identify the topic sentence in each case; or if it is implied, state it in your own words. Point out the organization of each paragraph.*

Coherence

Coherent writing flows smoothly and easily from one sentence and paragraph to another, clarifying the relationships among ideas and thus allowing the reader to grasp connections. Because incoherent writing fails to do this, it confuses, and sometimes even irritates, the reader.

Here is a paragraph that lacks coherence:

> I woke up late. I had been so tired the night before that I had forgotten to set the alarm. All I could think of was the report I had stayed up until 3 a.m. typing, and how I could possibly get twenty copies ready for next morning's 9 o'clock sales meeting. I panicked and ran out the door. My bus was so crowded I had to stand. Jumping off the bus, I raced back up the street. The meeting was already underway. Mr. Jackson gestured for me to come into the conference room. Inserting the first page of the report into the copier, I set the dial for twenty copies and pressed the print button. The sign started flashing CALL KEY OPERATOR. The machine was out of order. Mr. Jackson asked whether the report was ready. I pointed to the flashing red words. Mr. Jackson nodded grimly without saying anything. He left me alone with the broken machine.

This paragraph has some degree of unity: Most of its sentences relate to the writer's disastrous experience with the sales report. Unfortunately, though, its many gaps in logic create rather than answer questions, and in very bumpy prose, at that. Note the gap between the third and fourth sentences. Did the writer jump out of bed and rush right out the door? Of course not, but the reader has no real clue to the actual sequence of events. Another gap occurs between the next two sentences, leaving the reader to wonder why the writer had to race up the street upon leaving the bus. And who is Mr. Jackson? The paragraph never tells, but the reader will want to know.

Now read this rewritten version, additions italicized:

> I woke up late *because* I had been so tired the night before that I had forgotten to set the alarm. All I could think of was the report I had stayed up until 3 a.m. typing, and how I could possibly get twenty copies ready for next morning's 9 o'clock sales meeting. *When I realized it was 8:30,* I panicked. *Jumping out of bed, I threw on some clothes, grabbed the report,* and ran out the door. My bus was so crowded I had to stand *and could not see out the window. Two blocks beyond my stop, I realized I should have gotten off. "Stop!" I cried and,* jumping off the bus, raced back up the street. *When I reached the office, it was 9:15, and* the meeting was already underway. Mr. Jackson, *the sales manager, saw me and* gestured for me to come into the conference room. *"One*

moment," I said as calmly as I could and hurried to the copier. Inserting the first page of the report into it, I set the dial for twenty copies and pressed the print button. *Immediately,* the sign started flashing CALL KEY OPERATOR. The machine was out of order. *The next thing I knew,* Mr. Jackson *was at my side* asking whether the report was ready. I pointed to the flashing red words, *and* Mr. Jackson nodded grimly without saying anything. *Turning on his heel,* he *walked away and* left me alone with the broken machine.

As this example shows, correcting an incoherent paragraph may call for anything from a single word to a whole sentence or more.

EXERCISE   *Rewrite the following student paragraph to improve coherence. You may rearrange sentence order, combine and condense sentences, or add any connecting words that seem appropriate.*

> Many elderly people, as well as people that can no longer care for themselves, are placed in long-term care facilities. These surroundings can be unpleasant for many, and can cause residents to become very depressed. Within the last few years, animal therapy has become recognized as a way to improve health. Many of these facilities arrange weekly visits from a local handler and their best friend, which is usually a well-trained dog. These visits provide patients with something to look forward to. The presence of a loving animal companion can comfort lonely people. Visiting with animals helps to lower blood pressure. It also can reduce stress. In turn, many patients generally become more responsive to their treatment. Residents seem happier overall and feel better when animals are allowed to visit their facility.
>
> Alana Reekie, student

Coherence derives from a sufficient supply of supporting details and your firm sense of the way your ideas go together. If you brainstorm your topic thoroughly and think carefully about the relationships between sentences, incoherence isn't likely to haunt your paragraphs.

As you write, and especially when you revise, signal connections to the reader by using *transitions*—devices that link sentences to one another. These are the most common transitional devices:

1. Connecting words and phrases
2. Repeated key words
3. Pronouns
4. Parallelism

You can use them to furnish links both within and between paragraphs.

Connecting Words and Phrases   These connectors clarify relationships between sentences. The following list groups them according to function:

Showing similarity: in like manner, likewise, moreover, similarly

Showing contrast: at the same time, but, even so, however, in contrast, instead, nevertheless, still, on the contrary, on the other hand, otherwise, yet

Showing results or effects: accordingly, as a result, because, consequently, hence, since, therefore, thus

Adding ideas together: also, besides, first (second, third . . .), furthermore, in addition, in the first place, likewise, moreover, similarly, too

Drawing conclusions: as a result, finally, in brief, in conclusion, in short, to summarize

Pointing out examples: for example, for instance, to illustrate

Showing emphasis and clarity: above all, after all, again, as a matter of fact, besides, in fact, in other words, indeed, nonetheless, that is

Indicating time: at times, after, afterward, from then on, immediately, later, meanwhile, next, now, once, previously, subsequently, then, until, while

Conceding a point: granted that, of course, to be sure, admittedly

Don't overload your paper with connectors. In well-planned prose, your message flows clearly with only an occasional assist from them.

In the following excerpt, which clarifies the difference between workers and workaholics, the connectors are italicized:

> My efforts to define workaholism and to distinguish workaholics from other hard workers proved difficult. *While* workaholics do work hard, not all hard workers are workaholics. Moonlighters, *for example,* may work 16 hours a day to make ends meet, but most of them will stop working when their financial circumstances permit. Accountants, *too,* seem to work non-stop, but many slow down after the April 30 tax deadline. Workaholics, *on the other hand,* always devote more time and thought to their work than their situation demands. Even in the absence of deadlines to meet, mortgages to pay, promotions to earn, or bosses to please, workaholics still work hard. What sets them apart is their attitude toward work, not the number of hours they work.
>
> Marilyn Machlowitz, "Workaholism: What's Wrong with Being Married to Your Work?"

DISCUSSION QUESTIONS

1. What ideas do each of the italicized words and phrases connect?
2. What relationship does each show?

Repeated Key Words   Repeating key words, especially those that help convey a paragraph's central idea, can smooth the reader's path. The words may appear in different forms, but their presence keeps the main issues before the reader. In the following paragraph, the repetition of the phrase "*it adds*" and "*it is,*" along with the word "blandness" aids coherence.

What is the point of the battered fry? *It adds* crunch. *It adds* weight. *It adds* calories. *What it* does not *add* is flavour. *What it* removes *is* potato-ness. *It is* a blandifier. And *it is* its very *blandness* that makes it popular. *Blandness* is more tenacious than any virus: *It* will always conquer a host population, wherever *it is* introduced.

Russell Smith, "Battered by Blandness"

EXERCISE   *Write a paragraph using one of the following sentences as your topic sentence. Insert the missing key word and then repeat it in your paragraph to help link your sentences together.*

1. _____ is my favourite relative.

2. I wish I had (a, an, some, more) _____.

3. _____ changed my life.

4. _____ is more trouble than it's worth.

5. A visit to _____ always depresses me.

Pronouns   Pronouns stand in for nouns that appear earlier in the sentence or in previous sentences. Mixing pronouns and their nouns throughout the paragraph prevents monotony and promotes clarity. We have italicized pronouns that aid coherence in the following excerpt from an address about Canadian literature by Robertson Davies.

In psychological terms, Canada is very much an introverted country, and *it* lives cheek by jowl with the most extraverted country known to history. Let me explain the terms. In personal psychology, the extravert is *one* who derives *his* energy from *his* contacts with the external world; for *him*, everything lies outside and *he* moves outward toward *it*, often without much sensitivity to the response of that toward which *he* moves. The introvert, on the other hand, finds *his* energy within *himself*, and *his* concern with the outside world is a matter of what approach the outside world makes to *him*. It is absurd to say that one psychological orientation is superior to the other. Both have *their* values, but difficulties arise when *they* fail to understand one another.

Robertson Davies, "Living in a Country Without a Mythology"

Some words such as *this, that, those,* and *these* also may contribute to coherence, or flow, by referring back to something that has come just before. Sometimes they function as pronouns; at other times they may function as demonstrative adjectives.

Experience with diversity shows that inequities must be acknowledged and addressed for a diverse people to move forward together. *This* is a slow and sometimes painful process, but it is essential if all Canadians are to enjoy the same sense of belonging and attachment to their country. It also serves to familiarize Canadians with the history they share and the obligations that their history confers. *These* obligations include honouring the proclamations and negotiated arrangements made with First Nations peoples.

"Canadian Multiculturalism: An Inclusive Citizenship"

EXERCISE   *In a magazine, newspaper, textbook, or some other written source, find two paragraphs that use pronouns or demonstrative adjectives to increase coherence. Copy the paragraphs, underline the pronouns, and explain what each refers to.*

Parallelism   Parallelism uses repetition of grammatical form to express a series of equivalent ideas. Besides giving continuity, the repetition adds rhythm and balance to the writing. Note how the following italicized constructions tie together the unfolding definition of poverty:

> *Poverty is staying up* all night on cold nights to watch the fire, knowing one spark on the newspaper covering the walls means your sleeping children die in flames. In summer *poverty is watching* gnats and flies devour your baby's tears when he cries. The screens are torn and you pay so little rent you know they will never be fixed. *Poverty means* insects in your food, in your nose, in your eyes, and crawling over you when you sleep. *Poverty is hoping* it never rains because diapers won't dry when it rains and soon you are using newspapers. *Poverty is seeing* your children forever with runny noses. Paper handkerchiefs cost money and all your rags you need for other things. Even more costly are antihistamines. *Poverty is cooking* without food and cleaning without soap.
>
> Jo Goodwin Parker, "What Is Poverty?"

■ Paragraphs with Special Functions

Special-function paragraphs include introductions, transitional paragraphs, and conclusions. One-paragraph introductions and conclusions appear in short, multi-paragraph essays. Transitional paragraphs occur primarily in long compositions.

Introductions

A good introduction acquaints and coaxes. It announces the essay's topic and may directly state the thesis. In addition, it sets the tone—sombre, lighthearted, angry—of what will follow. An amusing anecdote would not be an appropriate opening for a paper about political torture.

With essays, as with people, first impressions are important. If your opening rouses interest, it will draw the reader into the essay and pave the way for your ideas. If, instead, you'd like to try your hand at turning the reader away, search for a beginning that is mechanical, plodding, and dull. Your success will astonish you. Here are some bad openings:

> In this paper I intend to . . .
>
> Wars have always afflicted humankind.
>
> As you may know, having too little time is a problem for many of us.
>
> In the modern world of today . . .

How would you respond to these openings? Ask yourself that same question about every opening you write.

Gear the length of the introduction to that of the essay. Although longer papers sometimes begin with two or more introductory paragraphs, generally the lead-in for a short essay is a single paragraph. Here are some possibilities for starting an essay. The type you select depends on your purpose, subject, audience, and personality.

A Directly Stated Thesis   This is a common type of opening, orienting the reader to what will follow. After providing some general background, the writer of our example narrows her scope to a thesis that previews the upcoming sections of her essay.

> An increasing number of midlife women are re-entering the workforce, pursuing degrees, and getting more involved in the public arena. Several labels besides "midlife" have been attached to this type of person: the mature woman, the older woman, and, more recently, the re-entry woman. By definition, she is between thirty-five and fifty-five years old and has been away from the business or academic scene anywhere from fifteen to thirty years. The academic community, the media, marketing people, and employers are giving her close scrutiny, and it is apparent that she is having a greater impact on our society than she realizes.
>
> Jo Ann Harris

A Definition   This kind of introduction works particularly well in a paper that acquaints the reader with an unfamiliar topic.

> You are completely alone in a large open space and are struck by a terrifying, unreasoning fear. You sweat, your heart beats, you cannot breathe. You fear you may die of a heart attack, although you do not have heart disease. Suppose you decide you will never get yourself in this helpless situation again. You go home and refuse to leave its secure confines. Your family has to support you. You have agoraphobia—a disabling terror of open spaces.
>
> "Controlling Phobias Through Behaviour Modification"

A Quotation   A beginning quotation, particularly from an authority in the field, can be an effective springboard for the ideas that follow. Make sure any quote you use relates clearly to your topic.

> Unhappiness with body image seems to be a national preoccupation. According to statistics compiled by the National Eating Disorder Information Centre in Toronto, 90 per cent of Canadian women are dissatisfied with some aspect of their bodies. One of the main battlegrounds in the fight for improvement, of course, is eating. According to the *Maclean's* year-end poll published in late December, 43 per cent of Canadian women—compared with 33 per cent of men—believe they are overweight. The eating disorder centre says that its surveys show that fully 70 per cent of Canadian women are preoccupied with their weight, and 40 per cent are

yo-yo dieting. "For most women, when they get together in a group a common topic is trying to lose weight," says Dr. Christine Davies, a family physician in Saint John, N.B., who is concerned about how that may rub off on their daughters. Margaret Beck, acting director of the eating disorder centre, affirms that danger: "The research," she says, "does seem to suggest that mothers who are food- and weight-preoccupied tend to have daughters who are the same."

Celia Milne, "Pressures to Conform"

An Anecdote or Personal Experience   A well-told personal anecdote or experience can lure readers into the rest of the paper. Like other introductions, this kind should bear on what comes afterward. Engle's anecdote, like the stories she reviews, demonstrates that "women also have dark hearts."

> My mother used to have a little china cream and sugar set that was given to her by a woman who later killed her children with an axe. It sat cheerfully in the china cabinet, as inadequate a symbol as I have ever seen of the dark mysteries within us. Yet at least it was there to remind us that no matter how much Jesus wanted us for a sunbeam, we would still have some day to cope with a deeper reality than common sense could explain. It stood for strange cars not to get into, running shoes to wear when you were out alone at night and the backs of Chinese restaurants you were not supposed to go into.

Marian Engle, review of The Goddess and Other Women by Joyce Carol Oates

An Arresting Statement   Sometimes you can jolt the reader into attention, using content, language, or both, particularly if your essay develops an unusual or extreme position.

> I no longer remember the first time I forced myself to throw up. What I do remember is how inexpert I was and how long it took before I succeeded in actually vomiting instead of just gagging and retching. I began by sticking my finger down my throat and wiggling it around, but this produced few results; it wasn't until articles about bulimia appeared in women's magazines that I finally thought to use the handle of a toothbrush instead of my forefinger. It became easy after that.

Evelyn Lau, "An Insatiable Emptiness"

Interesting Details   These details pique curiosity and draw the reader into the paper.

> A lot of people have theories as to just when this country peaked and started its inexorable slide into the sorry, divided state we find ourselves in today. My father's pet belief was that 1967 was the year we peaked. And it makes some sense: kids singing that obnoxious confederation ode *Canada* (pronounced "Caaaa-naaah-daaaah") from coast to coast, the French placated by Expo, the Leafs winning the Stanley Cup, our dollar strong and our deficit just a gleam in soon-to-be-dictator Pierre's eye.

P. T. Jensen, "Lament for the Short and Stubby"

A Question   A provocative question can entice the reader into the essay to find the answer.

> When you leave your apartment or house, do you begin to feel better? If you leave for a week-long trip, do you find your head clears, your migraine disappears, dizziness stops, your aches and pains subside, depression fades away, and your entire attitude is better? If so, chemical pollution of the atmosphere in your home may be making you ill.
>
> Marshall Mandell, "Are You Allergic to Your House?"

EXERCISE

1. **Explain why each of the preceding introductions interests or does not interest you. Does your response stem from the topic or the way the author introduces it?**

2. **Find magazine articles with effective introductory paragraphs illustrating at least three different techniques. Write a paragraph explaining why each impresses you.**

Transitional Paragraphs

In the midst of a lengthy essay, you may need a short paragraph that announces a shift from one group of ideas to another. Transitional paragraphs summarize previously explained ideas, repeat the thesis, or point to ideas that follow. In our example, Bruno Bettelheim has been discussing a young boy named Joey who has turned into a kind of human machine. After describing Joey's assorted delusions, Bettelheim signals his switch from the delusions to the fears that caused them.

> What deep-seated fears and needs underlay Joey's delusional system? We were long in finding out, for Joey's preventions effectively concealed the secret of his autistic behavior. In the meantime we dealt with his peripheral problems one by one.
>
> Bruno Bettelheim, "Joey: 'A Mechanical Boy'"

The following transitional paragraph looks back as well as ahead:

> ```
> Certainly these three factors--exercise, economy, convenience of
> shortcuts--help explain the popularity of bicycling today. But a
> fourth attraction sometimes overrides the others: the lure of the
> open road.
>
>                                                         Mike Bernstein
> ```

Conclusions

A conclusion rounds out a paper and signals that the discussion has been completed. Not all papers require a separate conclusion; narratives and descriptions, for example, generally end when the writer finishes the story or concludes the impression. But many essays benefit from a conclusion that drives the point home a final time. To be effective, a conclusion must mesh logically and stylistically with what comes earlier. A long, complex paper often ends with a summary of the main points, but any of several other options may be used for shorter papers with easy-to-grasp ideas. Most short essays have single-paragraph conclusions; longer papers may require two or three paragraphs.

Here are some cautions about writing your conclusion:

1. Don't introduce new material. Draw together, round out, but don't take off in a new direction.

2. Don't tack on an ending in desperation when the hour is late and the paper is due tomorrow—the so-called midnight special. Your reader deserves better than "All in all, skiing is a great sport" or "Thus we can see that motorcycle racing isn't for everyone."

3. Don't apologize. Saying that you could have done a better job makes a reader wonder why you didn't.

4. Don't moralize. A preachy conclusion can undermine the position you have established in the rest of your composition.

The following examples illustrate several common types of conclusions.

Restatement of the Thesis   The following conclusion reasserts Beyak's thesis that "the term *youth* has been co-opted by government and corporate interests as a means of evading responsibility for both their actions and their inactions—actions and inactions that are having an impact on a generation of young, and not-so-young, adults."

> By replacing the term *adult* with *youth,* governments, corporations, and the media can offer the majority of the electorate and the majority of society (baby boomers, if you will) an easy explanation for why those aged 18–35 are not receiving what they as adults need—namely employment, a living wage, and a minimal level of independence. At the same time, those with a vested interest in the status quo are creating a diversion from a multitude of other issues that will inevitably have to be addressed. All of this with one word.
>
> Andrew Beyak, "The Sweet Bird of Youth Is Showing Signs of Age"

A Summary   A summary draws together and reinforces the main points of a paper.

> Today, despite rampant consumerism, social problems of alienation, drug abuse, suicide, spousal violence, road rage and loneliness have become major concerns. But in our preoccupation with keeping the economy growing, we fail to ask fundamental questions like what is an economy for, how much is enough and what are the important things in our lives. I think it's time to ask those questions, to re-open the ideas about more leisure time and quality of life and get off this mindless and destructive path of hyper consumerism.
>
> David Suzuki, "How Much Stuff Is Enough?"

A Question   The paragraph below concludes an argument that running should not be elevated to a religion, that its other benefits are sufficient. A final question often prompts the reader to think further on the topic. If your essay is meant to be persuasive, be sure to phrase a concluding question so that the way a reasonable person would answer emphasizes your point of view.

> Aren't those gifts enough? Why ask running for benefits that are plainly beyond its capacity to bestow?
>
> James Fixx, "What Running Can't Do for You"

A Quotation   A quotation can capture the essence of your thought and end the essay with authority.

> "We had no idea of the emotional involvement and the commitment of these women," Richard says. "Suddenly a constituency arose. Suddenly there are thousands and thousands of women who don't care about your moral position or mine—they want a baby."
>
> David Zimmerman, "Are Test-Tube Babies the Answer for the Childless?"

Ironic Twist or Surprising Observation   These approaches prompt the reader to think further about a paper's topic. The following paragraph highlights the irony of the writer's regret after he has fulfilled a seemingly desirable dream. Although living now in a premium Vancouver locale, the author regrets that his son is missing out on the cultural and economic diversity of his own youth in Montreal.

> When I grew up I bought a house in the gentle forests of the Pacific and my son walks to school among the cherry blossoms. And sometimes I am sad for him.
>
> Moses Milstein, "Memories of Montreal—and Richness"

Clever or Lighthearted Ending   In our example, the writer, capitalizing on the essay's topic, ends by exaggerating the fault being criticized.

> Because using clichés is as easy as falling off a log, it goes without saying that it would be duck soup to continue in this vein till hell freezes over. However, since that would be carrying coals to Newcastle, let's ring down the curtain and bid adieu to the fair topic of the cliché. (No use beating a dead horse.)
>
> Student Unknown

Personal Challenge   A challenge often prompts the reader to take some action.

> And therein lies the challenge. You can't merely puff hard for a few days and then revert to the La-Z-Boy recliner, smugly thinking that you're "in shape." You must sweat and strain and puff regularly, week in and week out. They're your muscles, your lungs, your heart. The only caretaker they have is you.
>
> Monica Duvall

Hope or Recommendation   Both a hope and a recommendation may restate points already made in the essay or suggest actions to take in order to arrive at a solution.

A helpful response would be an amendment that would require these special antiterrorist measures to lapse automatically after one year unless re-enacted within that time. There would be nothing to lose and conceivably much to gain. The government already has its antiterrorist laws to do with them what it will. But, to whatever extent it wanted any of these measures to linger longer, it would feel effectively pressured to reintroduce them in more manageable segments so that, at long last, there could be a meaningful parliamentary and public debate. The current situation is simply unacceptable.

Alan Borovoy, "Security's Serpentine Coils"

I who am blind can give one hint to those who can see—one admonition to those who would make full use of the gift of sight: Use your eyes as if tomorrow you would be stricken blind. And the same method can be applied to the other senses. Hear the music of voices, the song of the bird, the mighty strains of an orchestra, as if you would be stricken deaf tomorrow. Touch each object you want to touch as if tomorrow your tactile sense would fail. Smell the perfume of flowers, taste with relish each morsel, as if tomorrow you could never smell and taste again. Make the most of every sense; glory in all the facets of pleasure and beauty which the world reveals to you through the several means of contact which Nature provides. But of all the senses, I am sure that sight must be the most delightful.

Helen Keller, "Three Days to See"

EXERCISE

1. Explain why each of the foregoing conclusions does or does not interest you. Does your response stem from the topic or from the author's handling of it?

2. Copy effective concluding paragraphs, illustrating at least three different techniques, from magazine articles. Then write a paragraph explaining why each impresses you.

Effective Sentences

A sentence is a group of words that begins with a capital letter; ends with a period, question mark, or exclamation point; and makes sense by itself. The elements that comprise sentences include subjects, predicates, direct objects, indirect objects, subject complements, object complements, phrases, and clauses.

Sentences take many forms, some straightforward and unadorned, others intricate and ornate, each with its own stylistic strengths. Becoming familiar with these forms and their uses gives you the option to

- emphasize or de-emphasize an idea
- combine ideas into one sentence or keep them separate in more than one sentence
- make sentences sound formal or informal
- emphasize the actor or the action
- achieve rhythm, variety, and contrast.

Effective sentences bring both exactness and flair to your writing.

■ Sentence Strategies

Effective sentences stem, at least in part, from selecting the right word order for independent clauses, coordinating and subordinating effectively, correctly positioning movable modifiers, using parallel structures, choosing the right verb voice, and avoiding fragments except for particular effects. Usually it's best to work on these different strategies as you revise rather than pausing to refine each sentence after you write it.

Word Order in Independent Clauses

Most independent clauses follow a similar arrangement. First comes the subject, then the verb, and finally any other element needed to convey the main message.

> Barney blushed. *(subject, verb)*

> They built the dog a kennel. *(subject, verb, indirect object, direct object)*

> Samantha is an architect. *(subject, verb, subject complement)*

This arrangement puts the emphasis on the subject, right where it's usually wanted.

But the pattern doesn't work in every situation. Occasionally, a writer wants to emphasize some element that follows the verb, create an artistic effect, or give the subject unusual emphasis. Enter inverted order and the expletive construction.

Inverted Order   To invert a sentence, move to the front the element you want to emphasize. Sometimes the rest of the sentence follows in regular subject-then-verb order; sometimes the verb precedes the subject.

> Lovable he isn't. *(subject complement, subject, verb)*

> This I just don't understand. *(direct object, subject, verb)*

> Tall grow the pines in the mountains. *(subject complement, verb, subject)*

Sentences that ask questions typically follow an inverted pattern.

> Is this your coat? *(verb, subject, subject complement)*

> Will you let the cat out? *(verb, subject, verb, direct object)*

Most of your sentences should follow normal order: readers expect it and read most easily through it. Furthermore, don't invert a sentence if the result would sound strained and unnatural. A sentence like "Fools were Brett and Amanda for quitting school" will only hinder communication.

Expletives   An expletive fills a vacancy in a sentence without contributing to the meaning. English has two common expletives, *there* and *it*. Ordinarily, *there* functions as an adverb, *it* as a pronoun, and either can appear anywhere in a sentence. As expletives, however, they alter normal sentence order by beginning sentences and anticipating the real subjects or objects.

Expletives are often used unnecessarily, as in the following example:

There were twenty persons attending the sales meeting.

This sentence errs on two counts: its subject needs no extra emphasis, and it is very clumsy. Notice the improvement without the expletive and the unneeded words:

Twenty persons attended the sales meeting.

When the subject or object needs highlighting, leading off with an expletive will, by altering normal order, call it more forcefully to the reader's attention.

Normal order:	A fly is in my soup.
	He seeks her happiness.
Expletive construction:	There is a fly in my soup. *(expletive anticipating subject)*
	It is her happiness he seeks. *(expletive anticipating object)*

Once in a while you'll find that something just can't be said unless you use an expletive.

There is no reason for such foolishness.

No other construction can express exactly the same thought.

> **EXERCISE**   *Indicate which of these sentences follow normal order, which are inverted, and which have expletive constructions. Rewrite so that all will be in normal order.*
>
> 1. Dick Lewis is a true friend.
> 2. May I go to the movie with you?
> 3. There are many dead fish on the beach.
> 4. The instructor gave the class a long reading assignment.
> 5. It is Leslie's aim to become a lawyer.

Coordination and Subordination

Coordination and subordination are ways to rank ideas in sentences. Coordination makes ideas equal; subordination makes them unequal. To understand coordination and subordination, you need to know about four kinds of sentences: simple, compound, complex, and compound–complex.

Simple Sentences A simple sentence has one subject and one predicate. Some simple sentences consist merely of a single noun and a single verb.

Millicent shouted.

Others can include elements such as compound subjects, compound verbs, direct objects, indirect objects, and subject complements.

Jim and Sue have bought a car. *(compound subject, direct object)*

Lucretia Borgia smiled and mixed her guests a cocktail. (*compound verb, indirect object, direct object*)

Autumn is a sad season. (*subject complement*)

Most simple sentences are rather short and easy to understand. This trimness can add punch to your writing, but it can also make your writing sound childish and may waste words.

The audience was young and friendly. It was responsive. It cheered for each speaker.

Combined into a single simple sentence, the information is easier to follow and more interesting to read:

The young, friendly, responsive audience cheered for each speaker.

Compound Sentences   A compound sentence contains two or more independent clauses, each holding the same (coordinate) rank. As a result, the idea in the first clause receives the same emphasis as the idea in the second. In some cases, a comma and a coordinating conjunction (*and, but, or, nor, for, yet, so*) link successive clauses.

Name the baby Huey, *or* I'll cut you out of my will.

The audience was young, friendly, and responsive, *so* it cheered for each speaker.

 In others, a semicolon and a conjunctive adverb (*for example, however, in fact, likewise, meanwhile, instead,* and the like) furnish the connection.

Tod wants to see the play; *in fact,* he's talked about it for weeks.

Today, many young women do not rush into marriage and motherhood; *instead,* they spend several years establishing careers.

Finally, a writer may omit any connecting word and separate the clauses with a semicolon.

The sky grew pitch black; the wind died; an ominous quiet hung over the whole city.

Be sure to read this Robertson Davies novel; it shows the ramifications of a single small event.

As the preceding sentences show, compound sentences allow writers to express simple relationships among simple ideas. However, such sentences have one important limitation: it is impossible to highlight one particular idea. To do this, we need to use complex sentences.

Complex Sentences   A complex sentence has one independent clause and one or more dependent clauses. Relegating an idea to a dependent clause shows that the writer wishes it to receive less emphasis than the idea in the main clause.

Because the young, friendly audience was responsive, it cheered for each speaker.

After the ball was over, Arthur collapsed on the sofa.

Once they had reached the lakeshore, the campers found a level spot *where they could pitch their tent.*

Unlike compound sentences, complex ones allow writers to vary the emphasis of ideas.

While I watered the grass, I discussed stock options with Liz.

I watered the grass *while I discussed stock options with Liz.*

The first sentence emphasizes the talk with Liz, the second watering the lawn. Often, shifting emphasis allows a writer to change the meaning of a sentence.

While his bicycle was damaged, Pat walked to work.

While Pat walked to work, his bicycle was damaged.

Furthermore, complex sentences signal *how* ideas relate. Note the various relationships in the following sentences:

Because she was swimming well, Millicent did 200 laps today. *(reason)*

The CN Tower is taller *than the Empire State Building. (extent)*

Ms. Yoshira is the executive *for whom I am working. (relationship between persons)*

Compound–Complex Sentences   This type of sentence features two or more independent clauses and one or more dependent clauses. Here are two examples with the dependent clauses italicized:

Ms. Harris works as an investment manager, and Mr. Williams, *who lives next door to her,* owns a jewellery store.

If you are to communicate properly, your thoughts must be clear and correct; thoughts are wasted *when language is muddled.*

Compound–complex sentences allow writers to present more intricate relationships than do other kinds of sentences. In the following example, three sentences—one compound and two simple—have been rewritten as a compound–complex sentence. Notice how subordination improves the compactness and smoothness of the final version.

Mary hated to be seen in ugly clothing, but she wore an ugly dress with red polka dots. She had received the dress as a Christmas present. Her Aunt Ida had given it to her.

Mary hated to be seen in ugly clothing; nevertheless, she wore an ugly red-polka-dot dress that her Aunt Ida had given her for Christmas.

The second version condenses thirty-five words to twenty-six.

EXERCISE

A. Label the independent and dependent clauses in the sentences below. Then identify each sentence as simple, compound, complex, or compound–complex.

1. A career in broadcasting requires good verbal skills, an extensive wardrobe, and a pleasant smile.

2. Because its bag was too full, the vacuum cleaner backfired, leaving the room dirtier than it had been before.

3. When Tom arrived home, his roommate asked him where he had really gone; six hours seemed too long a time to spend in the library.

4. My apple tree blossomed last week; however, the peach trees have withered, probably because of the freeze last month.

5. It's risky to confide in a co-worker because one can never be sure that the confidence will be kept.

B. Using coordination and subordination, rewrite the following passages to reduce words and/or improve smoothness.

1. He played the piano. He played the organ. He played the French horn. He did not play the viola.

2. Life on Venus may be possible. It will not be the kind of life we know on Earth. Life on Mars may be possible. It will not be the kind of life we know on Earth.

3. Albert lay in bed. He stared at the ceiling. Albert thought about the previous afternoon. He had asked Kathy to go to dinner with him. She is a pretty, blonde-haired woman. She sits at the desk next to his. They work at Hemphill's. She had refused.

4. I went to the store to buy a box of detergent. I saw Bill there, and we talked about last night's game.

5. Tim went to the newsstand. He bought a magazine there. While he was on the way home, he lost it. He had nothing to read.

Positioning of Movable Modifiers

Movable modifiers can appear on either side of the main statement or within it.

Modifiers After Main Statement   Sentences that follow this arrangement, frequently called loose sentences, occur more commonly than either of the others. They mirror conversation, in which a speaker first makes a statement and then adds on further thoughts. Often, the main statement has just one modifier.

> Our company will have to file for bankruptcy *because of this year's huge losses. (phrase as modifier)*

Or it can head up a whole train of modifiers.

> He burst suddenly into the party, *loud, angry, obscene. (words as modifiers)*

> The family used to gather around the hearth, *doing such chores as polishing shoes, mending ripped clothing, reading, chatting, always warmed by one another's presence as much as by the flames. (words and phrases as modifiers)*

Sally stared in disbelief, and then she smiled, *slowly, tremulously, as if she couldn't believe her good fortune.* (words and clause as modifiers)

There are three essential qualities for buzzard country: *a rich supply of unburied corpses, high mountains, a strong sun.* (noun-base groups as modifiers)

John D. Stewart, "Vulture Country"

A sentence may contain several layers of modifiers. In the following example, we've indented and numbered to show the different layers.

1. The men struggled to the top of the hill,
   2. thirsty,
   2. drenched in sweat,
   2. and cursing in pain
      3. as their knapsack straps cut into their raw, chafed shoulders
         4. with every step.

In this sentence, the terms numbered 2 refer to *men* in the item numbered 1. Item 3 is linked to *cursing* in the preceding item 2, and item 4 is linked to *cut* in item 3.

The modifiers-last arrangement works well for injecting descriptive details into narratives and also for qualifying, explaining, and presenting lists in other kinds of writing.

Modifiers Before Main Statement   Sentences that delay the main point until the end are called periodic. In contrast to loose sentences, they lend a formal note to what is said, slowing its pace, adding cadence, and making it more serious.

If you can keep your head when everyone around you is panicking, you probably don't understand the situation. (clauses as modifiers)

From the onset of his journey to the heart of darkness, Marlow witnesses many incidents that reveal the human capacity for evil. (phrases as modifiers)

The danger of sideswiping another vehicle, the knowledge that a hidden bump or hole could throw me from the dune buggy, both of these things added to the thrill of the race. (noun plus phrase and noun plus clause as modifiers)

When so large a percentage of our students admits to cheating, when so many professors practice grade inflation, when administrators fail to face up to these problems, our schools are in serious trouble. (clauses as modifiers)

1. *When the public protests,*
2. *confronted with some obvious evidence of the damaging results of pesticide applications,* it is fed little tranquilizing pills of half truth. (clause and phrase as modifiers)

Rachel Carson, *Silent Spring*

As shown in the Carson example, periodic sentences can also have layers of modifiers.

Positioning the modifiers before the main point throws the emphasis upon the end of the sentence, adding force to the main point. The delay also lets the writer create sentences that, like the first example, carry stings, ironic or humorous, in their tails.

Modifiers Within Main Statement   Inserting one or more modifiers into a main statement creates a sentence with *interrupted order.* The material may come between the subject and the verb or between the verb and the rest of the predicate.

The young girl, *wearing a tattered dress and looking anything but well-off herself,* gave the beggar a ten-dollar bill. *(phrases between subject and verb)*

Dewey declared, *in a loud, happy voice,* that the concert was the best he'd ever heard. *(phrase between verb and rest of predicate)*

The bedsprings, *bent and rusted, festooned with spider webs,* lay on top of the heap. *(words and phrase between subject and verb)*

The evolutionists, *piercing beneath the show of momentary stability,* discovered, *hidden in rudimentary organs,* the discarded rubbish of the past. *(one phrase between subject and verb, another between verb and rest of predicate)*

By stretching out the main idea, inserted modifiers slow the forward pace of the sentence, giving it some of the formality and force of a periodic sentence.

EXERCISE   *Identify each sentence as loose, periodic, or interrupted. Rewrite each as one of the other kinds.*

1. Victoria, rejected by family and friends, uncertain where to turn next, finally decided to start a new life in Halifax.

2. When told that she had to have her spleen removed, the woman gasped.

3. Tom missed the bus because his wife had forgotten to reset the alarm after she got up and he had cut himself several times while shaving.

4. Good health, warm friends, a beautiful summer evening—the best things cannot be purchased.

5. A customer, angry and perspiring, stormed up to the claims desk.

6. Stopping just short of the tunnel entrance, the freight train avoided a collision with the crowded commuter train stalled inside.

7. The new kid hammered away at the fading champ, determination in his eyes and glory in his fists.

8. The new tract house sparkled in the sunlight, pink and trim, its lawn immaculate, its two bushes and newly planted crab apple tree, by their very tininess, making the yard look vaster than its actual size.

9. Bright red and skin stinging after a day at the beach, Steve will remember the sunscreen next time.

10. Saloons, gaudily painted and beckoning with promises of extraordinary pleasures, lined the town's main street.

11. In being whisked from Lyons, France, to Tel Aviv to Sri Lanka for location shots, the Hollywood star gave new force to the phrase *international celebrity.*

12. The first graders stood in line, talking and giggling, pushing at one another's caps and pencil boxes and kicking one another's shins, unmindful of the drudgery that awaited them within the old schoolhouse.

Using Parallelism

Parallelism presents equivalent ideas in grammatically equivalent form. Dressing them in the same grammatical garb calls attention to their kinship and adds smoothness and polish. The following sentence pairs demonstrate the improvement that parallelism brings:

Nonparallel:	James's outfit was *wrinkled, mismatched,* and *he needed to wash it. (words and independent clause)*
Parallel:	James's outfit was *wrinkled, mismatched,* and *dirty. (words)*
Nonparallel:	Oscar likes *reading books, attending plays,* and *to search for antiques. (different kinds of phrases)*
Parallel:	Oscar likes *reading books, attending plays,* and *searching for antiques. (same kind of phrases)*
Nonparallel:	Beth performs her tasks *quickly, willingly,* and *with accuracy. (words and phrase)*
Parallel:	Beth performs her tasks *quickly, willingly,* and *accurately. (words)*
Nonparallel:	The instructor complimented me *for taking part in class discussions* and *because I had written a superb theme. (phrase and clause)*
Parallel:	The instructor complimented me *for taking part in class discussions* and *for writing a superb theme. (phrases)*

As the examples show, revising nonparallel sentences smooths out bumpiness, binds the ideas together more closely, and lends them a more finished look.

Parallelism doesn't always stop with a single sentence. Writers sometimes use it in a series of sentences:

He had never lost his childlike innocence. He had never lost his sense of wonder. He had never lost his sense of joy in nature's simplest gifts.

For an example of parallelism that extends over much of a paragraph, see page 199.

Repeating a structure through several sentences of a paragraph beats a tattoo that drums the points home more forcefully and adds rhythm to the prose.

But don't overuse the technique, or it will lose its impact and seem irritating and artificial.

Balance, a special form of parallelism, positions two grammatically equivalent ideas on opposite sides of some pivot point, such as a word or punctuation mark.

Hope for the best, and prepare for the worst.

Many are called, but few are chosen.

When I'm right, nobody ever notices; when I'm wrong, nobody ever forgets.

The sheep are in the meadow, and the cows are in the corn.

Like regular parallel sentences, balanced sentences sometimes come in series. Balanced sentences can be especially resonant in speeches.

> We want to live in a country in which French Canadians can choose to live among English Canadians and English Canadians can choose to live among French Canadians without abandoning their cultural heritage.
>
> Pierre Elliot Trudeau, "Statement on Introduction of the Official Languages Bill"

Balance works especially well for pitting contrasting ideas against each other. It sharpens the difference between them while achieving compactness and lending an air of insight to what is said.

EXERCISE   *Identify each sentence as nonparallel, parallel, or balanced; then rewrite each nonparallel sentence to make it parallel.*

1. Professor Bartlett enjoys helping students, counselling advisees, and participation in faculty meetings.

2. I can still see Aunt Alva striding into the corral, cornering a cow against a fencepost, try to balance herself on a one-legged milking stool, and butt her head into the cow's belly.

3. The city plans on building a new fishing pier and on dredging the channel of the river.

4. Michèle plans on vacationing in Quebec City, but Robert wants to golf in Charlottetown.

5. Being half drunk and because he was already late for work, Tom called his boss and said he was too ill to come in that day.

6. The novel's chief character peers through a tangle of long hair, slouches along in a shambling gait, and gets into trouble constantly.

7. You can take the boy out of the country, but you can't take the country out of the boy.

8. Joe's problem is not that he earns too little money but spending it foolishly.

9. The room was dark, gloomy, and everything was dusty.

10. The apparition glided through the wall, across the room, and up the fireplace chimney.

Choosing the Right Verb Voice

A sentence's verb voice derives from the relationship between the subject and the action. A sentence in the *active voice* has a subject that does something plus a verb that shows action.

> The boy hit the target.

> The girl painted the garage.

This pattern keeps the key information in the key part of the sentence, making it strong and vigorous and giving the reader a close-up look at the action.

The *passive voice* reverses the subject–action relationship by having the subject receive, rather than perform, the action. It is built around a form of the verb *to be,* for example, *is, are, was, were.* Some sentences identify the actor by using a prepositional phrase; others don't mention the actor at all.

> The target was hit by the boy. *(actor identified)*

> The federal debt is to be targeted for reduction *(actor unidentified)*

Demoting or banishing the actor dilutes the force of the sentence, puts greater distance between the action and the reader, and almost always adds extra words to the message.

Most writers who overuse the passive voice simply don't realize its effects on their writing. Read the following paragraph, written mainly in the passive voice:

> Graft becomes possible when gifts are given to police officers or favours are done for them by persons who expect preferential treatment in return. Gifts of many kinds may be received by officers. Often free meals are given to them by the owners of restaurants on their beats. During the Christmas season, they may be given liquor, food, or theatre tickets by merchants. If favoured treatment is not received by the donors, no great harm is done. But if traffic offences, safety code violations, and other infractions are overlooked by the officers, corruption results. When such corruption is exposed by the newspapers, faith is lost in law enforcement agencies.

This impersonal, wordy passage plods across the page and therefore lacks any real, persuasive impact. Now note the livelier, more forceful tone of this rewritten version.

> Graft becomes possible when police officers accept gifts or favours from persons who expect preferential treatment in return. Officers may receive gifts of many kinds. Restaurant owners often provide free meals for officers on the beat. During the Christmas season, merchants may give them liquor, food, or theatre tickets. If donors do not receive favoured treatment, no great harm is done. But if officers overlook traffic offences, safety code violations, and other infractions, corruption results. When the newspapers expose such corruption, citizens lose faith in law enforcement agencies.

Don't misunderstand: the passive voice does have its uses. It can mask identities—or at least try to. A child may try to dodge responsibility by saying, "Mother, while you were out, the living room lamp got broken." Less manipulatively, reporters may use it to conceal the identity of a source.

Technical and scientific writing customarily uses the passive voice to explain processes.

In the production of steel, iron ore is first converted into pig iron by combining it with limestone and coke and then heating the mixture in a blast furnace. Pig iron, however, contains too many impurities to be useful to industry, and as a result must be refined and converted to steel. In the refining process, manganese, silicon, and aluminum are heated with the pig iron in order to degas it, that is, to remove excess oxygen and impurities from it. The manganese, silicon, and aluminum are vaporized while the iron remains in the liquid state and the impurities are carried away by the vapours. Once this step has been completed, the molten steel is poured into ingots and allowed to cool. The steel is now ready for further processing.

Putting such writing in the passive voice provides a desirable objective tone and puts the emphasis where it's most important: on the action, not the actor. On occasion, everyday writing also uses the passive voice.

The garbage is collected once a week, on Monday.

These caves were formed about 10 million years ago.

In the first case, there's no need to tell who collects the garbage; obviously, garbage collectors do. In the second, the writer may not know what caused the formation, and saying "Something formed these caves about 10 million years ago" would sound ridiculous. In both situations, the action, not the actor, is paramount.

Unless special circumstances call for the passive voice, however, use the active voice.

EXERCISE   *After determining whether each sentence below is in active or passive voice, rewrite the passive sentences as active ones.*

1. Mary's parents gave her a sports car for her sixteenth birthday.
2. Fires were left burning by negligent campers.
3. The new ice arena will be opened by the city in about two weeks.
4. Harry left the open toolbox out in the rain.
5. Turkeys were introduced to Europe from North America.
6. Cyril took a trip to Whitehorse, Yukon.
7. We have just installed a new computer in our main office.
8. The club president awarded Tompkins the Order of the Golden Mace.
9. The sound of war drums was heard by the missionaries as they floated down the river.
10. Objections were raised by some members of the legislature to the ratification of the proposed amendment.

Using Fragments

A fragment is a part of a sentence that is capitalized and punctuated as if it were a complete sentence.

Although fragments are seldom used in formal prose, they form the backbone of most conversations. Here's how a typical bit of dialogue might go:

"Where are you going tonight?" *(sentence)*
"To Woodland Mall." *(fragment)*
"What for?" *(fragment)*
"To buy some shoes." *(fragment)*
"Alone?" *(fragment)*
"No, with Maisie Perkins." *(fragment)*
"Can I come too?" *(sentence)*
"Sure." *(fragment)*

As with most conversations, the sprinkling of complete sentences makes the fragments clear.

Writers of nonfiction use fragments to create special effects. In the following passage, the fragment emphasizes the importance of the question it asks and varies the pace of the writing:

> Before kidney transplants, people had an ethical unease about renal dialysis—the artificial kidney machine. Unquestionably it was a great technical advance making it possible to treat kidney dysfunctions from which thousands die. But the machine was, and is, expensive and involves intensive care of the patient by doctors and nurses. For whom the machine? In the United States the dilemma was evaded but not solved by having lay panels, like juries, making life-or-death choices. In Britain, where the National Health Service entitles everyone, rich or poor, to have access to any necessary treatment, the responsibility rests on the medical staff. It was (and still is) a difficult decision.
>
> Lord Ritchie-Calder, "The Doctor's Dilemma"

Once in a while, as in the following examples, a writer will use a whole series of fragments. In the Ciardi selection, the fragments heighten the ironic effect. In the following one, they create a kaleidoscopic effect that mirrors the kaleidoscopic impressions offered by the Jazz Age itself.

> Or look at any of the women's magazines. There, as Bernard DeVoto once pointed out, advertising begins as poetry in the front pages and ends as pharmacopoeia and therapy in the back pages. The poetry of the front matter is the dream of perfect beauty that must be hers. These, the flawless teeth. This, the baby skin that must be hers. This, the perfumed breath she must exhale. This, the sixteen-year-old figure she must display at forty, at fifty, at sixty, and forever.
>
> John Ciardi, "What Is Happiness?"

> The Jazz Age offers a kaleidoscope of shifting impressions. Of novelties quickly embraced and quickly discarded. Of flappers flaunting bobbed hair and short skirts. Of hip flasks and bootleg whisky, fast cars and coonskin coats, jazz and dancing till dawn. And overall a sense of futility, an uneasy conviction that all the gods were dead.
>
> Elliott L. Smith and Andrew W. Hart,
> *The Short Story: A Contemporary Looking Glass*

Before using any fragment in your own writing, think carefully about your intended effect and explore other ways of achieving it. Unless only a fragment will serve your needs, don't use one; fragments are likely to be viewed as unintentional—and thus errors—in the work of inexperienced writers.

EXERCISE   *The following passage includes one or more fragments. Identify each and explain its function.*

He [Richard Wagner] wrote operas; and no sooner did he have the synopsis of a story, but he would invite—or rather summon—a crowd of his friends to his house and read it aloud to them. Not for criticism. For applause. When the complete poem was written, the friends had to come again, and hear *that* read aloud. Then he would publish the poem, sometimes years before the music that went with it was written. He played the piano like a composer, in the worst sense of what that implies, and he would sit down at the piano before parties that included some of the finest pianists of his time, and play for them, by the hour, his own music, needless to say. He had a composer's voice. And he would invite eminent vocalists to his house, and sing them his operas, taking all the parts.

Deems Taylor, "The Monster"

■ Beyond the Single Sentence

What makes a team successful? Skilled players, to be sure, but teamwork as well. Most sentences are part of a team; and unless they work in harmony, the composition will suffer, however good each of them may be.

Harmony—the rhythmic interplay of sentences—demands, first of all, sentences of different lengths. If all your sentences drag on and on, your reader may bog down and lose the train of thought. If all are clipped, the ideas may seem simplistic, and the sentences will jerk along like a car with a misfiring engine. And if all of them are middling long, their plodding, monotonous pace may bring boredom and inattention.

Content sets the pattern of sentence lengths, and often your ideas will lead naturally to the proper mix of long and short sentences. But don't count on it. Chances are you will need to make adjustments. Once you have finished a draft of your paper, read it over, see how its rhythms strike your inner ear, and put check marks by stretches that "sound" wrong. For instance, you might need to condense a set of jolting primer-book sentences into one or two sentences that present their ideas in a series:

Original Version

Members of the Unification Church actively recruit converts. They do it in shopping malls. University and college campuses are also recruiting sites. They talk about the benefits of world unity and sell books as well as records. Donations are also solicited. Listeners receive invitations to a dinner. There the guests learn more about the sect.

Revised Version

Members of the Unification Church recruit converts in such places as shopping malls and university and college campuses. They talk about the benefits of world unity, sell books and tapes, ask for donations, and invite listeners to a dinner to learn more about the sect.

If a key point is submerged in a long sentence, highlight it as a separate thought, thereby giving it the recognition it deserves. Here is an example:

Original Version

Employers find mature women to be valuable members of their organizations. They are conscientious, have excellent attendance records, and stay calm when things go awry, *but unfortunately many employers exploit them.* Despite their desirable qualities, most remain mired in clerical, sales, and elementary teaching positions. On the average they earn two-thirds as much as men.

Revised Version

Employers find mature women to be valuable members of their organizations. They are conscientious, have excellent attendance records, and stay calm when things go awry. *Unfortunately, though, many employers exploit them.* Despite their desirable qualities, most remain mired in clerical, sales, and elementary teaching positions. On the average they earn two-thirds as much as men.

In the following paragraph, the sentences differ considerably in length.

To protest that some fairly improbable people, some people who could not possibly respect themselves, seem to sleep easily enough is to miss the point entirely, as surely as those people miss it who think that self-respect has necessarily to do with not having safety pins in one's underwear. There is a common superstition that "self-respect" is a kind of charm against snakes, something that keeps those who have it locked in some unblighted Eden, out of strange beds, ambivalent conversations, and trouble in general. It does not at all. It has nothing to do with the face of things, but concerns instead a separate peace, a private reconciliation.

Joan Didion, "On Self-Respect"

Much of the appealing rhythm of this passage stems from varied sentence length. The first two rather long sentences (forty-nine and thirty-six words) are followed by the very brief "It does not at all," which gains emphasis by its position. The last sentence adds variety by means of its moderate length (nineteen words), quite apart from its interesting observation on the real nature of self-respect.

Look to the structures of your sentences as well as their length. Do they resemble a street full of row houses built from the same blueprint? If they are all simple, with few modifiers, your readers may underrate the importance of your message. To correct row-house sentences, draw upon the patterns you learned about earlier in this chapter. Try inverting sentence order or positioning modifiers at different points. Combine sentences. Turn a statement into a question. Build from several blueprints. Try anything as long as the structures go together and you don't warp meanings.

The following example illustrates how sentence combining adds smoothness and interest to a piece of writing.

Original Version

Before deaf children can speak, they must learn the speech sounds of the English language. This is a process that requires them to practise breath control, to mouth vowels, and to study the speech positions of the mouth and tongue for many hours. A speech specialist helped my brother do these things. The specialist started with him before he was two years old. She built up his vocabulary by teaching him a series of related words. Each of these words identified something in his environment. My brother proved to be an apt student. He soon learned to talk.

Revised Version

Before deaf children can speak, they must learn the speech sounds of the English language, a process that requires them to practise breath control, mouth vowels, and study the speech positions of the mouth and tongue for many hours. A speech specialist helped my brother do these things. Starting before he was two years old, she built up his vocabulary by teaching him a series of related words, each identified with something in his environment. My brother proved to be an apt student and soon learned to talk.

EXERCISE   *Revise the following passage to improve its style.*

From 1868 to 1870 Louis Riel was the leader of the Métis. The Métis were the French-speaking majority of the North-West Territories. Riel was a skillful politician. He forced the Canadian government to protect his people's rights. He united his people against exploitative American and Canadian fur trading interests. As a result of his efforts, Canada was compelled to create the province of Manitoba in 1870. Riel fled Manitoba in 1870 to avoid prosecution for hanging a racial bigot, Thomas Scott. He fled to America and became a citizen. In 1885 he came to Northern Saskatchewan to lead another rebellion. He was caught and hanged in the fall of 1885. Many people view him as a symbolic French-Canadian victim of English Canada.

chapter 16

Diction, Tone, Style

Your decisions about words and sentences set the tone and style of your writing. Not only do you choose sentence strategies for correctness and effectiveness, but you also choose words for accuracy and effect. Sentences must be clear and effective; so must words. Diction deals broadly with words, not in isolation but as parts of sentences, paragraphs, and essays. Every time you write and revise, diction comes into play.

■ Toward Clear Diction

Clear diction stems from choosing words with the right meanings, using abstract and concrete words appropriately, and picking terms that are neither too specific nor too general. Dictionaries and thesauruses can help guide your choices.

Word Meanings

Make sure the words you use mean what you think they do, so that inaccurate words will not distort your message. Sound-alike word pairs often trip up unwary writers. Take *accept* and *except* for example. *Accept* means "to approve." *Except,* when used as a verb, means "to exclude or omit." If you want to indicate approval but you say, "The following new courses were *excepted* by the committee," think of the obvious consequences. Likewise, consider the distinction between *continual* (frequently or regularly repeated) and *continuous* (uninterrupted). If you illustrate your popularity by saying "My phone rings *continuously*," your reader will wonder why you never answer it and how you ever sleep.

Concrete and Abstract Words

A concrete word names or describes something that we can perceive with one or more of our five senses. A thing is concrete if we can weigh it, measure it, hold it in our hands, photograph it, taste it, sniff it, add salt to it, drop it, smash into it, or borrow it from a neighbour. If it's abstract, we can't do any of these things. *The Tragically Hip* is a concrete term, as are *Swiss cheese, petroleum, maple syrup,* and *Vancouver.* On the other hand, *jealousy, power, conservatism, size,* and *sadness* are abstract terms.

Concrete words evoke precise, vivid mental images and thus help convey a message. The images that abstract terms create differ from person to person. Try this test: ask several of your friends to describe what comes to mind when they think of *joy, hatred, fear,* or some other abstract term. To illustrate, the word *hatred* might call up images of a person with cold, slitted eyes, a grimly set jaw, and tightly clenched fists. As you can see, concrete terms help us specify what we mean and thus enhance communication.

In the following passage, the concrete diction is italicized:

> To do without self-respect . . . is to be an unwilling *audience of one* to an interminable *documentary* that details one's failings, both real and imagined, with *fresh footage spliced in* for every *screening.* There's *the glass you broke* in anger, there's *the hurt on X's face; watch now, this next scene, the night Y came back from Houston,* see how you muff this one. To live without self-respect is to *lie awake some night,* beyond the reach of *warm milk, phenobarbital,* and *the sleeping hand on the coverlet,* counting up the sins of commission and omission, the trusts betrayed, the promises subtly broken, the gifts irrevocably wasted through sloth or cowardice or carelessness. However long we postpone it, we eventually lie down alone in that notoriously *uncomfortable bed,* the one we make ourselves. Whether or not we sleep in it depends, of course, on whether or not we respect ourselves.
>
> Joan Didion, "On Self-Respect"

Now note how vague and colourless the passage becomes without the concrete diction:

> To do without self-respect is to be continuously aware of your failings, both real and imagined. Incidents stay in your mind long after they are over. To live without self-respect means being bothered by intentional or unintentional failings, trusts betrayed, promises subtly broken, and gifts irrevocably wasted through sloth or cowardice or carelessness. However long we postpone it, we eventually must come to terms with who we are. How we respond to this situation depends, of course, on whether or not we respect ourselves.

EXERCISE   *Underline the concrete terms in the following passage:*

> The fog which rises from the river has no color, no texture, no taste, smell, or sound. It is sheer vision, a vision of purity, a slow, mesmeric, inexorable erasure of the slate. You see fog mushrooming along the river's course. Gently, it obliterates the alders tangled on the banks, wipes out the road. Buildings without foundations, trees without trunks, hang in the air like mirages. Sun may be shining brightly on them, or rain drenching them, or stars twinkling above or among them. Slowly the fog reaches higher and spreads. Ridgepoles, small topmost branches, and your own dooryard vanish. There is nothing left now but shining mist. It is all, and you float on it, utterly alone, as one imagines he might in empty space if flung off by earth; as the mind does, drifting into sleep; as the spirit does, having escaped its mortal frame.

Gladys Hasty Carroll, *Sing Out the Glory*

Specific and General Terms

One concrete term can be more specific or more general than another. As we move from *Lassie* to *collie* to *dog* to *mammal* and finally to *animal*, we become less and less specific, ending with a term that encompasses every animal on earth. With each step we retain only those features that fit the more general term. Thus, when we move from *collie* to *dog*, we leave out everything that makes collies different from terriers, greyhounds, and other breeds.

The more specific the term, the less difference among the images it calls to mind. If you say *animal* to a group of friends, one may think of a dog, another of a horse, and a third of a gorilla. *Collie,* on the other hand, triggers images of a large, long-haired, brown and white dog with a pointed muzzle.

Ask yourself how specific you need to be and then act accordingly. Often, the more specific term will be the better choice. If, for instance, you're describing a wealthy jet-setter, noting that he drives a Ferrari, not just a car, helps establish his character. But if you're writing a narrative about your flight to Quebec City and your experience at the winter carnival, nothing is gained by naming the make of car you rented and used uneventfully during your stay.

EXERCISE

1. **Arrange each set of words from less specific to more specific.**

   a. man, ex-Prime Minister, human being, John A. Macdonald, Canadian

   b. Forest Hills Apartments, building, structure, condominium, dwelling

2. **Expand each of the following words into a series of four or more that become progressively more specific. Use 1a or 1b as a pattern.**

a. activity	**c.** political party	**e.** device
b. event	**d.** institution	**f.** reading matter

Dictionaries and Thesauruses

Get the dictionary habit and learn to use a thesaurus. They'll increase your vocabulary as well as your skill at using words you already know.

Dictionaries Dictionaries are storehouses of word meanings. In general, dictionary makers do not try to dictate how words should be used. Instead, they note current and past meanings. When a word gains or loses a meaning or a newly minted word enjoys wide circulation, dictionary makers observe and record. Most users, however, regard dictionaries as authorities on correctness.

Idioms Idioms express meanings that differ from those of the words that make them up. Here are two examples.

I won't *put up with* any foolishness.
The dowager *gave me the cold shoulder.*

Put up with means "tolerate"; *gave me the cold shoulder* means "snubbed me." Looking up the most prominent word of an unfamiliar idiom may lead you to a listing and a definition.

Irregular Forms Any irregular forms are indicated. In *The Canadian Oxford Dictionary,* the entry for the verb *spring* notes that the other forms are *sprang* and *sprung.* This information helps you use correct forms in your writing.

Usage Labels Usage labels help you determine whether a word suits the circumstances of your writing. Here are the most common labels:

Label	Meaning
Colloquial	Characteristic of informal writing and speaking; should not be considered nonstandard.
Slang	Informal, newly coined words and expressions or old expressions with new meanings.
Obsolete	No longer in use but found in past writing.
Archaic	Still finds restricted use; for example, in legal documents; otherwise not appropriate.
Poetic	Used only in poetry and in prose with a poetic tone.
Dialect	Used regularly only in a particular geographical location such as the southeastern United States or the Scottish Lowlands.

Supplementary Information While focusing primarily on individual words, dictionaries often provide several other kinds of information. These may include a history of the language, lists of standard abbreviations and of universities and colleges, biographical notes on distinguished individuals, and geographical notes on important locations.

While any dictionary is better than none, some clearly outrank others in usefulness. A pocket dictionary is handy but not as comprehensive as a desk dictionary. Excellent desk-sized dictionaries include the following:

The Canadian Oxford Dictionary
The American Heritage Dictionary
Funk and Wagnall's Standard College Dictionary
The Random House Dictionary of the English Language
Webster's Tenth New Collegiate Dictionary
Webster's New World Dictionary of the American Language

Unabridged (complete) dictionaries such as *Webster's Third New International Dictionary* and the *Oxford English Dictionary* can be found in most libraries. There you'll also find a variety of specialized dictionaries. Your librarian can direct you to dictionaries that list terms in particular fields.

EXERCISE   *Use a good desk dictionary to look up the specified information for each of the following lists of words:*

1. Variant spellings:

airplane	aesthete	grey	tornadoes
colour	gaily	theatre	usable

2. Syllabication and the syllable that receives the main stress:

anacrusis	cadenza	harbinger	misanthrope
baccalaureate	exclamation	ionize	sequester

3. Parts of speech:

before	fair	separate	to
deep	here	then	where

4. Etymology:

carnival	Icarian	phenomenon	supercilious
fiduciary	lethargy	sabotage	tawdry

5. Idiomatic phrases:

beat	get	jump	put
eat	high	make	set

6. Synonyms:

attack	ghastly	mercy	plot
distress	keep	object	range

Thesauruses   Thesauruses list synonyms for words but omit the other elements in dictionary entries. Figure 16.1, on the following page, shows a typical entry. Note that the items are grouped according to parts of speech, and some are cross-indexed.

A thesaurus will help you find a word with just the right shade of meaning or a synonym when you want to avoid repetition. But synonyms are never exactly equal, nor are they always interchangeable. To illustrate, *old* means "in existence or use for a long time"; *antiquated* conveys the notion that something is old-fashioned or outdated. Therefore, use the thesaurus along with the dictionary. Only then can you tell which synonym fits a specific sentence.

247. FORMLESSNESS

1. nouns **formlessness, shapelessness;** amorphousness, amorphism, amorphia; **chaos,** confusion, messiness, orderlessness; disorder 62; entropy; anarchy 740.2; **indeterminateness, indefiniteness,** indecisiveness, vagueness, mistiness, haziness, fuzziness, blurriness, unclearness, obscurity.
2. unlicked cub, diamond in the rough.
3. verbs **deform, distort** 249.5; unform, unshape; disorder, jumble, mess up, muddle, confuse; obfuscate, obscure, fog up, blur.
4. adjs **formless, shapeless,** featureless, characterless, nondescript, inchoate, lumpen, blobby *or* baggy [both informal], inform: amorphous, amorphic, amorph(o)-: **chaotic, orderless,** disorderly 62.13, unordered, unorganized, confused, anarchic 740.6; kaleidoscopic; **indeterminate, indefinite,** undefined, indecisive, vague, misty, hazy, fuzzy, blurred *or* blurry, unclear, obscure.
5. **unformed, unshaped,** unshapen, unfashioned, unlicked; uncut, unhewn.

Figure 16.1   A Typical Thesaurus Entry

From *Roget's International Thesaurus,* 5th edition, Peter Mark Roget. Copyright © 1992 by HarperCollins Publishers, Inc. Reprinted by permission of HarperCollins Publishers, Inc.

Excellent guides to synonyms include the following:

Roget's International Thesaurus
Webster's New Dictionary of Synonyms
Modern Guide to Synonyms and Related Words

■ Toward Rhetorical Effect

Rhetorical effect refers to the response that the manner of writing, not the message, generates in the reader. Successful writers create a desired response through the level of their diction and the tone of their writing.

Level of Diction

What level of diction is best? The answer depends upon the writer's audience and purpose. Think about a safety engineer who investigates a serious industrial accident on which she must write two reports, one for the safety director of the company, who represents a technical audience, and another for the local newspaper, read by a general audience. Although the two accounts would deal with the same matter, clearly they would use very different language: specialized and formal in the first case, everyday and more relaxed in the second. In each case, the language would reflect the background of the audience. As you write, always choose language suited to your audience and purpose.

Edited standard English follows the familiar grammatical rules maintained in most formal and academic writing. Generally, everything you write for university or college courses or on the job should be in edited standard English. *Nonstandard English* refers to any version of the language that deviates from these rules. Here is an example from Dionne Brand's short story, "Blossom: Priestess of Oya, Goddess of winds, storms and waterfalls":

> This was Blossom's most successful endeavour since coming to Canada. Every once in a while, under she breath, she curse the day she come to Toronto from Oropuche, Trinidad. But nothing, not even snarky white people could keep Blossom under. When she first come it was to babysit some snot-nosed children on Oriole Parkway. She did meet a man, in a club on Henry Street in Port-of-Spain, who promise she to take care of she, if she ever was in Toronto. When Blossom reach, the man disappear and through the one other person she know in Toronto she get the work on Oriole.

Nonstandard English does have a place in writing. Fiction writers use it to narrate the talk of characters who, if real, would speak that way. Journalists use it to report eyewitness reactions to accidents and crimes, and people who compile oral histories use it to record the recollections of people they interview.

Edited standard English includes four levels of usage: formal, informal, formal–informal, and technical. Another commonly recognized category is colloquial language and slang.

Formal Level The formal level, dignified and serious, is suitable for important political, business, and academic occasions. Its vocabulary is marked by many abstract and multisyllabic words but no slang or contractions. Long sentences and deliberately varied sentence patterns help give it a strong, rhythmic flow. Sentences are often periodic, and many have parallel or balanced structures. (See pages 214–15.) Overall, formal prose impresses the reader as authoritative, stately, and graceful.

The following excerpt from the introduction to the third edition of Susanna Moodie's *Roughing It in the Bush* illustrates the formal level:

> In most instances, emigration is a matter of necessity, not of choice; and this is more especially true of the emigration of persons of respectable connections, or of any station or position in the world. Few educated persons, accustomed to the refinements and luxuries of European society, ever willingly relinquish those advantages, and place themselves beyond the protective influence of the wise and revered institutions of their native land, without the pressure of some urgent cause. Emigration may, indeed, generally be regarded as an act of severe duty, performed at the expense of personal enjoyment, and accompanied by the sacrifice of those local attachments which stamp the scenes amid which our childhood grew, in imperishable characters upon the heart. Nor is it until adversity has pressed sorely upon

the proud and wounded spirit of the well-educated sons and daughters of old but impoverished families, that they gird up the loins of the mind, and arm themselves with fortitude to meet and dare the heart-breaking conflict.

In this address to the readers of the third edition of her journals recounting expatriate life in Canada during the nineteenth century, Susanna Moodie formally expresses her sense that "emigration is a matter of necessity, not of choice." This initial parallelism is characteristic of the contrast throughout the passage as Moodie notes the dire circumstances of life in the colony removed from "the protective influence of the wise and revered institutions" of Europe. All of the sentences utilize complex causal relationships and modification. The sense that the European emigrant performs a noble task in an ignoble place is reinforced by elevated diction—polysyllabic words like *educated, protective, revered, sacrifice, imperishable, impoverished,* and *fortitude,* along with shorter abstract words like *duty, proud, spirit,* and *mind.* The carefully controlled language and syntax lend an earnest, altruistic tone to this passage directed toward a largely European audience.

Informal Level   Informal writing resembles orderly, intelligent conversation. Earmarked by relatively ordinary words, loose sentences, and numerous shorter, less varied sentence structures than formal prose, informal writing may include contractions or even slang, and it is more likely than formal writing to use the pronouns I, me, my, you, and yours. Casual and familiar rather than dignified and rhythmic, informal writing does not usually call attention to itself. Nevertheless, the language is precise and effective. Here is an example:

> There was a distressing story in the paper a few months ago. I wish I'd clipped it out and saved it. As it is, I can only hope I remember it fairly accurately. There was a group of people who wanted a particular dictionary removed from the shelves of the local library because it contained a lot of obscenity. I think they said there were sixty-five or so dirty words in it. Some poor woman who was acting as a spokesman for the group had a list of offending words, which she started to read aloud at a hearing. She managed to read about twenty of them before she started sobbing uncontrollably and couldn't continue.
>
> Thomas H. Middleton, "The Magic Power of Words"

Unlike the Moodie excerpt, this one has relatively uncomplicated sentences. Three of them—the fourth, sixth, and seventh—are loose rather than periodic. The passage includes two contractions, *I'd* and *couldn't,* one casual expression, *a lot of,* and the pronoun *I.* Most of the words are very short, and none would be out of place in an ordinary conversation.

Formal–Informal Level   As life has become less formal, informal diction has become increasingly widespread. Today many articles and books, even ones on relatively serious topics, mix informal and formal elements. Here is an example:

> . . . faith in sports has been vigorously promoted by industry, the military, government, the media. The value of the arena and the locker room has been imposed on our national life. Coaches and sportswriters are speaking for generals and businessmen, too, when they tell us that a man must be physically and psychologically "tough" to succeed, that he must be clean and punctual and honest, that he must

bear pain, bad luck, and defeat without whimpering or making excuses. A man must prove his faith in sports and the American Way by whipping himself into shape, playing by the rules, being part of the team, and putting out all the way. If his faith is strong, he will triumph. It's his own fault if he loses, fails, remains poor.

Robert Lipsyte, Sports World

All these sentences except the next to last are loose. Two are quite long, four quite short, and only two have parallel phrases or clauses. Although a few expressions—*bear, the American Way, triumph*—echo formal diction, most of the words have an informal ring, and two expressions, *whipping himself into shape* and *putting out all the way*, skirt the edges of slang.

Technical Level A specialist writing for others in the same field or for sophisticated nonspecialists writes on the technical level, a cousin to the formal level. Technical language uses specialized words that may be unfamiliar to a general audience. Its sentences tend to be long and complex, but unlike formal diction it doesn't lean toward periodic sentences, parallelism, and balance. Read this example from the field of entomology, the study of insects:

> The light organs of fireflies are complex structures, and recent studies using the electron microscope show them to be even more complex than once supposed. Each is composed of three layers: an outer "window," simply a transparent portion of the body wall; the light organ proper; and an inner layer of opaque, whitish cells filled with granules of uric acid, the so-called "reflector." The light organ proper contains large, slablike light cells, each of them filled with large granules and much smaller, dark granules, the latter tending to be concentrated around the numerous air tubes and nerves penetrating the light organ. These smaller granules were once assumed by some persons to be luminous bacteria, but we now know that they are mitochondria, the source of ATP [adenosine triphosphate] and therefore of the energy of light production. The much larger granules that fill most of the light cells are still of unknown function; perhaps they serve as the source of luciferin.

Howard Ensign Evans, Life on a Little-Known Planet

Note the specialized vocabulary—*granules, uric acid, mitochondria,* and *luciferin*—as well as the length and complexity of the sentences. Five sentences make up the passage, the shortest having twenty-four words. None is periodic, and none has a parallel or balanced structure.

Every field has *jargon,* specialized terms or inside talk that provides a convenient shorthand for communication among its members. For an audience of biologists, you may write that two organisms have a *symbiotic relationship,* meaning "mutually beneficial"; for psychology majors, you might use *catalepsy* instead of "a temporary loss of consciousness and feeling, often accompanied by muscular rigidity." As a general rule, use technical terms only if your audience will know their meanings. If you must use unfamiliar words when writing for a general audience, define them the first time they appear.

Colloquial Language and Slang *Colloquial* originally meant "the language of ordinary conversation between people of a particular region." *Slang,* according to *The Canadian Oxford Dictionary,* is defined as "words, phrases, and uses that are regarded as very informal and are often restricted to special contexts." These two categories shade into each other, and even authorities sometimes disagree on whether to label a term *colloquial* or *slang*. The word *bender,* meaning "a drinking spree," seems firmly in the colloquial camp, and *bummer,* a term recently used by young people to mean "a bad time," is just as clearly slang. *Break a leg* is theatre slang used to wish a performer success. But what about *guy* and *kid?* Once they were slang, but so many people have used them for so long that they have now become colloquial.

Regardless of their labels, colloquial and slang terms are almost never appropriate in formal writing. They sometimes serve a useful purpose in informal writing by creating a special effect or increasing audience appeal. Even so, careful writers use them sparingly. Some readers may not understand some colloquial language, and slang usually becomes dated quickly. The following paragraph uses colloquial and slang expressions successfully:

> . . . When I was just a kid on Eighth Avenue in knee pants . . . [Big Bill] was trying to get himself killed. He was always in some fight with a knife. He was always cutting or trying to cut somebody's throat. He was always getting cut or getting shot. Every Saturday night that he was out there, something happened. If you heard on Sunday morning that somebody had gotten shot or stabbed, you didn't usually ask who did it. You'd ask if Big Bill did it. If he did it, no one paid much attention to it, because he was always doing something like that. They'd say, "Yeah, man. That cat is crazy."
>
> Claude Brown, *Manchild in the Promised Land*

Kid, yeah, and *cat* reflect the speech of Brown's characters and thus add authenticity to his account. Despite the informal diction, Brown uses parallelism in the second, third, and fourth sentences; repetition of *he was always* emphasizes the single-minded self-destructiveness of Big Bill's behaviour.

EXERCISE *Identify the level of diction in each of the following passages. Support your answers with examples from the passages. Point out slang or colloquial expressions.*

1. We may now recapitulate the reasons which have made it necessary to substitute "space-time" for space and time. The old separation of space and time rested upon the belief that there was no ambiguity in saying that two events in distant places happened at the same time; consequently it was thought that we could describe the topography of the universe at a given instant in purely spatial terms. But now that simultaneity has become relative to a particular observer, this is no longer possible. What is, for one observer, a description of the state of the world at a given instant, is, for another observer, a series of events at various different times, whose relations are not merely spatial but also temporal.

    Bertrand Russell, *The ABC of Relativity*

2. In some ways I am an exceptionally privileged woman of thirty-seven. I am in the room of a private, legal abortion hospital, where a surgeon, a friend of many years, is waiting for me in the operating room. I am only five weeks pregnant. Last week I walked out of another hospital, unaborted, because I had suddenly changed my mind. I have a husband who cares for me. He yells because my indecisiveness makes him anxious, but basically he has permitted the final choice to

rest in my hands: "It would be very tough, especially for you, and it is absolutely insane, but yes, we could have another baby." I have a mother who cares. I have two young sons, whose small faces are the most moving arguments I have against going through with this abortion. I have a doctorate in psychology, which among other advantages, assures me of the professional courtesy of special passes in hospitals, passes that at this moment enable my husband and my mother to stand in my room at a nonvisiting hour and yell at each other over my head while I sob.

Magda Denes, *In Necessity and Sorrow: Life and Death in an Abortion Hospital*

3.   I have just spent two days with Edward T. Hall, an anthropologist, watching thousands of my fellow New Yorkers short-circuiting themselves into hot little twitching death balls with jolts of their own adrenalin. Dr. Hall says it is overcrowding that does it. Overcrowding gets the adrenalin going, and the adrenalin gets them queer, autistic, sadistic, barren, batty, sloppy, hot-in-the-pants, charred-in-the-flankers, leering, puling, numb—the usual in New York, in other words, and God knows where else. Dr. Hall has the theory that overcrowding has already thrown New York into a state of behavioral sink. Behavioral sink is a term from ethology, which is the study of how animals relate to their environment. Among animals, the sink winds up with a "population collapse" or "massive die-off." O rotten Gotham.

Tom Wolfe, *The Pump House Gang*

Tone

Tone reveals the author's attitude toward the topic and the reader. Every piece of writing has a tone, intended or otherwise, that stems from the meanings and connotations of words, the sentence patterns, and the rhythm of the prose.

Denotation and Connotation   The denotation of a word is its direct, essential meaning: what the word always stands for. The word *book,* for example, denotes "a set of printed or blank sheets bound together along one edge to form a volume." This definition is objective and neutral: it does not assign any special value or convey any particular attitude toward the word or what the word stands for. Connotations are the values and emotional associations that accompany a word. When the self-made man snorts "book learnin'" at his better-educated junior partner, he assigns a value and an attitude—that he ranks experience higher than the knowledge gained from books.

Some words—*death,* for instance—almost always carry strong connotations or emotional associations. *The Canadian Oxford Dictionary* defines it as "the final cessation of vital functions" or "the ending of life," but it means much more. All of us have hopes, fears, and memories about death, feelings that colour our responses whenever we hear or read the word. Likewise, we have personal responses to words like *sexy, cheap, radical, politician,* and *mother.* Experience, to a considerable extent, conditions how we think and feel about a word. To an Olympic swimmer who has won a gold medal, *swimming* may stir pleasant memories of the victory and the plaudits that went with it. The victim of a near-drowning, however, might react to the same word with something approaching horror.

Nonetheless, cultural connotations are more important than personal ones. Cultural connotations develop the way individual ones do, but on a much larger scale, growing out of the common experiences of many speakers and writers and changing with usage and circumstances.

Context, the parts of a passage that precede and follow a word, also affects connotation. Note, for instance, the different associations of *dog* in these sentences:

That movie is a real dog.

I sure am putting on the dog!

It's a dog-eat-dog world.

Your dog-in-the-manger attitude makes you very unpopular.

Denotation is sometimes called the language of science and technology, connotation, the language of art. But we need both to communicate effectively. Denotation allows us to convey precise, essential meanings. Connotation adds richness, warmth, and bite. Without these qualities our language would be bland and sterile, our lives bleak and mechanical.

Objective Tone   An objective tone keeps the writer's personality and opinions out of the message. Here is an example:

```
Myopia is a condition of the eye that makes distant vision
blurry. In brief, the myopic individual is nearsighted. When the
eye is normal, rays of light pass through it and come to focus on
the retina, located at the back of the eye. In the myopic eye, how-
ever, the rays of light come together a little in front of the
retina. As a result, the distant image is not seen clearly. Myopia
may result from the eye itself being too long or the lens of the
eye being too flat. In either case, the rays converge in front of
the retina, and the nearsighted individual is likely to have diffi-
culty making out distant objects.
```

Janine Neumann

This tone suits a popular explanation of a medical condition. The prose is businesslike and authoritative, the sentence patterns uncomplicated, and nothing reveals the person behind the words.

Other Attitudes   Sometimes you write merely to inform, sometimes to persuade. In persuasive writing, let your attitude toward your topic set the tone. Decide how subtle, flamboyant, or formal your writing should be and what special tone—satiric, cynical, serious, mock pompous, bawdy, playful—will win your reader over.

Every essay has combined characteristics that give it a special tone. The following excerpts illustrate some of tone's many dimensions:

Unless you have led an abnormally isolated adulthood, the chances are excellent that you know many people who have at one time or another committed an act, or consorted with someone who was committing an act, for which they might have been sent to prison. We do not consider most of these people, or ourselves, criminals; the act is one thing, the criminality of it quite something else. Homicide, for example, is in our law not a crime; murder only is proscribed. The difference between the two is the intention, or to be more accurate, society's decision about the nature of that intention.

Bruce Jackson, "Who Goes to Prison: Caste and Careerism in Crime"

Here we have a sophisticated and rather formal tone. Terms like *consorted* and *proscribed,* while exactly suited to Jackson's meaning, do not form part of most people's word kits. The complexity of the first sentence and the varied patterns of the others add to the air of sophistication. The emphatic *quite,* meaning "entirely," is cultivated usage; and along with *society's decision,* it lends the tone a wry touch.

Cans. Beer cans. Glinting on the verges of a million miles of roadways, lying in scrub, grass, dirt, leaves, sand, mud, but never hidden. Piels, Rheingold, Ballantine, Schaeffer, Schlitz, shining in the sun or picked by moon or the beams of headlights at night; washed by rain or flattened by wheels, but never dulled, never buried, never destroyed. Here is the mark of savages, the testament of wasters, the stain of prosperity.

Who are these men who defile the grassy borders of our roads and lanes, who pollute our ponds, who spoil the purity of our ocean beaches with the empty vessels of their thirst? Who are the men who make these vessels in millions and then say, "Drink and discard"? What society is this that can afford to cast away a million tons of metal and to make a wild and fruitful land a garbage heap?

Marya Mannes, "Wasteland"

Rhythm and word choice contribute equally to the tone of this passage. The excerpt opens with imagistic sentence fragments that create a panoramic word picture of our littered roadways. Then complete sentences and sombre commentary follow. Words and patterns are repeated, mixing the dignified language of epic and religion with common derogatory terms—*testament, purity, vessels,* and *fruitful* set against *savages, wasters, defile,* and *garbage heap*—to convey the contradictions Mannes deplores. The rhetorical questions, used instead of accusations, add a sense of loftiness to her outrage, helping create a tone both majestic and disdainful.

Erethizon dorsatus, an antisocial character of the Northern U.S. and Canadian forest, commonly called a porcupine, looks like an uncombed head, has a grumpy personality, fights with his tail, hides his head when he's in trouble, attacks backing up, retreats going ahead, and eats toilet seats as if they were Post Toasties. It's a sad commentary on his personality that people are always trying to do him in.

R. T. Allen, "The Porcupine"

The tone of this passage is affectionately humorous. Allen sets this tone by noting the porcupine's tousled appearance, testy personality, and peculiar habits, such as eating outdoor toilet seats (for their salt content, as Allen later explains). The net effect is to personify porcupines, making them seem like the eccentric reprobate human that others regard with amused toleration.

The final passage begins by referring to "genuine love": the patience, sharing, forgiveness, trust, and acceptance necessary to reconcile Native cultures with the contemporary North American culture.

> The only thing that can truly help us is genuine love. You must truly love us, be patient with us and share with us. And we must love you—with a genuine love that forgives and forgets . . . a love that forgives the terrible sufferings your culture brought ours when it swept over us like a wave crashing along a beach . . . with a love that forgets and lifts up its head and sees in your eyes an answering love of trust and acceptance.
>
> Chief Dan George, "I am a Native of North America"

This writing speaks honestly and passionately about love and reconciliation. Its most obvious rhetorical strategy is the personification of love. Love takes on human form when it "lifts up its head and sees . . . an answering love." This personification reinforces the basic humanity, mutual respect, and love that Natives and non-Natives alike must recognize in each other for reconciliation to take place. The repetition of love throughout the passage reinforces the earnest emotional plea. Eloquence comes through parallelism, repetition, and words like *truly* and *genuine*. Vividness comes through the simile describing the impact of colonization on Native culture as akin to "a wave crashing along a beach."

Like George Orwell, Mark Twain, Joseph Conrad, and other masters of tonal effects, Chief Dan George uses both rhythm and diction to create a tone that infuses and invigorates his message.

EXERCISE   *Characterize the tone of each of the following paragraphs. Point out how word choice, sentence structure, rhythm, and other elements contribute to it.*

1.   When I awoke, dimly aware of some commotion and outcry in the clearing, the light was slanting down through the pines in such a way that the glade was lit like some vast cathedral. I could see the dust motes of wood pollen in the long shaft of light, and there on the extended branch sat an enormous raven with a red and squirming nestling in its beak.

   The sound that awoke me was the outraged cries of the nestling's parents, who flew helplessly in circles around the clearing. . . . And he, the murderer, the black bird at the heart of life, sat there, glistening in the common light, formidable, unperturbed, untouchable. The sighing died. It was then I saw the judgment. It was the judgment of life against death. I will never see it again so forcefully presented. I will never hear it again in notes so tragically prolonged. For in the midst of protest, they forgot the violence. There, in that clearing, the crystal note of a song sparrow lifted hesitantly in the hush. And, finally, after painful fluttering, another took the song, and then another, the song passing from one bird to another, doubtfully at first, as though some evil thing was being slowly forgotten. Till suddenly they took heart and sang from many throats joyously together as birds are known to sing. They sang under the brooding shadow of the raven. In simple truth they had forgotten the raven, for they were the singers of life, and not of death.

   Loren Eiseley, "The Judgment of the Birds"

2.   The great economic scandal of our times isn't the dotcom crash or even the criminal culture of the corporate oligarchy. It's an economic system that

measures the "goods" without the "bads." For every pound of pesticide we count the bushels of corn but not the cases of cancer; we see the burgers without the obesity, the cows but not the cowshit.

James MacKinnon and Jeremy Nelson, *Adbusters*

3.   Babe Ruth was *** The Sultan of Swat ***
Babe Ruth was *** THE BAMBINO ***
Babe Ruth was what you came to see!!!!

It was like going to a carnival, with Babe as both the star performer and the side-show attraction. Hell, that's what we called him: "You big ape." He was what a home-run hitter was supposed to look like. Wide, flat nose. Big feet. Little ankles. Belly hanging over his belt. All he had to do was walk on to the field and everybody would applaud. The air became charged with electricity. You just felt that something great was going to happen.

He'd twirl that big 48-ounce bat around in little circles up at the plate as if he were cranking it up for the Biggest Home Run Ever Hit—*you felt that*—and when he'd hit one he would hit it like nobody has hit it before or since. A mile high and a mile out. I can see him now, as I did so many times, just look up, drop the bat and start to trot, the little pitter-patter pigeon-toed, high-bellied trot that seemed to say, I've done it before and I'll do it again, but this one was for you.

Leo Durocher, *Nice Guys Finish Last*

■ Special Stylistic Techniques

The style of a piece of writing is its character or personality. Like people, writing can be many things: dull, stuffy, discordant, sedate, lively, flamboyant, eccentric, and so on. Figurative language and irony can contribute to your own distinctive writing style.

Figurative Language

Figurative language uses concrete words in a nonliteral way to create sharply etched sensory images that catch and hold the reader's attention. Besides energizing the writing, figurative language helps to strengthen the reader's grip on its ideas. Five figurative devices are especially important: simile, metaphor, personification, overstatement, and understatement.

Simile and Metaphor   A *simile* directly compares two unlike things by the use of *like* or *as*. "Todd is as restless as an aspen leaf in a breeze" and "Her smile flicked on and off like a sunbeam flashing momentarily through a cloud bank" are similes. A *metaphor* also compares unlike things, but without using *like* or *as*. Some metaphors include a linking verb (*is, are, were,* and so on); others do not. "The moon was a wind-tossed bark" and "The curtain of darkness fell over the land" are both metaphors. Here is an excerpt that contains similes and metaphors:

The field is a sea of deep, dark green, a sea made up of millions of small blades of grass blended together as one. Each blade

is a dark green spear, broad at the bottom and narrowing to a needle point at the tip. Its full length is arched so that, viewed from one end, it looks like a shallow trough with paper-thin sides. On the inner side of this trough, small ridges and shallow valleys run from base to tip. To a finger rubbed across them, they feel like short, bristly hairs.

Daniel Kinney

DISCUSSION QUESTIONS

1. Locate the similes in this passage and explain how they help the reader.
2. Locate the metaphors and point out how each heightens the sensory impact of the writing.

Writers too often snatch hastily at the first similes and metaphors that come to mind and end up strewing their pages with overused and enfeebled specimens. Johnny is "as blind as a bat," Mary runs around "like a chicken with its head cut off"—and the writing slips into trite gear. Other comparisons link items that are too dissimilar. For example, "The wind whistled through the trees like a herd of galloping horses" would only puzzle a reader.

Personification This is a special sort of metaphor that assigns human qualities or traits to something nonhuman: a plant, an abstraction, a nonliving thing. Here are some examples:

The vine clung stubbornly to the trunk of the tree.

May fortune smile upon you.

The waves lapped sullenly against the base of the cliff.

Each of these sentences assigns its subject a different emotional quality—stubbornness, friendliness, gloom—each figurative rather than literal: vines aren't stubborn, fortune doesn't smile, and waves aren't sullen.

Personification sometimes extends beyond a single sentence. To illustrate, from an essay comparing and contrasting the merits of long-neck and stubby beer bottles, the following passage personifies the short and stubby beer bottle as a proud, but unpretentious and egalitarian man.

> Mr. Long-neck will flop over like a bowling pin and, unless you've got a head on you like a tenpin bowling ball, Mr. Stubby will still be standing proud, if not tall.
> Stubby was unpretentious. No glamour, all function. Stubby was egalitarian. Millionaire or mooch, you got your brew in a stubby.

P. T. Jensen, "Lament for the Short and Stubby"

Personification works best when it is used in moderation and doesn't make outrageous comparisons. Dishes don't run away with spoons except in nursery rhymes.

Overstatement Overstatement, sometimes called hyperbole, deliberately and drastically exaggerates in order to make a point. In a humorous essay about the replacement of the stubby beer bottle in Canada by the long neck beer bottle, Perry Jensen writes:

> Time to take a stand, Canada. Let's demand the return of our national beer bottle, the stubby, and refuse to drink from foreign containers until the brewers come crawling on their hands and knees.

> P. T. Jensen, "Lament for the Short and Stubby"

Overstatement may contribute to a humorous effect. If it is used sparingly in persuasive essays, it can sometimes add force and punch. Writers must be careful, however, not to lose credibility through excessive exaggeration.

Understatement Understatement makes a quiet assertion in a matter-of-fact way, as when a sportscaster calls a team's 23–2 record "pretty fair." By drawing attention to the thing it appears to slight, this soft-spoken approach offers writers an effective strategy. Here is an example:

> To assume that Heidi Mansfield lacks the qualifications for this position is not unwarranted.

Without ever actually calling Mansfield unqualified, the statement suggests that she is. Similarly, when a meat company executive says, "It is not unlikely that beef prices will jump ten cents a kilogram in the next two months," we might as well count on spending another dime. As these statements show, understatement not infrequently has an ulterior motive.

EXERCISE   *Identify the similes, metaphors, personifications, overstatements, or understatements in these sentences.*

1. The old table greedily sucked up the linseed oil.
2. Russia's social and economic system is a giant staircase that leads nowhere.
3. Stanley has the bile of human meanness by the litre in every vein.
4. Their music sounds like the drumming of an infant's fists against the sides of a crib.
5. The foundations of our divorce are as strong as ever.
6. It is not unlike Muriel to be late.
7. You're the world's biggest liar!
8. "Fashion, though folly's child, and guide of fools,
   Rules e'en the wisest, and in learning rules."
9. Einstein's theories have had some impact on modern science.
10. I'm as tired as a farm horse at sunset.

Irony

Irony occurs when a writer intentionally states one thing but actually means something different or even opposite. The sportswriter who refers to the "ideal conditions" for a tennis tournament when rain has drenched the courts and forced cancellation of matches speaks ironically. In an article about government cutbacks, Charles Gordon uses irony to make a serious point:

> Welcome to Cutback World, ladies and gentlemen. We hope you enjoyed your flight. Sorry you had to walk so far in the rain, but spending reductions have made it possible for us to operate the same number of airplanes with fewer unloading ramps. You will notice complimentary newspapers on some of the seats of this bus. We hope you don't mind sharing them. While we wait to begin our tour, you might like to read some of the stories, just to get an introduction to the place we call home. If you turn to page 1, you'll see the little item about what we are doing for our homeless citizens. We have provided 300 beds for them in this city alone. According to the most recent estimates, this means that at least 10 percent of our homeless citizens will be able to find a bed tonight. So across the country, only 20,000 to 40,000 people are sleeping on the streets.

> Charles Gordon, "A Guided Tour of the Bottom Line"

The author never directly states that he disagrees with the government's spending reductions, but he uses details that highlight what he considers the injustice or absurdity of government spending cuts. When he states that "at least 10 percent" of the homeless have beds, he pretends to be self-congratulatory, but is in fact emphasizing the relatively tiny portion of the homeless population that has shelter.

■ Eliminating Flawed Diction

Diction flaws include wordiness, euphemisms, clichés, mixed metaphors, and sexist language. As you revise, stay alert for these culprits and eliminate any that you find.

Wordiness

Wordiness is verbal obesity, and like physical obesity it has more than one cause. Some writers overnourish their prose to make it sound more impressive, some to pad an assignment, and some simply because they don't realize they're doing it. Whatever the reason, the results are the same: ponderous, slow-moving papers that lack punch. To inject vigour, strip your prose down to fighting weight by cutting out every word that doesn't serve a purpose. If five words are doing the work of one, drop four.

The two major forms of wordiness, deadwood and gobbledygook, often occur together. *Deadwood,* which does nothing but take up space and clutter the writing, is bracketed in the following sentence:

> Responsible parents [of today] neither allow their children [to have] absolute freedom [to do as they please] nor severely restrict their children's activities.

Now read the sentence without the deadwood:

> Responsible parents neither allow their children absolute freedom nor severely restrict their children's activities.

Careful revision has increased the clarity and reduced the words from twenty-three to fourteen.

Gobbledygook consists of long, abstract, or technical words that help create unnecessarily long and complex sentences. Some people who write it mistakenly believe it "dignifies" their thoughts. Others want to conceal their meanings by clouding their statements. And some naively think that long words are better than short ones. All of these writers use gobbledygook, but none of their readers appreciates it. Here are some samples of gobbledygook followed by revised versions in plain English:

Original Version	**Revised Version**
The fish exhibited a 100 percent mortality response.	All the fish died.
We have been made cognizant of the fact that the experiment will be terminated in the near future.	We have learned that the experiment will end soon.

Euphemisms

Euphemisms take the sting out of something unpleasant or add stature to something humble. Familiar expressions include *pass away* for *die*, *preowned* for *used*, and *sanitation engineer* for *garbage collector*.

In most cases, the writer simply intends to cushion reality. But euphemisms also have grisly uses. Companies don't fire employees; they *restructure* or *downsize*. Mobsters don't *beat up* merchants who refuse *protection* (itself a euphemism); they *lean on* them. Hitler didn't talk about *exterminating the Jews* but about *the final solution to the Jewish problem*. These euphemisms don't just blur reality; they blot out images of horror. Of merchants with broken limbs and bloodied faces. Of cattle cars crammed with men, women, and children en route to death camps. Of barbed wire and gas ovens and starved corpses in the millions.

Any euphemism, however well-intentioned, probably obscures an issue. On occasion you may need one in order to protect the sensitive reader, but usually you will serve readers best by using direct expressions that present reality, not a tidied-up version.

Clichés and Mixed Metaphors

Clichés   Clichés are expressions that have become flat and stale from overuse. Rather than responding to experience with their own perceptions, writers sometimes resort to oft-repeated words or phrases that stem from patterned thinking. Dullness follows. Daily conversation abounds with stale, trite expressions because talk is unplanned, but writing allows you time to find invigorating and effective language. Your individual response is what draws the reader's interest, and only fresh thinking will produce that response. The list of clichés on the following page barely "scratches the surface":

acid test	burn the midnight oil	green with envy
almighty dollar	chip off the old block	last but not least
beat a hasty retreat	clear as a bell	nipped in the bud
better late than never	cool as a cucumber	rears its ugly head
black sheep	easier said than done	set the world on fire
blind as a bat	goes without saying	sick as a dog

Mixed Metaphors   Clichéd writing often suffers as well from mixed metaphors—inappropriate combinations that startle or amuse the reader. How would you respond if you came across this example?

When he opened that can of worms, he bit off more than he could chew.

Can you visualize someone chewing a mouthful of worms? The point is obvious.

Gender Inclusive Language

Non-inclusive language assigns roles to people according to gender. It is offensive because it demeans women and men or reinforces erroneous beliefs that limit the roles they can play. Deliberate or accidental, non-inclusive language must be eliminated from your writing. These guidelines will help you do just that:

1. Don't unnecessarily mention an individual's appearance, spouse, or family.

   Non-inclusive: The attractive new loan officer at the credit union is a real hit with customers.

   Non-inclusive: John Mercer, husband of local surgeon Leslie Mercer, won election to the Board of Education.

   Non-inclusive: After eight years of attending university part time, Gerald Denham, a three-time grandfather, was awarded a bachelor of science degree.

   Inclusive: The efficient new loan officer at the credit union is a real hit with customers.

   Inclusive: John Mercer, president of Bear Publishing, won election to the Board of Education.

   Inclusive: After eight years of attending university part time, Gerald Denham was awarded a bachelor of science degree.

   Note how, in each case, the sentence has been rewritten to include only relevant information.

2. Use the pronouns *she and he, her and him, her and his,* and *herself and himself* only when referring to antecedents that clearly indicate a specific gender.

   Non-inclusive: Each tourist must carry *his* passport with *him* at all times.

   Non-inclusive: If anyone doesn't understand the instructions, *she* should see me right away.

Correct this type of error by substituting plural antecedents and pronouns for the singular ones or by rewriting the sentence to eliminate the pronouns.

Inclusive: Tourists must carry *their* passports with *them* at all times.

Inclusive: Anyone who doesn't understand the instructions should see me right away.

3. Don't use occupational labels that imply the positions are held only by men.

Non-inclusive	**Inclusive**
chairman	chair
fisherman	fisher
fireman	fire fighter
policeman	police officer
mailman	letter carrier

A word of caution here. To avoid non-inclusive language, some writers substitute the suffix *-person* for *-man* in many job titles (such as *handyperson* for someone who does odd jobs). Such attempts, however, often create awkward expressions that you should avoid.

EXERCISE   *The following sentences are flawed by wordiness, euphemisms, clichés, mixed metaphors, and non-inclusive language. When you have identified the faults, revise the sentences.*

1. The very keen student, who was studying at school, asked focused, pertinent questions.
2. Last summer, I was engaged in the repair of automobiles.
3. You're looking as bright as a button this morning.
4. There was a large amount of collateral damage in the war.
5. Any student wishing to attend summer school must pay her tuition one week before registration day.
6. My brother is in the process of pursuing a curriculum of industrial chemistry.
7. The ball's in your court, and if you strike out, don't expect me to pick up the pieces.
8. The blonde, sultry-voiced clerk quickly filled the order.
9. Winning first prize for her essay was a real feather in Peggy's cap.
10. Our company plans to confer retirement on 200 employees by year's end.

The Essay Examination

Instructors use essay examinations to gauge your grasp of ideas, noting how well you apply, analyze, challenge, compare, or otherwise handle them. Facts and figures, on the other hand, are more often tested by objective examinations. Writing essay answers under pressure and with minimal time to rethink and revise differs from writing at home. Instructors expect reasonably clear, complete, and coherent answers but not models of style or neatness. They do expect legibility. They also expect you to follow directions carefully, and, of course, to practise academic honesty. Very occasionally instructors will allow you to bring in notes that you may use; be sure you understand exactly what is and is not allowed. In almost any class, an effective presentation with a well-defined thesis, relevant and specific support for the thesis, and an organizational plan will increase your chances for success.

Studying for the Examination

Here are some pointers for studying:

1. Allow adequate preparation time. For a comprehensive test, start reviewing several days in advance. For one that covers a small segment of the course, a day or two should be enough.

2. Reread the key points you've marked in your class notes and textbook. Use them to develop a set of basic concepts.

3. Try to anticipate what the instructor might ask by making up a set of sample questions related to these concepts. You could then do some freewriting to answer them, or discuss key ideas with others in the class in a collaborative study session. Even if none of your questions appears on the test, your efforts will ease pretest jitters and supply insights that apply to other questions.

4. Answer your questions by drawing upon your concepts and supplying details from your notes and textbook.

■ Types of Test Questions

Some instructors favour narrow, highly focused test questions with detailed answering instructions. Others like broad items, perhaps with simple directions such as "Write for twenty minutes." The sample questions below range from very broad to very narrow. Note how when answering them you can often use the writing strategies discussed in Chapters 4–12.

1. Analyze the *influences* of the industrial revolution on European society.

2. Discuss the most important *causes* of the First World War.

3. *Compare and contrast* the David statues of Michelangelo and Bernini.

4. Select three different camera shots used in the movie *Titanic*. Identify at least one scene that *illustrates* each shot; then explain how each shot functions by *describing* the relationship between the shot and the action or dialogue.

5. Analyze the huge drop in value of technology stocks in 2001 and 2002. Consider the major *factors* involved, such as the liberal lending practices of international banks, the questionable accounting practices of many companies, and the unbridled enthusiasm of investors, and how these *factors* interacted. Use a thesis statement that signals the points you will discuss.

A highly focused question such as item 5 suggests how to organize and develop the essay. If you know the answer, you can begin writing quickly. In contrast, item 1 forces you to focus and narrow the subject before you respond. Answering this type of item requires careful planning.

■ Preparing to Write

You can't get from Moncton to Montreal without knowing and following an appropriate route. The same principle applies to exam writing. Often students fail to read general directions or to answer what is asked. Low grades follow. To avoid penalizing yourself, scan the test items, noting how many must be answered and which ones, if any, are optional. When you have a choice, select the questions you can answer most thoroughly. Pay attention to any suggestions or requirements concerning length (one paragraph, two pages) or relative weight (25 points, 30 minutes, 40 percent), and budget your time accordingly.

The first requirement for most essay tests is to read the question for *key words*. Some instructors may want you to summarize and organize material that has been covered in class, while at other times you may be asked to formulate an argument of your own, selecting relevant evidence for your claims. Does the instructor want you to analyze, compare, criticize, defend, describe, discuss, evaluate, illustrate, explain, justify, trace, or argue? If you are asked to explain how Darwin's theory of evolution affected nineteenth-century thinking, do just that; do not simply summarize the theory, or stray from the question by arguing against the theory. Merely putting ideas on paper, even perceptive ideas, does not substitute for addressing the question.

EXERCISE   *Indicate what each of the following questions calls for. What is required? By what methods—arguing, describing, or the like—would you develop the answer?*

1. Distinguish between mild depression and severe depression. You might focus on the nature, the symptoms, or the potential treatments of each condition.

2. Support or refute the following statement: Because waste incineration generates stack gases and ash that contain high levels of toxic substances, it is not an acceptable solution to waste-disposal problems.

3. Explain how to clean an automobile carburetor.

4. Briefly relate the events in the Book of Job and then explain the significance of the tale. Could the tale be called symbolic? Why or why not?

When you have the essay question clearly in mind, don't immediately start writing. A jackrabbit start spells trouble. Instead, take a few moments to plan your answer. Following these steps will help you do this:

1. Jot down specific supporting information from your reading and lecture notes.

2. Make a rough outline that sketches the main points you'll cover and an effective order for presenting them.

3. Prepare a thesis statement that responds to the question and will control your answer.

Writing an essay exam, like writing an essay, is a front-end-loaded process. Much of the brain work occurs before you put your answer on paper.

■ Writing the Examination Answer

Here are some guidelines that will help you write a successful exam:

1. Position your thesis statement at the beginning of your answer. Make sure each paragraph is controlled by a topic sentence tied to the thesis statement.

2. Don't become excessively concerned about your wording. Focus on content and, if time permits, proofread and make stylistic changes later.

3. Fight the impulse to jot down everything you know about the general subject. Be focused, direct, and selective. The grader doesn't want to plow through verbiage to arrive at your answer.

The following essay illustrates these guidelines:

Question:	Discuss the various appeals described by classical rhetoric that an orator can use. Give a brief example of each kind of appeal.
Answer: *Thesis statement previews* *focus and order of answer*	Classical rhetoric defines three major appeals—logical, emotional, and ethical—that orators may use to win support from their audience.
Topic sentence:	Most rhetoricians agree that any argument must be based on logic; that is, it must appeal to the intellect of the listeners. Unless it does, the
Example 1:	orator will fail to convince them. For example, a speaker who is urging the election of a candidate and presents the candidate's voting record is appealing to logic, asking the audience to understand that the voting record predicts how the candidate will continue to vote if elected.
Example 2:	Likewise, a candidate for public office who describes how a tax cut will stimulate the economy and create new jobs is using a logical appeal.
Topic sentence:	In addition to logic, emotional appeals are a powerful means of swaying people, especially groups. Though emotional appeals work along with logical appeals, they are quite different because they are directed at the listener's hopes,
Example 1:	fears, and sympathies. The candidate for prime minister who indicates that a vote for an opponent is a vote to increase government spending and risk a financial crisis is making an emotional appeal. So, too, is the mayoral candidate
Example 2:	who asserts that her city's industry can be revitalized and serve as a model for all other cities.
Topic sentence:	The ethical appeal is more subtle than either of the other two but probably just as important. The orator must strike the audience as a sensible, good person if they are to believe the
Example 1:	message. Sometimes the speaker's logic and also the tone—moderate, sensible, or wise—
Example 2:	will convey sufficient ethical appeal. At other times, a speaker will use statements that are deliberately intended to create ethical appeal. "In developing this program, I will work closely

with all representatives in parliament, regardless of their party affiliations" and "Despite our
differences, I believe my opponent to be a decent, honest person" are examples of such
statements.

Restatement of thesis: In any speech, all these appeals—logical, emotional, and ethical—work together to convince
an audience.

Student Unknown

In contrast, the next two responses to the same question illustrate common
faults of examination essays.

Answer A

1   There are three basic appeals that a speaker can make to captivate an audience.
These are the ethical appeal, the logical appeal, and the emotional appeal.

2   The first of these—the ethical appeal—includes all the speaker's efforts to be
viewed as rational, wise, good, and generous. Needless to say, the ethical appeal is
very important. Without it, no one would pay attention to the speaker's argument.

3   The second appeal—logical—is also extremely important. It carries the burden
of the argument from speaker to listener and appeals to the intellect of the audience.

4   Emotional appeal—the third and final one—is made to the passions and feelings of the listeners. The significance of such an appeal is obvious.

5   A speaker often uses all three appeals to win an audience over.

Answer *A* starts with a thesis statement and includes brief definitions of the
three appeals; however, it omits any concrete examples and includes no specific details. As a result, the significance of the emotional appeal is not "obvious," as paragraph 4 claims, nor does the answer offer any hints as to why the other appeals are
important. This response resembles an outline more than an answer and suggests
the student lacked the knowledge to do a good job.

Answer B

1   Orators may make three different kinds of appeals to win favour from an audience: emotional appeal, logical appeal, and ethical appeal.

2   Let's start with emotional appeal because this is the one that is not essential to a
speech. Logical and ethical appeals are always included; emotional appeal may be
used to help sway an audience, but without logical and ethical appeals no argument
is accepted. This simply makes sense: if there is no logic, there is no argument; and
if the speaker doesn't come across as an ethical person—someone to be relied
upon—then no one will accept the message. But emotional appeal is different.
Unemotional arguments may be accepted.

3   Nevertheless, emotional appeal is important. It includes whatever a speaker
does to move the feelings of the audience. The speaker asks, "Don't you want to protect your families?" Such an appeal is emotional. A speaker may appeal to the prejudices or biases of listeners. Someone at a Ku Klux Klan rally does that. So does a
minister who exhorts people to be "saved." Both speakers address the emotions of
the groups they talk to.

4   There is a very fine use of emotional appeal in the "Letter from Birmingham Jail" by Martin Luther King, Jr. At one point King asks his audience of white clergy how they would feel if, like blacks, they had to deny their children treats such as amusement parks and had to fear for the lives of their families, and so on. He also describes the bombings and burnings that blacks are subjected to. All the details move readers emotionally, so that they come to sympathize with blacks who live in fear.

5   Logical appeal, as noted earlier, is crucial. The speaker must seem to have an intelligent plan. The listeners want the plan to meet their needs.

6   The other appeal is the ethical one. It is made when speakers make themselves seem generous, good and wise.

7   All three appeals can be used in one speech, although the logical and ethical appeals are essential to it.

Although the writer opens with an acceptable thesis statement, this answer shows little evidence of advance planning. Does it make sense to begin in paragraph 2 with an appeal tagged "not essential"? And note how the paragraph drifts from the emotional appeal to the other two types, despite its topic sentence. Paragraphs 3 and 4 do focus on the emotional appeal and ironically, through specific examples, make a good case for its importance. Paragraphs 5 and 6 shortchange logical and ethical appeals by saying next to nothing about them. The essay contradicts itself: if logical and ethical appeals are the essential ones and emotional appeals "not essential," why is more than half of the essay about emotional appeal?

Writing About Literature

Instructors of literature generally expect you to analyze some aspect of what you have read. Typically they might ask you to

- analyze how an author handled one element such as character, point of view, tone, theme, or a particular pattern of imagery in a literary work

- compare and contrast two characters in a work of fiction, or ways in which two different works treat a particular element

- analyze how several elements contribute to the unity or effectiveness of a literary work

- argue a particular interpretation of a work

Writing about literature offers several benefits. Weighing and recording your thoughts on literary elements, or arguing a particular interpretation of a work can sharpen your critical thinking ability. Careful reading and thoughtful writing about literature will also deepen your appreciation of the writer's craft. Furthermore, you'll feel a sense of accomplishment as you coherently express your perceptions. Finally, writing a literature paper offers yet another opportunity to apply writing skills of focusing, selecting relevant material, choosing a logical plan of organization, writing a draft, revising, and editing.

■ The Elements of Literature

Most writing assignments on literature will probably feature one or more of the following elements:

Plot   Setting   Theme
Point of view   Images or Symbols   Irony
Character

Depending on the work, some of these will be more important than others. Read the following story by Alice Munro, "An Ounce of Cure." The discussions that follow it point out the basic features of each element and offer useful writing suggestions.

An Ounce of Cure

Alice Munro

My parents didn't drink. They weren't rabid about it, and in fact I remember that when I signed the pledge in grade seven, with the rest of that superbly if impermanently indoctrinated class, my mother said, "It's just nonsense and fanaticism, children of that age." My father would drink a beer on a hot day, but my mother did not join him, and—whether accidentally or symbolically—this drink was always consumed outside the house. Most of the people we knew were the same way, in the small town where we lived. I ought not to say that it was this which got me into difficulties, because the difficulties I got into were a faithful expression of my own incommodious nature—the same nature that caused my mother to look at me, on any occasion which traditionally calls for feelings of pride and maternal accomplishment (my departure for my first formal dance, I mean, or my hellbent preparations for a descent on college) with an expression of brooding and fascinated despair, as if she could not possibly expect, did not ask, that it should go with me as it did with other girls; the dreamed-of spoils of daughters—orchids, nice boys, diamond rings—would be borne home in due course by the daughters of her friends, but not by me; all she could do was hope for a lesser rather than a greater disaster—an elopement, say, with a boy who could never earn his living, rather than an abduction into the White Slave trade.

But ignorance, my mother said, ignorance, or innocence if you like, is not always such a fine thing as people think and I am not sure it may not be dangerous for a girl like you; then she emphasized her point, as she had a habit of doing, with some quotation which had an innocent pomposity and odour of mothballs. I didn't even wince at it, knowing full well how it must have worked wonders with Mr. Berryman.

The evening I baby-sat for the Berrymans must have been in April. I had been in love all year, or at least since the first week in September, when a boy named Martin Collingwood had given me a surprised, appreciative, and rather ominously complacent smile in the school assembly. I never knew what surprised him; I was not looking like anybody but me; I had an old blouse on and my home-permanent had turned out badly. A few weeks after that he took me out for the first time, and kissed me on the dark side of the porch—also, I ought to say, on the mouth; I am sure it was the first time anybody had ever kissed me effectively, and I know that I did not wash my face that night or the next morning, in order to keep the imprint of those kisses intact. (I showed the most painful banality in the conduct of this whole affair, as you will see.) Two months, and a few amatory stages later, he dropped me. He had fallen for the girl who played opposite him in the Christmas production of *Pride and Prejudice*.

I said I was not going to have anything to do with that play, and I got another girl to work on Makeup in my place, but of course I went to it after all, and sat down in front with my girl friend Joyce, who pressed my hand when I was overcome with pain and delight at the sight of Mr. Darcy in white breeches, silk waistcoat, and sideburns. It was surely seeing Martin as Darcy that did it for me; every girl is in love with Darcy anyway, and the part gave Martin an arrogance and male splendour in my eyes which made it impossible to remember that he was simply a high-school senior, passably good-looking and of medium intelligence (and with a reputation slightly tainted, at that, by such preferences as the Drama Club and the Cadet Band) who happened to be the first boy, the first really presentable boy, to take an interest in me. In the last act they gave him a chance to embrace Elizabeth (Mary Bishop, with a sallow complexion and no figure, but big vivacious eyes) and during this realistic encounter I dug my nails bitterly into Joyce's sympathetic palm.

That night was the beginning of months of real, if more or less self-inflicted, misery for me. Why is it a temptation to refer to this sort of thing lightly, with irony, with amazement even, at finding oneself involved with such preposterous emotions in the unaccountable past? That is what we are apt to do, speaking of love; with adolescent love, of course, it's practically obligatory; you would think we sat around, dull afternoons, amusing ourselves with these tidbit recollections of pain. But it really doesn't make me feel very gay—worse still, it doesn't really surprise me—to remember all the stupid, sad, half-ashamed things I did, that people in love always do. I hung around the places where he might be seen, and then pretended not to see him; I made absurdly roundabout approaches, in conversation, to the bitter pleasure of casually mentioning his name. I daydreamed endlessly; in fact if you want to put it mathematically, I spent perhaps ten times as many hours thinking about Martin Collingwood—yes, pining and weeping for him—as I ever spent with him; the idea of him dominated my mind relentlessly and, after a while, against my will. For if at first I had dramatized my feelings, the time came when I would have been glad to escape them; my well-worn daydreams had become depressing and not even temporarily consoling. As I worked my math problems I would torture myself, quite mechanically and helplessly, with an exact recollection of Martin kissing my throat. I had an exact recollection of *everything*. One night I had an impulse to swallow all the aspirins in the bathroom cabinet, but stopped after I had taken six.

My mother noticed that something was wrong and got me some iron pills. She said, "Are you sure everything is going all right at school?" *School!* When I told her that Martin and I had broken up all she said was, "Well so much the better for that. I never saw a boy so stuck on himself." "Martin has enough conceit to sink a battleship," I said morosely and went upstairs and cried.

The night I went to the Berrymans was a Saturday night. I baby-sat for them quite often on Saturday nights because they liked to drive over to Baileyville, a much bigger, livelier town about twenty miles away, and perhaps have supper and go to a show. They had been living in our town only two or three years—Mr. Berryman had been brought in as plant manager of the new door-factory—and they remained, I suppose by choice, on the fringes of its society; most of their friends were youngish couples like themselves, born in other places, who lived in new ranch-style houses on a hill outside town where we used to go tobogganing. This Saturday night they had two other couples in for drinks before they all drove over to Baileyville for the opening of a new supper club; they were all rather festive. I sat in the kitchen and pretended to do Latin. Last night had been the Spring Dance at the High School.

I had not gone, since the only boy who had asked me was Millerd Crompton, who asked so many girls that he was suspected of working his way through the whole class alphabetically. But the dance was held in the Armouries, which was only half a block away from our house; I had been able to see the boys in dark suits, the girls in long pale formals under their coats, passing gravely under the street-lights, stepping around the last patches of snow. I could even hear the music and I have not forgotten to this day that they played "Ballerina," and—oh, song of my aching heart—"Slow Boat to China." Joyce had phoned me up this morning and told me in her hushed way (we might have been discussing an incurable disease I had) that yes, M.C. *had* been there with M.B., and she had on a formal that must have been made out of somebody's old lace tablecloth, it just *hung*.

When the Berrymans and their friends had gone I went into the living room and read a magazine. I was mortally depressed. The big softly lit room, with its green and leaf-brown colours, made an uncluttered setting for the development of the emotions, such as you would get on a stage. At home the life of the emotions went on all right, but it always seemed to get buried under the pile of mending to be done, the ironing, the children's jigsaw puzzles and rock collections. It was the sort of house where people were always colliding with one another on the stairs and listening to hockey games and Superman on the radio.

I got up and found the Berrymans' "Dance Macabre" and put it on the record player and turned out the living-room lights. The curtains were only partly drawn. A street light shone obliquely on the windowpane, making a rectangle of thin dusty gold, in which the shadows of bare branches moved, caught in the huge sweet winds of spring. It was a mild black night when the last snow was melting. A year ago all this—the music, the wind and darkness, the shadows of the branches—would have given me tremendous happiness; when they did not do so now, but only called up tediously familiar, somehow humiliatingly personal thoughts, I gave up my soul for dead and walked into the kitchen and decided to get drunk.

No, it was not like that. I walked in to the kitchen to look for a coke or something in the refrigerator, and there on the front of the counter were three tall beautiful bottles, all about half full of gold. But even after I had looked at them and lifted them to feel their weight I had not decided to get drunk; I had decided to have a drink.

Now here is where my ignorance, my disastrous innocence, comes in. It is true that I had seen the Berrymans and their friends drinking their highballs as casually as I would drink a coke, but I did not apply this attitude to myself. No; I thought of hard liquor as something to be taken in extremes, and relied upon for extravagant results, one way or another. My approach could not have been less casual if I had been the Little Mermaid drinking the witch's crystal potion. Gravely, with a glance at my set face in the black window above the sink, I poured a little whisky from each of the bottles (I think now there were two brands of rye and an expensive Scotch) until I had my glass full. For I had never in my life seen anyone pour a drink and I had no idea that people frequently diluted their liquor with water, soda, et cetera, and I had seen that the glasses the Berrymans' guests were holding when I came through the living room were nearly full.

I drank it off as quickly as possible. I set the glass down and stood looking at my face in the window, half expecting to see it altered. My throat was burning, but I felt nothing else. It was very disappointing, when I had worked myself up to it. But I was not going to let it go at that. I poured another full glass, then filled each of the bottles with water to approximately the level I had seen when I came in. I drank the second glass only a little more slowly than the first. I put the empty glass down on the counter with care, perhaps feeling in my head a rustle of things to come, and went and sat down on a chair in the living room. I reached up and turned on a floor lamp beside the chair, and the room jumped on me.

When I say that I was expecting extravagant results I do not mean that I was expecting this. I had thought of some sweeping emotional change, an upsurge of gaiety and irresponsibility, a feeling of lawlessness and escape, accompanied by a little dizziness and perhaps a tendency to giggle out loud. I did not have in mind the ceiling spinning like a great plate somebody had thrown at me, nor the pale green blobs of the chairs swelling, converging, disintegrating, playing with me a game full of enormous senseless inanimate malice. My head sank back; I closed my eyes. And at once opened them, opened them wide, threw myself out of the chair and down the hall and reached—thank God, thank God!—the Berrymans' bathroom, where I was sick everywhere, everywhere, and dropped like a stone.

From this point on I have no continuous picture of what happened; my memories of the next hour or two are split into vivid and improbable segments, with nothing but murk and uncertainty between. I do remember lying on the bathroom floor looking sideways at the little six-sided white tiles, which lay together in such an admirable and logical pattern, seeing them with the brief broken gratitude and sanity of one who has just been torn to pieces with vomiting. Then I remember sitting on the stool in front of the hall phone, asking weakly for Joyce's number. Joyce was not home. I was told by her mother (a rather rattlebrained woman, who didn't seem to notice a thing the matter—for which I felt weakly, mechanically grateful) that she was at Kay Stringer's house. I didn't know Kay's number so I just asked the operator; I felt I couldn't risk looking down at the telephone book.

Kay Stringer was not a friend of mine but a new friend of Joyce's. She had a vague reputation for wildness and a long switch of hair, very oddly, though naturally, coloured—from soap-yellow to caramel-brown. She knew a lot of boys more exciting than Martin Collingwood, boys who had quit school or been imported into town to play on the hockey team. She and Joyce rode around in these boys' cars, and sometimes went with them—having lied of course to their mothers—to the Gay-la dance hall on the highway north of town.

I got Joyce on the phone. She was very keyed-up, as she always was with boys around, and she hardly seemed to hear what I was saying.

"Oh, I can't tonight," she said. "Some kids are here. We're going to play cards. You know Bill Kline? He's here. Rom Armour—"

"I'm *sick*," I said trying to speak distinctly; it came out an inhuman croak. "I'm *drunk*. Joyce!" Then I fell off the stool and the receiver dropped out of my hand and banged for a while dismally against the wall.

I had not told Joyce where I was, so after thinking about it for a moment she phoned my mother, and using the elaborate and unnecessary subterfuge that young girls delight in, she found out. She and Kay and the boys—there were three of them—told some story about where they were going to Kay's mother, and got into the car and drove out. They found me still lying on the broadloom carpet in the hall; I had been sick again, and this time I had not made it to the bathroom.

It turned out that Kay Stringer, who arrived on this scene only by accident, was exactly the person I needed. She loved a crisis, particularly one like this, which had a shady and scandalous aspect and which must be kept secret from the adult world. She became excited, aggressive, efficient; that energy which was termed wildness was simply the overflow of a great female instinct to manage, comfort and control. I could hear her voice coming at me from all directions, telling me not to worry, telling Joyce to find the biggest coffeepot they had and make it full of coffee (*strong* coffee, she said), telling the boys to pick me up and carry me to the sofa. Later, in the fog beyond my reach, she was calling for a scrub-brush.

Then I was lying on the sofa, covered with some kind of crocheted throw they had found in the bedroom. I didn't want to lift my head. The house was full of the smell of coffee. Joyce came in, looking very pale; she said that the Berryman kids had wakened up but she had given them a cookie and told them to go back to bed, it was all right; she hadn't let them out of their room and she didn't believe they'd remember. She said that she and Kay had cleaned up the bathroom and the hall though she was afraid there was still a spot on the rug.

The coffee was ready. I didn't understand anything very well. The boys had turned on the radio and were going through the Berrymans' record collection; they had it out on the floor. I felt there was something odd about this but I could not think what it was.

Kay brought me a huge breakfast mug full of coffee.

"I don't know if I can," I said. "Thanks."

"Sit up," she said briskly, as if dealing with drunks was an everyday business for her, I had no need to feel myself important. (I met, and recognized, that tone of voice years later, in the maternity ward.) "Now drink," she said. I drank, and at the same time realized that I was wearing only my slip. Joyce and Kay had taken off my blouse and skirt. They had brushed off the skirt and washed out the blouse, since it was nylon; it was hanging in the bathroom. I pulled the throw up under my arms and Kay laughed. She got everybody coffee. Joyce brought in the coffeepot and on Kay's instructions she kept filling my cup whenever I drank from it. Somebody said to me with interest. "You must have really wanted to tie one on."

"No," I said rather sulkily, obediently drinking my coffee. "I only had two drinks."

Kay laughed, "Well it certainly gets to you, I'll say that. What time do you expect *they*'ll be back?" she said.

"Late. After one I think."

"You should be all right by that time. Have some more coffee."

Kay and one of the boys began dancing to the radio. Kay danced very sexily, but her face had the gently superior and indulgent, rather cold look it had when she was lifting me up to drink the coffee. The boy was whispering to her and she was smiling, shaking her head. Joyce said she was hungry, and she went out to the kitchen to see what there was—potato chips or crackers, or something like that, that you could eat without making too noticeable a dint. Bill Kline came over and sat on the sofa beside me and patted my legs through the crocheted throw. He didn't say anything to me, just patted my legs and looked at me with what seemed to me a very stupid, half-sick, absurd and alarming expression. I felt very uncomfortable; I wondered how it had ever got around that Bill Kline was so good looking, with an expression like that. I moved my legs nervously and he gave me a look of contempt, not ceasing to pat me. Then I scrambled off the sofa, pulling the throw around me, with the idea of going to the bathroom to see if my blouse was dry. I lurched a little when I started to walk, and for some reason—probably to show Bill Kline that he had not panicked me—I immediately exaggerated this, and calling out, "Watch me walk a straight line!" I lurched and stumbled, to the accompaniment of everyone's laughter, towards the hall. I was standing in the archway between the hall and the living room when the knob of the front door turned with a small matter-of-fact click and everything became silent behind me except the radio of course, and the crocheted throw inspired by some delicate malice of its own slithered down around my feet and there—oh, delicious moment in a well-organized farce!—there stood the

Berrymans, Mr. and Mrs., with expressions on their faces as appropriate to the occasion as any old-fashioned director of farces could wish. They must have been preparing those expressions, of course; they could not have produced them in the first moment of shock; with the noise we were making, they had no doubt heard us as soon as they got out of the car; for the same reason, we had not heard them. I don't think I ever knew what brought them home so early—a headache, an argument—and I was not really in a position to ask.

Mr. Berryman drove me home. I don't remember how I got into that car, or how I found my clothes and put them on, or what kind of a good-night, if any, I said to Mrs. Berryman. I don't remember what happened to my friends, though I imagine they gathered up their coats and fled, covering up the ignominy of their departure with a mechanical roar of defiance. I remember Joyce with a box of crackers in her hand, saying that I had become terribly sick from eating—I think she said *sauerkraut*—for supper, and that I had called them for help. (When I asked her later what they made of this she said, "It wasn't any use. You *reeked*.") I remember also her saying, "Oh, no, Mrs. Berryman I beg you, my mother is a terribly nervous person I don't know what the shock might do to her. I will go down on my knees to you if you like but *you must not phone my mother.*" I have no picture of her down on her knees—and she would have done it in a minute—so it seems this threat was not carried out.

Mr. Berryman said to me, "Well I guess you know your behaviour tonight is a pretty serious thing." He made it sound as if I might be charged with criminal negligence or something worse. "It would be very wrong of me to overlook it," he said. I suppose that besides being angry and disgusted with me, he was worried about taking me home in this condition to my strait-laced parents, who could always say I got the liquor in his house. Plenty of Temperance people would think that enough to hold him responsible, and the town was full of Temperance people. Good relations with the town were very important to him from a business point of view.

"I have an idea it wasn't the first time," he said. "If it was the first time, would a girl be smart enough to fill three bottles up with water? No. Well in this case, she was smart enough, but not smart enough to know I could spot it. What do you say to that?" I opened my mouth to answer and although I was feeling quite sober the only sound that came out was a loud, desolate-sounding giggle. He stopped in front of our house. "Light's on," he said. "Now go in and tell your parents the straight truth. And if you don't, remember I will." He did not mention paying me for my babysitting services of the evening and the subject did not occur to me either.

I went into the house and tried to go straight upstairs but my mother called to me. She came into the front hall, where I had not turned on the light, and she must have smelled me at once for she ran forward with a cry of pure amazement, as if she had seen somebody falling, and caught me by the shoulders as I did indeed fall down against the bannister, overwhelmed by my fantastic lucklessness, and I told her everything from the start, not omitting even the name of Martin Collingwood and my flirtation with the aspirin bottle, which was a mistake.

On Monday morning my mother took the bus over to Baileyville and found the liquor store and bought a bottle of Scotch whisky. Then she had to wait for a bus back, and she met some people she knew and she was not quite able to hide the bottle in her bag; she was furious with herself for not bringing a proper shopping-bag. As soon as she got back she walked out to the Berrymans'; she had not even had lunch. Mr. Berryman had not gone back to the factory. My mother went in and had a talk with both of them and made an excellent impression and then Mr. Berryman drove her home. She talked to them in the forthright and unemotional way she had, which was always agreeably surprising to people prepared to deal with a mother, and she told them that although I seemed to do well enough at school I was extremely backward—or perhaps eccentric—in my emotional development. I imagine that this analysis of my behaviour was especially effective with Mrs. Berryman, a great reader of Child Guidance books. Relations between them warmed to the point where my mother brought up a specific instance of my difficulties, and disarmingly related the whole story of Martin Collingwood.

Within a few days it was all over town and the school that I had tried to commit suicide over Martin Collingwood. But it was already all over school and the town that the Berrymans had come home on Saturday night to find me drunk, staggering, wearing nothing but my slip, in a room with three boys, one of whom was Bill Kline. My mother had said that I was to pay for the bottle she had taken the Berrymans out of my baby-sitting earnings, but my clients melted away like the last April snow, and it would not be paid for yet if newcomers to town had not moved in across the street in July, and needed a baby sitter before they talked to any of their neighbours.

My mother also said that it had been a great mistake to let me go out with boys and that I would not be going out again until well after my sixteenth birthday, if then. This did not prove to be a concrete hardship at all, because it was at least that long before anybody asked me. If you think that news of the Berrymans adventure would put me in demand for whatever gambols and orgies were going on in and around that town, you could not be more mistaken. The extraordinary publicity which attended my first debauch may have made me seemed marked for a special kind of ill luck, like the girl whose illegitimate baby turns out to be triplets: nobody wants to have anything to do with her. At any rate I had at the same time one of the most silent telephones and positively the most sinful reputation in the whole High School. I had to put up with this until the next fall, when a fat blonde girl in Grade Ten ran away with a married man and was picked up two months later, living in sin—though not with the same man—in the city of Sault Ste. Marie. Then everybody forgot about me.

But there was a positive, a splendidly unexpected, result of this affair: I got completely over Martin Collingwood. It was not only that he at once said, publicly, that he had always thought I was a nut; where he was concerned I had no pride, and my tender fancy could have found a way around that, a month, a week, before. What was it that brought me back into the world again? It was the terrible and fascinating reality of my disaster; *it was the way things happened*. Not that I enjoyed it; I was a self-conscious girl and I suffered a good deal from all this exposure. But the development of events on that Saturday night—that fascinated me; I felt that I had had a glimpse of the shameless, marvellous, shattering absurdity with which the plots of life, though not of fiction, are improvised. I could not take my eyes off it.

And of course Martin Collingwood wrote his Senior Matric that June, and went away to the city to take a course at a school for Morticians, as I think it is called, and when he came back he went into his uncle's undertaking business. We lived in the same town and we would hear most things that happened to each other but I do not think we met face to face or saw one another, except at a distance, for years. I went to a shower for the girl he married, but then everybody went to everybody else's showers. No, I do not think I really saw him again until I came home after I had been married several years, to attend a relative's funeral. Then I saw him; not quite Mr. Darcy but still very nice-looking in those black clothes. And I saw him looking over at me with an expression as close to a reminiscent smile as the occasion would permit, and I knew that he had been surprised by a memory either of my devotion or my little buried catastrophe. I gave him a gentle uncomprehending look in return. I am a grown-up woman now; let him unbury his own catastrophes.

Plot

Plot Factors Plot is the series of events that moves a narrative along. The opening of a story with a conventional plot introduces important characters and sets the stage for what happens. Then one or more conflicts develop, some pitting person against person, others setting characters against society, nature, fate, or themselves. Action gradually builds to a climax, where events take a decisive turn. The ending can do a number of things—clear up unanswered questions, hint at the future, state a theme, or reestablish some sort of relationship between two foes. The story "An Ounce of Cure" reveals a conflict between the narrator's desire to conform to the values of her conservative family and town, and her desire for greater independence and more worldly experience. In addition, the narrator experiences a conflict within herself over the defunct relationship with Martin Collingwood. When the narrator meets Martin Collingwood years later at funeral, and gives "a gentle, uncomprehending smile," we see that she has acquired adult wisdom and detachment.

To organize plots, writers use a number of techniques. In foreshadowing, for example, the writer hints at later developments, thus creating interest and building suspense. When the narrator of "An Ounce of Cure" mentions parenthetically that she hears a briskness in Kay Stringer's voice that she would recognize "years later, in the maternity ward," the reader is reassured by this hint that the narrator will overcome the embarrassment and indignity of this adolescent disaster with alcohol and will go on to become a parent herself.

When using a flashback, another organizational technique, the writer interrupts the flow of events to relate one or more happenings that occurred before the point at which the story opened, then resumes the narrative at or near the point of interruption. Near the beginning of "An Ounce of Cure," we read that the narrator's mother had a habit of emphasizing lessons with an air of "innocent pomposity" that "must have worked wonders with Mr. Berryman." The narrator then backs up to mention the evening she baby-sat for the Berrymans, and flashes back further to describe the short-lived romance with Martin Collingwood. A bit later the story narrates the baby-sitting incident at the Berrymans, after which it returns to detail the mother's visit to Mr. Berryman. Flashbacks fill in necessary information and either create or resolve suspense.

Not every plot unfolds in clear stages. Many modern stories lack distinct plot divisions and focus on psychological, not physical, conflicts. In extreme cases, writers may abandon the traditional plot structure and present events in a disorganized sequence that helps accomplish some literary purpose, such as reflecting the ambiguity and confusion of individual or historical perspective. Margaret Atwood's novel, *Alias Grace,* fits this mould. To dramatize the shifting complexity of history, Atwood develops her first person narrative with letters, poems, and excerpts from newspapers, transcripts, and books.

Writing About Plot   Of course, it is necessary to understand what happens in a narrative before you can analyze why or how it happens. However, most instructors will not want you to simply summarize what happens in the story in an academic paper, although they may ask you how the plot serves a larger purpose. Does it build suspense, mirror a character's confusion, shape a conflict, show how different lives can intersect, or help reveal a theme?

Before starting to write, answer the following questions:

What are the key events of the story? Do they unfold in conventional fashion or deviate from it in some way?

Does the writer use foreshadowing or flashback? If so, for what purpose?

Is the plot believable and effective, or does it display weakness of some sort?

Does it include any unique features?

Is it similar to the plot of another story or some type of story?

What plot features could I write about? What examples from the story would support my contentions?

As you prepare your analysis, determine the important events and how they relate to your topic. If the story is disjointed or incoherent, arrange the events so that they make sense and ask yourself why the writer chose that sequence. To mirror the main character's disordered state of mind? To show that life is chaotic and difficult to understand? Similarly, assess the reason for any use of foreshadowing or flashback. Does it build, create, or resolve suspense?

Not all plots are successful. A character's actions may not fit his or her personality or the situation. The plot might be too hard to follow or fail to produce the desired effect, as in a mystery where the clues are too obvious to create suspense. Or a writer might rely on chance or coincidence to resolve a conflict or problem: it's unacceptable to have the cavalry charge in gallantly out of nowhere and rescue the hero.

If there's something unique about the plot—perhaps a surprise event that works well—describe it and tell how it functions in the story, or perhaps you can compare the plot with one in another story in order to show how both develop some key insight.

The organization of a paper on plot is simple: you'll either present a thesis and then support it with examples taken from the text, or you'll write a comparison. Writing about "An Ounce of Cure," you could show how foreshadowing lets the reader know that the narrator will overcome her adolescent mishaps and will gain an adult perspective. More ambitiously, you might compare the ways in which the plots of this story and another Munro story, "How I Met My Husband," both unfold a movement from the naiveté of innocence to the wisdom of experience.

Point of View

Point-of-View Factors   The point of view is the vantage point from which the writer of a literary work views its events. A writer may adopt either a first-person or a third-person point of view. In *first-person* narration, someone in the work tells what happens and is identified by words like *I, me, mine,* and *my.* "An Ounce of

Cure" illustrates first-person narration. A *third-person* narrator stays completely out of the story and is never mentioned in any way.

The most common form of first-person narration features a narrator who takes part in the action. This technique puts the readers directly on the scene and is excellent for tracing the growth or deterioration of a character. Instead of participating in the action, the narrator may view it from the sideline, an approach that preserves on-the-scene directness and allows the narrator to comment on the characters and issues. The narrator, however, cannot enter the mind and reveal the unspoken thoughts of anyone else.

Third-person narrators don't participate in the action but can survey the whole literary landscape and directly report events that first-person narrators would know only by hearsay. Most third-person narrators reveal the thoughts of just one character. Others, with *limited omniscience,* can enter the heads of several characters, while still others display *full omniscience* and know everything in the literary work, including all thoughts and feelings of all characters. Omniscience allows the narrator to contrast two or more sets of thoughts and feelings and draw general conclusions from them.

Yet another type of third-person narration, *dramatic,* has emerged in contemporary fiction. A dramatic narrator, like a motion-picture camera, moves about recording the characters' actions and words but without revealing anyone's thoughts. Stories with surprise endings often use this technique.

Writing About Point of View   For a paper about point of view, ask and answer these questions:

> What point of view is used? Why is it used? What is the effect of having this particular character tell the story?
>
> If the story uses first-person narration, is the narrator reliable or unreliable? What textual evidence supports my answer? How does the narrator's vantage point affect the reader's interpretation of events or character?
>
> What focus would produce an effective paper? What textual evidence could support its discussion?

Various reasons might prompt the choice of a particular point of view. For example, an author might use the first person to show a character's mental deterioration. An unreliable first-person point of view may produce ironic ambiguity. A third-person narrator might provide a sense of impersonal distance, or allow glimpses into various characters' minds.

First-person narrators are sometimes unreliable; that is, they offer the reader a distorted or biased view of things. If there is a discrepancy between what the narrator says and what the work otherwise reveals, the narrator may seem naïve, psychologically warped, or too self-justifying to view events fairly. If so, speculate on the reasons. A naïve, unreliable narrator may be used, for example, to heighten the horror of events.

Although organization can vary, papers on point of view basically follow a cause-and-effect format, first identifying the point of view used and then demonstrating, with examples, its effect on the story and reader. In "An Ounce of Cure," first person narration provides a sense of vivid immediacy as the narrator recounts her experiences at the Berryman house, along with a sense of objectivity provided by the narrator's distance in time from her youthful follies.

Character

Character Factors   The characters in a literary work function in various ways. Some are centres of physical and mental action. Others furnish humour, act as narrators, provide needed information, act as *foils* who highlight more important characters by contrast, serve as symbols, or simply populate the landscape. In "An Ounce of Cure," the efficient and worldly Kay Stringer acts as a foil to the dreamy, naïve narrator. When the narrator is young, she at first sees Martin Collingwood as a symbol of male charisma and romance.

Writers present characters in several ways. Some tell the reader point-blank that a person is brave, stupid, self-serving, or the like. But most authors take an indirect approach by indicating how their characters look and act, what they think and say, how they live, and how other characters regard them.

Flat, one-dimensional characters remain static; more complex, *round* characters mature, gain insight, or deteriorate in some telling way. The narrator of "An Ounce of Cure" changes and grows. As an adolescent, she romanticizes the brief relationship with Martin Collingwood, but as an adult, she views it with wry detachment.

Writing About Character   Start the process by asking yourself these questions:

What characters seem most intriguing and offer most potential for in-depth analysis?

Do the characters undergo any changes? If so, how and why do the changes occur?

What motivates the characters? Do any characters have conflicting, or unconscious motivations? How are the characters influenced by their society or cultural context?

What textual evidence could support my argument?

Usually, you'll write about the main character, referred to as the *protagonist*, but at times you might choose the chief adversary or a secondary character whose significance could easily be overlooked. When writing about a central character, it may be interesting to explore why or how a character changes, or does not change, from beginning to end.

Think hard about what motivates fictional characters to act as they do. If they are round characters, they may, like many of us, be subject to inner and outer pressures, or have conflicting desires and motivations. They may be limited by their gender, culture, or socio-economic class; they may gain, in the course of a narrative, a wider awareness or freedom to act. Start your paper by identifying your character's role or personality; then back your contention with illustrations that support it, possibly following the sequence in which the writer presents them. If a character changes, say so, tell why, and indicate the results of the change, again using supporting examples. Such a paper is usually a cause-and-effect analysis. Papers that examine two characters are essentially comparisons.

Setting

Setting Factors   Setting locates characters in a time, place, and culture so they can think, feel, and act against this background. Writers can generate feelings and moods by describing settings. Sunny spring landscapes signal hope or happiness, dark alleys are filled with foreboding, and thunderstorms suggest violent possibilities. Poetry, especially, uses setting to create mood. In "Cannery Town in August," Lorna Dee Cervantes combines images of tired, work-stained employees, a noisy workplace, and dismal streets to evoke an unpleasant setting.

> All night it humps the air.
> Speechless, the steam rises
> from the cannery columns. I hear
> the night bird rave about work
> or lunch, or sing the swing shift
> home. I listen, while bodyless
> uniforms and spinach specked shoes
> drift in monochrome down the dark
> moon-possessed streets. Women
> who smell of whiskey and tomatoes,
> peach fuzz reddening their lips and eyes—
> I imagine them not speaking, dumbed
> by the can's clamor and drop
> to the trucks that wait, grunting
> in their headlights below.
> They spotlight those who walk
> like a dream, with no one
> waiting in the shadows
> to palm them back to living.

Setting can also help reveal theme and character. The narrator's naïveté in "An Ounce of Cure" is emphasized by the setting—a conservative Canadian small town, and a family household where the rare drink of beer must be consumed outside.

Writing About Setting   Begin your search for a topic by identifying the settings in the story and then asking these questions about each one:

What are its key features?

What does it accomplish? create a mood? reveal a character? serve as a symbol? reinforce the story's point? How does it accomplish these things?

In what ways does it support or interfere with the story?

Does the setting seem realistic? If not, why not?

What focus would produce an effective paper? What textual evidence would support it?

How does setting interact with mood, or character, or theme? Do changes in the setting reflect changes in character or theme? If the setting remains the same, point out any shifts in the way the character views it.

What larger significance does the setting have? In writing about "An Ounce of Cure," you might argue that Munro uses setting to highlight a theme of initiation into adult experience. For support, you might show that while the family home seems innocent and protected, the school, the Berryman household, and the neighbouring town of Baileyville hold temptations and distractions that suggest adult experience.

Images and Symbols

Images appeal to our senses such as sight, hearing, touch, taste and smell. Writers may use images to evoke different emotions or reinforce a theme; in Timothy Findley's book *The Wars*, for example, the recurrent imagery of fire suggests the devastation of war and destructive passions. Writers may also use symbols: names, persons, objects, places, colours, or actions that have significance beyond their surface meaning. A symbol may be very obvious—as a name like Mr. Grimm, suggesting the person's character—or quite subtle, as an object representing a universal human emotion.

Some symbols are private and others conventional. A private symbol has special significance within a literary work but not outside it. Conventional symbols are deeply rooted in our culture, and almost everyone knows what they represent. We associate crosses with Christianity and limousines with wealth and power. In "An Ounce of Cure," the narrator's first kiss from a boy seems a conventional symbol of experience, while the liquor bottles on the counter seem a more private symbol of dangerous allure.

Whether or not a recurring item is a symbol depends upon its associations. In Tomson Highway's play *Rez Sisters*, for instance, the game of bingo seems to symbolize alluring dreams of prosperity and a raucous community spirit; in Irving Layton's poem "Keine Lazarovitch" about his mother, the mother's dark eyebrows seem to symbolize vanity, beauty, dignity, and strength.

Writing About Symbols   When you examine the symbols in a literary work, think about these questions:

> What symbols are used and where do they appear?
>
> Are they private or conventional?
>
> What do they appear to mean?
>
> Do any of them undergo a change in meaning? If so, how and why?
>
> Which symbol(s) could I discuss effectively?
>
> What textual evidence would support my interpretation?

To locate symbols, read the literary work carefully, looking for items that seem to have an extended meaning. You might, for example, discover that the cracked walls of a crumbling mansion symbolize some character's disordered mental state or that a voyage symbolizes the human journey from birth to death. Sometimes a symbol changes meaning during the course of a work. A woman who regards her lover's large, strong hands as symbols of passion may, following an illness that leaves him a dangerous madman, view them as symbols of danger and brute strength. Note any changes you discover, and suggest what they signify.

A word of caution: don't let symbol hunting become an obsession. Before you assert that something has a different and deeper meaning than its surface application, make sure the evidence in the work backs up your claim.

Irony

Irony Factors   Irony signals some discrepancy between appearance and reality, between what is expected and what actually happens, or between what a character believes and what the reader knows is true. Sometimes a character says one thing but means something else. The critic who, tongue in cheek, says that a clumsy dancer is "poetry in motion" speaks ironically.

Irony also results when the reader or a character recognizes something as important, but another character does not. In "An Ounce of Cure," irony results from the discrepancy between the narrator's tragic view of her broken romance with Martin Collingwood and the mother's matter-of-fact dismissal of it: "'Well so much the better for that. I never saw a boy so stuck on himself." Irony may also result from a discrepancy between what the reader knows and what the character knows, as when the girl in "An Ounce of Cure" keeps drinking straight liquor in the mistaken notion that the alcohol is not affecting her yet.

Writing About Irony   Start by answering these questions:

Where does irony occur? How is it created?

What does it accomplish?

What could my thesis be, and how could I support it?

In probing for irony, check for statements that say one thing and mean something else, situations in which one character knows something that another doesn't, and contrasts between the ways characters should and do behave. Also, tell the reader what the irony accomplishes. In "An Ounce of Cure," it is ironic that someone as ordinary as Martin Collingwood should inspire such emotional turmoil, or again that someone as sheltered and unsophisticated as the narrator should develop one of "the most sinful reputations in the whole high school." These ironies are central to the theme of maturation in the story.

Theme

Theme Factors   The theme of a literary work is its controlling idea, some observation or insight about life or the conditions and terms of living, such as the prevalence of evil, the foolishness of pride, or the healing power of love. Many literary works suggest several themes: sometimes one primary motif and several related ones, sometimes a number of unrelated motifs. Theme is central to a work of literature; frequently all of the other elements help develop and support it.

On occasion, the writer or a character states the theme directly. Mrs. Alving, the main character in Henrik Ibsen's play *Ghosts,* notes that the dead past plays a powerful and evil role in shaping human lives:

> . . . I am half inclined to think that we are all ghosts, Mr. Manders. It is not only what we have inherited from our fathers and mothers that exists again in us, but all sorts of old dead ideas and all kinds of old dead beliefs and things of that kind. They are not actually alive in us; but there they are dormant, all the same, and we can never be rid of them.

Ordinarily, though, the theme remains unstated and must be deduced by examining the other elements of the literary work.

Writing About Theme   Before you begin writing, ask and answer these questions:

> What are the themes of this work? Are they obvious or subtle? Which of these should I write about?
>
> How is a particular theme revealed through imagery, action, character, or other elements?
>
> How does a particular theme relate to other elements in the work?

Check the comments of the characters and the narrator to see whether they refer to themes directly. If they don't, assess the interaction of characters, events, settings, symbols, and other elements to determine them.

A paper on theme is basically an argument, first presenting an interpretation and then supporting it with textual evidence. You might argue that the theme of "An Ounce of Cure" is the movement from youthful romanticism to adult realism. For support, you could cite the narrator's response to her first kiss from Martin Collingwood, her exaggerated response to the break-up, her unrealistic expectations about what alcohol will do to her; and then show how she has become a down-to-earth, respectable member of the community by the end, as shown in her calm glimpse of Martin Collingwood at a funeral. In addition, you might argue a related theme: youthful mistakes may be a necessary prelude to adult wisdom.

■ Ethical Issues

When you write about literature, you'll need to be aware of certain ethical considerations. Imagine someone reading only part of a short story and then writing a scathing analysis that suggests he has read the entire work. Imagine a thematic analysis of a novel that deliberately ignores large sections of the text in order to develop a twisted interpretation about the evils of capitalism. Imagine citing atypical quotations from the heroine of a play that deliberately create a distorted impression of her character. To help fulfill your ethical responsibility, ask and answer the following questions.

- Have I read the entire work carefully?

- Is my interpretation supported by most of the textual evidence? Does it avoid deliberate distortion?

- Have I avoided using quotations that are atypical or taken out of context?

- Is my interpretation fair to the text rather than distorting events to promote an agenda?

■ Writing a Paper on Literature

The Writing Procedure

Focusing, gathering information, organizing, writing, revising, and editing—the same procedure leads to success in a literature paper as in any other type.

First, make sure you *understand the assignment*. Let's assume you have been asked to do the following:

> Write an essay of about 700–750 words on how one of the literary elements in Alice Munro's story "An Ounce of Cure" relates to theme. For instance, you could show how character, setting, symbols, or irony helps illumine theme.

For this assignment, you realize that you are being asked to examine how one of the literary elements of fiction relates to a larger meaning in the story.

Next, *decide upon a suitable topic*. For papers on literature, your best approach is to reread the work carefully and then reflect on it. As you do this for the assignment on "An Ounce of Cure," you find yourself thinking about the character of the narrator. In class, you have touched on the theme of maturation in the story, and you are curious about what the story shows about growing up. The story reminds you of a somewhat similar incident from your own adolescence that you still feel embarrassed about. You wonder how the narrator has come to view her younger self with such a mixture of affection, humour, and distance. You decide to write about her character, and how it develops.

To complete the next stage, *gathering information*, read the story again, listing all pertinent information you can find about the character's development. Your efforts might yield these results:

1. Mother views her with despair, but there is hint that nothing terrible will happen, as mother hopes for "lesser rather than greater disaster" (434).*

2. Once she is kissed, narrator does not want to wash the kiss off (434).

3. When she sees Collingwood playing Mr. Darcy in the school play, she watches play with anguish, digging nails into friend's palm (435). Can't see Collingwood as just "a high-school senior."

4. Talks of her misery and "preposterous emotions" after the break-up (435).

5. Is so miserable she takes Aspirins to kill herself, but stops after six aspirins (435).

6. Does not go to spring dance because only Millerd Crompton asked her, but can watch boys and hear music: "oh, song of my aching heart" (436).

7. Berryman living room provides a stage for her emotions (436).

8. Says she decided to get drunk, then corrects herself (436).

9. Drinking whisky is like taking "the witch's crystal potion" (436).

*Page references from Munro, Alice. "An Ounce of Cure" in *The Bedford Introduction to Literature*. 5th ed. Ed. Michael Meyer. Boston: Bedford Press, 1999. 434–41.

10. Since she is disappointed not to feel much at first, she drinks more (436–37).

11. When Kay Stringer comes over with boys, she lies down passively (438).

12. When she tries to walk straight, she makes fun of herself before the others (439).

13. After Mr. Berryman takes her home, she confesses everything to her mother, "overwhelmed" by her lucklessness (440).

14. Story becomes a scandal in the school and town but is forgotten after new scandal arises (440–41).

15. Says that there was "a splendidly unexpected" result of this affair: she got over Martin Collingwood (441).

16. She comes back into the world through the "reality of her disaster," a sense of the absurdity of one of life's plots (441).

17. Sees Collingwood later at a funeral, but gives him a "gentle, uncomprehending look in return" (441). She claims to be a "grown-up woman now."

List in hand, you are now ready to organize your information. As you examine the items on your list, you start to realize that the narrator changes in the story from romanticizing and exaggerating her emotions to being more of a realist. To reflect your discovery, you prepare a formal topic outline

I. Evidence that girl romanticizes when young
   A. Early stage of romance with Collingwood
      1. Does not first wash kiss off
      2. Watches Collingwood play Mr. Darcy with great anguish
      3. Takes six Aspirins after break-up
   B. Incident while baby-sitting
      1. Living room provides "stage for her emotions"
      2. Drinking alcohol is like "drinking witch's potion"
      3. Makes fun of herself in front of others

II. Evidence girl changes later
   A. Aftermath of incident at Berrymans
      1. Story becomes a scandal in town
      2. Scandal gets erased by new town scandal
      3. Girl must pay for bottle of liquor as punishment
      4. She gets over Collingwood
   B. Maturation and distance later
      1. She comes back to the world "through the reality of her disaster"
      2. Gives Collingwood a gentle smile
      3. Is grown-up woman now

The next stage, *developing a thesis statement,* will be much easier now that you have an outline. After thinking about the outline for a while, you draft the following sentence:

> The story "An Ounce of Cure" shows how the narrator's youthful self-conscious romanticism gives way to an adult realism and wry detachment.

Drawing on your notes and following your outline, you now *write a first draft* of your essay, and then follow up with the necessary revising and editing. In addition, you review the story and verify your interpretation.

As you *prepare your final draft,* follow these guidelines.

Handling Quotations   In order to make your case, you need to support your claims with relevant quotations from the text. Quotations should be used when necessary, but not to excess. Cite brief, relevant passages to support key ideas, but fight the urge to quote huge blocks of material. Set up the quotation by cueing your reader as to the context of the quotation (who says it, to whom, when, where, and why) and alert the reader to the significance of the quotation. Do not assume that the point of the quotation is obvious. Introduce the quotation, and elaborate on its significance. Place short quotations, less than five lines long, within quotation marks and run them into the text. For longer passages, omit the quotation marks and indent the material ten spaces from the left-hand margin. When quoting poetry, use a slash mark (/) to show the shift from one line to the other in the original: "A honey tongue, a heart of gall, / Is fancy's spring, but sorrow's fall." Pages 350–353 provide added information on handling quotations.

Documentation   Document ideas and quotations from outside sources by following the guidelines on pages 345–353.

If your instructor wants you to document quotations from the work you're writing about, include the information within parentheses following the quotations. For fiction, cite the page number on which the quotation appeared: (83). For poetry, cite the word "line" or "lines" and the appropriate numbers: (lines 23–24). For plays, cite act, scene, and line numbers, separated by periods: (1.3.18–19). When discussing a work of fiction not in your textbook, identify the book you used as your source. Your instructor can then easily check your information. In short papers like the one below, internal documentation is often omitted.

Tense   Write your essay in the present rather than the past tense. Say "In *The Sound and the Fury,* William Faulkner uses four narrators, each of whom provides a different perspective on the events that take place," not ". . . William Faulkner used four narrators, each of whom provided a different perspective on the events that took place."

Example Student Essay on Literature

Maturation in "An Ounce of Cure"

1   Alice Munro's short story "An Ounce of Cure" shows the theme of maturation. As a teenage girl, the unnamed narrator seems more in love with her own emotions than with the supposed object of her affections, a certain Martin Collingwood. Her anguish when her brief relationship is broken off leads her to a foolish experiment with alcohol one night while she is baby-sitting. In the conservative small town where this story is set, her drinking gives rise to a scandal that is forgotten only when a bigger scandal erases the town's memory of her folly. By the end of the story, we see that the adult narrator has grown out of her early romanticism and become more of a realist.

2   As a teenager, the narrator's reaction to the first boy who takes notice of her suggests her immaturity. The narrator seems far more interested in the idea of romance than in Martin Collingwood as a person. When Collingwood kisses her, she is careful not to wash her face "that night or the next morning, in order to keep the imprint of those kisses intact." After the relationship is broken off, she is "overcome with pain and delight" to see Collingwood playing the role of Mr. Darcy in a school play. As an adult, the narrator can see her emotions as "preposterous," but as an adolescent, she has no such objectivity. The intensity of her anguish leads her into a swamp of emotion where she spends a great deal more time daydreaming, "thinking about Martin Collingwood--yes, pining and weeping for him" as she ever spent with him. She even flirts with the impulse toward suicide as she starts taking Aspirins from the bathroom cabinet, but stops herself after taking six. The tragic intensity the girl feels over this broken off relationship seems to reflect her lack of perspective.

3   When she is asked to baby-sit for the Berrymans, she has even more chance to dramatize and exaggerate her emotions. In contrast to her home, where "the life of the emotions" tended to get buried under everyday clutter, the Berrymans' "big softly lit room, with its green and leaf-brown colours, made an uncluttered setting for the development of the emotions, such as you would get on a stage."

The word "stage" suggests that she imagines herself as the romantic
heroine of a play or opera. Her naiveté is brought out more when
she goes into the kitchen and sees liquor bottles on the counter
that look "about half full of gold," and seems to enter the dreamy
state of a children's fairy tale. She compares herself to the
"Little Mermaid drinking the witch's crystal potion." She does not
know enough to dilute the whisky, and when the alcohol does not
take immediate effect, she pours out more. The reader, like the
adult narrator telling the story, recognizes her immaturity, what
she herself refers to later as "disastrous innocence."

4   Her handling of this disaster is further proof of her adolescent
immaturity. When she calls two girls over, they bring three boys
who clean up the mess in the house, then start dancing to the
radio. When one of the boys sits beside her and starts patting her
leg "through the crocheted throw," she reacts with discomfort and
nervousness. When she starts to walk, and lurches a little, she immediately makes fun of herself, exaggerating her drunkenness like a
clown. Yet when the Berrymans suddenly open the front door, the
evening that started on a note of tragic melodrama becomes transformed into "a well-organized farce." At home later, she confesses
everything to her mother, and a suitable punishment is found--
paying for the bottle of liquor the mother bought to compensate
the Berrymans.

5   The ending of the story shows that the narrator eventually over-
comes the embarrassment of what turns into a town scandal and gains
maturity. Just as the memory of the scandal fades in the town when
it is erased by the news of another, more interesting scandal, the
narrator manages to get "completely over Martin Collingwood." She
reflects later that what brought her back into the world again was
"the terrible and fascinating reality" of her "disaster; it was the
way things happened." She seems to have moved away from her early
romanticizing, where she saw herself as a character in a story, to
a sense of reality, where "the plots of life, though not of fiction, are improvised." She no longer seems to see her experience
as tragic, but as an example of "shameless, marvellous, shattering
absurdity."

6   When we read that the narrator sees Martin Collingwood years
later, and gives him "a gentle, uncomprehending look," we recognize

that the narrator has come a long way from her youthful romanticism. She says calmly, "I am a grown-up woman now; let him unbury his own catastrophes." By telling her story, the narrator has perhaps unburied it, but now she can let it fade into her own past as she gets on with her adult life. As readers who have no doubt suffered through our own adolescent trials, we can appreciate the way Alice Munro shows that we mature to become respectable members of adult society, looking at our younger selves with sympathy and humour.

Including the Views of Others

Obviously you are not the first one to write about an established piece of literature. To help deepen your understanding, your instructor may ask you to draw upon various sources that analyze the work you are discussing.

As you read these secondary sources, jot down any insights you find helpful. Be sure to record the name of the author and the source so that you can document appropriately and therefore avoid plagiarism. (For an explanation of plagiarism and when you need to document a source, see "Avoiding Plagiarism" in Chapter 20.) Keep track of where you disagree or have a different insight. Some students keep a reading journal in which they record useful quotes or information about both the piece of literature and the secondary source.

When you write the paper, you can synthesize (see pages 64–65) the views of the critics you've read and offer them as additional support for your view. Alternatively, you might summarize the conclusions, or perhaps the conflicting views, of critics and then offer your own observations along with appropriate support. Think of writing in response to others' views as entering a conversation with friends about a good book; they have their opinions, but your insights will add something to the discussion.

Research Guide

Much of your academic and workplace writing will require some type of research—obtaining information from one or more sources to help achieve your writing purpose. The nature of your writing task and the demands of the situation determine the format you use and the way you document your sources.

This section of the text explores in detail the research tools and procedures you will use to develop various types of papers and reports. Sometimes you'll draw upon books, magazines, newspapers, and other printed sources, as well as electronic sources, in order to prepare a longer library research paper; at other times you'll do the same for shorter papers. Still other situations call for using primary research—the type that you plan and carry out yourself—to accomplish your purpose. The three chapters in this section will help you to meet these writing demands.

Chapter 19 explains how to choose a suitable library research topic and then focuses on carrying out the necessary steps to write a research paper. The chapter includes a continuing case history that leads to a finished paper complete with margin notes that will provide guidance as you prepare your own paper.

Chapter 20 shows how to prepare correct references for your paper's bibliography. It also shows the correct formats for references within the body of the paper, explains how to handle quotations, and offers guidelines for avoiding plagiarism.

Chapter 21 explains and illustrates the most common types of primary research strategies—interviews, questionnaires, and direct observations. In each case, student models, annotated with margin notes, embody the key features of that strategy.

Together, the material in these three chapters should provide all the information you'll need to complete your writing assignments that require research.

The Library Research Paper

Scene: A dark, sinister-looking laboratory. In the centre of the stage stands a large laboratory bench crowded with an array of mysterious chemistry apparatus. Tall, cadaverous, and foreboding, Dr. Frankenslime leers as he pours the contents of a tube through a funnel and into a bubbling flask. A short, hunched-over figure looks on with interest. Suddenly the doctor spreads his arms wide and flashes a sardonic smile.

Frankenslime: Igor! At last! At last I've got it! With this fluid, I can control . . .

Research, yes. But not all researchers are mad scientists, or scientists, or even mad. You might not be any of these things, but no doubt you'll be asked to prepare a *library research paper* for your composition class. This assignment calls for you to gather information from a variety of sources and then to focus, organize, and present it in a formal paper that documents your sources. The procedure will familiarize you with the mechanics of documentation, and when you finish you'll have a solid grasp of your topic and pride in your accomplishment. In addition, the experience will help you learn how to meet the research demands of other courses and your job.

For many students, the thought of writing a research paper triggers feelings of anxiety and fears of drudgery. Some feel overwhelmed by the amount of material in a college library and the need to make a lengthy search for useful information.

Others doubt that they could have anything more to say about any topic they might choose: What's the point of simply rehashing what experts have already said much better? Still others are daunted by how much there might actually be to say about their topic.

But writing a research paper really isn't so formidable. You can acquaint yourself with the various library resources that will provide easy access to the information you need. Reading what others have written on a topic will give you a chance to draw your own conclusions. And as a writer you can limit your topic so that it doesn't balloon out of control.

Research writing is common both in the classroom and on the job. A history professor might require a long report on the causes of the War of 1812. A business instructor might ask you to trace the history of a company, evaluate an advertising campaign, or review the Japanese style of management. A building trades instructor might call for a short report that compares the effectiveness of several new insulating materials. At work, a marketing analyst might report on the development costs, sales potential, and competition for a product the company is considering introducing. An engineer might write a journal article that summarizes recent developments in plastic fabrication. A physical therapist might prepare a seminar paper that evaluates different exercise programs to follow arthroscopic surgery.

Whatever the writing project, let your purpose guide your research and determine the information you elect to use. When you write, the conclusions you have reached from thinking about what you have read and your purpose in communicating, not your notes, should dictate what you say.

■ Learning About Your Library

Before starting a library research paper, take time to familiarize yourself with your library. Many libraries offer guided tours, and almost all of them display floor plans that show where and how the books are grouped. If your library doesn't have tours, browse through it on your own and scan its contents. As you do, note the following features:

Card Catalogue: The card catalogue indexes the library's books and often most of its other holdings as well. Although most universities and colleges now have computerized card catalogues, a few use conventional catalogues, which consist of files of 3 x 5-inch cards. Pages 282–287 discuss computerized catalogues and pages 288–289 the conventional type.

Computerized Databases: These databases, like printed periodical indexes, provide listings of articles in magazines and newspapers, and some even provide the full text of the article. Information may be on compact discs or transmitted to the library by wire from another location. Pages 289–294 discuss databases.

Computers with Internet Access: These computers connect users to a worldwide network of organizations and individuals, providing access to an almost endless variety of information. Internet access to library catalogues and databases is widely available, allowing users to search and order materials online prior to picking them up at their local college, university, or public city library. Pages 294–298 discuss the Internet.

Stacks: These are the bookshelves that hold books and bound periodicals (magazines and newspapers). Stacks are either open or closed. Open stacks allow you to go directly to the books you want, take them off the shelf, and check them out. Closed stacks do not allow you direct access to shelved material. Instead, some staff member brings you what you want.

Periodical Area: Here you'll find current and recent issues of magazines and newspapers. If your topic calls for articles that have appeared within the last few months, you're likely to find them in this area.

Microfilm and Microfiche Files: Microfilm is a film strip bearing a series of photographically reduced printed pages. Microfiche is a small card with a set of photographically reduced pages mounted on it. Often, most of a library's magazine and newspaper collection is on film. Ask a librarian how to work the viewing machines. Once you can run them, you'll have access to many library resources.

Circulation Desk: Here's where you check materials in and out, renew books you want to keep longer, and pay overdue fines. If you can't find something you want, the desk clerk will tell you whether it's missing, on reserve, or checked out. If it's out, fill out a hold card, and the library will notify you when it is available.

Reserve Area: This area contains books that instructors have had removed from general circulation so students can use them for particular courses. Ordinarily, you can keep these books for only a few hours or overnight.

Reference Area: This area houses the library's collection of encyclopedias, periodical indexes, almanacs, handbooks, dictionaries, and other research tools that you'll use as you investigate your topic. You'll also find one or more reference guides—Eugene P. Sheehy's *Guide to Reference Books* (1996) for example—that direct you to useful reference tools. To ensure that these books are always available, they must be used in the library. Someone is usually on duty to answer questions.

■ Choosing a Topic

Instructors take different approaches in assigning library research papers. Some want explanatory papers, other want papers that address a two-sided question, and still others allow students a free choice. An explanatory paper takes no position but provides information that gives the reader a better grasp of the topic. For example, it may explain the key advantages of solar heating, thereby clearing up popular misconceptions. An argument paper, on the other hand, attempts to sway the reader toward one point of view—for instance, that solar heat is commercially feasible. Some instructors specify not only the type of paper but also the topic. Others restrict students to a general subject area, ask them to pick topics from lists, or give them free choice. If you have little say in the selection, take a positive view: At least you won't have to wrestle with finding a topic.

Whatever the circumstances, it's a good idea to follow a pacing schedule that establishes completion dates for the various stages of your paper. Such a timetable encourages you to plan your work, clarifies both your progress and the work remaining, and provides an overview of the entire project. You can use the following sample schedule as a guide, modifying the stages or adding other ones as necessary.

Sample schedule for a library research paper

Activity	Targeted Completion Date
Topic Selection	_____
Working Bibliography	_____
Research Question and Tentative Thesis	_____
Note Taking	_____
Working Outline	_____
First Draft	_____
Revised Drafts	_____ _____ _____
Date Due:	_____

Topics to Avoid

If you have free rein to pick your topic, how should you proceed? To begin, rule out certain types of topics.

- Those based entirely on personal experience or opinion such as "The Thrills I Have Enjoyed Waterskiing" or "Newfoundland Has More [or Less] Scenic Beauty than Ontario." Such topics can't be supported by library research. Don't hesitate, however, to include personal judgments and conclusions that emerge from your reading.

- Those fully explained in a single source. An explanation of a process, such as cardiopulmonary resuscitation, or the description of a place, such as the Gobi Desert, does not require coordination of materials from various sources. Although you may find several articles on such topics, basically they will repeat the same information.

- Those that are brand new. Often it's impossible to find sufficient source material about such topics.

- Those that are overly broad. Don't try to tackle such elephant-sized topics as "The Causes of World War II" or "Recent Medical Advances." Instead, slim them down to something like "The Advent of Jet Fighters" or "Eye Surgery with Laser Beams." The techniques discussed on pages 13–20 can help you reduce a topic to manageable size.

- Those that have been worked over and over, such as abortion and the legal drinking age. Why bore your reader with information and arguments that are all too familiar already?

EXERCISE   *Using the advice on topics to avoid, explain why each of the following would or would not be suitable for a library research topic:*

1. genetic counselling

2. neoconservatism

3. the home computer revolution

4. how last night's riot got started

5. building a rock garden

6. a Third World hot spot as described on the evening news

7. reforming the financing of provincial election campaigns

Drawing on Your Interests

Let your interests guide your choice. A long-standing interest in hockey might suggest a paper on the pros and cons of expanding the number of teams in the National Hockey League. An instructor's lecture might spark your interest in a historical event or person, an economic crisis, a scientific development, a sociological trend, a medical milestone, a political scandal, or the influences on an author. An argument with a friend might spur you to investigate latch-key children. A television documentary might arouse your curiosity about a group of aboriginal people. A recent article or novel might inspire you to explore the occult or some taboo.

Be practical in selecting a topic. Why not get a head start on a particular aspect of your major field by researching it now? Some management, marketing, or advertising strategy; the beginnings of current contract law; medical ethics—all of these topics, and many others, qualify. Think about your audience, the availability of information, and whether you can fit it into the guidelines for your paper.

To develop a focus for your paper, it's often helpful to brainstorm, skim encyclopedia articles and other materials, and utilize the branching or clustering technique. If you're exploring the topic of child abuse, preparing a clustering diagram like the one in Figure 19.1 can help you decide how to narrow your topic as well as provide a rough map of areas to research. The more you brainstorm, the richer your map will be. Brainstorming often results in a series of questions, perhaps based on the writing strategies discussed earlier, that will help guide your research. Often it is helpful to state your main research question, followed by a series of related questions that elaborate on it. From our cluster example, a student wishing to explore the topic of psychological abuse might develop the following set of questions:

What can be done to help victims of psychological abuse?

    What is psychological abuse?

    What long-term and short-term effects does it have on a child?

    How can a child living at home be helped?

        Are there services to help limit the abuse?

        Is family therapy an option?

            What is family therapy, and what does it do?

    What psychological help is available for an adult who experienced childhood abuse?

        What therapies work best?

        What do they do?

        How effective are they?

These questions make research easier. After all, the purpose of research is to answer questions. Later, as you examine source material, you will be seeking specific answers, not just randomly searching for information.

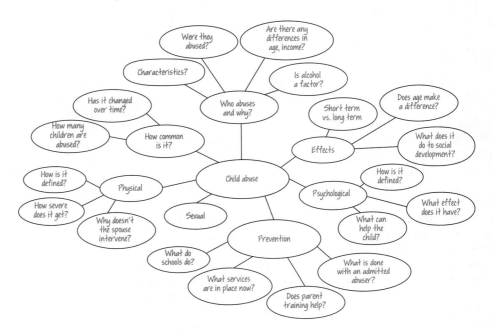

Figure 19.1 Clustering Diagram on Child Abuse

Encyclopedias are usually neither current enough nor sufficiently detailed to be major sources for a paper. They can, however, provide an overview of a topic's essential points and alert you to areas of controversy that you'll need to investigate in order to produce a thoughtful paper. You can consult both general and specialized encyclopedias, and other specialized publications are also available. If, for instance, you need material on a historical figure, you can check the *McGraw-Hill Encyclopedia of World Biography*. Your librarian can suggest other useful resources. Once you've found your focus, the branching technique will allow you to expand the list of items obtained by brainstorming.

More often than not, things won't fall neatly into place as you probe for a topic and then a focus. Don't be discouraged by false starts and blind alleys. Think of yourself as an explorer who will gradually become well versed in your chosen topic.

Case History

Keith Jacque was a first-year composition student majoring in criminal justice when he wrote the library research paper at the end of this chapter. The assignment was to write about a recent technological development or an innovative solution to a social problem. Intrigued by the possible solutions to the problem of prison overcrowding, Keith decided to explore several options: building more prisons, developing early release programs for the least dangerous criminals, setting up house-arrest programs verified by electronic monitoring systems, utilizing halfway houses, converting empty military bases into prisons, and re-evaluating legal codes to determine which offences should require incarceration. After a little thought, Keith realized that in order to develop his paper properly he would need to concentrate on only one option. Because he had recently watched a televised report on electronic monitoring and found it interesting, he decided to investigate this alternative.

To establish a focus for his paper, Keith drafted a series of questions suggested by the writing strategies discussed in Chapters 4–12. Here are the questions he developed:

> Could I *narrate* a brief history of electronic monitoring?
>
> Could I *describe* how a monitoring system works?
>
> Could I *classify* monitoring systems?
>
> Could I *compare* monitoring systems to anything?
>
> Could I explain the *process* involved in monitoring?
>
> What *causes* led to the development of monitoring?
>
> What kind of *effects* is monitoring likely to have?
>
> What systems best *illustrate* the essence of monitoring?
>
> Is there a widely accepted *definition* of electronic monitoring?
>
> Could I *argue* for or against the expanded use of monitoring?

These writing strategies can often help you narrow a subject down to a manageable topic.

For background reading, Keith consulted two general encyclopedias: the *Canadian Encyclopedia* and the *Encyclopaedia Britannica*. After preparing a list of possible entries that included "electronic monitoring," "electronic surveillance," "electronic incarceration," "home incarceration," and "house arrest," he began searching for those entries but found none of them. Next, he decided to look in more specialized publications. Not knowing how to proceed, he asked a reference librarian, who directed him to the latest editions of the *Encyclopedia of Crime and Justice* and the *McGraw-Hill Encyclopedia of Science and Technology*. These sources also contained no useful information.

At this point, drawing on what he had learned from his criminal justice instructor and the television report, Keith brainstormed in order to determine a possible focus for his paper. He came up with the following list:

1. Brief history of electronic monitoring
2. Technical problems in developing systems
3. Types of monitoring systems
4. Benefits of monitoring
5. Problems associated with monitoring

Upon reflection, Keith eliminated the second item because it would re-quire reading highly technical material, which he might not understand. The other items were interesting to him, and he believed that they would also interest his audience—fellow students at the vocationally oriented school he attended.

Next, Keith used branching to expand his list and guide his library search, concentrating on what he knew at this stage.

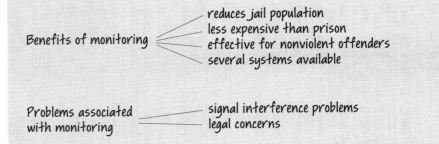

This case history continues on page 298.

■ Assembling a Working Bibliography

Once you have a topic, you're ready to see whether the library has the resources you'll need to complete the project. This step requires that you check additional reference tools and compile a working bibliography—a set of cards that list prom-ising sources of information. This section discusses these reference tools and how to use them.

Encyclopedias

What They Are   Encyclopedias fall into two categories, general and specialized. General encyclopedias, the *Canadian Encyclopedia* and the *Encyclopaedia Britannica*, for instance, offer articles on a wide range of subjects. Specialized encyclopedias cover one particular field, such as advertising or human behaviour. Here's a sam-pling of specialized encyclopedias:

Encyclopedia of Advertising
Encyclopedia of Education
Encyclopedia of Environmental Science

Encyclopedia of Human Behavior: Psychology, Psychiatry, and Mental Health
Encyclopedia of Social Work
Encyclopedia of World Art
Harper's Encyclopedia of Science
International Encyclopedia of the Social Sciences
McGraw-Hill Encyclopedia of Science and Technology

How to Use Them Encyclopedias are sometimes a convenient launching pad for your investigation because they provide an overview of the broad field your topic fits into. For a nonspecialized topic, like the impact of commercial television during the 1950s, check the articles on television in one or more general encyclopedias. For a specialized aspect of television, say the development of the picture tube, consult one or more specialized encyclopedias, such as *Harper's Encyclopedia of Science* and the *McGraw-Hill Encyclopedia of Science and Technology,* along with the general encyclopedias. During this search you'll re-encounter material you scanned while trying to focus on a topic.

Some instructors allow you to acknowledge encyclopedias as a source; others prohibit their use; and still others allow material from specialized, but not general, encyclopedias. As always, follow your instructor's wishes. If you will be using encyclopedia sources, jot down the following information for each note you take:

Title of article

Author(s) of article (Not always available. Sometimes only initials at the end of an article identify an author. In that case, check the list of contributors at the front of the first volume for the full name.)

Name of encyclopedia

Year of publication

For specialized encyclopedias, also include the number of volumes in the set, the encyclopedia editor, and the place of publication.

Most important, check for bibliographies at the ends of articles and copy down any reference that looks promising.

Computer-Based Encyclopedias Today, a number of encyclopedias, both general and specialized, are available on computer compact discs or over the Internet. They are easy to search and often allow you to search for a key phrase such as "Greek architecture." The results will guide you not only to articles devoted to your topic but also to others that refer to it, even if only in a paragraph. If you use an electronic encyclopedia, write down, in addition to the other source information, the publication medium, the name of the vendor (Microsoft, for example, for a Microsoft product), and the name and date of the electronic publication.

When you've finished your exploratory reading in encyclopedias, turn to the card catalogue and periodical indexes—the prime sources of information for library research papers.

Computerized Card Catalogue

What It Is A computerized card catalogue lists all the books in the library, usually along with other holdings like magazines, newspapers, government documents, and electronic recordings. It may also provide additional information, such as whether a book has been checked out and, if so, the return date. Some catalogues even include the holdings of nearby libraries. Books are usually catalogued using Library of Congress call numbers, although some libraries use the Dewey decimal system.

Several catalogue systems are available, all having similar terminals that consist essentially of a viewing screen and a keyboard on which to enter requests for information. Some terminals also have printers for copying material shown on the screen. To use the unit properly, read the instructions at the terminal or ask a librarian. Remember, a computer can't think. It can only match the string of letters you type to similar strings of letters in its database. If you misspell a word, you will not find any matches.

Most systems let you conduct searches by author, title, subject, and key terms—those appearing in book titles and descriptions. Typically, you'll begin by typing in a code—say A for "author," T for "title," S for "subject," and KT for "key term"—then an equal sign and your specific search request. Searching may require you to view a series of screens having increasingly specific information, with the final screen providing information about a single book. Figure 19.2 illustrates a two-screen subject search. Figures 19.3, 19.4, and 19.5 show the screens obtained in author, title, and key term searches. Note that all four screens provide identical information about the book. Most libraries have handouts and training programs that explain the different symbols and options of their specific system.

Often, a key term search (see Figure 19.5) can be the most helpful way to approach a topic. In this type of search, the computer checks the titles and descriptions of books for the key terms you enter and lists any that it finds. Different key terms will produce varying strings of articles, so it is a good idea to try different words or phrases for the same topic. For example, if you're searching for material on "electric cars," you might also try "electronic cars," "alternative fuels," and so on. Because such searches are very rapid, you can experiment with different combinations of terms to focus your search. If, for instance, you're asked to write a paper on some aspect of Japanese culture, you might investigate such combinations as "Japanese business," "Japan and education," and "Japanese feminists." Because key term searches allow you to use logical terms like *and, or, but,* and *not,* they are especially useful for narrowing a broad focus.

Obtaining the Books Start your search for useful books by looking up any promising titles found in encyclopedia bibliographies or other sources. Use the appropriate code and enter the title into the computer exactly. Once you've found the screen for a book that appears useful, write down any subject headings for it that appear on the screen. You can use these headings for a subject search.

Next, draw up a list of promising subject headings and check them in the computer. If you're investigating satanic cults, your headings might include "devil worship," "satanism," "diabolism," and "cult."

Successful subject and key term searches often turn up more book titles than a single screen can accommodate, a situation illustrated by the top screen in Figure 19.2.

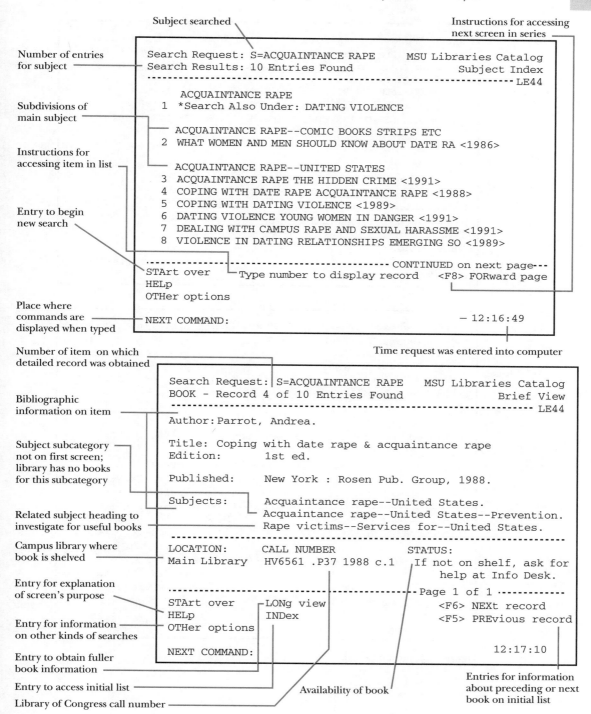

Subject searched

Instructions for accessing next screen in series

Number of entries for subject

Subdivisions of main subject

Instructions for accessing item in list

Entry to begin new search

Place where commands are displayed when typed

```
Search Request: S=ACQUAINTANCE RAPE      MSU Libraries Catalog
Search Results: 10 Entries Found                   Subject Index
----------------------------------------------------------- LE44
     ACQUAINTANCE RAPE
1  *Search Also Under: DATING VIOLENCE

   ACQUAINTANCE RAPE--COMIC BOOKS STRIPS ETC
2  WHAT WOMEN AND MEN SHOULD KNOW ABOUT DATE RA <1986>

   ACQUAINTANCE RAPE--UNITED STATES
3  ACQUAINTANCE RAPE THE HIDDEN CRIME <1991>
4  COPING WITH DATE RAPE ACQUAINTANCE RAPE <1988>
5  COPING WITH DATING VIOLENCE <1989>
6  DATING VIOLENCE YOUNG WOMEN IN DANGER <1991>
7  DEALING WITH CAMPUS RAPE AND SEXUAL HARASSME <1991>
8  VIOLENCE IN DATING RELATIONSHIPS EMERGING SO <1989>

---------------------------------------- CONTINUED on next page---
STArt over    Type number to display record   <F8> FORward page
HELp
OTHer options

NEXT COMMAND:                             - 12:16:49
```

Time request was entered into computer

Number of item on which detailed record was obtained

Bibliographic information on item

Subject subcategory not on first screen; library has no books for this subcategory

Related subject heading to investigate for useful books

Campus library where book is shelved

Entry for explanation of screen's purpose

Entry for information on other kinds of searches

Entry to obtain fuller book information

Entry to access initial list

Library of Congress call number

```
Search Request: S=ACQUAINTANCE RAPE   MSU Libraries Catalog
BOOK - Record 4 of 10 Entries Found              Brief View
--------------------------------------------------------- LE44
Author:Parrot, Andrea.

Title: Coping with date rape & acquaintance rape
Edition:    1st ed.

Published:    New York : Rosen Pub. Group, 1988.

Subjects:     Acquaintance rape--United States.
              Acquaintance rape--United States--Prevention.
              Rape victims--Services for--United States.
-----------------------------------------------------------
LOCATION:      CALL NUMBER           STATUS:
Main Library   HV6561 .P37 1988 c.1  If not on shelf, ask for
                                       help at Info Desk.

----------------------------------------Page 1 of 1 -----------
STArt over    LONg view              <F6> NEXt record
HELp          INDex                  <F5> PREvious record
OTHer options

NEXT COMMAND:                        12:17:10
```

Availability of book

Entries for information about preceding or next book on initial list

Figure 19.2 Subject Search
Screens courtesy of Michigan State University libraries' online "Magic" system.

```
Search Request: A=PARROT, ANDREA      MSU Libraries Catalog
Search Results: 3 Entries Found                  Subject Index
---------------------------------------------------------LE44
       PARROT ANDREA
   1   ACQUAINTANCE RAPE THE HIDDEN CRIME <1991>
   2   COPING WITH DATE RAPE ACQUAINTANCE RAPE <1988>
   3   HUMAN SEXUALITY CONTEMPORARY CONTROVERSIES <1984>




   -----------------------------------------------------------
STArt over     Type number to display record
HELp
OTHer options
                                            12:16:35

NEXT COMMAND:
```

```
Search Request: A=PARROT, ANDREA      MSU Libraries Catalog
BOOK - Record 2 of 3 Entries Found               Brief View
---------------------------------------------------------D3BB
Author:Parrot, Andrea.

Title: Coping with date rape & acquaintance rape
Edition:      1st ed.

Published:    New York : Rosen Pub. Group, 1988.

Subjects:     Acquaintance rape--United States.
              Acquaintance rape--United States--Prevention.
              Rape victims--Services for--United States.
   -----------------------------------------------------------
LOCATION:     CALL NUMBER          STATUS:
Main Library  HV6561 .P37 1988 c.1 If not on shelf, ask for
                                        help at Info Desk.
   ----------------------------------- Page 1 of 1 -----------
STArt over    LONg view              <F6> NEXt record
HELp          INDex                  <F5> PREvious record
OTHer options
                                            14:02:20

NEXT COMMAND:
```

Figure 19.3 Author Search

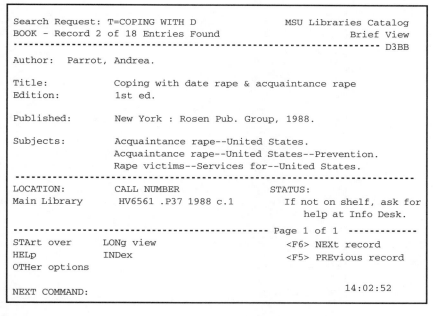

Repetition indicates that original title uses *&* instead of *and*

```
Search Request: T=COPING WITH D              MSU Libraries Catalog
Search Results: 18 Entries Found                       Title Index
------------------------------------------------------------- LE44
 1 COPING WITH DATE RAPE & ACQUAINTANCE RAPE. PARROT ANDREA <1988>
 2 COPING WITH DATE RAPE AND ACQUAINTANCE RAPE. PARROT ANDREA <1988>
 3 COPING WITH DATING VIOLENCE. RUE NANCY N <1989>
 4 COPING WITH DEATH. RAAB ROBERT A <1978>
 5 COPING WITH DEATH AND DYING AN INTERDISCIPLINARY APPROACH <1985>
 6 COPING WITH DEATH IN THE FAMILY. SCHNEIDERMAN GERALD <1979>
 7 COPING WITH DEATH ON CAMPUS <1985>
 8 COPING WITH DESTITUTION POVERTY AND RELIEF IN WESTERN EUROPE.
   MITCHISON ROSALIND <1991>
 9 COPING WITH DIFFICULT PEOPLE. BRAMSON ROBERT M <1981>
10 COPING WITH DIFFICULT TEACHERS. BERGREEN GARY <1988>
   COPING WITH DISABILITY INVENTORY A STUDY OF THE RELIABILITY AND
   VALIDITY OF AN INSTRUMENT DESIGNED TO MEASURE COPING B
11 KULKARNI MADHAV R <1985>

------------------------------------------- CONTINUED on next page --
STArt over      Type number to display record       <F8> FORward page
HELp
OTHer options

NEXT COMMAND:                                         12:15:07
```

```
Search Request: T=COPING WITH D              MSU Libraries Catalog
BOOK - Record 2 of 18 Entries Found                     Brief View
------------------------------------------------------------- D3BB
Author:   Parrot, Andrea.

Title:             Coping with date rape & acquaintance rape
Edition:           1st ed.

Published:         New York : Rosen Pub. Group, 1988.

Subjects:          Acquaintance rape--United States.
                   Acquaintance rape--United States--Prevention.
                   Rape victims--Services for--United States.
------------------------------------------------------------------
LOCATION:         CALL NUMBER            STATUS:
Main Library      HV6561 .P37 1988 c.1    If not on shelf, ask for
                                            help at Info Desk.

------------------------------------------- Page 1 of 1 ------------
STArt over     LONg view                   <F6> NEXt record
HELp           INDex                        <F5> PREvious record
OTHer options

NEXT COMMAND:                                         14:02:52
```

Figure 19.4 Title Search

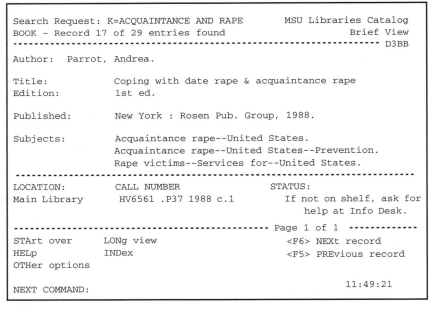

```
Search Request: K=ACQUAINTANCE AND RAPE        MSU Libraries Catalog
Search Results: 29 Entries Found                      Key Term Index
----------------------------------------------------------------- D3BB
     DATE  TITLE:                                    AUTHOR:
  15 1993  Beyond the legal definition: u <microfilm> Campbell, Rebecca M
  16 1993  Beyond the legal definition: understanding Campbell, Rebecca M
  17 1993  Coping with date rape & acquaintance rape  Parrot, Andrea
  18 1993  Date rape : the secret epidemic : what it  Boumil, Marcia M
  19 1993  When "I love you" turns violent : abuse in Johnson, Scott A
  20 1991  Acquaintance gang rape on campus           O'Sullivan, Chris S
  21 1991  Acquaintance rape : the hidden crime
  22 1991  Dating violence : young women in danger
  23 1991  Dealing with campus rape and sexual harass
  24 1990  The date rape epidemic : profitable myth   Anderson, James D
  25 1989  Coping with dating violence                Rue, Nancy N
  26 1989  Violence in dating relationships : emergin
  27 1988  Coping with date rape & acquaintance rape  Parrot, Andrea
  28 1988  I never called it rape : the Ms. report on Warshaw, Robin
  --------------------------------------------- CONTINUED on next page----
STArt over       Type number to display record      <F8> FORward page
HELp                                                 <F7> BACk page
OTHer options
                                                         11:14:18

NEXT COMMAND:
```

```
Search Request: K=ACQUAINTANCE AND RAPE        MSU Libraries Catalog
BOOK - Record 17 of 29 entries found                       Brief View
----------------------------------------------------------------- D3BB
Author:  Parrot, Andrea.

Title:           Coping with date rape & acquaintance rape
Edition:         1st ed.

Published:       New York : Rosen Pub. Group, 1988.

Subjects:        Acquaintance rape--United States.
                 Acquaintance rape--United States--Prevention.
                 Rape victims--Services for--United States.
--------------------------------------------------------------------
LOCATION:        CALL NUMBER              STATUS:
Main Library     HV6561 .P37 1988 c.1        If not on shelf, ask for
                                              help at Info Desk.

--------------------------------------------- Page 1 of 1 ------------
STArt over       LONg view                   <F6> NEXt record
HELp             INDex                        <F5> PREvious record
OTHer options
                                                         11:49:21

NEXT COMMAND:
```

Figure 19.5 Key Term Search

In this case, using a key designated at the bottom of the screen will let you review the rest of the list. With especially long lists, you may need to narrow your focus and start searching anew. For example, "Japan and education" might be narrowed to "Japan and primary education."

When a check of your subject headings yields nothing, don't give up. Perhaps your list doesn't include any headings that are actually used. To find the right headings, turn to the *Library of Congress Subject Headings,* if your library catalogues its books according to the Library of Congress system. If it uses the Dewey decimal system, then consult the *Sears List of Subject Headings.* If, for example, you're researching the subject of multiculturalism and your library uses the Library of Congress system, don't expect to find anything catalogued under that heading. Instead, as the *Subject Headings* guide shows, books on multiculturalism are catalogued under "Pluralism (social studies)."

When you have found a promising title, entering its number, or a command and the number, will call up a screen with relevant information. This is illustrated by the bottom screen in Figure 19.2. With some systems, this screen indicates whether the book is in the library or checked out and tells you how to proceed if you can't find it on the shelf. With other systems, you can get the information by entering a command. Some systems will even allow you to reserve a book by entering the request into the computer.

If your terminal has a printer, use it to make a copy of each promising reference. Otherwise, record the following information on an index card:

Author(s)
Title
Editor(s) and translator(s), as well as author(s) of any supplementary material
Total number of volumes (if more than one) and the number of the specific volume
    that you want to use
City of publication
Name of publisher
Date of publication

Also, copy the book's call number in the upper left-hand corner of the card.

Next, scan the books themselves. If your library stacks are closed, give the librarian a list of your call numbers and ask to see the books. If you can enter the stacks, locate the general areas where your books are shelved. Once you find a number range that includes one of your call numbers, follow the trail of guides on the book spines until you find your book. Spend a few extra minutes browsing in the general area of each book; you may discover useful sources that you overlooked in the card catalogue.

Skim each book's table of contents and any introductory material, such as a preface or introduction, to determine its scope and approach. Also check the index and note the pages with discussions that relate to your topic. Finally, thumb through any portions that look promising. If the book won't help you, throw away the card. If a book is missing from the shelf and the computer hasn't indicated that someone has checked it out, then it's probably on reserve. Check at the circulation desk; if the book is on reserve, go to that section and examine it there. If someone has checked the book out and the due date is some time away, perhaps a library nearby will have a copy.

Conventional Card Catalogue

What It Is Although their numbers are shrinking, conventional card catalogues are still used in some university and college libraries. A conventional card catalogue is a file of 3- x 5-inch cards that indexes all the books in the library and sometimes other holdings, such as magazines and newspapers. Some libraries have their catalogues on microfiche cards or microfilms, which are read with a special viewing device.

The card catalogue contains three kinds of cards—author, title, and subject—for each nonfiction item catalogued. Fiction has author and title cards only. Except for the top line, which differs for the different types of cards, all cards for the same book are identical. Figure 19.6 shows a typical author card. The cards are filed alphabetically, and the three kinds may be filed together, separately, or in some other manner, for example, title and author cards together, subject cards elsewhere. In alphabetizing the cards, librarians follow certain standard practices.

1. Title and subject cards are filed alphabetically according to the first word that is not an article (*a, an, the*).
2. Cards are filed word by word rather than strictly letter by letter. Thus, "Chicken and Turkey Tapeworms" precedes "Chicken Beacon," and "Chicken Raising Made Easy" precedes "The Chicken-bone Special."
3. "Mc" names are filed under "Mac."
4. Numbers and abbreviations are filed alphabetically as if they were spelled out. For example, the title card for the novel *Mr. Bridge* is filed under "Mister."
5. Names of people precede identical names of places and things. Thus, "Snow, C. P., *The Masters*" comes before *"Snow at Evening."*

Knowing these conventions will lessen tedious thumbing through the cards.

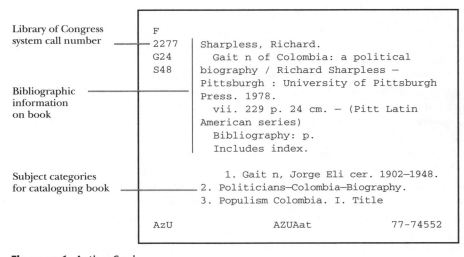

Figure 19.6 Author Card

How to Use It   Follow the procedure given on pages 282–287 for computerized card catalogues, making any needed modifications.

EXERCISE

1. **Select five of the following topics. Go to the card catalogue and find one book about each. List each book's call number, author, title, publisher, and date of publication. Because subject headings may vary, investigate related categories, if necessary, to find an entry. To illustrate, if you find nothing under "mountaineering," check "mountain climbing" or "backpacking."**

   1. Adolescence
   2. Balkan Peninsula
   3. Child abuse
   4. Flying saucers
   5. Mohandas Gandhi
   6. Internet
   7. Doris Lessing
   8. Mass transit
   9. Mountaineering
   10. Origami
   11. Plains of Abraham
   12. Parapsychological research
   13. Regional planning
   14. Glenn Gould
   15. Spin fishing
   16. Taxidermy
   17. Telecommunication
   18. Underwater exploration
   19. Volcanoes

2. **Provide your instructor with a list of the books you found that appear useful for developing your paper's topic. For each book, furnish the information specified in Exercise 1 above, along with a brief note indicating why you think the book will be useful.**

Periodical Indexes

What They Are   Periodical indexes catalogue articles in magazines and newspapers. Indexes may be in book form, on microfilm or microfiche, or computerized. Some are offered in two or more forms. Computerized indexes, called *databases,* are available to libraries through subscription. Depending upon the particular database, information may be furnished on compact discs or transmitted via wire from a mainframe computer to the library. The term *CD-ROM* (compact disc, read-only memory) designates the first type of system, and *online* designates the second type. Databases are accessed through terminals equipped with a keyboard and a viewing screen. Some have printers that can supply lists of references and even copies of articles.

In some cases, terminals are intended for student operation; others are operated by library personnel. If you use a database, you may have to pay a service fee, but it's likely to be small.

Updated frequently, sometimes every week, periodical indexes provide access to information that hasn't yet found its way into books and perhaps never will. Their listings allow you to examine new topics, follow developments in older ones, and explore your topic in greater depth than you could by using books alone. In short, indexes help you avoid doing a superficial paper.

The *Readers' Guide to Periodical Literature,* available since 1900 in printed form, is now available online and on compact discs. The *Guide* indexes the material in over 200 widely circulated magazines—articles by subject and author and other categories by title and author. The *Guide* is especially useful for finding material on historical events and on social, political, and economic developments. The *Guide* also includes scientific, technical, and even literary articles intended for a general audience rather than specialists, but such articles do not include all the available research.

The first pages in the printed version of the *Guide* identify the abbreviations used for the magazines indexed. Figure 19.7 shows the arrangement of the index and the "see also" cross-references that direct you to related subject headings.

The *Magazine Index,* available on microfilm or online, indexes some four hundred popular publications by author, title, and subject. Updated monthly, it covers a five-year period and includes references to articles no more than two weeks old. The viewing machines for units using microfilm resemble small television sets and have motorized controls that allow swift movement through the filmstrip. Accompanying the viewer are coded reels of microfilm containing the indexed articles, together with a reader/printer that allows you to read articles and obtain printed copies. Your librarian will demonstrate how these machines work. The producers of the index also publish a listing of recent articles on twenty to thirty current topics.

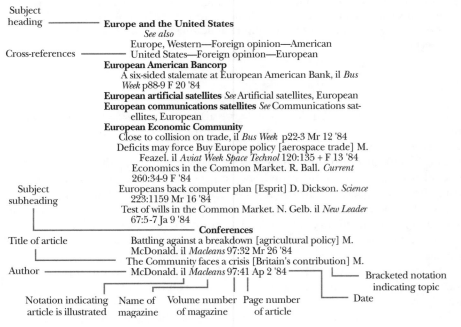

Figure 19.7 Arrangement of the Index

From *Readers' Guide to Periodical Literature,* May, 1984. Copyright ©1984 by the H. W. Wilson Company. Reproduced by permission.

The *National Newspaper Index* covers five national newspapers in the U.S.: the *Christian Science Monitor,* the *Los Angeles Times,* the *New York Times,* the *Wall Street Journal,* and the *Washington Post.* It is available on microfilm, on compact discs, and online. Each monthly issue covers two-and-one-half years of references, and back issues can be obtained on microfiche cards. Microfilm units have the same kind of viewer as the microfilm version of the *Magazine Index.*

NewsBank may be your best bet for a topic of regional interest. This CD-ROM database covers more than five hundred newspapers in the United States and Canada, indexing articles on politics, economics, business, the environment, and the entertainment world. It also offers the full text of many articles. A loose-leaf notebook version of *NewsBank,* accompanied by the articles on microfiche cards, is also available.

Two helpful periodical indexes that refer exclusively to Canadian sources are the *Canadian News Disc* and the *Canadian Business and Current Affairs Index.* The *Canadian News Disc* compiles articles from eleven major Canadian daily newspapers, including *The Globe and Mail, The Toronto Star,* and *The Vancouver Sun.* The *Canadian Business and Current Affairs Index* covers most major Canadian magazines and periodicals. Both of these indexes, and others like them, are accessible online at most university, college, and municipal libraries.

Periodical databases allow you to search quickly and effectively for articles in journals, magazines, and newspapers. Some databases such as *ERIC* (Educational Resources Information Center) or *Medline* (National Library of Medicine) give you access to citations of articles appearing in professional journals in a specific area. These articles, however, are usually aimed at a specialized audience and may be difficult to comprehend. Perhaps the best place to start a search is with a general periodical database such as *First Search* or *InfoTrac.* These databases provide access to listings of articles, arranged and subdivided by subject, that have appeared in over a thousand magazines and newspapers, including the entries in various other indexes. Articles are sometimes accompanied by abstracts—brief summaries of the articles' main points—and in some cases the full articles may be available on screen. *A word of caution: Don't mistake an abstract for the full article; an abstract is a 200–300 word summary of a journal article and should not be used as a source. Always take notes on the full article.* These databases are easy to operate. Your library probably has handouts that explain how to use your school's system and probably offers training sessions as well.

Because most periodical indexes, like *InfoTrac,* are organized around subject headings, it's a good idea to try a variety of subject terms since each will yield different articles. If your entry matches a subject heading or you are referred to a cross-reference, the computer will use a series of screens to direct you to a list of articles.

Along the way, one of the screens may list subdivisions of the request being searched, as in the following example:

Acquaintance Rape, subdivisions of

—analysis

—cases

—investigation

—laws, regulations, etc.
—media coverage
—moral and ethical aspects
—personal narratives
—prevention
—psychological aspects
—research
—social aspects
—statistics
—studying and teaching
—usage

Such a listing can uncover facets of your topic that you hadn't considered and that might enrich your final paper. For example, the subdivision "personal narratives" might contain an experience that would provide a powerful opening for the paper. Similarly, articles catalogued under "statistics" could provide information on the scope of the acquaintance rape problem.

If your entries don't match a subject heading, the computer may automatically switch to a key term search (see page 286) and display a list of articles. If your subject yields only a few articles, you can initiate a key term search that may uncover more. Just follow the instructions for beginning the search and then enter your key term. If, for example, your topic is "teenage suicide," type "teenagers and suicide" onto the screen that's already showing and press the search or enter key. The computer will check titles and abstracts for the key terms and provide a list of the corresponding articles. Allow ample time to explore a number of possibilities. If you try several terms related to your topic, you will find a wider variety of articles that serve your purpose.

The final result of any search is a listing of articles like the following one, obtained through *InfoTrac,* for the "psychological aspects" subdivision of the subject heading "acquaintance rape":

```
An open letter to a rape victim. Gail Elizabeth Wyatt.
Essence,
April 1992 v22 n12 p80(3). Mag. Coll.: 64B0749.
—Abstract Available—
Holdings: AS Magazine Collection

Between seduction and rape. (date rape) Kathy Dobie. Vogue,
Dec 1991 v181 n12 p154(4). Mag. Coll.: 62G6035.
—Abstract Available—
Holdings: AS Magazine Collection

Rape on campus: is your daughter in danger? Kate
Fillion.Chatelaine, August 1991 v64 n8 p33(5). Mag. Coll.:
61A5794.
Holdings: AS Magazine Collection
```

This listing shows that all three magazines are available in the library and that two articles are abstracted in the computer. (If the database provides the full text of an article, the notation "full text available" will appear after the citation.) The coded notation "Mag. Coll." indicates that the magazine is available on microfilm. The first two numbers and the letter in the code identify the number of the microfilm cassette. The remaining numbers indicate the microfilm page on which the article starts. The exact listings of your system may be somewhat different from what's shown here; the same kind of information, however, should be available. Besides the previously mentioned specialized indexes, many others are available that you could use to supplement your search of general indexes. Here is a brief sampling of some of them:

Applied Science and Technology Index, 1958–date (indexed by subject)

Education Index, 1929–date (indexed by subject and author)

Humanities Index, 1974–date (indexed by subject and author)

International Index to Periodicals, 1907–1964 (indexed by subject and author; entitled *Social Sciences and Humanities Index,* 1965–1974, and then separated into the *Humanities Index* and the *Social Sciences Index*)

Social Sciences and Humanities Index, 1965–1974 (indexed by subject and author)

Social Sciences Index, 1975–date (indexed by subject and author)

All come in printed form, and most are also available on compact discs and online.

With periodical indexes, as with the card catalogue, don't give up if a subject heading you're exploring yields few or no entries. Instead, explore related headings. For example, if your topic is teenage marriages, look also under "adolescence," "divorce," "teen pregnancies," and the like. Browse through the system and try a variety of options. Use this as an opportunity to gain different perspectives on your research project.

Obtaining the Articles   If the index is computerized and provides hard copies, print a copy of each promising reference you find. Otherwise, copy the following information on an index card.

Author(s), if identified

Title of article

Name of periodical

Volume or issue number (for professional and scholarly journals only)

Date of periodical

For newspapers, the edition name (city, metro) if more than one published, and section letter

The page range of the entire article

Obtain hard copies of whatever articles you can and check the topic sentences of paragraphs for essential points. Also, scan any accompanying abstracts or summaries. If an article appears useful, check to see whether it has a bibliography, which might include additional useful sources. Keep the cards for articles that seem promising—and any useful articles—and throw away the others.

Check the remaining references, including the ones from encyclopedia bibliographies, against the library's periodical catalogue to see which periodicals are available and where they are located. Libraries frequently keep current issues in a periodical room or some other special section. Back issues of magazines are often kept on microfilm or bound into hardcover volumes and shelved. Most newspapers are on microfilm. Check the articles for which you don't have hard copies in the same manner that you checked the others.

EXERCISE *Select five of the following topics and find one magazine article about each. Use at least three different periodical indexes to locate the articles. List the author, if given; the title of the article; the name of the magazine; its date; the page range; and the name of the index used.*

1. Acting schools
2. Aeronautical research
3. Black holes
4. Campaign funds
5. Collective bargaining
6. Fibre optics
7. Fundamentalism
8. Holography
9. Investment trusts
10. Leveraged buyouts
11. Louis St. Laurent
12. Nuclear fusion
13. Oral history
14. Roots Canada Co.
15. Television industry
16. Unemployment
17. Vegetarianism
18. Wayne Gretzky
19. X-ray astronomy
20. York University

The Internet

What It Is The Internet is a worldwide network that links the computer systems of educational institutions, government agencies, businesses, professional organizations, and individuals. The Internet offers a number of services, including the World Wide Web, electronic mail (e-mail), newsgroups, and listservs. It allows you to check the holdings of college, university and public city libraries; obtain information from online books, magazines, and newspapers; access research and government documents; gather viewpoints and information from numerous organizations and individuals; and communicate with people around the world or at the next computer station. This abundance of information and perspectives, sometimes not more than a day old, can greatly enhance your research. But remember that you'll still need to consult traditional sources in addition to using the Internet.

You can easily learn how to access the Internet and World Wide Web if you don't already know how. Your college or university may offer training sessions that you can attend. In addition, a number of excellent, easy-to-follow books are available. Whether enrolled in a training session or learning on your own, you'll need to obtain a log-on name, your own password, and an e-mail address if you plan to use your school's computers. If you encounter problems, personnel in the computer labs can probably answer many of your questions.

World Wide Web During the 1990s the World Wide Web exploded into international prominence. The Web gained quick popularity because it is easy to use and offers visuals, including many sites dedicated to art, and hypertext, that is, text with colour-coded words that can link you to other related sites. Web pages can include text, graphics, sound, video clips, entire computer programs, other files that can be downloaded, and even animated images.

To use the World Wide Web, you need access to a computer with a Web browser such as *Netscape Navigator* or *Microsoft Internet Explorer,* and you need *America Online, CompuServe,* or another Internet service provider to connect you to the Web. The format of these services is user-friendly and, in addition, most schools have training programs. The top of the screen on any browser features a tool bar that you can click on to save locations for future reference, stop the transfer of data, or initiate a search.

Each Web page has an address called a URL (uniform resource locator), which allows the browser to locate that page. Here is a sample address:

http://www.kwantlen.ca

How to Use It   The Internet includes millions of computers and offers a stupendous amount of information. As a result, finding just the material you want can be quite difficult. To solve this problem, several indexes, or *search engines,* have been developed that can connect any search term or terms with potentially millions of sites that include the key words. The easiest way to connect with these search engines is to simply select the search command or its nearest equivalent on your browser or Internet service. This will connect you with a specific search engine but also give you a choice of several others. You can also enter the direct address (URL) in the address window. Figure 19.8 provides the addresses of several popular search engines. Because the various search engines often select differently and produce different results, it's a good idea to use several engines while conducting your search.

Search Engine	Address
Google	http://www.google.ca
Alta Vista	http://www.altavista.digital.com
Lycos	http://www.lycos.com
Excite	http://www.excite.com
WebCrawler	http://webcrawler.com
Yahoo	http://www.yahoo.com

Figure 19.8   Popular Search Engines

While each search engine works in a slightly different manner, they all provide similar sorts of information. When prompted by the key words you enter, the engine searches and returns lists of links to information containing these words. Such engines reduce to a much more manageable size the job of finding what you want on the Internet. Still, expect the job to require patience, since search engines often provide information that isn't useful. For that reason, you'll often want to narrow your search when you begin. Single terms such as "health," "cancer," or "crime" could give you a million possible sites; instead, you may want to search for "ovarian cancer" or even "ovarian cancer cures." Most search engines also add more key words that will further narrow what has already been found. Different words or phrases can produce different results, so you'll want to try a variety of words for the same topic.

You can scroll through the list of sites the engine has found. The sites are usually accompanied by a short description that may help you decide whether they are useful. If you select any highlighted words, the search engine will transfer the data from that site and will connect you to a Web page.

When viewing a Web page, you may notice menus, highlighted words, or specially marked graphics. These features, called *hyperlinks,* will usually take you to a different location: another section within the original page, a different page within the same site, or even a new page on a computer in a different country. Following these hyperlinks allows you to explore related information from a variety of sources. As you move from Web page to Web page, browsers provide an easy way to navigate. *Netscape,* for example, has "back" and "forward" buttons that allow you to move to other sites. If you move back far enough, you will eventually get back to your main search site or even your home page. When you find an interesting site, you can print it out, or you can "bookmark" the site, allowing you easy future reference to the page. You'll need to keep track of any site addresses that you use since you'll include them in your bibliography.

Evaluating Internet Material   Because anyone can post virtually anything on the Internet, it is crucial that you check the accuracy and validity of any information you obtain from it. A source that sounds like a research centre, for example, the Institute for Social Justice, could be a political or even a cult organization giving out one-sided or false information for its own purposes. While articles for professional journals are reviewed by experts to ensure that the information is reliable, no such safeguard exists on the Internet. Carelessly researched or ethically questionable material can and does appear. Here are some guidelines for checking the validity of an Internet source:

1. Is the source identified as a reputable professional organization such as the Canadian Medical Association, a university like McGill, or a magazine like *Maclean's*? Keep in mind that anyone can use a professional-sounding name, so be alert.

2. Is there an identified author whose credentials can be checked? If there is no e-mail contact listed or if you can't find another way to verify the contents of the Web site, don't use it.

3. Is the tone of the site professional?

4. Is the information consistent with the other material you have found?

5. Does the site explain how the data were obtained?

6. Does the site appear to misuse any data? For instance, is the sample too small? Are the claims pushed too far? Are the statistics biased?

Sometimes, of course, you may want to check out pages that present the views of individuals or organizations with strong but slanted positions to gain a better understanding of their thinking, but don't consider such pages to be reliable sources. When using the Internet, "Reader beware" is a prudent attitude.

E-Mail   Once you get an e-mail address, you can communicate over the Internet with anyone else who has an address. It's a good idea to jot down the e-mail addresses of other students in your class so that you can exchange ideas. With some systems you can even exchange full drafts of your papers. Your instructor may create a distribution list that allows you to forward ideas and responses to the entire class by sending them to a single address.

You can also use e-mail to ask knowledgeable people about your research topic and get swift answers to your questions. Use this approach, however, as a last resort since busy people have limited time. If you must contact experts, don't bother them with questions that you could easily answer by reading background material. Reserve e-mail for specific queries that defy answer after extensive research. Most search engines have clearly identified directories that allow you to look up an e-mail address if you know a person's name. Sometimes you can find the name of an expert through the Web pages of major universities. If you do get a response to your query, evaluate it carefully; an overburdened expert may dash off a quick response while doing something else.

Newsgroups   A newsgroup is a group of people who discuss a common interest by posting their responses to a common address for everyone to read. These discussions can be informal and often are not monitored; as a result, they leave something to be desired as a source for research. Still, your university system will likely give you access to newsgroups, so ask your computer centre for an instruction sheet. A word of caution: Many newsgroups are intolerant of uninformed people intruding upon their conversation. Common *netiquette* (the etiquette of the Internet) calls for you to read what has already been written and to think before you write.

Listservs   A listserv consists of numerous e-mail addresses that make up a mailing list of people interested in a particular topic. Once you sign up, everything posted to that listserv will be sent to your e-mail address. People who subscribe to three or four listservs may receive thirty or forty e-mail messages every day. If you post a question on a listserv, you may get dozens of responses from professionals interested in the topic, and sorting out the validity of the different responses can be difficult. As with newsgroups, netiquette calls for you to acquire an understanding of your subject and follow the discussions on the listserv for some time before you post a question or a response. Your university computer professionals can probably supply you with instructions on how to find and sign up for a listserv. You can access a subject index of listservs at www.liszt.com.

FAQs   Whenever you find a promising Web site, newsgroup, or listserv, you will often see a line for FAQs (frequently asked questions). It's a good idea to read the FAQs first, since they may well answer your questions.

EXERCISE

1. **Using an appropriate search engine, find information on each of the following topics:**
    a. the United Nations
    b. current crime statistics
    c. sexual harassment
    d. current government immigration policy

2. **Enter the name of a major university into a search engine and then search. You should find that university's home page. Try to access the university's library to find what books are available on a topic of your choice. You might try Simon Fraser University, Queen's University, or the University of New Brunswick.**

Primary Research Findings

Besides relying on library materials, you may wish to use information obtained by conducting primary research. Chapter 21 provides detailed instructions for interviewing specialists, sending out questionnaires, and making direct observations. Before doing any type of primary research, always get your instructor's permission.

Adjusting Your Topic

After finishing your search for sources, you may need to adjust the scope and emphasis of your topic. If you start with "Early Nuclear-Powered Submarines" but fail to turn up enough sources, you might expand your emphasis to "Early Nuclear-Powered Warships." On the other hand, if you're working with "Early Nuclear-Powered Warships" and find yourself floundering in an ocean of sources, you might zero in on one type of vessel. Gathering evidence helps develop your judgment about how many sources you need to do the job.

Case History *(Continued from page 280)*

Once Keith Jacque had selected a focus for his paper on electronic monitoring, he began compiling his working bibliography. First he turned to the computerized card catalogue and began his search for books and government documents by typing in the subject entry "house arrest," but he found nothing. Next he tried "electronic monitoring of prisoners." This entry yielded a cross-reference directing him to the entries "punishment— United States" and "criminal statistics—analysis." These two entries yielded a list of seven books and eleven government documents. Further examination revealed that three of the books and four of the documents appeared promising.

Keith's search for periodical articles took him to the college's *InfoTrac* database. Using this system, he found three useful subject headings: "home detention," "electronic monitoring of prisoners," and "criminal statistics—analysis." A search of these subjects turned up twenty-four journal articles, all of which were available in the library. Eight looked as if they would be useful. Three newspaper articles seemed suitable, and a search of *NewsBank* revealed another promising newspaper article.

Since his library offered access to the Internet, Keith also searched the World Wide Web. He used the InfoSeek, Lycos, and Yahoo search engines and entered complete phrases such as "electronic incarceration," "home detention," "electronic monitoring," and "incarceration, electronic." Many of the Web sites he found were not relevant to his topic, but he persisted and finally found two that seemed promising. One, from an organization concerned with public policy, discussed the indirect costs of incarceration. The other, from the Probation Division of Georgia's Department of Corrections, discussed alternatives to jail sentences.

Keith realized that his sources were U.S.-based, and he still did not know much about how electronic monitoring was used in Canada. He sought and obtained his instructor's permission to conduct primary research on electronic monitoring in Canada. His instructor suggested he interview a criminology professor who could tell him about a 1989 pilot project on monitoring in British Columbia, the first of its kind in Canada. Keith was able to obtain the interview, which provided information not only on the B.C. pilot study results, but also on advantages and drawbacks of monitoring.

Satisfied that ample information was available, Keith carefully evaluated the content of the articles and of pertinent sections of the books and government documents he had located. His instructor had suggested that one good way to approach a topic is to pose a question about it and then draft a *tentative* answer, if possible. Here's how Keith proceeded:

Q.   What benefits does electronic monitoring offer jurisdictions that adopt it?

A.   Electronic monitoring is less expensive than incarceration, presents no serious problems, and offers a choice among several systems.

This answer provided a *tentative thesis,* an informed opinion that guided Keith's later note taking, giving him a sense of direction and indicating what information would probably prove useful and what was likely to be useless. Tentative theses can be altered slightly or changed completely if necessary. If later reading indicated that electronic monitoring can sometimes be more expensive than incarceration, Keith could alter his thesis accordingly.

This case history continues on page 306.

■ Taking Notes

To take notes, read your references carefully and record significant information. You might review or even expand your original research questions (page 277) so that you can read with a better sense of purpose. Notes are the raw materials for your finished product, so develop them accurately.

Evaluating Your Sources

Evaluate your sources by considering these factors.

The Expertise of the Author Judge an author's expertise by examining his or her professional status. Say you're searching for information on some new cancer-treating drug. An article by the director of a national cancer research centre would be a better bet than one by a staff writer for a magazine. Similarly, a historian's account of a national figure will probably have more balance and depth than a novelist's popularized account of that person's life. Gauging a writer's credentials is not difficult. Articles in periodicals often note authors' job titles along with their names. Some even supply thumbnail biographies. For a book, check its title page, preface, or introduction, and—if it's been left on—the dust jacket. Finally, notice whether the writer has other publications on this general subject. If your sources include two or more items by one person or if that person's name keeps cropping up as you take notes, you're probably dealing with an expert.

The Credibility of the Publication A book's credibility hinges on its approach and its reception by reviewers. Cast a cautious eye on books that take a popular rather than a scholarly approach. For research papers, scholarly treatments provide more solid fare. Weigh what reviewers said when a book first appeared. Two publications excerpt selected reviews and provide references to others. The *Book Review Digest* (1905–date) deals mainly with nontechnical works, while the *Technical Book Review Index* (1935–date) covers technical and scientific books. Turn first to the volume for the year the book came out. If you don't find any reviews, scan the next year's index. Often books published in the fall are not reviewed until the following year.

Periodical articles can also take a scholarly or popular tack. Editors of specialized journals and of some wide-circulation magazines—for example, *Equinox* and *The Atlantic Monthly*—publish only in-depth, accurate articles. Most newsstand publications, however, popularize to some extent, and some deliberately strive for sensationalism. Popularizing may result in broad, general statements, skimpy details, and a sensational tone.

Don't automatically reject a source because the writer lacks expertise or offers a popularized treatment. Often, especially when writing about a current topic, you'll need to use material that falls short in some way. Remember, though, that you undertake research to become more knowledgeable than general readers are about a topic. When information in popular periodicals provides less than adequate coverage, candidly acknowledge the shortcomings.

Mechanics of Note Taking

Generally your most effective approach to note taking is to use note cards. Copy each note on a large index card to avoid confusion with the smaller bibliography cards. Record only one note per card, even when you take several notes from a single page; you may use the notes at different points. If you can't fit a note on a single card, continue the note on a second card and paper-clip or staple the two together. Cards allow you to test different arrangements of notes and use the best one to write the paper.

Before you take a note, indicate its source at the bottom of the card. You will then have all the details necessary for documenting the information if you use it in your paper. Usually, the author's last name and the page number suffice, since the bibliography card contains all other details. To distinguish between two authors with the same last name or between two works by the same author, add initials or partial titles. *Don't forget to include the page number or numbers for each note.* Otherwise, you'll have to waste time looking them up when you cite your sources in the paper.

Summarize briefly the contents of the note at the top of the card. Later, when you construct an outline, these notations will help you sort your cards into categories and subcategories.

Responding to Notes

As you take notes, reflect on your topic and try to come up with new ideas, see connections to other notes, and anticipate future research. Think of yourself as having a conversation with your sources, and jot down your responses on the backs of your note cards. Ask yourself these questions: Does this information agree with what I have learned so far? Does it suggest any new avenues to explore? Does it leave me with questions about what's been said? Although it may take a few minutes to record your responses to a note, this type of analysis will help you write a paper that reflects *your* opinions, decisions, and evaluations, not one that smacks of notes merely patched together from different sources.

Types of Notes

A note can be a summary, paraphrase, or quotation. *Whenever you use any kind of note in your paper, give proper credit to your source. Failure to do so results in plagiarism—that is, literary theft—a serious offence even when committed unintentionally.* Pages 353–355 discuss plagiarism, and pages 329–353 explain proper documentation of sources.

Summary   A summary condenses original material, presenting its core ideas *in your own words*. In order to write an effective summary, you must have a good grasp of the information, and this comprehension ensures that you are ready to use the material in your paper. You may include brief quotations if you enclose them in quotation marks. A properly written summary presents the main points in their original order without distorting their emphasis or meaning, and it omits supporting details and repetition. Summaries, then, serve up the heart of the matter.

Begin the summarizing process by asking yourself, "What points does the author make that have an important bearing on my topic and purpose?" To answer, note especially the topic sentences in the original, which often provide essential information. Copy the points in order; then condense and rewrite them in your own words. Figure 19.9 summarizes the Bertrand Russell passage that follows. We have underscored key points in the original.

Necessity for law

About a century and a half ago, there began a still-existing preference for impulsive actions over deliberate ones. Those responsible for this development believed that people are naturally good but institutions have perverted them. Actually, unfettered human nature breeds violence and brutality, and law is our only protection against anarchy. The law assumes the responsibility for revenge and settles disputes equitably. It frees people from the fear of being victimized by criminals and provides a means of catching them. Without it, civilization could not endure.

Russell, pp. 63-65

Figure 19.9 Summary

Under the influence of the romantic movement, a process began about a hundred and fifty years ago, which has continued ever since—a process of revaluing the traditional virtues, placing some higher on the scale than before, and others lower. The tendency has been to exalt impulse at the expense of deliberation. The virtues that spring from the heart have come to be thought superior to those that are based upon reflection: a generous man is preferred to a man who is punctual in paying his debts. *Per contra,* deliberate sins are thought worse than impulsive sins: a hypocrite is more harshly condemned than a murderer. The upshot is that we tend to estimate virtues, not by their capacity for providing human happiness, but by their power of inspiring a personal liking for the possessors, and we are not apt to include among the qualities for which we like people, a habit of reflecting before making an important decision.

The men who started this movement were, in the main, gentle sentimentalists who imagined that, when the fetters of custom and law were removed, the heart would be free to display its natural goodness. Human nature, they thought, is good, but institutions have corrupted it; remove the institutions and we shall all become angels. Unfortunately, the matter is not so simple as they thought. Men who follow their impulses establish governments based on pogroms, clamour for war with foreign countries, and murder pacifists and Negroes. Human nature unrestrained by law is violent and cruel. In the London Zoo, the male baboons fought over the females until all the females were torn to pieces; human beings, left to the ungoverned impulse, would be no better. In ages that have had recent experience of anarchy, this has been obvious. All the great writers of the middle ages were passionate in their admiration of the law; it was the Thirty Years' War that led Grotius to become the first advocate of international law. Law, respected and enforced, is in the long run the only alternative to violent and predatory anarchy; and it is just as necessary to realize this now as it was in the time of Dante and Grotius.

What is the essence of law? On the one hand, it takes away from private citizens the right of revenge, which it confers upon the government. If a man steals your money, you must not steal it back, or thrash him, or shoot him; you must establish the facts before a neutral tribunal, which inflicts upon him such punishment as has seemed just to the disinterested legislators. On the other hand, when two men have a dispute, the law provides a machinery for settling it, again on principles laid down in advance by neutrals. The advantages of law are many. It diminishes the amount of private violence, and settles disagreements in a manner more nearly just than that which would result if the disputants fought it out by private war. It makes it possible for men to work without being perpetually on the watch against bandits. When a crime has been committed it provides a skilled machine for discovering the criminal.

Without law, the existence of civilized communities is impossible. In international law, there is as yet no effective law, for lack of an international police force capable of overpowering national armies, and it is daily becoming more evident that this defect must be remedied if civilization is to survive. Within single nations there is a dangerous tendency to think that moral indignation excuses the extra-legal punishment of criminals. In Germany an era of private murder (on the loftiest grounds) preceded and followed the victory of the Nazis. In fact, nine-tenths of what appeared as just indignation was sheer lust for cruelty; and this is equally true in other countries where mobs rob the law of its functions. In any civilized community, toleration of mob rule is the first step towards barbarism.

Bertrand Russell, "Respect for Law," *San Francisco Review,* Winter 1958, 63–65.

EXERCISE

A. **Select two passages that your instructor approves from an essay in the Reader and prepare summary note cards for them.**

B. **Submit summaries of three pieces of information that you plan to use in writing your paper; also submit complete versions of the original.**

Paraphrase   To paraphrase is to restate material *in your own words* without attempting to condense it. Unlike a summary, a paraphrase allows you to present an essentially complete version of the original material. A note of caution, however: don't copy the original source nearly verbatim, changing only a word here and there. To do so is to plagiarize. To avoid this offence, follow a read, think, and write-without-looking-at-the-original strategy when you take notes so that you concentrate on recording the information in your own words. Then verify the accuracy of your notes by checking them against the original source. Here is a sample passage; Figure 19.10 is its paraphrase.

Over time, more and more of life has become subject to the controls of knowledge. However, this is never a one-way process. Scientific investigation is continually increasing our knowledge. But if we are to make good use of this knowledge, we must not only rid our minds of old, superseded beliefs and fragments of magic, but also recognize new superstitions for what they are. Both are generated by our wishes, our fears, and our feelings of helplessness in difficult situations.

Margaret Mead, "New Superstitions for Old," *A Way of Seeing,* New York: McCall, 1970, 266.

> ### Combatting Superstitions
>
> As time has passed, knowledge has asserted its sway over larger and larger segments of human life. But the process cuts two ways. Science is forever adding to the storehouse of human knowledge. Before we can take proper advantage of its gifts, however, we must purge our minds of old and outmoded convictions, while recognizing the true nature of modern superstitions. Both stem from our desires, our apprehensions, and our sense of impotence under difficult circumstances.
>
> Mead, p. 266

Figure 19.10   Paraphrase

| **EXERCISE**   *Paraphrase a short passage from one of your textbooks. Submit a complete version of the passage with the assignment.*

Quotation   A quotation is a copy of original material. Since your paper should demonstrate that you've mastered your sources, don't rely extensively on quotations. You need practice in expressing yourself. As a general rule, avoid quotations except when

- the original displays special elegance or force
- you really need support from an authority
- you need to back up your interpretation of a passage from a literary work

Paraphrasing a passage as well written as the one below would rob it of much of its force.

> Man is himself, like the universe he inhabits, like the demoniacal stirring of the ooze from which he sprang, a tale of desolation. He walks in his mind from birth to death the long resounding shores of endless disillusionment. Finally, the commitment to life departs or turns to bitterness. But out of such desolation emerges the awful freedom to choose beyond the narrowly circumscribed circle that delimits the rational being.
>
> Loren Eiseley, *The Unexpected Universe*

Special rules govern the use of quotations. If, for clarity, you need to add an explanation or substitute a proper name for a personal pronoun, enclose the addition in *brackets*.

> The American Declaration of Independence asserts that "the history of the present King of Great Britain [George III] is a history of repeated injuries and usurpations. [. . .] "

If your keyboard doesn't have brackets, insert them neatly with a dark pen.

Reproduce any grammatical or spelling errors in a source exactly as they appear in the original. To let your reader know that the original author, not you, made the mistake, insert the Latin word *sic* (meaning "thus") within brackets immediately after the error.

> As Wabash notes, "The threat to our enviroment [sic] comes from many directions."

If you exclude an unneeded part of a quotation, show the omission with an ellipsis—three spaced periods—[. . .]. Indicate omissions *within sentences* in the following way:

> Writing in *Step by Step, 1936–1939,* Winston Churchill observed, "To France and Belgium the avalanche of fire and steel which fell upon them twenty years ago [. . .] [was] an overpowering memory and obsession."

When an omission comes *at the end of a sentence* and what is actually quoted can also stand as a complete sentence, use an unspaced period followed by an ellipsis.

> In his second inaugural address, Lincoln voiced his hopes for the nation: "With malice toward none, with charity for all, with firmness in the right as God gives us to see the right, let us strive on to finish the work we are in. [. . .] "

Do the same when you drop *a whole sentence* within a quoted passage.

> According to newspaper columnist Grace Dunn, "Williamson's campaign will undoubtedly focus primarily on the legalized gambling issue because he hopes to capitalize on the strong opposition to it in his district. [. . .] Nonetheless, commentators all agree he faces an uphill fight in his attempt to unseat the incumbent."

Don't change or distort when you delete. Tampering like the following violates ethical standards:

> *Original passage:*   This film is poorly directed, and the acting uninspired; only the cameo appearance by Laurence Olivier makes it truly worth seeing.
>
> *Distorted version:*   This film is [. . .] truly worth seeing.

You can summarize or paraphrase original material but retain a few words or phrases to add vividness or keep a precise shade of meaning. Simply use quotation marks but no ellipsis.

> Government spokesperson Paula Plimption notes that because of the "passionate advocacy" of its supporters, the push to roll back property taxes has been gaining momentum across the country.

When you copy a quotation onto a note card, put quotation marks at the beginning and the end so you won't mistake it for a paraphrase or a summary when you write the paper. If the quoted material starts on one page and ends on the next, use a slash mark (/) to show exactly where the shift comes. Then if you use only part of the quotation in your paper, you'll know whether to use one page number or two.

Don't expect to find a bonanza on every page you read. Sometimes one page will yield several notes, another page nothing. If you can't immediately gauge the value of some material, take it down. Useless information can be discarded later. Place a rubber band around your growing stack of note cards. Store them in a large envelope closed with a snap or string and labelled with your name and address. Submit them with your completed paper if your instructor requests.

Case History *(continued from page 299)*

Working bibliography in hand, Keith Jacque prepared note cards. Most of his notes were summaries of the source material, but in a few cases he chose quotations because of the importance of the source or the significance of the material. For example, one quotation cited a former U.S. Attorney General who pointed out the disproportionate number of crimes committed by habitual violent offenders. Another quotation cited a key reason for the growing use of electronic monitoring: the high cost of prisons. Still another detailed various difficulties encountered in transmitting signals.

As Keith took notes, a plan for his paper began to emerge. The introduction would explain the reasons behind the growing use of electronic monitoring. The body would present a brief history of monitoring and then detail the different kinds of available systems, examine the problems encountered when using them, and point out their effectiveness.

This case history continues on page 308.

■ Organizing and Outlining

Next comes your formal outline, the blueprint that shows the divisions and subdivisions of your paper, the order of your ideas, and the relationships between ideas and supporting details. An outline is a tool that benefits both writer and reader.

A formal outline follows the pattern shown below:

I.

   A.

   B.

      1.

      2.

         a.

         b.

II.

You can see the significance of an item by its numeral, letter, or number designation and by its distance from the left-hand margin; the farther it's indented, the less important it is. All items with the same designation have roughly the same importance.

Developing Your Outline

Developing an outline is no easy job. It involves arranging material from various sources in an appropriate manner. Sorting and re-sorting your note cards is a good way to proceed. First, determine the main divisions of your paper by checking the summarized notations at the tops of your cards, and then make one stack of cards for each division. Next, review each stack carefully to determine further subdivisions and sort it into smaller stacks. Finally, use the stacks to prepare your outline.

There are two types of formal outlines: *topic* and *sentence.* A topic outline presents all entries as words, short phrases, or short clauses. A sentence outline presents them as complete sentences. To emphasize the relationships among elements, items of equal importance have parallel phrasing. Although neither is *the* preferred form, a sentence outline includes more details and also your attitude toward each idea. Many students first develop a topic outline, do additional research, and then polish and expand this version into a sentence outline. While it's easy to be sloppy in a topic outline, forming a sentence outline requires you to reach the kinds of conclusions that will be the backbone of your paper. The following segments of a topic and a sentence outline for a paper on tranquilizer dependence illustrate the difference between the two:

Topic Outline

II. The tranquilizer abuse problem
    A. Reasons for the problem
        1. Overpromotion
        2. Overprescription
        3. Patient's misuse
          a. Dosage
          b. Length of usage
    B. Growth of the problem

Sentence Outline

II. Tranquilizers are widely abused.
    A. Several factors account for the abuse of tranquilizers.
        1. Drug companies overpromote their product.
        2. Doctors often unnecessarily prescribe tranquilizers.
        3. Patients often do not follow their doctors' instructions.
          a. Some patients take more than prescribed doses.
          b. Some continue to use tranquilizers beyond the prescribed time.
    B. The problem of tranquilizer abuse appears to be growing.

Note that the items in the sentence outline are followed by periods, but those in the topic outline are not.

Keying Your Note Cards to Your Outline

When your outline is finished, key your note cards to it by writing at the top of each card the letters and numbers—such as IIA or IIIB2—for the appropriate outline category. Now arrange the cards into one stack, following the order shown in the outline. Finally, start with the top card in the stack and number all of them consecutively. If they later fall off the table or slide out of place, you can easily put them in order again. You might have a few stragglers left over when you complete this keying. Some of these may be worked into your paper as you write or revise it.

Case History   *(Continued from page 306)*

Sorting and re-sorting was challenging and at times frustrating for Keith. Since some of his material could be arranged in different ways, he found himself experimenting, evaluating, and rearranging as he tried various options. After much thought and some trial and error, the following *initial draft* of his outline emerged:

I. Reasons why monitoring used
   A. Serious crime problem and number of people in prisons
   B. High cost of prisons
II. Brief history of electronic monitoring
III. Types of monitoring systems

   A. Programmed-contact systems
   B. Continuous-contact systems
   C. Hybrid systems
IV. Problems with these systems

   A. Practical problems
     1. Offenders' problems
     2. Transmission difficulties
   B. Legal problems
     1. Do the systems violate constitutional rights?
     2. "Net-widening" effect
V. Effectiveness of electronic monitoring
   A. Effectiveness with low-risk offenders
   B. Cost effectiveness
VI. Expanded use of monitoring likely

This version is marked by nonparallel structure and inadequate attention to some points. Despite these weaknesses, it provided an adequate blueprint for the first draft of Keith's paper.

This case history concludes on page 312.

Ethical Issues

When you present the information you've gathered from a variety of sources, you'll want to proceed in an ethically responsible way. Asking and answering the following questions will help you to do just that.

- Have I carefully researched my topic, making sure that my conclusions are well founded? Imagine the consequences if slipshod testing by an auto company led to the erroneous conclusion that the steering mechanism on one of its models met current safety standards.

- Have I adequately acknowledged any evidence that runs counter to the conclusions I draw? A paper that stresses the advantages of charter schools, but deliberately avoids mentioning their disadvantages, could be a form of deception.

- Have I properly documented my sources? Using someone else's words or ideas without giving proper credit is a form of academic dishonesty.

- Have I honestly represented the authority of my sources? If you read an article touting almond extract as a cure for cancer that was written by a practising foot doctor, it would be dishonest to suggest that the article was written by a "prominent research scientist." Refer to someone as an expert only when that person's credentials warrant the label.

- Could my information have an undesirable effect on the readers? If so, how can I address their concerns? A report describing a new antibiotic-resistant strain of tuberculosis might alarm some readers, and therefore the writer could provide appropriate reassurances of the limited risk to most people.

Writing Your Research Paper

Some students think of a library research paper as a series of quotations, paraphrases, and summaries, one following the other throughout the paper. Not so. Without question, you use the material of others, but *you* select and organize it according to *your purpose. You* develop insights, and *you* draw conclusions about what you've read. You can best express your conclusions by setting your notes aside, stepping back to gain some perspective, and then expressing your sense of what you've learned. Many students find it helpful to write two or three pages that summarize what they want to say as well as whom they want to reach with their message and why. Like all forms of writing, research papers are written for some purpose and aimed at some audience.

Writing the First Draft

Your final research results will be expressed in a thesis. You've already drafted a tentative thesis (see page 299), and now you'll probably refine or revise it to accommodate any changes in your perspective on the topic. Position the thesis in the introductory part of your paper unless you're analyzing a problem or recommending a solution; then you might hold back the thesis until later in the essay. If you do hold it back, state the problem clearly at the outset. Because of the paper's length, it's a good idea to reveal your organizational plan in your introductory section.

Write the paper section by section, following the divisions of your outline. But keep in mind that you're not locked into its pattern. If you see an opportunity to develop an important idea that you omitted from your outline, try it. If you discover that it might be better to introduce an item earlier than you intended, go ahead. Just be sure to check your organization later. As you write, think of yourself as supporting the conclusions you have reached with the appropriate material on your note cards, not just as stringing these cards together. You will then incorporate the material on your note cards with your own assessments and with transitional elements that clarify your information and orient the reader. As you proceed, here again you'll use the writing strategies presented earlier in the book.

Because of this paper's length, you will probably need to connect its major sections with transitional paragraphs that pull together the material already covered and prepare the reader for what follows. Don't fret if the style bumps along or connections aren't always clear. These problems can be smoothed out when you revise. You will, of course, need to know how to document your sources properly, handle quotations, and avoid plagiarism. Chapter 20 presents guidelines on these important subjects.

On occasion you may want to include supplementary information that would interrupt the flow of thought if you placed it in the paper. When this happens, use an *explanatory note*.[1] A typical explanatory note might clarify or elaborate upon a point, discuss some side issue, or define a term used in a specialized way.

When you finish writing, let this version sit for a day or two. Then revise it, just as you would with a shorter essay. Keep track of all your sources so that preparing the bibliography will go smoothly.

Preparing Your Finished Copy

Follow the revision guidelines in Chapter 3. In addition, verify that you have

- included all key information
- clearly organized your material
- not overloaded your paper with quotations

---

[1]This is an explanatory note. Position it at the bottom of the page, spaced four lines away from the main text. If more than one note occurs on a page, double-space between them. If the note carries over to the next page, separate it from your text with a solid, full-length line. Put two spaces above the line and two spaces below it.

- worked in your own observations

- put in-text documentation and source information in proper form

Prepare your final draft with a typewriter or word-processor printer that produces dark, readable copy. Double-space throughout, including indented block quotations and the list of works you used to prepare the paper.

Two systems for formatting and documenting library research papers are in common use: the Modern Language Association (MLA) system, favoured by many English and humanities instructors, and the American Psychological Association (APA) system, used by many social science and psychology instructors.

MLA System for Preparing Papers

- Number each page in the upper right-hand corner, one-half inch from the top. Precede each number with your last name.

- Starting one inch from the top of the first page, type your full name, the instructor's name, the course designation, and the date, all flush with the left-hand margin.

- Double-space below the date, and centre the title; then double-space before starting the first paragraph.

- Leave one-inch margins on all four sides except at the top of the first page. Indent the first line of each paragraph five spaces.

- The MLA system does not require a title page. If your instructor wants one, however, centre (1) the title of the paper about two inches below the top of the sheet, (2) your name in the middle of the sheet, and (3) the instructor's name, course designation, and date about two inches from the bottom. Use capital and lowercase letters for everything. Repeat the title, again in capital and lowercase letters, on the first text page, centred about two inches from the top.

- Begin the bibliography on a new page that follows the text of the paper, and give it the heading "Works Cited," without quotation marks. Centre the heading on the page.

- List each bibliography entry alphabetically according to the author's last name or, if no author is given, by the first significant word in the title. For a work with more than one author, alphabetize by the name that comes first. If there's more than one entry for an author, substitute three unspaced hyphens, followed by a period and a double space, for the author's name in the second and subsequent entries.

- Begin the first line of each entry at the left-hand margin and indent any subsequent lines five spaces.

APA System for Preparing Papers

- The APA system requires a title page. Centre (1) the title of the paper about four inches from the top and (2) your name, two spaces below the title. About three-quarters of the way from the top, provide the course designation, the name of your instructor, and the date, typed double-spaced and flush with the right-hand margin. Two inches from the top of the page, type the words "Running Head" without quotation marks, flush with the left-hand margin; then type a colon and a word or phrase that identifies the paper's topic. Type the running head in capital letters; type everything else in capital and lowercase letters.

- Repeat the title of the paper on the first text page, centred about one-and-a-half inches from the top and typed in capital and lowercase letters.

- Number every page of the text in the upper right-hand corner, starting with the title page. Position the first two or three words of the title five spaces to the left of the page number.

- Leave one-inch margins at the bottom and at both sides of each page. Indent the first line of each paragraph five spaces.

- Begin the bibliography on a new page that follows the text of the paper, and give it the heading "References," without quotation marks. Centre this heading on the page. Follow the alphabetizing and positioning guidelines for the MLA system except that if the listing includes more than one entry for an author, repeat the author's name.

- Indent the first line of each entry five spaces and begin any subsequent lines at the left-hand margin.

Case History   (Continued from page 309)

Using his outline and thesis statement as a guide, Keith prepared a first draft of his paper, following the MLA format required by his instructor. It didn't all come easily. In order to ensure an effective presentation, he checked his note cards carefully to determine which material would provide the strongest support for his conclusions. He was careful to use his own words except when he was quoting. To achieve smoothness, he tried to connect his major sections with transitions, aware that he could polish these connections when he revised the paper.

When he had completed the first draft, Keith set it aside for two days in order to distance himself from his writing. Then he returned to it and revised it carefully. Reading the paper from the perspective of a slightly skeptical critic, he looked for unsupported claims, questions that readers might have, sections that might be confusing or poorly organized, and weak transitions. Like most writers, Keith found sections that could be improved. Next, he revised his initial topic outline and followed it when drafting the sentence out-line that appears on pages 313–315. Keith then prepared the final draft of the paper itself, which is on pages 316–328. Direct your attention to its note-worthy features, which include italicized notations indicating where Keith used the writing strategies discussed earlier in the text.

Example Student Research Paper

Sentence Outline

Thesis statement: House arrest offers a choice of several monitoring systems, presents no insurmountable problems, proves effective in controlling low-risk offenders, and costs less than incarceration.

I. The use of house arrest stems from serious crime problems in both Canada and the United States.

   A. Extensive use of prisons in Canada and the U.S. has led to economic and social problems.

   B. Violent crimes committed by chronic offenders have led to tougher crime-control legislation.

   C. This legislation has increased the country's prison population and the cost of incarcera-tion.

   D. As a result, many jurisdictions have adopted house-arrest programs for low-risk offenders.

II. Electronic monitoring has a short history.

   A. The idea first appeared in the comic <u>Spiderman</u>.

   B. A New Mexico judge asked computer companies to develop an electronic bracelet.

   C. Monitoring was first used in 1984 to control offenders, and the concept quickly spread across the country.

Sentence outline: note use of complete sentences throughout, use of periods following section and subsection markers, and the indentation arrangement

III. Electronic monitoring devices fall into three categories.

    A. A programmed-contact system calls the offender's home during curfew periods and reports absences.

        1. A computer may simply record the offender's voice.

        2. A computer may compare the voice heard over the phone to a recording of the offender's voice.

        3. The offender may wear an encoded bracelet and insert it into a special telephone transmitter.

        4. A camera may transmit photos of the offender over telephone lines.

    B. A continuous-signal system requires the offender to wear a transmitter that sends uninterrupted electronic signals.

    C. A hybrid system combines programmed-contact and continuous-signal techniques.

        1. The programmed-contact component usually includes voice- and photo-transmission units.

        2. Jurisdictions can tailor systems to their needs.

IV. Electronic systems have created practical and legal problems.

    A. Practical problems include both difficulties experienced by offenders and transmission difficulties.

        1. Encoded bracelets can cause offenders discomfort and embarrassment.

        2. Telephone lines and objects in the offender's home can interfere with signal pickup.

    B. Legal problems include possible infringe-
       ment of rights and the net-widening
       effect.
       1. Charging surveillance fees and limiting
          surveillance to the least dangerous
          persons may infringe on offenders'
          equal-protection rights.
       2. Monitoring may violate the right to
          privacy of others in offenders' homes.
       3. Net-widening can result in an excessive
          number of individuals under house
          arrest.
 V. Electronic monitoring has proved effective
    with low-risk offenders.
    A. Offenders successfully completed monitor-
       ing programs in B.C.
    B. Monitoring costs less than incarceration.
VI. The advantages of house arrest over prison
    sentences should increase the use of this hu-
    mane alternative in Canada.

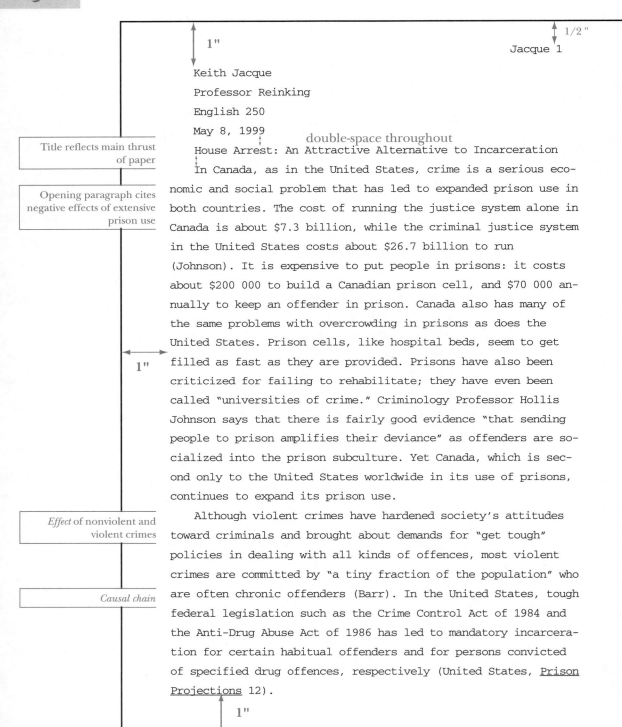

1"
1/2"
Jacque 1

Keith Jacque

Professor Reinking

English 250

May 8, 1999

double-space throughout

Title reflects main thrust of paper

House Arrest: An Attractive Alternative to Incarceration

Opening paragraph cites negative effects of extensive prison use

In Canada, as in the United States, crime is a serious economic and social problem that has led to expanded prison use in both countries. The cost of running the justice system alone in Canada is about $7.3 billion, while the criminal justice system in the United States costs about $26.7 billion to run (Johnson). It is expensive to put people in prisons: it costs about $200 000 to build a Canadian prison cell, and $70 000 annually to keep an offender in prison. Canada also has many of the same problems with overcrowding in prisons as does the United States. Prison cells, like hospital beds, seem to get filled as fast as they are provided. Prisons have also been criticized for failing to rehabilitate; they have even been called "universities of crime." Criminology Professor Hollis Johnson says that there is fairly good evidence "that sending people to prison amplifies their deviance" as offenders are socialized into the prison subculture. Yet Canada, which is second only to the United States worldwide in its use of prisons, continues to expand its prison use.

1"

Effect of nonviolent and violent crimes

Although violent crimes have hardened society's attitudes toward criminals and brought about demands for "get tough" policies in dealing with all kinds of offences, most violent crimes are committed by "a tiny fraction of the population" who are often chronic offenders (Barr). In the United States, tough federal legislation such as the Crime Control Act of 1984 and the Anti-Drug Abuse Act of 1986 has led to mandatory incarceration for certain habitual offenders and for persons convicted of specified drug offences, respectively (United States, <u>Prison Projections</u> 12).

Causal chain

1"

Jacque 2

The introduction of mandatory sentencing guidelines, now
common on the state as well as the federal level, provides consistent punishment for similar crimes. It has led, however, to
an explosion in the number of prison inmates, which by mid-1996
totalled over 1.1 million, according to the Justice
Department's Bureau of Justice Statistics ("BJS Reports" 1).
Between 1980 and 1995, the U.S. prison population increased by
242 percent ("Inmate Populations" 10). Many of these inmates
are guilty of nonviolent offences. In 1997, three-fourths of
all prisoners fell into the nonviolent category (Richey 3).

In the United States the prison population is expected to
keep growing. The National Council on Crime and Delinquency has
estimated that the total number of prisoners might reach 1.4
million by the year 2000, a jump of 24 percent over the 1995
level ("Inmate Populations" 10). The Bureau of Prisons has pro-
jected construction costs of some four billion dollars for new
federal prisons scheduled to open in the 1996-2006 decade and
between ten billion and fourteen billion dollars for the new
state prisons required to house the anticipated increase in
prisoners ("Inmate Populations" 10).

Even these figures don't tell the whole story. Director of
the Federal Bureau of Prisons J. Michael Quinlan (114) comments
that over the lifetime of a prison, "construction costs are
only 5-7 percent of the total expense. This means that from 15-
20 times the construction costs will have to be budgeted over
the life of each prison now being built." Underestimating operating costs can result in unused facilities as in Florida
where, in 1992, two newly constructed 900-person prisons and a
336-person death-row facility remained empty because the state
lacked the money to operate them (Katel 63).

Overcrowding and the high costs of prisons have seriously
undermined state spending on public services and created a number of hidden expenses. In Michigan, for example, corrections
spending increased over 300 percent between 1979 and 1989, as

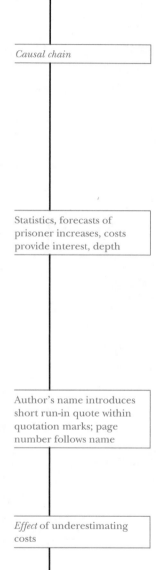

Causal chain

Statistics, forecasts of
prisoner increases, costs
provide interest, depth

Author's name introduces
short run-in quote within
quotation marks; page
number follows name

Effect of underestimating
costs

Jacque 3

compared to a 98 percent increase in social services spending and a 40 percent increase in education spending (Baird 122). And these figures do not include hidden costs such as welfare payments to the families of imprisoned offenders and the loss of tax revenues from prisoners removed from the job market (Lynch).

Faced with the social and educational consequences of current policy, many state legislators have recommended using prison space only for violent offenders and developing, for nonviolent ones, low-cost alternatives that provide adequate public protection. At times, results have been mixed. In the early 1980s, for example, the state of Georgia attempted to relieve severe prison overcrowding by greatly expanding the use of closely supervised probation. While significant cost savings were realized, tremendous work overloads on the probation staff resulted (Probation Division).

Definition of term

Omission within sentence, ellipsis

Another alternative to prison sentences besides probation is a form of house arrest that "confines an offender to a specific site ... during specific hours" and supervises the offender by means of an Electronic Monitoring System, sometimes referred to as EMS (BC <u>EMS Discussion Paper</u> 2–3). While this technology has been used in the United States since approximately 1984, it was introduced to Canada by some provinces in the late 1980s. Perhaps it is time for us to consider whether electronic monitoring should be promoted more widely in Canada, perhaps even on the federal level. It offers a choice of several monitoring systems, presents no insurmountable problems, is effective in controlling low-risk offenders, and costs less than incarceration.

Rationale for essay's focus

Thesis statement reflects paper's content, previews organization

Electronic monitoring[1] has curious roots--the comic <u>Spiderman</u>. The idea first occurred in 1979 to New Mexico Judge

Explanatory note

[1]This alternative is sometimes called electronic tethering, electronic surveillance, electronic house arrest, or electronic incarceration.

Jacque 4

Jack Love, who observed that Kingpin, Spiderman's nemesis, used an electronic bracelet to control his crime-fighter enemy. Love asked computer companies to develop a similar device (Scaglione, "Jails" 32; Sullivan 51). The first house-arrest program using electronic monitoring was implemented in 1984, and five years later programs had been established in over a hundred jurisdictions across more than thirty states (Peck 26; Scaglione, "Under Arrest" 26). By 1993, the number of offenders being electronically monitored throughout the United States totalled 65 650 (Carey and McLean 1).

The U.S. Department of Justice classifies electronic monitoring systems according to their signalling characteristics (United States, <u>Electronic Monitoring</u> 1). Types include programmed contact, continuous signal, and hybrid systems--a combination of the first two.

With a programmed-contact system, a computer calls an offender's residence on a random basis during established curfew periods and reports any unauthorized absence to correctional authorities. Various levels of sophistication are possible depending upon how much certainty is desired. In the simplest system, the computer merely records the offender's voice. Correctional authorities then review the taped responses the next day to determine any curfew violations. A variant approach uses a prerecording of the offender's voice, which the computer compares to the voice heard during random calls. If the two do not match, the computer can immediately notify authorities of a violation. Voice systems are comparatively inexpensive as no special equipment needs to be installed in the offender's home or worn by the individual (Hofer and Meierhoefer 36-37).

A more sophisticated means of checking on offenders makes use of an encoded bracelet worn by the offender. Again, a computer calls randomly during curfew. Instead of answering in the usual manner, however, the offender responds by inserting the bracelet into a special transmitter attached to the telephone.

Narrative relates brief history of monitoring

Double citations show two sources with essentially identical information; shortened titles distinguish between separate articles by same author

Classification of monitoring systems

Definition of system

Comparison of systems

Jacque 5

The bracelets can be made in such a way that unauthorized attempts to remove them will damage their transmitting ability (Hofer and Meierhoefer 36-37).

Process explained

Visual verification probably offers the best assurance against curfew violation. A special camera that can transmit photographs over telephone lines is installed in the offender's home. During calls, the computer can request the monitored individual to provide a variety of poses to the camera. These photographs can then be stored in the computer for later review or compared immediately to a reference key for the individual (Hofer and Meierhoefer 37).

Comparison of systems; *definition* of system

Continuous-signal systems, unlike programmed-contact systems, require the offender to wear a transmitter that sends a continuous sequence of electronic signals, often several times a minute, to his or her home telephone. If a break in transmission occurs during a detention period, the monitoring computer notifies authorities. The transmitters are relatively small and generally worn on a tamper-resistant strap around the ankle. Attempts to remove the strap could cause the unit to stop sending signals or could be detected during periodic inspections. These systems provide a greater degree of supervision than programmed-contact systems, which check on offenders only intermittently (Hofer and Meierhoefer 38-39).

Comparison of systems

Hybrid systems combine programmed-contact and continuous-signal techniques in order to realize the advantages of each (United States, Electronic Monitoring 1). Typically, the programmed-contact component includes both voice and video units. This component can function as a backup for continuous-signal monitoring or as a supplement to it. In the first case, the computer is programmed to call for voice-video identification whenever the offender's transmitter fails to send a continuous signal. In the second case, the computer randomly calls for voice-video verification as well as receives transmitter signals (Scaglione, "Jails" 36).

Jacque 6

Jurisdictions can develop hybrid systems tailored to their individual needs. For example, a house-arrest program for drunk drivers could employ a continuous-signal transmitter supplemented by random telephone verification. Home monitoring equipment could even include a Breathalyzer to determine and transmit to the computer the offender's blood-alcohol level during telephone verification calls (Scaglione, "Jails" 36). A variation of this type of system is used in Annapolis, Maryland, where video cameras have been installed in the homes of some convicted drunk drivers. The offenders are called periodically and required to give themselves a blood-alcohol test in front of the camera (Peck 28).

Not surprisingly, electronic monitoring has resulted in some practical problems and legal concerns. Most problems arise with those who wear encoded verification bracelets or transmitters. These offenders complain that the devices cause physical discomfort or embarrassment. Correction officials can adjust the fit of the device or suggest that offenders wear a cut-off tube sock, tennis-type wrist band, or other type of padding under the strap. Wearers, however, must find their own ways of coping with embarrassment. In studying the electronic monitoring of federal parolees, Beck, Klein-Saffran, and Wooten found that offenders could be quite innovative in explaining why they were wearing units. When questioned by strangers, "the majority told the truth, while other parolees stated that [the unit] was a heart monitor, pager, battery charger for a video camera, or a fish caller" (29).

Transmitting difficulties have created other practical problems. In some areas, existing telephone lines may be inadequate or incompatible with the transmitting characteristics of certain monitoring systems. In other cases, the offender's home may cause difficulties. Ford and Schmidt, who conducted research for the U.S. National Institute of Justice, point out that

Cites article with three authors; page number follows quotation

Brackets enclose explanatory words inserted into quotation

Examples of problems

The typical room has dead space in which the receiver
cannot pick up the transmitter's signal. In particular,
metal tends to limit the range of the transmitter;
kitchens are therefore an especially difficult environment. Transmission breaks have also been attributed to
metal furniture, faulty wiring, other electronic devices, bathroom fixtures, waterbeds, and even certain
sleeping positions. Mobile homes constitute a problem
for offenders trying to do yard chores: the range outside the building is as little as ten feet, as compared
to as much as 200 feet from a mainframe building. (3)

Other researchers have noted similar interference problems.
In one situation, authorities suspected noncompliance when they
discovered breaks in an offender's continuous signal transmis-
sions. These breaks always occurred during the same time period
and only on Sundays. Investigation revealed that a large rock
and metal coffee table was blocking the signal from the transmitter on the offender's ankle while he was watching football
on television (Beck, Klein-Saffran, and Wooten 27).

Most practical problems associated with electronic monitoring pose no serious challenge. Troublesome bracelets and transmitters can be adjusted or padded. Offenders often develop
ingenious explanations for the units they wear. Difficulties in
signal transmission can often be overcome by having trained
technicians install equipment or by having offenders slightly
modify their routine. Legal problems, on the other hand, pose a
greater challenge.

Electronic surveillance programs necessarily involve some
type of entry into offenders' homes. Therefore, they need careful examination to ensure that they don't violate the equal
protection and right to privacy provisions of the U.S.
Constitution. The American Civil Liberties Union is concerned
that two common practices--charging a fee to cover surveillance
costs and restricting surveillance to classes of offenders

Extended quotation indented ten spaces, without quotation marks, double-spaced

Period precedes citation

Transition paragraph summarizes solutions to practical problems, looks ahead to legal problems

Jacque 8

least likely to violate house arrest--may infringe on the equal protection clause of the U.S. Constitution. The first practice, the ACLU notes, can discriminate against young and indigent offenders by imprisoning them because they cannot pay their fees. The second, by singling out persons guilty only of property crimes and without serious criminal records or histories of drug abuse, may target disproportionately high numbers of white-collar offenders (Petersilia 3).

Because electronic monitoring programs are always voluntary, participants essentially waive their right to privacy. By agreeing to a program in lieu of prison, they have indicated their willingness to undergo surveillance. Still, as the Bureau of Justice Assistance notes, court rulings may uphold a convicted person's right to privacy if electronic surveillance "cannot be justified in terms of an articulated security interest, ability to deter future criminal conduct or ability to reduce the risk of flight" (United States, Electronic Monitoring 5). Furthermore, electronic monitoring can invade the privacy of others in the offender's home. Family members who have not committed an offence and have not waived their right to privacy can accidentally be photographed or recorded. To prevent such intrusions, Kentucky, Nevada, and West Virginia have banned the use of equipment that might accidentally record extraneous sights and sounds. And because North Carolina prohibits photographing juveniles, visual verification cannot be used in that state (Scaglione, "Jails" 34).

Besides protecting an offender's constitutional rights, correction officials must try to avoid a "net-widening" effect when electronic monitoring is used. This effect occurs when a judge approves surveillance for offenders who would formerly have received probation but denies it to anyone who would formerly have gone to prison. The result is a "widening of the net of social control" to encompass more individuals. When such abuses take place, the system does not provide an option for

Quotation indicates precise conditions that justify monitoring

Definition of term

those who would otherwise have gone to prison, and it serves as a new form of punishment for those who would otherwise have been placed on probation. Prison overcrowding is not reduced, and the costs of punishment actually rise because of the excess number of individuals under surveillance (Morris and Tonry 225). The net-widening effect has been avoided in some jurisdictions by establishing strict rules for the selection of participants. New Jersey, for instance, restricts alternative punishment programs to offenders who have already been sentenced to prison (Hofer and Meierhoefer 22).

Argument in favour of monitoring

A pilot project on electronic monitoring introduced in British Columbia in 1987 has provided convincing evidence that electronic monitoring works well in supervising low-risk prisoners. Candidates for this study were carefully screened, and those with a history of violence or those facing a charge of a violent nature were ineligible (BC EMS Pilot Project Evaluation 11). The 92 offenders assessed suitable and taken through the entire project all completed their sentences successfully (BC Pilot Project 16). In its report afterwards, the chair of the Canadian Bar Association (C.B.A.) John Conroy recommended going "on record supporting, in principle, the use of electronic monitoring as an alternative to imprisonment where imprisonment is not considered necessary in the public interest" (20). Conroy also called for legislative changes to the "bail and probation provisions in the Criminal Code of Canada" to encourage the use of electronic monitoring, though only as an alternative to imprisonment so that judges are not tempted to widen the net (21).

Qualification of thesis where necessary

Interview supplements library research

The British Columbia program was also a success on the level of public acceptance. In a personal interview, Criminologist Hollis Johnson said that groups like Mothers Against Drunk Drivers (M.A.D.D.) who were at first opposed to the program later became its greatest proponents. "Once they got involved in the development of the program, they began to see that these people would be placed under greater control

Jacque 10

than their counterparts who would be sent to prisons on week-
ends." Although the public may see electronic monitoring as
overly lenient at first, in fact it can provide an effective,
round-the-clock supervision of offenders who would otherwise be
contributing to the problem of prison overcrowding.

Argument in favour of
monitoring

Although electronic monitoring can reduce prison overcrowding, it is not, of course, a cure-all for the problems associated with our criminal justice system. It is also true that we
need to guard against the potential for widening the net "so
that increasing numbers of people are placed under . . . surveillance" (Johnson). It is important that we do not violate
our Charter of Rights and Freedoms in the implementation of
this technology. Still, electronic monitoring may help with
economic and human waste of our punitive prison system. While
the start-up costs associated with electronic monitoring may
seem high, these decrease later once the system is in longer
use. With prison sentencing, as Hollis Johnson pointed out,
there are hidden costs as well as the obvious ones. Prisoners
don't earn a wage, don't contribute to their families or society, and leave prison with a stigma that makes it difficult for
them to get hired later. Electronic monitoring offers advantages to prison sentences for nonviolent offenders. Several
systems are available; no insurmountable problems are evident;
low-risk offenders are effectively controlled; and the costs
are less than for incarceration. As we begin the twenty-first
century in Canada, we can look to electronic monitoring as a
humane, practical alternative to prison sentencing.

Independent conclusion
acknowledges and answers
possible objections

Independent conclusion
draws together and
reinforces main points of
paper; predicts future of
house-arrest programs in
Canada

Works Cited

Baird, Christopher. "Building More Prisons Will Not Solve
     Prison Overcrowding." America's Prisons: Opposing
     Viewpoints. Ed. David Bender, Bruno Leone, and Stacey
     Tipp. San Diego: Greenhaven, 1991. 118-24.

Barr, William. "Corraling the Hard-Core Criminal." Detroit News
     and Free Press 18 Oct. 1992, state ed.: B3.

Beck, James L., Jody Klein-Saffran, and Harold B. Wooten. "Home
     Confinement and the Use of Electronic Monitoring with
     Federal Parolees." Federal Probation Dec. 1990: 22-31.

"BJS Reports: Nation's Jail and Prison Incarceration Rate
     Almost Doubled During Last Decade." Corrections Digest 24
     Jan. 1997: 1-2.

British Columbia. Ministry of Attorney General. Corrections
     Branch. Electronic Monitoring System for Offender
     Supervision. Discussion Paper. 2nd edition. British
     Columbia: GPO, 1987.

--. Ministry of Solicitor General. Corrections Branch.
     Electronic Monitoring for Offender Supervision: Pilot
     Project Evaluation by Linda Neville et al. British
     Columbia: GPO, 1989.

Carey, Anne R., and Elys A. McLean. "Electronic Prison Bars."
     USA Today 30 Sept. 1993: A1.

Conroy, John. Electronic Monitoring: Report of the Special
     Committee on Imprisonment and Release. Canadian Bar
     Association. Ottawa: GPO, 1988.

Margin annotations (left column):

- Entry for collection containing several authors' contributions compiled by three editors
- Entry for newspaper article
- Entry for occupational journal article, with three authors
- Entry for occupational journal article, no author given
- Entry for government discussion paper, no author given
- Entry for government document with more than one author
- Entry for newspaper item with two authors
- Entry for legal report with one author

Jacque 12

Ford, Daniel, and Annesley K. Schmidt. <u>Electronically Monitored</u>
    <u>Home Confinement</u>. United States. National Institute of
    Justice, Department of Justice. Washington: GPO, 1989.

Georgia. Probation Division of the Georgia Department of
    Corrections. <u>Alternatives to Incarceration</u> 1 July 1997.
    3 Feb. 1998 <http://www.harvard.edu/~innovat/aiga87.html>.

Hofer, Paul J., and Barbara S. Meierhoefer. <u>Home Confinement:</u>
    <u>An Evolving Sanction in the Federal Criminal Justice</u>
    <u>System</u>. Washington: Federal Judicial Center, 1987.

"Inmate Populations, Costs and Projection Models." <u>Corrections</u>
    <u>Compendium</u> Jan. 1997: 10-11.

Johnson, Hollis. Personal interview. 16 Feb. 1999.

Katel, Peter. "New Walls, No Inmates." <u>Newsweek</u> 18 May 1992:
    63.

Lynch, Allen. <u>Cost Effectiveness of Incarceration</u>. Leroy
    Collins Institute for Public Policy. 1 July 1997
    <http://www.dos.state.fl.us/fgils/agencies/fcc/
    reports/crime.html>.

Morris, Norval, and Michael Tonry. <u>Between Prison and</u>
    <u>Probation: Intermediate Punishments in a Rational</u>
    <u>Sentencing System</u>. New York: Oxford UP, 1990.

Peck, Keenan. "High-Tech House Arrest." <u>Progressive</u> July 1988:
    26-28.

Petersilia, Joan. <u>House Arrest</u>. United States. National
    Institute of Justice, Department of Justice. Washington:
    GPO, 1988.

Entry for government
document, two
authors given

Entry for Internet report,
no author given

Entry for book with
two authors

Entry for personal interview

Entry for popular magazine
article with one author

Entry for Internet report,
one author given

Entry for government
document, one author given

Jacque 13

Quinlan, J. Michael. "Building More Prisons Will Solve Prison
    Overcrowding." <u>America's Prisons: Opposing Viewpoints</u>.
    Ed. David Bender, Bruno Leone, and Stacey Tipp. San
    Diego: Greenhaven, 1991. 112-16.

Richey, Warren. "Bulging Cells Renew Debate Over Prisons As
    Tools to Fight Crime." <u>Christian Science Monitor</u> 22 Jan.
    1997: 3.

Entry for occupational
journal article with
one author

Scaglione, Fred. "Jails Without Walls." <u>American City & County</u>
    Jan. 1989: 32-40.

Second entry for author;
three unspaced hyphens
substitute for author's name

---. "You're Under Arrest--At Home." <u>USA Today</u> Nov. 1988; 26-28.[1]

Sullivan, Robert E. "Reach Out and Guard Someone: Using Phones
    and Bracelets to Reduce Prison Overcrowding." <u>Rolling
    Stone</u> 29 Nov. 1990: 51.

Second entry for
government document,
no author given

United States. Department of Justice. Bureau of Justice
    Assistance, Office of Justice Programs. <u>Electronic
    Monitoring in Intensive Probation and Parole Programs</u>.
    Washington: GPO, 1989.

United States. Senate. Subcommittee on Federal Spending,
    Budget, and Accounting, Committee on Governmental
    Affairs. <u>Prison Projections: Can the United States Keep
    Pace?</u> 100th Cong., 1st. sess. Washington: GPO, 1987.

[1]The magazine <u>USA Today</u>, not the newspaper of that name.

Documenting Sources

In order to acknowledge and handle sources, you must know how to (1) prepare proper bibliographical references, (2) document sources within your text, (3) handle quotations, and (4) avoid plagiarism.

The kind of information included in bibliographical references depends on the type of source and the documentation system. Two systems are in common use: the Modern Language Association (MLA) system and the American Psychological Association (APA) system. The entries that follow illustrate basic MLA and APA conventions. For more information, consult the *MLA Handbook for Writers of Research Papers,* 6th ed., 2003, and the *Publication Manual of the American Psychological Association,* 4th ed., 1994. When documenting online sources, you can consult the Web sites noted on page 338.

■ Preparing MLA and APA Bibliographic References

Books

The basic bibliographic reference for a book includes the name of the author, the title of the book, the place of publication, the name of the publisher, and the date of publication. Other information is added as necessary. The order of presentation depends upon which system of listing sources, the MLA or APA, is used. Note that the APA system uses initials rather than first and middle names for authors, editors, and translators.

■ A Book with One Author

MLA   Ondaatje, Michael. <u>The English Patient</u>. Toronto: Vintage Books, 1993.

APA   Ondaatje, M. (1993). <u>The English patient</u>. Toronto: Vintage Books.

■ A Book with Two Authors

MLA   Finnbogason, Jack, and Al Valleau. <u>A Canadian Writer's Guide</u>. Toronto: Nelson, 1997.

APA   Finnbogason, J., & Valleau, A. (1997). <u>A Canadian writer's guide</u>. Toronto: Nelson.

Note that the APA system reverses the name of the second author and uses "&" instead of "and" between the names. In titles and subtitles, only the first word and proper nouns and adjectives are capitalized. Whereas the APA system indents the first line of each reference five spaces, the MLA system indents subsequent lines five spaces. The APA now also permits the use of a second indentation format that follows the general MLA practice but indents subsequent lines just three spaces. Here is an example:

APA   Finnbogason, J., & Valleau, A. (1997). <u>A Canadian Writer's Guide</u>. Toronto: Nelson.

Use the indentation format that your instructor specifies, and take care not to mix formats.

■ A Book with More Than Three Authors

MLA   Alder, Roger William, et al. <u>Mechanisms in Organic Chemistry</u>. New York: Wiley, 1971.

APA   Alder, R. W., Finn, T., Bradley, M. A., & Li, A. W. (1971). <u>Mechanisms in organic chemistry</u>. New York: John Wiley.

The MLA system uses "et al." for four or more authors or editors; the APA system gives all author or editor names in the reference list.

■ A Book with a Title That Includes Another Title

The MLA offers two options: You may omit underlining the embedded title, or you may set it off with quotation marks.

Tanner, John. Anxiety in Eden: A Kierkegaardian Reading of
    Paradise Lost. Oxford: Oxford UP, 1992.
MLA

Tanner, John. Anxiety in Eden: A Kierkegaardian Reading of
    "Paradise Lost." Oxford: Oxford UP, 1992.
MLA

The APA offers no guidelines for this situation. We suggest that you follow the first option.

    Tanner, J. (1992). Anxiety in Eden: A Kierkegaardian
Reading of Paradise Lost. Oxford: Oxford University Press.
APA

■ A Book with Corporate or Association Authorship

United Nations, Public Administration Division. Local Government
    Training. New York: UN, 1968.
MLA

    United Nations, Public Administration Division. (1968).
Local government training. New York: Author.
APA

When the author of the work is also the publisher, the APA system uses the word "Author" following the place of publication. If the work is published by another organization, its name replaces "Author."

■ An Edition Other Than the First

Waldman, Neil, and Sarah Norton. Canadian Content. 3rd ed.
    Toronto: Harcourt Brace, 1996.
MLA

    Waldman, N. & Norton, S. (1996). Canadian content. (3rd
ed.) Toronto: Harcourt Brace.
APA

■ A Book in Two or More Volumes

Bartram, Henry C. The Cavalcade of America. 2 vols. New York:
    Knopf, 1959.
MLA

    Bartram, H. C. (1959). The cavalcade of America (Vols.
1-2). New York: Alfred Knopf.
APA

■ A Reprint of an Older Work

MLA Matthiessen, F. O. <u>American Renaissance: Art and Expression in the Age of Emerson and Whitman</u>. 1941. New York: Oxford UP, 1970.

APA Matthiessen, F. O. (1970). <u>American renaissance: Art and expression in the age of Emerson and Whitman</u>. New York: Oxford University Press. (Original work published 1941)

■ A Book with an Editor Rather Than an Author

MLA Toye, William, ed. <u>The Oxford Companion to Canadian Literature</u>. Toronto: Oxford, 1983.

APA Toye, W. (Ed.). (1983). <u>The Oxford companion to Canadian literature</u>. Toronto: Oxford.

■ A Book with Both an Author and an Editor

MLA Conrad, Joseph. <u>Heart of Darkness</u>. Ed. Robert Hampson. London: Penguin, 1995.

APA Conrad, J. (1995). <u>Heart of darkness</u>. (R. Hampson, Ed.). London: Penguin. (Original work published 1902)

■ A Translation

MLA Beauvoir, Simone de. <u>All Said and Done</u>. Trans. Patrick O'Brian. New York: Putnam, 1974.

APA Beauvoir, S. de. (1974). <u>All said and done</u> (P. O'Brian, Trans.). New York: G. P. Putnam. (Original work published 1972)

■ An Essay or Chapter in a Collection of Works by One Author

MLA Woolf, Virginia. "The Lives of the Obscure." <u>The Common Reader</u>, First Series. New York: Harcourt, 1925. 111–18.

APA Woolf, V. (1925). The lives of the obscure In V. Woolf, <u>The common reader</u>, first series (pp. 111-118). New York: Harcourt Brace.

■ An Essay or Chapter in an Anthology

Blaise, Clark. "A Class of New Canadians." <u>Pens of Many Colours:</u> MLA
    <u>A Canadian Reader</u>. Ed. Eva C. Karpinski and Ian Lea.
    Toronto: Harcourt Brace Jovanovich, 1993: 218-26.

Blaise, C. (1993). "A class of new Canadians." In E.C. APA
Karpinski and I. Lea (Eds.), <u>Pens of many colours: a Canadian</u>
<u>reader</u> (pp. 218-226). Toronto: Harcourt Brace Jovanovich.

Periodicals

Periodicals include newspapers, popular magazines, and specialized occupational and scholarly journals. The basic information for a periodical article includes the name of the article's author, the name of the periodical, the title of the article, the date of publication, the page range of the entire article, and, for scholarly journals, the volume number of the periodical. Again, the order of presentation depends on the documentation system used. The MLA and APA systems capitalize periodical titles identically; however, the MLA style omits an introductory *the* from these titles. As illustrated by our example for a signed article in a daily newspaper, the two systems follow a different format for showing when an article does not appear on consecutive pages. Note also that the systems capitalize the titles of articles differently and that the APA system precedes page numbers for newspaper articles with "p." or "pp."

■ An Article in a Scholarly Journal Consecutively Paged Through the Entire Volume

Pfennig, David. "Kinship and Cannibalism." <u>Bioscience</u> 47 (1997): MLA
    667-75.

Pfennig, D. (1997). Kinship and cannibalism. <u>Bioscience</u>, APA
47, 667-675.

■ An Article in a Scholarly Journal That Pages Each Issue Separately

Block, Joel W. "Sodom and Gomorrah: A Volcanic Disaster." MLA
    <u>Journal of Geological Education</u> 23.5 (1976): 74-77.

Block, J. W. (1976). Sodom and Gomorrah: A volcanic APA
disaster. <u>Journal of Geological Education</u>, 23(5), 74-77.

■ An Unsigned Article in a Scholarly Journal

"Baby, It's Cold Inside." <u>Science</u> 276 (1997): 537-38. MLA

Baby, it's cold inside. (1997). <u>Science</u>, 276, 537-538. APA

■ **A Signed Article in an Occupational or a Popular Magazine**

MLA   Gopnik, Adam. "The Good Soldier." New Yorker 24 Nov. 1997:
106–14.

APA   Gopnik, A. (1997, November 24). The good soldier. The New
Yorker, 73, 106–114.

■ **An Unsigned Article in an Occupational or a Popular Magazine**

MLA   "Robot Productivity." Production Engineering May 1982: 52–55.

APA   Robot productivity. (1982, May). Production Engineering,
29, 52–55.

■ **A Signed Article in a Daily Newspaper**

MLA   Aird, Elizabeth. "Take Men as Sexual Victims, Please." The
Vancouver Sun 14 February 1998:A5.

APA   Aird, E. (1998, February 14). Take men as sexual victims,
please. The Vancouver Sun p. A5.

■ **An Unsigned Article in a Daily Newspaper**

MLA   "The Arithmetic of Terrorism." Washington Post 14 Nov. 1997:
A26.

APA   The arithmetic of terrorism. (1997, November 14). The
Washington Post, p. A26.

Encyclopedia Articles

When documenting familiar works, such as the *Canadian Encyclopedia,* the basic information for the MLA system includes the name of the article's author if known, the title of the article, the name of the encyclopedia, and the date of the edition.

MLA   Sobieszek, Robert A. "Photography." World Book Encyclopedia.
1991 ed.

The APA system requires additional information for all encyclopedia citations, as does the MLA system when less familiar publications are documented. Again, the order of presentation differs for the two systems.

MLA   Fears, J. Rufus. "Emperor's Cult." Encyclopedia of Religion. Ed.
Mircea Eliade. 16 vols. New York: Macmillan, 1987.

Fears, J. R. (1987). Emperor's cult. In <u>The encyclopedia</u>
<u>of religion</u> (Vol. 5, pp. 101–102). New York: Macmillan.

APA

For an anonymous article, references for both the MLA and APA systems begin with the article's title. With the APA system, position the publication date, within parentheses, after this title. The remaining format is identical to the citations with an author.

Government Documents

The basic information for a federal, provincial, or foreign government publication that is documented using the MLA system includes the name of the author, the title of the publication, the name of the government and the agency issuing the publication, the place of publication, the name of the printing group, if known, and the date. If no author is named, begin by identifying the government and then cite the government agency as the author. The APA system presents similar information but omits the government name, adds a cataloguing code where one exists, and follows a different order of presentation.

Helix, Jefferson. <u>Environmental Impact of Fish Farming in</u>
      <u>British Columbia</u>. British Columbia. Ministry of
      Environment. A Discussion Paper: Queen's Printer for
      British Columbia, 1997.

MLA

Helix, J. (1997). <u>Environmental Impact of Fish Farming in</u>
<u>British Columbia</u>. British Columbia, Ministry of Environment.
Victoria: Queen's Printer for British Columbia.

APA

Canada. Department of Finance. <u>Annual Report 1991–1992</u>. Ottawa:
      Queen's Printer, 1994.

MLA

Canadian Department of Finance. (1993). <u>Annual Report</u>
<u>1991–1992</u>. Ottawa: Queen's Printer.

APA

United States. Cong. Office of Technology Assessment. <u>The</u>
      <u>Biology of Mental Disorders</u>. 102nd Cong., 2nd sess.
      Washington: GPO, 1992.

MLA

U.S. Congress, Office of Technology Assessment. (1992).
<u>The biology of mental disorders</u> (SUDOCS No. Y3.T22/2:2/B57/10).
Washington, DC: U.S. Government Printing Office.

APA

Other Sources

The information presented and the order of presentation depend on the type of source and the documentation system.

■ Book Reviews

MLA

Koenig, Rhoda. "Billy the Kid." Rev. of <u>Billy Bathgate</u>, by E. L.
    Doctorow. <u>New York</u> 20 Feb. 1989: 20–21.

APA

    Koenig, R. (1989, February 20). Billy the Kid [Review of
the book <u>Billy Bathgate</u>]. <u>New York</u>, 21, 20–21.

If the review is untitled, follow the above formats but omit the missing element.

■ Published Interviews

MLA

Noriega, Manuel. "A Talk with Manuel Noriega." By Felipe
    Hernandez. <u>News Report</u> 20 March 1997: 28–30.

The APA system does not include a documentation format for published interviews. If you are using the APA format and your paper includes material from a published interview, we suggest that you document as follows:

APA

    Hernandez, F. (1997, March 20). A talk with Manuel
Noriega. [Interview with Manuel Noriega]. <u>News Report</u>, 15,
28–30.

If the interview is untitled, use, in place of a title, the word "Interview," without quotation marks or underlining, for the MLA system. For the APA system, follow the example above, omitting any mention of a title.

■ Personal Interviews

If you conducted the interview yourself and are using the MLA system, start with the name of the person interviewed and follow it with the kind of interview and the date conducted.

MLA

Newman, Paul. Personal interview. 19 May 1997.

For the APA system, a personal interview is considered personal correspondence and is not included in the References list. Instead, use an in-text parenthetical citation. Include the name of the person interviewed, the notation "personal communication," and the date: (P. Newman, personal communication, May 19, 1997).

■ Films

MLA

<u>Frankenstein</u>. Dir. James Whale. Perf. Boris Karloff, John Boles,
    Colin Clive, and Mae Clarke. Universal, 1931.

If you are interested in the contribution of a particular person, start with that person's name.

Whale, James, dir. <u>Frankenstein</u>. Perf. Boris Karloff, John
    Boles, Colin Clive, and Mae Clarke. Universal, 1931.

MLA

In the APA system, the citation begins with an individual's name and his or her contribution to the film.

    Whale, J. (Director). (1931). <u>Frankenstein</u> [Film].
Hollywood, Universal.

APA

■ Television and Radio Programs

Basic citations follow the formats below:

<u>The Independent Eye</u>. Prod. M. Paris and J. Robertson. Knowledge
    Network. Know, Burnaby. 13 Feb. 1999.

MLA

    Paris, M., & Robertson, J. (Producers). (1999, February
13). <u>The independent eye</u>. Burnaby, B.C.: Knowledge Network.

APA

Use these formats when additional information is pertinent:

<u>Peril at End House</u>. By Agatha Christie. Dir. Renny Rye. Prod.
    Brian Eastman. Perf. David Suchet and Hugh Fraser.
    Mystery. Introd. Diana Rigg. PBS. WKAR, East Lansing. 12
    Aug. 1993.

MLA

    Exton, C. (1993). <u>Peril at end house</u> (R. Rye, Director).
In B. Eastman (Producer), Mystery. Washington, DC: Public
Broadcasting Service.

APA

With the APA system, the scriptwriter's name appears in the author's position. In-text references begin with the first name in the bibliographical reference (for example, Exton, 1993).

■ Sound Recordings

If the recording is on a CD, you do not need to indicate the medium. If the recording is on any other medium, such as an LP or an audiocassette, you must indicate the medium just before the name of the manufacturer. See the example below indicating an LP.

Smith, Bessie. <u>The World's Greatest Blues Singer</u>. LP. Columbia,
    1948.

MLA

If you mention the name of a particular item on the sound recording, set it off with quotation marks and position it as shown:

Smith, Bessie. "Down Hearted Blues." <u>The World's Greatest Blues
    Singer</u>. LP. Columbia, 1948.

MLA

The APA system calls for these formats:

> Smith, B. (1948). <u>The world's greatest blues singer</u>. [LP.] New York: Columbia Records.

> Smith, B. (1948). Down hearted blues. On <u>The world's greatest blues singer</u>. [LP.]. New York: Columbia Records.

■ Computer Software

<u>Data Desk</u>. Vers. 6.0. Computer software. Ithaca, NY: Data Description, 1997.

> <u>Data Desk</u> (Version 6.0) [Computer software]. (1997). Ithaca, NY: Data Description, Inc.

■ CD-ROMs

Norman, J. L. "Barcelona." <u>Software Toolworks Multimedia Encyclopedia</u>. CD-ROM. Software Toolworks, 1992.

> Norman, J. L. (1992). Barcelona. In <u>Software Toolworks Multimedia Encyclopedia</u> [CD-ROM]. Available: Software Toolworks, Inc.

<u>Digital Resource Library for Introductory Psychology</u>. Release 2.0. CD-ROM. Prentice Hall, 1996.

> Prentice Hall. (1996). <u>Digital Resource Library for Introductory Psychology</u>, Release 2.0. [CD-ROM].

Online Sources

The most recent edition of the *Publication Manual of the American Psychological Association* provides only limited recommendations for documenting online sources. However, you can consult the association's Web site for up-to-date information about citing sources from the Internet and the World Wide Web:

> http://www.apa.org/journals/webref.html

The examples here follow the latest guidelines for the MLA and APA Web sites. Be sure to ask your instructor which format to follow, and then use that format consistently. Often data from the Internet are incomplete, perhaps lacking an author or even a title. Include all the available information. Remember: Your goal is to enable your reader to find the source.

■ **Books**

The basic information for a book documented by the MLA system includes the name(s) of the author(s), if known; the title of the book; the place and date of original publication, if applicable; the electronic site, if named; the date of electronic publication if the online version has never been published in print, or if it is part of a scholarly project; the sponsor of the site; the date the material was retrieved; and the online address.

Locke, John. <u>An Essay Concerning Human Understanding</u>. London,
    1690. Institute of Learning Technologies. 1955. Columbia
    University. 24 June 2000
    <http://www.ilt.columbia.edu/projects/digitexts/locke/
    understanding/title.html>.

MLA

The APA provides no specific guidelines for documenting online books. We suggest that you follow the general guidelines for a printed book and conclude with appropriate electronic source information.

Locke, John. (1995). <u>An essay concerning human
understanding</u>. New York: Columbia University. (Original work
published 1690). Retrieved June 24, 2000, from the World Wide Web:
http://www.ilt.columbia.edu/projects/digitexts/locke/
understanding/title.html

APA

When some of the basic information is not provided, use whatever is available.

Chaney, Walter J., William J. Diehm, and Frank Seeley. <u>The
    Second 50 Years: A Reference Manual for Senior Citizens</u>.
    Weed, CA: London Circle, 1999. 8 August 2000
    <http://londoncircle.com/2d50.html>.

MLA

Chaney, W. J., Diehm, W. J., & Seeley, F. (1999). <u>The
second 50 years: A reference manual for senior citizens</u>. Weed,
CA: London Circle. Retrieved August 8, 2000, from the World Wide
Web: http://londoncircle.com/2d50.html

APA

When you cite part of an electronic book, place the citation right after the name(s) of the author(s) or, for an APA citation, right after the date of original publication.

Dawson, Marie. Introduction. <u>Methods of Sociological
    Investigation</u>. New York: Harmon, 1997. 6 Sept. 2000
    <http://www.harmon.edu/edu-books.html>.

MLA

Dawson, M. (1997). Introduction. <u>Methods of Sociological
Investigation</u>. New York: Harmon. Retrieved Sept. 6, 2000, from
the World Wide Web: http://www.harmon.edu/edu-books.html

APA

■ **Periodicals on the World Wide Web**

Periodicals online include specialized occupational and scholarly journals, popular magazines, newspapers, and newsletters. The basic information for a periodical includes the author's name, if known; the title of the article; the title of the periodical; the volume number; the date the article was published; the number of paragraphs in the article or its page numbers; the date the material was retrieved; and the online address. Because the APA provides no specific guidelines for documenting online articles, we recommend that you follow the guidelines for printed versions and add the online source information. Note the omission of volume numbers and pagination from the documentation for some popular publications.

MLA

Cervetti, Nancy. "In the Breeches, Petticoats, and Pleasures of Orlando." <u>Journal of Modern Literature</u> 20.2 (1996): 32 pars. 8 Jan. 1998 <http://www.indiana.edu/~iupress/journals/mod-art2.html>.

APA

Cervetti, N. (1996). In the breeches, petticoats, and pleasures of Orlando. <u>Journal of Modern Literature</u>, 20(2). Retrieved January 8, 1998 from the World Wide Web: http://www.indiana.edu/~iupress/journals/mod-art2.html

MLA

Navarro, Mireya. "Women in Sports Cultivating New Playing Fields." <u>New York Times on the Web</u> 13 Feb. 2001. 22 Feb. 2001 <http://www.nytimes.com>.

APA

Navarro, M. (2001, February 13). Women in Sports Cultivating New Playing Fields. <u>New York Times on the Web</u> Retrieved February 22, 2001, from the World Wide Web: http://www.nytimes.com

MLA

"No Link Found in Violence, Videos." <u>Boston Globe Online</u> 8 Aug. 2000. 27 Aug. 2000. <http://www.boston.comdailyglobe2/ ... nk_found_in_violence_videos+.shtml>.

APA

No Link Found in Violence, Videos. (2000, August 8). <u>Boston Globe Online</u>, p. A14. Retrieved August 27, 2000, from the World Wide Web: http://www.boston.comdailyglobe2/ ... nk_found_in_violence_videos+.shtml

MLA

Oakes, Jeannie. "Promotion or Retention: Which One Is Social?" <u>Harvard Education Letter</u>. Jan.-Feb. 1999. 7 pars. 8 Aug. 2000 <http://www.edetter.org/past/issues/ 1999-jf/promotion.shtml>.

Oakes, J. (1999, January-February). Promotion or
retention: Which one is social? <u>Harvard Education Letter</u>.
Retrieved August 8, 2000, from the World Wide Web:
http://www.edetter.org/past/issues/1999-jf/promotion.shtml

■ Periodicals Accessed Through an Online Library Service or Large Network Provider

Increasingly, full-text articles are available online at libraries or at home through services provided by private institutions such as Lexis-Nexis or public institutions like governments, who maintain extensive databases. These services may or may not provide an online address for accessed material. If you know the service's home page, and you're documenting by the MLA system, cite the author's name, if known; the title of the article; the title of the periodical; the date the article was published; the page numbers for the article; the name of the database; the name of the library service; the name of the library; the date the material was accessed; and the online address of the service's home page.

Clemetson, Lynette. "A Ticket to Private School." <u>Newsweek</u> 27
    Mar. 2000. Lexis-Nexis. Ferris State University Library
    Web Database Access. 5 May 2000
    <http://libray.ferris.edu/databaseframes.html>.

The APA documentation system provides the same information but omits any online addresses except World Wide Web addresses.

Clemetson, L. (2000, March 27). A ticket to private
school. <u>Newsweek</u>. Retrieved May 5, 2000, from Ferris State
University Library Web Database Access. (Lexis-Nexis)

For MLA style, when no online address is provided, it is necessary to identify the key word/s you used to find the material you accessed.

Wilson-Smith, Anthony. "Hockey Night in Reality." <u>Maclean's</u> 14
    Oct. 2002:4. <u>EBSCO Host Research Databases</u>. Kwantlen
    University College Online Article Index. 18 Oct. 2002. Key
    words: Hockey; Canada.

Wilson-Smith, A. (2002, October 14). Hockey night in
reality. <u>Maclean's</u>. Retrieved October 18, 2002, from Kwantlen
University College Online Article Index (EBSCO Host Research
Databases). Key words: Hockey; Canada.

■ Encyclopedia Articles

The basic information for an encyclopedia article accessed through the World Wide Web includes the author's name, if known; the title of the article; the name of the encyclopedia; and the date of the edition, and the online address. MLA style also names the vendor.

MLA

```
Daniel, Ralph Thomas. "The History of Western Music." Britannica
     Online: Macropaedia. 1995. Encyclopaedia Britannica. 14
     June 1995
     <http://www.eb.com:180/cgi-bin/g:DocF=macro/5004/45/0.html>.
```

APA

```
     Daniel, R. T. (1995). "The history of western music." In
Britannica Online: Macropaedia. Retrieved June 14,1995, from the
World Wide Web:
http://www.eb.com:180/cgi-bin/g:DocF=macro/5004/45/0.html
```

For encyclopedia articles accessed through a CD-ROM, name the media after the title of the database.

■ Government Documents

The basic information for a government document includes the name of the author, if known; the title; the name of the government and agency issuing the document; the place of publication and printing group, if known; the date of publication; the date the material was retrieved; and the online address. If no author is given, begin by identifying the government and then give the government agency as the author. For the APA system, omit the government name, and add a cataloguing code if one is available.

MLA

```
Georgia State. Probation Division of the Georgia Department of
     Corrections. Alternatives to Incarceration. 1 July 1997.
     3 Feb. 1998 <http://www.harvard.edu/~innovat/aiga87.html>.
```

APA

```
     Probation Division of the Georgia Department of
Corrections. (1997, July 1). Alternatives to Incarceration (CSP
No. 239875). Retrieved February 3, 1998 from the World Wide Web:
http://www.harvard.edu/~innovat/aiga87.html
```

■ Personal Home Page

The basic information for a personal home page documented according to the MLA style system includes the name of its originator, if known; the title of the site, if any (use Home page or other such description if no title is given); the date the material was retrieved from the site; and the online address.

MLA

```
Lanthrop, Olin. Home page. 24 June 2000
     <http://www.cognivis.com/olin/photos.htm>.
```

The APA system offers no documentation guidelines for personal home pages. We suggest that you follow the pattern below, which conforms to general APA practice. Note that the APA system, unlike the MLA, includes the date of the latest Web page revision, if known, in parentheses.

> Lanthrop, O. (2000, May 28). Home page. Retrieved June 24, 2000, from the World Wide Web: http://cognivis.com/olin/photos.htm

APA

■ Newsgroups, Listservs, and E-mail

MLA gives guidelines for including newsgroups, listservs, and e-mail within the Works Cited list. APA format uses only in-text parenthetical citations for personal communications within the body of the paper and omits the citation in the Reference list at the end of the paper.

> Corelli, Aldo. "Colleges and Diversity." Online posting. 20 Apr.1993. <learninghouse.michigan.edu>.

MLA

> Nicholson, Brad. "Casino Gambling." E-mail to author. 2 Feb. 2001.

MLA

> . . . as reported in his study (B. Nicholson, personal communication, February 2, 2001).

APA

EXERCISE

A. **Using the MLA system, write a proper reference for each of the following sets of information:**

1. A book titled Gas Conditioning Fact Book. The book was published in 1962 by Dow Chemical Company in Midland, Michigan. No author is named.

2. An unsigned article titled Booze Plays a Big Role in Car Crashes. The article was published in the November 28, 1997, state edition of the Detroit News. It appears on page 2 of section C.

3. An essay written by C. Wright Mills and titled The Competitive Personality. The essay appeared in a collection of Mills's writings entitled Power, Politics, and People. The collection was published in 1963 by Ballantine Books in New York. The book is edited and introduced by Irving Louis Horowitz. The essay appears on pages 263 through 273.

4. An unsigned article titled Global Warming Fears on Rise. The article was published in the October 25, 1997, issue of Newswatch magazine. It appears on pages 29 to 31.

5. A book written by Guy Vanderhaeghe and titled The Englishman's Boy. The book was published in 1996 by McClelland & Stewart Inc. in Toronto.

6. A book written by Kate Chopin and titled The Awakening. The book, edited by Margaret Culley, was published in 1976 by W. W. Norton and Company in New York.

7. An article written by James E. Cooke and titled Alexander Hamilton. The article appears on pages 31 and 32 of the World Book Encyclopedia, Volume 9, published in 1996.

8. An article written by Sarah McBride and titled Young Deadbeats Pose Problems for Credit-Card Issuers. The article was published in the November 28, 1997, Toronto edition of The Globe and Mail. It appears on pages 1 and 6 of section B.

9. A book written by Magdalena Dabrowski and Rudolph Leopold and titled Egon Schiele. The book was published in 1997 by the Yale University Press in New Haven, Connecticut.

10. A book written by Jean Descola and titled A History of Spain. The book, translated by Elaine P. Halperin, was published in 1962 by Alfred A. Knopf in New York.

11. An article written by John T. Flanagan and Raymond L. Grimer and titled Mexico in American Fiction to 1850. The article was published in 1940 in a journal called Hispania. It appears on pages 307 through 318. The volume number is 23.

12. A Canadian government document titled Marine Fisheries Review. It was published by the Federal Department of Fisheries in 1993. No author is given.

13. A book written by David Kahn and titled The Codebreakers. The second edition of the book was published in 1996 by Scribner's in New York.

14. A book written by Joseph Blotner and titled Faulkner: A Biography. The book was published in two volumes in 1974 by Random House in New York.

15. An article written by Calvin Tompkins and titled The Importance of Being Elitist. The article was published in the November 24, 1997, issue of the New Yorker. It appears on pages 58 through 69.

16. A book written by Thomas Beer and titled Stephen Crane: A Study in American Letters. The book was published in 1923 and reprinted in 1972 by Octagon Books in New York.

17. A review of a book written by Jacques Barzun and titled The Culture We Deserve. The review, by Beth Winona, appeared in the March 1989 issue of American Issues magazine and was titled Barzun and Culture. It appeared on pages 46 through 50.

18. An interview of playwright Neil Simon. The interview was titled Neil Simon on the New York Theater and appeared in the September 3, 1997, issue of the Long Island News, on pages C4–5. The interviewer was Pearl Barnes.

19. A film titled Casablanca. The film was directed by Michael Curtiz and starred Humphrey Bogart, Ingrid Bergman, Claude Rains, and Paul Henreid. It was released in 1942 by Warner Brothers.

20. A television program titled Grizzly. It appeared on CBUT, Vancouver, on February 3, 1997. The station is part of the CBC.

B. Prepare a proper MLA entry for each of the works you plan to use in writing your paper.

Handling In-Text Citations

Both the MLA and APA systems use notations that appear within the text and are set off by parentheses. The systems are illustrated by the following examples.

Basic Citation Form

For the MLA system, the citation consists of the last name of the author and the page numbers of the publication in which the material originally appeared. The APA system adds the year to the citation. At the writer's option, the items may be grouped together or separated, as shown in the following examples. The bibliographic references preceding the passages follow the MLA format.

■ Bibliographic Reference

Rothenberg, Randall. "Life in Cyburbia." <u>Esquire</u> Feb. 1996:
        56-63.

■ Passage and Citation

A mania for the Internet has invaded many important aspects of our culture. Newspapers run stories on it, businesses have rushed to set up Web sites, and the Speaker of the House of Representatives has stated that even our poorest children have a stake in the Internet (Rothenberg 59).

MLA

Rothenberg states that a mania for the Internet has invaded many important aspects of our culture. Newspapers run stories on it, businesses have rushed to set up Web sites, and the Speaker of the House of Representatives has stated that even our poorest children have a stake in the Internet (59).

MLA

. . . our poorest children have a stake in the Internet (Rothenberg, 1996, p. 59).

APA

Rothenberg (1996) states . . . have a stake in the Internet (p. 59).

APA

■ Bibliographic Reference

Weider, Benjamin, and David Hapgood. <u>The Murder of Napoleon</u>. New
        York: Congdon, 1982.

■ **Passage and Citation**

MLA

Four different autopsy reports were filed. All the reports agreed that there was a cancerous ulcer in Napoleon's stomach, but none of them declared that the cancer was the cause of death. Nevertheless, cancer has become accepted as the cause (Weider and Hapgood 72).

APA

. . . Nevertheless, cancer has become accepted as the cause (Weider & Hapgood, 1982, p. 72).

If a source has more than three authors (more than six for the APA), use "et al.," meaning "and others," for all but the first-named one.

■ **Bibliographic Reference**

Baugh, Albert C., et al. A Literary History of England. New York: Appleton, 1948.

■ **Passage and Citation**

MLA

Although no one knows for certain just when Francis Beaumont and John Fletcher started collaborating, by 1610 they were writing plays together (Baugh et al. 573).

APA

. . . writing plays together (Baugh et al., 1948, p. 573).

Authors with the Same Last Name

If your citations include authors with the same last name, use the initials of their first names to distinguish them.

■ **Bibliographic References**

Adler, Jerry. "Search for an Orange Thread." Newsweek 16 June 1980: 32–34.

Adler, William L. "The Agent Orange Controversy." Detroit Free Press 18 Dec. 1979, state ed.: B2.

■ **Passage and Citation**

MLA

As early as 1966, government studies showed that dioxin-contaminated 2,4,5-T caused birth defects in laboratory animals. Later studies also found that this herbicide was to blame for miscarriages, liver abscesses, and nerve damage (J. Adler 32).

```
. . . miscarriages, liver abscesses, and nerve damage (J. Adler,
1980, p. 32).
```

APA

Separate Works by the Same Author

If your references include two or more works by the same author, add shortened forms of the titles to your in-text citation if you follow the MLA system. Underline shortened book titles and use quotation marks around article and essay titles. For the APA system, use the conventional name–date–page number entry.

■ Bibliographic References

```
Mullin, Dennis. "After U.S. Troops Pull Out of Grenada." U.S.
     News & World Report 14 Nov. 1983: 22-25.
---. "Why the Surprise Move in Grenada--and What Next." U.S.
     News & World Report 7 Nov. 1983: 31-34.
```

■ Passage and Citation

```
As the rangers evacuated students, the marines launched another of-
fensive at Grand Mal Bay, then moved south to seize the capital and
free the governor (Mullin, "Why the Surprise" 33).
```

MLA

```
. . . and free the governor (Mullin, 1983b, p. 33).
```

APA

As the APA example illustrates, if the two works appeared in the same year, put an "a" or a "b," without quotes, after the date to identify whether you are referring to the first or second entry for that author in the bibliography.

Two Separate Sources for the Same Citation

If two sources provide essentially the same information and you wish to mention both in one parenthetical citation, alphabetize them according to their authors' last names, group them together with a semicolon between them, and position the citation as you would any other citation.

■ Bibliographic References

```
Bryce, Bonnie. "The Controversy over Funding Community
     Colleges." Detroit Free Press 13 Nov. 1988, state ed.: A4.
Warshow, Harry. "Community College Funding Hits a Snag." Grand
     Rapids Press 15 Nov. 1988, city ed.: A2.
```

■ **Passage and Citation**

MLA

In contending that a 3 percent reduction in state funding for community colleges would not significantly hamper their operations,
the governor overlooked the fact that community college enrollment
was expected to jump by 15 percent during the next year (Bryce A4;
Warshow A2).

APA

. . . enrollment was expected to jump by 15 percent during the next
year (Bryce, 1988, p. A4; Warshow, 1988, p. A2).

Unsigned References

When you use a source for which no author is given, the in-text citation consists of
all or part of the title, the appropriate page numbers, and, for the APA system,
the date.

■ **Bibliographic Reference**

"Money and Classes." <u>Progressive</u> Oct. 1997: 10.

■ **Passage and Citation**

MLA

According to the General Accounting Office, repairing the country's
dilapidated school buildings would carry a price tag of over
110 billion dollars. Furthermore, constructing the 6,000 buildings
needed to end classroom overcrowding would cost many billions more
("Money and Classes" 10).

APA

. . . many billions more ("Money and classes," 1997, p. 10).

Citing Quotations

When the quotation is run into the text, position the citation as shown below.

■ **Bibliographic Reference**

Schapiro, Mark. "Children of a Lesser God." <u>Harper's Bazaar</u> Apr.
1996: 205–6+.

■ **Passage and Citation**

MLA

U.N. investigators who have studied the extent of child labour
in third-world countries estimate that "as many as 200 million

children go to work rather than to school . . . making everything
from clothing and shoes to handbags and carpets" (Schapiro 205).

". . . handbags and carpets" (Schapiro, 1996, p. 205).

APA

With longer, indented quotations, skip two horizontal spaces after the end punctuation and type the reference in parentheses.

■ **Bibliographic Reference**

Newhouse, John. "The Diplomatic Round: A Freemasonry of
    Terrorism." New Yorker 8 July 1985: 46–63.

■ **Passage and Citation**

One commentator offers this assessment of why foreign terrorist
groups don't operate in the United States:

MLA

> The reason that America has been spared so far, apparently,
> is that it is less vulnerable than Europe, especially to
> Middle Eastern extremists. Moving in and out of most European
> countries isn't difficult for non-Europeans; border controls
> are negligible. But American customs and immigration authori-
> ties, being hyper-alert to drug traffic, tend to pay atten-
> tion to even marginally doubtful people, and a would-be
> terrorist . . . could come under surveillance for the wrong
> reason. (Newhouse 63)

. . . come under surveillance for the wrong reason. (Newhouse,
1985, p. 63)

APA

Indirect Citations

If you use a quotation from person A that you obtained from a book or article written by person B, or you paraphrase such a quotation, put "qtd. in" before the name of the publication's author in the parenthetical reference.

■ **Bibliographic Reference**

Klein, Joe. "Ready for Rudy." New York 6 Mar. 1989: 30–37.

■ **Passage and Citation**

Rudolph Giuliani favors the death penalty for "the murder of a law-
enforcement officer, mass murder, a particularly heinous killing"

MLA

but would impose it only "when there is certainty of guilt well beyond a reasonable doubt" (qtd. in Klein 37).

APA

". . . there is certainty of guilt well beyond a reasonable doubt"
(qtd. in Klein, 1989, p. 37).

Authors Identified in Text

Sometimes you'll want to introduce a paraphrase, summary, or quotation with
the name of its author. In this case the page number may be positioned immediately after the name or follow the material cited.

■ Bibliographic Reference

Jacoby, Susan. "Waiting for the End: On Nursing Homes." New York
        Times Magazine 31 Mar. 1974, city ed.: 80.

■ Passage and Citation

MLA

Susan Jacoby (80) sums up the grim outlook of patients in bad nursing homes by noting that they are merely waiting to die.

MLA

Susan Jacoby sums up the grim outlook of patients in bad nursing
homes by noting that they are merely waiting to die (80).

APA

Susan Jacoby (1974, p. 80) sums up . . .

APA

Susan Jacoby (1974) sums up . . . waiting to die (p. 80).

> **EXERCISE**   *Using the MLA system, write a proper in-text citation for each of the biblio-
> graphic references you prepared for part B on page 344. Assume that you
> have not used the author's name to introduce the material you cite.*

■ Handling Quotations

Set off quotations fewer than five lines long (fewer than forty words long for the
APA system) with quotation marks and run them into the text of the paper. For
longer quotes, omit the quotation marks and indent the material ten spaces from
the left-hand margin (five spaces for the APA system). Double-space the typing. If
you quote part or all of one paragraph, don't further indent the first line. If you
quote two or more consecutive paragraphs, indent each one's first line three additional spaces (five for the APA system). Use single quotation marks for a quotation
within a shorter quotation and double marks for a quotation within a longer, indented quotation. The following examples illustrate the handling of quotations.
The documentation and indentation follow the MLA guidelines.

■ Short Quotation

Ellen Goodman offers this further observation about writers who peddle formulas for achieving success through selfishness: "They are all Doctor Feelgoods, offering placebo prescriptions instead of strong medicine. They give us a way to live with ourselves, perhaps, but not a way to live with each other" (16).

■ Quotation Within Short Quotation

The report further stated, "All great writing styles have their wellsprings in the personality of the writer. As Buffon said, 'The style is the man'" (Duncan 49).

■ Quotation Within Longer, Indented Quotation

Barbara Tuchman's The Proud Tower presents a somewhat different view of the new conservative leaders:

> Besides riches, rank, broad acres, and ancient lineage, the new government also possessed, to the regret of the liberal opposition, and in the words of one of them, "an almost embarrassing wealth of talent and capacity." Secure in authority, resting comfortably on their electoral majority in the House of Commons and on a permanent majority in the House of Lords, of whom four-fifths were conservatives, they were in a position, admitted the same opponent, "of unassailable strength." (4)

Always provide some context for material that you quote. Various options exist. When you quote from a source for the first time, you might provide the author's full name and the source of the quotation, perhaps indicating the author's expertise as well. The passage just above omits the author's expertise; the passage below includes it.

> Writing in Newsweek magazine, Riena Gross, chief psychiatric social worker at Illinois Medical Center in Chicago, said, "Kids have no real sense that they belong anywhere or to anyone as they did ten or fifteen years ago. Parents have loosened the reins, and kids are kind of floundering" (74).

Or you might note the event prompting the quotation and then the author's name.

> Addressing a seminar at the University of Toronto, Dr. Joseph
> Pomeranz speculated that "acupuncture may work by activating a neu-
> ral pain suppression mechanism in the brain" (324).

On other occasions you might note only the author's full name and expertise.

> Economist Richard M. Cybert, president of Carnegie-Mellon
> University, offers the following sad prediction about the steel in-
> dustry's future: "It will never be as large an industry as it has
> been. There are a lot of plants that will never come back and many
> laborers that will never be rehired" (43).

When quoting from a source with no author given, introduce the quotation with the name of the source.

> Commenting upon the problems that law enforcement personnel have in
> coping with computer crime, Credit and Financial Management maga-
> zine pointed out, "A computer crime can be committed in three hun-
> dredths of a second, and the criminal can be thousands of miles
> from the 'scene,' using a telephone" ("Computer Crime" 43).

After first citing an author's full name, use only the last name for subsequent references.

> In answering the objections of government agencies to the Freedom
> of Information Act, Wellford commented, "Increased citizen access
> should help citizens learn of governmental activities that weaken
> our First Amendment freedoms. Some administrative inconvenience
> isn't too large a price to pay for that" (137).

Page numbers are not helpful when you cite passages from plays and poems since these literary forms are available in many editions. When you quote from a play, identify the act, scene, and line numbers. Use Arabic numbers separated by periods. Here's how to cite Act 2, Scene 1, lines 295–300 of Shakespeare's *Othello:*

> That Cassio loves her, I do well believe it; That she
> loves him, 'tis apt, and of great credit: The Moor, how
> be it that I endure him not, Is of a constant, loving,
> noble nature; And I dare think he'll prove to Desdemona
> A most dear husband. (Othello 2.1. 295-300)

When quoting from a short poem, use "line" or "lines" and the line number(s).

> In "Dover Beach," Matthew Arnold offers this melancholy assessment
> of the state of religion:
>
> > The Sea of Faith
> > Was once, too, at the full, and round earth's shore
> > Lay like the folds of a bright girdle furl'd.

```
But now I only hear

Its melancholy, long, withdrawing roar. (lines 21-25)
```

In quoting poetry that has been run into the text, use a slash mark (/) to indicate the shift from one line to the next in the original:

```
In his ode "To Autumn," Keats says that Autumn is the "Season of
mists and mellow fruitfulness, / Close bosom-friend of the maturing
sun" (lines 1-2).
```

■ Avoiding Plagiarism

While documenting your sources properly strengthens the authority of your writing, failing to document properly weakens your personal and academic or professional credibility. This failure to document, whether intentional or not, may be regarded as plagiarism.

Plagiarism is a form of academic dishonesty. It occurs when a writer uses another person's material without properly acknowledging the debt. Almost all students know that the most obvious forms of plagiarism—such as buying a paper from a paper mill—are wrong. Often, however, plagiarism happens because students are careless in their note taking, or because they simply don't understand what must be acknowledged and documented. In our computerized worlds, where we become used to downloading music, or sharing software, it might be tempting to rationalize that material from the Internet is free for the taking. Some students might imagine that they can escape the obligation to cite sources by changing a word here or there, or cutting and pasting information from different sources. However, unless the material is clearly common knowledge that will not ever be questioned or challenged, any material from external sources, including the Internet, must be cited. Both intentional and unintentional plagiarism are unacceptable.

Plagiarism is a serious ethical breach. It degrades the quality of education for students and for institutions. It is unfair to the majority of students who are struggling to learn the challenging task of incorporating relevant research into their own writing in a responsible way. Students who plagiarize cheat themselves of genuine learning; they are also robbing the original writer of due recognition.

The consequences of plagiarism are often severe. Depending on the school policy, students caught plagiarizing risk getting a zero for that assignment, failing the course, or even being suspended or expelled. In 2002, 44 business and economics students at a major B.C. university were suspended for plagiarizing a tutor's work; the suspensions were noted on the students' transcripts. Large groups of students at other Canadian universities have been suspended for academic dishonesty. Instructors who are used to reading student essays can usually notice when the voice of the writer changes, or when the quality of the writing is inconsistent. In addition, many schools have plagiarism detection software that helps instructors track plagiarism, even if it is just a few sentences that have been raided from a source.

Any summary, paraphrase, quotation, statistics, or graphics you include in your paper must be documented. The only types of information escaping this requirement are those listed below:

1. Common knowledge. Common knowledge is information that most educated people would know. For instance, there's no need to document a statement that the Pacific National Exhibition attracts thousands of visitors each year. However, if you include precise daily, monthly, or yearly figures, then documentation is necessary.

2. Your own conclusions. As you write your paper, you'll incorporate your own conclusions at various points. Such comments require no documentation. The same holds true for your own research. If you polled students on a campus issue, simply present the findings as your own.

3. Facts found in many sources. Facts such as the year of Shakespeare's death, the size of the national debt, and the location of the Taj Mahal need not be documented.

4. Standard terms. Terms widely used in a particular field require no documentation. Examples include such computer terms as *mouse, floppy disk,* and *download.*

Any piece of information not set off with quotation marks must be in your own words. Otherwise, even though you name your source, you are plagiarizing by presenting the original phrasing as your own.

The following passages illustrate the improper and proper use of source material.

Original Passage

One might contend, of course, that our country's biological diversity is so great and the land is so developed—so criss-crossed with the works of man—that it will soon be hard to build a dam anywhere without endangering some species. But as we develop a national inventory of endangered species, we certainly can plan our *necessary* development so as to exterminate the smallest number possible . . .

James L. Buckley, "Three Cheers for the Snail Darter,"
National Review, September 14, 1979: 1144–45.

■ Plagiarism

Our country's biological diversity is so great and the land is so developed that it will soon be hard to build a dam anywhere without endangering some species. But as we develop a national inventory of endangered species, we certainly can plan our necessary development so as to exterminate the smallest number possible.

This writer has clearly plagiarized. The absence of Buckley's name and the failure to enclose his words in quotation marks create the impression that this passage is the student's own work.

■ Plagiarism

<u>Our country's biological diversity is so great and the land so de-</u>
<u>veloped</u> that in the near future we may pose a threat to some crea-
ture whenever we construct a dam. By <u>developing a national</u>
<u>inventory of endangered species</u>, however, <u>we can plan necessary de-</u>
<u>velopment so as to</u> preserve as many species as possible (Buckley
1144).

This version credits the ideas to Buckley, but the student has plagiarized by failing to put quotation marks around the phrasing (underlined above) that was copied from the original. As a result, readers will think that the passage represents the student's own wording.

■ Proper Use of Original

America has so many kinds of plants and animals, and it is so built
up, that in the near future we may pose a threat to some living
thing just by damming some waterway. If, however, we knew which of
our nation's plants and animals were threatened, we could use this
information to preserve as many species as we can (Buckley 1144).

This student has identified the author and used her own words. As a result, she has not plagiarized.

Students who are uncertain about what constitutes plagiarism are responsible to educate themselves. They may consult online sources such as:

- How Not to Plagiarize (from the University of Toronto)

- Avoiding Plagiarism: Mastering the Art of Scholarship (from the University of California at Davis)

- plagiarism.org

Whenever you are unsure whether material requires documentation, supply a reference. And always handle direct quotations by following the guidelines beginning on page 350.

Additional Research Strategies: Interviews, Questionnaires, Direct Observations

The library isn't the only source of information for research writing. Investigators also gather information through *primary research,* which includes such activities as consulting public records in local, provincial, and federal archives, performing experiments, conducting interviews, sending out questionnaires, and making direct observations of various kinds.

This chapter focuses on the latter three types, the most common primary research strategies.

The Value of Primary Research

What makes primary research so valuable? First, it allows individuals and organizations to collect recent information, often unavailable elsewhere, that precisely suits their needs. A company that has developed a new product can't turn to published data to estimate its sales prospects; such information simply doesn't exist. But polling test users with a well-crafted questionnaire could suggest some answers and perhaps also some tips for improving the product. Similarly, someone wanting to gauge the success of an ongoing clothing drive by a local charitable organization might interview its director.

Even when published material exists, it may not contain desired information. Although numerous articles discuss student attitudes about required courses, you probably wouldn't find a report that explores student reaction to a new general-education requirement at your school. You could, however, assemble this information by distributing a questionnaire. The findings might even contradict, and therefore cause you to question, the conclusions of others.

Primary research can also yield unexpected and significant material. Suppose you're investigating adult illiteracy, and you interview a professor with a specialty in this area of study. She explains the reasons why people who can't read resist help and supplies several relevant examples. Such information might not appear anywhere in print. Certainly the resulting report would carry more weight and elicit more interest than one without such insights.

You can integrate primary research into a report that consists largely of *secondary research,* the kind that depends on library materials. The student who wrote the research paper on electronic monitoring (see pages 316–328) incorporated the results of a personal interview with a criminology professor knowledgeable about a pilot program in British Columbia. This interview provided information on the scope, operation, success rate, and cost advantage of the program. Often, however, writers detail the findings of primary research in separate reports. This would be the case if, for example, your employer asked you to interview users of a new computer system in order to determine their degree of satisfaction with it.

■ General Principles for Primary Research

Primary research, like all research, requires well-formulated questions. Such questions must be specifically focused, contain clearly defined terms, and be answerable by the actual research. A vague, general question such as "What attitudes do Canadians have about their government?" lacks the necessary precision and therefore can't be resolved. What kind(s) of attitudes? What level or branch of government? Which Canadians? How would you gather their opinions? A more realistic question might be "According to the Kwantlen University College faculty, how adequate is the new government proposal for funding of academic research in this country?" You could easily develop and distribute to faculty members a questionnaire addressing the different provisions of the proposal. In addition, you can't resolve ethical or philosophical questions through primary research. While you could use a questionnaire to determine student attitudes about the police using sobriety check lines, such information won't decide the ethical issue of whether the police should use such check lines.

For valid results, conduct your primary research in an impartial manner. Always aim to determine facts rather than to justify some belief you hold. This means, first of all, that you must develop questions that have no built-in bias. If you poll other students and ask them to tell you "how teachers on this campus marked their papers unreasonably hard," those responding might falsify their answers to give you what you want. Instead, use neutral phrasing such as "Do you believe teachers on this campus marked your papers fairly or unfairly? Explain." Second, don't rely on atypical sources and situations for your data. If you investigate the adequacy of parking space on campus, don't deliberately observe the parking lots on a day when some special event has flooded the campus with visitors. Careful readers will see what you have done and reject your findings.

Just as you avoid bias when gathering information, so also should you report your results fairly. For one thing, don't use inaccurate interpretations of your findings to make them agree with the conclusions you're after. If you believe peer editing produces questionable results, don't claim that the students in a class you observed spent their time sneering at one another's work when in fact they offered constructive criticism. Similarly, don't report conclusions that are unsupported by your actual research. If you observe a large number of violent acts while watching Saturday cartoons, don't leap to the conclusion that the violence in the cartoons causes violent behaviour in children. You simply don't have the evidence needed to support that assertion. Finally, don't cover up results that you don't like. If your survey of teachers' marking practices shows that most of your respondents believe instructors mark fairly, don't hide the fact because it doesn't match what you expected to discover. Instead, report your findings accurately and rethink your original position. The following section further explores ethical matters.

■ Ethical Issues

Today most people chuckle at an advertising ploy for a product recommended by "nine out of ten doctors." We recognize that the doctors were hand-picked and don't represent an objective sample of adequate size. As a result, little harm occurs. With primary research, however, distorted investigating and reporting are sometimes hard to detect and can have significant consequences.

Say the officials of Hanford, Saskatchewan, alarmed at a sharp rise in auto accidents caused by distracted drivers, schedule a meeting attempting to ban cell phone calls by those driving within city limits. It would be unethical for a reporter opposed to the ban to write a supposedly objective feature article on the issue but include interviews only with people who share his views. Now suppose a presumably neutral group in the city of Winnipeg, Manitoba distributes a questionnaire to residents to gauge their reaction to a proposed gambling casino. It would be unethical to include a biased question such as "Should the city deprive its residents of the revenue that a casino can provide?" Finally, imagine that a city manager, concerned by reports of motorists running a red light at a major intersection, gets the Department of Motor Vehicles to investigate. A department employee conducts a twenty-minute observation and then writes a report indicating that surveillance cameras are not needed there. Clearly, the employee has acted unethically in drawing a conclusion after such a limited observation. To help ensure that your primary research reports are ethically responsible, ask and answer the following questions.

- Have I attempted to avoid bias in gathering and evaluating information?
- Are my data based on an adequate sample size? If not, have the limitations of the sample been indicated clearly?
- Is my information printed objectively and completely without any intentional effort to omit findings that run counter to my position?

- Are the people involved, whether I'm preparing an interview, questionnaire, or direct observation report, aware that they are part of a study and how the information will be used? Are they protected from harm that might result from their inclusion?

- Do I have permission to name in my report persons interviewed or observed?

- In an interview report, would the interviewee recognize and accept statements attributed to him or her?

- Have I noted any apparent bias in the interviewee?

- In a questionnaire report, have I avoided any biased questions?

■ Interviews

During an interview, questions are asked and answered. Some interviews amount to little more than brief, informal chats. Others, like those discussed here, may feature extended conversations, involve a series of questions, and require careful preparation. Interviewing an informed person provides you with first-hand answers to your queries, lets you ask follow-up questions, and gives you access to the most up-to-date thinking.

If you major in a business program, an instructor may require you to question a personnel manager about the company's employee relations program. If your field is social work, you might have to interview a case worker as part of your study of some kind of family problem. On the job, you might have to talk with prospective employees and then assess their suitability for a position in the company. Police officers routinely interview witnesses to accidents and crimes, and journalists do the same in pursuit of stories.

Choosing the Interviewee

Professional and technical personnel are a rich source of interview candidates. The faculty of any university can provide insights into a wide range of subjects. Doctors, pharmacists, and other health professionals can draw upon their expertise to help you, as can lawyers, engineers, researchers, corporation managers, and employees at every level of government—federal, provincial, and municipal.

Whom you interview depends, of course, on what you wish to know. For information on the safe disposal of high-level nuclear waste, you might consult a physics professor. If you want an expert view on the causes of homelessness, contact an authority such as a sociologist, who could provide objective information. If, however, you want to gain a sense of what it's like to be homeless, you might interview the manager of a shelter or (in a safe place) one or more homeless people.

Preparing for the Interview

If you don't relish the thought of phoning to request an interview, keep in mind that most interviewees are eager to discuss their areas of expertise and are often flattered by the opportunity. The worst that can happen is a turndown, and in that event you can always find someone else in the same field.

Before you phone, review your own upcoming commitments and try to determine which ones you could reschedule if necessary. You may need to make an adjustment to accommodate the schedule of a busy person. When you call, indicate who you are, that you are requesting an interview, the subject of the interview, and how much time you'd like.

If the person agrees to meet with you, then ask when it would be convenient. Carefully record the time, day, and place of the interview, and if for any reason you need to cancel be sure to call well in advance.

Before the interview, do as much background reading as possible. This reading will help you develop a list of key questions and avoid those with obvious and readily available answers. Write out your questions to help ensure that the interview will proceed smoothly.

Good questions permit elaboration and don't call for simple "yes" or "no" answers. To illustrate:

Poor: Is it difficult to work with adult illiterates?
            (The obvious answer is "yes.")

Better: What have you found most challenging about working with
            adult illiterates?

On the other hand, don't ask overly broad questions that can't be answered in a relatively brief interview.

Poor: What's wrong with primary-school education?

Better: Why do you think so many children have trouble learning to
            read?

Avoid questions that are biased and may insult the interviewee.

Poor: Why do you bother to work with adult illiterates?

Better: Why did you decide to work with adult illiterates?

Likewise, avoid questions that restrict the interviewee's options for answering.

Poor: What do you think accounts for the poor academic perform-
            ance of so many Canadian secondary-school students—too
            much TV watching or overly large classes?

Better: People often blame the poor academic performance of so
            many Canadian students on too much TV watching or overly
            large classes. What importance do you attach to these factors?
            Do you think other factors contribute to the problem?

The number of questions you prepare depends on the length of the interview. It's a good idea to draft more questions than you think you'll have time to ask, then arrange them from most to least important. If the interviewee keeps to the schedule, you'll obtain your desired information. If the interviewee grants you extra time, your written follow-up will have even more substance.

Conducting the Interview

Naturally you'll want to arrive on time and to bring a notepad and a pen. Sometimes you can tape-record an interview but only if you ask permission first. Because most people warm up slowly, you might start with one or two brief, general questions that provide you with useful background. Possibilities include "What is the nature of your specialty?" and "How long have you been employed in this field?"

Proceed by asking your most important questions first. If you believe that a question hasn't been answered or that an answer is incomplete, don't hesitate to ask follow-up questions.

As the interview unfolds, take notes but don't attempt to copy everything that's said. Instead, jot down key phrases and ideas that will serve as memory prompts. If you want to capture an essential explanation or some other important material in the interviewee's own words, ask the person to go slowly while you copy them down. When the interview is over, thank the person for talking to you. You may also offer to supply a copy of the finished report. With the answers to your questions fresh in your mind, expand on your notes by filling in details, supplying necessary connections between points that were made, and noting your reactions.

Writing About the Interview

The project you're working on determines how to handle your interview information. If you're preparing a library research paper, include the material, suitably presented, at the appropriate spot and document it according to whatever system, MLA or APA, you're using (see page 336).

Often, however, you'll be asked to prepare a separate report of the interview. Then, as with any other report, you'll need to organize and present the material in an effective order. Your topic, purpose, and audience will determine the arrangement you select. In any event, remember to establish the context for the report, identify the interviewee and his or her position, and present the information accurately.

Example Student Interview Report

Budget Cuts Affect Police:

An Interview Report with Officer Robert Timmons

Holly Swain

Confronted with a billion-dollar budget deficit, the provincial government has been forced to make sharp budget cuts. One of these cuts is the allocation to the police. This decision has threatened the loss of some police jobs and aroused considerable controversy.

> Paragraph 1: establishes context for interview

How, many ask, will the police, who were already on a tight budget, be able to provide the public with adequate protection when they have even less money and fewer personnel?

Sentence 1, paragraph 2: identifies interviewee and his position

Remainder of report: presents information provided by interviewee

When Officer Robert Timmons first heard that the premier might call for police cutbacks, he didn't believe they would become a reality. Timmons thought the premier was just making "political noise." Actually, the chief of police did at first propose cutting 350 jobs, Timmons' among them, to help meet a $19 million cutback. This proposal was rejected in favour of one that combined demotions, pay cuts, and the elimination of special programs. In addition, the amounts allotted for other purposes were also cut.

All of these actions, Timmons says, have had an unfortunate effect on the operations of the police. As an example, he mentions a sergeant who was demoted to "accident reconstructionist," a job requiring him to review severe accidents and reconstruct what happened for the court. This demotion, Timmons says, has taken an excellent police officer out of the field, where he's most needed, and put him behind a desk.

Timmons notes several bad effects of cuts in the allocation for gasoline. Because of these cuts, police officers are expected to drive just one hundred and fifty kilometres a night. Timmons thinks this limitation has a "direct effect on the public." A motorist stranded on a highway might not be spotted and aided by an officer who is unable to make another run through that territory. Late-night accidents might go undiscovered, with serious or fatal consequences for those involved. Many more speeders and drunk drivers will escape being caught.

As of now, Timmons says, there are only 3000 provincial police, about 400 fewer than needed. Each year, 100 to 200 officers retire. These vacancies need to be filled, but according to Timmons the police academy has been closed for over a year. The personnel shortages that already exist and the cutbacks resulting from the budget troubles are making it harder and harder for the police to do an adequate job of protecting the public.

Officer Timmons understands that the government needs to control its spending. However, he believes that the present budget cutbacks for a department that is already understaffed are very unwise. "I feel the premier should have given the matter more thought," he says.

Questionnaires

A questionnaire consists essentially of a series of statements or questions to which recipients are asked to respond. Questionnaires help individuals and organizations determine what select groups of people think about particular products, services, issues, and personal matters. You yourself have probably completed a variety of questionnaires, including teacher evaluations and market surveys.

Questionnaires are used extensively both on campus and in the workplace. A social science instructor might ask you to prepare a survey that explores community reaction to a recently implemented penalty for graffiti artists. A business instructor might want you to survey a test-market group to determine its response to some new product. In fact, some marketing classes focus on survey techniques. But even if marketing isn't your specialty, learning how to construct questionnaires can serve you well in your career. If you work in the hotel, restaurant, or other service field, you could use a questionnaire to gauge customer satisfaction. The same holds true if you manage or own a small repair service. As a landscape specialist, you might survey the people in your community to learn what planting and maintenance services they desire.

Developing the Questionnaire

When you develop a questionnaire, you need to target precisely what you want to know and what group you intend to survey. You could survey restaurant customers to determine their attitudes about the service and the quality of the food or to assess the types of food they prefer. Zero in on only one area of interest and then explore it with appropriate questions.

Begin the questionnaire with a clear explanation of what you intend to accomplish, and supply brief but clear instructions on how to respond to each part. Keep the questionnaire as short as possible, preferably no longer than a page or two. The longer the survey is, the less likely that people will answer all the questions.

As you draw up your questions, take care to avoid these common errors:

1. Don't ask two questions in the same sentence. Their answers may be different.

   Unacceptable: Do you find that this year's Ford Taurus has better acceleration and fuel economy than last year's model?

   To correct this fault, use separate sentences.

   Better: Do you find that this year's Ford Taurus has better acceleration than last year's model?

   Better: Do you find that this year's Ford Taurus has better fuel economy than last year's model?

2. Don't include vague or ambiguous questions. Since people won't understand your intent, their answers may not reflect their beliefs.

   Unacceptable: Is assisted suicide a good idea?

> *Better:*   Should assisted suicide be permitted for terminally ill patients?

3. Avoid biased questions. They might antagonize those who don't share your views and cause them not to complete the questionnaire.

> *Unacceptable:*   Should taxpayers continue to waste money on renovating the North Park Bridge?

> *Better:*   Should taxpayers spend an additional $100 000 to complete the North Park Bridge renovation?

Most questionnaire items fall into the categories that follow. The information you want determines which you choose. Often you'll need to include several or all of the categories in your questionnaire.

Two-Choice Items Some items have two possible responses: yes/no, true/false, male/female.

> *Example:*   Do you plan to repaint your house during the summer months?
>
> ☐ yes
> ☐ no

Multiple-Choice Items Often there are several possible responses to a questionnaire item. When you prepare this type of item, make sure that you include all significant choices and that the choices share some common ground. Don't ask if someone's primary vehicle is a subcompact, compact, full-size, or manual car as size and type of transmission are unrelated. To determine whether the vehicle is automatic or manual, use a separate item.

> *Example:*   Check the income group that describes your combined family income.
>
> ☐ less than $10 000 a year
> ☐ $10 000–$20 000 a year
> ☐ $20 000–$30 000 a year
> ☐ $30 000–$40 000 a year
> ☐ $40 000–$50 000 a year
> ☐ over $50 000 a year

Checklists Checklists allow respondents to mark more than one option. They can help you determine the range of factors that led to a decision.

> *Example:*   Please check any of the following factors that help explain why you decided not to re-enroll your child in Good Growth Private School:

☐ can no longer afford tuition
☐ moved
☐ dissatisfaction with child's progress
☐ disagree with school's educational approach
☐ conflict with teacher
☐ conflict with other staff
☐ child unhappy with school
☐ child had conflict with other children

Ranking Lists Sometimes you may need to ask people to rank their preferences. This information will help you select the most suitable option from among several possibilities.

Example: Designating your first choice as "1," please rank your preferences in music from 1 through 5.

☐ classical
☐ country and western
☐ jazz
☐ rock and roll
☐ rap

Using the responses to this item, the manager of a local radio station could broadcast the type of music that listeners clearly prefer.

Scale Items When you are trying to determine the extent to which members of a group support or oppose some issue, using a scale can be helpful. Be sure to have people respond to a statement, *not* a question.

Example: Please circle the response that best reflects your feelings about the statement below.

SA = strongly agree, A = agree, N = no opinion,

D = disagree, SD = strongly disagree

Women should be allowed to fly combat aircraft in time of war.

SA   A   N   D   SD

Open-Ended Items When you want to gather ideas from other people, you might turn to open-ended items—those that don't limit the reader's response. If you do, keep such items narrow enough to be manageable. You should know, however, that readers are less likely to complete open-ended items and that they are difficult to sort and tally.

Example: Please list the three improvements that you would most like to see in Lowden's high school curriculum.

_____

_____

_____

_____

_____

_____

Example Student Questionnaire

Survey on Public Smoking

Kelly Reetz

Please take a few minutes to fill out this questionnaire. My purpose is to determine the smoking habits and attitudes toward public smoking of Bartram College male smokers.

Two-choice item

1. Do you smoke cigarettes? (check one)

    _____ yes

    _____ no

Multiple-choice item

2. If you smoke, indicate how many cigarettes each day. (check one)

    _____ less than half a pack

    _____ between a half and a whole pack

    _____ between one and two packs

    _____ more than two packs

Multiple-choice item

3. If you smoke, what are you likely to do upon entering a public place with no posted smoking restrictions? (check one)

    _____ smoke freely

    _____ check to see whether your smoking is bothering others

    _____ ask others whether they would be bothered if you smoke

    _____ not smoke

Checklist

4. Check the statements you believe are true.

    _____ My health is at risk only if I am a smoker.

    _____ Secondhand smoke contains the same ingredients as directly inhaled smoke.

    _____ Secondhand smoke poses no health risk to nonsmokers.

_____ Secondhand smoke poses a health risk to nonsmokers.

_____ Secondhand smoke poses less of a health risk than directly inhaled smoke.

5. Please rate each of the statements below, using the following scale: SA = strongly agree, A = agree, N = no opinion, D = disagree, SD = strongly disagree

_____ There should be no restrictions on public smoking.

_____ Smoking should be prohibited in stores, banks, offices, and workshops.

_____ Smoking and nonsmoking sections in restaurants should be separated by a barrier that smoke cannot penetrate.

_____ Smokers and nonsmokers should have separate workplace lounges.

_____ All public smoking should be prohibited.

6. Please add one or two comments you might have regarding public smoking. _____

_____

| Scale items |

| Open-ended item |

Testing and Administering the Questionnaire

When you have finished making out the questionnaire, ask several people to respond to the items and gauge their effectiveness. Are any items vague, ambiguous, biased, or otherwise faulty? If so, rewrite and retest them.

To ensure that you obtain an accurate assessment, make certain that you select an appropriate cross-section of recipients. To illustrate, assume that you and many of your campus friends dislike early morning classes. You decide to draw up a questionnaire to sample the attitudes of other students. You suspect that many students share your dislike, and you plan to submit your findings to the college president for possible action. To obtain meaningful results, you'll have to sample a sizable group of students. Furthermore, this group will need to include representative numbers of first-year and upper-year students, as these classes may not share a uniform view. Failure to sample properly can call your results into question and cause the administration to disregard them. Proper sampling, on the other hand, pinpoints where dissatisfaction is greatest and suggests a possible response. Thus if first-year students register the most objections, the administration might decide to reduce the number of first-year classes meeting at 8 A.M.

Totalling the Responses

When the recipients have finished marking the questionnaire, you will need to total the responses. Even without computer scoring, this job is easier than you might think. Simply prepare a table that lists the questionnaire items and the possible responses to each; then go through the questionnaire and add up the number of times each response is marked.

When you finish, turn your numbers into percentages, which provide an easier-to-understand comparison of the responses. Simply divide the number of times each possible response is checked by the total number of questionnaires and then multiply the result by 100.

Writing the Questionnaire Report

When you write your report, don't merely fill it with numbers and responses to the questionnaire items. Instead, look for patterns in the responses and try to draw conclusions from them. Follow the order of the questionnaire items in presenting your findings.

Typically, a report consists of two or three sections. The first, "Purpose and Scope," explains why the survey was performed, how many questionnaires were distributed and returned, and how the recipients were contacted. The second section, "Results," reports the conclusions that were drawn. Finally, if appropriate, a "Recommendations" section offers responses that seem warranted based on the survey findings.

Example Student Questionnaire Report

Findings from Smoking Questionnaire Distributed to
Bartram College Students

Kelly Reetz

Purpose and Scope of Survey

Provides background details on project, profile of respondents

This survey was carried out to determine the smoking habits and attitudes toward public smoking of Bartram College's male students. The assignment was one of my requirements for completing Public Health 201. Each of the 240 male students in Crandall Hall received a copy of the questionnaire in his mailbox, and 72 completed questionnaires were returned. This latter number equals 10 percent of the college's male student population and therefore can be considered a representative sample. Of those responding, 37, or 51 percent, were cigarette smokers. Thirty-five, or 49 percent, were nonsmokers. Of the smokers, all but 11 percent smoked over a pack of cigarettes a day.

Results of Survey

Smokers seemed fairly considerate of nonsmokers in public places. Only 16 percent said they would smoke freely. In fact, 51 percent said they wouldn't smoke at all. The remaining 33 percent indicated they would either look around to see whether they were bothering others or ask others whether they objected to cigarette smoke.

Discusses responses to questionnaire item 3

In general, respondents seemed aware that secondhand smoke poses a health risk. Seventy-six percent believe that such smoke contains the same ingredients as directly inhaled smoke, and an amazing 96 percent believe that anyone exposed to secondhand smoke may be at risk. Only 3 percent think no health risk is involved.

Discusses responses to questionnaire item 4

Opinions were strongly divided on the matter of banning all public smoking, with 79 percent strongly opposed and 21 percent strongly in favour. As might be expected, all of the smokers fell in the first group, but a surprising 51 percent of the nonsmokers did too. A sharp division was equally apparent between supporters and opponents of restaurant barriers, with 81 percent for or strongly for them and 19 percent against or strongly against them. In contrast to the findings on a smoking ban, all of the smokers favoured barriers. Respondents overwhelmingly endorsed, 90 percent to 10 percent, prohibiting smoking in stores and banks and providing separate workplace lounges. Nobody registered a "no opinion" vote on any of the statements under item 5.

Discusses responses to questionnaire item 5

Responses to items 3-5 reveal an awareness among smokers of the dangers posed by secondhand cigarette smoke, a concern for the well-being of nonsmokers, and a willingness to accept restrictions, though not an outright ban, on public smoking. This attitude was consistent for both light and heavy smokers. For their part, about half the nonsmokers showed a tolerant attitude by supporting smoking restrictions but rejecting an outright ban.

Discusses patterns in responses to items 3–5

No smokers, but 71 percent of the nonsmokers, responded to the request to provide one or two additional comments. All of these comments dealt with how the respondents would act if bothered by someone else's smoke. Two-thirds said they would move to another spot, half of the remainder said they would ask the smoker to stop, and the other half said they would remain silent rather than risk an argument.

Discusses responses to item 6

<u>Recommendations</u>

As noted previously, this survey included only male students. To determine how its results compare with those for females, the same questionnaire should be administered to a similar group of female students.

■ Direct Observations

Often direct observation is the most effective means of answering research questions. If you want to know the extent and nature of violence in children's TV cartoons, watching a number of shows will tell you. Similarly, a researcher who seeks information about living conditions in a poor area of some city can obtain it by visiting that locale. Such observations furnish firsthand answers to our questions.

At school and on the job, you may need to report your own observations. If you're majoring in business, an instructor might require a report on the work habits of employees at a small local company. If your field is biology, you might need to assess and report on the environmental health of a marsh, riverbank, or other ecological area. On the job, a factory superintendent might observe and then discuss in writing the particulars of some problem-plagued operation. Police officers routinely investigate and report on accidents, and waste-management specialists inspect and report on potential disposal sites.

The following suggestions will help you make your observations, record them, and then write your report.

Preparing to Make the Observations

First, determine the purpose of your observations and keep the purpose firmly in mind as you proceed. Otherwise, you'll overlook important details and record less-than-helpful information. Obviously, observing a classroom to assess the interaction of students calls for a different set of notes than if you were observing the teacher's instructional style or the students' note-taking habits.

Next, establish the site or sites that will best supply you with the information you need. If you're trying to determine how students interact in the classroom, then the time of day, kind of class, and types of students will all make a difference. You might have to visit more than one class in order to observe the different types of behaviour.

If your observations will take place on private property or will involve an organized group such as a legislative body, you'll need to obtain permission and to make an appointment. Also, you might want to supplement your observations with an interview. Ordinarily, the interview will take place after you make your observations so that you can ask about what you've seen. However, if technical information is needed in advance, the interview should precede the observations.

Because you'll probably be making a great many individual observations, try to develop a chart and a code for recording them. Suppose you're comparing the extent to which students interact with one another and with the instructor in first-year and third-year composition courses. After much thought, you might develop a chart like the one following:

Class Designation: English 1100				
Minutes into observation when inter-action occurred	Classroom location of interacting students	Number and sex of students	Subject of interaction	Length of interaction

With certain kinds of observations, using a chart will not be possible.

In developing your code, you would undoubtedly use M = male and F = female to distinguish the sexes. To show the location of the interacting students, FC = front of class, MC = middle of class, and BC = back of class would probably work quite well. Coding the kinds of interactions presents a more difficult task. Here, after considering several possibilities, you might decide upon these symbols: CR = class related, SR = school related, SP = sports, D = dating, O = other matters. To save writing time, you'd probably want to use "min." for "minutes" and "sec." for "seconds" when recording the lengths of the interactions.

Making the Observations

If your visit involves a scheduled appointment, be sure to arrive on time and be ready to take notes. Select a location where you can observe without interfering. If you are observing people or animals, remember that they need to adjust to you before they will behave naturally.

Before you begin taking notes, record any pertinent general information. If you're observing a class, you might note the time it is meeting, its size, the name of the instructor, and whether he or she is present when you arrive. If you're observing an apartment, pertinent information would include the location and condition of the building, the time of the visit, and the general nature of the environment. Note also whether the landlord as well as the tenant knew you were coming: It is amazing how much cleanup landlords can carry out when they know an observer will soon arrive.

Don't feel as though you must take extensive notes. Do, however, record enough details to ensure that you won't forget any events, activities, or features that are important. If you have a chart and coding system, rely on it as much as possible when recording information. Refer to the chart on page 372 for how the coded notes for part of a classroom visit might look.

If you haven't developed a chart, take enough notes so that you can produce a thorough report. Try to follow some note-taking pattern. When observing the condition of an apartment, you could proceed from room to room, jotting down observations such as "Front hallway, entranceway: paint peeling in large strips from wall, paint chips on floor. Hallway dark, bulb burned out. Linoleum curling up along sides. Cockroaches running along lower moulding." Remain as objective as possible as you take notes. Record what you see, hear, and smell, and avoid judgmental language. If you must record a subjective impression, identify it as such.

Class Designation: English 1100				
Minutes into observation when inter- action occurred	Classroom location of interacting students	Number and sex of students	Subject of interaction	Length of interaction
0 3 Instructor arrived	FC MC	M-M F-F	SP D	1 min. 30 sec.
5 20	FC, MC, BC FC, MC	M-M-M-F-F M-F-M	CR CR	3 min. 45 sec. 1 min.

Ask questions if necessary, but rely primarily on what you observe, not what you're told. If the landlord of a run-down apartment you're visiting tells you that he's repainting the building but you see no signs that this is happening, ignore what he says or report it along with an appropriate cautionary comment. When you finish, thank the person(s) who made your observations possible or helped you in other ways.

When you leave the observation site, expand your notes by adding more details. Supply any needed connections and record your overall impressions. To illustrate, suppose you are expanding your notes on student interactions in an English class. You might note that the greatest number of interactions occurred before and immediately after the instructor arrived, that all student-student interactions involved individuals seated together, that student-instructor interactions included students in all parts of the room, and that all the latter interactions were about subject-related matters. This information might stimulate interesting speculation concerning the student-student and student-teacher relationships in the class, causing you to conclude that the students were hesitant about having exchanges with the instructor. As you proceed, record only what you actually observed, not what you wanted or expected to observe.

If upon reviewing your notes you find that you require more information, you may need to arrange a second or even a third visit to the observation site.

Writing the Report

Once your notes are in final form, you can start writing your report. On the job your employer may specify a certain form to follow. As a general rule, all such reports reflect their purposes, focus on relevant information, and remain objective.

Usually you begin by explaining the reason for the investigation, noting any preliminary arrangements that were made, and if appropriate, providing an overview of the observation site. Depending upon the nature of the report, the primary means of organization may be as follows:

1. *Narration.* A report on the changing conduct of a child over a three-hour period in a daycare centre would probably be organized by narration.
2. *Description.* A report assessing the storm damage in a large urban area could present its details in spatial order.
3. *Classification.* A visit to a toxic-waste dump suspected of violating government regulations might produce a report classifying the types of wastes improperly stored there.
4. *Point-by-point comparison.* If you're comparing two possible sites for a baseball stadium, shopping mall, or other structure, a point-by-point comparison will probably best suit your purpose.
5. *Cause and effect.* This pattern works well for reporting events whose effects are of special concern, such as the testing of a new siren intended to scare birds from an airport runway.
6. *Process.* This arrangement is indicated when readers will want to know step-by-step how some process—for example, a new test for determining the mineral content of water—is carried out.

Conclude the report by discussing the significance of the findings and making any other comments that seem justified.

Example Student Observation Report

Observations of a Run-Down Apartment Building

Caleb Thomas

To fulfill part of the requirements for Social Service 321, I observed the housing conditions in a poor residential area in our city. The building I selected is located at the corner of Division Avenue and Hall Street, an area where most of the residents hold minimum-wage jobs or receive some form of public assistance.

> Gives reason for visit, location of site

I met the building superintendent, who had agreed to this visit, at 9:30 A.M. on Friday, April 17, 1998. The brick sides of the three-storey apartment building appeared to be in good repair, but one second-storey window was broken out and boarded up. Most windows had standard window shades, but a few were blocked with sheets or black plastic bags. Two had no coverings of any kind. Overall,

> Notes preliminary arrangements, provides overview of site location

the building's appearance was similar to that of several nearby apartment buildings.

Heavy traffic clogged Division Avenue at the time of my visit. Next to the apartment building stood three single-storey wooden buildings housing an adult video store, a bar, and a novelty shop, all with boarded windows and peeling paint. Across the street, a single-storey Salvation Army Store occupied the entire block. In front of it, three women in short skirts walked slowly back and forth, eyeing the cars that passed. Two men sat on crates, their backs to the building, drinking something out of paper bags.

The superintendent opened the unlocked metal door of the apartment building, and we went in. The hallway was lighted by a single dim bulb located on the wall toward the rear. Other bulbs along the wall and in two light fixtures hanging from the ceiling appeared burned out. Scraps of newspaper and chips of paint that had peeled from the ceiling and walls littered the floor. A strong urine-like smell pervaded the air.

Stating that he couldn't show me an occupied apartment because he "respected the privacy of the tenants," the supervisor took me to an unoccupied apartment on the first floor. He had trouble unlocking the wooden door; the key appeared to stick in the lock. The inside of the door had two bolt locks, one a few inches above the door handle and the other one near the floor. The door opened into a short hall with rooms off either side. Here, as in the building entrance, paint chips from the peeling walls and ceiling littered the floor. A battered socket on the wall held a single bulb, but when I flicked its switch, the bulb did not light. On the hall floor, linoleum curled at the edges. When I bent down to examine it more closely, several cockroaches scurried under the curl.

The first door on the right-hand side of the hall led into a 10-by-12-foot room that the supervisor identified as the living room. Here the walls had been recently painted--by a former tenant, the supervisor said--and a strong paint smell was still apparent. However, nothing else had been done to the rest of the room. The radiator was unshielded, several nail heads protruded from the stained and uncovered wooden floor, and the sagging ceiling had several long cracks. Plaster chips dotted the floor.

Continues overview of site location

Describes building's hallway

Describes apartment hallway

Describes apartment living room

A small kitchen was situated behind the living room. Again, linoleum floor covering curled from the baseboard, and cockroaches scurried for cover. The kitchen was furnished with a battered-looking gas stove, but there was no refrigerator (the superintendent said one was on order). The surface of the sink was chipped and had many brownish stains. When I turned on the faucet, a rusty brown stream of water spurted out. I asked for a sample to be tested for lead content, but the superintendent refused.

Describes apartment kitchen

The bathroom, located at the end of the hall, had no radiator. Its floor tiles, broken in a number of places, exposed a foot-long section of rotted wood. The toilet, with seat missing, would not flush when I tried it but simply made a hissing noise. A brown stain spread over the bottom of the bathtub and a large portion of its sides. The wall tiles around the tub bulged outward and appeared ready to collapse into the tub. The superintendent offered the observation that there had been "some trouble with the plumbing."

Describes apartment bathroom

Two small bedrooms opened off the left side of the hall. Like the living room both had unprotected radiators, uncovered wooden floors, and cracked ceilings. Walls were papered rather than painted, but long strips of the wallpaper were missing. In one bedroom a piece of plasterboard hung on the wall as if covering a hole. The windows in both bedrooms were covered with sheets tacked to the wall.

Describes apartment bedrooms

When I had finished looking at the bedrooms, the superintendent quickly escorted me from the apartment and the building, declaring that he was too busy to show me any other vacant apartments. He also said he had no time to answer any questions.

Clearly the building I visited fails to meet the city housing code: The living conditions are not what most people would consider acceptable. A careful investigation, including a test of the water and of the paint for lead content, seems called for to determine whether this apartment constitutes a health risk.

Discusses significance of findings

Reader

Strategies for Successful Reading

Effective reading is not the passive process that many people imagine. On the contrary, it requires the ongoing interaction of your mind and the printed page. Bringing your own knowledge and experience to bear on a piece of writing can help you assess its events, ideas, and conclusions. For example, an understanding of marriage, love, and conflict, as well as experience with divorce, can help readers comprehend an essay that explores divorce. As you read, you must also understand each point that's made, consider how the various parts fit together, and try to anticipate the direction the writing will take. Successful reading, then, requires work. Fortunately, you can follow specific strategies to help yourself read better.

Following an Effective Reading Strategy

Different purposes require different approaches to reading. When reading for pleasure, you can relax and proceed at your own pace, slowing down to savour a section you especially enjoy, speeding up when you encounter less interesting material, and breaking off when you wish. Even so, you will get more satisfaction out of the material if you can relate it to your own knowledge and experience.

Reading for information/evaluation and critiquing the writing call for a more methodical approach. Most of your academic reading will require this kind of attention.

Strategies When Reading for Information/Evaluation

Because of the challenging nature of most university and college level reading assignments, you should plan on more than one reading. A good first reading should orient you to the material. Before you begin, scan any accompanying biographical sketch and try to determine the writer's expertise and views on the topic.

Next, see what the title tells you. Most titles identify the topic and often the viewpoint as well. Thus "The Sweet Smell of Success Isn't All That Sweet" (pages 488–490) suggests that the author isn't overly impressed with conventional attitudes toward success. Some titles signal the writer's primary strategy: "Should Human Cloning Be Permitted?" (pages 501–507) indicates development by argument and "How to Adopt a Stray" (pages 413–415) development by process analysis. After evaluating the title, read the introductory paragraph(s) to see if you can determine the writer's main thesis.

Read the body of the essay quickly, noting any likely topic sentences that stand out (often the first or last sentence in a paragraph). Try to gain an idea of the essay's main thrust, the key ideas that support it, and the ways that they are organized. In your first reading, you can skim over the more difficult sections without trying to understand them fully. When you've finished, and before you reread the essay, think about what you've learned and then, either by saying it to yourself or jotting it down, express it *in your own words. For effective reading to take place, this activity is crucial.* You can hardly be said to understand what you've read, and you will be less likely to remember it, until you can state its essence in your own words. Next, go back and underline the thesis statement or, if one is not included, try to formulate one in your own words. Also look for any writing strategies the author has used. Finally, jot down questions that the first reading has raised in your mind.

On the second reading, which will take more time, you carefully absorb the writer's ideas. Read at a pace suitable to the material. Underline significant topic sentences as well as other key sentences, but keep in mind that underlining in itself doesn't ensure comprehension. Restating the ideas in your own words is more effective. As you proceed, carefully examine the supporting sentences to see how well they back up the main ideas. In addition, underline or note in the margin any ideas or facts you feel are important.

Consider reading as a kind of conversation with the text. Develop the habit of asking questions about facts, reasons, ideas—practically anything in the essay. Jot your queries and their answers in the margins. (On page 382 you can see how a student interacted with the first page of Amy Gross's essay "The Appeal of the Androgynous Man.") Good writers anticipate your questions and answer them; and because you have posed the questions yourself, you are more likely to see the connections in the text. If the author hasn't answered your questions, there may be problems with the work.

At times, unfamiliar words can hinder your grasp of the material. Whenever you encounter a new word, circle it, use context to help gauge its meaning, check the dictionary for the exact meaning, and then record it in the margin or some other convenient place. If the writing is peppered with words you don't know, you may have to read the whole piece just to figure out its general drift, then look up key words, and finally reread the material.

When the ideas of a single section prove difficult, restate the points of those sections you do understand. Then experiment by stating in your own words different interpretations of the problem section and see which one best fits the writing as a whole. When an entire essay is troublesome, state the ideas that are easier for you to understand and use them as keys to help unlock meanings that are difficult but not unintelligible. Save the most difficult sections until last. You might also want to discuss a difficult essay with others who are reading it.

Whenever you finish a major section of a lengthy essay, express your sense of what it means. If you have trouble seeing the connections between ideas, try outlining them, using as a starting point the topic sentences you've noted. When you finish an essay, do an overall summary.

To strengthen your grasp of material you'll need to remember for some time, try restating its main points a couple of days after the second reading. If anything has become hazy or slipped your mind, reread the appropriate section(s).

Strategies When Reading to Critique

In university or college you usually read not only to understand but also to judge. Your instructors will want to know what you think about what you've read.

Much of what written work conveys isn't always immediately apparent. Every writer makes assumptions, implies attitudes and values not directly stated, and has biases. For each major point that you encounter, ask yourself, "Why does the writer think this?" Then examine the supporting material for an answer.

Often, you'll be asked whether you agree or disagree with a piece of writing. Merely because information and ideas are in print does not mean that they are true or acceptable. An essay, for example, might include faulty logic, unreasonable ideas, suspect facts, or unreliable authorities. Don't hesitate to dispute the writer's information. Does it match your experience? Do the pieces of evidence support the claims? Do the ideas appear reasonable? Note any objections that you have. When you agree, try to suggest why, perhaps by citing additional support. Knowledge of the various reasoning fallacies can also help you critique a piece of writing. These fallacies are discussed on pages 158–162.

Amy Gross

*both male and
female in one*

The <u>Appeal</u> of the (Androgynous) Man

Amy Gross, a native of Brooklyn, New York, earned a sociology degree at Connecticut College. Upon graduation, she entered the world of fashion publishing, holding editorial positions on the staffs of Glamour, Mademoiselle, Vogue, *and* Mirabella. *She is now editorial director of* Elle *magazine. In 1990, she and Dee Ito coauthored a book on women and breast surgery and, in the following year, one on women and gynecological surgery. In this selection, which first appeared in* Mademoiselle, *Gross compares androgynous men favourably to macho "all-men."*

1   James Dean was my first androgynous man.[1] I figured I could talk to him. He was anguished and I was 12, so we had a lot in common. With only a few exceptions, <u>all the men I have liked or loved have been a certain kind of man: a kind who doesn't play football or watch the games on Sunday, who doesn't tell dirty jokes featuring broads or chicks, who is not contemptuous of conversations that are philosophically speculative, introspective, or otherwise foolish according to the other kind of man.</u> He is more self-amused, less inflated, more quirky, vulnerable and responsive than the other sort (the other sort, I'm visualizing as the guys on TV who advertise deodorant in the locker room). He is more like me than the other sort. <u>He is what social scientists and feminists would call androgynous: having the characteristics of both male and female.</u>

2   Now the first thing I want you to know about the <u>androgynous man is that he is neither effeminate nor (hermaphroditic.)</u> All his primary and secondary sexual characteristics are in order and I would say he's all-man, but that is just what he is not. He is more than all-man.   *both male and female sex organs*

3   The merely all-man man, for one thing, never walks to the grocery store unless the little woman is away visiting her mother with the kids, or is in the hospital having a kid, or there is no little woman. All-men men don't know how to shop in a grocery store unless it is to buy a 6-pack and some pretzels. Their ideas of nutrition expand beyond a 6-pack and pretzels only to take in steak, potatoes, scotch or rye whiskey, and maybe a wad of cake or apple pie. All-man men have absolutely no taste in food, art, books, movies, theatre, dance, how to live, what are good questions, what is funny, or anything else I care about. It's not exactly that the all-man's man is an uncouth illiterate. He may be educated, well-mannered, and on a first-name basis with fine wines. One all-man man I knew was a handsome individual who gave the impression of being gentle, affectionate, and sensitive. He sat and ate dinner one night while I was doing something endearingly feminine at the sink. At one point, he mutely held up his glass to indicate in a primitive, even ape-like, way his need for a refill. This was in 1967, before Women's Liberation. Even so, I was disturbed. Not enough to break the glass over his handsome head, not even enough to mutely indicate the whereabouts of the refrigerator, but enough to remember that moment in all its revelatory clarity. No androgynous man would ever brutishly expect to be waited on without even a "please." (With a "please," maybe.)

---

[1]James Dean (1931–1955) was a 1950s film star who gained fame for his portrayals of restless, defiant young men.

Margin notes:

Does she favour androgynous men? What kind of appeal?

She will give a woman's perspective. She writes for and edits women's magazines.

Seems like she is going to talk about the advantages of androgynous men as compared to other men. Sees them as better.

Attempt to counter stereotype? Can't androgynous men also be effeminate?

Suggests "All-men" men reject behaviours and interests they consider feminine, but isn't she stereotyping? Are all these men like this? She seems to be exaggerating.

4   The brute happened to be a doctor—not a hard hat—and, to all appearances, couth. But he had bought the whole superman package, complete with that fragile beast, the male ego. The androgynous man arrives with a male ego too, but his is not as imperialistic. It doesn't invade every area of his life and person. Most activities and thoughts have nothing to do with masculinity or femininity. The androgynous man knows this. The all-man man doesn't. He must keep a constant guard against anything even vaguely feminine (*i.e.,* "sissy") rising up in him. It must be a terrible strain.

5   Male chauvinism is an irritation, but the real problem I have with the all-man man is that it's hard for me to talk to him. He's alien to me, and for this I'm at least half to blame. As his interests have not carried him into the sissy, mine have never taken me very far into the typically masculine terrains of sports, business and finance, politics, cars, boats and machines. But blame or no blame, the reality is that it is almost as difficult for me to connect with him as it would be to link up with an Arab shepherd or Bolivian sandalmaker. There's a similar culture gap.

6   It seems to me that the most masculine men usually end up with the most feminine women. Maybe they like extreme polarity. I like polarity myself, but the poles have to be within earshot. As I've implied, I'm very big on talking. I fall in love for at least three hours with anyone who engages me in a real conversation. I'd rather a man point out a paragraph in a book—wanting to share it with me—than bring me flowers. I'd rather a man ask what I think than tell me I look pretty. (Women who are very pretty and accustomed to hearing that they are pretty may feel differently.) My experience is that all-men men read books I don't want to see paragraphs of, and don't really give a damn what I or any woman would think about most issues so long as she looks pretty. They have a very limited use for women. I suspect they don't really like us. The androgynous man likes women as much or as little as he likes anyone.

7   Another difference between the all-man man and the androgynous man is that the first is not a star in the creativity department. If your image of the creative male accessorizes him with a beret, smock and artist's palette, you will not believe the all-man man has been seriously short-changed. But if you allow as how creativity is a talent for freedom, associated with imagination, wit, empathy, unpredictability, and receptivity to new impressions and connections, then you will certainly pity the dull, thick-skinned, rigid fellow in whom creativity sets no fires.

8   Nor is the all-man man so hot when it comes to sensitivity. He may be true-blue in the trenches, but if you are troubled, you'd be wasting your time trying to milk comfort from the all-man man.

9   This is not blind prejudice. It is enlightened prejudice. My biases were confirmed recently by a psychologist named Sandra Lipsetz Bem, a professor at Stanford University. She brought to attention the fact that high masculinity in males (and high femininity in females) has been "consistently correlated with lower overall intelligence and lower creativity." Another psychologist, Donald W. MacKinnon, director of the Institute of Personality Assessment and Research at the University of California in Berkeley, found that "creative males give more expression to the feminine side of their nature than do less creative men. . . . [They] score relatively high on femininity, and this despite the fact that, as a group, they do not present an effeminate appearance or give evidence of increased homosexual interests or experiences. Their elevated scores on femininity indicate rather an openness to their feelings and emotions, a sensitive intellect and understanding, self-awareness and wide-ranging interests, including many which in the American culture are thought of as more feminine. . . ."

10   Dr. Bem ran a series of experiments on college students who had been categorized as masculine, feminine, or androgynous. In three tests of the degree of nurturance—warmth and caring—the masculine men scored painfully low (painfully for anyone stuck with a masculine man, that is). In one of those experiments, all the students were asked to listen to a "troubled talker"—a person who was not neurotic but simply lonely, supposedly new in town and feeling like an outsider. The masculine men were the least supportive, responsive or humane. "They lacked the ability to express warmth, playfulness and concern," Bem concluded. (She's giving them the benefit of the doubt. It's possible the masculine men didn't express those qualities because they didn't possess them.)

11   The androgynous man, on the other hand, having been run through the same carnival of tests, "performs spectacularly. He shuns no behaviour just because our culture happens to label it as female and his competence crosses both the instrumental [getting the job done, the problem solved] and the expressive [showing a concern for the welfare of others, the harmony of the group] domains. Thus, he stands firm in his opinion, he cuddles kittens and bounces babies and he has a sympathetic ear for someone in distress."

12   Well, a great mind, a sensitive and warm personality are fine in their place, but you are perhaps skeptical of the gut appeal of the androgynous man. As a friend, maybe, you'd like an androgynous man. For a sexual partner, though, you'd prefer a jock. There's no arguing chemistry, but consider the jock for a moment. He competes on the field, whatever his field is, and bed is just one more field to him: another opportunity to perform, another fray. Sensuality is for him candy to be doled out as lure. It is a ration whose flow is cut off at the exact point when it has served its purpose—namely, to elicit your willingness to work out on the field with him.

13   Highly masculine men need to believe their sexual appetite is far greater than a woman's (than a nice woman's). To them, females must be seduced: Seduction is a euphemism for a power play, a con job. It pits man against woman (or woman against man). The jock believes he must win you over, incite your body to rebel against your better judgment: in other words—conquer you.

14   The androgynous man is not your opponent but your teammate. He does not seduce: he invites. Sensuality is a pleasure for him. He's not quite so goal-oriented. And to conclude, I think I need only remind you here of his greater imagination, his wit and empathy, his unpredictability, and his receptivity to new impressions and connections.

■ Reading as a Writer

All of us who write can use reading as a springboard for improving our writing. You can do several things to make your reading especially useful.

As you read, the views of others, the experiences they relate, and the information they present often deepen your understanding of yourself, your relationships, and your surroundings. In turn, this broadened perspective can supply you with writing ideas. When possibilities surface, be sure to record them. Some writers keep a reading journal in which they summarize what they've read and jot down writing ideas that come to mind. In addition, you can take down specific ideas, facts, and perhaps even a few particularly telling quotations that you discover. You may want to incorporate this material into your own writing at a later time. Carefully record the source so that you can document it properly in order to avoid plagiarism (see pages 353–355). When you read various sources that explore the same topic or related topics, you may notice connections among their ideas. Since these connections can be fertile ground for a paper of your own, don't neglect to record them. Once you have jotted down these ideas, circle and label related thoughts. You can also draw a line linking the different thoughts to one another and to the main point that relates them. Express as a thesis statement your view of how these ideas fit together. Interacting with various sources and using their ideas to advance the purpose of your writing is a form of synthesis (see page 64). When you proceed in this fashion, as in writing any paper, review your information, determine the points you want to make, and experiment until you find the order that works best. As you write, use the material from your sources as you would any support; be careful, however, to credit the authors properly in order to avoid plagiarism. If you will be writing a paper that synthesizes material from various sources, review pages 329–343 and 345–350 on how to document your sources properly.

Because writers solve problems, you'll want to pay attention to the techniques and strategies that other writers use. If you find an introduction, an organizational pattern, a transition, a certain description or comparison unusually engaging, study the writer's technique. Perhaps you can use it yourself. Similarly, observe when a piece of writing fails and try to determine why.

Narration

James Alexander Thom

The Perfect Picture*

James Alexander Thom (born 1933) is a native of Gosport, Indiana, where his parents were physicians, and a graduate of Butler University. Before becoming a freelance writer in 1973, he worked as an editor for the Indianapolis Star *and the* Saturday Evening Post. *In addition, he has been a lecturer at Indiana University. He has authored one volume of essays,* Let the Sun Shine *(1976), and four historical novels:* Long Knife *(1979),* Follow the River *(1981),* From Sea to Shining Sea *(1984), and* Panther in the Sky *(1989), for which he earned the Best Novel Award from the Western Writers of America. He is a contributor to many popular magazines and an editor for* Nuggets *magazine. "The Perfect Picture," which first appeared in* Reader's Digest, *depicts an incident and an ethical dilemma that Thom experienced as a cub reporter.*

<table>
<tr><td>Introduction notes time, locale, and cause of action; first-person point of view</td></tr>
</table>

1   It was early in the spring about 15 years ago—a day of pale sunlight and trees just beginning to bud. I was a young police reporter, driving to a scene I didn't want to see. A man, the police-dispatcher's broadcast said, had accidentally backed his pickup truck over his baby granddaughter in the driveway of the family home. It was a fatality.

<table>
<tr><td>Body: paragraphs 2–12; action begins</td></tr>
</table>

2   As I parked among police cars and TV-news cruisers, I saw a stocky white-haired man in cotton work clothes standing near a pickup. Cameras were trained on him, and reporters were sticking microphones in his face. Looking totally bewildered, he was trying to answer their questions. Mostly he was only moving his lips, blinking and choking up.

<table>
<tr><td>Time signal
Key event</td></tr>
</table>

3   After a while the reporters gave up on him and followed the police into the small white house. I can still see in my mind's eye that devastated old man looking down at the place in the driveway where the child had been. Beside the house was a freshly spaded flower bed, and nearby a pile of dark, rich earth.

*Reprinted with permission from the August 1976 *Reader's Digest*. Copyright © 1976 by The Reader's Digest Assn., Inc.

4   "I was just backing up there to spread that good dirt," he said to me, though I had not asked him anything. "I didn't even know she was outdoors." He stretched his hand toward the flower bed, then let it flop to his side. He lapsed back into his thoughts, and I, like a good reporter, went into the house to find someone who could provide a recent photo of the toddler.

> Dialogue

5   A few minutes later, with all the details in my notebook and a three-by-five studio portrait of the cherubic child tucked in my jacket pocket, I went toward the kitchen where the police had said the body was.

> Time signal
> Secondary event

6   I had brought a camera in with me—the big, bulky Speed Graphic which used to be the newspaper reporter's trademark. Everybody had drifted back out of the house together—family, police, reporters and photographers. Entering the kitchen, I came upon this scene:

7   On a Formica-topped table, backlighted by a frilly curtained window, lay the tiny body, wrapped in a clean white sheet. Somehow the grandfather had managed to stay away from the crowd. He was sitting on a chair beside the table, in profile to me and unaware of my presence, looking uncomprehendingly at the swaddled corpse.

> Key event

8   The house was very quiet. A clock ticked. As I watched, the grandfather slowly leaned forward, curved his arms like parentheses around the head and feet of the little form, then pressed his face to the shroud and remained motionless.

> Time signal

9   In that hushed moment I recognized the makings of a prize-winning news photograph. I appraised the light, adjusted the lens setting and distance, locked a bulb in the flashgun, raised the camera and composed the scene in the viewfinder.

10   Every element of the picture was perfect: the grandfather in his plain work clothes, his white hair backlighted by sunshine, the child's form wrapped in the sheet, the atmosphere of the simple home suggested by black iron trivets and World's Fair souvenir plates on the walls flanking the window. Outside, the police could be seen inspecting the fatal rear wheel of the pickup while the child's mother and father leaned in each other's arms.

11   I don't know how many seconds I stood there, unable to snap that shutter. I was keenly aware of the powerful story-telling value that photo would have, and my professional conscience told me to take it. Yet I couldn't make my hand fire that flashbulb and intrude on the poor man's island of grief.

> Conflict

12   At length I lowered the camera and crept away, shaken with doubt about my suitability for the journalistic profession. Of course I never told the city editor or any fellow reporters about that missed opportunity for a perfect news picture.

> Time signal
> Action ends

13   Every day on the newscasts and in the papers, we see pictures of people in extreme conditions of grief and despair. Human suffering has become a spectator sport. And sometimes, as I'm watching news film, I remember that day.

14   I still feel right about what I did.

> Conclusion: paragraphs 13 and 14; indirectly states point; notes writer's reaction

DISCUSSION QUESTIONS

1. Thom notes in his opening paragraph that he is "driving to a scene I didn't want to see." How does this statement help explain what happens later?

2. Paragraph 10 contains several descriptive details. What bearing do these details have on Thom's decision?

3. Do you think that Thom made the right decision? Why or why not?

TOWARD KEY INSIGHTS

How have the media affected our sense of privacy?

Is their influence good or bad?

To answer these questions, consider the role of the newspaper photographer in "The Perfect Picture," TV crews at disasters, and talk shows built around very personal revelations.

SUGGESTION FOR WRITING

Write a personal narrative that features a conflict over a choice between an advantageous and a morally satisfying decision. State your point directly or indirectly, and use time signals and dialogue as necessary.

Philip Ross

The Boy and the Bank Officer

Philip Ross (born 1939) is a native of New York City. After earning degrees at Princeton (1961) and Columbia (1962), he became a newspaper reporter and then, in 1965, a writer for the American Museum of Natural History. Between 1969 and 1983, he worked as a freelance writer, after which he began his present career as a Manhattan psychotherapist. While a freelance writer, he authored one book-length nonfiction work, The Bribe *(1976), about a failed attempt at municipal bribery, and contributed numerous articles to such periodicals as* New York, Reader's Digest, *and the* New York Times. *This essay details an episode with an unexpected and highly embarrassing outcome.*

1   I have a friend who hates banks with a special passion. "A bank is just a store like a candy store or a grocery store," he says, "except that a bank's merchandise happens to be money which is yours in the first place. If banks were required to sell wallets and money belts, they might act less like churches."

2   I began thinking about my friend the other day as I walked into a small, overlighted branch office on the West Side. I had come to open a checking account.

3   It was lunchtime and the only officer on duty was a fortyish black man with short, pressed hair, a pencil mustache, and a neatly pressed brown suit. Everything about him suggested a carefully groomed authority, an eager determination to define himself through his vaulted surroundings.

4   This officer was standing across a small counter from a young white boy who was wearing a crew-neck sweater, khakis, and loafers. He had sandy hair, and I think I was especially aware of him because he looked like he belonged more on the campus of a New England prep school than in a West Side bank.

5   The boy continued to hold my attention because of what happened next.

6   He was clutching an open savings-account book and wearing an expression of open dismay. "But I don't understand," he was saying to the officer. "I opened the account myself, so why can't I withdraw any money?"

7   "I've already explained to you," the officer told him, "that bank regulations prohibit someone who is fourteen years old from withdrawing any funds without a letter from his parents."

8   "But that doesn't seem fair," the boy said, his voice breaking. "It's my money. I put it in. It's my account."

9   "I know it is," the officer said, "but those are the rules. Now if you'll excuse me."

10   He turned to me with a smile. "May I help you, sir?"

11   I didn't think twice. "I was going to open a new account," I said, "but after seeing what's going on here, I think I've changed my mind."

12   "Excuse me?" he said.

13   "Look," I said, "if I understand what's going on here correctly, what you're saying is that this boy is old enough to deposit his money in your bank but he's not old enough to withdraw it. And since there doesn't seem to be any question as to whether it's his money or his account, the bank's so-called policy is patently ridiculous."

14   "It may seem ridiculous to you," he replied in a voice rising slightly in irritation, "but that is the bank's policy and I have no alternative but to abide by the rules."

15   The boy had stood hopefully next to me during this exchange, but now I was reduced to his helplessness. Suddenly I noticed that the open savings book he continued to grasp showed a balance of about $100. It also showed that there had been a series of small deposits and withdrawals.

16   I had my opening.

17   "Have you withdrawn money before by yourself?" I asked the boy.

18   "Yes," he said.

19   I moved in for the kill.

20   "How do you explain that away?" I zeroed in on the officer. "Why did you let him withdraw money before but not now?"

21   He looked exasperated. "Because the tellers were not aware of his age before and now they are. It's really very simple."

22   I turned to the boy with a pained shrug. "You're really getting ripped off," I said. "You ought to get your parents to come in here and protest."

23   The boy looked destroyed. Silently, he put his savings book in a rear pocket and walked out of the bank.

24   The officer turned to me. "You know," he said, "you really shouldn't have interfered."

25   "Shouldn't have interfered?" I shouted. "Well, it damn well seemed to me that he needed someone to represent his interests."

26   "Someone was representing his interests," he said softly.

27   "And who might that be?"

28   "The bank."

29   I couldn't believe what this idiot was saying. "Look," I concluded, "we're just wasting each other's time. But maybe you'd like to explain exactly how the bank was representing that boy's interests?"

30   "Certainly," he said. "We were informed this morning that some neighborhood punk has been shaking this boy down for more than a month. The other guy was forcing him to take money out every week and hand it over. The poor kid was apparently too scared to tell anyone. That's the real reason he was so upset. He was afraid of what the other guy would do to him. Anyway, the police are on the case and they'll probably make an arrest today."

31   Uh.

32   "You mean there is no rule about being too young to withdraw funds from a savings account?"

33   "Not that I ever heard of. Now, sir, what can we do for you?"

DISCUSSION QUESTIONS

1. In his opening paragraph Ross cites a friend's attitude toward banks, and in paragraph 3 he describes the bank officer. What does he accomplish by presenting these two aspects of the story?

2. Examine the dialogue in this essay and then point out examples of incomplete sentences and slang. Why are these included?

3. This story has very few time signals. Why are they unnecessary?

4. This narrative features two conflicts: the first between the boy and the bank officer, the second between the officer and the narrator. In which paragraphs does Ross present each conflict? Why does the second conflict receive more extended treatment?

5. Ross provides a good example of a narrative with an unstated point. What is the point? Refer to specific parts of the story when answering.

6. Do you find the lying of the bank officer objectionable, even under the circumstances? Discuss.

TOWARD KEY INSIGHTS

Was either the narrator or the bank officer right in intervening unasked in the boy's affairs?

When is it appropriate and when inappropriate to intervene in another person's affairs?

Are we ever *obligated* to do so?

SUGGESTION FOR WRITING

Narrate an experience whose outcome was not at all what you expected. Include material that points toward an ending different from the one that in fact occurred.

Write a narrative about a time you chose to intervene in a situation involving others. Include details that suggest whether, on reflection, your intervention seems to have been wise or unwise.

Moses Milstein

Memories of Montreal—and Richness

Moses Milstein was born in 1947 in Austria and grew up in Montreal. He received degrees from McGill University, Université de Montreal, and Guelph University. He now makes his living in British Columbia as a veterinarian and is a regular contributor to the North and West Voice. *In this essay, originally published in* The Globe and Mail, *Milstein recounts memories of growing up in Montreal. He reflects with subtle nostalgia on how his experience of urban, economic, and cultural diversity growing up in Montreal will not be duplicated for his son, who is growing up in a more homogeneous, upper-middle class area of Vancouver. The essay may prompt discussion of generational, class, or ethnic differences, or of gains that may entail losses.*

1   In the April of his youth, my son walks to school in a gentle shower of cherry blossoms. Down the slopes of West Vancouver's Hollyburn Mountain he can see the houses nestled among tall cedars. Bursts of rhododendrons guard the yards and over their tops he can see the sun glinting on the placid waters of Howe Sound. He walks through this serene neighbourhood unmolested, the quiet punctuated by the thwonk of tennis balls coming from cozy courts nearby.

2   And I blame myself.

3   In the April of my childhood in the Montreal of the fifties, the way to school was still studded with chunks of sandy moraine from winter's retreating ice. With the threat of blizzards gone, I could shed my heavy winter boots, and feel the sidewalk strangely close beneath the thin soles of my shoes.

4   The corners of our street, like every street then, were held by the four corner stores. The one we used, the "Jewish" store, could be counted on for an emergency box of matzohs, or kosher Coca Cola during Passover. Although Mr. Auerbach practically lived in his store, he did, in fact, go home at night. His French competitors across the street, though, lived amidst their crowded displays of potato chips, soft drinks and fly-paper rolls – cooking, sleeping, arguing, watching TV, just behind the curtain in the back of the store.

5   You could buy a tiny bag of potato chips for a penny. My mother insisted that it was filled with sweepings.

6   Around the corner was Wing Ling, the Chinese laundry, like all Chinese laundries painted green on the outside. Within, great vats seethed with steam where Mr. Lee and his family washed and ironed our sheets, which he would then hand to me in a package wrapped in brown paper and string.

7   Next to the laundry, across the alley, which ran like a sparkling river of broken glass and urine produced by the hordes of feral cats, giant rats and stumbling drunks who waded therein, was the Jewish Tailor. His narrow house, barely a door and a window wide, extended backwards from his work room and housed his wife and daughter, a sewing machine and a steam iron. An air of sadness, like the tape measure he wore around his neck, enveloped the place.

8   His old, thick-legged wife shared his melancholic mien. Their daughter was my age and wore braces on her legs. I often wondered whether they were her parents or her grandparents, so great was the difference in their ages. According to rumour, they were, like our family, survivors of the "Krieg," the Holocaust.

The tailor and his wife had each had families of their own, children and spouses. They perished somehow, I don't remember the details. Every family I knew then had a story of death and they were all mixed up in my mind. In a DP camp after the war, the tailor met and married this woman and she was able to give birth to one more child, with crippled legs, and then no more.

9   I would rush by their sad house, and in one block was on St. Lawrence Street, noisy and bursting with commerce. Two long blocks before I reached my school.

10   My father worked on St. Lawrence Street at the Junior Trend Factory, which he pronounced "Jooniohtren." One April, when school was closed for Passover, I brought him his lunch. The elevator in his building passed floor after floor of angrily buzzing sewing machines. On some floors anonymous contractors were making clothes under other manufacturer's labels; on others I could see fancy offices where men with cigars, manicured fingers and pomaded hair struggled for ascendancy in the *shmatte* business.

11   My father worked among his friends from back home. They would usually greet me with jokes, smiles and much cheek-pinching. But when I saw them at their sewing machines their faces were closed and dark and they worked feverishly at piecework, sewing linings, sleeves, buttonholes under the critical eyes of the foreman. I left quickly.

12   Between these rows of tall, brown brick buildings, I would pass the restaurants that fed the workers. Delicatessens beckoned, their windows steamed from the smoked meat briskets waiting within, festooned with hanging salamis, rows of jars of pickled tomatoes and long banana peppers, green and red. Inside, the esteemed smoked-meat cutter stood resplendent on his pedestal, dispensing thick, greasy, spicy slices of meat onto golden rounds of rye bread. A good cutter was rumoured to be worth his substantial weight in gold and was held in reverential awe by my friends and me. Unhappily, the price of 25 cents, an hour's wages for my father, was beyond our reach.

13   The smells of the delicatessen mixed with the forest of urban smells welling out of each block–fruit stores, bakeries, taverns (for men only), poultry and egg stores, fish stores, bagel bakeries, steak houses, all of which would have me slavering until I reached that pinnacle of sensual delights, the Rachel Market. Here, the smells and sights merged as the French farmers, some able to speak Yiddish, backed their trucks up to the wide sidewalks where they set up their tables and displayed their produce. Beneath the market, down a spiral of stone steps slicked with blood, was a subterranean chamber of death. If you stood halfway down the stairs, you could see the hell waiting for the birds below. An open fire to singe their pin feathers burned in an alcove. Hooks covered the walls from which the chickens were suspended by their feet while men in bloodied aprons cut their throats, drained their blood and plucked their feathers which floated in the air until they settled among the clots of gray droppings on the floor and walls.

14   Across the street, the large bakery, Richstones, held a secret known only to the few. On Fridays, if you went to the door at the top of the loading bays, you could ask for the seconds, the crumbled cakes, broken doughnuts, smeary cupcakes. Sometimes they would give you some and sometimes they would chase you away angrily. Another example of the incomprehensible capriciousness of adults.

15   As if to remind me of my destination, I would ultimately come to the offices of Der Kanader Adler, one of three local Yiddish papers. Occasionally, one of my teachers would publish a poem there, truly the last song of the Last of the

Mohicans. The Jewish Peretz School was just around the corner on Duluth Street. We were educated in Yiddish, spoke to each other in English and lived in a French neighbourhood.

16   I can recall every building and business along the two blocks to school. Many of the proprietors knew me and my family. I felt as safe and happy on the streets as in my own home and would often linger until dusk on the return home.

17   When I grew up I bought a house in the gentle forests of the Pacific and my son walks to school among the cherry blossoms. And sometimes I am sad for him.

DISCUSSION QUESTIONS

1. What contrast does the writer introduce in the first three paragraphs? What details are especially effective in highlighting the contrast? Why do you suppose that the second paragraph is only one sentence long?

2. Point out sensory details that reflect sight, sound, taste, smell, touch. Comment on the effect of these sensory impressions.

3. Why does Moses Milstein spend so much time describing the Jewish Tailor (paragraphs 7–9), whose place was enveloped by "an air of sadness"? What is the larger significance of the reference to the Holocaust?

4. How does the writer reveal a kind of double perspective, as a child and an adult? Consider the fragment that ends paragraph 14: "Another example of the capriciousness of adults." Is this the child or the adult speaking? What does the writer mean here?

5. In the last paragraph the father states that he is sad for his son sometimes even though his son "walks to school among the cherry blossoms." What is the paradox here? Do you think the boy would understand if his father tried to explain to him that he was missing something?

6. Does this essay have a stated or an unstated point? If it is stated, indicate where. If it is unstated, express it in your own words.

TOWARD KEY INSIGHTS

What are the advantages of living in a place of cultural and economic diversity? Are there any disadvantages?

What are the possible losses and/or gains associated with moving away from the place where you grew up?

What does Moses Milstein reveal about the nature of parent/child relationships?

Whose childhood would you prefer—the father's or the son's? Explain.

SUGGESTION FOR WRITING   *Create a sense of paradox by recounting a memory of a time or place that at first glance seemed far from perfect, but which has given you riches that you have come to appreciate.*

Daniel Francis

My Life with Riley

Daniel Francis originally published this article in the Fall 1996 issue of Geist *magazine. In the following essay, Francis narrates a lively, even humorous, account of the relationship he had with his blind dog. The essay, which shows the effects of the discovery of his dog's blindness on himself initially and then on other people, may allow for the discussion of ethical issues relating to disabilities.*

1   We were driving through Stanley Park, talking about what to call the new dog when my son piped up from the back seat, "Why not Stanley Bark?" It was his first joke (a pretty good one, too) and we all laughed appreciatively, but in the end, families being what they are and democracy being what it is, we settled on Riley.

2   Collectors of political trivia will recall that in 1990 Barbara Bush's dog Millie published her first book. Titled simply *Millie's Book,* it was a heartwarming dog's-eye view of life in the White House, illustrated with many colour photographs of Millie going about her daily activities as the most powerful dog in the free world.

3   Millie was a springer spaniel. So was Riley. A coincidence, but when I learned about it I took it as a sign that we had chosen the right breed. The Dog of Presidents. But this was as far as the similarity went. Millie was obviously a gifted dog. After all, she had written a book. Riley, on the other hand, did not write books. To be honest, he could not even read them. Riley was blind.

4   Until Riley came into my life, I was not what is commonly called a dog lover. Not like the President and Mrs. Bush. My only other canine encounter was with a yappy, anorexic Chihuahua purchased by my parents when I was a boy. They called him Rex. I suppose it was meant to be a joke. Rex had a serious problem with continence and soon moved on to alternative accommodation where white rugs were not an issue. This brief experience in no way prepared me for the implications of Riley's disability.

5   We did not realize that Riley was blind until some time after we purchased him. I remember looking into his eyes. They seemed completely blank, like Orphan Annie's dog in the comic strip, but it did not occur to me that there was nobody there looking back. Finally, when Riley began walking into walls and falling off the back porch, we began to suspect there was something wrong. Still, it came as a complete shock when the dog ophthalmologist diagnosed two detached retinas. They were floating in his eyeballs like small collapsed trumpets, the doctor said. Riley couldn't see a thing.

6   The world immediately divided into two camps. On one side were those who counselled us to replace Riley with a "healthy" dog. They argued that any dog, but especially a natural-born retriever, could not be happy blind. For the sake of the animal, for the sake of our children, we should try again. Which, of course, meant having Riley euthanized. And we had better do it soon before we grew attached to him.

7   The other camp argued that there was nothing wrong with a blind dog, that it was a kind of insane consumerism that treated a dog like a faulty vacuum cleaner to be traded in for a better model. One friend said, "When the dog's time comes, it will come, but it's not now." Life seemed to be filled with conversations like that. In the end we decided, for better or worse, not to kill the dog.

8   I acquired one of those long retractable leashes which extend to a reasonable distance and began taking Riley for strolls through the neighbourhood. His walk was erratic; he tacked from side to side like a sailboat heading into the wind. Of course, his handicap remained invisible to people we met along the way, many of whom were reluctant to accept the fact when told. I did not want to be a mendicant begging for sympathy on Riley's behalf, but when an obvious dog lover stopped us to make conversation about Riley I usually let drop the fact that he was blind. As a matter of mutual interest. On more than one occasion these strangers tried to convince me that I was wrong. I recall an elderly gentleman who dropped to his knees on the sidewalk and began passing his finger back and forth in front of Riley's eyes, claiming that Riley was actually following the movement and therefore could not be blind. It is too absurd to think that he thought I was lying, that I was so desperate for sympathy that I spent my time cruising the neighbourhood with a cockamamie story about a blind dog. I guess he just thought I had made a horrible mistake.

9   (And then there was the neighbour who emerged from her house one day and, seeing Riley and me standing in the front yard, cheerily called out, "Is he still blind?" as she got into her car and drove off.)

10   When it wakes up, how does a blind dog remember where it went to sleep? This question occurred to me one evening when I arrived home and found Riley snoozing in the living room. At the sound of my voice he wakened, totally disoriented. First he stepped onto the hearth and stared into the fireplace for a few seconds. Then he spun around and trotted into the far corner of the room where he became entangled in the legs of a table. I called him and he came back across the room and stumbled into a chair. Finally it occurred to me that this would work better if I went to him.

11   We strove to treat Riley as a normal, sighted dog whenever possible. To this end, my wife enrolled him in obedience class. But he was overstimulated by the smells and sounds of movement around him and proved impossible to discipline. Eventually my wife began going to obedience class by herself, leaving Riley at home. I guess the idea was that we would convey all the information to him at some later time, but it never happened. He remained completely untrained, though my wife became very good at fetching the newspaper.

12   In the end, Riley developed intractable ear infections which we could not seem to eradicate. The operation was going to cost more money than we had, and might leave him deaf anyway. After another prolonged moral struggle, we concluded that we were not doing this dog a favour. The vet agreed that perhaps it was time to put him down.

13   It fell to me, of course, to deliver Riley to his own execution. He came happily; he had always trusted me completely, which just made it worse. The vet explained that I could remain with Riley and hold his head as he drifted out of consciousness but such stoicism was beyond my emotional range. As it was I dissolved in tears in the parking lot. It was a scene out of *Lassie*, except Lassie always recovered from her injuries to do another show.

14   For a long time afterward, I was burdened with a deep sense of guilt. I wondered if perhaps instead of giving Riley the final injection the vet might have passed him on to a more caring owner who would not put his own convenience ahead of the welfare of a loyal pet. I began eyeing other black and white spaniels in the street, wondering if perhaps one of them was actually Riley, his sight and hearing restored through the intervention of expensive surgery.

15   Eventually the irrationality subsided, the grieving process came to an end. I am not sure what I learned from this episode. I know only that I will never own another dog. The emotional and moral demands are too extreme.

16   And Riley, if you're out there reading this, forgive me.

DISCUSSION QUESTIONS

1. What is the effect of the references to dogs that are not the focus of the essay—Millie and Rex (paragraphs 1–4)?

2. Why does the author withhold the information that "Riley was blind" until the end of the third paragraph? How does the subject of Riley's blindness bring up ethical implications that extend beyond this particular family's dilemma (paragraphs 6–7)?

3. Why do you suppose "strangers tried to convince" the writer that he was wrong about Riley's blindness (paragraph 8)? What other responses do people have to information about Riley's blindness, and what is the larger significance of their reactions?

4. How does the narrator avoid sentimentality in the treatment of Riley's blindness (paragraphs 8–11) and Riley's death (paragraph 13)? What is the tone, or attitude, of the writer in the essay as a whole? Consider what the references to *Millie's Book* (paragraph 2), Orphan Annie's dog (paragraph 5), and the *Lassie* show (paragraph 13) contribute to the tone.

5. What does the writer mean when he says that he will "never own another dog" because "the emotional and moral demands are too extreme" (paragraph 15)?

TOWARD KEY INSIGHTS

After learning that Riley is blind, the narrator finds the world "divided into two camps"—those who believe that Riley should be euthanized, and those who argue that Riley should not, in effect, simply "be traded in for a better model." What do you imagine the arguments would be for or against keeping the dog? To what extent are similar arguments applied to humans?

SUGGESTIONS FOR WRITING

If you or someone you are close to has a visible or invisible disability, write about an experience that illustrates the effects of this disability on you, or on others.

If you have lost a pet for any reason, write a narrative about what you learned from this experience without falling into sentimentality.

Write a narrative about an instance in which people have challenged a personal decision that you felt ethically or emotionally committed to.

Description

David Helwig

The Quiet of the Backstretch

David Helwig

David Helwig is a poet who lives in Belfast, P.E.I. "The Quiet of the Backstretch" first appeared in the September/October 1998 issue of Canadian Geographic. *In this essay, David Helwig gives an evocative, affectionate description of a local horse track on Prince Edward Island. The uncommercial aspect of racing could be contrasted with the commercial emphasis of powwows, as portrayed in a later essay, "Native Postmodern."*

1   Pinette Raceway is hidden in a small patch of woods not far from our big frame house. You get there by turning down a clay road just past Mike's Lobster Pound on the Trans-Canada Highway, about 40 kilometres east of Charlottetown. There's a handmade sign for the track, the outline of a horse, driver and sulky.

2   The raceway has a wooden grandstand, a frame building with a snack bar, and, farther off, a longer, lower building with stalls for the horses. Everything is painted white with green trim. The oval of the track is the red ochre of Prince Edward Island earth. When you climb into the grandstand, you look across at a stand of tall spruce that runs half the length of the backstretch. The other half opens across fields to the shining surface of the Pinette River. Sometimes I have seen the quick, short beat of an osprey's wings as it circles over the water, hunting, waiting to dive. On the quiet of the backstretch between races I have seen a fox trot by on its dainty feet, out of the spruce woods and back in.

3   Most of those who come to the track live close by. A girl of 16 takes your dollar admission on the way in, and a few minutes later she turns up in the grandstand selling tickets for the night's raffle. There's no rush to the betting windows here; there are no betting windows. No purse for the winner either. The races are just for the fun of racing, for the pleasure of seeing the long delicate legs moving in harmony, pulling the slender wheels of the carts twice around the oval.

4   When they want to groom the track after the first couple of races, a tractor pulls out from behind the horse barn with the trunk of a good-sized spruce tree on a chain behind it, and the log is dragged over the bright earth to level it.

Title identifies dominant impression: quiet

Introduction: paragraphs 1 and 2; identifies what, when, where, who, why. Sight impression

Addresses reader directly

Vivid language

Moving vantage point

Contrast

Sight impression

Taste impressions

5   The snack bar has hot dogs and chips and homemade muffins, sold by the kind of women you might run into at a church tea. In fact, the worlds aren't far apart. A woman just along the row in the grandstand is talking about a minister she's just heard, some kind of a Baptist, she's certain, she could tell by the way he preached, and as the horses in the third race battle toward the wire, the announcer calls out, "Sing your favourite hymns."

Time signal
Touch impression

6   A Wednesday evening, and we are sitting in the stands. It is late summer, the end of the season, a chill is in the air. One of the horsemen, a familiar face from earlier Wednesdays, jokes that he's coming up into the seats to get warm.

7   "That one's a good little goer," he says of a two-year-old pacing down the back-stretch. No one comments, and he says it again. "That one's a good little goer."

8   The race card is not planned too much in advance. A driver will stop his horse in front of the grandstand to shout up to the race announcer the name of a new arrival, then tell those of us watching that he has to go back to the stables to get his whip since someone's mislaid it.

9   Between races the driver who won the first appears among the spectators, still in the helmet which is his only racing gear. He's a small, thin man with a smiling face. When they find themselves short of entries for the third race, he takes his horse out again. He wins again. Tonight, the second race had only two horses in it, and neither driver was carrying a whip. You could hear their voices across the darkening air shouting encouragement at their horses as they came down the home stretch.

Time signal

Sound impression

Conclusion: paragraphs
10–12 follow time sequence

10   There are no lights on the Pinette track, so the races have to be over before dark comes up out of the east over the river and the tall trees. Will there be races next week? Maybe, but the days are getting short. The air is sharp with cold. After the last race, everyone is quick to get up and move to the cars.

Contrast
Time signal

11   The sun is setting over the cove at Pinette, and the beach where we dug clams in the summer is empty. At this time of year the lobster boats are brought ashore and set on blocks to pass the winter, then to be painted and cleaned up when the weather warms up in spring. It is part of the poetry of fall here, the boats appearing in the yards of houses down every country road.

Conclusion points ahead
to future; returns to
"red earth" from
introduction;
sight and sound impression

12   Soon, they'll be taking down the sign announcing the races, but in a few months, when the ice is out, among the others signs of spring on the island, the horses will be back, their hooves banging along over the red earth.

Discussion Questions

1. In paragraphs 1 and 2, does the writer use a fixed or moving vantage point? Explain.

2. Examine the first three and last three paragraphs in order to see how details are arranged and organized. Does the writer use spatial organization, time sequence, or any other principle of organization?

3. In paragraph 3, Helwig says "There's no rush to the betting windows here." What implied contrast is he suggesting?

4. Even though he is describing a place he has visited many times rather than a particular experience, why does Helwig zero in to describe a "Wednesday evening" (paragraphs 6–7) on which nothing especially significant happened?

5. Cite examples of places where Helwig appeals to the five primary senses. Are there other ways that Helwig conveys a sense of vivid immediacy?

6. How does Helwig provide the sense of an ending? Consider in particular what he accomplishes with the last sentence.

TOWARD KEY INSIGHTS

David Helwig says that the races he enjoys watching are "just for the fun of racing" (paragraph 3). Are you familiar with any places or events in your community that are unspoiled by commercialization? What is lost to a community when places like Pinette Raceway get developed?

SUGGESTION FOR WRITING

Describe a place, gathering, or event that you have seen at different seasons. Make your account vivid by providing specific details that appeal to the senses, or perhaps to one key sense. Consider writing in the present tense.

Rohinton Mistry

Lend Me Your Light

Born in Bombay in 1952, Rohinton Mistry came to Canada in 1975 and has lived since then near Toronto. He has won a number of prestigious literary prizes for his fiction, including the Governor General's Award for his novel Such a Long Journey. *"Lend Me Your Light" is a story in* The Tales of Firozsha Baag, *an anthology of Mistry's short stories. Rohinton Mistry's account of growing up in an upper-middle class family in India and then coming to Canada presents interesting ambiguities surrounding cultural and class differences, and explores the necessary contradiction between dreams and reality.*

. . . your lights are all lit—then where do you go with your lamp? My house is all dark and lonesome—lend me your light.

Rabindranath Tagore
Gitanjali

1   We both left Bombay the same year. Jamshed first, for New York, then I, for Toronto. As immigrants in North America, sharing this common experience should have salvaged something from our acquaintanceship. It went back such a long way, to our school days at St Xavier's.

2   To sustain an acquaintance does not take very much. A friendship, that's another thing. Strange, then, that it has ended so completely, that he has erased himself out of our lives, mine and Percy's; now I cannot imagine him even as a mere bit player who fills out the action or swells a procession.

3   Jamshed was my brother's friend. The three of us went to the same school. Jamshed and my brother, Percy, both four years older than I, were in the same class, and spent their time together. They had to part company during lunch, though, because Jamshed did not eat where Percy and I did, in the school's drill-hall-cum-lunchroom.

4   The tiffin carriers would stagger into the school compound with their long, narrow rickety crates on their heads, each with fifty tiffin boxes, delivering lunches from homes in all corners of the city. When the boxes were unpacked, the drillhall would be filled with a smell that is hard to forget, thick as swill, while the aromas of four hundred steaming lunches started to mingle. The smell must have soaked into the very walls and ceiling, there to age and rancify. No matter what the hour of the day, that hot and dank grotto of a drillhall smelled stale and sickly, the way a vomit-splashed room does even after it is cleaned up.

5   Jamshed did not eat in this crammed and cavernous interior. Not for him the air redolent of nauseous odours. His food arrived precisely at one o'clock in the chauffeur-driven, air-conditioned family car, and was eaten in the leather-upholstered luxury of the back seat, amidst his collection of hyphenated lavishness.

6   In the snug dining-room where chauffeur doubled as waiter, Jamshed lunched through his school-days, safe from the vicissitudes of climate. The monsoon might drench the tiffin carriers to the bone and turn cold the boxes of four hundred waiting schoolboys, but it could not touch Jamshed or his lunch. The tiffin carriers might arrive glistening and stinking of sweat in the hot season, with scorching hot tiffin boxes, hotter than they'd left the kitchens of Bombay, but Jamshed's lunch remained unaffected.

7   During the years of high school, my brother, Percy, began spending many weekend afternoons at his friend's house at Malabar Hill. Formerly, these were the afternoons when we used to join Pesi *paadmaroo* and the others for our most riotous times in the compound, the afternoons that the adults of Firozsha Baag would await with dread, not knowing what new terrors Pesi had devised to unleash upon the innocent and the unsuspecting.

8   But Percy dropped all this for Jamshed's company. And when he returned from his visits, Mummy would commence the questioning: What did he eat? Was Jamshed's mother home? What did the two do all afternoon? Did they go out anywhere? And so on.

9   Percy did not confide in me very much in those days. Our lives intersected during the lunch routine only, which counted for very little. For a short while we had played cricket together with the boys of Firozsha Baag. Then he lost interest in that too. He refused to come when Daddy would take the whole gang to the Marine Dri *maidaan* on Sunday morning. And soon, like all younger brothers, I was seen mainly as a nuisance.

10   But my curiosity about Percy and Jamshed was satisfied by Mummy's interrogations. I knew that the afternoons were usually spent making model airplanes and listening to music. The airplanes were simple gliders in the early years; the records, mostly Mantovani and from Broadway shows. Later came more complex models with gasoline engines and remote control, and classical music from Bach and Poulenc.

11   The model-airplane kits were gifts from Jamshed's itinerant aunties and uncles, purchased during business trips to England or the U.S. Everyone except my brother and I seemed to have uncles and aunties smitten by wanderlust, and Jamshed's supply line from the western world guaranteed for him a steady diet of foreign clothes, shoes, and records.

12   One Saturday, Percy reported during question period that Jamshed had received the original soundtrack of *My Fair Lady*. This was sensational news. The LP was not available in Bombay, and a few privately imported or "smuggled" copies,

brought in by people like Jamshed's relatives, were selling in the black market for two hundred rupees. I had seen the records displayed side by side with foreign perfumes, chocolates, and cheeses at the pavement stalls of smugglers along Flora Fountain.

13   Sometimes, these stalls were smashed up during police raids. I liked to imagine that one day a raid would occur as I was passing, and in the mêlée and chaos of the clash, *My Fair Lady* would fly through the air and land at my feet, unnoticed by anyone. Of course, there wasn't much I could have done with it following the miracle, because our old gramophone played only 78 rpms.

14   After strenuous negotiations in which Mummy, Percy, and I exhausted ourselves, Percy agreed to ask his friend if I could listen to the album. Arrangements were made. And the following Saturday we set off for Jamshed's house. From Firozsha Baag, the direction of Malabar Hill was opposite to the one we took to go to school every morning, and I was not familiar with the roads the bus travelled. The building had a marble lobby, and the lift zoomed us up smoothly to the tenth floor before I had time to draw breath. I was about to tell Percy that we needed one like this in Firozsha Baag, but the door opened. Jamshed welcomed us graciously, then wasted no time in putting the record on the turntable. After all, that was what I had come for.

15   The afternoon dragged by after the sound-track was finished. Bored, I watched them work on an airplane. The box said it was a Sopwith Camel. The name was familiar from the Biggles books Percy used to bring home. I picked up the lid and read dully that the aircraft had been designed by the British industrialist and aeronautical engineer, Thomas Octave Murdoch Sopwith, born 1888, and had been used during the First World War. Then followed a list of parts.

16   Later, we had lunch, and they talked. I was merely the kid brother, and nobody expected me to do much else but listen. They talked of school and the school library, of all the books that the library badly needed; and of the *ghatis* who were flooding the school of late.

17   In the particular version of reality we inherited, *ghatis* were always flooding places, they never just went there. *Ghatis* were flooding the banks, desecrating the sanctity of institutions, and taking up all the coveted jobs. *Ghatis* were even flooding the colleges and universities, a thing unheard of. Wherever you turned, the bloody *ghatis* were flooding the place.

18   With much shame I remember this word *ghati*. A suppurating sore of a word, oozing the stench of bigotry. It consigned a whole race to the mute roles of coolies and menials, forever unredeemable.

19   During one of our rare vacations to Matheran, as a child, I watched with detachment while a straining coolie loaded the family's baggage on his person. The big metal trunk was placed flat on his head, with the leather suitcase over it. The enormous hold-all was slung on his left arm, which he raised to steady the load on his head, and the remaining suitcase went in the right hand. It was all accomplished with much the same approach and consideration used in loading a cart or barrow–the main thing was balance, to avoid tipping over. This skeletal man then tottered off towards the train that would transport us to the little hill station. There, similar skeletal beings would be waiting with rickshaws. Automobiles were prohibited in Matheran, to preserve the pastoral purity of the place and the livelihood of the rickshawallas.

20   Many years later I found myself at the same hill station, a member of my college hikers' club, labouring up its slopes with a knapsack. Automobiles were still not permitted in Matheran, and every time a rickshaw sped by in a flurry of legs and wheels, we'd yell at the occupant ensconced within: "Capitalist pig! You bastard! Stop riding on your brother's back!" The bewildered passenger would lean forward for a moment, not quite understanding, then fall back into the cushioned comfort of the rickshaw.

21   But this type of smug socialism did not come till much later. First we had to reckon with school, school uniforms, brown paper covers for textbooks and exercise books, and the mad morning rush for the school bus. I remember how Percy used to rage and shout at our scrawny *ghaton* if the pathetic creature ever got in his way as she swept and mopped the floors. Mummy would proudly observe; "He has a temper just like Grandpa's." She would also discreetly admonish Percy, since this was in the days when it was becoming quite difficult to find a new *ghaton*, especially if the first one quit due to abuse from the scion of the family and established her reasons for quitting among her colleagues.

22   I was never sure why some people called them *ghatons* and others, *gungas*. I suppose the latter was intended to placate—the collective conferment of the name of India's sacred river balanced the occasions of harshness and ill-treatment. But the good old days, when you could scream at a *ghaton*, kick her and hurl her down the steps, and expect her to show up for work next morning, had definitely passed.

23   After high school, Percy and Jamshed went to different colleges. If they met at all, it would be at concerts of the Bombay Chamber Orchestra. Along with a college friend, Navjeet, and some others, my brother organized a charitable agency that collected and distributed funds to destitute farmers in a small Maharashtrian village. The idea was to get as many of these wretched souls as possible out of the clutches of the village money-lenders.

24   Jamshed showed a very superficial interest in what little he knew about Percy's activities. Each time they met, he would start with how he was trying his best to get out of the country. "Absolutely no future in this stupid place," he said. "Bloody corruption everywhere. And you can't buy any of the things you want, don't even get to see a decent English movie. First chance I get, I'm going abroad. Preferably the U.S."

25   After a while, Percy stopped talking about his small village, and they only discussed the concert program or the soloist's performance that evening. Then their meetings at concerts ceased altogether because Percy now spent very little time in Bombay.

26   Jamshed did manage to leave. One day, he came to say goodbye. But Percy was away working in the small village: his charitable agency had taken on the task full time. Jamshed spoke to those of us who were home, and we all agreed that he was doing the right thing. There just weren't any prospects in this country; nothing could stop its downhill race towards despair and ruin.

27   My parents announced that I, too, was trying to emigrate, but to Canada, not the U.S. "We will miss him if he gets to go," they told Jamshed, "but for the sake of his own future, he must. There is a lot of opportunity in Toronto. We've seen advertisements in newspapers from England, where Canadian Immigration is encouraging people to go to Canada. Of course, they won't advertise in a country like India—who would want these bloody *ghatis* to come charging into their fine land?—but the office in New Delhi is holding interviews and soliciting highly qualified applicants." In the clichés of our speech was reflected the cliché

which the idea of emigration had turned into for so many. According to my parents, I would have no difficulty being approved, what with my education, and my westernized background, and my fluency in the English language.

28   And they were right. A few months later things were ready for my departure to Toronto.

DISCUSSION QUESTIONS

1. Consider the descriptions of the school lunch in the drillhall and Jamshed's lunch in the "air-conditioned family car" (paragraphs 4–6). What impressions do the sensory details create? What is the effect of the contrast between the two kinds of lunches?

2. Why are the narrator and his mother so curious about Jamshed's daily life (paragraphs 8–10)?

3. What does the original soundtrack of *My Fair Lady* seem to symbolize (paragraphs 12–14)?

4. When the narrator hears his brother talk with Jamshed about the ways that "*ghatis* were always flooding places," he remembers the word *ghati* "with much shame" (paragraphs 15–17). Why does the word *ghati* bring a sense of shame to the narrator? How do we infer that his attitude toward the *ghatons* has changed since he was a child (paragraphs 18–21)?

5. How does this essay move in time and space? Find examples of places where the narrator provides time signals to orient the reader. Examine especially the movements forward in time in paragraphs 20–21. What is the effect on you of these different time frames?

6. Explain how Jamshed's criticism of India (paragraph 24) relates to our impression of Jamshed, or to the larger point of this essay.

7. What criticisms and ironies does the conclusion suggest (paragraphs 27–28)?

TOWARD KEY INSIGHTS

What possible reasons are suggested for the narrator's own callousness toward the ghatons in the past, or for his brother's rage toward the "scrawny *ghaton*" getting in his way (paragraph 21)? Can you remember examples from your childhood of your own insensitivity, or even cruelty toward those who were in a different social grouping? How was your attitude similar to or different from the narrator's?

What does the West represent to the narrator when he is in India? How do we infer that his attitude toward the West changed since he began living in Canada?

Drawing from Mistry's essay, comment on the challenges of adaptation facing those who immigrate to Canada from post-colonial countries such as India.

SUGGESTION FOR WRITING

Describe a relationship with a friend or acquaintance from a different socioeconomic level or culture. Use details that highlight the contrast.

Evelyn Lau

An Insatiable Emptiness

Evelyn Lau, born in 1970 in Vancouver, British Columbia, is the author of Runaway: Diary of a Street Kid. *She has also written five volumes of poetry and prose. In Lau's essay, "An Insatiable Emptiness," which first appeared in* The Georgia Straight, *she uses vivid detail to describe the effects of an eating disorder that she eventually overcame.*

1   I no longer clearly remember the first time I forced myself to throw up. What I do remember is how inexpert I was and how long it took before I succeeded in actually vomiting instead of just gagging and retching. I began by sticking my finger down my throat and wiggling it around, but this produced few results; it wasn't until articles about bulimia appeared in women's magazines that I finally thought to use the handle of a toothbrush instead of my forefinger. It became easy after that.

2   In my mid-teens, I was too young to believe I was anything but immortal. It didn't occur to me that what I was doing was dangerous—instead, it seemed a smart and practical way of coping with things. I went through months of throwing up once or twice a day, then brief periods when I did not throw up at all, when I seemed to have broken the pattern. Surely this meant I was in control. But by the time I turned 18, the months of not throwing up had diminished to weeks, and when I *was* vomiting I was doing it four, five, six times a day. I had become addicted to the sensation. It was no longer a penance I had to perform after eating, but the reward at the end of a binge. I loved the feeling I had after purging, of being clean and shiny inside like a scrubbed machine, superhuman. I would rise from the bathroom floor, splash my face with cold water, vigorously brush the acid from my mouth. I would take a wet cloth, wipe off the vomit that had spattered my arms, and feel as energized as someone who had just woken from a nap or returned from an invigorating jog around the block. I felt as if everything disgusting inside me had been displaced so that it was now outside myself. Not only all the food I had eaten, but my entire past.

3   No one could tell me to stop, not even my friends who eventually knew what I was doing. They could not control this part of my life or any other. This was mine alone—the chemical flower smell of the blue water in the toilet, the vomit that shot out as a burning liquid, drenching the sides of the bowl. After a session in the bathroom, a certain emptiness would sing inside me, a sensation of having become a cage of bones with air rushing through it. I craved this feeling so much I no longer cared what I had to eat in order to vomit—I would cram clusters of bananas into my mouth, or tubs of ice cream that lurched back up my throat in a thin and startlingly sweet projectile.

4   When I left the bathroom, I felt like someone who had achieved some great thing—climbed a mountain, written a book—and survived. I was overweight by only 10 pounds or so, but when I looked in the mirror all I saw was buttery flesh covering my body. My stomach had become swollen and globular from the gorging and purging; I had earned it the way other women earn washboard stomachs and lean waists from hours of sit-ups and crunches at the gym.

5   As a child, I had been thin and healthy, with a flat belly and limbs that turned brown in the summer. I had my first period when I was 11, and for the next several years the blood welled out of me in thick, rust-coloured gouts that no tampons or pads could contain. My body had somehow become a vessel filled with secret, terrible workings, and I longed to make it translucent, pared-down, clean as a whistle.

But the blood spread in the shapes of clouds on my skirts and pants, for 10 or 12 days each month, and my hips and breasts pressed outwards. I hated what was happening to my body, once so straight and uninflected. I attracted the attention of one of my parents' friends, who stared at the fuzzy-dark crook at the top of my thighs when I sat cross-legged in front of him, who asked me to perform somersaults and splits while his thick lips hung open with desire. My own father grew awkward around me, refusing to touch me or meet my eyes, driven away by this growing body that forced him out like a giant balloon expanding in a small room. I was in despair. I wanted to trick my body back into childhood by starving it, but I was hungry all the time; I craved food during the week prior to my traumatic periods. Sometimes I would consume a whole bag of shortbread cookies or three chocolate bars; the sugar and fat would induce a heavy, mucousy lethargy.

6   My breasts continued to develop, horrifying my mother, who frequently made me undress in front of her so she could ridicule them. Her actions convinced me there was something wrong with my body. She decided to put the whole family on a diet, serving small portions of steamed fish and vegetables, chicken with the skin removed. During dinner, and in the hungry hours of the evening that followed, she would say over and over again, "It's because of you we didn't get enough to eat, that we're going to bed hungry. Look at the sacrifices we're making for you." I would sit at the dinner table, staring down at my plate with tears in my eyes, grief forming a hot, choking knot in my throat. I would watch my father slowly raise his fork to his mouth while my eagle-eyed mother watched me triumphantly, eating only half of what was on her plate in order to set an example.

7   My mother was so thin and white that whenever I glimpsed her undressing behind a half-closed door, her thighs looked like those of the Holocaust survivors I examined in photographs in history class at school. Meanwhile, I began to put on weight, growing chubby beneath sweatshirts and loose jeans. I stole chocolates from the drugstore, bought greasy bags of day-old cookies from the bakery, consumed candies in a blind rush on the mile-long walk from school to home. I crammed myself with food, yet I hated food: its veils of grease, its sauces like paste. I hated its fragility beneath my hands, could not bear the delicacy of pastry. But once I started eating, I could not stop, and after I gave in I would again have to cope with the horrible feeling of satiation—a feeling so uncomfortable and guilt-ridden it threatened to annihilate me.

8   I hated the unaccustomed thickness of my body, yet I took a secret, perverse pride in the space I was filling up, the air I was pushing aside in the family home in order to make room for myself. I looked in scorn upon my mother, who wore tiny pink sweaters with pearl buttons, size XS. Her legs were like bleached sticks, the skin white and crepey; her hipbones jutted visibly beneath her skirts, and she reminded me of a starving cow, its ribs and hips holding up the tent of skin. At 13, I had grown to match my father's weight. But at 130 pounds, he was small for a man, his arms straight, the biceps undefined. He was weak, useless in the battle that had sprung up between my mother and myself. He would not protect me, he took no sides in the daily tug-of-war for power. He merely absented himself, took the coward's way out. For this, I knew, one day I would make him suffer.

9   I thought that if I were to physically fight my mother I could break her dry arms like twigs. I could twist her skeleton between my hands; I could sit on her and suffocate her. But it never came to that. Instead, with each pound I gained, my mother became more controlling. I felt that in my entire world there was only one thing my mother could not take away from me: my body. She was trying, of course, with her diets and carefully calibrated meals and calorie counters set up around the kitchen. She wanted to watch me day and night, but in this she in-

evitably encountered frustration and failure: she could not see the junk food I snuck between meals and hid between textbooks and in my locker at school.

10   And it was driving my mother crazy, I began to realize. She turned to the only thing she could control 24 hours a day: her own body. For every pound I gained, she lost one. In Grade 9, when I came home from school I found her doing jumping jacks and skipping rope in the living room, or following an aerobics show on television. She had virtually stopped eating, complaining that I was doing enough eating for us both. Her eyes grew large in her face, and her hair began to fall out in swirls that clogged up the drain in the sink and the shower. When I stood up from the table and looked down at my mother's skull, I could see the wide, white swathe of the part in her hair.

11   For a while, my father insisted that she eat, but he soon gave up and came home less and less, always too late for the dinner hour, fraught as it was with its agonizing tensions: my mother staring at me with fascination as I ate, her eyes transfixed with hunger. I thought I could no longer stand it; I was as guilty as a murderer with every bite. At night, I lay in my room contemplating suicide and listening to the footsteps of my father pacing his study, waiting for his wife to fall asleep before daring to enter their bedroom. When I trespassed there, I saw pink walls, pink curtains, a pink throw on the queen-sized bed. The bedroom faced south, and all day the sun shone relentlessly through the gauze curtains, revealing the motes of dust in the air. When I opened the dresser drawers, I found beautiful, tiny clothes, beaded and jewelled, carefully folded and wrapped in plastic, as if their owner had already died. I knew these clothes would never again be worn by my mother, and I would never be small enough to wear them. I knew this was a source of bitterness in my mother's life—she could not pass herself on to me; she could not live her life again through me. In order to survive, I would have to deny my mother this second life and claim my own.

12   In the en suite bathroom I found orange lipsticks dried to hard, wax nubs, cakes of powder that crumbled at a touch, an old tube of KY Jelly squeezed from the bottom like toothpaste. All of it seemed a shrine to my mother's glamorous past. She had been a beauty in her youth, with thick hair that hung down to her waist, so much hair it was almost impossible to bind into ponytails. She had pale skin and pink cheeks like apple blossoms, and she wore short skirts and high heels to work.

13   What my mother didn't know was that I was already beginning to incorporate her inside me. She didn't know that she was winning and that for the rest of my life I would contain aspects of her—both the young beauty turning men's heads and the wasted figure doing sit-ups on the living room floor. I would grow up to wear contact lenses and to put a wave in my hair; I would admire myself in mirrors and spend small fortunes on clothes and cosmetics. Beneath this evidence of self-esteem, though, I would learn to cultivate a parallel self-hatred: my thoughts would repeat themselves obsessively; I would become compulsive in my behaviour, desperate for control; I would avoid other women because I was afraid they would be like my mother; and I would live at the mercy of my emotions, the endless stream of hatred that poured out of my mouth when I bent over the toilet.

14   "You will never succeed at anything," my mother told me day after day. "You're like your father—spineless, weak, good for nothing."

15   The last time I saw them, when I was 17 and they were in their 50s, he seemed bewildered by what had happened to our family. She had become a confused, agitated woman who plucked ceaselessly at the strap of her purse with an anguished tic. She had become powerless to control me, this piece of herself that had separated from her. She had lost me in her attempt to keep me forever.

16   I was 20 years old when I began to lose the feeling of immortality. I thought my body would regenerate itself in time, that once again everything would be new and resilient. But it only got worse. My body began showing sings of wear— my throat constantly ached from throwing up, and when I opened my mouth I saw in the mirror a red, inflamed pendulum dangling behind rows of teeth softened and eroded by acid. My own teeth, once so enamel white—the sort of teeth parents thank God for; the sort of teeth a man meeting me for the first time would go away remembering—had, overnight it seemed, turned pitted and yellow, the back ones worn down to shrunken saddles. When I looked in the mirror, they were translucent as X-rays, made, it seemed, of water and putty. I began to brush more vigorously after each purge, not knowing then that I was accelerating the process, scrubbing my teeth with my own stomach acid.

17   I waited for the day when I would throw up blood. Already I could taste it at the back of my throat, inching farther upward with each heartbeat. Now after vomiting, I would rise shakily from my knees, gripping the edge of the counter for balance, my heart knocking wildly in my chest. A column of flame speared me from my stomach to my throat—my esophagus a two-edged blade in my chest, a tunnel set on fire, a steel pole thrust through me.

18   Now when I threw up, I reeled from the pain. I was not throwing up half-digested food, as I had for years, but what felt like complete objects—plastic balls, pieces of Lego, nuts and bolts that tore at me as they came out of my body. Afterwards, my stomach would hurt so much that for the rest of the evening any sustenance I sought would have to be the sort given to a convalescent or a starvation victim: thin porridge, vegetable soup, herbal tea.

19   I no longer thought of myself as a girl or a woman. I no longer felt sexual desire. I was an "it," a conduit for a constant stream of ugliness that had to pass through it in order for me to stay pure.

20   In some dim part of me, I knew that when I left my apartment to go out into the street, other people did not see me as I saw myself. They did not recoil from me in horror, as I expected. I knew I was a reasonably attractive young woman, like so many young women in the city, neither fat nor thin. But I felt somehow grotesque and abnormal. Strangers knew nothing of my secret; friends were helpless; my dentist would only shake his head over my open mouth and tap his pencil along my teeth to track the path of corrosion the vomit had left in its wake.

21   Once, in a determined moment, I called the Eating Disorder Clinic at St. Paul's Hospital, but the waiting list meant I would not get in for a year. At that time, a year seemed forever, so I did not add my name to the list. Surely in a year's time everything would change, resolve itself. Twelve months later I called again, but by this time the list was even longer, and again I did not add my name.

22   I finally stopped being bulimic nearly two years ago, when I was 22. It ended not because of willpower or therapy or something so banal as an increased sense of self-esteem. It ended because the pain from throwing up rendered the pleasure slight by comparison. It ended when my softened teeth cringed at every mouthful and when I woke several times each night with cramps wracking my stomach from one side of my waist to the other. It ended when I arrived at the point where I could no longer feel my feet. Months later, when I went to the doctor, he would diagnose it as an electrolyte imbalance caused by the vomiting up of so many vitamins and minerals. But for a long time, I didn't know what it was, and it frightened me—sometimes when I stood up, I nearly fell over. My feet were like dead fish, cold and clammy, disconnected from the rest of my body. Once in a while they flared suddenly to life, a constellation of pins and needles, so that I could not

bear to press my soles to the floor. When I tried to go to the bathroom in the middle of the night, I felt in the underwater light of that hour as if I had transformed into the fairy-tale mermaid who had chosen her lover over the sea: with each step, I landed on knife points.

23   By then I had also developed a hiatus hernia—a portion of my stomach protruded through my esophagus—and my teeth became so compromised that one day one of them simply disintegrated under pressure.

24   "Your tooth isn't going to grow back," the dentist said flatly, and it was then I understood for the first time that my body did not possess some secret store of replacement parts, that physical damage, like its psychological counterpart, left marks that could remain a lifetime.

25   The last time I forced myself to throw up, it felt like internal surgery. Grief, love, rage, pain—it all came pouring out, yet afterwards it was still there inside me. I had been bulimic off and on for eight years, and in all that vomiting I had not purged myself of any of the things that were making me sick.

DISCUSSION QUESTIONS

1. Examine the ways that Evelyn Lau describes the sensations associated with her former compulsion in paragraphs 1–3. What is the effect of the different sensory details and images? How does she use comparisons, or metaphors, to make her experiences vivid to the reader?

2. What impression does Lau convey about crossing into puberty? What associations does she suggest between her eating disorder and sexuality?

3. What connection is implied between the daughter's hunger and the mother's hunger (paragraphs 5–11)? How do you interpret the reference to "the daily tug-of-war for power" (paragraph 8)?

4. What does the writer mean when she says that she "began to lose the feeling of immortality" at a certain age (paragraph 16)?

5. After referring to paragraph 22, explain in your own words why Lau stops being bulimic. Why do you suppose her compulsion continued as long as it did?

6. What is your emotional reaction to this essay? Do you feel sympathy or empathy for the writer? Explain your answer.

TOWARD KEY INSIGHTS

Do you or does someone you know have a compulsion or addiction? What are the reactions of others to this compulsion? What is the effect of these reactions?

What rewards or compensations did Lau receive from the addiction at first? Does her essay suggest that cultural pressures caused her eating disorder, or does it imply that there were other contributing factors?

SUGGESTIONS FOR WRITING

Write an essay that describes the overcoming of a compulsion—even a minor one.

Write an essay describing how you lost your feeling of immortality.

Lesley Hazleton

Assembly Line Adventure*

Lesley Hazleton (born 1945) is a native of England who earned a B.A. degree from Manchester University and an M.A. degree from the Hebrew University of Jerusalem before emigrating to the United States in 1979. Hazleton is a nationally known automotive journalist with wide-ranging interests that include baseball, psychology, and politics. She has authored six nonfiction books, and her numerous shorter pieces have appeared in a variety of major newspapers and popular magazines. Our essay is excerpted from her latest book, Driving to Detroit *(1998). In it she describes her brief introduction to auto assembly-line work and the lessons she learned from the experience.*

1   I'd toured many auto plants before, and physically this was not much different. That is, it was an assault on the senses: an enclosed, windowless world of harsh artificial light and hard concrete floors ringing with the discordant cacophony of industrial production. Metal rang on metal. Stamping presses clanked, power tools whined, pulleys groaned, hoists clanged, welding robots whooshed, sparks crackled, lasers beeped, compressed air hissed, bolts banged into place, trolleys rumbled down the aisles, and all the while, conveyor belts carried cars in one stage or another of production, from bare metal frames to fully painted bodies, clattered and clanketed beside us and behind us and even over our heads.

2   At five in the afternoon, I started work, joining three other workers stationed around a huge rotating machine. Our job was to feed a robot.

3   Officially, we were preparing dashboard molds for foam injections. In fact, we were simply loading and unloading the machine for the robot, which injected the foam and then wiped its own nozzle as though it were wiping its nose—one of those infuriatingly human gestures that make you think, "Cute," and then hate yourself for having thought it.

4   This was one of the simplest tasks on the whole assembly line. Squirt some filler release into a hole. Lift a light plastic mold and place it on a protruding lip of the machine. Bang a board with your knee to drop three locks to hold the mold in place. Check the locks. Push a black button to bring the lift down into the right position for the next guy. Wait for the machine to rotate and present you with a new lip. And that was it. A ten-second job to be repeated ad infinitum.

5   Two hours later, I moved from one of the simplest jobs on the line to one of the most complicated: assembling the whole instrument panel. Steering wheel, indicator and wiper wands, gauges, dashboard line, the lot.

6   Audrey, the woman whose task it was to teach me this job had a tough challenge ahead of her.

7   I guessed she was in her mid-thirties. Despite a mass of long brown curly hair, she had a boyish way to her, maybe because of the leather builder's apron she was wearing, its pockets so full of connectors and screws and bolts that it took me a while to realize she was six months pregnant.

8   "Is this your first?" I asked.

9   She burst out laughing. "Honey, I'm forty-three years old. And a grandmother. I married again not long ago, and"—she spread her arms wide and stared at her belly—"just look what happened. This sure is the last thing I ever expected."

*Editors' title.

10   "How long will you go on working?"

11   She laughed again. "Do you know how much kids cost? I'm staying right here till the day I pop."

12   She hadn't stopped working for a moment as we talked. She couldn't. The line was rolling, and it was either keep up or bring everything to a halt. We were standing on the line, a wide conveyor belt rumbling past an array of shelves piled high with parts, and beneath an overhead rack dangling power tools and bins of screws. On the line with us, every six feet or so, was a workstand holding an empty dashboard shell, placed upside down on the stand so that it was easy to work on. Audrey's job was to make it into a complete instrument panel.

13   For the first few moments, standing on the moving belt was almost childishly fun. The world was reversed: you stood still and it went past you. Your mind knew it was you moving, not the world, but your senses told you otherwise. And all the time, the belt vibrated gently underfoot: if it weren't for the noise, it might even have been pleasantly sexy.

14   "Watch your head," Audrey said, and I ducked as a power wrench came dangling past my right ear. Followed by another. And yet another. Even though I reminded myself that it was me moving, not them, every time I looked up they seemed to be aiming for my brains with a certain inexorable malevolence.

15   I spent the first half-hour watching Audrey and figuring out how to stay out of the way. So far as I could make out, she had a total of some fifty separate procedures to complete in a logic-defying sequence of about three minutes. Each step had to be performed in perfect timing, so that the right parts and tools were at hand exactly when she needed them. And to add to the pressure, this job was what they called a "show-stopper."

16   Farther on down the line, the completed instrument panel would be lowered into the "smile joint"—a large lazy U going from side to side of the cars' frame. If it didn't fit, the line would stop, and the whole plant would start running behind. "You can't go back and do it again," Audrey said. "You got to do it perfect the first time."

17   I knew I'd never be able to do this job. Yet Audrey seemed convinced that I was educable. She talked each movement out loud as she worked, with me following her around like a pet dog. Somehow, she convinced me to do a bit here and a bit there, until within an hour, I had the beginning of it down pat.

18   Walk six stands down the line, past other team members at different stages of the job, and read the manifest hanging on the dashboard shell. Pick up different parts from the shelves alongside the line, depending on whether this is to be a sedan or a wagon, an automatic or a manual shift. Jam a leather sheath over the sharp metal edge to the side of the module. Ease the parts into place. Snap-connect electrical wires: gray to the right, blue to the middle, white to the left.

19   So far so good. I was feeling quite proud of myself. Trouble was, this was only the beginning of the beginning.

20   The rest began to blur: Snap-connect a black fastener, then a yellow one. Don't delay. If you go too slow, the line will take you past the parts you need, and you'll have to start running back and forth for them. Pick up the steering shaft from a shelf and ease its thirty-pound weight down through the center of the module. Arrange the wires to run over the top of the shaft. Slip on and snap a green fastener . . .

21   Or were those last two steps the other way round? "Here," said Audrey, redoing my work.

22   Okay, now pick up two bronze-covered bolts and screws, two black bolts, a circular piece, and two silver bolts from those big bins alongside the line. Insert the silver bolts. Fine. Place the bronze-colored ones in one place, the black ones in another. Great. Pull down a power wrench from the overhead line . . .

23   I grabbed for it and missed. It began to recede from me. I stretched and yanked it down just in time to tighten the bolts. I had no idea of what I was bolting to what, or why. Neither, it turned out, did Audrey.

24   Right, you've got those bolts nice and tight. Now pick different bronze-colored bolts from another bin. No, not alongside the line—right here, hanging overhead. Fine. Insert them and tighten them by hand for now. What about the wrench? Not there yet, that comes soon. First, thread the electrical wires through the back of the module and out through this flap, then loop them over and under the shaft like so, and then . . .

25   Then what? I couldn't remember. And I was only a third of the way through the job.

26   "Don't worry," said Audrey. "It takes most people four days to learn this job. You're doing real good."

27   That was sweet of her, but it didn't feel real good to me. My attention strayed for a moment, I lost a beat, and suddenly the power tools and screw bins were bearing down on me way before I was ready for them. I worked as fast as I could, one eye on my hands, the other on the dangling wrench going past. I swore, lunged for it, and yanked at the cord as though if I pulled hard enough I could pull back the whole line and slow things down to my pace. I remembered Charlie Chaplin's desperation in *Modern Times*, and suddenly there was nothing remotely funny about it. I dropped a bolt, reached for the wrong wrench, and watched pathetically as Audrey stepped in and put everything to rights. I hadn't felt quite this incompetent since I was a kid trying to thread a sewing machine at school. I never did master that.

28   Every time I thought I had the hang of it all, another two steps somehow reversed themselves in my mind, or one slipped out of existence altogether. My ears were ringing, my mind was reeling, and my hands had never felt clumsier. I began to fumble the screws, inserting them at an angle so that they wouldn't tighten properly and had to be taken out and inserted anew. Audrey was working as hard as I was by now; we stood shoulder to shoulder, me fouling things up, her fixing them.

29   And suddenly it was ten o'clock, and there was a half-hour break for lunch. Ten at night, this is. By now, I was squinting to stop from seeing double. I was convinced that if I could just work through to the end of the shift, I'd get this job down pat. But as the line came to a halt and everything stopped moving, some remote part of my brain managed to signal a weak but just decipherable message that the pressure was getting to me. It was time to call it quits before I damaged a car, or myself, or worse still, somebody else.

30   "Don't you want some lunch before you go?" said Audrey. But I was too exhausted to even look at food. I needed fresh air. And solitude. And silence. I made my excuses, stuffed my yellow Kevlar gloves into my pocket as a memento, got lost twice trying to find the way out, and finally emerged into the parking lot.

31   Never had a parking lot seemed so beautiful: so quiet, so peaceful, so serene. Even the buzzing yellow of the sodium vapor lights seemed soothing. Behind me, the plant hummed gently, its skylights glowing into the night. Mid-shift, I was the only person out here, and I had a flash of guilt mixed with giddy freedom, the kind that comes from playing hooky.

32   I found the truck, climbed in, made to start it up. Then stopped, hand in midair, and sat staring at the instrument panel. Something was wrong. I took a moment to figure it out: I'd spent the past few hours working on upside-down instrument panels, and now I was seeing this one the right way up.

33   I reached out and examined it for its component parts, thinking of the man or the woman who'd put it together, and appreciating the way it had been done. This thing I usually took so for granted that I'd never before paid a moment's attention to it, was now an astounding piece of man-made—woman-made—complexity.

34   I started the truck and drove slowly out of the lot, wondering how long I'd keep this awareness that cars are not merely machines, but things put together by human beings, products of real men and real women doing the kind of work that would drive most people crazy. Not long enough, for sure.

DISCUSSION QUESTIONS

1. Comment on the effectiveness of the essay's title.
2. Which of the five sensory impressions does Hazleton include? Refer to specific paragraphs when answering.
3. What is the dominant impression of this essay?
4. What time signals does Hazleton use? Refer to specific paragraphs when answering.
5. This description takes the form of a narrative with the action moving forward until a turning point is reached. Where does this turning point occur?
6. Identify the conclusion of the essay and what it accomplishes.
7. After reading Hazleton's description, how do you think you would tolerate working on an assembly line as a summer job? Discuss.

TOWARD KEY INSIGHTS

What jobs have you done or heard about that you would consider unbearable? What characteristics make them unbearable?

What jobs have you done or heard about that you would find enjoyable? What characteristics make them enjoyable?

SUGGESTION FOR WRITING

Write an essay describing your introduction to some new job. Use an appropriate number of sensory details that create a dominant impression and indicate your reaction to what you learned.

Process Analysis

Kathy Roth

How to Adopt a Stray

Kathy Roth is a cat fancier with special concern for the plight of homeless animals. In this essay, which first appeared in The Cat Catalog *(1976), she tells how to go about turning a stray cat into a healthy, contented house cat.*

1   Did you know that for every cat with a home there are twelve strays? We have all seen them—huddled in doorways, foraging through garbage, frightened, sick, unwanted. The average street cat has a limited life expectancy; poorly fed, he risks death from untreated ailments, automobiles, and the cold. It is of no help to think someone else will do something about the stray. In most cases no one does. The A.S.P.C.A. can do no more than pick up some of them. What stray cats need are *homes.*

2   Adopting a stray can be rewarding and fun for you and the cat, but be aware before you bring the cat home of what the costs will be. Every stray will need at least a check-up, shots and neutering as soon as possible after adoption. Many veterinarians (not all, but many) will reduce fees if you tell them that the animal you have adopted was a stray. If your veterinarian cannot help with costs, find one who can—they do exist. Your local A.S.P.C.A. or humane society can probably make recommendations.

3   The first step in adopting a stray is, of course, getting him home. Approach the cat slowly; talk to him reassuringly. Touch him, pet him. Pick him up by placing your right hand under his rib cage between his two sets of legs, your left hand around his rump supporting his back legs, and lifting gently. If you have a distance to go, wrap him inside your coat or sweater, for a sudden noise on the street might cause him to start and jump from your arms. Hold him close to your body so that he will be comforted by your body heat.

4   The stray in need of help is often the most docile, the most trusting. The seriously injured stray needs help most, yet because people dislike the problems this situation creates, this is the cat most often ignored. Take the injured cat to a

Title indicates set of directions

Introduction: paragraphs 1 and 2

Emotional appeal

Notes rewards, requirements of adoption

Body: paragraphs 3–13; uses polite commands, addressing reader as "you"

First step and its actions

Reasons for actions

veterinarian immediately. Even if it must be euthanized, it is far worse to walk away and leave a cat to suffer.

5 Pregnant cats present other problems, particularly if they are strays. You will not help reduce the stray population by taking in the mother and then plan to abandon the newborn kittens. If you assume responsibility for a cat's welfare, you should be prepared to assume total responsibility. Therefore, if you are unable to deal with the difficulties of finding good homes for kittens (as anyone who has tried knows, it is nearly an impossible job), then it is best to have the kittens aborted.

Warning

Second step and its actions

6 If you are bringing the stray into a household where there is another cat, totally isolate the stray on arrival and until it has been examined by your vet. The most frequent health problems one confronts in strays are parasites—ear mites, worms and fleas. Although these can be treated quickly and effectively, they are easily transmitted to other cats. Strays may also suffer from upper respiratory ailments—symptoms are running eyes, sneezing and nasal discharge. Do not think of this as "just a cold." Upper respiratory ailments can kill cats.

Warnings

7 If you already have a cat, you probably know about feline distemper. This is a virus which may be fatal to cats. If your cat has been inoculated, he runs no risk of catching this virus from a stray (nor do you, since it affects only cats). During the past two years, I have rescued fourteen strays. None of these had distemper and only one died from an upper respiratory illness. Do not be overly concerned about the possibilities of the stray being seriously sick. Just follow two simple precautions: keep the stray isolated from other cats for the first few days and have him examined by a doctor as soon as possible.

8 Once treated for ailments and restored to good health, strays require no more special care than any other cat. Some people think that stray cats, like dogs, should be bathed. It is best to let the cat take care of himself unless he has gotten into some terrible mess that only a scrubbing, and not a self-licking, will clean up. Secure in a new home, even the dingiest stray will soon make himself shine again.

9 Stray cats, like all cats, do not need much training to be house-broken. Introduce the stray to the litter pan and he will quickly get the idea. If your stray seems slow catching on, put him in the pan and help him make digging motions in the litter with his front paws, as you would a kitten. One or two lessons should be sufficient.

10 Because of poor diet, strays often suffer from constipation or diarrhea when first picked up. If your cat is suffering from constipation, feed him a half-teaspoon of nonmedicated petroleum jelly. If he is suffering from diarrhea, mix a little cooked white rice with his food. If you notice blood in the cat's stool, it may be the result of the stray's having eaten bones or sharp objects or having gotten worms while living outside on the street. Don't panic; take a stool sample to your veterinarian to be analyzed.

Warning

11 The adoption of a stray should be enjoyable, but it is no fun living with a cat who has not been spayed or neutered. Adult males tend to spray furniture with urine; females cry all night long, particularly when in heat. Do not believe the old stories about how neutering or spaying will change the disposition of a cat. It does not, as your veterinarian will tell you.

Third step and its actions

12 Once you have provided the physical comforts and medical necessities of your new pet, you may begin to worry about his adjustments to his new life. The best advice is not to worry. If this is your first cat, relax and enjoy getting to know

him. He will be nervous and shy for a few days, but gradually he will begin to come to you for petting and play sessions. You are providing him with food and shelter, and in a short time he will begin to show his appreciation of your care. If you already have a cat, let the new cat adjust gradually. Do not try to force the cats to accept each other—they will want to maintain distance for a time. No matter how much explaining you do, your original cat will feel threatened and jealous. Reassure him by giving him extra attention. There will be growling and hissing, but ignore everything for at least three days. In most cases, by the end of this period the original cat usually tires of hostilities and begins to establish a negotiated peace.

Warning

13   As soon as your new cat begins to feel at home, he will sleep a lot. A little food, a little quiet, and you may not see much of your new pet for a few days. I have known strays to sleep almost uninterruptedly for a week after being rescued from the rigors of street life. If the vet found the cat healthy, do not worry. Let him rest and, in a few days, he will feel more sociable.

14   People often mistakenly think that cats who have lived on the streets must be permitted to go outside. A former street cat will quickly adjust to life in the home and come to depend on the food and comforts he has been deprived of for so long. To let your cat back out on the streets is to expose him once more to the risks of becoming a stray again. You are not breaking natural laws; you are establishing a new, happy life the stray deserves.

Conclusion: corrects misconception

Warning

DISCUSSION QUESTIONS

1. Explain why the steps in this process could or could not be arranged in a different order.
2. Characterize the tone (see pages 232–235) of Roth's essay.

TOWARD KEY INSIGHTS

Is it a good deed to adopt and neuter a stray animal as Roth suggests? Why or why not?

From the animal's perspective, why might it prefer to remain a stray?

SUGGESTION FOR WRITING

Write an essay that provides directions for selecting a riding horse, hunting dog, or household pet other than a cat. Be sure to include the reason for any action whose purpose is not obvious, and provide cautionary warnings whenever necessary.

Rod McQueen

Millionaire Questionnaire

Born in Guelph, Ontario, in 1944, Rod McQueen has worked as a reporter, editor, director of public affairs at the Bank of Nova Scotia, and managing business editor at Maclean's. *He has won many awards for his writing, including the National Business Book Award for* Who Killed Confederation Life? The Inside Story. *He has authored six other books, including* The Last Best Hope—How to Start and Grow Your Own Business. *He is now a Toronto-based senior writer at* The Financial Post. *Rod McQueen's clear, tightly structured essay "Millionaire Questionnaire" might also have been called "Steps to Starting a Small Business" or "Setting a Goal and Succeeding."*

1   Lottery tickets are a waste of money. Everybody knows the improbable odds—one in 13 million.

2   There's a better way to become a millionaire. You've already got everything you need—right inside.

3   Here's the four-word secret: Start your own business.

4   Have you got what it takes?

5   After five years of interviewing the presidents of Canada's 50 Best Managed Private Companies, I've identified the top 10 steps to success.

6   **1.   Find a need and fill it.** Have a plan and follow it. Newfoundland's Lorraine Lush concluded that her neighbors needed work skills. For 14 years she'd been a secretary so she taught the first 65 students what she knew best: secretarial skills.

7   Today, The Career Academy has 22 programs, 3,000 students and 15 campuses.

8   **2.   Believe in yourself.** If you don't who will? When free trade arrived in 1989, observers predicted the demise of Morrison Lamothe Inc., an Ottawa bakery begun in the 1930s. Third-generation president John Morrison didn't heed the so-called experts.

9   The firm focused on private-label frozen dinners. Almost half of the product line is new in the last four years and the firm is tackling the U.S.

10   **3.   Exude optimism.** Nobody wants to deal with a dud. Geoff Chutter runs Whitewater West Industries Ltd., of Richmond, B.C., making waterslides and wave pools.

11   Talking to this man is like taking a tonic. Despite having the best job in the world, Chutter has twice run for Parliament because he believes he can make a public policy difference.

12   **4.   Be flexible.** Bend the rules. Take chances. Mining exploration fell two-thirds from 1987 to 1992 and with it went the drilling tool business of Fordia, in St. Laurent, Que.

13   Fordia's Alain Paquet took a chance and chased customers in South America. "Your life is at risk when traveling in those areas," he says after being robbed in Venezuela. "You can get killed for nothing if you're not careful." He and the company both survived. Fordia now sells in 28 countries.

14   **5.   Exercise vision.** This is the capacity to see the invisible. In September, 1996, a stranger arrived at Crila Plastic Industries Ltd., in Mississauga, Ont., promoting an unlikely product, a plastic that looked and acted like wood.

15   Intrigued, Crila president Peter Clark flew to Britain, obtained North American rights and now sells two million board feet of Extrudawood per month in an industry where a million board feet of anything in a year is a good sale.

16 **6. Accept help and advice.** Honor what people have to offer. Edmonton-based Fountain Tire doesn't just wait to hear ideas, it goes looking.

17   Says CEO Brian Hesje: "It's more productive to be humbled by those that succeed rather than have the false sense of security that comes from visiting the less successful."

18 **7. Tap the passion within.** Be resourceful. Trust your instincts. "I believe entrepreneurs are being visited by divine inspiration," says clothing designer Linda Lundström. "I also believe an entrepreneur can visualize something and make it happen."

19   How else to explain the moment when a bird-dropping spattered her car windshield while Lundström drove on an expressway. She combined that unhappy impact with a message she read on a passing truck and concluded that her La Parka line would do well. Her instincts were accurate.

20 **8. Fulfill customers' needs and exceed their expectations.** Glegg Water Conditioning, of Guelph, Ont., shipped a key component to a U.S. client but customs problems meant a 24-hour delay.

21   A Lear jet was chartered to deliver the item that very day. "We'll do whatever it takes to look after our clients," says president and CEO Robert Glegg.

22 **9. Never give up.** True character means never accepting defeat. Robert Mills and his son, Ray, of Calgary, spent nine months in 1989 making 1,000 sales calls. They sold only two of their pumps.

23   In the tenth month, Ray sold 15 pumps to one company. Today, Kudu Industries Inc., employs 100 and has annual sales of $35 million.

24 **10. Dream it and do it.** Olympic cyclist Louis Garneau's racing gear and helmet business, based in St-Augustin, Quebec, began with one sewing machine in his father's garage. Montreal's Karel Velan filled his order book using a four-page leaflet before he'd manufactured his first valve.

25   Not every start-up succeeds; annual failure rates run to 20%.

26   But what that also means is that out of 100 new businesses launched tomorrow, 30 will still be alive in five years.

27   Of those, 20% will be scraping by, 60% will be doing middling well, but 20% will be spectacularly successful.

28   Each of those six firms will have anywhere from 30 to 100 employees plus annual sales as high as $50 million.

29   And each of those individual founders will be millionaires.

30   Six millionaires for every 100 entrants.

31   I like those odds. Don't you?

32   You have the power to make of tomorrow exactly what you want.

DISCUSSION QUESTIONS

1. Why do you suppose the writer uses examples to illustrate each step? What examples do you find especially vivid?

2. Consider the brevity of the paragraphs in this article, especially the introductory and concluding paragraphs. Why do you think the writer has written such short paragraphs?

3. Find examples of the writer's use of numbers and statistics, quotations, and rhetorical questions. Comment on their effect.

4. Do you trust the writer's advice in this essay? Why or why not?

Toward Key Insights

What reasons besides financial ones might people have for starting a small business? If you were to "find a need and fill it," what business would you start?

If you were to go into business immediately after leaving school, would you prefer to start a small business or join a corporation? Explain.

Some people believe that superstores, large chains, and shopping malls make it difficult for small businesses to compete successfully. What is your view? Where do you prefer to take your business?

Suggestion for Writing

Think of an endeavour outside of the business realm where it is important to "believe in yourself," and write an essay explaining how to be successful in this activity.

Beth Wald

Let's Get Vertical!

Beth Wald (born 1960) first felt the attraction of the mountains when, at age sixteen, she took a backpacking trip to Canada. A native of Minnesota, she studied botany and Russian at the University of Minnesota and then, in the mid-1980s, began a dual career as a freelance writer and photographer. Her career and her love of climbing have taken her around the world. Her articles have appeared in a variety of climbing and outdoor magazines, as have her photographs, which include environmental and cultural subjects as well as sports and travel. From 1988 to 1992, she was a contributing editor for Climbing Magazine. *In our selection, Wald acquaints potential recruits with the sport of rock climbing.*

1   Here I am, 400 feet up on the steep west face of Devil's Tower,[1] a tiny figure in a sea of petrified rock. I can't find enough footholds and handholds to keep climbing. My climbing partner anxiously looks up at me from his narrow ledge. I can see the silver sparkle of the climbing devices I've jammed into the crack every eight feet or so.

2   I study the last device I've placed, a half-inch aluminum wedge 12 feet below me. If I slip, it'll catch me, but only after a 24-foot fall, a real "screamer." It's too difficult to go back; I have to find a way up before my fingers get too tired. I must act quickly.

3   Finding a tiny opening in the crack, I jam two fingertips in, crimp them, pull hard, and kick my right foot onto a sloping knob, hoping it won't skid off. At the same time, I slap my right hand up to what looks like a good hold. To my horror, it's round and slippery.

---

[1] A large, flat-topped formation, 876 feet high, in northeastern Wyoming.

4   My fingers start to slide. Panic rivets me for a second, but then a su·
adrenalin snaps me back into action. I scramble my feet higher, lunge w.
left hand, and catch a wider crack. I manage to get a better grip just as my ⅰ
hand pops off its slick hold. My feet find edges, and I regain my balance. Whippir.
a chock (wedge) off my harness, I slip it into the crack and clip my rope through
a carabiner (oblong metal snaplink). After catching my breath, I start moving
again, and the rest of the climb flows upward like a vertical dance.

5   ***The Challenges and Rewards***   I've tried many sports, but I haven't found any to
match the excitement of rock climbing. It's a unique world, with its own language,
communities, controversies, heroes, villains, and devoted followers. I've lived in
vans, tepees, tents, and caves; worked three jobs to save money for expenses;
driven 24 hours to spend a weekend at a good rock; and lived on beans and rice
for months at a time—all of this to be able to climb. What is it about scrambling
up rocks that inspires such a passion? The answer is, no other sport offers so many
challenges and so many rewards.

6   The physical challenges are obvious. You need flexibility, balance, and strength.
But climbing is also a psychological game of defeating your fear, and it demands
creative thinking. It's a bit like improvising a gymnastic routine 200 feet in the
air while playing a game of chess.

7   Climbers visit some of the most spectacular places on earth and see them
from a unique perspective—the top! Because the sport is so intense, friendships
between climbers tend to be strong and enduring.

8   ***Anyone Can Climb***   Kids playing in trees or on monkey bars know that climbing is
a natural activity, but older people often have to relearn to trust their instincts. This
isn't too hard, though. The ability to maintain self-control in difficult situations is
the most important trait for a beginning climber to have. Panic is almost automatic when you run out of handholds 100 feet off the ground. The typical reaction
is to freeze solid until you fall off. But with a little discipline, rational thinking,
and/or distraction tactics such as babbling to yourself, humming, or even screaming, fear can change to elation as you climb out of a tough spot.

9   Contrary to popular belief, you don't have to be superhumanly strong to
climb. Self-confidence, agility, a good sense of balance, and determination will
get you farther up the rock than bulging biceps. Once you've learned the basics,
climbing itself will gradually make you stronger, though many dedicated climbers
speed up the process by training at home or in the gym.

10   Nonclimbers often ask, "How do the ropes get up there?" It's quite simple; the
climbers bring them up as they climb. Most rock climbers today are "free climbers."
In free climbing, the rope is used only for safety in case of a fall, *not* to help pull
you up. (Climbing without a rope, called "free soloing," is a *very* dangerous activity
practiced only by extremely experienced—and crazy—climbers.)

11   First, two climbers tie into opposite ends of a 150-foot-long nylon rope. Then
one of them, the belayer, anchors himself or herself to a rock or tree. The other,
the leader, starts to climb, occasionally stopping to jam a variety of aluminum
wedges or other special gadgets, generically referred to as protection, into cracks
in the rock. To each of these, he or she attaches a snaplink, called a carabiner,
and clips the rope through. As the leader climbs, the belayer feeds out the rope,
and it runs through the carabiners. If the leader falls, the belayer holds the rope,
and the highest piece of protection catches the leader. The belayer uses special techniques and equipment to make it easy to stop falls.

12   When the leader reaches the end of a section of rock—called the pitch—and sets an anchor, he or she becomes the belayer. This person pulls up the slack of the rope as the other partner climbs and removes the protection. Once together again, they can either continue in the same manner or switch leaders. These worldwide techniques work on rock formations, cliffs, peaks, even buildings.

13   ***Rocks, Rocks Everywhere***   Some of the best climbing cliffs in the country are in the Shawangunk Mountains, only two hours from New York City. Seneca Rocks in West Virginia draws climbers from Washington, D.C., and Pittsburgh, Pennsylvania. Chattanooga, Tennessee, has a fine cliff within the city limits. Most states in the U.S. and provinces in Canada offer at least one or two good climbing opportunities.

14   Even if there are no large cliffs or rock formations nearby, you can climb smaller rocks to practice techniques and get stronger. This is called bouldering. Many climbers who live in cities and towns have created climbing areas out of old stone walls and buildings. Ask someone at your local outdoor shop where you can go to start climbing.

15   ***Get a Helping Hand***   There's no substitute for an expert teacher when it comes to learning basic techniques and safety procedures. One of the best (and least expensive) ways to learn climbing is to convince a veteran climber in your area to teach you. You can usually meet these types at the local crag or climbing shop.

16   As another option, many universities and colleges, some high schools, and some YMCAs have climbing clubs. Their main purpose is to introduce people to climbing and to teach the basics. Other clubs, such as the Appalachian Mountain Club in the eastern U.S. and the Mountaineers on the West Coast, also provide instruction. Ask at your outdoor shop for the names of clubs in your area.

17   If you live in a place completely lacking rocks and climbers, you can attend one of the fine climbing schools at the major climbing area closest to you. Magazines like *Climbing, Rock & Ice,* and *Outside* publish lists of these schools. Once you learn the basics, you're ready to get vertical.

18   In rock climbing, you can both lose yourself and find yourself. Life and all its troubles are reduced to figuring out the puzzle of the next section of cliff or forgotten in the challenge and delight of moving through vertical space. And learning how to control anxiety, how to piece together a difficult sequence of moves, and how to communicate with a partner are all skills that prove incredibly useful back on the ground!

DISCUSSION QUESTIONS

1. Discuss the effectiveness of Wald's title.

2. At the beginning of the essay, Wald notes that she is 400 feet up one side of Devil's Tower and positioned above her climbing partner. What do you think these statements accomplish?

3. In which paragraphs does Wald detail the actual process of climbing? What do the remaining paragraphs in the body of the essay accomplish?

4. Point out two places in the first four paragraphs where Wald cites reasons for her actions.

5. What attributes does Wald believe a rock climber must have? Refer to the essay when answering.

6. After reading this essay, are you ready to begin rock climbing? Does your answer stem from Wald's content, the manner of presentation, or both? Discuss.

What challenging activities appeal to you?

What level of risk are you willing to accept in an activity?

How do you account for your attitude about taking risks?

SUGGESTION FOR WRITING   *Write a process paper in which you explain the attributes required and the steps involved in one of your recreational activities.*

Ian Dunbar

Fast Track to Perfection

Ian Dunbar is a veterinarian and behaviourist who has an international reputation for his "lure and reward" method of training animals. Born in England, he holds degrees from the Royal Veterinarian College of London University and in psychology from the University of California. He now heads the Center for Applied Animal Behavior at his California alma mater. Dunbar has written extensively about his specialty, most recently (1999) coauthoring a series of volumes on different breeds of dogs. In this selection, he shows readers how to apply his methods to training puppies.

1   Puppies mature at an astounding rate. Don't let yours fall behind on the developmental curve. Nearly everything a puppy needs to learn must be taught in 12 weeks—between the ages of 2 and 5 months. You can buy yourself time by knowing what and how to teach the puppy before you bring it home. Go to puppy classes, read behavior and training books, watch instructional videos and consult your veterinarian. Then raise your puppy perfectly by meeting these six training deadlines.

Deadline 1: Before You Bring Home a Puppy

2   Your puppy should be accustomed to a domestic environment before you bring it home—at around 8 weeks of age. Make sure it has been raised indoors and in close contact with people. It should be prepared for the clamor of everyday life—the noise of the vacuum cleaner, the hoopla surrounding sports programs on the television, children crying, adults arguing. Early exposure—before the pup's eyes and ears have fully opened—allows the puppy to gradually assimilate sights and sounds that otherwise might frighten.

3   The window for socializing begins to close by the time the pup turns 3 months of age, and its most impressionable learning period starts to fade by its fifth month.

Deadline 2: Puppy's First Day at Home

4   Misbehavior is the most common reason dogs end up in shelters. This is especially sad because owners can prevent most behavior problems. For instance, if you avoid leaving the pup unsupervised, it won't chew furniture and belongings or soil your house; while teeny accidents do little damage in themselves, they may set a precedent for habits in months to come.

5   When you cannot watch your pup, confine it to a crate or a puppy-proofed room, which should contain:

- a comfortable bed
- a bowl of fresh water
- a doggie toilet placed away from the bed and which simulates the indoors. Lay down a sheet of linoleum and cover it with a disposable plastic sheet. Next lay newspaper or something absorbent. Top the three layers with dirt or sod to teach the pup to relieve itself on grass (or concrete slabs for city pups that relieve themselves curbside)
- hollow chew toys with kibble inside to reward your puppy for chewing toys rather than furniture. During its first few weeks at home, a marvelous training ploy is to serve your puppy's food only in chew toys. After it's a chew toy-aholic—and has not had a chewing mishap for at least three months—begin to serve its dinner in a bowl.

6   At least every hour, release your puppy from its crate, quickly leash it and hurry it to its outdoor toilet area. Stand still and give the pup three minutes to produce. When it does, lavishly praise and offer *three* extra special treats. Freeze-dried liver treats work well because dogs love their strong smell.

7   If your puppy eliminates, it may be allowed supervised exploration of the house. If it does not eliminate, lead it back to its crate or puppy-proof room and try again in half an hour.

8   Keep up the once an hour schedule until your pup is at least 3 months old to make certain it never eliminates indoors. After 3 months of age pups start to develop the bladder control necessary for longer waits between potty breaks, but you must still be vigilant. One mistake can set a bad precedent.

9   Always reward your puppy for using its outdoor toilet area, but wait until it has completed its shots before taking it to public property; otherwise it can pick up other dogs' diseases. A pup must not walk or sniff where other dogs have been until it has developed sufficient immunity (between 3 and 4 months old).

Deadline 3: Puppy at 3 Months

10   By 3 months your pup must master socialization and basic manners. Pups that do not will have a hard time picking up these skills later in life. Unfortunately, the risk of disease means dog-to-dog socialization must wait. Meanwhile, teach your pup to be people-friendly.

11   As a general rule, your pup should socialize with at least 100 people before it is 3 months old. This is easier than it sounds. Invite eight friends over each Sunday to watch sports on the television. Each Monday invite eight different friends to watch *Ally McBeal* and *Dateline*. Catch up on outstanding social obligations by inviting family, friends and neighbors to weekly puppy parties. On another night, invite some neighborhood children. Socializing a puppy is great because it does wonders for *your* social life.

12   Show your guests how to hand feed the puppy's kibble to encourage and reward it for coming, sitting and lying down. Ask your puppy to come. Praise profusely as it approaches and offer a piece of kibble when it arrives. Back up, then do it again—and again and again. Then say "Puppy, Sit" and slowly move a piece of kibble from in front of the puppy's nose to between its eyes. As the puppy raises its nose to sniff, it will lower its rear and sit. If the puppy jumps up, you're holding the food too high. When your puppy sits, say "Good dog" and offer the kibble. Now say "Puppy, Down" and lower a piece of kibble in front of the puppy's nose

to between its forepaws. As the puppy lowers its head to follow the food, it will usually lie down. If your puppy stands, hide the kibble in your palm until it lies down. Then say "Good dog" and offer the food. Coach your guests until each can get the puppy to come, sit and lie down three times for a piece of kibble.

13   When a puppy approaches promptly and happily, it is a sign the dog is people-friendly. Sitting and lying down on request indicates respect for the person issuing instructions. If your puppy is regularly hand-fed by guests, it will learn to enjoy people's company.

Deadline 4: Puppy at 4¹/₂ Months

14   Seemingly overnight, puppies become adolescents. Enroll in a training class before yours is 14 weeks old—that is, before it starts to test your limits. A professional will teach it to stop nipping and other behavior no-no's, as well as temper its hyper-turbo energy.

15   Most puppies can start classes at 3 months. Classrooms are generally safe places; the puppies are vaccinated, the floors regularly sterilized. I advise delaying walks in public places until your puppy is 4 months old because of the risk of disease.

16   Puppy classes develop canine social savvy through play with other puppies in a controlled setting. Most classes are family-oriented, offering pups opportunities to socialize with all sorts of people—men, women and children. The number of behaviors your pup learns in its first training lesson will amaze you. Shy and fearful pups gain confidence. Bullies tone it down and become gentle. All dogs learn to come, sit and lie down when requested and listen to their owners and ignore distractions.

Deadline 5: Puppy at 5 Months

17   Take your dog everywhere—errands around town, car trips to visit friends, picnics in the park and especially to explore the neighborhood. And bring a little bag of kibble. Give a couple of pieces to each stranger who wants to meet your dog. Ask each person to offer the kibble only after your pup sits to say hello.

18   At this point, you may come to believe the canine weight-pulling record exceeds 10,000 pounds. Your dog also may begin to ignore you. A few tips:

- **Make your dog walk for its dinner.** With kibble in hand, stand still and wait for the dog to sit. Ignore everything else your dog does; it will sit eventually: When it does, say "Good dog," offer the kibble, take another step forward, stand still and wait for your dog to sit again. Repeat this until your dog sits each time you stop. Now take two giant steps before your stop. Then three steps, five, eight, 10, 20 and so on. *Voilà*—your dog walks calmly and attentively by your side and sits each time you stop.
- **Take a few time-outs on each walk.** Sit down, relax and allow the dog to settle down and watch the world go by. If your pup is not the sit-still type, take along a treat-stuffed chew toy as an incentive.
- **Never take your dog's sound temperament for granted.** Outdoors can be scary and offer the occasional surprise. Give your dog a piece of kibble every time a big truck, noisy motorcycle or child on a skateboard whizzes by and your dog doesn't overreact.
- **Don't make a habit of letting your dog off-leash to run and play with other dogs;** your dog may eventually refuse to come when called. Instead, take your dog's dinner to the park and, throughout its play session, call your dog every

minute or so and have it sit for a couple of pieces of kibble. It will soon get the idea and its enthusiastic response will be the talk of the park.

Deadline 6: Now and Forever

19   Continue walking your dog at least once a day and take it to a dog park several times a week. Find different walks and dog parks to meet a variety of dogs and people. If your dog always sees the same people and dogs, it may regress socially and become intolerant of strangers.

20   Now enjoy life with your good-natured, well-mannered companion. Give your dog a special bone—Good dog!—and yourself a pat on the back—Good owner!

DISCUSSION QUESTIONS

1. Point out why Dunbar's title is appropriate. Refer to the essay when answering.

2. In paragraph 18 Dunbar states that the owner might "believe the canine weight-pulling record exceeds 10,000 pounds." Explain what he means.

TOWARD KEY INSIGHTS

Given the choice, what animal would you prefer to train? Why?

What animal would you least like to train? Why?

SUGGESTION FOR WRITING

Write an essay that provides instructions for training a riding horse, hunting dog, or guard dog. Be sure to include the reason for any action for which the purpose is not obvious, and provide cautionary warnings whenever necessary.

Illustration

Andrew Struthers

How Spell-Check Is Destroying English: With No Governing Body, Our Language Now Lies Prone to Market Forces

Andrew Struthers is a frequent contributor to The Mix, *the arts and entertainment section in the weekend edition of* The Vancouver Sun, *where his article first appeared. His essay uses a wide variety of detailed examples in order to demonstrate how spell-checking tools have influenced our language usage.*

1   The word "bizarre" is a remnant of the stone age, a verbal coelacanth swimming in the depths of modern English. It comes from Basque, Europe's only aboriginal tongue. The rest were long ago supplanted by Indo-Germanic.

     Example shows how words contain history

2   "Bizarre" began as "bisare," the Basque word for beard. It was appropriated by the Spanish as "bizarre" (dashing), wended into French as "bizarre" (angry or unstable), and by the time it reached England it meant "just plain weird." So this ancient word's journey tells us how the Spanish saw the Basques, how the French saw the Spanish, and how the English saw the French. <u>As Emerson said, "Language is the archives of history.</u>"

     Topic sentence at end of paragraph

3   In a bizarre twist, these archives have fallen into the hands of Bill Gates.

     One sentence transition to subject of essay

4   I'm talking about <u>Spell-check, the helpful tool that underlines words it doesn't recognize in red, tacitly pressuring you to change them.</u> A red line is a subtle pressure. But even the strongest swimmer can only buck the tide 'til his arms get tired. Consider the fate of " founder." Time was, when a ship went down we said it "foundered"—from the Latin "fundus" meaning bottom. Today we say it "flounders," because we've confused "founder" with "flounder," the bottom-dwelling fish—probably because it thrashes around then lies down in the mud. The original word and its history are lost, swept into oblivion by the tide of common usage, its only crime having a homonym that was also a synonym.

     Ironic statement of thesis

     Example shows how words can be lost

5   <u>Thanks to Spell-check, Canadian spelling now bucks a similar tide.</u> Because of market forces even my Canadian-made (Corel) Spell-check was factory-set on U.S.

     Topic sentence

English, so it encouraged me to love my "neighbor." I changed the setting to Canadian English, but every time I booted up the Yankees were back. I set out to track the problem to its source, but it was easier said than done. I'm no Bill Gates. Last time I tried anything south of the toolbar I accidentally deleted a program file. Next thing I know I'm trying to wangle a Windows 98 product key out of a support technician down in Florida called "Dixie 343629." For problems with Spell-check I was advised to read "Knowledge Base Article Q178238."

6   Pass.

7   I could turn Spell-check off, but the ugly truth is, I can't live without it. At 3 a.m., fumbling towards deadline, I no longer care whether "theatre" is Canadian or incorrect, I just change the darn word till I get the red out.

Example shows pressure on Canadian spelling

8   Thousands of kids today are doing the same thing without even realizing it. Eventually Bill Gates' spelling will prevail. It's a triumph of the individual over the collective.

Topic sentence

9   The situation has a precedent. Spelling was standardized around 1500 by a single individual—William Caxton, the first English printer. He learned his trade in Germany, where "g" and "h" often appear together, which meant he had lots of "gh" blocks lying around his print shop. To cut costs (market forces again) he arbitrarily inserted the "h" in "ghost," which it haunts to this day. And because he worked in London, Southeast dialect was used to determine spelling, supplanting the more widespread East Midlands dialect. So you might say Bill Gates is the William Caxton of our time.

Example shows historical influence of market forces on spelling

10   Such power should be wielded wisely. Our forbears ascribed a power to spelling that was downright mystical. It's no coincidence we speak of magic "spells." Even the word glamour (originally "to enchant")—is an 18th-century pun on "grammar," a tacit reference to occult practices associated with the rules of language.

Topic sentence illustrated with examples

11   Here's a "glamorous" experiment. Write out the alphabet, then underneath write it in reverse:

ABCDEFGHIJKLMNO . . .
ZYXWVUTSRQPONML . . .

12   The letters of certain short words—like the biblical interjection "lo"—land in the same positions in both alphabets, but in the second alphabet the sequence is reversed. The "l" and "o" in the first set of letters line up perfectly over the "o" and "l" of the second set. A handful of two-letter "mirror words" exist, but there are very few with more letters. The odds against a six-letter word working both ways are nearly infinite, so only one has been found: Wizard.

13   This might be sheer coincidence, but remember that the people who decided on the spelling of "wizard" also finalized the order of the alphabet. Perhaps this game offers a glimpse of the deep connection between spelling and history. At the very least, wholesale overhauls of such a delicate and ancient ecosystem should be handled with care.

Repetition of phrase adds coherence

14   L'Academie Francais at the Sorbonne in Paris handles French with care. No changes can be made in their lexicon until they've had a few hundred meetings. In Iceland words are government-regulated. In Japan, state control of language is extreme. When the Imperial Army lost WWII the brass blamed it on spelling. There are more than 20,000 characters in Japanese. Only linguists know them all. When generals wrote orders they used around 5,000 characters. But the leadbiters in the trenches could read only 2,000. Chaos ensued. When the radioactive dust settled the government reduced the number of characters allowed for mass communication to 1,945 (a little reminder of their shame).

Examples of state control of language

Illustration 427

15 That degree of government control is unthinkable in English. We immediately flash on Orwell's *1984* and its abbreviated lexicon, Newspeak. Every new edition of the *Newspeak Dictionary* contained fewer words than the one before. The government's evil plan was to control what its citizenry thought by subtracting nouns that described the proscribed.

16 So English has no governing body, and with Spell-check programs vying for eyeballs, our language now lies prone to market forces.

> Loops back to thesis

17 Rule #1 of the free market: never offend the marks. To accommodate the strait-laced, <u>Spell-check redlines profanity as a matter of course</u>. Too bad. "Fuck" can teach us things. Fuck, from the Scandinavian "fock," was not written down until the early 16th century, but a 1278 reference to one "John le Fucker" tells us people were saying it at least 300 years prior—proof of the resilience of slang.

> Topic sentence
>
> Examples of pressures exerted by Spell-check

18 <u>Corel even finds some words guilty by association</u>: "bugger"(how else do I refer to a person who is bugging me?), "cock" (perchance I'm speaking of that herald of the dawn), and the lowly "ass," which is legitimate even in pejorative mode, deriving from the Old English term "oers"—to play the fool.

> Topic sentence

19 <u>The market forces that drive Spell-check programs toward smaller, faster, more *ruthless* efficiency also threaten obscure words that describe very specific things</u>. *Lordosis,* that mysterious twisting of the spine. *Deinosis,* the ability to see things at their worst, surely a word Eminero fans might cherish. *Poxphyma,* the purple-pissing malady that caused the madness of King George III.

> Topic sentence

20 There's a belief that with bigger hard drives this problem will just go away. But I call this "mumpsimus"—a "bigoted adherence to an exposed but customary error."

21 Because simply increasing the size of the program will not help. I own a *Random House Encyclopedic Dictionary* the size of a small couch that has no entry for "mandala," "racist" or "coven," and I'm not convinced lack of space is the reason.

22 An inordinate share of the unwanted words in my Spell-check describe the proscribed—which brings us back to *1984*.

23 The interesting verb "frag"—when soldiers kill an unpopular officer—gets no shrift, even though this four-letter word does more to break down "us and them" stereotypes of war than a stack of Catch-22s. The dark side of the moon is missing from my software ("occultation"), as is the "Antichrist," who's been around since the third century AD. The only way to get the red out is to spell it anti-Christ, which has a whole different meaning.

> Examples of words that Spell-check does not recognize

24 "Hocus-pocus" is trapped in a twilight zone—"hocus" is acceptable, "pocus" is not—like siamese twins who won't survive surgery. "Widdershins," a most excellent term for anti-clockwise, left-handed or God-cursed, is banished.

25 If Orwell was right about words, and it's impossible to think certain things without their help, the New Age will be nipped in the bud. Zen "koans" (what is the sound of one hand clapping?) didn't make the cut. Forget about balancing your kundalini or your ki, because they no longer exist. Nor do the Suds. Mandala has become manana.

26 Perhaps we are facing a word die-off like the one that claimed the megafauna of the paleolithic, a farewell to the "wiccans," the "homos," the "half-assed twats" and "schlongs" of this world, who must now slouch off to the vast tundra of words that never were, like "queendom," and the word for "male muse," whatever that might be.

> Examples of "word die-off"

27 Or perhaps this arbitrary pruning of Shakespeare's tongue will quicken the sap.

Topic sentence makes
political point

Examples support topic
sentence

Examples reinforce
connection between words
and market forces

28   Because when all's said and done and run through Spell-check, <u>English has fared better than those state-controlled tongues</u>. Despite centuries of hard work by l'Academie Francais, fewer people speak French every year. The only people who still speak Icelandic are Bjork and her immediate family. And Japanese is now 30 per cent English (their word for velcro is "majiku tapu"—magic tape). In fact, I once tutored a Japanese banker so that he could understand board meetings between Dutch, Thai and Nihon businessmen, all trying to converse in English.

29   So it looks like English is the lingua franca of the future. But before we celebrate we'd best give a smidgen of thought to what our language will look like once market forces have whittled it so that it fits inside the mall. Here are some words not ostracized by Spell-check: Coca-cola, Pepsi, velcro, Big Mac, Taco Bell.

DISCUSSION QUESTIONS

1. Why do you think that the writer uses such an archaic word as "*coelacanth*," which readers are unlikely to recognize in the first sentence? What point is the writer illustrating at the outset by tracing the history of the word "*bizarre*"?

2. How can you tell that this essay is directed to a Canadian audience? Explain what the writer means when he says that "eventually Bill Gates' spelling will prevail" (paragraph 8) or that "our language now lies prone to market forces" (paragraph 16).

3. What examples does the writer use to illustrate his claim (paragraph 10) that spelling has a magical, even mystical power?

4. What is the point of Andrew Struthers's references to Orwell's "Newspeak" in the novel *1984* (paragraphs 15, 22, 25)?

5. What examples does the writer use to demonstrate that we may be "facing a word die-off" (paragraph 26)? In your own words, explain why the writer is concerned that there are many words that Spell-check does not recognize.

6. Find examples of irony or humour in this essay (paragraphs 4, 5, 29). What is the effect of using humour?

TOWARD KEY INSIGHTS

What frustrations have you found with computer editing tools such as Spell-check?

What benefits have you found?

What other examples can you think of to illustrate differences between the spelling, pronunciation, or even word meanings from Canada and another English-speaking country?

What other market forces, especially from the United States, are threatening Canadian distinctiveness?

SUGGESTIONS FOR WRITING

Consider some other aspect of technology (e-mail, computer upgrades, microwaves, cell phones, etc.) that is supposed to make life easier, and write an essay illustrating the drawbacks of this technology.

Illustration

429

*Using a number of examples, write an essay show-
ing how language is enriched or impoverished by
the use of slang and/or profanity. If you are interested in the history of words, you may wish to consult the* Oxford English Dictionary, *or a
dictionary of etymology.*

Bill Bryson

Idiosyncrasies, Anyone?[*]

*A native Iowan, Bill Bryson was born into a Des Moines newspaper family. After complet-
ing his education, he moved to England, where he is now a freelance writer. He has authored four books—three on travel and one on the English language—and his short pieces
have appeared in a wide-ranging group of British and American periodicals. In the following selection, Bryson offers several examples to support his belief that some countries lack
the ability to get certain things right.*

1   Seeking the Perfect Union Between Custom and Country, I recently discovered
a phenomenon that I call the Copenhagen movie house syndrome. I call it that because it was in a Copenhagen movie house that I first thought of it. What I thought
was this: Every country in the world does some things far better than every other
country and some things far worse, and I began to wonder why that should be.
Sometimes a nation's little practices and inventions are so instantly engaging that
we associate them with that country alone—double-decker buses in Britain, wind-
mills in Holland, sidewalk cafés in France. But at the same time, there are some
things most countries do without difficulty that some can scarcely do at all. Consider
the Copenhagen movie house.

2   When you went into a movie theater in Denmark, at least until recently, you
were given a ticket for an assigned seat. On the occasion of my visit, I found that
my ticket directed me to sit beside the only other people in the place, a young
couple locked in the sort of impassioned embrace associated with dockside re-
unions at the end of very long wars. I could no more have sat right beside them
than I could have asked to join in—it actually would have come to much the same
thing—so I took a place a few discreet seats away.

3   People came into the theater, examined their tickets, and filled the adjacent
seats. By the time the movie started, there were about thirty of us sitting together
in a tight pack in the middle of a vast and otherwise empty auditorium. A woman
laden with shopping bags came in and made her way with difficulty down my row,
stopped beside me, and announced in a stern Danish voice, full of glottals and indignation, that I had taken her seat. This caused much play of flashlights by a
corps of usherettes and fretful re-examining of tickets by everyone in the vicinity
until it became generally realized that I was an American tourist with an evident
inability to follow simple seating instructions and was escorted in some shame
back to my assigned place.

[*] Editors' title.

4   So we sat all together, thirty or so of us, in crowded discomfort, like refugees in an overloaded lifeboat, rubbing shoulders and sharing small noises, and watched the movie. And I would submit, with all respect to Denmark and her long and noble history as a sovereign state, that that is a pretty nerdy way to run a movie house.

5   The phenomenon, I hasten to add, is not exclusive to the Danes, even with regard to the movies. The Germans can be equally insensate when it comes to the silver screen. Once, caught in a downpour in Munich, I spied a movie theater across the street showing a Charlie Chaplin silent picture. No language problems there, I thought brightly, and dashed in. Barely had I seated myself and wiped the steamy mist from my glasses than the film concluded, and everyone departed.

6   An usherette came and told me that I must go too. I explained that I had only just arrived and would hang on for the next showing. The usherette indicated severely that this was against the rules. I explained again that I had only just arrived and showed her that the rain was even now dripping from my brow and chin. But this cut *kein* ice with the lady, who conducted me to the back door with the efficiency of a bouncer and left me standing blinking in an alleyway.

7   The Germans are, of course, famous for such officiousness. I've never been entirely sure whether we notice this streak of Teutonic inflexibility in them because we have been conditioned to look for it or because it genuinely exists. But I do know a couple renting a cottage in the Black Forest who were ordered by their landlady to take down their washing from the clothesline and rehang it in a more orderly and regimented manner before they were allowed to go out for the day.

8   The great British failing, on the other hand, is a strange uncomfortableness with regard to food, particularly mass catering, a fact that can become evident to the traveler almost from the moment he sets foot in the country. In his book *Flying Visits,* the Australian critic Clive James describes the food at Heathrow Airport as not fit for a dog to eat. That is perhaps a little unfair—you could certainly feed it to a dog—but it is true that the most charitable thing that can be said of the food there, and at many other public gathering places like train stations and motorway service areas, is that it won't kill you.

9   More than that, there is among the British a curious inability to grasp the basic idea of many foods—as evidenced by the persistent British habit of eating hamburgers with a knife and fork. In fact, there isn't much to do with dining in Britain that isn't mildly odd to foreign eyes, from the types of food eaten (baked beans on toast) to the manner of their eating (holding the fork upside down and balancing the food precariously on its back). As I write, a commercial is running on British television that shows a man enthusiastically spreading his favorite brand of peanut butter across an ear of sweet corn. I would suggest that this alone is evidence of a kind of national dementia where eating is concerned.

10   On the credit side, however, the British are consummate queuers—so much so that during riots in Liverpool in 1981 looters formed a line outside the store. I swear it. This is in stark contrast to the French, who have never quite come to terms with the concept of queuing. Wherever you go in Paris, you see orderly lines waiting patiently at bus stops. But as soon as the bus arrives, the line instantly disintegrates into something reminiscent of a fire drill at an insane asylum as everyone scrambles to be the first aboard.

11   The most bewildering French custom, however, is the practice of putting timers on light switches in hotel corridors and staircases. These are designed, with uncanny precision, to plunge you into darkness the moment you get near your room, so that you must complete the last stages of the process—feeling your way along the walls, finding the door and doorknob, fumbling with the key—without benefit of vision.

Illustration   431

12   To the casual observer there may seem little point in providing illumination if it's going to poop out at the critical moment, or in forming an orderly line at bus stops if it's just going to lead to anarchy once the bus heaves into view. But that is a crucial feature of the syndrome: The behavior must seem largely inexplicable to any rational outsider, yet be accepted without question by the natives. In its most extreme form, it can even take on a kind of bizarre logic.

13   Consider the matter of dining out in Norway. I once made the mistake in that country of not thinking about dinner until about dinnertime. This, I discovered, was several hours too late. Finding myself in Bergen on a Sunday, I ventured out onto the streets at about 5:30 with that agreeable pang of anticipation that comes with having a large appetite in a strange city. I wandered through the empty lanes of the old town and far out into the suburbs, but at every restaurant I came across the windows showed only darkened premises with chairs stacked on the tables.

14   At one place, I turned forlornly from the window to find an elderly woman watching me. "There's no one there," I croaked in bewilderment. "Yes," she replied in perfect English, "I expect the staff have all gone home to eat. It *is* dinnertime, you know." But of course.

15   In Spain, the problem comes at the other extreme of the clock. The Spanish wait until all the visitors to the country have put on their pajamas and gone to bed before they eat. For a long time I supposed that this was so they could talk about us, but I am assured by a Spanish friend that it is an ancient practice and there's nothing personal in it. Nonetheless, it is a strange sensation to wander to the hotel desk in the small hours, half expecting to see the night clerk in his bathrobe and everyone else sensibly tucked up in bed, only to find the hotel restaurant packed with laughing people, with children running around and aged grannies plowing into large platters of paella.

16   Outbreaks of the Copenhagen movie house syndrome can be found in all countries. One of the most prolific, if improbable, sources is the automobile light. In most parts of the world, people work from the assumption that when it is dark you put your car lights on and when it is light you switch them off. This seems pretty basic to most of us. Yet in Sweden there is a law that all drivers must put their lights on all the time, even in brilliant sunshine.

17   You would think the Swedes would be embarrassed to have saddled themselves with such an ineffably silly law ("It was a bad week; we don't know what came over us"), but evidently not. It is equivalent to making pedestrians wear miners' helmets, yet the Swedes appear to see nothing strange in it.

18   The British, conversely, use their car lights as sparingly as possible, as if fearful of running up a large quarterly bill for their use. At dusk throughout Britain, you see the strange phenomenon of gray, unilluminated shapes sweeping at you out of the gloom, their drivers peering intently through the windshields, unable to see much of anything. Why, you wonder, don't they put their lights on? It is a mystery that no one can answer. The British, of course, are particularly skilled at doing silly things (viz., requiring their judges to wear little mops on their heads).

19   And as for us Americans, what are our national shortcomings? Since one of the requirements of the Copenhagen movie house syndrome is that we be blind to our own faults, I am not entirely sure. An informal survey among foreign friends elicited a host of suggested shortcomings, ranging from Tammy Bakker's eyelashes[1] to a misguided affection for plaid pants. But in my view perhaps the most fundamental of all our faults is simply the complete inability to follow simple seating instructions in foreign movie houses.

---

[1] The wife of former televison evangelist Jim Bakker, who was convicted of misappropriating viewer contributions.

DISCUSSION QUESTIONS

1. Point out the thesis statement of this essay.

2. Why do you think Bryson chose numerous examples rather than a single extended one to illustrate his point?

3. Comment on the order in which Bryson arranges his examples.

4. State your understanding of the term "Teutonic inflexibility" in paragraph 7. Show how this trait is revealed in the illustrations in paragraphs 6 and 7.

5. How do you account for Bryson's use of slang expressions such as "nerdy" (paragraph 4) and "poop out" (paragraph 12)?

6. Think about the essay as a whole and then discuss the significance of its closing sentence.

TOWARD KEY INSIGHTS

Do you believe that Canada, like other countries, lacks the ability to get certain things right? Why or why not?

What foibles, if any, do you see in Canadian society?

How would you suggest that we correct them?

Despite his disclaimers, do you think Bryson could be accused of stereotyping? Why or why not?

SUGGESTION FOR WRITING

Write an essay that illustrates customs or habits of your peers that you regard as strange. Focus your paper on three or four examples.

Candace Fertile

The Oldest Profession: Shopping

Candace Fertile has a Ph.D. in English Literature from the University of Alberta. She wrote her dissertation on the novels of Lawrence Durrell. She now teaches English at the University of Victoria and Camosun College and reviews books for several Canadian newspapers, mainly to support her addiction to reading. And yes, she loves to shop.

1   My shopping career began in earnest when I was seven. My currency was time and deceit. My boutiques were the garbage cans in the alley behind our apartment house in Edmonton.

2   I could not believe that people threw out such wonderful stuff. What a deal— something for nothing. Perhaps like the first-time gambler who wins and is forever hooked on that adrenaline rush, my love of shopping began with that first magical exposure, on a day when I was wandering home from school, taking my usual route through back alleys. To my extreme delight, I saw peeking out of a

Illustration   433

galvanized-steel garbage pail what looked like a blue three-ring binder. Acquisition grabbed my seven-year-old soul, and to this day it hasn't let go, fuelled no doubt by relentless advertising and the creation of more and more stuff that announces to the world who we are. Or perhaps who we want to be.

3   In that alley, my paper-loving self honed in on that blue binder like a cat streaking up from the basement at the sound of a can opener, and I started to understand the power of objects. As a second-grader, I was (unjustly, I thought) required to use despised scribblers. The covers were barely more substantial than the rather nasty paper within them. The booklets had three staples in the middle holding the whole ugly mess together. I hated these scribblers, and I hated their name. And I particularly hated the fact that the teacher would stalk around the room, checking to see if we were properly holding our pencils (another affront—I longed to use a pen). Periodically she would sneak up and grab our yellow HBs to make sure that we were not gripping them too tightly. Her actions made me clutch my pencil as if it were keeping my heart pumping. And the choke-hold I had on my pencil meant that I frequently made holes in the flimsy paper of the scribbler. With grim regularity the teacher and I would get into a tug-of-war over my pencil.

4   It was after such a dismal war (I always had to lose) that the bright blue plastic corner of the binder caught my eye. I debated for sometime about whether or not I was allowed to look in the can, or if taking something from a garbage can was stealing. I should mention: not only was I polite, but I was also Catholic. I knew God was watching my every move, and should I be so vile as to commit a mortal sin, lightning bolts would descend and incinerate my evil little soul, so that all that would be transported to Hell would be something the size of a barbecue briquette. The possibility of owning a binder seemed worth the risk.

5   I inched closer, then looked up and down the alley to make sure no one was watching me. I carefully removed the lid, which was already precariously perched to one side, and laid it on the ground. A perfect, blue, three-ring binder glowed at me. I was in Heaven. I picked it up and with disbelief discovered an unopened packet of three-hole paper inside. The narrow blue (not even the more babyish wide) lines on the stark white paper with the margins marked with a thin pink line were everything my crummy scribbler wasn't. This paper and binder were for grownups, not little kids.

6   I could hardly wait to write in my new binder. With a pen. I felt instantly grown-up, more important, more substantial, the tug-of-war over my pencil forgotten. I had gained a new status. And this emotional boost into the stratosphere was accomplished by the simplest of means: I had acquired a new object. And it was free. No drug would ever reproduce the rush I felt as my concept of myself and the world tilted.

7   On subsequent shopping expeditions down the back alleys I never found anything as great as the binder and paper, but sometimes I found stuff for my little brother. At two, he would play with just about anything. I enjoyed his delight, and finding free stuff meant saving my allowance. I now suspect my kid-sized version of dumpster-diving sparked my career as a bargain shopper.

8   Once I found a scarf—a sophisticated, almost sheer, leopard-spotted scarf. It spoke of glamour, beauty, and fashion, with just an edge of wildness. It was a scarf worn by elegant and capable women on television. It was perfect for my mother, who set off for work each morning with her matching high heels and handbag.

9   Maybe the scarf wasn't even supposed to have been thrown out, but there it was, dangling from a garbage can a few blocks away from home. (In the space of a few weeks, I had increased my territory substantially.) My mother would love this scarf, I thought, but I had no idea how I would explain the acquisition of such a treasure. I didn't have that kind of money. I had finally revealed the binder to her, as it was too difficult trying to write in it without being found out. Even that was hard, as I'd had to commit what I hoped was a venial sin by lying that a friend's older sister had given me the stuff. I knew that wouldn't work again with a scarf. And I still felt a bit singed around the edges from the lie. For a week I had imagined everyone thought I smelled like a campfire. And while I knew what the wrath of God entailed, I was absolutely sure that the wrath of my mother was worse.

10   I decided to come clean. I took the scarf home, and when my mother got home from work, I presented it to her. She was astonished, and then asked where I got it. I told her. To my bafflement, she burst into gales of laughter, nearly hiccupping herself into a coma while trying to catch her breath.

11   When she regained control, she announced that my garbage-looting days were over. Nice girls didn't do such things. And there could be dangerous things in the garbage. Like what, I wanted to know, but she wouldn't tell me. These events happened decades ago—I'm sure my mother was worried I'd cut myself on a tin can or broken bottle, not get jabbed by some hypodermic needle. Garbage was safer then, but not safe enough for my mother's daughter to play in it.

12   But what sticks indelibly in my mind is that my mother carefully washed and ironed the scarf and wore it faithfully, even proudly, a splash of jungle against her ever-so-fashionable green wool coat with the fur around the sleeves. She would fling one end over her shoulder as she headed out the door in the morning, as if to announce her formidable presence in the universe.

13   Scavenging no longer an option, I had to find another way to satisfy the desire for acquisition now flowing through my veins. Little did I know that I was turning into a good little twentieth-century consumer. According to Lauren Langman, an academic who studies human development:

> In the contemporary world, the signifying and celebrating edifice of consumer culture has become the shopping mall which exists in [a] pseudo-democratic twilight zone between reality and a commercially produced fantasy world of commodified goods, images, and leisure activities that gratify transformed desire and provide packaged self-images to a distinctive form of subjectivity. (40)

14   Langman's thesis certainly helps to explain not only the label-consciousness of shoppers but also the desire of many shoppers to become apparent walking billboards for name-brand products. How much difference, if any, is there between my girlish desire for white go-go boots and the current stampede to wear T-shirts emblazoned with "Roots" or "Nike"?

15   I prefer to think the difference is significant. I could be wrong, in which case, Langman's argument is unassailable. But another academic offers me some hope. In an article in *Vogue* titled "The Professor Wore Prada," Elaine Showalter, professor of English at Princeton and recently president of the Modern Language Association, comments on her love of fashion and shopping. She does so in a humorous way, defending her intellectualism, femininity, and feminism. As she says, "For years I have been trying to make the life of the mind coexist with the day at

Illustration   435

the mall, and to sneak the *femme* back into feminist" (80). Showalter delineates the various ways female academics (herself included) have dressed in an effort to be taken seriously, and ends her essay by saying, "if you want to deconstruct my feminist criticism, go right ahead. But you'd better not sneer at my angel backpack or step on my blue suede shoes. I've paid my dues dressing 'feminist,' and now I'm going to wear what I like" (92). Showalter's essay is full of the pleasure one can gain from shopping, both the activity of looking and actual purchase. Throughout history and likely before, human beings have been drawn to objects of beauty (although certainly the concepts of beauty change).

16   The acquisition of objects, beautiful or otherwise, is usually an economic transaction. As a child prevented from plundering garbage bins, I needed a new way to get the stuff I wanted. So from time and deceit as currency, I turned to the more usual one: money. Getting that required work. My first job was ironing for my mother. I had seen a T-shirt in Sears, and my mother refused to buy it for me because, as she said, "You don't need it." It's no wonder that nowadays when I buy yet another object I don't need I think of King Lear's "Oh, reason not the need."[1] The other object that captured my fancy was a particular lava lamp. I loved that lava lamp, but it was out of the realm of financial possibility. And my mother was right about the T-shirt. I didn't need it. I wore a uniform to school, and I had sufficient play clothes. Incessant pestering of my mother resulted in the ironing agreement. I ironed like a demon, encouraging my beleaguered mother to change clothes frequently so I could have something to iron. Eventually I saved enough to buy the T-shirt, and I wore it to shreds. It was the first thing I bought for myself with my own money, and I remember it in every detail. Still. It had short white sleeves, a white back, and a front in four coloured squares of red, yellow, blue, and green. If I had had white go-go boots to match, life would have achieved its pinnacle. (Elaine Showalter, by the way, wore white go-go boots to her Ph.D. defence.)

17   Since those very early days, my shopping has expanded in terms of money, objects, and range. Like many middle-class Canadians, I have more material goods than some small nations, and I am constantly acquiring more. What is interesting is that none of us needs all these things, but lemming-like we hurl ourselves at the nearest mall, which has acquired the status of a cathedral for some. Or else we seek out independent and unique shops in downtowns and other shopping areas. We go to outlets and discount centres. We are the consumer society of which much has been written. Thorstein Veblen's *The Theory of the Leisure Class* (1934), Christopher Lasch's *The Culture of Narcissism* (1979), and Hilary Radner's *Shopping Around: Feminine Culture and the Pursuit of Pleasure* (1995) are just three of the many works written to explore humans' need to shop even when we are way beyond buying what is necessary for our survival. Veblen's term "conspicuous consumption" indicates that the purchase of many unnecessary items is a performance. It's interesting to imagine what the performance means. If we examine advertising, which certainly fuels consumer desire, we see that Langman's view of buying an identity is accurate. To wear a certain brand (a "Roots" or "Nike" T-shirt is infinitely more desirable to certain groups than, say, a "K-Mart" T-shirt) or to drive a certain car or to drink a certain beer is presumably a statement of who we are. Or is it?

---

[1] When King Lear's daughters Goneril and Regan challenge the necessity of Lear's keeping an army after he has given away his kingdom, Lear protests, saying that for human life to have value, humans need more than the basics of survival (King Lear 2.4. 264).

18   In his essay "The Individual, Consumption Cultures and the Fate of Community," Rob Shields attends to the performative aspect of purchasing and gives consumers some credit: "Many consumers are now ironic, knowing shoppers, conscious of the inequalities of exchange and the arbitrary nature of exchange value. As social actors, they attempt to consume the symbolic values of objects and the mall environment while avoiding the inequalities of exchange" (100). Shields's essay notes that public spaces have changed and that the mall serves as a gathering place. Thus, the activity of shopping (whether or not a purchase is made) plays a significant social role. Shields argues: "It is necessary to recognize that consumption itself is partly determined by the non-rational, cultural element of society. Shopping is not just a functional activity. Consumption has become a communal activity, even a form of solidarity" (110). It appears to me that shopping plays a number of roles, and one of these is certainly a communal one, as Shields argues. But it can also be said that in addition to having a connective importance, shopping—and more specifically the purchased goods—can fulfill people's desires both to join a group and to differentiate themselves from one another. For example, clothing choices are laden with meaning, even if the message is inaccurate.

19   Shoppers, as Shields notes, are becoming more sophisticated and particular, if the growth in thrift stores is any indication. A CBC newscast in July 1998 noted that the thrift store business is so popular that charities depending on donations have to be much more competitive. We are still conspicuously consuming, but we want a bargain. Certain sections of the population have always needed to shop for sale goods, but the practice is now losing any stigma it might have had. In fact, getting a bargain, or a "steal," marks one as a consummate shopper. Getting a deal has become a selling point for much commercial activity. I'd like to mention sales, for example. Anyone in western Canada familiar with Woodward's $1.49 Day will remember the thrust and parry of grabbing for the goodies on this once-a-month sale extravaganza. The deals were often extraordinary, and people didn't want to miss this opportunity. Encountering sharp elbows was common. In contrast, the former frenzy of Bay Day has abated now that the sale lasts for ages and has lost any special air. No need to dive in a scrum for the merchandise. No, it's all there in stacks, and then we stand in line to pay. Infrequent sales events such as Boxing Day sales create line-ups hours before the stores open. The sale must appear to be an unusual event or it garners little excitement. I once worked at Harrods, and the annual sale was marked by the sound of crashing crockery as maniacal shoppers stormed the aisles.

20   But what are we doing when we shop, and why do I refer to it as the oldest profession? The answer is simple. Well, sort of. In *Shopping Around: Feminine Culture and the Pursuit of Pleasure,* Hilary Radner argues the following: "Feminine culture emphasizes a process of investment and return, of negotiation, in which the given articulation of pleasure is always measured against its costs, the inevitable price of an invitation that is never extended freely, never absolutely, the terms of which change from day to day, from place to place" (178). While the terms and values change, it is surely the case that a shopper considers the relative costs (whether in time, effort, or money) and the benefits of the object gained. And these judgments will differ from person to person even within the same socio-economic group.

21   Shopping is our contemporary form of hunting and gathering. Men may have hunted, and women may have gathered, but both processes resulted in main-

Illustration　　437

taining life. And if the effort expended exceeded what was gained—the result was death. Such an obvious relationship between acquisition (shopping in a sense) and survival is still evident in the world today. But in rich countries like Canada, hunting and gathering is largely done at the mall, and our survival is not in question. In "Dressed to Kill," Don Gillmor makes fun of men at a clothing sale, and he uses the metaphor of the hunt:

> The big game is on the suit rack, though. Some of the men simply drape a dozen business suits over one arm and then try to find a little room in which to sort and sniff them, like lions defending their kill. But to bring down a three-button, blue wool crepe 42R Donna Karan (reg. $2,295, now $395) in open country requires keen eyesight, stealth, and a burst of cheetah-like speed . . . . [Men] are taking home cashmere and silk and cotton that feels like whipped butter. They have hunted well and they are filled with the self-knowledge that comes with risk and death and loss and dramatic savings. (75)

22   Whether the hunting is done in an exclusive boutique or a thrift store, it's the thrill of the chase that drives shoppers. It could be the lure of low prices, or exclusive merchandise, or the media-created buzz about something completely useless like Cabbage Patch Dolls or Beanie Babies that gets everyone out there, roaming, foraging, stalking, pouncing, occasionally even wrestling another shopper for the item.

23   Then we bag our prize and take it back to our cave, er, home. I bet those cavepeople never stopped and said to each other, "Listen, honey, I think we have too many acorns or dried fish or fur blankets." I think they were out there scooping up whatever they thought might come in handy for survival.

24   And so while many of us shop for a variety of reasons, including pleasure, but rarely need (even grocery stores are full of stuff no one needs to survive; in fact, some of that junk probably shortens lives), perhaps somewhere at the heart of the endeavour is a genetic link to our past, when tracking and locating food was essential for survival. Now different needs drive our shopping expeditions. And survival is perceived in ways beyond the merely physical.

REFERENCES

Gillmor, Don. "Dressed to Kill: What Really Happens When Men Go Hunting for Deep Discounts." *Saturday Night* 113, no. 5 (June 1998: 75).

Langman, Lauren. "Neon Cages: Shopping for Subjectivity." In *Lifestyle Shopping: The Subject of Consumption,* ed. Rob Shields, 40–82. London: Routledge, 1992.

Radner, Hilary. *Shopping Around: Feminine Culture and the Pursuit of Pleasure.* New York: Routledge, 1995.

Shields, Rob. "The Individual, Consumption Cultures and the Fate of Community." In *Lifestyle Shopping: The Subject of Consumption,* ed. Rob Shields, 99–113. London: Routledge, 1992.

Showalter, Elaine. "The Professor Wore Prada." *Vogue,* December 1997: 80, 86, 92.

DISCUSSION QUESTIONS

1. How does the writer use irony in the title and the first paragraph? What does the writer mean when she says that her "currency was time and deceit"?

2. Why does the writer spend so much time describing the "blue binder" she discovers (paragraphs 3–6)? How does the writer suggest the significance of this binder through overstatement or exaggeration, and through metaphorical comparisons?

3. What is the relevance of her religious background (paragraphs 4–5, 9) and the distinction between a "mortal sin" (paragraph 4) and a "venial sin" (paragraph 9)?

4. What is the significance of the scarf (paragraphs 8–12) that the writer presents to her mother? What image of the mother is created in this brief narrative? Why does the mother's response to the scarf mean that "scavenging is no longer an option" (paragraph 13)? How does the image of scavenging early on connect to the image of bargain hunting (paragraphs 15–16) toward the end of the essay?

5. How does the writer shift from a personal story to a more academic tone in paragraph 13? What different perspectives on shopping are offered by scholars Lauren Langman (paragraph 13) and Elaine Showalter (paragraph 15)? Which perspective does the author Candace Fertile seem to prefer?

6. The writer refers to a theory that "the purchase of many unnecessary items is a performance" (paragraphs 17). In your own words, explain what this means (paragraphs 17–18).

7. In paragraphs 14, 16, and 19 the writer illustrates general points with concrete examples. Locate places where she uses illustration, and explain the point of these illustrations.

TOWARD KEY INSIGHTS

When she was young, Candace Fertile did ironing jobs for her mother so that she could earn the money to acquire unnecessary but desired possessions: a T-shirt and a lava lamp. When have you been motivated to work in order to buy what might be considered unnecessary but desirable possessions? What different reasons did you have for these purchases? How did you come to view the possessions later?

To what extent do you agree that shopping helps people feel connected to others, as well as "differentiated" from others (paragraph 18)?

In your experience, does "getting a bargain . . . [mark] one as a consummate shopper" (paragraph 19)?

SUGGESTION FOR WRITING

After reading Candace Fertile's essay, reflect on what underlying reasons you might have for going to the mall, or for purchasing unnecessary items. Then, using illustrations of your own, write an essay showing that the reasons for shopping often go beyond obvious survival needs.

Illustration

439

Ellen Goodman

The Company Man

Ellen Goodman (born 1941) is a native of Massachusetts and a 1963 graduate of Radcliffe College. A journalist since graduation, she has worked as a researcher and reporter for Newsweek, *a feature writer for the* Detroit Free Press *and the* Boston Globe, *and a columnist for the* Washington Post Writers Group, *as well as a commentator on CBS Radio's* Spectrum *show and NBC-TV's* Today Show. *She has also contributed articles to* Ms., McCall's, *and the* Village Voice. *Book-length publications include* Turning Points *(1979) and three collections of newspaper columns:* Close to Home *(1979),* At Large *(1981), and* Making Sense *(1989). She has received numerous writing awards, including a 1980 Pulitzer Prize for distinguished commentary. Our selection, taken from* At Large, *depicts a workaholic whose total dedication to his job killed him.*

1   He worked himself to death, finally and precisely, at 3:00 a.m. Sunday morning.

2   The obituary didn't say that, of course. It said that he died of a coronary thrombosis—I think that was it—but everyone among his friends and acquaintances knew it instantly. He was a perfect Type A, a workaholic, a classic, they said to each other and shook their heads—and thought for five or ten minutes about the way they lived.

3   This man who worked himself to death finally and precisely at 3:00 a.m. Sunday morning—on his day off—was fifty-one years old and a vice-president. He was, however, one of six vice-presidents, and one of three who might conceivably—if the president died or retired soon enough—have moved to the top spot. Phil knew that.

4   He worked six days a week, five of them until eight or nine at night, during a time when his own company had begun the four-day week for everyone but the executives. He worked like the Important People. He had no outside "extra-curricular interests," unless, of course, you think about a monthly golf game that way. To Phil, it was work. He always ate egg salad sandwiches at his desk. He was, of course, overweight, by 20 to 25 pounds. He thought it was okay, though, because he didn't smoke.

5   On Saturdays, Phil wore a sports jacket to the office instead of a suit, because it was the weekend.

6   He had a lot of people working for him, maybe sixty, and most of them liked him most of the time. Three of them will be seriously considered for his job. The obituary didn't mention that.

7   But it did list his "survivors" quite accurately. He is survived by his wife, Helen, forty-eight years old, a good woman of no particular marketable skills, who worked in an office before marrying and mothering. She had, according to her daughter, given up trying to compete with his work years ago, when the children were small. A company friend said, "I know how much you will miss him." And she answered, "I already have."

8   "Missing him all these years," she must have given up part of herself which had cared too much for the man. She would be "well taken care of."

9   His "dearly beloved" eldest of the "dearly beloved" children is a hardworking executive in a manufacturing firm down South. In the day and a half before the funeral, he went around the neighborhood researching his father, asking the neighbors what he was like. They were embarrassed.

10   His second child is a girl, who is twenty-four and newly married. She lives near her mother and they are close, but whenever she was alone with her father, in a car driving somewhere, they had nothing to say to each other.

11   The youngest is twenty, a boy, a high-school graduate who has spent the last couple of years, like a lot of his friends, doing enough odd jobs to stay in grass and food. He was the one who tried to grab at his father, and tried to mean enough to him to keep the man at home. He was his father's favourite. Over the last two years, Phil stayed up nights worrying about the boy.

12   The boy once said, "My father and I only board here."

13   At the funeral, the sixty-year-old company president told the forty-eight-year-old widow that the fifty-one-year-old deceased had meant much to the company and would be missed and would be hard to replace. The widow didn't look him in the eye. She was afraid he would read her bitterness and, after all, she would need him to straighten out the finances—the stock options and all that.

14   Phil was overweight and nervous and worked too hard. If he wasn't at the office, he was worried about it. Phil was a Type A, a heart-attack natural. You could have picked him out in a minute from a lineup.

15   So when he finally worked himself to death, at precisely 3:00 a.m. Sunday morning, no one was really surprised.

16   By 5:00 p.m. the afternoon of the funeral, the company president had begun, discreetly of course, with care and taste, to make inquiries about his replacement. One of three men. He asked around: "Who's been working the hardest?"

DISCUSSION QUESTIONS

1. Goodman says that Phil was "a perfect Type A" (paragraph 2). After reflecting on her essay, explain the characteristics of this type.

2. Why do you think Goodman doesn't supply Phil's last name or the name of the company he works for?

3. What idea is Goodman trying to put across?

4. Goodman's essay uses one longer illustration rather than several shorter ones. Why?

5. What is the significance of Phil's oldest son going "around the neighborhood researching his father, asking the neighbors what he was like" (paragraph 9)? Why were they embarrassed?

6. How do you account for Goodman's relatively short paragraphs?

TOWARD KEY INSIGHTS

What social values would cause individuals to work themselves to death?

In that regard, what is the significance of the company president asking "Who's been working the hardest?"

Illustration

441

Are these values basically good, or should we make some changes in our attitudes toward work and success? If so, what kinds of changes?

SUGGESTION FOR WRITING   *Using one extended example, write an essay that illustrates the lifestyle of a laid-back employee or friend. Your paper need not, of course, feature a death.*

Classification

Eve Golden

Dangerous Curves

Eve Golden's work appears monthly in Movieline, Classic Images, *and* Across the Board *magazines. She is the author of the books* Platinum Girl: The Life & Legends of Jean Harlow *(1991) and* Vamp: The Rise and Fall of Theda Bara *(1996), and is currently working on a biography of turn-of-the-century musical comedy star Anna Held. In this essay she takes a lighthearted look at several kinds of women that men should avoid at all costs.*

1   My girlfriends and I spend an inordinate amount of time grousing about the terrible guys we fall for. So far the winner is Marie, who dated a guy who (1) lived in a trailer park because he liked it; (2) slept with a gun under the pillow; and (3) kept holy water in the freezer to *keep it holy longer.*

Introduction: paragraphs 1–3; indicates author's specific purpose for classifying these women; notes expertise author will rely on; previews tone and style of essay

2   But—as the guys in my life are constantly making clear to me—men make the exact same mistakes, and fall for just as many of the wrong women. So in an effort to "C'mon, be fair about this, okay?" I've gone in search of *Five Women You Should Never Fall For. . . .*

3   I spoke with Atlanta psychiatrist Frank Pittman, M.D., author of *Man Enough: Fathers, Sons and the Search for Masculinity.* After I described some of the terrible romances the men I know have wound up in, Dr. Pittman, who spends much time counseling couples with dysfunctional relationships, didn't let me down. "The women you mention are all Incomplete Women," he told me, making me feel nicely superior. "They seem safe to incomplete men," he added, thus explaining my current lack of social life: A complete, dangerous woman, that's me.

4   In fact, all of the women you're going to learn to avoid have some very attractive qualities, qualities that many men instinctively fall for. That's what makes it so critical for you to avoid them. So without further ado, let's meet our contestants in the Dating Game from Hell.

The Damsel in Distress

Body: paragraphs 5–21

5   She's the woman you see on those made-for-TV movies starring Barry Bostwick or Stephen Collins, about a good-natured guy who winds up entangled with some

442

woman from the *Twilight Zone* (usually played by Meredith Baxter). She's help-less and heartbroken and just waiting for a big, strong man like you to come and sweep her off her feet. Does that sound a little anti-feminist, coming from a card-carrying NOW member? Remember, these women do exist. And they should all come equipped with big signs reading "Dangerous Curves Ahead."

First category: paragraphs 5–8

6   "She is a disaster for everybody," Dr. Pittman states flat out. "Damsels in distress are never capable of knowing who is St. George and who is the dragon. If she is being abused by everyone in her life and you try to rescue her, I promise you it will only be a matter of time before you're seen as the next abuser."

7   My friend Rick agrees, having been the Stephen Collins character in one of those relationships. He tells me a sob story about his personal Damsel. "Ultimately, I stayed with her because she needed rescuing. I stuck around for a year and a half and never did rescue her. I learned from her, though: If there's a problem, get out early before it starts to affect your psyche."

8   How can you recognize the Damsel type? Dr. Pittman referees a lot of these re-lationships. "Any woman who falls in love with you too quickly, too desperately, too completely, must be nuts." Gee, there goes the plot of every movie made between 1929 and 1950. If you're married, you'll be able to spot her easily—she's the one making eyes at you from across the room. "These women are the sort of people who fall into affairs with married men," Dr. Pittman says. "Normal women don't do that." What makes a guy dumb enough to fall back? "A victim—a woman with more problems than you've got—will distract you from your problems. Briefly. Men are all too eager to believe that they're heroes, and that someone has finally noticed it." The lesson: Don't think too highly of yourself, and don't think too highly of anyone who thinks too highly of you.

The (S)motherer

Second category: paragraphs 9–11

9   You know how sometimes a man and a woman will have the exact same cold, yet the woman's up making hot tea and the man's in bed moaning, "Call a priest"? Some men just invite mothering, and some women (not me, not on your life) love playing Mama. Maybe 100 years ago, when women didn't have actual lives, that was a good way to vent emotional and physical energy. But nowadays, any woman who puts 100 percent of her hopes, dreams, fears and desires on her man's life rather than her own is not someone you need.

10   Dr. Pittman, of course, agrees. "A motherer doesn't require that you give any-thing back. She's so constantly giving that you end up feeling like a child." Surprisingly, this kind of woman still exists in the 1990s. I have to admit, I couldn't find any Big Mamas or their admirers around my New York digs, so I called my friend Norman, whose Deep-South sister is June Cleaver II. "Oh, she bought a vac-uum cleaner for one boyfriend," says Norman. "She made payments on his truck, she did his laundry. He just ate it up."

11   You can see how this kind of relationship can be wonderful for a guy, at least for a while. But it can't be permanent. Eventually, you'll want to give something back, and she won't want what you have to offer. All she wants, Dr. Pittman says, is to live vicariously through you, and living two people's lives is a little bit more of a burden than most anyone would want to tackle. What ever happened to Norman's sister's boyfriend? "He got some other girl pregnant and married her," Norman says. "The guys who are attracted to my sister tend to be young and immature." Which reinforces my belief: that guys who fall for motherly types are entirely too much in touch with their inner child. Do us all a favour, will you, and get in touch with your inner adult?

The Chameleon

Third category:
paragraphs 12–14

12   You know the type: Suddenly she has a Boston accent, and suddenly she loves touch football, just because she's dating a Kennedy. "She's never an equal partner," Dr. Pittman says of this clinging vine, "because she gets her identity from adapting to the guy."

13   Oh, and I do know one or two chameleons. Very nice gals, but not with the best of self-images. Blanche was understandably defensive when I approached her on the topic, though she happily admitted that she indeed fit the bill. "I dress like my boyfriend. I think it's good," she says philosophically. "We can share clothes." Blanche went on to try and explain herself. "Guys' opinions and ways of doing things just rub off from being around them. It's an ego thing for them." But doesn't it show kind of a lack of ego on Blanche's part? So far, Blanche and her boyfriend seem happy, though she is starting to look more and more like him every day and everyone's pretty much hoping he doesn't start sporting a mustache.

14   Yet this type of one-sided relationship will eventually drag a man under. "The guy finds it flattering for a while, but neither the man nor the woman has the possibility of give-and-take, of being able to adapt to the other," Dr. Pittman says. "They naturally begin to feel something's missing." I talked to one of Blanche's ex-boyfriends, Max. Why did they break up? "We were just bored," he said. "We fell into a rut. Doing the same thing"—his thing, I might add—"night after night." Didn't the fact that Blanche brought nothing to the ball game have something to do with this? Max claimed not to know what I was talking about. "Well, yeah, we had a lot of the same interests, that's why we had such a great time together, isn't it?" I've known Blanche for years, I told him, and she was never the slightest bit interested in basketball, Van Damme films or Japanese food before they met. "Yeah?" His eyes light up; he's obviously delighted. "Well, I guess she got a few things out of the relationship, then, right?"

The Uptown Girl

Fourth category:
paragraphs 15–18

15   You know her, or at least you've seen her: She's Sharon Stone, Geena Davis, whoever's on the cover of *Sports Illustrated* this year. Happily, most men don't go around shooting U.S. presidents to impress her. But it's hard not to fall for a woman who's just—let's face it—out of your league.

16   The most insidious thing about this unattainable glamour girl is that she thinks she's Just Folks. I tried to reach Sharon Stone, Drew Barrymore and Kelly Lynch for their opinions on the topic, but they proved to be, well, unattainable. I did, however, get my friend Lauren, a successful film producer, to comment. Lauren has natural red hair, looks like a more glamorous Jodie Foster, as sweet as you'd wish. But she started back in horror when I described her as Unattainable. "But I'm not!" she squealed, as a male friend rolled his eyes helplessly behind her. "I mean, I'm not gorgeous or anything like that!" She does admit that men seem afraid to approach her, but puts that down to shyness. She's utterly wrong. My not-too-terribly-shy friend Rick admits even he's intimidated by women like Lauren. "I just gaze at them with sheep eyes."

17   "There are women who just don't notice the guys who are pursuing them: that's what makes them unattainable," Dr. Pittman says. The men who pursue these glamorous ghosts "don't really want a woman. They're like dogs chasing cars. It's great exercise, as long as you know you'll never catch one. This is the perfect set-up for the guy who wants to be in love without all the problems of having

a relationship. It's safe. Plus, he gets an identity from feeling the love he holds for her."

18   On the other hand, if you have normal, mutual relationships with other women, there's nothing wrong with having a crush on someone now and then. Dr. Pittman sheepishly admits that "I have that relationship with Susan Sarandon—whom I've never met, of course."

The Cruise Director

19   Okay, I have a confession. When my editor described this kind of Woman to Avoid, I thought he was being sarcastic and describing me: opinionated, always in control, bossy, having to make all the plans and double-check them afterward. This type of woman may be nerve-racking, but I hasten to add she always gets her stories in on deadline.

Fifth category: paragraphs 19–21

20   "She sounds real nice," agrees Dr. Pittman. "I have entirely too many pleasures in life to waste time running my life. I prefer having someone else do it for me. A Cruise Director can be someone who frees you up to be successful, to be creative."

21   That's fine as long as you're happy to leave your social life up to someone else's whims, and as long as she's willing to play cruise director for an extended tour. But it doesn't always work out that way. My friend Walter refused to talk about his ex-wife, but his new wife, Carol, was delighted to help. "Oh, she was such a pushy type," Carol enthused. "She ran everything, which was fun for both of them, at least for a while. But then the challenge was over, and she and Walter split up." Dr. Pittman says there can indeed be downsides to dating a Cruise Director. "If you're scared of women and you've got one who runs your life, you're going to feel controlled, that your autonomy is impinged upon, like an adolescent. She's for a guy who's got something to do that's more important than proving that women can't tell him what to do. But for the guy who's scared of female control, she'd be a disaster."

22   So maybe you're smart enough to avoid the above bachelorettes. Or maybe you're the type who clings to one after the other like Tarzan swinging through the vines. What's Dr. Pittman's advice for guys who keep falling for the wrong woman? "Get into a permanent, full-time committed relationship with someone with whom you don't get along terribly well and are basically incompatible." Yikes! He continues: "That puts you in the position of having to constantly examine yourself, develop new skills, learn to see the world from another perspective— it's a great maturing process." So is running away to join the circus, but I wouldn't recommend it for everyone.

Conclusion: paragraphs 22–25; perspective on male–female relationships

23   "Seriously," Dr. Pittman explains, "you need incompatibility in a relationship. Of course, you need compatibility, too—to make you feel comfortable, safe, understood. But compatibility is never complete, and never permanent. It takes a certain amount of conflict to give a relationship life."

24   If that's the hard way, here's the easy one: Guys, if you want to have a relationship in the worst way, take it from me, you will. There's this odd notion today that if you're not involved in a romantic/sexual relationship, you're somehow half a person and cannot possibly be happy.

25   Bull. How many hours have you spent on the phone with friends, moaning to your barkeep or to your therapist about how unhappy you are in one relationship or another? Take my advice and think long and hard next time you fall. As my wise old Aunt Ida once told me, "It's better to be alone than to wish you were."

DISCUSSION QUESTIONS

1. Discuss the nature and effectiveness of Golden's title.

2. Why does Golden identify herself in paragraph 5 as "a card-carrying NOW member"?

3. Does Golden offer a complete classification in which all categories of women are discussed?

4. The content of the essay indicates that Golden is writing for a male audience. Do you think her general purpose is to inform? to entertain? to persuade? Discuss.

5. Dr. Pittman notes in paragraph 23 that "compatibility is never complete, and never permanent. It takes a certain amount of conflict to give a relationship life." Reflect on your own dating and/or marital experience and then discuss the extent to which you agree.

TOWARD KEY INSIGHTS

Do you think Golden is guilty of stereotyping? Why or why not?

What differentiates a truthful portrayal from an offensive stereotype?

SUGGESTION FOR WRITING

Write an essay classifying several types of desirable women, desirable men, or undesirable men. Use whatever type of support seems appropriate.

Marion Winik

What Are Friends For?

Marion Winik (born 1958) is a graduate of Brown University and of Brooklyn College, where she earned a master of fine arts degree in creative writing. Since graduation, she has pursued a career in education, writing, and marketing. Her writings include poems, short stories, essays, and books, and the shorter pieces have appeared in a variety of major newspapers and popular magazines. Her most recent book, Lunch-Box Chronicles: Notes from the Parenting Underground *(1998), discusses her experiences in raising her sons after her husband's death. In this selection, Winik takes a humorous look at the different categories of friends and the benefits derived from each one.*

1   I was thinking about how everybody can't be everything to each other, but some people can be something to each other, thank God, from the ones whose shoulder you cry on to the ones whose half-slips you borrow to the nameless ones you chat with in the grocery line.

2   Buddies, for example, are the workhorses of the friendship world, the people out there on the front lines, defending you from loneliness and boredom. They call you up, they listen to your complaints, they celebrate your successes and curse your misfortunes, and you do the same for them in return. They hold out through innumerable crises before concluding that the person you're dating is no good, and even then understand if you ignore their good counsel. They accompany you to

a movie with subtitles or to see the diving pig at Aquarena Springs. They feed your cat when you are out of town and pick you up from the airport when you get back. They come over to help you decide what to wear on a date. Even if it is with that creep.

3   What about family members? Most of them are people you just got stuck with, and though you love them, you may not have very much in common. But there is that rare exception, the Relative Friend. It is your cousin, your brother, maybe even your aunt. The two of you share the same views of the other family members. Meg never should have divorced Martin. He was the best thing that ever happened to her. You can confirm each other's memories of things that happened a long time ago. Don't you remember when Uncle Hank and Daddy had that awful fight in the middle of Thanksgiving dinner? Grandma always hated Grandpa's stamp collection; she probably left the window open during the hurricane on purpose.

4   While so many family relationships are tinged with guilt and obligation, a relationship with a Relative Friend is relatively worry-free. You don't even have to hide your vices from this delightful person. When you slip out Aunt Joan's back door for a cigarette, she is already there.

5   Then there is that special guy at work. Like all the other people at the job site, at first he's just part of the scenery. But gradually he starts to stand out from the crowd. Your friendship is cemented by jokes about co-workers and thoughtful favors around the office. Did you see Ryan's hair? Want half my bagel? Soon you know the names of his turtles, what he did last Friday night, exactly which model CD player he wants for his birthday. His handwriting is as familiar to you as your own.

6   Though you invite each other to parties, you somehow don't quite fit into each other's outside lives. For this reason, the friendship may not survive a job change. Company gossip, once an infallible source of entertainment, soon awkwardly accentuates the distance between you. But wait. Like School Friends, Work Friends share certain memories which acquire a nostalgic glow after about a decade.

7   A Faraway Friend is someone you grew up with or went to school with or lived in the same town as until one of you moved away. Without a Faraway Friend, you would never get any mail addressed in handwriting. A Faraway Friend calls late at night, invites you to her wedding, always says she is coming to visit but rarely shows up. An actual visit from a Faraway Friend is a cause for celebration and binges of all kinds. Cigarettes, Chips Ahoy, bottles of tequila.

8   Faraway Friends go through phases of intense communication, then may be out of touch for many months. Either way, the connection is always there. A conversation with your Faraway Friend always helps to put your life in perspective: when you feel you've hit a dead end, come to a confusing fork in the road, or gotten lost in some crackerbox subdivision of your life, the advice of the Faraway Friend—who has the big picture, who is so well acquainted with the route that brought you to this place—is indispensable.

9   Another useful function of the Faraway Friend is to help you remember things from a long time ago, like the name of your seventh grade history teacher, what was in that really good stir-fry, or exactly what happened that night on the boat with the guys from Florida.

10   Ah, the Former Friend. A sad thing. At best a wistful memory, at worst a dangerous enemy who is in possession of many of your deepest secrets. But what was it that drove you apart? A misunderstanding, a betrayed confidence, an unrepaid loan, an ill-conceived flirtation. A poor choice of spouse can do in a friendship just

like that. Going into business together can be a serious mistake. Time, money, distance, cult religions: all noted friendship killers . . . .

11   And lest we forget, there are the Friends You Love to Hate. They call at inopportune times. They say stupid things. They butt in, they boss you around, they embarrass you in public. They invite themselves over. They take advantage. You've done the best you can, but they need professional help. On top of all this, they love you to death and are convinced they're your best friend on the planet.

12   So why do you continue to be involved with these people? Why do you tolerate them? On the contrary, the real question is, What would you do without them? Without Friends You Love to Hate, there would be nothing to talk about with your other friends. Their problems and their irritating stunts provide a reliable source of conversation for everyone they know. What's more, Friends You Love to Hate make you feel good about yourself, since you are in so much better shape than they are. No matter what these people do, you will never get rid of them. As much as they need you, you need them too.

13   At the other end of the spectrum are Hero Friends. These people are better than the rest of us, that's all there is to it. Their career is something you wanted to be when you grew up—painter, forest ranger, tireless doer of good. They have beautiful homes filled with special handmade things presented to them by villagers in the remote areas they have visited in their extensive travels. Yet they are modest. They never gossip. They are always helping others, especially those who have suffered a death in the family or an illness. You would think people like this would just make you sick, but somehow they don't.

14   A New Friend is a tonic unlike any other. Say you meet her at a party. In your bowling league. At a Japanese conversation class, perhaps. Wherever, whenever, there's that spark of recognition. The first time you talk, you can't believe how much you have in common. Suddenly, your life story is interesting again, your insights fresh, your opinion valued. Your various short-comings are as yet completely invisible.

15   It's almost like falling in love.

DISCUSSION QUESTIONS

1. Comment on the effectiveness of Winik's title.

2. Characterize the level of diction that Winik uses in her essay

3. What elements of Winik's essay interest you the most? What elements interest you the least?

TOWARD KEY INSIGHTS

What traits characterize the various types of friends that you have?

In what ways are these friendships mutually beneficial?

SUGGESTION FOR WRITING

Write an essay classifying the various types of people that you consider undesirable. Choose an appropriate number of categories and support them with appropriate specific details.

Stephen Perrine

The Crystal Healer Will See You Now

Stephen Perrine is the executive editor of Cosmopolitian *magazine and editor at large for* Men's Health *magazine. Formerly the deputy editor of* Men's Health, *he has written for* M, Parents, Elle, *and the Japanese art and architecture magazine* Diamond Design. *A graduate of Ithaca College, Perrine lives in New York City and rural Pennsylvania with his wife and two daughters.*

1   David introduces himself. He is a tall, jocular man in a flannel shirt and corduroy pants, with red hair that has begun to give way on top. He reminds me of a chunky Ron Howard—the kind of fellow you might see in the booth next to you at Shakey's, finishing off the last of his frappé. Despite the Oriental screens and Chinese lettering on the walls, despite the faint smell of incense and the exotic strumming of guitars over the loudspeaker, I find his casual smile familiar and reassuring. Which is nice, because very shortly David will begin inserting long, sharp needles into my body.

2   He will be attempting to cure a mysterious inflammation of my wrist and middle knuckle, one that left my regular physician at a loss. David has quickly surmised that I am suffering from "a blockage in the energy flow along one of my meridians." We'll get to that later. He has also learned, from examining my tongue, that I don't properly metabolize my food. ("This is how I see inside you," he says, gazing down my throat and starting to make me nervous.) He advertises himself as an acupuncturist, but, like most practitioners of alternative healing, he wears many hats. In his reception room is a display of herbal remedies and nutritional supplements; in the treatment room he takes me to is a shelf of homeopathic remedies—mixtures of water and alcohol that supposedly contain the essences of various toxic substances, designed to stimulate the body into healing itself.

3   My treatment consists of five needles inserted into my right arm and hand: two on each side of the knuckle, one in my wrist and two in my forearm. I also receive a bottle of herbal medicine called San Qi 17, a massage of my sore arm with a substance called Po Sum On oil and, for a bruise on my elbow, a plaster patch of musk and tiger bone. The whole encounter takes more than two hours. I leave feeling, if not healed, at least well tended to.

4   I'm told my experience is not unique. More and more Americans—some with illnesses that modern medicine can't cure, others simply fed up with the impersonal culture of mainstream care—have begun seeking out healing methods that fall outside the expertise of, say, your average Marcus Welby, M.D. Whether they're practiced by doctors, by laypersons, or by those mysterious individuals in between who call themselves herbalists or homeopaths or hypnotists, alternative treatments are becoming big business: Consumers spent an estimated $13.7 billion on unconventional therapies in 1990.

5   What exactly is alternative medicine? "That's a question that's very simple to answer: I don't know," says Daniel Eskinazi, Ph.D., D.D.S. It's a pretty honest reply, considering Dr. Eskinazi is the deputy director of the National Institutes of Health's Office of Alternative Medicine, a recently established branch of the government's primary health-research organization. In fact, a recent study in *The New England Journal of Medicine* caused a great brouhaha when it reported that a third of the 1,500 Americans surveyed had used some form of alternative therapy in 1990.

But under the heading "alternative" was lumped everything from acupuncture and energy healing to simple exercise, prayer and commercial weight-loss programs. (Richard Simmons, spiritual healer? We don't think so.)

6   "'Alternative' is a political weasel word," explains John Renner, M.D., president of the Consumer Health Information Research Institute. "We're talking about things that run the gamut from harmless folklore to organized and extremely dangerous quackery. Some physicians feel it's a lot of bull—." But not all fringe medicine is practiced in incense-filled basements; sometimes it's used in brightly lit hospitals and doctors' offices. How can you tell where scientific method ends and the Twilight Zone begins? Here's a look at some popular healing methods, and just when, how and if they work.

7   *Chiropractic.*   Doctors of chiropractic treat patients by manipulating the spinal column and joints, a technique often referred to as an "adjustment." The chiropractic and mainstream medical communities have long been at odds. The American Medical Association traditionally viewed chiropractic as an unscientific cult. But in 1987, a court ruling prohibited the AMA from actively discouraging its members from referring patients to chiropractors. Since then, chiropractors have been increasingly welcomed into the fold of conventional medicine. Today it's not uncommon to see group practices shared by M.D.'s and chiropractors, and many hospitals include chiropractic care. Chiropractic treatment is now covered by many insurance policies; in fact, 45 states require policies underwritten by health-insurance providers to reimburse for chiropractic care.

8   *The Claims.*   Even within the field, there are vast disagreements on how far chiropractic can go toward healing a variety of physical ailments. Upwards of 80 percent of chiropractic patients are seeking relief from back and neck pain, usually through a manipulation of the spinal column and joints. Some chiropractic organizations feel chiropractors should do nothing more. The majority of practitioners, however, also utilize massage, ultrasound, heat treatments and physical therapy. And then there's a minority who still adhere to a theory called "subluxation," the belief that minor misalignments of the spine are the source of all illness. These chiropractors may claim they can relieve everything from allergies and digestive trouble to high blood pressure, heart disease, cancer and diabetes simply by manipulating the spine.

9   *The Research.*   There's little doubt that chiropractic medicine is effective for acute lower-back pain. A review of literature in the *Annals of Internal Medicine* reported consistent findings of acute back-pain relief. However, there is no hard evidence of chiropractic's use for treating more serious conditions.

10   *The Bottom Line.*   Chiropractors are winning increased acceptance from the medical community and the public at large; in fact, they treat about twice as many people for back pain as medical doctors do. Most chiropractors receive four years' training at accredited schools, including instruction in diagnostics, radiology and physical therapy. A good one will treat mainly lower-back and related pains and will be able to recognize illnesses and refer you to a physician if your problem falls outside his area of expertise. If you decide to consult a chiropractor, look for one who's certified by the National Board of Chiropractic Examiners, the national standard for practitioners, and who has graduated from a school accredited by the Council on Chiropractic Education. (Not all states require these two criteria.) Back away from anyone who claims to cure disease or treat allergies, who routinely recommends full-body X-rays, or who tries to sell you medicines or nutritional supplements.

11 **_Homeopathy._** The practice of homeopathy originated in Europe in the late 1700s, the brainchild of German physician Samuel Hahnemann. His theory, still abided by today, is that like cures like: A disease can be cured by giving the patient an infinitesimal amount of a substance that, in a healthy person, might cause the same symptoms—arsenic, for example, or belladonna, or snake venom, or tarantula poison. The toxic substance is diluted until perhaps not even one molecule of the original toxin remains. But the belief is that the solution somehow retains the "memory" of the original substance and stimulates the body to cure itself.

12 _The Claims._ There seems no end to the ailments homeopathy purports to cure. Besides the common cold and various other diseases deemed incurable by mainstream medicine, homeopathy has also been applied to alcoholism and chronic fatigue syndrome. "We don't know how it works," admits Thomas Kruzel, N.D., a doctor of naturopathic medicine who teaches urology at the National College of Naturopathic Medicine in Portland, Oregon. (Naturopathy is a discipline whose followers may use homeopathy as well as a variety of alternative and mainstream treatments.)

13 The homeopath will treat an individual not by disease, but by how the disease manifests itself, says Kruzel. One of the most common problems he treats is sexually transmitted disease. "Let's say that a man comes in with genital herpes, and that the sore is causing an aching pain, and that it is spreading and weeping," Kruzel proposes. "That would be an indication for the homeopathic remedy mercurius, which is made from mercury." Why? Because someone who suffers from mercury poisoning will develop weeping sores on his body. If, instead of weeping sores, the herpes were to manifest itself as sharp, radiating pain surrounded by dry skin, Kruzel would administer homeopathic nitric acid. You guessed it—nitric acid poisoning creates sore, dry skin.

14 _The Research._ Homeopathy is far more prevalent in parts of Europe than it is in the U.S, where not much legitimate research has been done. Homeopaths, however, point to a long history of "provings," extremely dangerous experiments in which healthy people were given higher doses of a substance and developed various reactions to it—belladonna, for example, was "proven" for strep throat by demonstrating that someone taking the potentially fatal substance would develop a sore throat and high fever.

15 _The Bottom Line._ Mainstream doctors strenuously refute homeopathic claims. A homeopathic herpes treatment has no rational basis, says Stephen Kurtin, M.D., assistant professor of dermatology at Mount Sinai School of Medicine. A herpes lesion starts as a blister, then usually becomes a weeping sore before finally crusting over. Dr. Kurtin speculates that the homeopathic approach accommodates people at different stages of a breakout. But even with no treatment, the average herpes sore disappears in 7 to 10 days. "[The drug] acyclovir is the treatment," says Dr. Kurtin. "It has taken what was once a horrendous disease and made it a minor nuisance."

16 Depending on which state they practice in and what training they've received, homeopaths can offer an array of treatments in addition to the homeopathic cures. In some states they may prescribe most of the same medications mainstream doctors use. Counseling and nutrition also factor into care. Homeopathic remedies are available not only from practitioners but also at some holistic pharmacies and through mail order. While the FDA requires prescriptions for homeopathic treatments for conditions like cancer and AIDS, it does not guarantee the safety or effectiveness of any homeopathic remedy. But because they contain such small doses of active ingredients, most are considered harmless.

17   ***Energy Healing.***   Is your energy centered, or have you misplaced your *chi?* A vital question, some say. The idea of healing through energy, or life force, or chi, runs through a number of holistic medical techniques—the most familiar of which may be crystals. You won't find many complicated theories surrounding this form of healing, but you will find plenty of believers. And they're not all relegated to the New Age gift shops. One popular exercise specialist uses energy healing in her Hollywood clients' training. Naturopath Kruzel says he alters his course of treatment depending on his perception of the patient's "vital force," but so do mainstream doctors. "I might call it vital force, but an M.D. might call it 'will to live,'" he says. "And an M.D. might not perform an operation on a patient he perceives as having a weaker will to live." The question, however, is whether that force can be harnessed for healing.

18   *The Claims.*   Since your life force is what keeps you healthy, a disruption of it is what makes you ill. In her book *Stone Power,* a guide to crystals and their healing properties, author Dorothee Mella (a "noted color specialist in nonverbal communications") claims that precious and nonprecious gems have their own special effects on your life energy. Amethyst will relieve headaches, garnet will balance thyroid disorders, ivory will protect the body from injury. (Quick, send some to Joe Montana.)

19   *The Research.*   Has the medical community rushed out to investigate these claims? No, and it's not likely to unless Shirley MacLaine coughs up some big bucks to finance a study. But Dr. Eskinazi of the NIH says his organization won't rule out an investigation into such fields if an intelligent study is proposed.

20   *The Bottom Line.*   Keep the snickering down. Someone you know is probably fingering a crystal right now.

21   ***Herbal Medicine.***   For many people, the allure of herbal medicine lies in taking a natural remedy grown in their own garden instead of a concentrated, synthetic drug from a bottle covered with warnings about side effects. Herbal remedies, which may sound as innocuous as Grandma's chicken soup, have grown into a $1 billion-a-year industry. There are two different approaches to herb therapy: a Western (or European) application, which uses specific herbs to attack specific problems, and the Chinese style, which uses a variety of herbs in combination to create a balanced remedy whose whole is somehow more effective than its parts.

22   *The Claims.*   According to traditional Chinese medicine, disease is viewed as an imbalance of two opposing energies, yin and yang, in the major organ systems. Concoctions of Chinese herbs are therefore used to restore these forces to proper proportions. According to Western thinking, herbs used on an individual basis in standardized preparations are touted as natural replacements for their synthetic or processed counterparts—willow bark in place of aspirin, for example, or foxglove instead of the heart medication digitalis.

23   *The Research.*   Claims about Chinese herbology are almost impossible to verify using Western science. Because traditional Chinese medicine uses the herbs in complex combinations, the active ingredients in the remedies can be difficult to analyze because they may not be present at detectable levels.

24   Scientists think that many low-dose complex herbs probably work through the immune system. A Japanese researcher recently reported that studies of an herbal blend used in his country for centuries seemed to improve both the immune responses and general health of some patients with chronic viral hepatitis.

25   Studies into the salutary effects of specific herbs are more widely available. Garlic extracts, for example, have been linked with improved ratios of "good" to

"bad" cholesterol in the bloodstream, and a large population study of Chinese provinces showed that those areas with a higher consumption of garlic had markedly lower death rates from colon cancer.

26   *The Bottom Line.*   Research is continuing into the effects of a variety of herbal remedies—if only in the hopes that they'll yield more effective pharmacological cures. The World Health Organization estimates that 75 percent of mainstream drugs were discovered through the use of plants in traditional medicine. But that doesn't mean that most herbal medicines sold at health-food stores are effective. "Many herbal products can be useless if they're not standardized," says Ara Der Marderosian, Ph.D., professor of pharmacognosy and medicinal chemistry at Philadelphia College of Pharmacy and Science. Even a heart-healthy herb like garlic may be rendered useless if it's processed or diluted improperly. For example, Der Marderosian conducted one study of commercial ginseng products and found that as many as 10 percent contain absolutely none of ginseng's active ingredient. His recommendation: "If you have a medical condition, probably the best thing to do is to use the standard, proven medication." If you do want to try an herbal remedy, look for one that's standardized. The label should describe the active ingredient in the herb and how much of it is in each dose. (For example, the number of garlic pills you must take to get the same amount of the active ingredient, allicin, found in a single clove of raw garlic.) And tell your physician, so he or she can monitor its effects.

27   ***Hypnosis.***   After 20 years of using hypnotherapy to help her young patients tolerate the discomfort of medical procedures, pediatrician Karen Olness, M.D., got a chance to test out the method herself. After being injured in a skiing accident, Dr. Olness, professor of pediatrics and family medicine at Case Western Reserve University in Cleveland, decided to undergo surgery without anesthesia. Instead, she used relaxation techniques and her imagination to block the pain impulses while her disbelieving doctor went to work repairing her injured hand. What is this strange power that enables people to endure grueling pain without breaking a sweat?

28   *The Claims.*   Despite what you saw in that magic show at the comedy club, hypnotherapists will not make you quack like a duck, speak Japanese, or fall asleep whenever somebody says "Walter Mondale." But what they may try to do is offer pain relief, help you quit smoking, or even train your immune system to fight disease. And hypnosis is also used by some professional sports trainers to boost their athletes' performances.

29   *The Research.*   Substantial anecdotal evidence, such as Dr. Olness's experience, demonstrates that for some people, hypnotherapy may offer relief from acute and chronic pain. When witnessed by medical doctors, this phenomenon is pretty hard to refute. And scientists are now examining another aspect of hypnotherapy: the technique's effect on the immune system. In a study at Tulane Medical School in New Orleans, hypnotic suggestion was used on a group of adults and children who suffered from warts. Almost all of the children were cured, although the immediate success rate among adults was not as high. Still, the researchers were eventually able to cure 80 percent of the subjects with hypnotherapy. Another study, conducted by Dr. Olness, compared three groups of children. One group was taught self-hypnosis, a second was taught the same exercise but also given a hypnotic suggestion to boost an immune-system substance found in the saliva, and the third was not exposed to hypnosis. When the children's saliva was

measured, the group given the suggestion showed a striking increase in the amount of the immune substance found in their saliva.

30   *The Bottom Line.*   "It is far too early to say for sure that hypnotherapy can be used to stimulate the immune system," concedes Dr. Olness. But for those suffering from chronic illness or from pain due to ongoing medical procedures, or for those who cannot tolerate anesthesia, hypnotherapy is a widely available and effective technique. What it may not be so effective at is what it is more commonly identified with: weight-loss and stop-smoking programs. Many of these courses are one-shot deals, and Dr. Olness says the reason most people fail is that patients need to clearly imagine their lives without the cigarettes or the extra weight in order for the treatment to be effective—and that level of concentration often takes a substantial amount of time to learn.

31   It's possible to learn self-hypnosis with instructional tapes, but as with golf, a few lessons from a professional can go a long way. If you're seeking help for a specific medical problem, choose a doctor who is knowledgeable about your specific condition as well. Some dentists, for example, teach the technique to people who need root-canal work but cannot tolerate anesthesia.

32   **Guided Imagery.**   The use of imagery is part and parcel of almost all therapies that involve relaxation. Patients are taught to envision themselves in a calm, peaceful place like the beach or the woods. "If I simply said, 'Relax your muscles,' you might not be able to do it," says Martin L. Rossman, M.D., clinical associate in the department of medicine at the University of California–San Francisco. "But if I say, 'Imagine yourself in a calm, tranquil place,' and I ask you to describe it—what you see, hear, smell, feel—you can reach a deeper state of relaxation." This technique is called *sensory recruitment* because it calls on areas of the brain that control each different sense. But relaxation is only the first step in guided imagery.

33   *The Claims.*   Many practitioners claim imagery can be used for both diagnostic and therapeutic purposes. *Receptive imagery* involves entering a relaxed state, then concentrating on the area of the body that is ailing. The idea is to envision some embodiment of the illness—a little troll perhaps, or a mischievous demon...—and ask it why it is causing the trouble. "On the surface it sounds kind of crazy," admits Dr. Rossman, "but the unconscious provides a great deal of information about what the body needs."

34   *Active imagery* involves envisioning an illness being cured. This may mean anything from imagining your immune system attacking a tumor to picturing shoulder pain as a ball that rolls down your arm and out of your body. Gerald Epstein, M.D., author of *Healing Visualizations,* claims the use of images can help treat at least 80 physical and psychological disorders, from high blood pressure and acne to diabetes, cancer and addictions.

35   *The Research.*   While there is no hard scientific data on the curative powers of imagery, the theory is that the brain responds the same to a vivid imagining as it does to an actual stimulation of a sense. In other words, if you imagine hearing music, your brain reacts the same way as if you were actually hearing it; if music relaxes you, so should imagining music.

36   Physiological responses have been demonstrated, too. A small study from Penn State University and Case Western Reserve University found that imagery coupled with relaxation significantly reduced the recurrence of canker sores in seven chronic sufferers. Envisioning a series of guided images of white blood cells attacking the sores, subjects cut their individual numbers of cankers by as much as two thirds.

37   *The Bottom Line.*   Dr. Rossman says that as a diagnostic tool, guided imagery is best used to supplement conventional medical efforts. He believes that many ailments are really the body's way of responding to one's life and lifestyle.

38   Not everyone is capable of undergoing this type of treatment. Subjects must be able to suspend disbelief. And an active imagination is also a must, as the vividness of the envisioned image may play a role in the treatment's effectiveness. But, says Dr. Rossman, "If you can imagine something sexual and it gives you an erection, you can probably use guided imagery. Do we know exactly how a particular thought increases blood flow to the penis? No, but it does." At the very least, imagery is a nontoxic treatment that can give the patient an active role in his own healing.

39   *Acupuncture.*   In addition to mistrust of government, the mess in Cambodia and a constant stream of books by Bob Woodward, we have Richard Nixon to blame for one more thing: acupuncture. The technique was relatively unknown in the U.S. until Nixon visited China in the early 1970s; there to cover his arrival, *New York Times* reporter James Reston came down with an acute case of appendicitis and relayed back to the States how a Chinese doctor miraculously relieved his post-appendectomy pain through a series of strategically placed needles.

40   *The Claims.*   Although considered a panacea in China, acupuncture is mainly used in the U.S. for pain relief. In traditional Oriental acupuncture, numerology plays a big role. There are 365 acupuncture points, one for each day of the year, and these points are connected along "meridians," lines through which life energy flows—that chi stuff again. A traditional acupuncturist will insert needles into these points to stimulate the flow of energy in the right direction. A true practitioner of the Chinese technique may even claim to cure all ills, since the meridians are said to govern the various organ systems.

41   Modern acupuncture is accompanied by the use of electrical stimulation. To relieve pain, needles are inserted into "motor points," spots in the body where nerve enters muscle. (These often correspond to traditional acupuncture points.) The electrical current then stimulates the brain to release natural painkillers, similar to those that cause "runner's high."

42   *The Research.*   Most of the studies on both traditional and electrically stimulated acupuncture treatments have been conducted in China, where the methodology is far different from that of Western medicine. Chinese researchers reportedly found positive results among patients with clinically diagnosed depression who were treated twice a day with acupuncture. But what few Western studies exist have proven inconclusive. A Canadian study, while not endorsing the method, did note that using specific acupuncture sites seemed to have a more positive effect on gastrointestinal function than random "control" sites.

43   *The Bottom Line.*   Some experts believe that mainstream medicine has turned its back on acupuncture, despite the fact that many M.D.'s practice the technique. One practitioner is George Ulett, M.D., Ph.D., clinical professor of psychiatry at the University of Missouri School of Medicine and author of *Beyond Yin and Yang: How Acupuncture Really Works.* "There's a clear distinction between using neuro-electrical acupuncture and the ancient ways," he says. But the medical and insurance industries see them as one and the same. However, some doctors will perform acupuncture and bill it as TENS treatment, an approved treatment that uses electrodes on the skin in a similar way.

44   *Biofeedback.*   Of all the alternative healing techniques, biofeedback is perhaps the most accepted by the mainstream medical community. Maybe that's because

expensive, high-technology gadgets are involved. A patient using biofeedback is connected with sensors to a machine that monitors one or more of his vital signs, then translates them into audio or visual cues. Using the machine's signals as guides to his progress, the patient then attempts to alter his vital signs in order to attack a physical problem.

45   *The Claims.* Biofeedback machines can be programmed for treatment of different disorders, depending on which bodily process is involved. Among the most common vital signs monitored (alone or in any combination) are muscle tension (used to treat tension headaches, muscle pain, incontinence and partial paralysis and to promote general relaxation); skin temperature (used to treat Raynaud's syndrome, migraines, hypertension, anxiety); perspiration (anxiety, sweat-gland disorders); pulse (hypertension, anxiety, arrhythmia); and breathing rate (asthma, hyperventilation, anxiety).

46   *The Research.* A great deal of research has shown biofeedback to be effective. A study at the Medical College of Ohio in Toledo found that when patients with hypertension were given a particular blood-pressure medication, only 1 in 10 was helped. But when the medication was combined with biofeedback-assisted relaxation, more than half the subjects lowered their blood pressure. Another study at Johns Hopkins University deemed thermal biofeedback can be effective for irritable bowel syndrome and some forms of chronic constipation. And researchers at San Francisco State University reported reductions in symptoms, medication use and emergency-room visits among asthmatics using the technique.

47   *The Bottom Line.* Biofeedback is being used by all manner of health professionals—physicians, psychologists, social workers and nurses. One reason it's still not considered a proven mainstream treatment is that biofeedback is seldom used by itself; it's usually combined with medications and lifestyle changes, as well as other relaxation techniques. In addition, there's a human factor involved: The treatment doesn't work for everyone; the best biofeedback candidates are usually those willing to make changes to improve their conditions.

48   So what were the results of my journey into the New Age? Well, that bruise on my elbow that had been lingering for two weeks did clear up pretty quickly, and perhaps the tiger bone and musk did help. But I can't say that my sore wrist or inflamed knuckle are much improved, and after three treatments (the number originally recommended by David—he suggested a fourth visit; I said I'd call *him*), I'm ready to move on to more proven methods.

49   Does anyone know a good crystal healer?

DISCUSSION QUESTIONS

1. Consider the essay as a whole and then comment on the effectiveness of Perrine's title.

2. Identify the sentence fragment in paragraph 1. How do you account for its inclusion?

3. In paragraph 4, Perrine notes that consumers spent nearly $14 billion on unconventional therapies in 1990, and in paragraph 5 he cites a 1990 study showing that one-third of those surveyed had tried alternative therapies. Why do you think Perrine points out these facts?

4. Discuss the function of paragraph 6 in the essay.

5. What purpose do Perrine's headings and subheadings serve?

TOWARD KEY INSIGHTS

What is your attitude toward alternative medicine?

Would you consider using any of the kinds Perrine discusses?

Why do you think alternative forms of medicine have become popular with many people?

Why do you think the mainstream medical profession generally disapproves of these therapies?

SUGGESTION FOR WRITING   *Some instructors use the lecture format in the classroom; some use a variety of alternative approaches. Write an essay classifying some alternative approaches that you have found effective or ineffective.*

Kerry Banks

As a Dad, Will I Do Right by My Daughter?

Kerry Banks is a freelance journalist. He has written six books and has won nine writing awards for his feature magazine work. He has written articles for numerous publications, including Equinox, Harrowsmith, Maclean's, *and* Chatelaine. *Since 1992, he has written a weekly sports column for the Vancouver news-and-entertainment weekly,* The Georgia Straight. *Banks's essay, "As a Dad, Will I Do Right by My Daughter?" reflects on the contemporary pitfalls of being a first-time father of a daughter. Having read a book about the different kinds of fathers who affect their daughters' self-image in different, sometimes troubling ways, Banks questions women he knows about their experiences of fathers. Banks presents the results of his research in a way that is sympathetic and engaging.*

1   My daughter's first word was "Da-Da." At least, that's how I remember it. Her mother, Anne, insists it was actually "dog." Whatever the true order, it was a thrill to hear her identify me by name. I think the bond between us grew a little closer at that moment. I know the weight of responsibility suddenly gained several pounds.

2   Riley is our first child and she is full of surprises. As she nears one year of age, we are amazed to discover how much she enjoys books, how quickly she can ransack a room and how deeply she is attached to the TV remote control. The first surprise, though, was her sex.

3   Both Anne and I come from families dominated by male progeny, and the odds seemed to suggest a son. When he turned out to be a she, it immediately struck me how little I knew about girls. With a son, I would be on familiar turf; I would instinctively know where he was heading and how he would feel when he got there. With a daughter, I would only be guessing. Each stage of her development would be a mystery to me.

4   Being a first-time parent is never easy, but I think it is especially tough for fathers these days. Our role is in flux. The "good provider" and "stern father" figures are as out of style as the hula hoop. Modern dads are expected to be more actively

involved in child-rearing. We are supposed to change more diapers, spend more time at home, be more sensitive and avoid gender stereotyping of our children at all costs.

5   Unfortunately, we have no role models on whom to base our behaviour. It is hard to feel confident when you are making things up as you go along. Pressured by society to be different from our fathers and struggling to achieve domestic equilibrium with our wives, we cannot help but feel anxious. So, as I confronted the reality of having a daughter, I could only wonder: what sort of father was I going to be?

6   As I was mulling over this conundrum, a book entitled *Women and Their Fathers: The Sexual and Romantic Impact of the First Man in Your Life* came across my desk. Contrary to popular wisdom, the author, New York journalist Victoria Secunda, contends it is the father, not the mother, who has the more profound impact in shaping a daughter's self-image. According to Secunda, the way dad and daughter get along largely determines how the daughter will see herself as an adult, and what she will expect from men.

7   Secunda classifies fathers into categories—"templates for their daughters' future attachments," she calls them. Fathers are doting, distant, demanding, absent or seductive. She classifies daughters too. A particular type of father does not necessarily produce a single type of daughter, but the way the relationship plays out produces daughters who are favoured, good, competitive, fearful or maverick. As I read the sobering litany of the ways in which each father type can damage his daughter's psyche, little Riley began to assume the fragility of a package of gelignite. Did so much of what she would become depend on me?

8   I began questioning women I knew about the impact of their fathers on their lives. Few of their relationships fit Secunda's categories precisely, but some patterns were evident. It was, for example, not difficult to find examples of the **distant father**—most of the women I spoke with had fathers who were remote in some way. But it was harder to correlate cause and effect. According to Secunda, distant fathers can produce a myriad of emotional consequences. Their daughters may or may not become sexually promiscuous, suffer from anorexia nervosa, be unable to achieve orgasm or marry men who don't notice them.

9   Sometimes, women raised by distant fathers deliberately seek out men who are diametrically different. Terrie Orr is a case in point. Orr, a soft-spoken but strong-willed 39-year-old Vancouver homemaker, says she has always been drawn to men with dynamic outgoing characters—men quite unlike her father, who is a quiet, unemotional reserved man. Orr refers to her dad as an "armchair father." His main interest, she recalls, was his job on the Canadian Pacific Railway. He occupied most of his leisure time with solitary pursuits, such as watching TV, doing carpentry and gardening. Orr says it was her effervescent mother who kept the family's five kids in line. "It was strange. Even though Dad was around a lot, you never had the feeling that he was really there."

10   Orr's most vivid memory of her father was one rare occasion when he stepped out of character. On Mother's Day, when Orr was 10, her father suggested that his wife sleep in as a treat while he took the kids out for a stroll in the woods near their home in Winnipeg. "We walked for two or three hours. I remember sunshine and open fields and laughing and skipping along. It was one of the only times he initiated something with the family."

11   Orr still finds her father an enigma, although she knows that her own reserved personality somewhat resembles his. Ironically, her relationship with her sales manager husband, Laurie Stein, is in some respects a mirror image of her

own parents' merger of opposites. But, in this case, it is her husband who is the socializer.

12   Orr says that one of the things that attracted her to Laurie was his natural affinity for children: "He likes to play and fool around with our two boys and be naughty."

13   Orr's distant father does not sound much like me, but I do tend to be the introspective type. In fact, my wife does not hesitate to describe me as "moody." And truth be told, I exhibit other "distant father" danger signs—obsession with my work and a reluctance to discuss my feelings on personal subjects openly. Uptight, macho, WASP, self-obsessed: as I read Secunda's book, these psychological buzz-words began doing a noisy dance in my male psyche.

14   Maybe it's just self-justification, but I think some of the distance that exists between fathers and daughters is a product of our sexual blueprints. Men tend to deal with their emotions differently from women. It does not mean we do not have any. The challenge I will face with Riley is to make sure our differences never destroy the bonds between us.

15   At the other end of the emotional spectrum is the **doting father**—the daddy who makes everything all right. Annemarie Beard, 35, a stylish, sassy production manager with a Vancouver advertising firm, says she was "always the light in my fa-ther's eye." In sharp contrast to her two brothers, she was "spoiled and treated like a princess." Beard says her father, a chemical engineer, was always physically affectionate and ready to play. Only when she reached puberty did "the bubble burst," as her father began to pull away.

16   This is evidently a common reaction among fathers, according to Vancouver family therapist Mary Trokenberg. "As daddy's little girl grows into womanhood and becomes more sexually aware, many men don't know how to handle it. When men feel fragile and in doubt, they withdraw, and as a result, children feel aban-doned."

17   Today, Annemarie Beard says the bond with her father has been restored. Yet, she admits that her early idealization of him had its consequences. "It took me a long time to grow up. I had to discover that not all men are like my father."

18   Author Secunda says many women with doting fathers are drawn to men who resemble their fathers—men who will protect them and keep them in the pam-pered style to which they are accustomed. Often, they tend to be older men. This is certainly true of Beard. "I had my first date at 15," she says. "He was 35." Today, she continues to feel most comfortable with older men. She likes their secure na-ture and the attentive manner in which they treat her. "Older men seem delighted just to have a younger woman around."

19   Doting and distant are polar opposites. Logically, therefore, I can't possibly be the doting type. So, why is it that Anne and I are already divided over the issue of protectiveness, which is one of the characteristics Secunda attributes to doting dads? I think Anne is too carefree with Riley; she feels I worry too much. And yet, how can I not worry? Our once benign household has suddenly become a nest of dangers—electrical outlets, open staircases, hot liquids, bottled poisons. So, if I am doting now, it is only for Riley's own good. This stage will surely pass. Once she is old enough to take care of herself, I will let her climb trees and play tackle football. Maybe.

20   Another of Secunda's archetypes, the **demanding father,** casts a dual-edged shadow over his daughter's life. Secunda says the best sort of demanding fathers are those who are stern but fair—they inspire confidence and ambition in their

daughters. But when the sternness is not balanced by tenderness and support, daughters may be left with painful legacies.

21   Bonita Thompson, a vivacious, high-energy, 45-year-old Vancouver lawyer, traces much of what she has accomplished in life to her demanding father's influence. A chartered accountant, he was wrapped up in his career and spent little time with her three sisters and one brother. But Thompson forged a bond with him through sports. "From age 6 to 16, I was dad's caddie on the golf course. He taught me a sense of gentlemanly conduct, sportsmanship, ethics and setting high standards for yourself."

22   But some of his standards were impossibly high. "I'd bring home my report card with an average of 94 percent, and he'd say, 'Why isn't it 100 percent?' He was joking, but there was a barb underneath it."

23   As far back as she can recall, Thompson always had a strong desire to achieve. Yet, even as her law career flourished, she sensed there was something lacking. "After each of my achievements, I'd feel empty." Eventually, Thompson realized that "all I had done in life was a continuing effort to elicit my father's praise."

24   Thompson's failed first marriage was to a man very similar to her father. Her current husband is the antithesis. "He's a free spirit, a warm, outgoing humorous person. And he's a bit of a rascal and a rule breaker. He's the nurturer in our family. He stayed home and raised our child."

25   The problem of fathers who are grudging with praise often surfaced in my conversations with women. I may be in dangerous waters here too. Neither of my parents expressed support easily, and it's going to be hard for me to break the mould.

26   The discussions with my female friends did little to relieve my angst. I kept seeing bits of my character reflected in the darker side of their fathers' images. As for Secunda's book, I was left wondering whether a healthy relationship between a father and a daughter is possible at all.

27   Mary Trokenberg, the therapist, helped me put it in perspective: "Some of the ways in which daughters develop has to do with their fathers, but not all. The danger with these sorts of self-help books is that people will think one-dimensionally. When you divide people into categories, you lose the nuances and fail to see other possibilities."

28   This makes sense to me. While I will undoubtedly have a major influence on Riley, I suspect her view of men will also be shaped by what she sees in the relationship between my wife and me, and in her mother's attitudes toward men generally.

29   As for being distant, doting or demanding, I will try to keep my conflicting impulses in balance. Like any new parent, I have hopes. I want Riley to be an independent thinker, confident and creative. I want her to be a woman who is involved in the world, a woman who likes men and who can tell a joke. Most of all, I want her to be happy.

30   I don't know yet how I will deal with the familiar crises of fatherhood, such as when Riley begins dating boys with green hair and nose rings. But there is time to learn, and I will need to trust my instincts. For now, I am content simply to share the extraordinary discoveries of Riley's young life—and her awe at seeing the night stars for the first time, the giddy tingle of walking barefoot on a freshly mown lawn, the magical spell of a street musician's guitar. For now, just being Da-Da is enough.

DISCUSSION QUESTIONS

1. Why does the writer think that being a father today is more difficult for him personally than it might be for other people? (See paragraphs 2–3.) Why is being a father generally more difficult today than it might have been for fathers in the past? (See paragraphs 4–5.) How does this discussion of difficulties with the paternal role make the reader receptive to what follows?

2. In paragraph 7, Kerry Banks reports about the way that reading a book about fathers and daughters affected him: "As I read the sobering litany of the ways in which each father type can damage his daughter's psyche, little Riley began to assume the fragility of a package of gelignite" (paragraph 7). What does he mean?

3. Why does Kerry Banks follow his description of the "distant father" with the description of the "doting father" (paragraph 15)? Explain the three main categories of fathers that the writer deals with in your own words. Why do you suppose that Banks does not discuss two other categories of fathers—the absent or seductive father—(paragraph 7) in detail? What is the principle for classification of fathers in the essay?

4. Why does Kerry Banks talk to women he knows about their relationships with their fathers (paragraph 8)? What does he find out from these women? How do these interviews influence the writer's attitude toward fathering?

5. Study the conclusion of this essay. How does Kerry Banks expand the scope of his essay outwards, enlarging the context and significance of what he has been discussing? How does he also come full circle?

TOWARD KEY INSIGHTS

From your own experience, or from your observations of gender roles in other families, do you also conclude that the roles of fathers are "in flux" (paragraph 4)? Why or why not?

Kerry Banks writes that "men tend to deal with their emotions differently from women" (paragraph 14). How does he qualify this claim? To what extent do you agree with this generalization? Is it possible to make meaningful generalizations about such gender differences? Why or why not?

Kerry Banks quotes a therapist as saying, "When you divide people into categories, you lose the nuances and fail to see other possibilities" (paragraph 27). Do you also see problems with classifying people? Why or why not? What are the reasons that we put people into categories?

SUGGESTION FOR WRITING

Write an essay that classifies a certain group of people into categories according to a clear principle—kinds of university students, instructors, coaches, dates, concert-goers, clothes shoppers. In your essay, acknowledge any potential problems with classifying in this way.

Comparison

Douglas Todd

Title sets up differences, suggests direction

In a Girl's World, It Can Be Tough Being a Boy

Douglas Todd writes a regular column on religion and ethics for The Vancouver Sun. *In the following essay Todd argues that boys are now on the losing end of the gender battle, particularly in education.*

Introduction: paragraphs 1–4; background and social context; significance of following contrasts

1   "Girl Power!" "Girls Rule!" These slogans now appear weekly as educators, the entertainment industry and the media celebrate spunky young women's rising successes.

2   Girls now do better in school than boys. Many employers are patting themselves on the back for hiring more females than males. Vancouver's Sarah McLachlan, who organized a big money-making all-women concert festival called Lilith Fair, is becoming an international icon for "Girl Power."

3   Unfortunately, the cheering for girls' triumphs is drowning out the quiet worries of a bunch of others—boys. Just as girls were stereotyped as sweet low-achievers in the '50s, now boys seem to be suffering from being pigeon-holed as unruly good-for-littles.

4   The notion of gender inequity has been turned on its head. While some commentators declare it's now a good time to be a girl, they're not dropping the other shoe: it's a troublesome, even crummy, time to be a boy.

Body: paragraphs 5–17; alternating pattern throughout

Differences in elementary school

5   A recent *Globe and Mail* column is typical of the current blindness. Education writer Jennifer Lewington analysed an Ontario study that found Grade 3 girls were doing better than boys at writing, as well as being more confident than boys about writing. Grade 3 girls were also doing better than boys at math, but weren't quite as confident as boys about numbers.

6   What angle did the *Globe* column pursue? It explored ways to improve girls' confidence in math—even though they were already doing better than boys in the subject. It didn't focus on the more pressing problem: helping Grade 3 boys catch up in both math and writing.

7   Lewington's column is just one small example of an education bias that drives at least one Vancouver school teacher to distraction. The teacher says many of

her colleagues, like much of the public, generally view girls as delightful, boys as trouble.

8   The teacher was at a recent conference where a female education specialist told the audience the only things boys are better at than girls is sports. As a mother of boys and a teacher, she could barely contain herself. (As a father of boys, I can also tell you this is increasingly becoming a topic among pro-feminist mothers and fathers of boys, at least those not afraid to discuss such spicy issues.)

9   It's a mug's game to try to figure out whether boys or girls are more hard-done-by today. Both are undoubtedly having a tough time, particularly because of meaner economics, higher divorce rates and greater role confusion. But girls, at least, are winning the fight for attention.

10   We see a flood of lifestyle articles about girls who lose confidence when they become adolescents.

Compares boys and girls in adolescence

11   But we see little about a similarly devastating emotional slide for boys. We hear a lot about how parents and teachers with low expectations for girls will ful-fill their own prophecies; we don't hear how the same attitude can doom boys to mediocrity or worse.

12   One of the few people to raise the alarm for boys is B.C. Teachers Federation professional development specialist Patrick Clarke. He believes the public hasn't noticed what's befallen boys because the switch has happened so fast—within the past 10 years.

13   Clarke's research has found almost 80 per cent of B.C. honor-roll students now are girls. B.C.'s education ministry also says about 60 per cent of current graduates with honors are girls (with the highest marks going to Asian girls, who, prevailing wisdom falsely argues, should be twin victims, of both their ethnicity and gender), which reverses test results of the early '80s.

Research and statistics reinforce claims

14   What's more, girls dominate school clubs and student councils. "To put it bluntly, the girls are running the place," says Clarke, who, rightly or wrongly, care-fully avoids blaming teachers or feminism for boys' crisis.

Contrasts level of participation in extra-curricular activities

15   Confirming the trend, British and Australian studies show at least one out of three boys succumbing to mass images that say the only way to glory lies in pro-fessional sports, or Beavis and Butthead-style laziness and mischief.

16   In Britain, while girls 15 to 17 are becoming more optimistic, boys are be-coming more pessimistic and introverted, suffering from low self-esteem and lack of ambition, which lead to poor study habits. A large minority of Britain's young men may be forming a new rogue under-class, writes Edward Balls in *Danger: Men Not at Work*.

Broadens scope of discussion

17   As a father of girls, Clarke says part of him recognizes that every boy who drops off the career path opens up another place for his daughters in an in-creasingly competitive marketplace. But his sense of social justice tells him he can't give in to such self-interest.

18   And while many others declare it's about time girls ruled the world, or at least the Western world (where girls' advances are far more pronounced), they might not enjoy telling that directly to a struggling 12-year-old boy. After all, he had absolutely nothing to do with centuries-old customs that confined women to nar-row roles.

Conclusion: paragraphs 18–20; recommends change in educational policy

19   While it's undeniable the top echelon of the business world is still dominated by men in suits, that doesn't mean much for boys (and the vast majority of men) who are just trying to get by, who weren't raised among the wealth and privilege that often opens the doors to such million-dollar positions. Young women are now doing fine in most professions.

20   Although it might seem shocking to some people stuck in outdated gender trenches, it could be time for affirmative-action education programs for boys similar to those that encouraged girls in the maths and sciences.

DISCUSSION QUESTIONS

1. Identify the thesis statement. Why do you think it is located where it is?

2. Consider colloquialisms such as the word "crummy" as Todd declares "it's a troublesome, even crummy, time to be a boy" (paragraph 4). What other examples of colloquialisms or slang can you find? Given that this article was originally written for a newspaper, comment on how Todd can use such an informal, casual writing style without losing authority.

3. How does the writer support his claim that girls are now "winning the fight for attention" (paragraph 9)?

4. How is the writer careful to qualify his argument by acknowledging the problems that females have faced? What does he mean when he refers to "outdated gender trenches" (paragraph 20)?

TOWARD KEY INSIGHTS

To what extent do you think that the problems for boys that Todd alludes to may be an inevitable result of feminist gains? What disturbing implications about gender equity are raised by this article?

Do you agree that for many boys today, "the only way to glory lies in professional sports, or Beavis-and-Butthead-style laziness and mischief" (paragraph 15)? Why or why not?

In your view, what different issues do males and females face in adolescence?

What do you think of Todd's suggestion that it could be time "for affirmative-action education programs for boys" (paragraph 20)?

SUGGESTION FOR WRITING

Drawing from your own experience, compare and contrast the treatment of males and females in a specific context such as sports or a specific sport, a place of employment, the news media, or Hollywood.

Nancy Masterson Sakamoto

Conversational Ballgames

Nancy Masterson Sakamoto graduated Phi Beta Kappa from UCLA with a degree in English. Married to a Japanese artist and Buddhist priest, she lived in Japan for twenty-four years before moving with her husband and two sons to Honolulu in 1982. While in Japan, she was visiting professor at the University of Osaka. She gave in-service training to Japanese junior and senior high school English teachers and talks on intercultural topics, both in English and in Japanese, to various business, educational, and women's groups. In addition to her book, Polite Fictions: Why Japanese and Americans Seem Rude to Each Other, *still used as a textbook in Japanese universities, she coauthored a research project report sponsored by the Japanese Ministry of Education and wrote various articles for Japanese English-teaching publications. In Hawaii, she has been a speaker and seminar leader for many educational, business, and professional organizations. Her current position is professor of American Studies, Shitennoji Gakuen University (Hawaii branch). In this essay, she discusses the divergent conversational styles of Americans and Japanese, just one example of the many differences that distinguish different cultures.*

1   After I was married and had lived in Japan for a while, my Japanese gradually improved to the point where I could take part in simple conversations with my husband and his friends and family. And I began to notice that often, when I joined in, the others would look startled, and the conversational topic would come to a halt. After this happened several times, it became clear to me that l was doing something wrong. But for a long time, I didn't know what it was.

2   Finally, after listening carefully to many Japanese conversations, I discovered what my problem was. Even though I was speaking Japanese, I was handling the conversation in a western way.

3   Japanese-style conversations develop quite differently from western-style conversations. And the difference isn't only in the languages. I realized that just as I kept trying to hold western-style conversations even when I was speaking Japanese, so my English students kept trying to hold Japanese-style conversations even when they were speaking English. We were unconsciously playing entirely different conversational ballgames.

4   A western-style conversation between two people is like a game of tennis. If I introduce a topic, a conversational ball, I expect you to hit it back. If you agree with me, I don't expect you simply to agree and do nothing more. I expect you to add something—a reason for agreeing, another example, or an elaboration to carry the idea further. But I don't expect you always to agree. I am just as happy if you question me, or challenge me, or completely disagree with me. Whether you agree or disagree, your response will return the ball to me.

5   And then it is my turn again. I don't serve a new ball from my original starting line. I hit your ball back again from where it has bounced. I carry your idea further, or answer your questions or objections, or challenge or question you. And so the ball goes back and forth, with each of us doing our best to give it a new twist, an original spin, or a powerful smash.

6   And the more vigorous the action, the more interesting and exciting the game. Of course, if one of us gets angry, it spoils the conversation, just as it spoils a tennis game. But getting excited is not always the same as getting angry. After all,

we are not trying to hit each other. We are trying to hit the ball. So long as we attack only each other's opinions, and do not attack each other personally, we don't expect anyone to get hurt. A good conversation is supposed to be interesting and exciting.

7   If there are more than two people in the conversation, then it is like doubles in tennis, or like volleyball. There's no waiting in line. Whoever is nearest and quickest hits the ball, and if you step back, someone else will hit it. No one stops the game to give you a turn. You're responsible for taking your own turn.

8   But whether it's two players or a group, everyone does his best to keep the ball going, and no one person has the ball for very long.

9   A Japanese-style conversation, however, is not at all like tennis or volleyball. It's like bowling. You wait for your turn. And you always know your place in line. It depends on such things as whether you are older or younger, a close friend or a relative stranger to the previous speaker, in a senior or junior position, and so on.

10   When your turn comes, you step up to the starting line with your bowling ball, and carefully bowl it. Everyone else stands back and watches politely, murmuring encouragement. Everyone waits until the ball has reached the end of the alley, and watches to see if it knocks down all the pins, or only some of them, or none of them. There is a pause, while everyone registers your score.

11   Then, after everyone is sure that you have completely finished your turn, the next person in line steps up to the same starting line, with a different ball. He doesn't return your ball, and he does not begin from where your ball stopped. There is no back and forth at all. All the balls run parallel. And there is always a suitable pause between turns. There is no rush, no excitement, no scramble for the ball.

12   No wonder everyone looked startled when I took part in Japanese conversations. I paid no attention to whose turn it was, and kept snatching the ball halfway down the alley and throwing it back to the bowler. Of course the conversation died. I was playing the wrong game.

13   This explains why it is almost impossible to get a western-style conversation or discussion going with English students in Japan. I used to think that the problem was their lack of English language ability. But I finally came to realize that the biggest problem is that they, too, are playing the wrong game.

14   Whenever I serve a volleyball, everyone just stands back and watches it fall, with occasional murmurs of encouragement. No one hits it back. Everyone waits until I call on someone to take a turn. And when that person speaks, he doesn't hit my ball back. He serves a new ball. Again, everyone just watches it fall.

15   So I call on someone else. This person does not refer to what the previous speaker has said. He also serves a new ball. Nobody seems to have paid any attention to what anyone else has said. Everyone begins again from the same starting line, and all the balls run parallel. There is never any back and forth. Everyone is trying to bowl with a volleyball.

16   And if I try a simpler conversation, with only two of us, then the other person tries to bowl with my tennis ball. No wonder foreign English teachers in Japan get discouraged.

17   Now that you know about the difference in the conversational ballgames, you may think that all your troubles are over. But if you have been trained all your life to play one game, it is no simple matter to switch to another, even if you know the rules. Knowing the rules is not at all the same thing as playing the game.

18   Even now, during a conversation in Japanese I will notice a startled reaction, and belatedly realize that once again I have rudely interrupted by instinctively trying to hit back the other person's bowling ball. It is no easier for me

to "just listen" during a conversation, than it is for my Japanese students to "just relax" when speaking with foreigners. Now I can truly sympathize with how hard they must find it to try to carry on a Western-style conversation.

19   If I have not yet learned to do conversational bowling in Japanese, at least I have figured out one thing that puzzled me for a long time. After his first trip to America, my husband complained that Americans asked him so many questions and made him talk so much at the dinner table that he never had a chance to eat. When I asked him why he couldn't talk and eat at the same time, he said that Japanese do not customarily think that dinner, especially on fairly formal occasions, is a suitable time for extended conversation.

20   Since westerners think that conversation is an indispensable part of dining, and indeed would consider it impolite not to converse with one's dinner partner, I found this Japanese custom rather strange. Still, I could accept it as a cultural difference even though I didn't really understand it. But when my husband added, in explanation, that Japanese consider it extremely rude to talk with one's mouth full, I got confused. Talking with one's month full is certainly not an American custom. We think it very rude, too. Yet we still manage to talk a lot and eat at the same time. How do we do it?

21   For a long time, I couldn't explain it, and it bothered me. But after I discovered the conversational ballgames, I finally found the answer. Of course! In a western-style conversation, you hit the ball, and while someone else is hitting it back, you take a bite, chew and swallow. Then you hit the ball again, and then eat some more. The more people there are in the conversation, the more chances you have to eat. But even with only two of you talking, you still have plenty of chances to eat.

22   Maybe that's why polite conversation at the dinner table has never been a traditional part of Japanese etiquette. Your turn to talk would last so long without interruption that you'd never get a chance to eat.

Discussion Questions

1. Sakamoto notes in paragraph 1 that she "had lived in Japan for a while" and in paragraph 2 that she has listened "carefully to many Japanese conversations." Why does she note these facts at the outset of her essay?

2. What purpose is served by the first two sentences of paragraph 3?

3. Why do you think Sakamoto uses various games—tennis, volleyball, bowling—to help explain the differences between American and Japanese conversational styles?

4. Point out specific supporting details that help make this comparison successful.

5. For what audience is Sakamoto writing? Refer to the essay when answering.

6. Sakamoto ends paragraph 17 with the assertion that "Knowing the rules is not at all the same thing as playing the game." Explain what she means.

Toward Key Insights

In what ways other than conversational style might cultures exhibit pronounced differences?

What problems might these differences create, and how can we best deal with them?

SUGGESTIONS FOR WRITING *Write a paper that explores a misunderstanding between you and someone else that arose because of a difference in cultures, generations, or outlooks.*

If you have come to Canada from another country or are familiar with the customs of another culture, compare and contrast two different kinds of cultural values or attitudes in a specific area: dating, gift-giving, teacher/student relationships, entertaining, etc.

Trevor Herriot

Generation unto Regeneration

Trevor Herriot is an accomplished prairie naturalist, illustrator, and writer. His award-winning book, River in a Dry Land, *is a personal reflection on life and landscape in the Qu'Appelle Valley, where he grew up. As is evident in "Generation unto Regeneration," Trevor Herriot's respect and enthusiasm for people and the natural environment is a prominent feature of his writing.*

1   Yesterday, 90-kilometre-per-hour winds blew glacial loess onto my desk through a crack in the window but this afternoon the rain has finally come. For the first time this spring, the kale and lettuce in my front-yard patch will be plunging root hairs into moisture that has come from the skies instead of the city's water system.

2   The need for rain has lately become something urban and rural people in Saskatchewan can agree upon, though we have more in common than we generally admit. To be a thoroughgoing urbanite in even the largest cities of this, the most rural of provinces, one has to go out of one's way to cultivate the illusion.

3   I live in central Regina, where I can walk downtown in 20 minutes or turn the other way and walk to fields on the western outskirts in 15 minutes. (I clocked myself the other day: 12 minutes from my front porch to the first meadowlark song.) Most of us living here grew up on farms, in villages, or on reserves, yet we talk about one another—urban and rural—as though we still had walls to keep the pagans at bay.

4   Our disprivileging of rural people is at least that old: Pagan, from the Latin paganus, means "of the country." It entered our lexicon when Christianity, a persecuted cult on the fringes of the Roman polis, snuck past the walls of civilization to become the Church of Emperors. When the marginal make it to the centre, their first act is to declare a new margin.

5   In this city, our "pagan" roots surface now and then, no matter how long we've lived away from the farm. You meet people here who garden by the moon and the fuzz on caterpillars. Office and government employees commonly give up vacation days each spring and fall to help with seeding and harvest on a relative's farm.

6   And when conversation shifts from the weather to the latest blow to rural community, stories and opinions come easily. Some are damning, others compassionate; most are discouraging, some manage to console.

7   "We might be the last generation of people who will remember days spent killing and plucking geese to make a feather tick." This from a friend, Joanne, who moved to Regina decades ago from the village of Limerick in south-central Saskatchewan.

8   I was suggesting that, as the rural economy slips, community-building skills and traditional lifeways become all the more vital. I asked how Limerick was getting by. In reply she told me about the system they use to keep community events going—fairs, weddings, funerals, feasts and dinners of all kinds.

9   The village's families, about 150 people, are divided into four work groups, and they do all the catering and organizing on a rotation, apportioning the labour among three of the groups. The fourth group gets a break and then at the next event it cycles to the "A" position responsible for the main load of work—cooking the food.

10   I had to ask the urban question: What if someone doesn't want to help? There isn't really any choice, she said. If you want to be well regarded and included in the community, you participate. The system finds a way for everyone to help; even young men are in there pinching perogies and basting turkeys.

11   Older citizens, like Joanne's father, 81 and long retired from active farming, have their role too in maintaining the well-being of Limerick. People are holding onto their cash more than ever in rural areas, but a fundraiser who has local knowledge and the respect of his neighbours can charm, beg, guilt and cajole enough money out of savings accounts and mattresses to bring almost any community dream into the light of day. Con, as Joanne's father is known throughout the district, has been Limerick's chief arm-twister until poor health recently forced him to quit.

12   A modest man, he won't stand up in front of a small gathering of family and neighbours to receive community service awards (Joanne suspects he has them mail the certificate), but as a fundraiser he'll wade in where others fear to tread, pin the most parsimonious of old bachelors against the wall and talk them into donating to the rink-building fund. "What do I want a rink for?" they'd say. "I ain't got kids or even a niece or a nephew to use it." Con's reply: "That doesn't matter. You live here, don't you?"

13   A simple notion that, but it works because Con and everyone else in Limerick knows that to live in a place is to be responsible for its welfare. Forgetting that truth, I will admit, is easier here in the city, where we protect the Prairie polis with walls made of all we choose to forget: that the country surrounds the city and not the reverse, that a civilization's social and spiritual renewal almost always comes from the margins, and that we ourselves are marginal and therefore more pagan than Roman. Perhaps worst of all, we forget that to keep a culture vital, its seed stock of lifeways must be resown in situ in the new soil of each generation.

14   Thomas Cahill has argued, convincingly I think, that after Rome fell Western civilization was saved by a few Roman-educated monks living among Celtic pagans just beyond the reach of the empire. When our current dispensation finally goes the way of all empires, the seeds that will keep our cultural practices, subsistence skills, and communal values alive will come from places far from the centre where pagans and Romans have been quietly mixing and planting their lifeways, sowing the old amongst the new.

15   A new day now and my garden is consoled by the rain, as I am by the thought of people living in places as far-flung as Limerick who still know how to get things done.

16   And one of them, bless his soul, is named Constantine, after the Roman emperor who let the Christians into the city in the first place.

DISCUSSION QUESTIONS

1. Why does the writer emphasize his position as an urban person in a primarily rural setting (see paragraphs 1–3, 5, and 10)? How might his perspective be different if he had never moved to a city, or if he had never lived in the country? What similarities and differences between rural and city people are suggested? Can you locate other, less obvious examples of comparison in these paragraphs?

2. What is the significance of the writer's references to "pagans" and to ancient Roman civilization (paragraphs 3–5, 13, 16)? Explain what the author means when he says, "When the marginal make it to the centre, their first act is to declare a new margin"(paragraph 4).

3. Why does the writer zero in on one community member, the older citizen named Con (paragraphs 11–13, 16)?

4. Identify the thesis statement, and speculate about why you think it comes so late in the essay (paragraph 13).

5. Explain how the title could be read in more than one way. Find examples of references, whether stated or implied, to the idea of "generation" or "generations" in the essay. Where does the writer use images or metaphors from farm life?

TOWARD KEY INSIGHTS

If you have experienced life on a farm or in a small village, how much of this essay can you identify with? If you have lived only in cities, what is your response to this portrait of rural life?

What is your view of the argument that as rural and village life falters, "community-building skills" become increasingly important?

What experiences have you had of community-building events or customs, and how are they similar to, or different from, the ones described in the essay?

SUGGESTIONS FOR WRITING

Reflect on two different cultures or ways of life (urban/rural; working class/middle class; East/West, etc.) you may have experienced. Write an essay that compares and contrasts the different perspectives on community, or nature, or a particular custom associated with each culture.

Compare this essay with either "Memories of Montreal" (page 391) or "The Quiet of the Backstretch" (page 397) in order to show how different writers convey regret for lost values of community and tradition.

Perry Jensen

Lament for the Short and Stubby

Perry Jensen is a former journalist who now makes his living as a corporate communicator in the financial services industry. He still writes humorous, opinionated freelance articles from time to time. Perry lives with his wife, child, and cat in Toronto and now drinks beer from a mug. Jensen's humorous essay "Lament for the Short and Stubby," which compares the long-necked beer bottle and the stubby one of yesteryear, could be used as a jumping-off place for discussing Canadian identity, commodification, or American influences on Canadian trends.

1   A lot of people have theories as to just when this country peaked and started its inexorable slide into the sorry, divided state we find ourselves in today. My father's pet belief was that 1967 was the year we peaked. And it makes some sense: kids singing that obnoxious confederation ode *Canada* (pronounced "Caaaa-naaah-daaaah") from coast to coast, the French placated by Expo, the Leafs winning the Stanley Cup, our dollar strong and our deficit just a gleam in soon-to-be-dictator Pierre's eye.

2   However, with apologies to the old man, I think the real moment of truth came several years later, with the introduction of the long-necked beer bottle. Thus began our long descent from happy, unified mediocrity into squabbling tribalism, for this was the beginning of the end of our national brew dispenser—the stubby beer bottle.

3   For those readers too young to remember this precious symbol of our national character, an explanation: The stubby was for many years the only acceptable container for our national drink. Taking a leaf from Henry Ford, who once said you could have your car in any colour you wanted, so long as it was black, our major brewers (Molson's, Labatt and Carling O'Keefe) decreed that all beers would be sold in the same interchangeable package.

4   And what a package! The bottle was short enough so that a 24-pack fit snugly at your side held by one hand angled up into your body, or on the average man's shoulder. Try that with a crate of long-necks if you're under 6 foot 3 and you'll soon be buckling from the discomfort of the awkwardly designed load.

5   The stoutness of the bottle was another advantage. Try this experiment. Get out an old stubby, if you're lucky enough to still have one of the little darlings, and a long-neck. Place them on a table in front of you; then, simulating the effects of one brew too many, drop your head to the table with a crash. Do it as many times as you want (well, not too often; the world has enough *Sun* readers) and the result will be the same. Mr. Long-neck will flop over like a bowling pin and, unless you've got a head on you like a tenpin blowing ball, Mr. Stubby will still be standing proud, if not tall.

6   Stubby was unpretentious. No glamour, all function. Stubby was egalitarian. Millionaire or mooch, you got your brew in a stubby. Moms even liked stubby because its short, air-trapping neck occasionally encouraged you to pour beer into a glass.

7   So what killed off the stubby? As you might have guessed, it started with the Yanks and the international rise of the Yuppie. First came the introduction of Miller into the Canadian market. Miller, like most American suds, is vile, over-carbonated bilge water. But, hey, said the average trendy, it comes in a neat bottle

with—gasp—a long neck. Pretty soon, the lumber-like flavour of Budweiser was also being extolled by packs of taste-challenged know-nothings who really fell in love with its Americanized dispenser.

8   The worst thing about this? The alien American bottles were invited into the country by our own brewers, the very people who should have been guarding our gates. Sure we'd had some regional differences before. Who can forget the famed quart bottles in Quebec of their souped-up Brador with its 6.2-percent alcohol blast? But by and large, we were united from coast to coast: Whether we drank Export or 50, Blue or Canadian, O'Keefe Ale or Golden, it came out of a stubby.

9   Today, that unity is gone forever. People drink out of long-necks, aluminum cans, kegs of all sizes, even—oh, the horror—plastic jugs.

10   And it's not just the variety of dispensers that has increased exponentially. Go to the beer store and check out the brands. Foreign beers formerly exiled to the LCBO are taking up shelf space once proudly occupied by Canadian brews. Does Don Cherry know about this? Foreign beers, dry beers, light beers, ice beers, wheat beers, red beers, dark beers and micro brews have divided this once-great nation into hundreds of different little groups. At times it seems there's a brand per Canadian, even though they often taste so similar it's reminiscent of the classic *Simpsons* episode where Duff, Duff Light and Duff Dry flow from three spigots connected to one pipe.

11   Time to take a stand, Canada. Let's demand the return of our national beer bottle, the stubby, and refuse to drink from foreign containers until the brewers come crawling on their hands and knees. However, in typically Canadian fashion, we must not be too radical: drinking jugs of draft will be allowed, nay encouraged, during this great Canadian protest.

Discussion Questions

1. What does Jensen accomplish in his first two paragraphs? Who is "the old man" referred to in paragraph 2? What is the connection between the first two paragraphs and the rest of the essay?

2. How does the writer move easily from one paragraph to another? Examine the first sentence in paragraphs 3 through 11, and explain how the writer uses bridges, or transitions, from one paragraph to the next.

3. What is the point of the experiment described in paragraph 5? What is the effect of the writer's personification of the two beer bottles as "Mr. Stubby" and "Mr. Long-neck"?

4. What details does the writer use to contrast the stubby bottle and the long-neck bottle (paragraphs 4, 5, 7)? How does the writer move into a contrast between foreign and Canadian beers (paragraphs 7, 8, and 10) without moving away from his main focus?

5. Why does the writer suddenly, in paragraph 10, ask whether Don Cherry knows about the foreign beers in Canadian markets? What is the effect of the allusion to the *Simpsons* episode in this paragraph? Does it matter if you know who Don Cherry is, or if you have seen the TV episode the writer refers to? Why or why not?

6. Why does the writer address Canada in the last paragraph? What does the writer mean by the last sentence? What is the tone here? Does the essay have a serious point, or is it written simply to entertain? Explain.

TOWARD KEY INSIGHTS

How does the short, stubby beer bottle function here as a Canadian symbol? What characteristics of the bottle does the writer associate with Canada at its best?

What products or services, if any, seem uniquely Canadian to you? Are there any that you remember from childhood that are no longer available? Explain.

Jensen implies that Canadians might well regret the ways in which Canadian products have been lost to global and American market influences. To what extent do you agree with the implied argument?

SUGGESTION FOR WRITING

Write a comparison essay that emphasizes the advantages of one type of product over another, at the same time suggesting a larger point. You might compare and/or contrast a Canadian product with an American one, or one that you remember from your childhood with one that is available today.

Cause and Effect

Deborah Tannen

Gender Gap in Cyberspace[*]

Deborah Tannnen (born 1945) earned a B.S. degree from the State University of New York in 1966 and a Ph.D. from the University of California in 1979. She is now a member of the linguistics department of Georgetown University. Tannen has authored a number of books on speaking and writing as well as numerous shorter pieces that have appeared in the New York Times, Newsweek, People, *and the* Harvard Business Review. *In this section, Tannen investigates the causes and effects of the differing male and female attitudes toward e-mail.*

1   I was a computer pioneer, but I'm still something of a novice. That paradox is telling.

2   I was the second person on my block to get a computer. The first was my colleague Ralph. It was 1980. Ralph got a Radio Shack TRS-80, I got a used Apple II+. He helped me get started and went on to become a maven, reading computer magazines, hungering for the new technology he read about, and buying and mastering it as quickly as he could afford. I hung on to old equipment far too long <u>because</u> I dislike giving up what I'm used to, fear making the wrong decision about what to buy, and resent the time it takes to install and learn a new system.

3   My first Apple came with videogames; I gave them away. Playing games on the computer didn't interest me. If I had free time I'd spend it talking on the telephone to friends.

4   Ralph got hooked. His wife was often annoyed by the hours he spent at his computer and the money he spent upgrading it. My marriage had no such strains—until I discovered E-mail. Then I got hooked. E-mail draws me the same way the phone does: it's a souped-up conversation.

| Introduction gives background narrative |
| Word "because" signals causes |
| Effects of E-mail on marriage |

---

5   <u>E-mail deepened my friendship with Ralph</u>. Though his office was next to mine, we rarely had extended conversations because he is shy. Face to face he mumbled so, I could barely tell he was speaking. But when we both got on E-mail, I started receiving long, self-revealing messages: we poured our hearts out to each other. A friend discovered that E-mail opened up that kind of communication with her father. He would never talk much on the phone (as her mother would), but <u>they have become close since they both got on line</u>.

Examples of effects of E-mail on male/female relationships

6   Why, I wondered, would some men find it easier to open up on E-mail? It's a combination of the technology (which they enjoy) and the obliqueness of the written word, just as many men will reveal feelings in dribs and drabs while riding in the car or doing something, which they'd never talk about sitting face to face. It's too intense, too bearing-down on them, and once you start you have to keep going. With a computer in between, it's safer.

Cause and effect

7   <u>It was on E-mail, in fact, that I described to Ralph how boys in groups often struggle to get the upper hand whereas girls tend to maintain an appearance of co-operation</u>. And he pointed out that this explained why <u>boys are more likely to be captivated by computers than girls are</u>. Boys are typically motivated by a social structure that says if you don't dominate you will be dominated. Computers, by their nature, balk; you type a perfectly appropriate command and it refuses to do what it should. Many boys and men are incited by this defiance: "I'm going to whip this into line and teach it who's boss! I'll get it to do what I say! (and if they work hard enough, they always can). Girls and women are more likely to respond, "This thing won't cooperate. Get it away from me!"

Topic sentence sets up contrast

Central idea

Cause and effect blended

8   Although no one wants to think of herself as "typical"—how much nicer to be *sui generis*—my relationship to my computer is—gulp—fairly typical for a woman. Most women (with plenty of exceptions) aren't excited by tinkering with the technology, grappling with the challenge of eliminating bugs or getting the biggest and best computer. These dynamics appeal to many men's interest in making sure they're on the top side of the inevitable who's-up-who's-down struggle that life is for them. E-mail appeals to my view of life as a contest for connections to others. When I see that I have fifteen messages, I feel loved.

Causes (reasons for) computer appeal

9   I once posted a technical question on a computer network for linguists and was flooded with long dispositions, some pages long. I was staggered by the generosity and the expertise, but wondered where these guys found the time—and why all the answers I got were from men.

10   Like coed classrooms and meetings, discussions on E-mail networks tend to be dominated by male voices, unless they're specifically women-only, like single-sex schools. On line, women don't have to worry about getting the floor (you just send a message when you feel like it) but, according to linguists Susan Herring and Laurel Sutton, who have studied this, they have the usual problems of having their messages ignored or attacked. The anonymity of public networks frees a small number of men to send long, vituperative, sarcastic messages that many other men either can tolerate or actually enjoy, but that turn most women off.

Effects of networks on men and women

11   The anonymity of networks leads to another sad part of the E-mail story: there are men who deluge women with questions about their appearance and invitations to sex. On college campuses, as soon as women students log on, they are bombarded by references to sex, like going to work and finding pornographic posters adorning the walls.

12   Most women want one thing front a computer—to work. This is significant counterevidence to the claim that men want to focus on information while women are interested in support. That claim I found was most often true in

casual conversation, in which there is no particular information to be conveyed. But with computers, it is often women who are more focused on information, because they don't respond to the challenge of getting equipment to submit.

| Topic sentence indicates effects |

13   <u>Once I had learned the basics, my interest in computers waned</u>. I use it to write books (though I never mastered having it do bibliographies or tables of contents) and write checks (but not balance my checkbook). Much as I'd like to use it to do more, I begrudge the time it would take to learn.

| Effects of computer expertise |

14   Ralph's computer expertise costs him a lot of time. Chivalry requires that he rescue novices in need, and he is called upon by damsel novices far more often than knaves. More men would rather study the instruction booklet than ask directions, as it were, from another person. "When I do help men," Ralph wrote (on E-mail, of course), "they want to be more involved. I once installed a hard drive for a guy, and he wanted to be there with me, wielding the screwdriver and giving his own advice where he could." Women, he finds, usually are not interested in what he's doing; they just want him to get the computer to the point where they can do what they want.

| Conclusion comes full circle |

15   Which pretty much explains how I managed to be a pioneer without becoming an expert.

DISCUSSION QUESTIONS

1. Does Tannen deal with causes, effects, or both? Refer to the essay when answering.
2. Characterize the level of diction in this essay.
3. Why do you think Tannen cites the two linguists in paragraph 10?
4. Point out the connecting devices that link the paragraphs in this essay.
5. Does your experience in cyberspace bear out Tannen's assertion about a gender gap? Discuss, citing specific examples.

TOWARD KEY INSIGHTS

How do you account for the differences that Tannen describes? Do you believe that they are inborn or stem mainly from cultural patterns?

What steps might be taken to reduce these differences?

SUGGESTION FOR WRITING

Write an essay exploring how gender affects dating done through the Internet. Support your answers.

Kristine Nyhout

Send in the Clowns

Kristine Nyhout is a freelance writer living in London, Ontario. She frequently writes on family issues, particularly the joys and challenges of raising a special-needs child. "Send in the Clowns" traces the physical and emotional benefits of laughter in a highly accessible essay that could well serve as a model of simplicity and clarity.

1   You exercise, eat the right foods and take vitamins. If you really want to stay healthy, try laughing more each day. It may sound silly, but health professionals are taking laughter seriously and using it to help people heal. Twenty years ago, the best-seller *Anatomy of an Illness* inspired the first research. When author Norman Cousins was diagnosed with a rare arthritis-like disease, he refused to accept pain as a fact of life. With his physician's approval, he checked in to a hotel and watched funny movies. He timed the effects: a belly laugh kept pain at bay for two hours. Now mainstream scientists are investigating humor's effects on health: it's no joke because jocularity has real psychological and physiological effects—from reducing stress to affecting production of hormones.

2   So the next time you visit a hospital, you may well see a red-nosed therapeutic clown or humor specialist—health professionals trained to get laughs—among white-coated doctors. Comedy carts filled with doses of satirical verse or slapstick films roll down the corridors. Consultants even bring the comedy preventive to workplace wellness seminars—apparently laughter also boosts creativity and productivity. Regina therapist Catherine Ripplinger Fenwick recognized the importance of humor when she battled breast cancer eight years ago. "I didn't laugh enough." She outfitted herself with a laughter first aid kit, took up clowning during her chemotherapy, and noticed the "wows" of life. Now she lectures government employees and others in the benefits of mirth.

3   Bringing humor into hospital helps defuse patient anxiety and change attitudes. One of the new healing clowns, registered nurse Dee Preikschas of Kitchener, Ont., tuned in to humor's healing power when her husband became ill. Now she's one of a number of therapeutic clowns in Canada who often work with children. Once Preikschas was dispatched to the bedside of a 10-year-old boy recovering from an appendectomy—he hated his IV and wasn't eating. By giving the kid a "magic" hammer that made a smashing noise at the offending IV, the clown got the boy to laugh—and cooperate. Clowns also bring comfort. Joy Van Herwaarde, who calls herself Joybells when she's clowning, says, "Humor can make someone less aware of the pain and can make them feel less lonely." Indeed, when a 101-year-old woman at Good Samaritan Hospital in Edmonton neared death, she asked for Joybells's brand of comfort. In Hamilton, Ont., nurse Sharon Orovan is using and studying humor to fend off panic attacks.

4   Humor also packs a physical punch. A sort of pharmacist of silliness, humor specialist Barbara Wetmore-Patel of London, Ont., dispenses videos and joke books from her comedy cart. How does it work? The laughing response can lower both heart rate and blood pressure, increase T-cell activity to fend off illness, and may improve digestion. Wetmore-Patel has seen how humor helps seniors in retirement homes and palliative care hospitals feel better physically. Laughing may release endorphins—chemicals in the brain responsible for the feeling of well-being known as runner's high—into the bloodstream, taking the edge off pain.

5   What's more, laughter may actually help keep you from getting sick. When you laugh, an antibody called immunoglobulin A travels from the bloodstream to the salivary glands where it blocks viruses from their usual port of entry, explains Herb Lefcourt, a psychology professor at the University of Waterloo. Lefcourt's research found that people who used humor more in their daily lives had higher levels of immunoglobulin A in their saliva. And when your body is under stress (as in a fight-or-flight confrontation), your immune system is suppressed. Lefcourt found humor defuses that state of arousal, allowing the immune system to continue doing its job.

6   Laughter can also lead to deeper breathing and relaxed muscles, according to physiologist David Garlick at the University of New South Wales in Sydney, Australia. Tense muscles can mean increased heart rate and blood pressure. Adrenaline levels and mental stress may also go up, Garlick adds. You may not be able to meditate during a meeting, but as Garlick points out, "Laughter is the usual way of helping to relieve muscle tension."

7   You don't have to be a stand-up comic to reap the health benefits of a chuckle—just look on the light side of life.

DISCUSSION QUESTIONS

1. Study the introductory paragraph and the concluding paragraph. What is the relationship between these two paragraphs? Identify the thesis statement. Where do you find out that the essay will focus on effects?

2. Identify five or six positive effects of laughter that are discussed in paragraphs 2–6.

3. How are paragraphs 4, 5, and 6 related? On what basis did the writer make the decision to separate these paragraphs?

4. What examples, or brief anecdotes, does the writer use to illustrate the benefits of laughter?

5. While this essay focuses on the effects of laughter, it also has a persuasive, or argumentative, slant. What strategies does the writer use to persuade you that laughter is beneficial for health? Why do you suppose the writer does not cite statistics to strengthen her argument?

TOWARD KEY INSIGHTS

To what extent do you agree with Kristine Nyhout that physical health and emotional health may be related?

Can a person decide to seek out opportunities for laughter? Why or why not?

How can humour help with other stressful situations besides physical illness? Are there ever times when humour could strike the wrong note?

SUGGESTION FOR WRITING

Interview three or four people who are knowledgeable about some aspect of health, and write an essay persuading your reader of the positive effects of a specific healthful practice, such as weight lifting, vegetarian eating, or meditation. Explain the benefits with short anecdotes, examples, and quotations from your interviewees.

Allen Abel

Sweet Nothings

Allen Abel is the author of three books and has been an on-air host for the CBC. He has also received the National Newspaper Award. Abel's article "Sweet Nothings," which first appeared in Saturday Night *magazine, shows how damaging patronizing language, referred to as "Elderspeak," may be to senior citizens. Students may be surprised to learn that social stereotyping may be quite subtle, and may even stem from good intentions. The essay could easily be paired with another essay in the book that brings up issues related to stages of life: "The Sweet Bird of Youth Is Showing Signs of Age."*

1   Somewhere between ambition and extinction, between Whitman's "exquisite realization of health" and Browning's "last of life, for which the first was made," stretches a shifting, invisible frontier—the boundary of old age.

2   On one side of this customs house, we stockpile growth and advancement; on the other, we store retreat and decline. We assume that those who cross the border can never reverse their journey, and that, once beyond it, they have entered the realm of darkness. A look, a shrug, a word is enough to hold them there, for they are old and helpless, and we are young and strong. Both sides are complicit in the game—a conspiracy of shunning and surrender.

3   "There is a global time when old age happens," a much younger woman tells me. "It may happen when you move into a nursing home. It may be when you are already in the nursing home and they move you onto the full-time-care floor. It may be when you are retiring, or after a heart attack or a stroke, or when your spouse dies.

4   "When this happens, you ask yourself, 'How is it going to be now?' You look in the social mirror and the social mirror says, 'You are old.' The negative stereotype is so ingrained that, if there's any decline at all, we assume that this is the new you."

5   "Why are we so afraid of old people?" I ask.

6   "It is our cultural fear of death," Dr. Ellen Bouchard Ryan replies. "In the nursing home, and within the family, there is a fear of ageing and the aged that creates a distance between the old and the young. Our behaviour and our language perpetuate this distance. But the irony is, most of the diminishment of old people's competence is done with a nurturing intent."

7   Dr. Ryan's life's work is the study of how the way we talk to the old helps make them old. (Within her academic discipline, the condescending, exaggerated baby talk often used with older adults is known as "elderspeak.") She is a professor of psychology at McMaster University in Hamilton, Ontario, and one of Canada's foremost gerontologists. Her ancestry on the Bouchard side can be traced back to eighth-century France. One of her Québécois progenitors sailed with Champlain. She has an uncle named Lucien. (But not *that* Lucien.)

8   "There are things we do to be nice to dear old people that aren't good for them," she says, summarizing nearly twenty years of work in one sentence. Then she immediately retracts the word "dear."

9   Ryan's research papers are unequivocal: terms such as *dearie* and *sweetie;* patronizing directives (*Shall we get our pants on?; Let's get you into bed*); commands (*Move it, lady*); and even praise (*Good girl!*) can ravage an older person's self-esteem as surely as a fractured hip. Non-verbal communication can be just as damaging—family members rolling their eyes as Grandmother begins to tell yet another story about the Dirty Thirties; a restaurant server asking the youngest person at the table what the oldest will have to eat.

10   The academic investigators of elderspeak pepper their papers with microscopic dissections of intergenerational conversations that count "left-branching clauses" and "repetitions per utterance" and "percentage of Long Words." Researchers pair student and senior volunteers, record the interactions, and count the *honeys* and *sweeties* and *dearies.*

11   The scholars' conclusions are hardly surprising. In one journal article, Dr. Ryan announces that "stereotyped expectations about elderly adults' cognitive decline" can create "a self-fulfilling prophecy." Passivity continues the downward spiral, she writes.

12   "Just when you need extra encouragement to stay active, society encourages you to lie down and rest," Dr. Ryan says. "If we are young, and we're having a really good day and somebody puts us down, we react by saying 'That person has a problem.' But when we're vulnerable, those comments go deep down."

13   "Older people *know* that old age is going to hit. They know the face of the person in the mirror is ageing, but they don't *feel* like that person. They use expressions such as 'Those old people in the nursing homes.' But then, on a bad day, they forget where their car is parked in the lot at the mall. Or they want to introduce someone and they forget that person's first name and then they suddenly feel old.

14   "It's like hearing yourself in a tape recorder for the first time—it's a different voice. Suddenly, it's not you. You're hurt, and then you start to get this negative feedback from society. The older person thinks, 'I know I need a hearing aid but I don't want to wear one. I *know* I need a cane but [then] when I go in a shop, the clerk will call me Dearie.'

15   "The problem in the nursing home," Dr. Ryan says, "is that the staff tend to give off so many clues that the older person is not competent—'I'm in control and you're not'—and for people who may have few other adult contacts, that has a tremendously debilitating effect.

16   "But when I talk to service providers about this, they *line up* to defend themselves. They say, 'I'm communicating to them that I love them.' Then it sort of dawns on them that they wouldn't like it either."

17   "What should service providers do?" I inquire.

18   "*Listen!*" the professor replies.

19   "I have heard it many times in the hospital," a seventy-eight-year-old fireball named Katie Allen tells me. "'*Put this leg in your pants, darling.' 'Come on, dear, we'd better go to bed now.'* Well, I think you get what you deserve. I never let it slide, not even *once.*"

20   Katie Allen is the founder of a group of older memoirists who meet every other Tuesday at the police station in Dundas, Ontario, and call themselves Writer's Cramp. When I meet her at her home in a wide spot in the road called, aptly, Copetown, she has just finished firing off an e-mail message to the president of the

United States. She and her associates, some of whom take part in Dr. Ryan's studies of young-old speech patterns, do not intend to go gently.

21   "You're *letting* them patronize you," she asserts. "Older people should make it plain that they are *not* children. They're *adults* and capable of doing it themselves—and even if they're *not* capable, they shouldn't be talked down to. I'm aggressive enough *not* to be put down. I *don't* accept it. I tell them, 'I am *not* your sweetie, sir.'"

22   Unprompted, she begins to quote Browning: "Grow old along with me, the best is yet to be . . . "

23   "What should older people do?" I ask.

24   "Get *out* of the damn rocking chair and *quit* watching TV."

25   On August 13, 1995, the automobile carrying Ellen Bouchard Ryan, her husband Patrick (a mathematician and computer scientist at McMaster), and two of their three children was halted at a stop sign not far from their home when it was rear-ended by another vehicle travelling eighty kilometres an hour. Three of the Ryans were unhurt. Ellen suffered a neck injury so severe that, two years later, she still needs the support of a walking stick.

26   Some days, the overachieving scholar—chair of the Department of Psychology at the University of Notre Dame in Indiana before she was thirty—is "close to what I was." More often, a horrible pain above her right eye, vertigo, and nausea are crippling. An attempt at yoga left her hardly able to move her head. Aquatic exercise made it even worse. Only acupuncture seems to help, and then only for a few hours.

27   Halfway to one hundred, her "exquisite realization of health" suddenly gone, perhaps forever, Dr. Ryan has had no shortage of time to ponder the metaphysics of her own predicament. She speaks of spiritual and emotional development, inspirational books: *Chicken Soup for the Soul.*

28   "Do you feel like the universe has provided you with a taste of old age?" I ask her, thinking myself insightful, as she sinks into her recliner in her sunken living room.

29   "It is unfortunate that, in our society, when people feel *ill*, we say they feel *old*," she replies. "There are many, many, many, many ways to be old. Just as in childhood—you can have a good old age or a bad old age. And, just as in childhood, what makes the difference is a sense of meaning and purpose in life.

30   "I am trying to teach the diversity of old age. The message is, there is pain and suffering—and glory—in the human condition, no matter how old you are."

DISCUSSION QUESTIONS

1. Analyze paragraph 2. Paraphrase what the writer is saying in your own words. What does Abel mean when he says "Both sides are complicit in the game"?

2. What reasons does the writer suggest for negative stereotypes of old age (paragraphs 5–6)? Why is it ironic that we may have a "nurturing intent" when we diminish "old people's competence" (paragraph 6)?

3. What are the verbal and nonverbal ways that Dr. Ryan claims we patronize old people (paragraphs 7–10)? What is meant by the term "elderspeak" (paragraph 7)? In your own words, summarize how the "academic investigators of elderspeak" conducted their research and what they found (paragraphs 10–11).

4. According to Dr. Ryan, what are the effects on older people of realizing the inevitable fact of their old age? (paragraphs 13–14)?

5. Why do you suppose the writer includes the story about the effects of a severe automobile accident on Dr. Ryan (paragraphs 25–29)? How is this story relevant to the overall point of the article?

6. What is the significance of paragraphs 19–24? How do you respond to the allusions to poetry (paragraphs 20, 22) here?

7. What does Dr. Ryan mean by "the diversity of old age" in the last paragraph? How effective is the conclusion?

TOWARD KEY INSIGHTS

Have you seen examples of "elderspeak"—or any other kinds of condescending, simplified language to certain kinds of people? What, in your view, might be the reasons that people speak this way? What might be the effects of this kind of language on others?

Drawing on your own experiences in school, with family, or in other social relationships, comment on whether you think people tend to meet others' expectations, falling into a downward or an upward spiral depending on what is expected of them.

How is it possible that a person's apparently good intentions may have damaging effects?

SUGGESTION FOR WRITING

Write an essay tracing the effects of a subtle form of negative stereotyping at school or in another social grouping you are familiar with.

Christopher Dewdney

After Deep Blue

Christopher Dewdney has published twelve books of poetry, two of which were nominated for Governor General's Awards. A first-prize winner of the CBC Literary Competition, Christopher Dewdney is also the author of three books of popular nonfiction about culture and technology: The Immaculate Perception *(1986),* The Secular Grail *(1993), and* Last Flesh: Life in the Transhuman Era *(1998). Dewdney's substantive essay, "After Deep Blue," highlights significant social and philosophical issues related to computer technology and artificial intelligence.*

1   Over the past three billion years, life on earth has undergone two major metamorphoses: the first linking together of complex molecules into self-reproducing units, and the emergence of human consciousness. Neurologists studying brain casts moulded from prehistoric human skulls place the attainment of consciousness at approximately 50,000 years ago. Julian Jaynes, the maverick American neurophilosopher, places it much more recently, at about 4,000 years ago. Whichever estimate is more accurate, all researchers agree on one thing: the emergence of consciousness was intimately connected to the development of language. Language

then became, as Marshall McLuhan pointed out, the fount of all subsequent technology. The acquisition of consciousness and language still overshadows any subsequent technological gains we have made, but all that is about to change.

2   We are on the verge of the next stage in life's evolution, the stage where, by human agency, life takes control of itself and guides its own destiny. Never before has human life been able to change itself, to reach into its own genetic structure and rearrange its molecular bases; now it can. Perhaps we are already entering the last few generations of our embodiment as carbon-based life forms. What is relatively certain is that we are about to enter the transition period between the human and the posthuman eras—the transhuman age. The goal of transhumanism is to surpass our current biological limitations, be it our life span or the capabilities of our brain.

3   On a planetary scale, most of us are already transhuman to some degree. We are the products of bioengineering. Our immune systems have been altered by decoy viruses injected via vaccines. We consume genetically altered food. We use mood-altering psychopharmaceuticals, from fermented grape juice to Prozac. More recently, our bodies have become sites for more than 250 types of artificial implants: synthetic heart valves, pacemakers, artificial hip and knee joints, synthetic arteries, and eye lenses, not to mention those used in plastic surgery.

4   Biotechnology is modifying us as well. We are becoming organic symbionts, with baboon hearts, porcine livers, porcine skin grafts. The transplanting of human organs—particularly blood—is already routine. Hormone-replacement therapy has become commonplace, and human trials with artificial organs, called "neo-organs," have already begun in France. This process will not stop; it will gather momentum, and shortly it will blossom into a panoply of discoveries, interventions, and breakthroughs.

5   There are many setbacks, as well as innovations of dubious safety, along the way, but the exponential effect of cumulative scientific data, doubling and then tripling, will accelerate the progress of research, resulting in a cascade of inventions. And, as the separate fields of bioengineering, artificial intelligence, and robotics converge, the division between carbon-based life (as we currently know it) and artificial life will become less and less detectable.

6   Arguably this convergence is still some distance in the future, but strong progress in artificial intelligence (a necessary forerunner of these technologies) is being made. The recent unprecedented expansion of computational power has already had some startling payoffs, including a challenge to human dominance in a game once considered beyond the ability of computers.

7   In February, 1996, and then again in May, 1997, the world's best chess player competed against a computer. The matches were between an IBM supercomputer nicknamed "Deep Blue" and Garry Kasparov, the reigning world champion. The first match ended in one win for Deep Blue, three wins for Kasparov, and two draws. Some of the games lasted six hours. Garry Kasparov won the first match, but towards the end of that series his adviser said, "Garry is more exhausted than I've ever seen him." Kasparov, after studying Deep Blue's weaknesses, agreed to the rematch in 1997. However, IBM programmers had also fine-tuned Deep Blue's RS/6000 SP parallel processing software. The rematch was disastrous for Kasparov, ending in two wins for the computer, one win for Kasparov, and three draws. The posthuman era had dawned.

8   Chess was one area of human expertise thought safely beyond machine capabilities. That is no longer the case. Although computers like Deep Blue rely on brute speed and processing volumes, their programs will soon be modified to

include pattern recognition. Strategy, foresight, and psychology, hitherto believed to be intrinsically human attributes, can be duplicated, and even exceeded, by a computer program. The 1997 Deep Blue match was possibly the last time a human would ever win against a computer.

9   Sceptics can say that the games won by Deep Blue were actually won by the half dozen IBM programmers who worked on the software, that the computer contains no innate intelligence or chess ability but is merely the sum of its instructions. This logic is compelling at first, until you consider that were the same group of programmers to play collectively against Kasparov, they would lose. When the program plays chess, it *exceeds* the programmers' collective abilities. Certainly Kasparov took Deep Blue's abilities seriously when he called their first match "species-defining."

10   Also, to say that the computer or the program didn't win the match because it wasn't thinking for itself is to fall into the trap of presuming that there is something magical about human thought that allows us to think for ourselves. We cannot operate the "machinery" of our neurons. Since we don't think for ourselves any more than a computer does, how cognition gets done is irrelevant if the end result is identical.

11   We could be complacent about losing primacy in this singular area of human competence if it weren't that computers are quickly gaining in other areas as well. When Doug Lenat's CYC project (entering common sense and general knowledge into computers) is completed in several years, computers will graduate out of the idiot-savant stage. They will no longer be bulk number-crunchers capable of astounding speed but possessing little insight; rather, they will have the rudiments of human savvy. Eventually, all subroutines of our highest attributes, such as language and pattern perception, will be duplicated, and perhaps exceeded, by computers. The final fusion of these diverse skills will be artificial intelligence. We might then console ourselves with the notion that, in art at least, machines (which are, after all, unemotional and unfeeling) will not be able to rival us. But this is falling into the trap of anthropomorphizing the basis of our own consciousness, our complex primate brain. If artificial intelligence is modelled on our consciousness, it will, at the very least, possess a rudimentary emotional repertoire as part of its self-governing reward-and-punishment circuits. The emotional foundation for true art will be laid alongside them.

12   The central question facing us here, on the eve of machine consciousness, is how will it be achieved? There are two main strategies for attaining artificial intelligence: the first consists of making such a detailed likeness of the human brain that the property of consciousness is achieved; the second enlists artificial biology—self-guiding "evolutionary programmes" which might eventually produce sentient intelligences.

13   If artificial intelligence is moulded in the likeness of its creators (as the former strategy would have it), the first artificial intelligence will be imprinted, behaviourally and emotionally, with the character of its human/scientific birth. Sheer joy of cognition and fierce curiosity about the world around it will be its prime motivations. The first artificial intelligence may well be science made conscious.

14   If the second technique, synthetic evolution, produces the first artificial intelligence (even though it will exist only virtually at first), then this entity may turn out to be profoundly alien to our mode of consciousness. Evolution is a powerful primal force that until now has been in nature's hands. All that, it would seem, is about to change. Not only are we taking over our genetic development,

but we are also using computers to simulate the very fundamental mechanisms of evolution.

15   A new scientific discipline has sprung up over the past few decades. Called "artificial biology," it uses simulations to study life. Its most important discovery is the ability to model and perpetuate evolution within a computer simulation. These simulations go beyond pure research; applications have already been found. Artificial evolution was used, for example, to create several of the software modules within Windows 95. These artificial evolutions are every bit as active and creative as real evolution is in nature, the only difference being that these artificial evolutions can be directed into areas completely untried by nature. If we can "harness" this evolutionary force, then computers will be able to innovate in ways we can neither conceive or predict.

16   Hugo de Garis, a computer scientist working for ATR laboratories in Japan, is coordinating the creation of a computer he calls a "silicon brain" and, when it is completed in the year 2001, it will have more than a billion artificial neurons. What is extraordinary about this brain is the fact that it is designing itself. Its neurons are "cellular automata," every one of which has its own computer programme. Each automaton grows its own linkages with the other automata; once interconnected in a neural network, the automata will form a massively parallel computer. De Garis calls this form of self-directed, internally constructed neural network a "Darwin Machine" because the computer is using evolutionary engineering to design itself.

17   This project is just one example of dozens of research programmes in laboratories throughout the world that are racing towards artificial intelligence.

18   Shortly after the creation of the first computer, ENIAC, over fifty years ago, the mathematician John Von Neumann used the term "singularity" to describe the point at which humans will create an artificial super-intelligence. It was during a conversation at a mathematics conference that, as he later recalled, he first articulated the idea that "the ever accelerating progress of technology and changes in the mode of human life . . . give the appearance of approaching some essential singularity in the history of the race beyond which, human affairs, as we know them, could not continue."

19   Optimistic computer scientists predict that the singularity will occur within four decades in any of several ways. The most obvious and direct route will be the symbiotic union of humans and computers. With neural implants (a concept so overused in science fiction that it already seems outdated), the performance of the human mind could be boosted well beyond current capabilities. On the other hand, we might create, *fait accompli*, a single supercomputer that becomes spontaneously conscious, a new and sophisticated life form. Possibly, we will link computing networks into a supercomputer that spawns emergent consciousness. Finally, biotechnology might enhance the cellular structure of our brains to boost our own organic intelligence.

20   Whatever its genesis, superhumanity is probably inevitable (barring catastrophe). The advent of the posthuman era will be poignant because humans, as we currently know ourselves, will be superseded and will pass from centre stage. As one scientist replied when asked whether he was worried that intelligent machines might one day replace humans, "I'll throw my chips in on the side of intelligence, whatever form it may take." But this process will not be abrupt, and we will not be pushed aside like assembly-line workers being replaced by robots. It would be foolish to think we would design machines to supplant us. We *will*, however, design machines that will bootstrap our species into the next, self-guided evolutionary state.

This will be an incremental and wholly voluntary process. It is in our best interests to accept our intellectual progeny, our "mind children," as Hans Moravec calls the future generations of artificially intelligent beings, because they are a natural extension of our own evolution.

21   In the sixties, the mathematician I. J. Good wrote, "an ultraintelligent machine could design even better machines; there would unquestionably be an 'intelligence explosion'; and the intelligence of man would be left far behind. Thus the first ultraintelligent machine is the last invention that man need ever make." But we must ask ourselves: if we are able to achieve immortality and inconceivable intelligence, what would be our relation (as posthumans) to our original selves? Would self, as we currently know it, become an empty sign? Ego, as neuroscientists would have it, is simply an illusion anyway. But what happens when your self can be copied or duplicated? Or what happens if parts of your "self" can be merged with other beings or supercomputers? What happens to language when you can communicate directly without words, by neurotelepathy facilitated by technology? What will become of our sense of self when, with genetic engineering, we can change our bodies into almost any shape?

22   Also, if the posthuman sensibility is finer and more sophisticated than our own, would today's finest artistic creations seem, to our successors, like the incoherent grunting of baboons? And if the new consciousness grows out of the old, what of those who are left behind? What of those who, for religious, personal, or socio-economic reasons, do not join the exodus? What will become of them?

23   The introduction of transhuman technologies will have profoundly revolutionary, perhaps politically destabilizing, effects on the new world order. Even now, as new technologies are being introduced, we are entering an ominous period of growing scientific illiteracy, an age of superstition and dangerous credulity. The time is ripe for a new dark age.

24   It is important at this point in our history, when we are about to take our most momentous step, possibly leaving our DNA-based substrate behind, to prepare our psychology for the next phase. It may well transpire that, after the transhuman era, humans will cease to exist—at least as we currently know them. But consciousness will certainly not end. We are approaching a terrifying, intoxicating, and possibly dangerous threshold, a border of awareness on whose other side is a mystery as imponderable as anything we have yet wondered about.

DISCUSSION QUESTIONS

1. Explain in your own words what Christopher Dewdney means when he claims we are in a "transhuman age" (paragraph 2). What support does the writer give for his claim that "most of us are already transhuman to some degree" (paragraph 3)?

2. What are the effects of biotechnology on humans as a species (paragraph 4), according to the writer, and what will be the effects of "cumulative scientific data" (paragraph 5)?

3. What does the writer consider to be the significance of Deep Blue's win against the chess master Kasparov in 1997 (paragraphs 7–10)?

4. Dewdney explores two different hypotheses of how "machine consciousness" or "artificial intelligence" might be achieved (paragraphs 12–14). What are they? Explain the fundamental distinction between these two methods of creating artificial intelligence.

5. What is meant by "artificial evolution" (paragraphs 15–16)? What might be the effects of using artificial evolution, according to the writer?

6. What four possible results might there be of the artificial super-intelligence called "singularity" (paragraphs 18–19)?

7. What attitude does Dewdney seem to have toward the prospect of "superhumanity" in the "posthuman era" (paragraphs 20–22)? What is the point of his many questions in paragraphs 21 and 22?

8. What possible dangers does Dewdney associate with "the introduction of trans-human technologies" (paragraphs 23–24)?

TOWARD KEY INSIGHTS

To what degree do you accept Dewdney's argument that "superhumanity is probably inevitable" (paragraph 20)? Explain.

How do you react to Dewdney's claim that machines could "possess a rudimentary emotional repertoire" (paragraph 11), or that "humans, as we currently know ourselves, will be superseded and will pass from centre stage"?

Dewdney asks many questions about what might happen to our sense of self in an era of machine consciousness (paragraphs 21–22). What additional questions can you imagine? Is there any way to answer these questions? If not, what is the point of raising them? If so, what possible answers would you suggest?

SUGGESTION FOR WRITING

Write an essay explaining the effects of accelerating technological advances on your life. Use at least one extended example.

Definition

Laurence Shames

The Sweet Smell of Success Isn't All That Sweet

Laurence Shames (born 1951) is a native of Newark, New Jersey, and a graduate of New York University. After completing his education, he began a career as a nonfiction writer, contributing to such publications as Playboy, McCall's, Esquire, Vanity Fair, *and the* New York Times. *A 1986 book,* The Big Time: The Harvard Business School's Most Successful Class and How It Shaped America, *explores the contributions of the 1949 graduating class to the worlds of business and public service. A later work,* The Hunger for More *(1991), focuses on the search for values in a world of greed. This concern for values is also apparent in the following selection, which attacks contemporary attitudes about success.*

1   John Milton was a failure. In writing "Paradise Lost," his stated aim was to "justify the ways of God to men." Inevitably, he fell short of accomplishing that and only wrote a monumental poem. Beethoven, whose music was conceived to transcend Fate, was a failure, as was Socrates, whose ambition was to make people happy by making them reasonable and just. The inescapable conclusion seems to be that the surest, noblest way to fail is to set one's own standards titanically high.

2   The flip-side of that proposition also seems true, and it provides the safe but dreary logic by which most of us live: The surest way to succeed is to keep one's strivings low—or at least to direct them along already charted paths. Don't set yourself the probably thankless task of making the legal system better; just shoot at becoming a partner in the firm. Don't agonize over questions about where your talents and proclivities might most fulfillingly lead you; just do a heads-up job of determining where the educational or business opportunities seem most secure.

3   After all, if "success" itself—rather than the substance of the achievements that make for success—is the criterion by which we measure ourselves and from which we derive our self-esteem, why make things more difficult by reaching for the stars?

Introduction: paragraphs 1–4; captures attention by ironically attacking high success standards, defending low standards

4   What is this contemporary version of success really all about?

5   According to certain beer commercials, it consists in moving up to a premium brand that costs a dime or so more per bottle. Credit-card companies would have you believe success inheres in owning their particular piece of plastic.

Body: paragraphs 5–12

Development by examples and brief definitions

6   If these examples sound petty, they are. But take those petty privileges, weave them into a fabric that passes for a value system and what you've got is a national mood that has vast motivating power that can shape at least the near future of the entire country.

Development by effect

7   Under the flag of success, modern-style, liberal arts colleges are withering while business schools are burgeoning—and yet even business schools are having an increasingly hard time finding faculty members, because teaching isn't considered "successful" enough. Amid a broad consensus that there is a glut of lawyers and an epidemic of strangling litigation, record numbers of young people continue to flock to law school because, for the individual practitioner, a law degree is still considered a safe ticket.

Development by comparison, examples, and causes

8   The most sobering thought of all is that today's M.B.A.'s and lawyers are tomorrow's M.B.A.'s and lawyers: Having invested so much time and money in their training, only a tiny percentage of them will ever opt out of their early chosen fields. Decisions made in accordance with today's hothouse notions of ambition are locking people into careers that will define and also limit their activities and yearnings for virtually the rest of their lives.

Development by effects

9   Many, by external standards, will be "successes." They will own homes, eat in better restaurants, dress well and, in some instances, perform socially useful work. Yet there is a deadening and dangerous flaw in their philosophy: It has little room, little sympathy and less respect for the noble failure, for the person who ventures past the limits, who aims gloriously high and falls unashamedly short.

Development by effects and argument

10   That sort of ambition doesn't have much place in a world where success is proved by worldly reward rather than by accomplishment itself. That sort of ambition is increasingly thought of as the domain of irredeemable eccentrics, of people who haven't quite caught on—and there is great social pressure not to be one of them.

Development by effects

11   The result is that fewer people are drawn to the cutting edge of noncommercial scientific research. Fewer are taking on the sublime, unwinnable challenges of the arts. Fewer are asking questions that matter—the ones that can't be answered. Fewer are putting themselves on the line, making as much of their minds and talents as they might.

Development by effects

12   The irony is that today's success-chasers seem obsessed with the idea of *not settling*. They take advanced degrees in business because they won't settle for just a so-so job. They compete for slots at law firms and investment houses because they won't settle for any but the fastest track. They seem to regard it as axiomatic that "success" and "settling" are opposites.

Development by effect, cause, and comparison

13   Yet in doggedly pursuing the rather brittle species of success now in fashion, they are restricting themselves to a chokingly narrow swath of turf along the entire range of human possibilities. Does it ever occur to them that, frequently, success is what people settle for when they can't think of something noble enough to be worth failing at?

Conclusion: argues against contemporary notions of success

DISCUSSION QUESTIONS

1. Shames notes in paragraph 3 that "'success' itself—rather than the substance of the achievements that make for success—" seems to be the touchstone by which we measure our worth. What do you think he means? Why is the distinction positioned at this point?

2. Why do you think Shames ends his essay with a rhetorical question, that is, one for which no answer is expected?

3. To what extent do you agree with Shames's idea of success? Discuss.

TOWARD KEY INSIGHTS

What evidence do you find that not all people are consumed by the desire for money?

What qualities do you consider crucial to living a "good" life? to happiness?

SUGGESTION FOR WRITING

Write a definition essay explaining how the popular view of responsibility, greed, marriage, single life, friendship, or some other concept needs redefining. Use whatever writing strategies advance your purpose.

Andrew Beyak

The Sweet Bird of Youth Is Showing Signs of Age

Andrew Beyak was born in Toronto in 1971. After studying Zoology at the University of Western Ontario, Beyak moved to Montreal for graduate work at Concordia University. While his educational background was in the sciences, he also has had a lifelong interest in literature, journalism, and music. Beyak's article "The Sweet Bird of Youth" has appeared previously in both The Hour, *the Montreal arts weekly, and* The Georgia Straight, *the Vancouver arts and entertainment weekly. "The Sweet Bird of Youth Is Showing Signs of Age" argues that the definition of "youth" is too elastic when it includes people from 18 to 30. Beyak suggests that there may be a political or economic agenda for those who would extend the period of "youth," enabling us collectively to dismiss the problem of unemployment as "youth unemployment."*

1   According to my 1956 edition of *Webster's New World Dictionary*, youth is: "1. the state or quality of being young. 2. the period of life coming between childhood and maturity; adolescence. 3. an early stage of growth or existence."

2   More recently, according to corporate, political, and media interests, youth is: "1. not employed; without work. 2. not being used; idle."

3   In case you haven't noticed, the term *youth* is increasingly becoming a euphemism for *unemployed and underemployed adults*. It no longer has anything to do

with age or maturity. Rather, the term *youth* has been co-opted by corporate and government interests as a means of evading responsibility for both their actions and their inactions—actions and inactions that are having an impact on a generation of young, and not-so-young, adults.

4   Virtually all of the programs in the federal government's current Youth Employment Strategy are available to "youths" under the age of 30. All of these programs are aimed at attacking the relatively recent problem of "youth unemployment," a problem that used to go by the name of "unemployment." Meanwhile, the Youth Employment Services Centre in Montreal offers services to "youths" between the ages of 16 and 35. Yes, that's right. Thirty-five. These days, you are considered a "youth" until you have lived almost one-half of the average male life, which is currently around 75 years long. Or, to give this some historical perspective, today you are a youth for what was the entire duration of the average life just over a century ago. With the ever-expanding usage of the term *youth,* I am sure you would not have to look very far to find some youths out there with youths of their own.

5   On CBC Television's *Youth Town Hall* program during the last federal election campaign, 18- to 25-year-olds had a go at the politicians. Prior to this, I had taken it for granted that the idea behind the age of majority was to officially recognize an age at which citizens are considered mature enough to decide the fate of our country. In other words, they are no longer youths, but adults. Unfortunately, none of the leaders of our official political parties seem to share this view, as was evidenced by their absence from the *Youth Town Hall* forum. Were these leaders absent due to conceit, or did they simply fear the wrath of an increasingly ostracized group? Whatever the reason, today 18- to 25-year-olds are routinely separated from the rest of the clear-thinking, mature adults and are labelled "youths," not because of their state of maturity or development, but because of their economic circumstances.

6   Many people in their 20s and early 30s may enjoy the term *youth* and be somewhat reluctant to give it up. Thus, many of us in this age bracket are accomplices in the escalating abuse and misuse of this word, for it suggests that we are still hip, beautiful, vibrant, and intimately in touch with the nuances of popular culture. However, there is something far more sinister than mere flattery going on here.

7   By referring to a segment of the most-educated generation of adults to date as "youth," older generations, corporations, and governments have succeeded in leaving the impression that these people are not getting ahead in life because, "well, it's just not quite time yet." They would have you believe that it has nothing to do with employee-taxation laws. It has nothing to do with the fact that many salaried employees are logging more than 60 hours a week. It is not that CEOs' salaries have skyrocketed since the 1960s. It is not a lack of job-sharing. It is not that many corporate leaders are given bonuses based on short-term, rather than long-term, performance. It is not greed. Not the unrealistic expectations of relatively unskilled university graduates. Not demographics. Not resource scarcity. Not automation. Not NAFTA. Not globalization. No, that's not it. It's just that the "youths" in our society, those in the 18-to-35 bracket, have a little more growing up to do. In other words, it is just a matter of time.

8   Unfortunately, there is something of a self-fulfilling prophecy here, in that many young adults only aspire to live up to their recently attenuated expectations. The consequences of this go beyond economics; they are also social in scope. Furthermore, these consequences will likely carry over to the next generation. Moving away from home, marriage, and parenthood, as well as many other

rites of passage in adults' lives, are increasingly being put off until people are well into their 30s. These events are now postponed until careers are firmly established and new cars and houses are bought. And why not, in a society that equates money with maturity, and full employment with adulthood?

9   By replacing the term *adult* with *youth*, governments, corporations, and the media can offer the majority of the electorate and the majority of society (baby boomers, if you will) an easy explanation for why those aged 18 to 35 are not receiving what they as adults need—namely employment, a living wage, and a minimal level of independence. At the same time, those with a vested interest in the status quo are creating a diversion from a multitude of other issues that will inevitably have to be addressed. All of this with one word.

DISCUSSION QUESTIONS

1. How does Beyak rewrite the traditional definition of "youth"? Why does he begin with a dictionary definition?

2. In paragraph 7, Beyak uses a number of negative statements beginning with "It is not," "Not," or "No." What is the effect of the many negatives?

3. According to the author, how does our society define maturity or adulthood (paragraphs 8–9)?

4. What are the negative social and economic consequences of calling people aged 18–35 "youth"?

5. Find the thesis statement, and paraphrase it. Why is it located where it is?

6. What is the tone of this article? Explain.

TOWARD KEY INSIGHTS

What does Beyak mean when he says that "the term youth has been co-opted by corporate and government interests"? Can you think of another term or concept that has been re-defined or co-opted by certain interests?

What do you consider to be the dividing line between youth and adulthood? Do you consider people between 18 and 35 adults? Explain.

What rites of passage do you associate with maturity?

What is your response to Beyak's suggestion that one cause of unemployment or underemployment is "unrealistic expectations of relatively unskilled university graduates" (paragraph 7)?

SUGGESTION FOR WRITING

Write an essay exploring how a word or term that once seemed relatively simple has taken on "ever-expanding usage" or changed its meaning according to a changing political, social, or economic climate.

Stephen L. Carter

The Insufficiency of Honesty

Stephen L. Carter (born 1954) earned a B.A. degree from Stanford University in 1976 and a law degree from Yale University in 1979. Between 1979 and 1982, he worked as a law clerk, first for the U.S. Court of Appeals, District of Columbia circuit, and then for Justice Thurgood Marshall of the U.S. Supreme Court. Since 1982, he has served on the faculty of the Yale Law School. Carter has authored three books: Reflections of an Affirmative Action Baby *(1991),* The Culture of Disbelief *(1993), and* Integrity *(1996), from which our selection was adapted. The first of these books critiques affirmative action policies, the second attacks current political and legal attitudes toward religion, and the third examines the nature of integrity. In our selection, Carter defines integrity by distinguishing it from honesty.*

1   A couple of years ago I began a university commencement address by telling the audience that I was going to talk about integrity. The crowd broke into applause. Applause! Just because they had heard the word "integrity": that's how starved for it they were. They had no idea how I was using the word, or what I was going to say about integrity, or, indeed, whether I was for it or against it. But they knew they liked the idea of talking about it.

2   Very well, let us consider this word "integrity." Integrity is like the weather: everybody talks about it but nobody knows what to do about it. Integrity is that stuff that we always want more of. Some say that we need to return to the good old days when we had a lot more of it. Others say that we as a nation have never really had enough of it. Hardly anybody stops to explain exactly what we mean by it, or how we know it is a good thing, or why everybody needs to have the same amount of it. Indeed, the only trouble with integrity is that everybody who uses the word seems to mean something slightly different.

3   For instance, when I refer to integrity, do I mean simply "honesty"? The answer is no; although honesty is a virtue of importance, it is a different virtue from integrity. Let us, for simplicity, think of honesty as not lying; and let us further accept Sissela Bok's definition of a lie: "any intentionally deceptive message which is *stated*." Plainly, one cannot have integrity without being honest (although, as we shall see, the matter gets complicated), but one can certainly be honest and yet have little integrity.

4   When I refer to integrity, I have something very specific in mind. Integrity, as I will use the term, requires three steps: discerning what is right and what is wrong; acting on what you have discerned, even at personal cost; and saying openly that you are acting on your understanding of right and wrong. The first criterion captures the idea that integrity requires a degree of moral reflectiveness. The second brings in the ideal of a person of integrity as steadfast, a quality that includes keeping one's commitments. The third reminds us that a person of integrity can be trusted.

5   The first point to understand about the difference between honesty and integrity is that a person may be entirely honest without ever engaging in the hard work of discernment that integrity requires: she may tell us quite truthfully what she believes without ever taking the time to figure out whether what she believes is good and right and true. The problem may be as simple as someone's foolishly saying something that hurts a friend's feelings; a few moments of thought would have revealed the likelihood of the hurt and the lack of necessity for the comment.

Or the problem may be more complex, as when a man who was raised from birth in a society that preaches racism states his belief in one race's inferiority as a fact, without ever really considering that perhaps this deeply held view is wrong. Certainly the racist is being honest—he is telling us what he actually thinks—but his honesty does not add up to integrity.

Telling Everything You Know

6   A wonderful epigram sometimes attributed to the filmmaker Sam Goldwyn goes like this: "The most important thing in acting is honesty; once you learn to fake that, you're in." The point is that honesty can be something one *seems* to have. Without integrity, what passes for honesty often is nothing of the kind; it is fake honesty—or it is honest but irrelevant and perhaps even immoral.

7   Consider an example. A man who has been married for fifty years confesses to his wife on his deathbed that he was unfaithful thirty-five years earlier. The dishonesty was killing his spirit, he says. Now he has cleared his conscience and is able to die in peace.

8   The husband has been honest—sort of. He has certainly unburdened himself. And he has probably made his wife (soon to be his widow) quite miserable in the process, because even if she forgives him, she will not be able to remember him with quite the vivid image of love and loyalty that she had hoped for. Arranging his own emotional affairs to ease his transition to death, he has shifted to his wife the burden of confusion and pain, perhaps for the rest of her life. Moreover, he has attempted his honesty at the one time in his life when it carries no risk; acting in accordance with what you think is right and risking no loss in the process is a rather thin and unadmirable form of honesty.

9   Besides, even though the husband has been honest in a sense, he has now twice been unfaithful to his wife: once thirty-five years ago, when he had his affair, and again when, nearing death, he decided that his own peace of mind was more important than hers. In trying to be honest he has violated his marriage vow by acting toward his wife not with love but with naked and perhaps even cruel self-interest.

10   As my mother used to say, you don't have to tell people everything you know. Lying and nondisclosure, as the law often recognizes, are not the same thing. Sometimes it is actually illegal to tell what you know, as, for example, in the disclosure of certain financial information by market insiders. Or it may be unethical, as when a lawyer reveals a confidence entrusted to her by a client. It may be simple bad manners, as in the case of a gratuitous comment to a colleague on his or her attire. And it may be subject to religious punishment, as when a Roman Catholic priest breaks the seal of the confessional—an offense that carries automatic excommunication.

11   In all the cases just mentioned, the problem with telling everything you know is that somebody else is harmed. Harm may not be the intention, but it is certainly the effect. Honesty is most laudable when we risk harm to ourselves; it becomes a good deal less so if we instead risk harm to others when there is no gain to anyone other than ourselves. Integrity may counsel keeping our secrets in order to spare the feelings of others. Sometimes, as in the example of the wayward husband, the reason we want to tell what we know is precisely to shift our pain onto somebody else—a course of action dictated less by integrity than by self-interest. Fortunately, integrity and self-interest often coincide, as when a politician of integrity is rewarded with our votes. But often they do not, and it is at those moments that our integrity is truly tested.

Error

12   Another reason that honesty alone is no substitute for integrity is that if forthrightness is not preceded by discernment, it may result in the expression of an incorrect moral judgment. In other words, I may be honest about what I believe, but if I have never tested my beliefs, I may be wrong. And here I mean "wrong" in a particular sense: the proposition in question is wrong if I would change my mind about it after hard moral reflection.

13   Consider this example. Having been taught all his life that women are not as smart as men, a manager gives the women on his staff less-challenging assignments than he gives the men. He does this, he believes, for their own benefit: he does not want them to fail, and he believes that they will if he gives them tougher assignments. Moreover, when one of the women on his staff does poor work, he does not berate her as harshly as he would a man, because he expects nothing more. And he claims to be acting with integrity because he is acting according to his own deepest beliefs.

14   The manager fails the most basic test of integrity. The question is not whether his actions are consistent with what he most deeply believes but whether he has done the hard work of discerning whether what he most deeply believes is right. The manager has not taken this harder step.

15   Moreover, even within the universe that the manager has constructed for himself, he is not acting with integrity. Although he is obviously wrong to think that the women on his staff are not as good as the men, even were he right, that would not justify applying different standards to their work. By so doing he betrays both his obligation to the institution that employs him and his duty as a manager to evaluate his employees.

16   The problem that the manager faces is an enormous one in our practical politics, where having the dialogue that makes democracy work can seem impossible because of our tendency to cling to our views even when we have not examined them. As Jean Bethke Elshtain has said, borrowing from John Courtney Murray, our politics are so fractured and contentious that we often cannot even reach *disagreement*. Our refusal to look closely at our own most cherished principles is surely a large part of the reason. Socrates thought the unexamined life not worth living. But the unhappy truth is that few of us actually have the time for constant reflection on our views—on public or private morality. Examine them we must, however, or we will never know whether we might be wrong.

17   None of this should be taken to mean that integrity as I have described it presupposes a single correct truth. If, for example, your integrity-guided search tells you that affirmative action is wrong, and my integrity-guided search tells me that affirmative action is right, we need not conclude that one of us lacks integrity. As it happens, I believe—both as a Christian and as a secular citizen who struggles toward moral understanding—that we *can* find true and sound answers to our moral questions. But I do not pretend to have found very many of them, nor is an exposition of them my purpose here.

18   It is the case not that there aren't any right answers but that, given human fallibility, we need to be careful in assuming that we have found them. However, today's political talk about how it is wrong for the government to impose one person's morality on somebody else is just mindless chatter. *Every* law imposes one person's morality on somebody else, because law has only two functions: to tell people to do what they would rather not or to forbid them to do what they would.

19   And if the surveys can be believed, there is far more moral agreement in America than we sometimes allow ourselves to think. One of the reasons that

character education for young people makes so much sense to so many people is precisely that there seems to be a core set of moral understandings—we might call them the American Core—that most of us accept. Some of the virtues in this American Core are, one hopes, relatively noncontroversial. About 500 American communities have signed on to Michael Josephson's program to emphasize the "six pillars" of good character: trustworthiness, respect, responsibility, caring, fairness, and citizenship. These virtues might lead to a similarly noncontroversial set of political values: having an honest regard for ourselves and others, protecting freedom of thought and religious belief, and refusing to steal or murder.

Honesty and Competing Responsibilities

20   A further problem with too great an exaltation of honesty is that it may allow us to escape responsibilities that morality bids us bear. If honesty is substituted for integrity, one might think that if I say I am not planning to fulfill a duty, I need not fulfill it. But it would be a peculiar morality indeed that granted us the right to avoid our moral responsibilities simply by stating our intention to ignore them. Integrity does not permit such an easy escape.

21   Consider an example. Before engaging in sex with a woman, her lover tells her that if she gets pregnant, it is her problem, not his. She says that she understands. In due course she does wind up pregnant. If we believe, as I hope we do, that the man would ordinarily have a moral responsibility toward both the child he will have helped to bring into the world and the child's mother, then his honest statement of what he intends does not spare him that responsibility.

22   This vision of responsibility assumes that not all moral obligations stem from consent or from a stated intention. The linking of obligations to promises is a rather modern and perhaps uniquely Western way of looking at life, and perhaps a luxury that only the well-to-do can afford. As Fred and Shulamit Korn (a philosopher and an anthropologist) have pointed out, "If one looks at ethnographic accounts of other societies, one finds that, while obligations everywhere play a crucial role in social life, promising is not preeminent among the sources of obligation and is not even mentioned by most anthropologists." The Korns have made a study of Tonga, where promises are virtually unknown but the social order is remarkably stable. If life without any promises seems extreme, we Americans sometimes go too far the other way, parsing not only our contracts but even our marriage vows in order to discover the absolute minimum obligation that we have to others as a result of our promises.

23   That some societies in the world have worked out evidently functional structures of obligation without the need for promise or consent does not tell us what *we* should do. But it serves as a reminder of the basic proposition that our existence in civil society creates a set of mutual responsibilities that philosophers used to capture in the fiction of the social contract. Nowadays, here in America, people seem to spend their time thinking of even cleverer ways to avoid their obligations, instead of doing what integrity commands and fulfilling them. And all too often honesty is their excuse.

DISCUSSION QUESTIONS

1. Discuss the effectiveness of Carter's title.
2. Identify the thesis statement of this essay.

3. What writing strategies does Carter use to develop his essay? Refer to specific parts of the essay when answering.

4. In paragraph 8, Carter notes that the husband's deathbed confession "carries no risk." Explain what he means.

5. Point out the linking devices that Carter uses to connect paragraphs.

6. Identify what paragraphs constitute Carter's conclusion and explain why it is effective.

7. Discuss examples of situations you have known when people displayed honesty without integrity and also situations when people displayed honesty with integrity.

TOWARD KEY INSIGHTS

To what extent do you believe that our moral obligations extend beyond our promises and stated intentions?

Do North Americans typically try to fulfill their "absolute minimum obligation?" What evidence can you cite to support your answer?

SUGGESTION FOR WRITING

Write an essay defining loyalty. Use appropriate examples and whatever writing strategies will further your purpose.

Bob Harvey

Loyalty: A Last Virtue; Me-First Attitude Is Stripping Away Our Sense of Community

Bob Harvey is a journalist for the Ottawa Citizen, *in which this article first appeared. This essay provides an extended definition of loyalty, partly by saying what it is not. True loyalty, the allegiance to something larger than the self, has faded in the West, eroded by our emphasis on subjectivity and individualism. This essay could be fruitfully paired with Stephen Carter's essay "The Insufficiency of Honesty."*

Loyal: 1. Steadfast in support and devotion to and never betraying the interests of one's homeland, government, or sovereign.
2. Faithful to a person, ideal or custom; constantly supporting or following. (French, from Old French loyal, loial, leial, fait
—*Reader's Digest Illustrated Encyclopedic Dictionary*

1   The Roman senator, Seneca, called it "the holiest virtue in the human head." For most of the 2,000 years since, few would have disagreed with his call for loyalty to the gods, to the state, to family and to duty.

2   But loyalty, that once-essential virtue, is fading fast, and our sense of community and identity is disappearing with it.

3   Recent headlines tell some of the story. Last month, actor Elizabeth Taylor filed for divorce from husband No. 8, and all it merited was a news brief. We've become used to the breakdown in marital loyalty. The Canadian divorce rate has shot up by 400 per cent since 1970.

Everyone's Not Doing It

4   This month, it was Wayne Gretzky who quit on a relationship. He pushed the Los Angeles Kings to trade him to the St. Louis Blues because he wants to be on a winning team. But it's not only athletes who'd rather switch than commit. In the last year, the owners of the Quebec Nordiques, the Winnipeg Jets and the Cleveland Browns have all chosen cash over their loyal fans.

5   Loyalty's gone in almost every sphere. Canadian voters have deserted the Tories and the New Democrats. Many Quebecois want to quit Canada. Consumers are dumping brand names. Believers are switching denominations and even bigger numbers are quitting organized religion altogether.

6   Today's new version of loyalty, according to people who've thought about this issue, is loyalty to self, as summed up by what was originally meant to be ironic advice to Hamlet: "To thine own self be true."

7   Philosopher Donald De Marco says what's happened is that "we've lost the sense of a common good. We've made an invalid of loyalty."

8   He says that without an accepted common good, or allegiance to something beyond the self, loyalty crumbles.

9   "If you're saying the highest loyalty is to self, you can't get beyond self. Therefore you're missing an essential element of loyalty. It's not a virtue to be loyal to oneself. It's a vice to be selfish," says De Marco, who teaches in St. Jerome's College at the University of Waterloo.

10   Graeme Hunter, who teaches philosophy at the University of Ottawa, says that in the West, Christianity kept me-first individualism in check for hundreds of years.

11   "Religious commitments weren't just restricted to the sphere of the church. They affected one's whole life. You had a responsibility to your community, to your employer and to the State."

12   In fact, the sacred scriptures of all the major faiths not only teach that God is loyal and faithful, but also urge we follow that divine example: "Those who faithfully observe their trust and their covenants will inherit Paradise," says the Koran.

13   Loyalty has been valued in all cultures, as witness this 16th-century advice to the Japanese samurai warrior: "The business of the samurai consists in discharging loyal service to his master, in devoting himself to duty above all."

14   But secularism and individualism are making inroads in all cultures, and taking away not only the religious backing for loyalty to others, but also some of the cultural emphasis on it. "If there is no God, there is no absolute foundation to anything," says Hunter.

First Fading Hints

15   The notion of loyalty began to fade first in the West, in the late 19th century, as exemplified by this 1889 musing by diarist Alice James: "When will women begin to have the first glimmer that above all other loyalties is the loyalty to Truth, i.e. to yourself, that husband, children, friends and country are as nothing to that."

16   Will Sweet, who teaches philosophy at St. Francis Xavier University in Antigonish, N.S., says, however, that this tendency to value self above community

or duty began at least 400 years ago. Rene Descartes, the father of modern philosophy, wrote *cogito ergo sum* (I think therefore I am) and began the shift from an emphasis on absolute values and absolute truths to an emphasis on subjectivity and the value of the individual.

But Which Good?

17   A hundred years later, Adam Smith and other economists speeded up the shift to me-first individualism by teaching that if we just pursued our own economic self-interest, all would benefit. Suddenly the common good was equated with the individual good. Only now are we beginning to see some of the problems with this notion, including the spread of poverty in spite of continuing increases in the production of goods.

18   Pollster Andrew Grenville says many aspects of modern life also contribute to the decline in loyalty. Greater prosperity makes divorce more possible when relationships break down, and *technology* makes it possible to market not only thousands of different products, but also thousands of different ideas.

19   Grenville, vice-president of the Angus Reid polling firm, says that along with these new choices comes a fragmentation in identities.

20   Instead of identifying with our neighbors, or our nation, we're developing new micro-identities as Internet surfers or evangelical Christians that transcend old boundaries, says Grenville.

21   Greg Walters teaches *ethics* at Ottawa's Saint Paul University and says loyalty got a bad name during the Second World War, when it became clear that not all loyalties are good loyalties.

22   The Nazis and other totalitarian regimes made us suspicious of authority and less willing to give uncritical loyalty to a State, or an institution;

23   However, he says the yearning for loyalty hasn't gone away. In spite of the current high divorce rate, surveys by Alberta sociologist Reg Bibby show that 97 per cent of Canadian teens still confidently expect to marry only once.

24   *Technology* and the breakdown of tradition have made it necessary to re-define ourselves and our loyalties, says Walters. And although we're still groping for new structures and new ways of thinking to help us to do it, he says history teaches us that it's probably just a matter of time until we do.

Terrible Tribalism

25   Sweet says the resurgence of nationalism and tribalism is more evidence of this yearning for enduring connections.

26   In some nations, like Rwanda and the former Yugoslavia, this new assertion of tribal or national identity community has turned psychopathic. In places like Quebec, the process is more peaceful. Like other thinkers, Sweet is philosophical about the new stain on our loyalties,

27   "It's the effect of a process that's been going on for 400 years. We can't expect any sudden changes in a lifetime."

DISCUSSION QUESTIONS

1. What is accomplished by introducing a dictionary definition of loyalty, followed by an ancient Roman senator's definition of loyalty, at the beginning of this essay?

2. How does the author define loyalty partly through negation?

3. How does the author make the subject of loyalty seem of universal and contemporary significance?

4. Find places where methods of development such as cause and effect analysis, contrast, or illustration are used. What larger purpose does the author have in using each of these strategies?

5. What connections does the author make between loyalty and religious faith? loyalty and economic philosophy? loyalty and technology?

6. In your own words, explain why Nazi and other totalitarian regimes might have contributed to the decline of loyalty (paragraphs 24–26).

TOWARD KEY INSIGHTS

The author quotes a philosopher who says that loyalty needs "allegiance to something beyond the self." Do you agree that "loyalty to self" is not true loyalty? Why or why not?

Do you agree with the author's claim that we are "developing new micro-identities" rather than "identifying with our neighbors"? Can you think of examples of "micro-identities" that people you know have formed?

Compare and contrast the way that Bob Harvey defines "loyalty" and the way that Stephen Carter defines "integrity" in the essay in this section, "The Insufficiency of Honesty." How do both essays include an element of argument? Which essay do you find more effective? Why?

SUGGESTION FOR WRITING

Write an essay in which you develop an expanded definition of a concept such as "commitment" or "faith" or "discipline." Draw from personal observation or experience in order to make a statement about this concept, showing, for instance, that the principle of commitment is alive and well, in decline, or simply changing.

Argument

Dr. Patricia Baird

Should Human Cloning Be Permitted?

Patricia Baird was trained as a pediatrician and then specialized in medical genetics. She has been Head of the Department of Medical Genetics at the University of British Columbia for over a decade and has been a member of numerous national and international bodies, among them the National Advisory Board on Science and Technology chaired by the Prime Minister; the Medical Research Council of Canada (and its Standing Committee on Ethics in Experimentation); and International Ethics Committees. She headed the Canadian Royal Commission on New Reproductive Technologies and has served as an Advisor to the World Health Organization in recent years. Since the mid-'80s she has been associated with the Canadian Institute for Advanced Research, where she currently chairs the Advisory Committee for the Population Health and Human Development Programs. She has received three honorary degrees and the Order of British Columbia. She is also an Officer of the Order of Canada, a Fellow of the Royal Society of Canada, and a "University Distinguished Professor" at the University of British Columbia. The following article, from Annals *33(4), June 2000, can be found on the Web.* [*]

Introduction and Background

1   In 2001, a California state legislature committee invited individuals to present their recommendations on what position should be taken on human cloning, and outline their reasons. This article is an abridged version of an invited presentation in January 2000 to that committee.

A Qualitatively Different Type of Reproduction

2   Producing humans by somatic-cell nuclear-transfer cloning differs from sexual reproduction—it separates reproduction from recombination. Normally, in an outbred species such as humans, we cannot predict what the overall characteristics

Introduction includes background, extended definition, and comparison

of an embryo will be. In sexual reproduction, it is unpredictable which combination of the parents' thousands of genes will occur. To date, in creating the next generation, we have had to give ourselves over to chance. But if nuclear transfer is used, the nucleus can be taken from an adult whose characteristics are known—and the process reproduces the biology of the former individual. It becomes possible to select by known characteristics which humans will be copied. The new technology allows the asexual replication of a human being, the ability to predetermine the full complement of a child's nuclear genes, and the easier alteration of the genes of prospective individuals. Cloning is a change in the integrity of our species, and we must think about the long-term consequences.

Indication of writer's attitude: forecasting statement	

Public Reaction to Human Cloning

Topic sentence	3

Cloning used to produce a human is rejected by the overwhelming majority of people. Polls on new scientific developments have limitations, but *The Economist* reported that over 90 per cent of Americans were opposed to human cloning.[1]

Rational appeal: statistics, citation of study	

Other polls have shown similar results.[2,3] Polls, however, are affected by how the questions are asked, so an in-depth approach is needed. Many experts believe that lay people cannot understand complicated scientific topics, but there are data showing that they can assimilate and make judgments about complex issues. The Wellcome Trust did a qualitative focus-group study, and reported that opposition to human cloning was "nearly universal" among participants.[4] Most were against the idea of using cloning for reproductive purposes, stemming from concerns for the children and society, as much as from fears about interfering with nature. When over 90 per cent of citizens in a democracy oppose human cloning, it is difficult for a government to justify a policy that permits it. There are a few people, however, who would pursue cloning because they see potential advantages for themselves.

Foreseeable Requests for Cloning

Topic sentence	4

There are foreseeable situations where individuals may want to pursue cloning, for example, for couples where both are infertile and have neither eggs nor sperm, or where the male produces no sperm.

Refutation	

Given that there are new treatment techniques using cells from testicular biopsy, such problems are rare.

Development by example	

A second example is where a lesbian couple might wish to use one partner's body cell and the enucleated egg of the other to produce a child together.

Refutation	

In these scenarios, there are other options available to form a family—such as sperm donation, egg and embryo donation, or adoption. Other situations where cloning may be pursued is when a couple's child is dying or is killed, and they want to replace him or her by using one of his or her cells in nuclear-transfer cloning; or when a clone could provide a genetically compatible organ for transplantation. There will be instances where people wish to pursue cloning for particular reasons.[5,7]

Topic sentence combines two claims	5

The arguments about physical and psychological harm to clones have also been well delineated.[8,9]

Support for first claim	

For example, with regard to possible physical harms, congenital malformations, handicap, early death, increased risk of cancer, premature aging, and death have all been raised.

Support for second claim	

Possible psychological harms to cloned individuals (replicands) have also been outlined, including diminished individuality, a sense of foreclosed future, or a disturbed sense of identity. An important part of human identity is the sense of arising from a maternal and a paternal line while at the same time being a unique individual. Many children who are adopted, or conceived from donor insemination, show a deep need to learn about their biological origins. Making children by cloning means that they do not have this dual genetic origin; they are not connected to others in the same biological way as the rest of humanity. The first person born this way would have to cope with being the first not to come from the union of egg and sperm. Social, family, and kinship relationships that support human flourishing have evolved over millennia—but there is no way to place replicands. Is the DNA source the twin? The mother? The father?

Widening the Frame

6   Most debate on human cloning focuses on a weighing of harms and benefits to individuals. This is a dangerously incomplete framing. Looking at the issue as a matter of reproductive technology choice, although it focuses on individual autonomy, reproductive freedom, and protection of children, means that other issues are omitted.[10] We need to shift from the framing as individual choice, to a framing that reveals how permitting cloning affects future generations and society. I am reminded of one of the consultations of the Royal Commission on New Reproductive Technologies with an aboriginal group in Canada. They told the commission about their seventh-generation rule. They said that when they had to make a big decision in their community, they always considered what the consequences were likely to be in the seventh generation. This is a useful perspective to have, because viewing cloning as a personal matter inappropriately minimizes potentially serious social consequences. Individual choices in reproduction are not isolated acts—they affect the child, other people, and future generations. The wider consequences must be considered because we all have a stake in the type of community that we live in. We do not want it to be one where the use of cloning commodifies children, commercializes family formation, or increases social injustice. Cloning raises issues about the future of our species. We have not yet found the wisdom to deal with hunger, poverty, and environmental degradation—we are unlikely to have the wisdom to direct our own evolution.

Ethical and emotional appeal

Established truth

Established truth

7   Nuclear-transfer cloning allows third parties to choose the genotypes of people who will be cloned. Before, when two people mated, no one could control which genes the child received out of a myriad of possibilities. This lottery of reproduction has been a protection against people being predetermined, chosen, or designed by others—including parents.

Development through comparison

8   Cloning directs the production of human beings in an unprecedented way. When a child of a particular genetic constitution is "made," it is easier to look on him or her as a product, rather than a gift of providence. If we can, and some people do, make children "to order," it is likely to change the way we view children.

Topic sentence

Development through effects

9   An impetus to developing nuclear-transfer cloning for producing animals has been that it could then be combined with genetic enhancement—genes could be added to give the animals desired traits. Genes are inserted into cells in culture, then the cells screened to pick the ones that have incorporated the desired genes. These altered cells are used as the donors of nuclei for cloned animals. It is then possible to create transgenic cloned animals with commercially desirable genetic traits (for example, heavier meat yield or production of insulin in the milk).[11]

Definition of key term: scientific fact

10   Reproduction by nuclear-transfer cloning makes it possible to think about genetically enhancing humans. A person's cells could be cultured, genes inserted, and those cells taking up the desired genes used to produce a cloned "improved" individual. We could insert genes for viral-disease resistance, or to protect against baldness or degenerative diseases, or insert genes related to height or intelligence. If nuclear-transfer cloning is permitted, what will stop genetic enhancement being used eventually? There would be strong individual motivation to have a taller or disease-resistant child. We would then be taking human evolution into our own

Refutation of argument for genetic enhancement

hands. Are we wise enough to manage it or the social consequences? Most people will want their child to be brighter, taller, disease-resistant—so this technology could make people more standard, based on individual choices and market forces. <u>If it works, it is likely to become used more often than just occasionally.</u>

Qualification of claim

11   Who would have access to cloning or genetic improvements? Everyone? It is likely that those with financial resources would have access, but not other people, because cloning or enhancement would have to be provided as a socially under-written "good" if it were to be available to everyone. And it is unlikely that most countries would provide publicly supported cloning, given that there are few social benefits and many potential harms.

12   If cloning or enhancement technology were provided as a public good to ensure equality of access, the government would have to decide in what circumstances people may clone themselves, and what traits were desirable. Docility? Height? Ability to provide a tissue transplant? Unless the market is to decide, criteria as to who may clone themselves, and a regulatory body will be needed.

Examples of traits

13   If cloning is used, will we undermine the unconditional parental acceptance of offspring that is central to nurturing human beings? Parental acceptance is likely to become conditional when we are able to program for certain characteristics. If cloning technology or genetic enhancement is permitted, people with disabilities, or members of racial or ethnic minorities, will be affected differently, and in a way unlikely to lead to greater equality and respect.

Ethical appeal

14   There are forces favouring the use of cloning—particular individuals will pursue it, and it will benefit financially those who provide it, so it is likely to be marketed to the public.

Deductive claim

15   Many issues arising from cloning cannot be resolved in the framework of individual autonomy and reproductive choice. The focus on autonomy leads us to overlook the collective and transgenerational consequences of leaving the use of reproductive technologies to individual choices.[12] The use of scientific technology focused on individual wishes may result in social harms because individual interests differ from the public good at times. It is analogous to the tragedy of the commons,[13] which is exemplified by ranchers sharing grazing land, or fishers sharing a fishing ground. There is an incentive for individuals to overgraze or overfish because the benefits of doing so accrue to the individual, whereas the costs and harms occur to the community. The aggregate effect of individually beneficial choices may harm the long-term common good, and the cumulative impact of individual choices can result in an unethical system. Public policy-making differs from individual-based decision-making—because the moral unit of a physician is the patient, while the moral unit of public policy is all citizens.[14] If there is a conflict between the total social good and the good of an individual, public policy must uphold the public interest.

Rational appeal: analogy

16   All members of the public have a stake in whether cloning is permitted, because if cloned people exist, the changes affect everyone. Even though a majority do not want to allow it, if it is permitted, we would all live in a world where people are cloned. Even though initially, individuals on whom cloning technology had a direct impact would be a minority, their collective experiences would influence social values. In public policy-making, it is inappropriate to subordinate every consideration to the question of whether it helps a couple to have a family. Society has a legitimate role in deciding whether cloning will be used. The far-reaching nature of this choice means more voices must be involved in making decisions. The decisions should not be taken preemptively by a clinical facility or a group of

scientists who ignore the wishes of the rest of the community. We need the perspectives not just of those who are knowledgeable in biology or science; we also need the perspectives of sociologists, humanists, and citizens from a variety of life experiences. On something that affects our species' future, it would be valuable to have the perspectives of people from many countries.

Conclusions Regarding Policy

17   There is no compelling case to make people by asexual means; human reproductive cloning is without potential benefits to almost all citizens, and other options are available in most situations. Many institutions have come to this conclusion; the prospects of making human beings by cloning have elicited concern in many countries, and there have been calls for a worldwide ban on cloning used to produce humans by many political and religious leaders, and by organizations such as the World Health Organization, the World Medical Organization, the American Medical Association, and UNESCO. Nineteen countries in the Council of Europe have signed an agreement that bans human cloning. Medicine, science, and technology are worldwide endeavours, so this is an issue facing humans as a species. For this reason, WHO is making an international effort to co-operate on guidelines for cloning in humans.

18   History shows that where there is a demand for a new service and the ability of a few to pay for it, unless there is legislation, there will be professionals willing to provide it. There is licensing of fertility clinics in several European countries, but in some other countries, reproductive technologies are highly commercialized and little regulated. If human cloning were permitted in the United States, it would likely proceed in the billion-dollar private reproductive-medicine sector. In this market-driven context, its use is unlikely to be controlled. It is now possible to peruse catalogues if you wish to buy eggs or surrogate pregnancies, so it seems likely that if human cloning is permitted in the United States, it is only a matter of time before pressure from individuals with specific interests would open up the field. Legislation is needed to ban the implantation into a woman of an egg cell that has had its nucleus transferred from a body cell. When such legislation is written, its wording should not inadvertently ban non-reproductive cloning research, or animal cloning research that may be of benefit, and that many people see as acceptable.

19   How we use cloning is not an individual or medical matter. It is a matter of social policy that cannot be viewed in a narrow framework of reproductive technology and individual choice. How we choose to use this technological capacity will shape society for our children, their children, and after. How it is used is likely to entrench existing inequalities, and create new ones.

Ethical appeal

20   In conclusion, using nuclear-transfer cloning to allow people to have a child introduces a different way of reproduction for our species. Once we breach this barrier, it leaves us with no place to stop. Given all the problems outlined, the reasons for permitting cloning to produce a person are insufficiently compelling. Even in the few circumstances where the case for human cloning seems justified, there are alternative solutions. We are at an appropriate stopping place on a slippery slope. Not all reasons why a person might wish to copy his or her cells are unethical, but given there are other options open to people wishing to form a family, concerns about individual and social harms from cloning are strong enough that it is not justified to permit it. These issues affecting the creation of the next generation are important for the future of our species; we must deal with them wisely. I hope we can.

Conclusion

Thesis statement

Ethical appeal

References

Please note that these References follow the Chicago style, not the MLA style usually recommended for essays in English classes.

1. Whatever next? *The Economist* 1997 March 1; 79–81.
2. Time/CNN poll. 1997 March.
3. International Food Information Council. *Wirthlin group quorum survey,* 1997 March 21–24.
4. *Public perspectives on human cloning, medicine in society program.* The Wellcome Trust, 1999 June (http://www.wellcome.ac.uk/en/1/awtpubrepcln.html).
5. McGee G. *The human cloning debate.* Berkeley: Berkeley Hills Books, 1998.
6. Hummer J, Almeder R. Human cloning. *Biomedical Ethics Reviews.* Ottawa: 1998.
7. Andrews L. *The clone age: 20 years at the forefront of reproductive technology.* New York: Henry Holt, 1999.
8. Wilson JQ, Kass L. *The ethics of human cloning.* Washington: American Enterprise Press, 1999:10(2).
9. Cloning human beings. Report of the national bioethics advisory commission. *Hastings Centre Report* 1997:27(5).
10. Baylis F. Human cloning: three mistakes and a solution. Unpublished manuscript.
11. Pennis E. After Dolly, a pharming frenzy. *Science* 1998:279; 646-8.
12. Baird PA. Individual interests, societal interests, and reproductive technologies. *Perspectives Biology Medicine* 1997; 40(3): 440-51.
13. Hardin G. The tragedy of the commons. *Science* 1968; 162:1243-8.
14. Lamm RD. Redrawing the ethics map. *Hastings Centre Report* 1999; 29(2): 28–9.

DISCUSSION QUESTIONS

1. What use does the writer make of polls on people's attitudes toward cloning? What possible objection to the use of polls does the writer anticipate and counter?

2. According to Baird, what are three reasons that people might wish to pursue cloning? How does she support her claim that cloned individuals may feel "a disturbed sense of identity" (paragraph 5)?

3. What does Baird imply by her call to "shift the framing" of the debate about human cloning? In her ethical appeal, what undesirable consequences does she imagine could result from cloning (paragraph 6)?

4. Locate the questions that Baird asks the reader (paragraphs 9, 10, 11, 12, 13). Why do you suppose that most of the questions are positioned later in the paper? What effect does Baird create through the asking of these questions?

5. Explain the point of the analogy which Baird uses in paragraph 15. Does this analogy help persuade you to Baird's point of view? Why or why not?

6. What concerns does Baird express about letting market forces decide whether or not cloning should be permitted (paragraphs 10–14)?

7. As in many arguments, the thesis statement comes in the last paragraph. Why do you suppose it comes toward the end?

8. What kinds of sources does Baird cite? To what extent does the use of sources bolster her argument?

9. Baird's views on cloning differ from those of Chris MacDonald set forth on the following pages. Read MacDonald's argument and summarize the main points of difference.

TOWARD KEY INSIGHTS

How do you respond to Baird's emphasis on the psychological harm to individuals that might result from cloning?

Do you believe that cloning would be more psychologically harmful than other forms of reproductive technology that are currently permitted? Why or why not?

In your view, what additional problems—or benefits—might result from genetic enhancement of human beings?

SUGGESTION FOR ORAL ARGUMENT

After researching both sides of the argument on the Internet or elsewhere, come to class prepared to argue either side of the following proposition:

As a society, we should support stem cell research.

SUGGESTION FOR WRITING

Write an essay that emphasizes either the potential benefits or the potential drawbacks in one type of reproductive or medical technology such as embryo research, genetic testing, pre-natal diagnostic screening, in-vitro fertilization, or surrogacy (pre-conception arrangements). Convey a sense of balance by considering opposing arguments as well. A useful starting point might be any of the sources cited in the article by Patricia Baird, or an electronic weekly digest of news stories related to assisted repro-duction: http://www.progress.org.uk, *or a related link that contains an annotated bibliography:* http://www.keele.ac.uk/depts/sttt.

Dr. Chris MacDonald

Yes, Human Cloning Should Be Permitted[*]

Chris MacDonald is a Canadian philosopher whose research interests include business ethics, health-care ethics, professional ethics, and ethical theory. Some of his most recent publications have been related to ethical issues in the biotechnology industry. As you read the following article, note how he responds to specific points in Patricia Baird's argument calling for a ban on human cloning.

1   Patricia Baird's discussion of human cloning (*Annals RCPSC*, June 2000) challenges the prospect of nuclear-transfer cloning for the purposes of human reproduction. Baird reviews a long list of familiar worries about human cloning, but the most striking feature of her discussion is its frankness in placing the onus of justification on the shoulders of those who would permit human cloning. The reasons for permitting cloning, she argues, are "insufficiently compelling," so cloning should be prohibited. The implication is that any new technology should be forbidden unless and until enough justification can be found for allowing its use.

2   Baird is to be commended for her frankness. But the onus is misplaced, or at least too severe. One need not be a single-minded defender of liberty to think that, contrary to Baird's implication, we need good reasons to limit the actions of others, particularly when those actions do no clear and specific harm. The fact that a portion of society—even a majority—finds an activity distasteful is insufficient grounds for passing a law forbidding it. For example, it is presumably true that at one point, roughly 90 per cent of the public (the same proportion that Baird says is against human cloning) was opposed to homosexuality. Does (or did) this justify action on the part of government to ban homosexual lifestyles? Surely not.

3   There may be a flaw in my analogy. Human cloning, according to critics, has harmful effects (or at least risks). Indeed, Baird suggests that the arguments regarding potential physical and psychological harm to clones have been "well delineated." In fact, a convincing case has yet to be made for the claim that the physical and psychological risks to clones are more severe than, or different in kind from, those faced by children produced in more traditional ways. Identical twins live with the psychological "burden" of not being genetically unique. Children born to women over 35 are at an increased risk of genetic illness. Children resulting from in-vitro fertilization or other reproductive technologies live with the knowledge that their origins were unusual. They may even live with the knowledge that their genetic profile has been manipulated (for example, through pre-implantation selection of embryos). Human cloning for reproductive purposes is another novel—and as yet untested—medical technology. As such, it should be approached with caution. Thorough animal trials should be completed before attempts on humans are contemplated. But this is true of any new medical technology.

4   Baird worries about the shift that human cloning might provoke in the way that we view children. This in turn would change the type of community that we are. The central worry is that human cloning "commodities" children (i.e. that cloning may make us think of children as a commodity or product to be bought and sold). Why would cloning have this effect? Is it simply because it is likely to be expensive, so that it costs money to have children? Surely this is insufficient to worry us. Raising children already costs money—the statistics show us how many hundreds

of thousands of dollars it costs to raise a child through to adulthood. Yet no one has suggested that we see our children as products, or love them any less. (In the mid-1940s—before publicly funded health care—my grandparents sold their car to pay the hospital bill related to my father's birth, so "purchasing" the birth of a child is nothing new!)

5   Baird argues that an "important part of human identity is the sense of arising from a maternal and a paternal line while at the same time being a unique individual." Yet without supporting evidence, this sounds like pop psychology. And we can reply in kind: most people I know do not identify with both their maternal and paternal lineages. One of my friends, who was raised by a single mother, identifies with her maternal eastern European heritage, and not with the French paternal heritage implied by her surname. Another friend identifies with his father's black heritage, rather than with his maternal Chinese lineage, despite his Asian physical features. Such patterns are not unusual. Dual heritage may be normal, but it hardly seems central to our conception of ourselves as humans. And identical twins seem none the worse for the knowledge that they are not genetically unique individuals. Claims about challenges to what makes us "human" may be powerful rhetorical devices, but they must be substantiated if they are to be convincing.

6   Baird is correct to exhort us to look beyond harms to identifiable individuals, to the social implications that human cloning might have. As a comparison, think of fetal sex selection. Most of us think that sex selection is a bad thing—not because of any purported harm to the child, but because we worry about the social implications of valuing children of one sex over those of another. So Baird rightly reminds us that focusing on potential harms to individuals constitutes a "dangerously incomplete framing" of the problem. Furthermore, cloning (and genetic technology in general) is sufficiently new—and its implications sufficiently poorly understood—to warrant a healthy respect, and even the allowance of a margin of safety. But this does not suggest the need for the ban that Baird (with others) proposes. What these worries suggest is a need for caution, for discussion, and for regulation. For instance, laws limiting the number of clones that might be created from one individual, restricting the combination of cloning with genetic modification, and defining lines of parental obligation, would alleviate many of the concerns associated with human cloning. (Françoise Baylis argues that cloning is so likely to be used in combination with gene transfer that we should think of cloning as an enhancement technology rather than as a reproductive technology, in her article "Human cloning: three mistakes and a solution," which has been accepted for publication in the *Journal of Medicine and Philosophy*.)

7   What I have said here should not be taken as an absolute defence of human cloning in all circumstances. (Indeed, there may be only a few circumstances in which cloning is appropriate.) Nor have I suggested that public monies should be spent on cloning research. All I have suggested is that a ban on research leading toward human cloning is unwarranted by the arguments raised thus far. Caution and discretion are warranted; a ban is not.

8   Finally, I worry that Baird's point of view exemplifies the way in which human reproductive cloning is being singled out, among cloning-related techniques, as a bogeyman. Almost in chorus, scientists are pleading with regulators not to place restrictions on cloning experimentation per se. At the same time, most scientists seem to be more than willing to swear off reproductive cloning, and indeed to wring their hands over the moral implications of its use. Yet this has the air of a too-hasty concession. The scientific community seems to be too willing to condemn one unpopular application of cloning technology, on the basis of too little convincing argumentation, to appease those who oppose cloning technology in general.

But human cloning for reproductive purposes has legitimate, morally acceptable applications—for example, for infertile couples, and for gay couples. And none of the criticisms have been convincingly made. We should not let reproductive human cloning be abandoned as the moral sacrificial lamb of the cloning debate.

DISCUSSION QUESTIONS

1. Chris MacDonald's essay is a rebuttal to the arguments offered by Patricia Baird, in her essay "Should Human Cloning Be Permitted?" What major premise of Baird's argument does MacDonald think is "misplaced, or at least too severe" (paragraph 2). Explain MacDonald's objection and the major argumentative premise of his essay.

2. While taking issue with many of Baird's claims, MacDonald acknowledges the strengths of her argument as well. Find an example showing how MacDonald praises an aspect of Baird's argument and then adapts it to serve his own argument.

3. Identify the main claims of Baird's argument to which MacDonald responds. Are his responses compelling? Does he succeed in raising doubt about Baird's conclusion?

4. Unlike Baird, MacDonald (except through one parenthetical reference to an un-published article by Françoise Baylis) does not refer to the scholarship of others to reinforce his position. Is his argument weakened by this lack of secondary scholarly support? Explain why or why not.

5. While Baird's essay is written almost entirely in the third-person voice, MacDonald's is written almost entirely in the first-person voice. How does this first-person point of view enhance or diminish MacDonald's persuasive appeal? Explain, using examples from the essay.

6. What rational, emotional, and ethical appeals does MacDonald use in the two concluding paragraphs of this essay?

TOWARD KEY INSIGHTS

How do you respond to MacDonald's assertion that there is no clear evidence that our humanity is predicated on being able to recognize and identify with our parental lineages? Do you believe that human cloning for reproductive purposes could be appropriate in some circumstances? Why or why not?

SUGGESTION FOR ORAL ARGUMENT

After researching both sides of the argument on the Internet or elsewhere, come to class prepared to argue either side of the following propositions:

As a society, we should support research into human cloning.

SUGGESTIONS FOR WRITING

After considering the issue of animal cloning, develop an argument that makes a strong ethical appeal for or against animal cloning. Use specifics in your argument.

After evaluating the two essays in this book on cloning, compare and contrast the ways in which each writer uses persuasive appeals or techniques, and evaluate which essay you find to be most successful, and why.

Paul Wells

A Justifiable Power Grab[*]

Paul Wells is the parliamentary columnist of the National Post. *In his article "A Justifiable Power Grab" Wells argues that even though the anti-terror legislation compromises the Charter of Rights, it is a justifiable "power grab" by Ottawa in order to protect Canadian democracy.*

1   The government's antiterror laws are medicine suited to the disease.

2   Joe Clark's powers of diagnosis, at least, remain acute. The Progressive Conservative leader has called Bill C-42, the federal government's second catchall antiterrorism bill, a "power grab." It's the most concise description of what the federal government is seeking to do with both C-42 and Bill C-36, the other law it has proposed to deal with terrorism: grab power, hoard it at the executive level to the detriment of Parliament and reduce the individual citizen's power to go about life in a predictable way, protected by a solid framework of rights and legal protections.

3   The interesting question is whether power grabbing is justified in the wake of the Sept. 11 atrocities. I think it is. There's plenty of room in the antiterror bills for abuse. Shortly after Sept. 11, a French diplomat sat me down and lectured me about what Canada needs to do if it is serious about stopping terrorists. Her list of measures included arrest for "suspicion of intent" to commit a terrorist act. In France cops have been arresting people for years on the basis of their best guess about what they might soon do. Great, I said, but we have a Charter of Rights in Canada, and we will not be doing anything that drastic.

4   Silly me. Bill C-36 provides those same preventive-arrest measures and much more. It boldly expands wiretap and surveillance powers and allows the feds to remove the evidence justifying such acts from any real public scrutiny.

5   With C-42, the alarming news keeps on coming: Defense Minister Art Eggleton could designate, for up to a year, "military security zones" of any size anywhere in Canada, from which his armed forces and any designated police could remove unauthorized personnel. Handy for shutting down protests outside international summits, critics warn, or for occupying Quebec if it tries to secede, the Bloc Quebecois says. Then there is C-42's enormous expansion of ministers' ability to issue "interim orders" that allow them to sidestep all kinds of laws governing public health, the environment, transport and borders.

6   What on earth is going on here? How can any of this be defended? Well, let's give it a try. The least important, but not unimportant, justification for passing laws like these is that everyone's doing it: all the big Western democracies, including our allies in the U.S. and Britain, have massively beefed up the power of

the state to catch bad guys who would prefer to hide in the thickets of the law. The Americans, in particular, are keeping an eye on us to ensure that Canada doesn't become a uniquely safe haven for terrorists. This was the subtext of U.S. Attorney General John Ashcroft's visit to the Canada-U.S. border. Ashcroft is developing quite a reputation at home for preferring effective policing over fastidious regard for civil liberties. Any decision he makes affecting the flow of traffic at the border will reflect the same hierarchy of priorities.

7   More important than keeping up with the Joneses are two lessons that governments have drawn from Sept. 11. First, it's exceedingly difficult to predict what the bad guys will do. Yet second, the cost of failing to catch them could be catastrophic. This makes the terrorist threat different from the public-security emergencies Canada is used to, like the 1990 Oka uprising or the separatist kidnappings of October 1970.

8   Those previous events were big, public, limited in duration. There were military secrets woven through both, but basically everyone knew in broad outline what was going on. So there was time to consult Parliament, debate in public, broadcast the government's response. That's the kind of situation the old War Measures Act and its replacement, the Emergencies Act, were written for.

9   The sleepers of al-Qaeda represent a different kind of threat: longer in duration, essentially permanent, which is why Bill C-36 implements permanent changes in Canada's national-security regime (and why sticklers like me dislike the idea of sunset clauses that could cancel some of its provisions after five years).

10   Within that permanent context there will be sudden and unpredictable stealth clashes, secret government responses to clandestine terrorist operations. When those happen, there will be no time to brief Joe Clark, no justification to go before the TV cameras, no way to know which complacent, profoundly bureaucratized routine will need an emergency detour traced around it by a Cabinet minister's pen.

11   The need for Parliamentary or judicial oversight of the new legal tools to be used in this ugly kind of conflict remains, but it will sometimes have to come after an immediate crisis has passed. Democracy's new enemy is swift and quiet and entirely ruthless; democracies must be faster and stealthier in their self-defense than they are used to being. This makes us more like our enemy than we like to be. There is no joy in such a situation, but neither, any longer, is there really a choice.

DISCUSSION QUESTIONS

1. Discuss the meaning of the title. How does it relate to the writer's thesis and purpose?

2. Illustrate and explain the author's main arguments in support of Bills C-36 and C-42.

3. How does the author demonstrate his understanding of viewpoints contrary to his own? Does he supply adequate support for his contention that "power grabbing is justified in the wake of the Sept. 11 atrocities" (paragraph 3)? Explain why or why not.

4. Do terrorist attacks such as the bombing in Bali or other world events, including the situation in Iraq, that have happened since this article was published in December, 2001 affect your response to Wells's article? Why or why not?

5. Cite examples of rational, emotional, and ethical appeals used in the argument. What is the main kind of appeal that the argument relies upon?

6. Examine the conclusion in the last two paragraphs. What do they reveal about the author's purpose in writing? Why does the author personify democracy?

TOWARD KEY INSIGHTS

How persuasive do you find this argument? Are there additional arguments or appeals that the writer might have used? Do you have any objections to the arguments that have not been adequately addressed? Are there any additional arguments that the writer might have included?

Consider other cases that demonstrate tension between the need for security and the need to uphold democratic rights of the individual. Can you think of examples where you think police or other governmental agencies have not been given enough authority to preserve an adequate level of safety for individuals in our society?

SUGGESTION FOR ORAL ARGUMENT

Research the arguments for and against the following proposition, and come to class prepared to argue either side:

Canada should strengthen its immigration laws.

SUGGESTION FOR WRITING

Write an essay that argues that Canada should have more (or less) airport, port, or border security. Bring in as many different kinds of evidence as you can.

Alan Borovoy

Security's Serpentine Coils*

Alan Borovoy has been General Counsel for the Canadian Civil Liberties Association since 1968. In that capacity he has spoken at public inquiries and before parliamentary committees on diverse issues such as campus speech codes, wiretapping, drug-testing, capital punishment and national security. Alan Borovoy has also worked as a columnist for the Toronto Star, *and has been a visiting professor in the Faculty of Law at Dalhousie University and the University of Windsor, as well as a part-time lecturer in the Faculty of Social Work at the University of Toronto and the Political Science Department at York University. He is the author of many articles on the topic of civil liberty and two books,* Uncivil Disobedience: The Tactics and Tales of a Democratic Agitator *and* When Freedoms Collide: The Case for Our Civil Liberties. *The latter was nominated for the Govenor General's Award in 1988.*

---

* *The Globe and Mail,* Thursday, August 1, 2003, A19.

1   Every day, we are deluged with news about the war on terrorism. On the home front, we have just learned that the Canadian Security Intelligence Service (CSIS) facilitated the transfer of a Canadian citizen, Mansour Jabarah, to the United States where he is currently being held. We don't now know whether this man went there voluntarily or against his will. But there is reason for concern: As necessary as it is to root out, and defeat terrorism, it is essential that our government obey the law and comply with the principles of fairness.

2   Just last week, the media carried stories about certain new additions to the government's list of terrorist entities. This news has evoked some lopsided responses. Why, some are asking, is the list so small? Why don't the additions include more of the Palestinian or any of the Asian extremists?

3   But what hasn't been questioned enough is the nature of the listing power itself. At the recommendation of the Solicitor-General, the federal government has wide powers to put people on the list. Although such action requires "reasonable grounds," it does not require the government to convene a hearing or produce any evidence. In addition to being stigmatized, perhaps irreparably, those on the list are headed for financial ostracization. The rest of us are explicitly prohibited from dealing with their property.

4   Why should people be transformed into legal pariahs without being found guilty of anything unlawful? Even though a court may ultimately remove such people from the list, their redemption may come too late to be helpful. Even if no one is bothered by the listing of such obvious terrorists as al-Qaeda and Osama bin Laden, it's important to note again the sheer breadth of the listing power.

5   Indeed, it appears that such power has already been misapplied. Consider the case of Liban Hussein, a Canadian citizen from Somalia who has been living in this country since 1991. He operated a business that supported himself, his wife, children, and several relatives.

6   In the fall of 2001, the bottom suddenly fell out of his life. Mr. Hussein learned that his name was on Canada's list of terrorist entities. Apparently the government decided on this action just a few hours after it learned that he appeared on the United States' terrorist list.

7   Shortly after his listing became public, Mr. Hussein was arrested, jailed and had his assets frozen. It then became a crime for anyone to have financial dealings with him. Worse, Mr. Hussein was made the target of extradition proceedings at the instigation of the United States.

8   In early June, this legal harassment ended as suddenly as it had begun. The government of Canada declared that there was no evidence linking this man to terrorism. But, although he was cleared, he was reportedly also ruined. According to his lawyer, Mr. Hussein lost his business, his income, his job and his prospects.

9   If one person could suffer such an injustice, why not others? Even if there might be an argument for the listing of certain organizations, why should the power apply to individuals—especially citizens and permanent residents? After all, organizations have limited functions to perform but individuals have ordinary lives to lead.

10   Moreover, to what extent does the legitimate fight against terrorism really require such an intrusive power? After all, those slated for the list are likely to be under intense surveillance already. This would be likely to increase the prospects for intercepting their harmful behaviour.

11   There are additional problems regarding the government's list. The new antiterrorist laws require all of us to tell the authorities if and when we come into possession of property belonging to a listed entity. This is a relatively unprecedented

obligation. With few exceptions, Canada has avoided compelling people to inform on one another. Among other things, it is believed that a climate of compulsory informing would erode social harmony.

12   Again, how necessary is this measure? Without it, the antiterrorist laws would still bar contributing to, raising money for, and, in many other ways serving, the interests of terrorist entities. Moreover, in light of Sept. 11, we could expect a substantial increase in voluntary reporting.

13   Unfortunately, such issues have received too little scrutiny. The government's antiterrorist measures were rammed through Parliament at such breakneck speed that there was never an adequate assessment of their costs and benefits. The major antiterrorist bill, C-36, containing more than 100 pages of complex measures, was introduced in mid-October and passed before the end of December. This is hardly the way a mature democracy should even discuss, let alone decrease, the fundamental civil liberties of its people.

14   A helpful response would be an amendment that would require these special antiterrorist measures to lapse automatically after one year unless re-enacted within that time. There would be nothing to lose and conceivably much to gain. The government already has its antiterrorist laws to do with them what it will. But, to whatever extent it wanted any of these measures to linger longer, it would feel effectively pressured to reintroduce them in more manageable segments so that, at long last, there could be a meaningful parliamentary and public debate.

15   The current situation is simply unacceptable.

DISCUSSION QUESTIONS

1. Discuss the meaning of the title. How does it relate to the writer's thesis and purpose? Find a sentence that you would identify as the thesis sentence.

2. Give examples of how the author presents himself as temperate and reasonable at the outset—anticipating and countering possible reader resistance, for instance. How does he qualify his argument (paragraphs 1, 4, 8)?

3. In your own words, explain what the writer means when he says, "What hasn't been questioned is the nature of the listing power itself" (paragraph 3)? What principal objections does he put forward (paragraphs 3–5)? What support does the writer give for his claim that the listing power of the court under new legislation "has been misapplied"(paragraph 5)?

4. What logic does the author use when he questions the necessity of the new antiterrorist measure (paragraphs 9–12)?

5. Cite examples of rational, emotional, and ethical appeals used in the argument. What is the main kind of appeal that the argument relies upon?

6. Examine the conclusion in the last three paragraphs. What do these paragraphs suggest about the author's purpose in writing? What recommendations does the writer include? Why is the last sentence in a paragraph by itself?

TOWARD KEY INSIGHTS

How persuasive do you find this argument? Are there additional arguments or appeals that the writer might have used? Do you have any objections to the arguments that have not been adequately addressed? Do you find yourself more persuaded by Borovoy's argument here or by Wells's argument that precedes this one? Explain why you find one more compelling than the other.

Consider other cases—near or far from home, historical, contemporary, or even fictional—that demonstrate tension between the need for state or national security and the need to uphold democratic rights of the individual. Can you think of examples where you think the centralized power of the state has been granted too much authority, or not enough authority? How applicable are Borovoy's arguments to these other cases?

SUGGESTION FOR ORAL ARGUMENT

Research the arguments for and against the following proposition, and come to class prepared to argue either side of the proposition:

Canada should strengthen its antiterrorist measures.

SUGGESTION FOR WRITING

Read recent news reports (within the last two or three months) on topical issues related to civil rights, human rights, terrorism, or war. Find one or more cases where you believe that civil liberties were not sufficiently respected, or where you think the powers of enforcement were overly constrained. Write an argument that points out dangers you see with the current approach, and recommend another course of action.

Martin Luther King, Jr.

I Have a Dream

Martin Luther King, Jr. (1929–1968) has earned lasting fame for his part in the civil rights struggles of the 1950s and 1960s. Born in Atlanta, Georgia, he was ordained a Baptist minister in his father's church in 1947. A year later, he graduated from Morehouse College, then went on to take a Bachelor of Divinity degree at Crozier Theological Seminary (1951) and a Ph.D. in Philosophy at Boston University (1954), after which he accepted a pastorate in Montgomery, Alabama. King's involvement with civil rights grew when he organized and led a boycott that succeeded in desegregating Montgomery's bus system. In 1957, he founded and became the first president of the Southern Christian Leadership Conference and assumed a leading role in the civil rights movement. King advocated a policy of nonviolent protest based on the beliefs of Thoreau and Gandhi and never veered from it despite many acts of violence directed at him. The success of King's crusade helped bring about the passage of the Civil Rights Act of 1964 and the Voting Rights Act of 1965 and won him the Nobel Peace Prize in 1964. King was assassinated on April 4, 1968, in Memphis, Tennessee. The speech "I Have a Dream" was delivered August 28, 1963, at the Lincoln Memorial in Washington, D.C., before a crowd of 200 000 people who had gathered to commemorate the centennial of the Emancipation Proclamation and to demonstrate for pending civil rights legislation. It stands as one of the most eloquent pleas ever made for racial justice.

1   I am happy to join with you today in what will go down in history as the greatest demonstration for freedom in the history of our nation.

2   Five score years ago, a great American, in whose symbolic shadow we stand today, signed the Emancipation Proclamation. This momentous decree came as a great beacon light of hope to millions of Negro slaves who had been seared in the flames of withering injustice. It came as a joyous daybreak to end the long night of their captivity.

3   But one hundred years later, the Negro still is not free; one hundred years later, the life of the Negro is still sadly crippled by the manacles of segregation and the chains of discrimination; one hundred years later, the Negro lives on a lonely island of poverty in the midst of a vast ocean of material prosperity; one hundred years later, the Negro is still languishing in the corners of American society and finds himself in exile in his own land.

4   So we've come here today to dramatize a shameful condition. In a sense we've come to our nation's capital to cash a check. When the architects of our republic wrote the magnificent words of the Constitution and the Declaration of Independence, they were signing a promissory note to which every American was to fall heir. This note was the promise that all men, yes, black men as well as white men, would be guaranteed the unalienable rights of life, liberty, and the pursuit of happiness.

5   It is obvious today that America has defaulted on this promissory note in so far as her citizens of color are concerned. Instead of honoring this sacred obligation, America has given the Negro people a bad check; a check which has come back marked "insufficient funds." But we refuse to believe that the bank of justice is bankrupt. We refuse to believe that there are insufficient funds in the great vaults of opportunity of this nation. And so we've come to cash this check, a check that will give us upon demand the riches of freedom and the security of justice.

6   We have also come to this hallowed spot to remind America of the fierce urgency of now. This is no time to engage in the luxury of cooling off or to take the tranquilizing drug of gradualism. Now is the time to make real the promises of democracy; now is the time to rise from the dark and desolate valley of segregation to the sunlit path of racial justice; now is the time to lift our nation from the quicksands of racial injustice to the solid rock of brotherhood; now is the time to make justice a reality for all of God's children. It would be fatal for the nation to overlook the urgency of the moment. This sweltering summer of the Negro's legitimate discontent will not pass until there is an invigorating autumn of freedom and equality.

7   Nineteen sixty-three is not an end, but a beginning. And those who hope that the Negro needed to blow off steam and will now be content will have a rude awakening if the nation returns to business as usual. There will be neither rest nor tranquility in America until the Negro is granted his citizenship rights. The whirlwinds of revolt will continue to shake the foundations of our nation until the bright day of justice emerges.

8   But there is something that I must say to my people, who stand on the worn threshold which leads into the palace of justice. In the process of gaining our rightful place, we must not be guilty of wrongful deeds. Let us not seek to satisfy our thirst for freedom by drinking from the cup of bitterness and hatred. We must forever conduct our struggle on the high plain of dignity and discipline. We must not allow our creative protests to degenerate into physical violence. Again and again we must rise to the majestic heights of meeting physical force with soul force. The marvelous new militancy, which has engulfed the Negro

community, must not lead us to a distrust of all white people. For many of our white brothers, as evidenced by their presence here today, have come to realize that their destiny is tied up with our destiny. And they have come to realize that their freedom is inextricably bound to our freedom. We cannot walk alone. And as we walk, we must make the pledge that we shall always march ahead. We cannot turn back.

9   There are those who are asking the devotees of Civil Rights, "When will you be satisfied?" We can never be satisfied as long as the Negro is the victim of the unspeakable horrors of police brutality; we can never be satisfied as long as our bodies, heavy with the fatigue of travel, cannot gain lodging in the motels of the highways and the hotels of the cities; we cannot be satisfied as long as the Negro's basic mobility is from a smaller ghetto to a larger one; we can never be satisfied as long as our children are stripped of their selfhood and robbed of their dignity by signs stating "For White Only"; we cannot be satisfied as long as the Negro in Mississippi cannot vote and a Negro in New York believes he has nothing for which to vote. No! No, we are not satisfied, and we will not be satisfied until "justice rolls down like waters and righteousness like a mighty stream."

10   I am not unmindful that some of you have come here out of great trials and tribulations. Some of you have come fresh from narrow jail cells. Some of you have come from areas where your quest for freedom left you battered by the storms of persecution and staggered by the winds of police brutality. You have been the veterans of creative suffering. Continue to work with the faith that unearned suffering is redemptive. Go back to Mississippi. Go back to Alabama. Go back to South Carolina. Go back to Georgia. Go back to Louisiana. Go back to the slums and ghettos of our Northern cities, knowing that somehow this situation can and will be changed. Let us not wallow in the valley of despair.

11   I say to you today, my friends, that even though we face the difficulties of today and tomorrow, I still have a dream. It is a dream deeply rooted in the American dream. I have a dream that one day this nation will rise up and live out the true meaning of its creed, "We hold these truths to be self-evident, that all men are created equal." I have a dream that one day on the red hills of Georgia, sons of former slaves and the sons of former slaves owners will be able to sit down together at the table of brotherhood. I have a dream that one day even the state of Mississippi, a state sweltering with the heat of injustice, sweltering with the heat of oppression, will be transformed into an oasis of freedom and justice. I have a dream that my four little children will one day live in a nation where they will not be judged by the color of their skin, but by the content of their character.

12   I HAVE A DREAM TODAY!

13   I have a dream that one day down in Alabama—with its vicious racists, with its Governor having his lips dripping with the words of interposition and nullification—one day right there in Alabama, little black boys and black girls will be able to join hands with little white boys and white girls as sisters and brothers.

14   I HAVE A DREAM TODAY!

15   I have a dream that one day every valley shall be exalted, every hill and mountain shall be made low. The rough places will be plain and the crooked places will be made straight, "and the glory of the Lord shall be revealed, and all flesh shall see it together."

16   This is our hope. This is the faith that I go back to the South with. With this faith we will be able to hew out of the mountain of despair, a stone of hope. With this faith we will be able to transform the jangling discords of our nation into a beautiful symphony of brotherhood. With this faith we will be able to

work together, to pray together, to struggle together, to go to jail together, to stand up for freedom together, knowing that we will be free one day. And this will be the day. This will be the day when all of God's children will be able to sing with new meaning, "My country 'tis of thee, sweet land of liberty, of thee I sing. Land where my fathers died, land of the pilgrim's pride, from every mountain side, let freedom ring." And if America is to be a great nation, this must become true.

17   So let freedom ring from the prodigious hilltops of New Hampshire; let freedom ring from the mighty mountains of New York; let freedom ring from the heightening Alleghenies of Pennsylvania; let freedom ring from the snowcapped Rockies of Colorado; let freedom ring from the curvaceous slopes of California. But not only that. Let freedom ring from Stone Mountain of Georgia; let freedom ring from Lookout Mountain of Tennessee; let freedom ring from every hill and molehill of Mississippi. "From every mountainside, let freedom ring."

18   And when this happens, and when we allow freedom to ring, when we let it ring from every village and every hamlet, from every state and every city, we will be able to speed up that day when all of God's children, black men and white men, Jews and Gentiles, Protestants and Catholics, will be able to join hands and sing in the words of the old Negro spiritual: "Free at last. Free at last. Thank God Almighty, we are free at last."

Discussion Questions

1. Why do you think King begins with a reference to Lincoln?

2. Does this speech have a stated or an implied proposition? What is the proposition?

3. What does King hope to accomplish by the speech? How does he go about achieving his aim(s)?

4. What is the audience for the speech?

5. How does King organize his speech? How does this organization advance his purpose?

6. Which type(s) of argumentative appeal does King use? Cite appropriate parts of the speech.

7. What kinds of stylistic devices does King use? Where do they occur? How do they increase the effectiveness of the speech?

Toward Key Insights

To what extent do people of all races relate to King's message today? Explain your answer.

Suggestion for Oral Argument

Research the following proposition, and come to class prepared to argue either side:

In order to promote more social justice, the Canadian government should institute an affirmative action program for racial minorities.

| SUGGESTION FOR WRITING | *Write an essay calling for some major social or political change. For example, you might recommend federally funded day-care centres for working parents, increased tuition subsidies for university students, increases or cuts in military spending.* |

Neil Bissoondath

No Place Like Home*

Neil Bissoondath has written several critically acclaimed books of fiction and nonfiction that explore themes of migration, alienation, and identity. His works of fiction include Digging Up Mountains, A Casual Brutality, *and* The Worlds Within Her. *Neil Bissoondath's provocative discussion of identity politics and multiculturalism,* The Cult of Multi-Culturalism in Canada *(1994), provides a broader and more in-depth discussion of the ideas and concerns raised in his essay "No Place Like Home," which is reproduced below.*

1   Three or four years into the new millennium, Toronto, Canada's largest city, will mark an unusual milestone. In a city of three million, the words "minorities" and "majority" will be turned on their heads and the former will become the latter.

2   Reputed to be the most ethnically diverse city in the world, Toronto has been utterly remade by immigration, just as Canada has been remade by a quarter century of multiculturalism.

3   It is a policy which has been quietly disastrous for the country and for immigrants themselves.

4   The stated purpose of Canada's *Multiculturalism Act* (1971) is to recognize "the existence of communities whose members share a common origin and their historic contribution to Canadian society". It promises to "enhance their development" and to "promote the understanding and creativity that arise from the interaction between individuals and communities of different origins." The bicultural (English and French) nature of the country is to be wilfully refashioned into a multicultural "mosaic."

5   The architects of the policy—the Government of then-Prime Minister Pierre Elliot Trudeau—were blind to the fact that their exercise in social engineering was based on two essentially false premises. First, it assumed that "culture" in the large sense could be transplanted. Second, that those who voluntarily sought a new life in a new country would *wish* to transport their cultures of origin.

6   But "culture" is a most complex creature; in its essence, it represents the very breath of a people. For the purposes of multiculturalism, the concept has been reduced to the simplest theatre. Canadians, neatly divided into "ethnic" and otherwise, encounter each other's mosaic tiles mainly at festivals. There's traditional music, traditional dancing, traditional food at distinctly untraditional prices, all of which is diverting as far as it goes—but such encounters remain at the level of a folkloric Disneyland.

* *New Internationalist*, September 1998, Issue 305, p. 20+.

7   We take a great deal of self-satisfaction from such festivals; they are seen as proof of our open-mindedness, of our welcoming of difference. Yet how easily we forget that none of our ethnic cultures seems to have produced poetry or literature or philosophy worthy of our consideration. How seductive it is, how reassuring, that Greeks are always Zorbas, Ukrainians always Cossacks: we come away with stereotypes reinforced.

8   Not only are differences highlighted, but individuals are defined by those differences. There are those who find pleasure in playing to the theme, those whose ethnicity ripens with the years. Yet to play the ethnic, deracinated and costumed, is to play the stereotype. It is to abdicate one's full humanity in favour of one of its exotic features. To accept the role of ethnic is also to accept a gentle marginalization. It is to accept that one will never be just a part of the landscape but always a little apart from it, not quite belonging.

9   In exoticizing and trivializing cultures, often thousands of years old, by sanctifying the mentality of the mosaic-tile, we have succeeded in creating mental ghettos for the various communities. One's sense of belonging to the larger Canadian landscape is tempered by loyalty to a different cultural or racial heritage.

10   When, for instance, war broke out between Croatia and Serbia, a member of the Ontario legislature, who was of Croatian descent, felt justified in declaring: "I don't think I'd be able to live next door to a Serb." That he was speaking of a fellow Canadian was irrelevant. *Over there* mattered more than *over here*—and the cultural group dictated the loyalty. Ironic for a country that boasted about its leading role in the fight against apartheid.

11   Often between groups one looks in vain for the quality that Canadians seem to value above all—tolerance. We pride ourselves on being a tolerant country, unlike the United States, which seems to demand of its immigrants a kind of submission to American mythology. But not only have we surrendered a great deal of ourselves in pursuit of the ideal—Christmas pageants have been replaced by "Winterfests"; the antiracist Writers Union of Canada sanctioned a 1994 conference which excluded whites—but tolerance itself may be an overrated quality, a flawed ideal.

12   The late novelist Robertson Davies pointed out that *tolerance* is but a weak sister to *acceptance.* To tolerate someone is to put up with them; it is to adopt a pose of indifference. Acceptance is far more difficult, for it implies engagement, understanding, an appreciation of the human similarities beneath the obvious differences. Tolerance then is superficial—and perhaps the highest goal one can expect of Canadian multiculturalism.

13   Another insidious effect of this approach is a kind of provisional citizenship. When 100-metre sprinter Ben Johnson won a gold medal at the Seoul Olympics, he was hailed in the media as the great Canadian star. Days later, when the medal was rescinded because of a positive drug test, Johnson became the Jamaican immigrant—Canadian when convenient, a foreigner when not. Tolerated, never truly accepted, his exoticism always part of his finery, he quickly went from being one of *us* to being one of *them.*

14   This makes for an uneasy social fabric. In replacing the old Canada, based on British and French tradition, with a mosaic (individual tiles separated by cement), we have shaken our sense of identity. In a country over 130 years old, we are still uncertain who we are.

15   A major 1993 study found that 72 per cent of the population wants, as one newspaper put it, "the mosaic to melt." Canadians were found to be "increasingly intolerant" of demands for special treatment made by ethnic groups—a Chinese

group who wanted a publicly funded separate school where their children would be taught in Chinese by Chinese teachers; a Muslim group who claimed the right to opt out of the Canadian judicial system in favour of Islamic law. Canadians wanted immigrants to adopt Canada's values and way of life.

16   Many immigrants agree. They recognize that multiculturalism has not served their interests. It has exoticized, and so marginalized, them, making the realization of their dreams that much harder. The former rector of the University du Quebec a Montreal, Claude Corbo, himself the grandson of Italian immigrants, has pointed out that multiculturalism has kept many immigrants "from integrating naturally into the fabric of Canadian and Quebec society . . . We tell people to preserve their original patrimony to conserve their values, even if these values are incompatible with those of our society."

17   Which leads to the other false premise on which multiculturalism is based. It assumes that people who choose to emigrate not only can but also *wish to* remain what they once were.

18   The act of emigration leaves no-one unscathed. From the moment you board a plane bound for a new land with a one-way ticket, a psychological metamorphosis begins—and the change occurs more quickly, more deeply and more imperceptibly than one imagines.

19   I arrived alone in Toronto from Trinidad in 1973, an 18-year-old with dreams but no experience of the world. A year later, I returned to Trinidad to visit my parents. Within days I realized the extent of the change that had come not only to me, but to all I had left behind. Even after so short a time, old friends had become new strangers, and old places remained only old places. Already Trinidad—its ways, its views, its very essences—was receding, becoming merely a memory of place and childhood experience. *Feeling* had already been wholly transferred to the new land, to this other country which had quickly become my home. Certainly, for others the process is slower and often less evident—but it is inexorable. The human personality is not immutable.

20   Multiculturalism, which asked that I bring to Canada the life I had in Trinidad, was a shock to me. I was seeking a new start in a land that afforded me that possibility. I was *not* seeking to live in Toronto as if I were still in Trinidad—for what would have been the point of emigration? I am far from alone in this. As the political scientist Professor Rias Khan of the University of Winnipeg put it: "People, regardless of their origin, do not emigrate to preserve their culture and nurture their ethnic distinctiveness . . . Immigrants come here to become Canadians; to be productive and contributing members of their chosen society . . . Whether or not I preserve my cultural background is my personal choice; whether or not an ethnic group preserves its cultural background is the group's choice. The state has no business in either."

21   The immigrant dream—of financial and social success; of carving out a place within the larger society—is grand in its simplicity. Requiring great courage, it is self-limiting on no level. All one asks is the freedom and fairness—through anti-discrimination legislation, if necessary—to fulfil one's potential. A vital part of that freedom is the latitude to recognize and welcome inevitable change in society and the migrant. One may treasure a private, personal identity built from family lore and experience, all the while pursuing the public integration vital to wider success. To be put in the position of either obliterating the past or worshipping it is, for the individual, an unnecessary burden that leads to a false and limiting theatre of the self.

22   Not long ago, my daughter's teacher wanted to know what kind of family the children in her first-grade class came from. For most of the children, born in Quebec City into francophone families that have been here for over 200 years, the answer was straightforward.

23   Then it was my daughter's turn. Her father, she explained, was born in Trinidad into an East Indian family; having lived in Canada for a long, long time, he was Canadian. Her mother was born in Quebec City, a francophone. She herself was born in Montreal.

24   "Ahh!" the teacher exclaimed brightly, "So you're from a West Indian family!"

25   My daughter returned home deeply puzzled. At six years of age she had been, with the best of intentions, handed an identity crisis.

26   In some ways she was lucky. We were able to sort out her confusions. In other parts of the country—in Toronto or Vancouver—where ethnic identity has become a kind of fetish, my daughter would have had to deal with a far more complex proposal. To be true to her inherited ethnicities, she would be: Franco-Quebecoise-First Nations-Indian-Canadian. Indeed, for her to describe herself as simply "Canadian" with no qualifying hyphen would be almost antagonistic.

27   The weight of this hyphen was signalled as far back as 20 years ago by the feminist writer Laura Sabia when she said: "I was born and bred in this amazing land. I've always considered myself a Canadian, nothing more, nothing less, even though my parents were immigrants from Italy. How come we have all acquired a hyphen? We have allowed ourselves to become divided along the line of ethnic origins, under the pretext of the 'Great Mosaic.' A dastardly deed has been perpetuated upon Canadians by politicians whose motto is 'divide and rule' . . . I am a Canadian first and foremost. Don't hyphenate me."

28   Or, one might add, future generations.

29   Canadian multiculturalism has emphasized difference. In so doing, it has retarded the integration of immigrants into the Canadian mainstream while damaging Canada's national sense of self. Canada has an enviable record in dealing with racism; our society, while hardly perfect (we too have our racists of all colours), remains largely free of racial conflict. And yet we do ourselves a disservice in pursuing the divisive potential in multiculturalism. With an ongoing battle against separatism in Quebec, with east-west tensions, we are already a country uncomfortably riven. Our "mosaic" does not help us.

30   In recognition of its growing unpopularity, official multiculturalism has had its status downgraded from a ministry, to a directorate, to a department. Canada, for the foreseeable future, will continue to be a nation open to immigrants—and one committed to combating racism, sexism and the various other forms of discrimination we share with other societies. Beyond this, because of the damage already inflicted by multiculturalism, we need to focus on programs that seek out and emphasize the experiences, values and dreams we all share as Canadians, whatever our colour, language, religion, ethnicity or historical grievance. And pursue *acceptance* of others—not mere *tolerance* of them.

31   Whatever policy follows multiculturalism, it should support a new vision of Canadianness. A Canada where no-one is alienated with hyphenation. A nation of cultural hybrids, where every individual is unique and every individual is a Canadian, undiluted and undivided. A nation where the following conversation, so familiar and so enervating to many of us, will no longer take place:

32   "What nationality are you?"

33   "Canadian."

34   "No, I mean, what nationality are you *really*?"

35   The ultimate goal must be a cohesive, effective society enlivened by cultural variety; able to define its place in the world. Only in this way might that member of the Ontario legislature and his neighbour no longer see each other as Serb and Croat but as Canadians with a great deal more in common than their politically sanctioned blindness allows them to perceive.

36   In the end, immigration is a personal adventure. The process of integration that follows it is a personal struggle within a social context that may make the task either more or less difficult. Multiculturalism in Canada has the latter effect but it may matter very little, because integration—the remaking of the self within a new society with one's personal heritage as invaluable texture—is finally achieved in the depths of one's soul. Many Canadians, like me, have simply ignored multiculturalism, by living our lives as fully engaged with our new society as possible, secure in the knowledge of the rich family past that has brought us here.

37   I will never forget the bright summer evening many years ago when, fresh off the plane from a trip to Europe, I stood on my apartment balcony gazing out at the Toronto skyline, at the crystal light emanating off Lake Ontario and beyond. I took a deep breath of the cooling evening air and knew, deep within my bones, that it was good to be home.

DISCUSSION QUESTIONS

1. In your own words, explain the rationale for Canada's *Multiculturalism Act* (paragraph 4). Why does the writer say the policy is an "exercise in social engineering" (paragraph 5)?

2. What does the writer see as the "two false premises" (paragraph 5) or flawed assumptions embedded in the policy of multiculturalism? Identify places where he uses rational, emotional, and ethical appeals throughout the essay to convince readers that these premises are mistaken.

3. What is the distinction that the writer makes between "tolerance" and "acceptance" (paragraph 12)? How does the example of Ben Johnson (paragraph 13) support his claim that tolerance does not necessarily translate into acceptance?

4. How does the writer gain credibility and authority from the inclusion of his personal background (paragraphs 19–20)? How might his point of view be affected by his country of origin, his marriage, and his social class? How might you have read this essay differently if the writer did not have the experience of being an immigrant?

5. What is the point of Bissoondath's anecdote about his daughter's school experience (paragraphs 22–25)? What does Bissoondath mean when he refers to "the weight of this hyphen" (paragraph 27)?

6. What positive alternatives to multiculturalism does Bissoondath envision (paragraphs 30–36)?

TOWARD KEY INSIGHTS

Do you agree that ethnic festivals are a kind of "folkloric Disneyland" (paragraph 6), or do you think they have value that Bissoondath does not discuss?

How do you respond to the idea of melting the cultural mosaic?

What, in your view, has Bissoondath left out of his argument that might have made it more persuasive?

SUGGESTIONS FOR WRITING   *After reading "Canadian Multiculturalism: An Inclusive Citizenship" at* http://www.pch.gc.ca/progs/multi/inclusive_e.cfm, *write an essay weighing the claims of both Bissoondath and the statement put out by the Canadian government. Demonstrate that you understand the arguments for and against the policy of multiculturalism, but take a position, and emphasize either the advantages or disadvantages. You may choose to elaborate on, or to refute, arguments made in either piece of writing.*

If you or your parents have come to Canada from a different country, write a persuasive essay directed to people in a particular community, about one of the following:

The value, for the individual, or for the larger Canadian society, of people retaining their ethnic heritage.

The need for more inclusiveness and acceptance of cultural differences.

The need for more governmental support of English language training and/or other services for immigrants.

Celia Milne

Pressures to Conform

Celia Milne writes for Maclean's *magazine. Her article "Pressures to Conform," which first appeared in* Maclean's, *points out how women have paid dearly for their unhappiness with their body image. Low self-esteem associated with body insecurities has contributed to the prevalence of eating disorders and a boom in plastic surgery. The essay's recommendation of body acceptance should generate lively discussion among students.*

1   "Lose 20 lb. by Christmas!" screams the headline on the cover of a popular women's magazine. Beside it is a picture of a gorgeous, typically stick-thin model. And below her is a photo of . . . guess what? A turkey dinner with all the trimmings. In vivid color, the cover neatly illustrates the body-image dichotomy: the twin obsessions with thinness and indulgence. Between the extremes of women intentionally so underweight they risk death and others overweight enough to be candidates for cardiovascular disease and adult-onset diabetes, there are millions

whose body mass index—relating height and weight—is in the normal range. Yet most of them feel fat.

2   "Oh my God, we are so sick in this society," fumes Dr. Joan Johnston, 48, an Edmonton family physician who suffered from anorexia from her late teens until well into adulthood. As a child, she was surrounded by messages about the importance of thinness. "I don't remember a time when my mother wasn't on a diet," she says. "My cousin and my aunt were always dieting." Johnston traces her eating disorder from the day when she was 19 and her mother patted her on the backside and said: "Better watch out, girl. You're getting a little broad across the beam!"

3   Johnston has recovered from what she now sees as an addiction to dieting. "I am five feet, three inches and I weigh 133 lb., the same as I did before anorexia," she says. "I am extremely comfortable with my body, and it is so liberating to not have to put energy into that. But I'm very atypical." Now, she puts her energy into helping young women who have eating disorders—a societal problem that is not getting any better.

4   Unhappiness with body image seems to be a national preoccupation. According to statistics compiled by the National Eating Disorder Information Centre in Toronto, 90 per cent of Canadian women are dissatisfied with some aspect of their bodies. One of the main battlegrounds in the fight for improvement, of course, is eating. According to the *Maclean's* year-end poll published in late December, 43 per cent of Canadian women—compared with 33 per cent of men—believe they are overweight. The eating disorder centre says that its surveys show that fully 70 per cent of Canadian women are preoccupied with their weight, and 40 per cent are yo-yo dieting. "For most women, when they get together in a group a common topic is trying to lose weight," says Dr. Christine Davies, a family physician in Saint John, N.B., who is concerned about how that may rub off on their daughters. Margaret Beck, acting director of the eating disorder centre, affirms that danger. "The research," she says, "does seem to suggest that mothers who are food- and weight-preoccupied tend to have daughters who are the same."

5   Public awareness of eating disorders got a big boost in 1995 when Diana, Princess of Wales, began talking openly about her struggles with bulimia. That bingeing and vomiting condition affects three to five per cent of young Canadian women aged 14 to 25. The other main manifestation of food preoccupation is anorexia, affecting one to two per cent of that group. And the problems occur among younger girls, too. "There are girls younger than 10, even as young as 6, being admitted to hospital programs," says Beck. "It is still a small number, but it is growing."

6   Another popular route in the quest for a better body is plastic surgery. There are no national statistics on esthetic surgery in Canada, but the trends are visible in figures kept by the American Society of Plastic and Reconstructive Surgeons. From 1994 to 1996, the number of people having tummy tucks rose 103 per cent, breast augmentation went up 123 per cent, breast lifts increased 60 per cent, chemical peels rose 47 per cent, retin-A anti-wrinkle treatments grew by 256 per cent, buttock lifts rose by 146 per cent and thigh lifts went up 93 per cent. Dr. Thomas Bell, president of the Canadian Society of Aesthetic Plastic Surgery in Toronto, also notices a trend towards younger patients wanting plastic surgery. "The median age has moved from the mid-50s to the late or mid-40s," he says. "This is part and parcel of body image issues."

7   Perhaps it was media images of ample, perky breasts that persuaded more than 100,000 Canadian women to undergo silicone implant surgery between 1969

and 1992. That type of implant was banned in 1993, and at least 10,000 Canadians blame them for health problems including arthritis, lupus and scarring.

8   Saline implants in a silicone shell are now the norm, and women are still seeking breast enlargement. Vancouver plastic surgeon Kimit Rai says they generally come in two age-groups: the younger women aged 19 or 20 who have never been happy with their breasts, and others who have finished breastfeeding their children and want a pick-me-up. The cost is steep—between $5,000 and $10,000—and there are possible, well-documented, risks. Yet for many women, the importance of looking full-figured seems to outweigh the need to feel good. "About five or six per cent are unhappy with their implants because they cause discomfort," says Rai, "but because they look good, they don't want them out."

9   In fact, women will go to frightening lengths to achieve their body ideal, according to an extensive reader survey published last year in the U.S. magazine *Psychology Today*. A troubling 24 per cent of women said they would give up three years of their life to achieve their weight goals. A few were willing to forgo motherhood because pregnancy would ruin the trim bodies they had worked so hard to achieve. Young women "are being initiated into feelings of body dissatisfaction at a tender age," reported the magazine, "and this early programming may be difficult to undo."

10   The same willingness to pay a high price for an enhanced image is evident in the fact that young women are now the fastest growing group of smokers in Canada. The reason appears to have a lot to do with low self-esteem. Studies indicate that young women who take up smoking consider themselves significantly less attractive than do their peers who never take up the habit.

11   Part of the esteem problem is inevitably related to the impossible ideals with which women are bombarded. "We are constantly shown images of very sick, anorexic women and that's what we are striving for," says Davies. "The average woman is five feet, five inches and 145 lb. The average model is five feet, 11 inches and 110 lb. Ninety-five percent of us don't match up and never will." Ironically, she adds, the average North American's weight has been rising over the past few decades, so most women are moving further away from the physique they seek.

12   Striving for the unattainable creates insecurity among women, says Davies. And that, in turn, leads them to try to please even an unreasonable partner. "A woman is more likely to stay with a man who is abusive if she has low self-esteem," Davies says. "She just doesn't have the confidence to leave." Among teens, low self-esteem can lead to unsafe activities designed to show their worth, such as having sex before they are ready to, which carries with it the risk of HIV and other sexually transmitted diseases.

13   Those tendencies alarm Dr. Sarah Kredentser, who sees a lot of young women in her Winnipeg family practice. "People judge themselves against others and through the eyes of others," she notes with regret. "It is not experience, personality skills and character that counts, but image." According to Kredentser, society's preoccupation with body image has worsened over the past decade. A 65-year-old woman recently asked about liposuction. "If you haven't solved your body image problems by the time you are 65, then you've got problems," Kredentser says.

14   On the other hand, it can sometimes be a positive step for a woman to have something "done" that has been bothering her for years. "I have seen instances where minor plastic surgery such as nose reshaping has made an enormous difference in self-esteem," Kredentser says. "My concern is that this can become the slippery slope. Then it's, 'Now I'll get my breasts done the way I want them,' and what next?"

15   Women simply have to become comfortable with the fact that their bodies are going to age, she says. "If you don't, you will have a chronic struggle with unhappiness and low self-esteem," says Kredentser. "You can never win this battle." Instead of surgery, women are much better off doing the psychological work necessary to accept the aging process, she says.

16   Acceptance is a vital key to dealing with body insecurities. As an administrative assistant at a student residence at the University of Waterloo, Angela Kelman, 23, has an interesting perspective. At five feet, six inches and weighing between 135 and 140 lb., she says she is not wrapped up in body image issues herself, yet sees those obsessions all around her. First-year students are worried about putting on pounds—"the freshman ten," as they call it. "What I see most is over-exercising," she says. "A couple of my friends do it to maintain a model look." Another trend among female university students is vegetarianism. "They say it is because of allergies, religion or animal rights," says Kelman, "but I think it is to lose weight."

17   Kelman credits her upbringing in Waterloo for her lack of concern about body image. "I come from a very close, large family with five children," she says. "My mother loves to cook, and I cook the way she does. We enjoy very balanced meals, and never a lot of prepackaged foods. I don't worry about it much. I'm lucky."

18   There is no doubt the way a woman views herself can affect those around her, particularly children. A mother-daughter competition to lose weight by dieting and going to the gym is not a healthy new year's resolution, says Beck. Instead, she suggests such pleasurable activities as walks in the park or games of touch football that do not have to do with food or weight loss.

19   A family life focused on looking good contributed to Joan Frère's obsession with body weight. The 35-year-old Edmonton social worker began to diet about 15 years ago, thinking it would make her a better person. "I thought thinness was equated with intelligence, success, being a good worker, achievement," she says. Over the years, she travelled the long and difficult journey from the depths of anorexia and bulimia, through the ups and downs of healing, and into a healthy way of thinking. Her coping mechanisms include reaching out to friends, taking long walks, focusing on things other than her weight, and listening to her body. "I am five feet, three inches and 128 lb., I will never be five-feet-six and 110 lb.," Frère says. "I eat what I want and I don't beat myself up. I have learned that I have the same feelings as everyone else, and I have acquired the tools to deal with life."

DISCUSSION QUESTIONS

1. In the first paragraph, Celia Milne describes a magazine cover that "illustrates the body-image dichotomy: the twin obsessions with thinness and indulgence." What does she mean? How does her point here relate to her overall argument?

2. What support does the writer give for her claim that "unhappiness with body image seems to be a national preoccupation" (paragraph 4)?

3. While the argument seems largely to emphasize "the frightening lengths" (paragraph 9) that women will go to achieve their body ideal, how does the essay also concede that sometimes changing one's body image through surgery "may be a positive step" (paragraph 14)? What is meant by the term "slippery slope" in this paragraph?

4. Examine paragraph 10. How does it act as a kind of bridging, or transitional, paragraph between what has come before and what comes after? How does the issue of self-esteem (paragraphs 10–16) relate to the essay's larger point about body image?

5. Cite examples of different kinds of rational appeals used in this essay—including expert opinions, primary source information, and statistical findings.

6. What positive recommendations does the writer make about ways to promote body acceptance (paragraphs 16–19)?

TOWARD KEY INSIGHTS

This essay cites a *Maclean's* poll that reports that more women than men believe they are overweight (paragraph 4). How do you account for this difference?

Compare and contrast this essay with Evelyn Lau's descriptive essay entitled "An Insatiable Emptiness." How does Celia Milne approach the subject of eating disorders in a different way than Evelyn Lau does? How is the purpose of this essay different from Evelyn Lau's?

Celia Milne recommends acceptance as the best way to deal with body insecurities. How realistic do you think this advice is? What, in your opinion, is the best way to promote body acceptance, both within the individual and within the larger society?

SUGGESTION FOR ORAL ARGUMENT

Research the arguments for and against the following proposition, and come to class prepared to argue either side of the proposition:

Plastic surgery for breast enhancement should be more strictly regulated.

SUGGESTION FOR WRITING

Write an essay that argues that males are increasingly subject to body insecurities too. Bring in as many different kinds of evidence as you can.

Brad Evenson

Native Postmodern

Brad Evenson has worked in journalism for 13 years and is currently the medical writer for the National Post *newspaper. He won the National Newspaper Award for investigative reporting in 1997 and was a National Magazine Award nominee in 1998 for an article about Prime Minister Jean Chrétien's speech disorder. Based in Ottawa, he studied theology before becoming a journalist. Evenson's essay entitled "Native Postmodern" raises questions about the ways in which the modern, government-supported powwow has created a "homogeneous culture" far removed from authentic aboriginal traditions. While acknowledging that powwows can foster a sense of identity and even self-esteem among some natives, the essay uses irony to highlight problems with commercialization and stereotyping.*

1   A feather is down. The aboriginal dancers freeze on the grass. The aboriginal Vietnam War veterans in camouflage pants freeze, too, in the shade of a vinyl tent. The woman selling aboriginal Arizona silver jewellery and aboriginal Harley-Davidson T-shirts falls silent. The aboriginal kid wearing L.A.-style baggy pants and a black Raiders cap stares in the sweltering Sunday heat. On the grill, a traditional buffalo burger sizzles untended. "All dancers, we have an eagle feather down," cries a man on the loudspeaker. "Everybody stop."

2   It is the National Aboriginal Day powwow in Ottawa and a feather is down, but nobody knows what to do about it. The aboriginal dancers, about two dozen of them, most in street clothes, crane their necks to spot it. The white spectators in the bleachers look on, concern etched on their sunburned foreheads. The loud-speaker guy says, we have to ask an elder. A conference. Muted voices emerge from a spruce-bough shelter where powwow officials are clustered. Long moments pass. After all, an eagle feather is some kind of sacred aboriginal symbol, isn't it?

3   "It's okay," he says finally. "It's not an eagle feather . . . . "

4   Thirty years ago, most North American natives had only heard of powwows from old stories or the movies, wistful memories of great gatherings in the prideful time before Canadian Christian residential schools and the U.S. cavalry wiped out their traditional way of life. Powwows all but disappeared for a century. But in the past few decades, resurgent interest in native culture has resurrected them on an extraordinary scale.

5   Powwow culture is burning brightly across North America, with powwows held every weekend, some attended by as many as 60,000 people. Casinos put up millions in prize money for dance competitions, powwow videos are sold over the Internet at twenty-five dollars a pop, colleges offer courses in drumming and beadwork, traditional foods and herbal remedies are in unprecedented demand. The modern powwow is a mix of country fair and spiritual revival, at a cost of up to twenty dollars a person. The annual Grand River powwow at Ontario's Six Nations Reserve is one of Canada's biggest, pulling in a quarter million dollars at the gate—before the government subsidy.

6   There is little argument powwows foster a sense of identity. They draw natives together and break down the isolation they can feel in a largely white culture. But the modern powwow has also created a homogeneous culture, a blend of the kitschy and the outright phoney that is no more authentic than a plastic tomahawk in a Tokyo duty-free shop. Powwow culture is a stew of dozens of native cultures, a sort of Disney version of the ultimate tribe that some traditional native leaders, academics, and artists find distressing.

7   Then add to that mix a New Age brand of native spiritualism so overwrought it elevates a feather from a token of respect to the status of consecrated icon. If a feather falls in the forest, does anyone hear it? And if so, should he stop dancing?

8   The term powwow originated in the U.S. with the Chickasaw people, and means, literally, the burning of tobacco, a communal ceremony practised when bands came together. Similar gatherings took place across much of North America for centuries for a variety of reasons: for trade, to speak about the dead, to discuss the needs of the community, or even to discuss war. During the 1960s, many natives realized powwows were also a terrific way to earn money from tourists, and soon the mass production of medicine wheels, pipes, and skin drums began. "We were making tomahawks, all kinds of things," recalls Michael Doxtater, a Mohawk now teaching Indian studies at Cornell University in Ithaca, New York. "We put ourselves through school with the medicine-wheel craze."

9   The problem was tourists weren't the only ones buying. Natives scooped up the Indian kitsch in equal numbers, but instead of hanging the stuff over their basement minibars, many took it seriously. Many still do. And that rankles a number of native leaders who fear the hucksterism common at powwows is eroding their ancient traditions. "There are too many phoney elders, too many phoney spiritual people, medicine people," says Rene Tenasco, grand chief of the Algonquin Anishinabeg Nation. Today, many self-described medicine people charge a hefty fee to pass on their wisdom. "It's a money-making thing at all levels," says Tenasco.

10   Tenasco still winces at the memory of a powwow he attended two years ago. With storm clouds threatening, a group of "elders" offered to ward off the rain with chants and prayers. "What is that all about?" he groans. "You have fakes that come along and exploit the goodwill of young people or people in general who are searching. And once these people find out the truth, they generally walk away."

11   For now, however, few are walking away. Powwow culture holds natives in a seductive embrace best described by what it is not. It's not traditional Indian culture. It's not unique to individual tribes or nations, although it has regional nuances. It's neither urban nor reservation-based. "It's our version of fast-food culture, I guess," says Doxtater.

12   No modern powwow is complete without shawl-making contests, sweat-lodge ceremonies (with entry fees), clothing and jewellery bazaars, story-telling sessions, and crafts festooned with enough coloured feathers to fill a tropical aviary. In powwow culture, looking native is the crucial first step. But what's native? A headband? A cowboy hat? Braids? "You look at some of the outfits and you know that it comes from watching Indian movies," sighs Shelley Niro, an Ontario Mohawk filmmaker who recently completed a film which features a powwow, *Honey Moccasin.* "For years everybody was wearing headdresses, but not every tribe wore headdresses."

13   Natives mix and match and embellish the art, dances, songs, and spiritual beliefs of different bands. Mohawks do Sioux sun dances, Micmacs paint Blackfoot images on paddles, Crees make and sell Navajo blankets, Algonquins fry buffalo burgers. It is virtually impossible to attend a powwow anywhere in Canada without smelling burning sweet grass, seeing Hopi-style beadwork, Haida-style salmon and raven motifs, grass dancing, and hearing the tattoo of an enormous skin drum. Then there is the dream catcher, the most ubiquitous powwow prop of all.

14   A willow hoop woven with string, a dream catcher is a good-luck charm of the Lakota people, a Plains tribe. According to the traditional story, Iktomi, the trickster and teacher of wisdom, appeared before an old Lakota spiritual leader in the form of a spider. While he wove a perfect web, Iktomi explained, "If you believe in the great spirit, the web will catch your good ideas and the bad ones will go through the hole in the middle." The Lakota would hang dream catchers above their beds to sift their dreams.

15   Dream catchers have become as common as Amway products across North America—a kind of universal symbol of native spirituality. There are dream catcher Web pages, earrings, and air fresheners. New Age magazines advertise dream-catcher kits and audio tapes narrating the dream catcher legend. In Regina, natives hang them from their rear-view mirrors so their cars won't be stolen by the Oldsmobile Gang, a notorious group of native car thieves operating in the area. "It's better than the Club," laughs Tom Doré, referring to the widely used anti-theft device. Doré, a Mohawk who teaches introductory Indian studies at Saskatchewan Indian Federated College in Regina, says people actually believe

that dream catchers show native solidarity. "If I put a dream catcher on my mirror the kids who steal cars won't steal mine because it's one of the brother's."

16   During the Christian residential-school era, which reached its peak in the late-1800s, native culture was all but extinguished. "For nearly a century, parents and grandparents in reserve communities were legally compelled to turn their children over to the custody of residential school authorities," notes the *Report of the Royal Commission on Aboriginal Peoples*. "Children were beaten for speaking their own language, and Aboriginal beliefs were labelled 'pagan.'" When the schools began to close in the 1950s, many natives from smaller, isolated, "fly-in" communities were drawn towards the larger tribes that seemed to hold onto their language and customs, such as the Lakota, the Blackfoot, and the Plains Cree. Young Sioux men travelled the country teaching the sun dance and drumming. This explains the prevalence of the dream catcher, the grass dance, the big drum, and the medicine wheel—all Plains Indian traditions—and goes a long way towards explaining the curious sameness of powwow culture. "A lot of Indian people were seeking a sense of Indianness," says Stephen Augustine, a Canadian Museum of Civilization ethnologist and hereditary Micmac chief.

17   Even larger nations have been drawn to the extravagant practices of the Plains tribes. "In a lot of tribes on the East coast, the chief, when he gets elected to office, will opt to be crowned with a Plains Cree headdress, which is totally out of whack with our culture," says Augustine.

18   Many natives believe governments have for decades promoted a kind of pan-Indian nation, with a common spiritual belief system, cultural hallmarks, and aspirations. After all, it is easier to deal with a homogeneous group than with a fractious collection of tribes with different political goals. For example, last year the federal government declared June 21 to be National Aboriginal Day. This irks many natives who value the uniqueness of their cultures. "The idea of pan-Indianism is seen in a negative light because it's like pan-Europeanism," says Augustine. "I mean, do you speak European or what language do you speak? Do you speak white? There's fifty-two different indigenous languages in Canada and each of us have different spiritual belief systems that are not congruent with each other."

19   Governments have regarded powwows as at worst benign, and possibly even useful—for example, as a panacea after the tensions of Oka and Douglas Lake. They spend millions each year on cultural grants to fund what are essentially profitable events. Art King, a Heritage Canada official in charge of native issues, says he sees a new grant request to fund a powwow once a week. In 1979, Mike Doxtater joined the organizing committee of the Grand River powwow at Ontario's Six Nations Reserve. He quit not long after, annoyed that the committee went looking for a provincial grant. "Powwows have been, right from the start, supported by government as what they perceive to be the approved cultures for Indians," says Doxtater. "The question among people is, well, if that's the case, is it really an Indian thing?"

20   This issue of authenticity is central to the bitter controversy surrounding B.C. Bishop Hubert O'Connor. The now seventy-one-year-old O'Connor was the highest-ranking Roman Catholic official in Canada ever convicted of a sex crime. In 1996 he was found guilty of rape and indecent assault for offences taking place while he was the principal of a residential school in Williams Lake, B.C., in the mid-sixties, but after serving six months, filed an appeal. The appeal court set aside his conviction, ordering an acquittal on the charge of indecent assault and a new trial

on the charge of rape. Last June, that charge was stayed in return for O'Connor's apology at a native healing ceremony in Alkali Lake, not far from where the offences occurred. While his victim, Marilyn Belleau, was satisfied by O'Connor's participation, many natives were outraged both at the leniency shown and at the inappropriateness of the ritual. Viola Thomas, of the United Native Nations of British Columbia, said the healing circle is not even part of B.C. native culture, but was copied from Manitoba natives.

21   The development of a pan-Indian nation also troubles Tom Doré because it creates a stereotype that many natives feel they must live up to. "Like every Indian has a medicine pouch, every Indian likes powwow music, every Indian burns sweet grass," he says sarcastically. "When I smell burning sweet grass, it gives me a headache. Does that mean I can't be an Indian?" Powwow culture sometimes merely replaces one stereotype with another.

22   In downtown Regina, says Doré, the way to look like a real Indian is to wear a baseball cap backwards, a black leather or jean jacket, Nike T-shirt, and "home-boy" pants with baggy crotch. They call each other "Bro," like American blacks. "They're so unsure of their own culture," he says, "they have to latch on to what somebody else has done."

23   Criticizing powwows is easier, of course, for people like Doré who are secure with their own identity. For those natives whose addictions and poverty are rooted in their lack of identity and low self-esteem, the powwow is strong medicine. "A lot of it is tacky and cliché-ridden and it gets a bit much after a while, but I just think that it allows you to contribute or participate," says filmmaker Shelley Niro. "My dad came from an age where you had to be really ashamed of being an Indian. He didn't speak his language, he went through that experience where [an Indian] couldn't go to a wine store and buy a bottle of wine, and you were sort of treated like servants. And then, when the powwow scene started, he was always invited to carry the flag as a war veteran, and doing that, even though he was paid for doing it, I think it really meant a lot to him."

24   Something that troubles Niro, as well as other native critics, is that powwow culture isn't just for natives any more. Many New Age whites are showing up, and the sight of beaded moccasins on plump, alabaster legs with blue veins annoys many natives. "If you look in any of the New Age sections of bookstores, half of them are all native spirituality books, and it's kind of gross," she says, adding that the New Age invasion diminishes her art by making it seem trendy and flaky instead of rooted in something authentic. "You know, it's like I'm doing this airhead art." Doxtater calls it "shake-and-bake shamanism."

25   Augustine, who's an ethnologist, says centuries of Christian influence and education have led to natives trying to become priest-like figures themselves, which runs counter to native traditions. "What our teachings tell us usually is that we are simple, we are common people. There's no mysticism, there's no magic in our spirituality; it's everyday, it's down-to-earth, and all it does is talk about truth, and honesty, and respect and those things. So people who go around charging [money] and saying I'm going to get you in a sweat-lodge ceremony and you'll see all these visions, and lights . . . I mean, that's hinging on evangelism in a native context."

26   So what about when an eagle feather falls? Stop dancing?

27   "Actually, the reverence for the eagle feather is part of Indian teachings, but it's not presented that way by the powwow practitioners," says Doxtater, who hosts annual spiritual gatherings near Oka, Quebec.

28   "[There's] a teaching that asks young people to be very careful and look after eagle feathers," Doxtater explains. "What they're saying, really, is this: if you can honour the feather from a dead bird, if you can respect these inanimate objects, you may do all right with your neighbours."

29   Most tribes give different symbolic meaning to the eagle feather. Some regard it as a fallen warrior; others as a token of respect; a few tribes don't consider it anything special at all. Perhaps the only appropriate postmodern response may be what merchant Billy Desjarlais did after the Ottawa powwow when he dropped a box of eagle feathers in a shallow puddle in the parking lot. "You've gotta dry-clean them," he said wearily. "If they're stained, they're not worth nearly as much."

DISCUSSION QUESTIONS

1. What seems to be the writer's tone in the first two paragraphs? How does the frequent repetition of the word "aboriginal" affect the tone?

2. What is the thesis, or argument? What possible counter-arguments does the writer acknowledge?

3. How does Evenson define the "powwow culture" (paragraphs 6–8)?

4. What problems does the writer suggest are associated with native participation in "powwow culture" (paragraphs 8–11)?

5. Explain the significance of the reference to "residential schools" (paragraph 16). How does the residential school history relate to the "powwow culture," according to the author?

6. What is meant by the claim that "powwow culture sometimes merely replaces one stereotype with another" (paragraph 21)? What support is provided for this claim?

7. Explain how the reference to the eagle feather takes on expanded meaning or significance each time it is mentioned (paragraphs 1–3; 7; 26–29). How do you respond to the question about what to do when an eagle feather falls? What is the effect of the last sentence?

TOWARD KEY INSIGHTS

Do you agree with Evenson's main objection to modern powwow culture? Why or why not?

What is the relevance of the controversy surrounding the sentencing of Bishop O'Connor to the main argument? Do you think that participation in a healing ceremony could be an appropriate punishment for a sex offender in the context described? Why or why not?

Brad Evenson says that filmmaker Shelly Niro is disturbed by the participation of "New Age whites" in "powwow culture" (paragraph 23). How do you respond to these comments?

How is the point of view toward cultural identity in this essay strikingly different from the viewpoint expressed in Martin Luther King's "I Have a Dream" speech? How do you account for the difference?

SUGGESTION FOR ORAL ARGUMENT

Research the following proposition, and come to class prepared to argue either side:

Cultural events such as powwows within aboriginal communities should be subsidized by the government.

SUGGESTIONS FOR WRITING

Drawing from a specific ethnic or cultural context you are familiar with, write an essay arguing in favour of mixing various cultural traditions. In your essay, be sure to acknowledge possible objections to your point of view.

After reading Neil Bissoondath's essay "No Place Like Home" (page 520), write an essay that contrasts Bissoondath's argument with Evenson's here. Evaluate the strengths and weaknesses of these arguments and explain why you find one more persuasive than the other.

Mixing the Writing Strategies

As we noted on page 176, most essays mix various writing strategies for assorted purposes. This section features three examples. Margin notations on the Lasn essay point out the interplay of several strategies, and the discussion questions following the Pevere/Dymond and Cobb essays direct your attention to the strategies these writers use.

Chris Cobb

Conspiracy Theories Spin out of Control on the Web

Chris Cobb is a journalist for the Ottawa Citizen*, in which this article first appeared. This essay points to the gullibility of conspiracy theorists on the Internet, and also makes the broader argument that we all need to be careful about what we read in cyberspace.*

1   There are, to put it bluntly, some real weirdos out there. They refuse to believe the most convincing evidence if it doesn't conform to their prejudice. But feed them some flimsy, half-baked notion they agree with and they swallow it whole.

2   They are humanity's conspiracy theorists and they have found a common home on the Internet, where they swarm in the thousands, swapping their ideas about a bizarre array of government and corporate coverups. Occasionally, information on the electronic grapevine leaks into the real world and creates havoc.

3   Nutty though much of it is, a staggering number of people believe what they read in cyberspace. Normal people, that is, not just the weirdos.

4   According to a random poll in the latest issue of the U.S. political magazine *George*, American citizens are predisposed to believing in conspiracies. About 75 per cent of respondents said their government is likely involved in some kind of conspiracy. Ten per cent of suspicious minds think Elvis is still alive. Forty per cent think the authorities are covering up evidence in the crash of TWA flight 800 that crashed shortly after take off in New York City this year.

5   Enter former high-profile television journalist Pierre Salinger, a one-time press secretary to President John Kennedy. He told a group of airline industry executives in Paris recently he had evidence that an errant U.S. navy missile downed the TWA jumbo jet last July 17. He had received a document, written by an American "linked to the U.S. Secret Service." He got the document from a European intelligence source.

Argument supported by illustration

6   Because of Salinger's reputation and profile, his theory was given some credibility by mainstream news media across the world. For a day, at least, it was serious news. The friendly fire theory, investigated and dismissed by the FBI and other investigators, has been around since the plane went down near Long Island, N.Y.

Cause and effect

7   Salinger's "evidence" began to crumble when a CNN television crew showed him a discredited document from the Internet's conspiracy camp. It was the same.

8   "Where did you get it?" asked Salinger, 71, who had received the "evidence" third or fourth hand.

9   Where indeed?

10   If somebody of Salinger's supposed sophistication can be suckered in by "evidence" born in the mind of an Internet conspiracy theorist, something strange must be happening. Conspiracy theorists might not believe what they read in newspapers but they will embrace without question fanciful notions posted in a newsgroup by an anonymous correspondent tapping away at a computer keyboard.

11   Carleton University communications specialist Paul Attallah says people, weird or otherwise, are easily fooled by the power of Internet technology.

Argument: opinion of authority

12   "The whole notion that technology empowers gives some people the foolish notion that they too are powerful," he says. "In fact, the Internet has been made popular by graphic interface which disguises its complexity. It makes us dumber but gives us the illusion of knowledge and control."

Effect of technology

13   Attallah's point is that Netscape, a particularly user-friendly interface, has eliminated the need for users to learn UNIX, which is the original, complex language that became the Internet. UNIX was developed by the U.S. military 30 years ago as a communications device to be used during and after a nuclear war.

Definitions: contrast between Netscape and UNIX

14   "It's a thrill to think you can have all the information you want and go anywhere you want," Attallah says. "You can go to Finland, Russia or anywhere in the world. It's a thrill, and you feel powerful, even though you find nothing of value. And if you find something you think might be valuable, how do you know it's accurate? How do you know who put it there? You don't.

15   "With legitimate journalism, there is an institution with resources, a reputation and a code of ethics which demands that facts are checked. If there is an error or deliberate manipulation, the newspaper or TV station will traditionally admit to it. If they don't, a competitor will. There are no such checks and balances on the Internet."

Comparison: argumentative claim with ethical appeal

16   So the next time you learn that Elvis, Jim Morrison, Kurt Cobain and John Lennon are the house band on some alien spacecraft and Paul McCartney is really dead, think twice.

Examples

17   The truth isn't always out there.

Light-hearted concluding statement

Discussion Questions

1. How does the opening sentence set the tone for this piece? Why do you suppose the writer has such short paragraphs? Consider especially the function of paragraph 8.

2. What point is the extended example about Pierre Salinger meant to illustrate (paragraphs 5–10)?

3. What is the reason, according to Carleton University's communications specialist, that people are so easily fooled by Internet technology (paragraphs 10–14)? Why should readers be even more careful about evaluating information found through the Internet than about that obtained through more traditional media?

4. What different strategies of development does the writer use? Explain.

5. What is the humorous reference, as well as the serious point, of the last sentence? How important is it for the reader to understand the allusion here?

TOWARD KEY INSIGHTS

Have you been exposed to strange rumours or hoaxes on the Internet or elsewhere? If so, how do you respond to them? What do you think motivates people to start conspiracy theories or hoaxes?

What evidence does the writer use to support the claim that "American citizens are predisposed to believing in conspiracies" (paragraphs 4–10)? Do you think Canadians are equally credulous? Explain.

SUGGESTION FOR WRITING

Write an essay warning Internet users, newspaper readers, television viewers, or students to be skeptical about information they consume. Use at least one extended example to support your argument.

Geoff Pevere and Greig Dymond

From *Mondo Canuck*

The authors, who live in Toronto, have written Mondo Canuck, *a book on Canadian popular culture. Geoff Pevere, who is now a film critic with the* Toronto Star, *is also the author of* Roots: A Field Guide to Team Spirit. *Their fresh perspective on the question of Canadian identity proposes that we can most easily recognize a true Canadian sensibility in popular culture.*

1   To grow up in those parts of this country called "English Canada" is to grow up with a peculiar certainty of the in-betweenness of things. It is to come to define yourself more readily as what you aren't than what you are, and to learn to register constant equivocation merely by the simple rhetorical attachment of a tentative "eh" to the end of otherwise declarative statements, as in "Hey, give back my damned wallet, eh?" Because neither your measuring nor monetary systems correspond with the most influential cultural, political and economic presence on your continent, as a Canadian you learn to do metric and financial conversions almost as early as you learn to skate. Though your background may be Chinese, Romanian, Ojibway or Haitian, you know the proper French phrase for things like "high in dietary fibre," and "now enriched with six essential vitamins" from staring daily at bilingual cereal boxes. You grow up psychically strafed by the relentless

barrage of American media, yet every time you reach for change you realize you still share a queen with the tiny, distant island which was once your colonial master. To be Canadian is to live in the space between certainties, to dwell in the gap that separates conviction from speculation. To be Canadian, in other words, is to exist in a state of constant becoming.

2   This explains why there may be no other country which has managed to turn the process of self-definition into such an industrious national pastime: next to hockey, watching TV and making long-distance phone calls, Canadians seem to enjoy nothing more than sitting around and fretting about who they are. And even more so lately: what with the unsettling prospect of Quebec separation, the continued depletion of the public sector and the post-multicultural distrust of nationalism generally, the process of anxious self-examination has reached a feverish pitch. Indeed, so much of our indigenous cultural activity—from *Morningside* panel discussions to *Maclean's* readers' polls—seems preoccupied with the question of defining Canada, one wonders if we'd have any indigenous cultural activity without the question to ask. Imagine it: if Canada were actually defined to the satisfaction of everyone involved, what would Canadians do for rhetorical amusement? After all, it may only be uncertainty, but it's *our* uncertainty. The fact is, in the absence of any other unanimously endorsed cultural characteristic, it's all we've got. Without doubt, we're nothing.

3   We believe that Canadians are different, and that knowing how and why we are distinct is somehow vital to our cultural health and well-being, if not survival, but where we break with tradition is over the arena of cultural reflection. While the vast bulk of national self-scrutiny has been circumscribed geographically—"Canadian" being what Canadians do in Canada—or limited in interest to activities and practices which are so unmistakably Canuck as to verge on national clichés, we'd like to suggest another approach. It's an approach which to us, as a pair of Anglo-Canadians who grew up between strip malls and TV screens, is obvious, but which has nonetheless only rarely been invited on the voyage of national self-definition.

4   Not that there's anything wrong with studying Canada through the Group of Seven, CanLit, politics, canoe trips or regional folk music heard on CBC-Radio. (Tiresome, redundant and mind-numbingly dull maybe, but not wrong.) Just that, for us, such things merely doubled that deeply Canadian sense of alienation: while we knew beyond doubt we were "Canadian"—and, as children of Expo and Trudeau, were unquestioningly *proud* to be so—we also knew that our "Canadian" experience wasn't necessarily reflected in the icy phallic peaks of Lawren Harris, the textured verse of Earle Birney, the spiritually cleansing act of portaging or, god knows, the foreign policy of Lester Pearson. Nope, it was right there, right in front of our little suburban faces: on TV. To be told that being Canadian meant sapping trees or digging documentaries amounted to being told one was not Canadian at all. On the other hand, to kick back after an invigorating game of road hockey by watching *The Forest Rangers* while eating packaged butter tarts off the back of the first Guess Who LP cover was to just know you were up to something culturally distinct. If it didn't make you feel proud to be Canadian, it left you with absolutely no doubt that you were one.

5   The fact was, if, like several million Canadians by this point, you grew up transfixed in the high beams of popular culture, much of the anxiety over national self-definition could just seem downright irrelevant. While the various gate-keepers of national identity would clasp hands and moan skyward over Canada's imminent cultural obliteration, we who watched too much TV knew better. We could spot "Canadian" in an instant, simply with a flick of the channel, and we knew it was different. We knew *Forest Rangers,* an "adventure" show with a polite

emphasis on collective problem-solving, was different from *Lost In Space,* and we knew that *Don Messer's Jubilee* would never be confused with *The Dean Martin Show.* As for The Guess Who, well, try to find a top-40 band across those entire fifty states down there which was quite so arrogantly indifferent to fashion and diet as Canada's first genuine hoser-rock superstars.

6   In pop culture at least there was no doubt: Canadian was distinct. Indeed, because the country was otherwise largely dominated by various forms of American media, the contrast was all the more stark: in the noisy din of U.S. network programming, the Canadian stuff stuck out like a stunned moose in the middle of the trans-Canada highway.

7   Our point is, it still does, perhaps now more than ever. Certainly, there is more Canadian popular culture now than ever, but it's also more *popular* that it ever was. Indeed, when one begins to list the names of Canadians who have made an impact on global entertainment over just the past few years, the results are nothing short of staggering: Bryan Adams, James Cameron, Jim Carrey, Doug Coupland, Celine Dion, Atom Egoyan, David Foster, k.d. lang, Pamela Anderson Lee, Alanis Morissette, Mike Myers, Matthew Perry, Shania Twain, Steve Williams. And we repeat: that's just the past few years.

8   Here's our suggestion. What if, for a moment, we were to drop that conventional Canadian middlebrow disinclination toward popular culture—a disinclination which is still very much alive and well—to suggest that Canada is every bit as distinct in its approach to schlock as it is to art, and that the former may indeed reveal vastly more of a national distinction than the latter. That it's possible to see as much of ourselves (if not more) in Mike Myers as it is in Margaret Atwood. That The Tragically Hip have as much to tell us (if not more) about the experience of living in post-Mulroney Canada as Peter Gzowski does. Moreover, what if, contrary to the established Canadian tradition of disowning anyone who dares to seek and find success elsewhere, we were to expand and ventilate our notion of what's Canadian to include what Canadians are doing on the global pop-culture stage? If one agrees first that there is something distinct about the way Canadians view and engage with the world, then why not allow for the possibility that our sensibility is a portable, flexible and resilient one, which influences what Canadians do no matter where we do it? Moreover, what is revealed about living in this strained Confederation when you examine Canada's parallel but distinct pop-cultural strains—the domestic (*Singalong Jubilee, King of Kensington*) and the international (*Ghostbusters,* Alanis Morissette)—side by side? If one does begin to think about Canada in terms of the pop culture it produces, both nationally and internationally, one not only begins to move away from the us-versus-them national-victimhood model of the past, one in fact starts to see something so different as to be strikingly so: a "Canada" which is not only sly, dynamic, intelligent and resourceful, but one that's also a helluva lot more fun than the old one.

DISCUSSION QUESTIONS

1. What concrete examples do the authors provide to illustrate their claim that "To be Canadian is to live in the space between certainties, to dwell in the gap that separates conviction from speculation" (paragraph 1)? In your own words, explain what you think the authors mean here.

2. How do the authors define Canadian identity (paragraph 4)? Why does part of their definition include mention of what, in their view, the "Canadian experience" is not?

3. How is this essay also an argument? Where does the essay use contrast, cause-and-effect analysis, and illustration?

4. What characteristics of the show *The Forest Rangers*, or the band The Guess Who (paragraph 5) seem Canadian to the authors? Can you think of additional examples of distinctively Canadian television shows or musical artists? Explain.

5. What is meant by the claim that "if one does begin to think about Canada in terms of the pop culture it produces, both nationally and internationally," one sees a different face of Canada, "a 'Canada' which is not only sly, dynamic, intelligent and resourceful, but one that's also a helluva lot more fun than the old one" (paragraph 8)?

TOWARD KEY INSIGHTS

The authors of this essay say that "the question of defining Canada" (paragraph 2) has become an important cultural activity. Do you think it is possible or desirable to define an essential Canadian identity? Why or why not?

Consider the comparison the authors use in paragraph 6: "In the noisy din of U.S. network programming, the Canadian stuff stuck out like a stunned moose in the middle of the trans-Canada highway." Do you agree that Canadian television is recognizably different from American television?

SUGGESTION FOR WRITING

Drawing from your knowledge of Canadian and American popular culture (television, movies, or popular music), write an essay in which you argue that Canadian popular culture does, or does not, have a significant cultural distinctness that should be recognized. In your essay, bring in contrast and illustration as part of your argument.

Kalle Lasn

Media Carta

Kalle Lasn is publisher of Adbusters *magazine and founder of the Adbusters Media Foundation and Powershift Advertising Agency. He has dedicated himself to launching social marketing campaigns like Buy Nothing Day and TV Turnoff Week, and to fighting legal battles for the right to public airwaves. "Media Carta" is a chapter from his recent book,* Culture Jam: The Uncooling of America, *which examines and resists the "media trance" of our TV-addicted age. Kalle Lasn, whose documentaries have been broadcast on PBS, on CBC, and around the world, has won fifteen international awards. He and his wife, Masako, make their home in Vancouver, Canada. Visit the author at* www.adbusters.org.

1   In the past twenty years, an unprecedented situation has developed with grave implications for democracy and freedom of speech: the emergence of a global communications cartel. The flow of information worldwide is controlled by an ever-shrinking number of transnational media corporations led by a handful of

giants—Tele-Communications Inc. (T.C.I.), Time Warner, Disney, Bertelsmann, General Electric, Viacom and Rupert Murdoch's News Corporation. The great power of these organizations lies in their vertical integration. They can produce a film and distribute it through their own partially or fully owned theater chain, promote it through their own TV networks, play the soundtrack on their own radio stations and sell the merchandising spinoffs at their own amusement parks. A property can enter this vertical chain at any point and be spun in either direction. A film becomes a book, a hit single, then a TV show, a video game, a ride. Among them, the media giants have the means to produce a never-ending flow of social spectacles, and to nurture them, feed them, massage them and keep them resonating in the public mind. With the exception of a few wild domains still left here and there (public-access TV, pirate radio, zines, some unexplored reaches of cyberspace), the media megacorps have pretty well colonized the whole global mindscape and "developed" it into a theme park—a jolly, terrifyingly homogenized Las Vegas of the mind.

2   What does freedom of speech mean in this kind of mental environment?

3   What can you as an individual do if you don't like an ad campaign, the violence on TV, the way your local TV station covers the news, or the way a corporation or the government is manipulating the public agenda? Well . . . you can send a letter to the editor of your local newspaper, call in to a radio talk show or take your complaint to an advertising industry association like the American Association of Advertising Agencies (AAAA) or the Canadian Advertising Association (CAA). You can phone a TV station or vent your spleen to the media watchdogs, the Federal Communications Commission (FCC) and the Canadian Radio-Telecommunications Commission (CRTC). If you're really angry (and somewhat organized), you can attend FCC hearings and try to revoke a TV license. Or you can become a media producer, write your own script and try to break into the information chain with your own documentary. If you're rich, you can bankroll your own films and documentaries. If you're very rich, you can buy a TV station. If you're filthy rich, you can amass a media empire. Each stage of participation takes you higher on what I call the "ladder of truth." Only a very few people ever get beyond the bottom rungs.

4   On the lower rungs, our democracy seems to work quite well. Newspapers print lots of letters to the editor, radio talk shows debate the hot issues of the day, media and advertising watchdogs deal with hundreds of complaints every year. But how do you climb the ladder of truth and get your voice heard in the higher echelons of public discourse?

5   David Grossman has thought a lot about this. A former U.S. Army officer and the author of the Pulitzer Prize-nominated *On Killing: The Psychological Cost of Learning to Kill in War and Society,* he has made a personal crusade of spreading the word on the incontrovertible link between TV violence and real-world crime. More than two hundred studies have identified a clear cause-and-effect relationship, and every credible agency from the American Medical Association to the Surgeon General's Office to the United Nations has accepted the conclusion. Yet this news has somehow escaped most American parents. If they realized the impact of TV violence on their kids, they would hardly be so cavalier about their kids' viewing habits (or for that matter their own), Grossman suspects.

6   These people cannot be warned effectively, because the most powerful and far-reaching delivery system for the message won't broadcast it. Even though Grossman has been contacted many times by apparently enthusiastic television producers, no story on him or the TV-crime link has ever aired on network TV (with one

exception, when *CNBC* gave him the hook after twenty seconds). "Every time the story gets to a higher level, it's killed," he says plainly. Grossman happens to live in Jonesboro, Arkansas, where a local student recently went on a schoolyard shooting rampage. As an expert on the psychology of assassination, Grossman was besieged by the media, did many international radio and newspaper interviews; and was contacted by more than a dozen network TV producers. But his TV spots never ran. "Without fail, remorse or hesitation, when the networks found out where I was coming from (that is, ready to implicate TV as a probable culprit in the tragedy) they'd have nothing to do with me," Grossman says. "The magnitude of the stonewalling is staggering."

7   What to do then? How do you get the message out when you have no access to the messenger? Grossman's long-term strategy involves three points of attack: education, legislation and litigation. Educate by every other means but TV "until there's a groundswell of outrage," until the conspicuous absence of TV coverage of an enormous national story becomes the obvious story in itself. Legislate change by lobbying for major amendments to broadcast regulations, or the wholesale replacement of the FCC. Institute class-action suits for damages against the industry, much like the ones that have been brought against the tobacco industry. "The broadcasters may be powerful enough to buy candidates and influence elections, but they can't buy every jury of twelve people in the U.S. When a jury sees the unassailable evidence, we've won." Grossman imagines a group of people who have already been victimized in a high-profile incident like the one in Jonesboro banding together and launching an action that simply cannot be ignored. "Parents of the shooter and the parents of the victims have to both agree that one of the criminals here is the TV networks. And then we hold the networks' feet to the fire."

8   Grossman is proof that a committed individual can climb the ladder of truth, but his dilemma points to a disturbing lack of democracy at the heart of our mass media. Nor is TV violence the only subject too taboo for the networks to touch. Think of TV addiction, arguably North America's number one mental health problem. Or unsustainable overconsumption by the affluent people of the First World. When is the last time you saw a network show (or a citizen-produced advocacy ad) on these subjects?

9   Here's the point: The ideas, expressions and concerns of individual citizens no longer matter very much. Culture isn't created from the bottom up by the people anymore—it's fed to us top-down by corporations. Under current conditions, real debate is impossible. Real democracy is impossible. Real change is impossible.

10   Media Carta is a media reform movement to take back the cultural power to which all citizens are entitled—to reclaim our airwaves and the rest of our mental environment so that we can start telling our own stories and learn how to talk to each other again.

11   Occasionally, we get a glimpse of how this new paradigm might work. In December 1996, the worst snowstorm in a century hit the Pacific Northwest. In Victoria, British Columbia, home to Canada's mildest climate, five feet of snow fell. A dead calm settled over the paralyzed city. Victoria was about as prepared for this as Troy was for the Greeks. The city had only a couple of snowplows. For days, no cars moved. People were trapped in their houses. Virtually no stores were open because the employees couldn't get to work. The brave ventured out, pulling supplies on sleds. A city of 300,000 was essentially plunged back to pre-Industrial Revolution days.

12   I mention this because a fascinating media story grew out of that storm. What happened at a local radio station called CFAX emerged as an example of

the potential use (and long-forgotten past use) of public airwaves as a democratic medium.

13   A couple of CFAX employees who had been marooned in the building by the snow decided to open up a kind of jungle telegraph of emergency information. Any citizens who could trudge to the station were put on the air, to tell the city what they had seen out there: someone needed help in saving a greenhouse on the Island Highway. An old couple was stranded and in trouble on Pandora Avenue. A family harboring two dozen refugee motorists in Fernwood was running out of food.

14   Soon everyone knew that CFAX (and, to a lesser extent, the Internet) was the source of breaking news, delivered by individual sets of eyes and ears. Every newscast contained information valuable to someone. Every broadcast, in the widest possible sense, served the public interest.

15   It struck many Victorians that this was the way the world was supposed to work. The private voices that came over the Victoria airwaves may not have been broadcasting-school smooth, but they rang with the clarity of the real. They weren't flacking some story that commercial interests wanted to propagate. They had something to tell and nothing to sell. The citizens responded. Isolated individuals suddenly felt part of the larger chain; in the Buddhist sense, everyone became enlightened.

16   The CFAX case is obviously a unique one—you couldn't repeat it, wouldn't want to repeat it, on a national scale. But it does contain the essence of what we're trying to reclaim here. Victorians never felt more part of a community than they did during that storm, when, for a brief time, the media fulfilled a social agenda and everyone's two cents were welcome and equal. I wonder how many of those people, when the snow had melted and their lives had returned to normal and the commercial pap was back on the air, looked at radio—or media in general—differently. I wonder if any of them thought, this is the way our mass media could be if they had taken a different evolutionary fork in the road.

17   I told the CFAX tale to a friend of mine who plays devil's advocate to many of my ideas. "So what's your point?" he asked.

18   "My point is, there needs to be a way to get people talking to each other on radio and TV without commercial mediation."

19   "There is," he said. "It's called public radio. And public television." He looked into the middle distance. "I can see it now. Kalle's World: all public broadcasting all the time. Commercialism has been weaned from the airwaves. And all these public stations are funded by ever-so-conscientious private listeners and viewers with nothing better to do with their time or money than phone in pledges. Remind me to come over to your place sometime and we'll catch what's on the tube: First we'll watch the puppet show and then we'll watch the half-hour documentary on mulch."

20   "Congratulations," I replied. "You've managed to completely miss the point. Look, this isn't about enforcing a diet of PBS. It's about opening TV up and letting the commercial memes duke it out with the noncommercial memes until a new balance is reached. I don't want commercialism to be completely purged from broadcasting. But it can't be the one and only voice."

21   What happens when the commercial voice monopolizes the information delivery systems for years and years? We get used to it. That voice becomes the norm. We cease questioning it. Indeed, we have a hard time even imagining other voices.

22   When President Clinton made a diplomatic trip to China in June 1998, high-level politicians held a debate to determine whether to allow him to address

human-rights issues or to debate President Jiang Zemin live on national TV. Eventually, it was decided that Clinton could have TV access if he agreed, among other things, not to meet later with dissidents in Hong Kong.

23 Most North Americans find this kind of thing fairly astonishing. That TV access by the world's most powerful leader would need the host government's approval seems ludicrous. That, however, is (as of this writing, at least) the Chinese way. Of course, if China were to scrap its state-controlled media, and citizen-owned media were to be installed in its place, the country would be instantly transformed. Chinese culture would heave.

24 American broadcasting isn't an Orwellian state-controlled system. It's a commercial, corporate-controlled system, but that control can be, in its own Huxleyan way, just as undemocratic and uncompromising as the Chinese system. If Americans suddenly decided to break up the media monopolies with powerful antitrust legislation; or to reserve a few minutes of every TV broadcast hour for public-generated advocacy messages; or to deploy some other participatory strategy that gives individuals and groups a voice on the public airwaves, American culture would heave, too.

25 On the surface, the battle for Media Carta—the struggle for who will control the production and distribution of information in the twenty-first century—looks like a very unfair fight. On one side stand the mighty media megacorporations, the government regulators, and a half-century tradition of managing the airwaves as a commercial enterprise. On the other side stands a motley collection of writers, artists, academics, politicized communications professors and high school media-literacy teachers, and a loose global network of NGOs and media and environmental activists. Nevertheless, the underdog has some effective tactical tools at its disposal. On several fronts there are "leverage points," and if we commit to working them simultaneously, they will bring results. Here are some of those leverage points:

26 **TV Turnoff Week.** A social ritual every April where citizens reclaim a little time and tranquillity by staying away from the set for one week. The short-term goal is to get enough abstainers on board to depress the Nielsen ratings for that week—a powerful gesture of consumer sovereignty. The broader goal is simply to improve the quality of people's lives.

27 **The Two-Minute Media Revolution.** As citizen-produced advocacy uncommercials challenge the status quo on TV, a cyberpetition gathers signatures. The petition demands that the broadcast industry's governing bodies (in the U.S., the FCC; in Canada, the CRTC), when granting broadcast licenses, give two minutes out of every broadcast hour back to the people (advocacy messages would be chosen on a first-come first-served basis from among those who wish to speak). If enough people sign the petition, this strategy will open a hairline crack in the media monopoly.

28 **Antitrust Lawsuits.** The U.S. attorney general's 1998 suit against Microsoft is a good example of how potent a tool antitrust legislation can be. If enough fed-up citizens demanded a freer, more diverse cultural environment, the government could be pressured to go after Time Warner, News Corporation and Disney, and limit the number of TV stations, newspapers and radio stations each is allowed to own.

29 **The Revocation of Television Licences.** Thirty years ago, local residents in Boston filed a petition to the FCC to protest the shoddy nightly news broadcasts

of their local station. They wanted WHDH-TV to have its license revoked—and they succeeded. WHDH faded to black and a new station under new management was born.

30   No one since has repeated the Bostonians' success. These days it's almost impossible to unplug trashy TV stations: Licenses only come up for renewal every eight years, the dates aren't advertised and for decades now, whenever a case does come before them, both the FCC and CRTC always come down in favor of the broadcasters.

31   None of this has deterred Paul Klite, the executive director of the Denver-based Rocky Mountain Media Watch.

32   Like many others, Klite believes a lot of network programming is unnecessarily, destructively violent, so he put Denver-area newscasts through a sophisticated content analysis he called the "mayhem test." What he found is no surprise: excessive coverage of murders, terrorism, war and disaster. One station's evening news was 47 percent "mayhem." With this data and citizens' petitions in hand, Klite's group lobbied the FCC to deny the renewals of the broadcast licenses of four local stations. Klite argued that Denver TV news is "harming the citizens of Colorado," and that they deserve some protection from such programming.

33   Klite struck out. In the FCC's view, TV news is protected by the First Amendment, and the networks are free to air whatever news they please.

34   Despite this setback, Klite's work has pumped new blood into media activism and created an example that other media watchdogs can follow. His work points to a whole new attitude of personal propriety toward the public airwaves, and reminds us that they belong to *us,* not the networks. Most important, he reminds us that we need regulators at the FCC and the CRTC to stop cozying up to broadcasters and start taking some courageous and independent stances in the public interest.

35   **Legal Action.** In 1995, Adbusters Media Foundation launched a Canadian Charter legal action against the Canadian Broadcasting Corporation (CBC) for refusing to sell us airtime for our citizen-produced advocacy messages. The case wound its way through the courts until the Supreme Court of Canada threw it out in 1998. The highest court in the land refused to hear it as a constitutional, freedom of speech issue. The Media Foundation will now take its case to the World Court in The Hague, under Article 19 of the Universal Declaration of Human Rights.

36   In the U.S., the Media Foundation has been trying since 1993 to launch a First Amendment legal action against NBC, CBS and ABC for routinely refusing to sell us airtime for any of the twenty-odd messages we have tried to air since 1991. We have files full of letters from the networks, plus transcripts of phone conversations with network executives, which prove that not just single thirty-second spots, but *whole classes of information* about transportation, nutrition, fashion and sustainable consumption are systematically being kept off the public airwaves simply because they threaten big-money sponsors.

37   A First Amendment victory in the U.S. Supreme Court would immediately transform television as we know it today. It would set up a new level playing field between citizens and corporations, and give people and groups a powerful new platform to speak out on the issues that concern them. TV would no longer just transmit commercial propaganda to a passive population

but, instead, would become a key site of struggle over the production of meaning. Bit by bit the emptiness of our spectacular culture would be revealed and our currently enforced menu of packaged fun, beauty, heroes and myths would fade. A vibrant new media culture would be born.

38   Given what's at stake here, you'd think there would be dozens of crusading lawyers eager to sink their teeth into this crucial, high-profile freedom-of-speech case. Unfortunately, that's not so.

39   Recently, I placed a call to one of America's most powerful litigators, a specialist in First Amendment issues. I explained our position. When citizens cannot walk into their local TV station and buy airtime, then surely their First Amendment rights are being violated. Aren't they?

40   His reaction was immediate and almost visceral. He was a fierce defender of the First Amendment, true, but chiefly with respect to how it applies to broadcasters. He seemed to hold their right to free choice above all others.

41   "In America, I don't think you can compel a publisher or broadcaster to carry a particular message," he said.

42   "But if a network decides that Nike or McDonald's can buy thirty seconds of airtime and say, 'Buy hamburgers' or 'Buy shoes,' why don't I have the right to buy airtime for my side of the story?"

43   "You do have your rights, but you can't diminish their rights in order to enforce yours."

44   I told him I thought my right to speak out on TV was fairly basic, given that these are public airwaves that legally belong to everyone.

45   "I think that's a fiction," he said. "The air may belong to you, but not the studios and broadcasting facilities of ABC."

46   I placed a call to another lawyer, this time a high-profile Los Angeles media attorney and former president of the Beverly Hills Bar Association, who turned out to be equally circumspect.

47   "Networks have the right to quality control," he said. "They have a right to say, 'We won't carry a message that would be offensive to the other sponsors, because we don't want to lose those sponsors.'"

48   That's the way it all boils down: The broadcaster's right to run a commercial business stands in direct opposition to my right to freedom of speech. I was looking for an advocate who believed that my cause—the cause of the people—had at least equal merit. The Beverly Hills attorney gave me the number of another lawyer to try, and he cordially hung up. The hunt for the First Amendment grail continues.

49   Media Carta is the great human-rights battle of our information age—a great personal, intellectual, social, cultural and legal test. The infrastructure for this battle is already in place. Culture jammers around the world are preparing for the showdown. In the early years of the new millennium, we will spearhead a media reform movement to enshrine the right to communicate as a fundamental human right in the constitutions of all free nations and in the Universal Declaration of Human Rights.

50   We will save the most precious of all our natural resources: the peace and clarity of our own minds.

DISCUSSION QUESTIONS

1. Discuss the meaning of the title. How does it relate to the writer's thesis and purpose?

2. The writer utilizes many rhetorical modes throughout his essay—narration, description, illustration, process analysis, comparison and contrast, cause and effect, definition. Find at least one example of the various modes utilized by the author and then explain how they contribute to his argument.

3. In your own words, explain what the writer means when he says that the experience of Grossman "points to a disturbing lack of democracy at the heart of our mass media" (paragraph 8). What explanations and evidence does he offer in support of this claim? What actions does he advocate in response to the monopoly of the "commercial voice" (paragraph 21)?

4. What appeals to authority does the writer make in support of his argument? What counterclaims to his argument does the writer present, and how does he respond to them?

5. Explain the relevance to the writer's argument of the extended narrative example of what occurred at the CFAX radio station in Victoria, B.C., during an extreme snowstorm in December, 1996.

6. In the writer's view, why are legal challenges to the World Court and the U.S. Supreme Court necessary steps to ensure the fundamental right to free communication is preserved?

TOWARD KEY INSIGHTS

How persuasive do you find this argument? Are there additional arguments or appeals that the writer might have used? Do you have any objections to the arguments that have not been adequately addressed? Are there any additional arguments that the writer might have included?

Consider other cases that demonstrate the lack of democracy and diversity of expression in mainstream media. Can you think of examples that show individuals and/or groups have suffered as a direct result of media manipulation or control? How applicable are Lasn's arguments to other phenomena of popular culture: fashion, music, and professional sports?

SUGGESTIONS FOR WRITING

Write an essay arguing that people should have the right to purchase airtime on television or radio, provided they do not break the law. Bring in as many different kinds of evidence as you can.

Write an essay illustrating the dangers to civil society that result from the pervasive influence of "the commercial voice" in our culture.

Handbook

Sentence Elements

Learning the parts of English sentences won't in itself improve your writing, but it will equip you to handle errors at the sentence level. Before you can identify and correct unwarranted shifts from past to present time, for example, you need to know about verbs and their tenses. Similarly, recognizing and correcting pronoun case errors require a knowledge of what pronouns are and how they are used. In this section we first cover subjects and predicates, then complements, appositives, and the parts of speech, and finally phrases and clauses.

■ Subjects and Predicates

The subject of a sentence tells who or what it is about. A *simple subject* consists of a noun (that is, a naming word) or a noun substitute. A *complete subject* consists of a simple subject plus any words that limit or describe it.

The predicate tells something about the subject and completes the thought of the sentence. A *simple predicate* consists of one or more verbs (words that show action or existence); a *complete predicate* includes any associated words also. In the following examples the simple subjects are <u>underlined once</u> and the simple predicates <u>twice</u>. The subjects and predicates are separated with slash marks.

<u>William</u>/<u>laughed</u>.

<u>Mary</u>/<u>has moved</u>.

<u>Sarah</u>/<u>painted</u> the kitchen.

<u>The student</u> over there in the corner/<u>is majoring</u> in art.

A sentence can have a compound subject (two or more separate subjects), a compound predicate (two or more separate predicates), or both.

The <u>elephants</u> and their <u>trainer</u>/<u>bowed</u> to the audience and <u>left</u> the ring.

Sentences that ask questions don't follow the usual simple subject–simple predicate order. Instead, the order may be reversed; or if the simple predicate consists of two verbs, the simple subject may come between them.

When <u>is</u>/your/<u>theme</u> due? (Simple subject follows simple predicate.)

<u>Has</u>/<u>Joan</u>/<u>walked</u> her pygmy goat yet? (Simple subject comes between verbs.)

Usage Considerations   Because subjects are such important sentence elements, think carefully about each one you write so that your sentences won't be vague or misleading. Read the example below:

Our government has failed to repeal the Goods and Services Tax.

This statement can be expressed more precisely:

The *House of Commons* has failed to repeal the Goods and Services Tax.

The *Prime Minister* has rejected proposals to repeal the GST.

Paying close attention to subjects lets you present your ideas more accurately and clearly.

> **EXERCISE**   *Place a slash mark between the complete subject and the complete predicate; then underline the simple subject once and the verb(s) twice. If a subject comes between two verbs, set it off with two slash marks.*
>
> **1.** The full moon rose majestically over the mountain peak.
> **2.** John was ill on the day of the big test.
> **3.** The boys and girls laughed and splashed happily in the pool.
> **4.** That man by the door is my uncle.
> **5.** The judge revoked Rudy's parole and ordered him to jail.
> **6.** The tall oak shaded almost the entire backyard.
> **7.** My favourite subject is history.
> **8.** Mr. Eames has bought a wicker chair for his living room.

■ Complements

A complement is a word or word group that forms part of the predicate and helps complete the meaning of the sentence. Complements fall into four categories: direct objects, indirect objects, subject complements, and object complements.

A *direct object* names whatever receives, or results from, the action of a verb.

The millwright repaired the *lathe*. (Direct object receives action of verb *repaired*.)

Hilary painted a *picture*. (Direct object results from action of verb *painted*.)

They took *coffee* and *sandwiches* to the picnic. (Direct objects receive action of verb *took*.)

As the last sentence shows, a sentence may have a compound direct object—two or more separate direct objects.

An *indirect object* identifies someone or something that receives whatever is named by the direct object.

> Doris lent *me* her calculator. (Indirect object *me* receives *calculator*, the direct object.)

> Will and Al bought their *boat* new sails. (Indirect object *boat* receives *sails*, the direct object.)

An indirect object can be converted to a prepositional phrase that begins with *to* or *for* and follows the direct object.

> Doris lent her calculator *to me*.

> Will and Al bought new sails *for their boat*.

A *subject complement* follows a linking verb—one that indicates existence rather than action. It renames or describes the subject.

> Desmond is a *carpenter*. (Complement *carpenter* renames subject *Desmond*.)

> The lights are too *bright* for Percy. (Complement *bright* describes subject *lights*.)

An *object complement* follows a direct object and renames or describes it.

> The council named Donna *treasurer*. (Object complement *treasurer* renames direct object *Donna*.)

> The audience thought the play *silly*. (Object complement *silly* describes direct object *play*.)

Usage Considerations Direct objects can be revised for greater precision, as these examples show:

> John sent *a gift*.

> John sent *a giant colouring book as a birthday gift*.

Often, you can carry the revision one step further by adding an indirect object, subject complement, or other complement to the sentence.

> John sent his *niece* a giant colouring book as a birthday gift. (Indirect object added.)

◼ Appositives

An appositive is a noun, or word group serving as a noun, that follows another noun or noun substitute and expands its meaning. Appositives may be restrictive or nonrestrictive. Restrictive appositives distinguish whatever they modify from other items in the same class. They are written without commas.

> My sister *Heidi* is a professional golfer. (Appositive *Heidi* distinguishes her from other sisters.)

I have just read a book by the novelist *Henry James*. (Appositive *Henry James* distinguishes him from other novelists.)

Nonrestrictive appositives provide more information about whatever they modify. This sort of appositive is set off by a pair of commas, except at the end of a sentence; then it is preceded by a single comma.

Anatoly Karpov, *the Russian chess player,* was interviewed on TV. (Appositive names *Karpov's* occupation.)

Todd plans to major in paleontology, *the study of fossils.* (Appositive defines the term *paleontology.*)

Usage Considerations When a brief definition is necessary, appositives can help you improve your sentences.

John Cage wrote hundreds of pieces for prepared piano.

John Cage, *a twentieth-century avant-garde composer,* wrote hundreds of pieces for prepared pianos, *instruments with odds and ends stuck between their strings to provide unusual effects.*

Don't, however, clutter your writing with appositives that provide unneeded information; the overload will impede and irritate your reader.

EXERCISE   *Identify each italicized item as a direct object (DO), an indirect object (IO), a subject complement (SC), an object complement (OC), or an appositive (AP).*

1. Harry is a *student* in business administration.
2. Mr. Ames gave his *son* money for the movies.
3. The study group found Kant's philosophy *difficult.*
4. Dan lost his *umbrella* in the subway.
5. Speed Spedowski, *our best pitcher,* won twenty-three games last season.
6. Bill borrowed several *tapes* for the party.
7. The newspaper named Melissa *editor.*
8. Nelson was *overjoyed* at winning the essay contest.

■ Parts of Speech

Traditional English grammar classifies words into eight parts of speech: *nouns, pronouns, verbs, adjectives, adverbs, prepositions, conjunctions,* and *interjections.* This section discusses these categories as well as verbals, phrases, and clauses, which also serve as parts of speech.

Nouns

Nouns name persons, places, things, conditions, ideas, or qualities. Some nouns, called *proper nouns,* identify one-of-a-kind items like the following:

France	Christmas
Pacific Ocean	Quebec
Maurice Richard	Mona Lisa
Booker Prize	Stanley Cup
Canadarm	Wyandotte Corporation
Charter of Rights	Douglas College

Mount Everest, on the border of *Tibet* and *Nepal,* was named for *Sir George Everest,* an Englishman.

Common nouns name general classes or categories of items and include abstract, concrete, and collective nouns.

Abstract Nouns   An abstract noun names a condition, idea, or quality—something we can't see, feel, or otherwise experience with our five senses.

arrogance	harmony	sickness
envy	liberalism	understanding
fear	love	

His *desire* to win caused him to cheat.

Mary felt great *loyalty* to her family.

Concrete Nouns   A concrete noun identifies something that we can experience with one or more of our senses.

man	desk	pillow	needle
bicycle	lemon	airplane	pan
building	piston	carton	smoke

The *air* was thin at the *peak* of the *mountain.*

The *hammer* had a broken *handle.*

Collective Nouns   A collective noun is singular in form but stands for a group or collection of items.

assembly	committee	crowd	flotilla	herd
bunch	congregation	delegation	gang	tribe
class	convoy	family	group	troop

The *jury* filed into the courtroom to announce its verdict.

The *flock* of geese settled onto the lake.

Usage Considerations   Good writing demands precise, potent nouns. If you carefully select your nouns, you can help sharpen your message. Ill-chosen nouns, on the other hand, suggest poor thinking. Note how the vague word *freedom* robs the following sentence of any specific meaning:

Our *freedom* needs to be protected.

What did the writer have in mind? Here are a few possibilities:

Our *right to free speech* needs to be protected.

Our *private behaviour* needs to be protected.

Our *national sovereignty* needs to be protected.

Even when meaning does not present problems, sentences can be sharpened by careful attention to nouns. Note the greater precision of the second sentence below:

Our *dog* has a savage bite.

Our *pit bull* has a savage bite.

EXERCISE   *Identify the nouns in the following sentences:*

1. Jeremy has undertaken the task of learning conversational German this summer.
2. Scrabble is a pleasant game to play on a cold, wet evening.
3. The chairperson will tell you about the decision of the committee.
4. The tree was covered with blossoms around which many bees buzzed.
5. My new apartment is in St. John's, Newfoundland.
6. His intelligence and humour make him a very popular lecturer.
7. A Rolls-Royce will provide decades of transportation for its owner.
8. Marcy Johnson jumped in her car, revved its engine, and roared off down the road.

Pronouns

Pronouns, which take the place of nouns in sentences, help you avoid the awkward repetition of nouns.

If Brad doesn't like the *book,* take *it* back to the library.

There are eight categories of pronouns: *personal, relative, interrogative, demonstrative, reflexive, intensive, indefinite,* and *reciprocal.*

Personal Pronouns   Personal pronouns refer to one or more clearly identified persons, places, or things.

Subjective	Objective	Possessive
I	me	my, mine
you	you	your, yours
he	him	his
she	her	her, hers
it	it	its
we	us	our, ours
you	you	your, yours
they	them	their, theirs

Subjective pronouns serve as the subjects of sentences or clauses, objective pronouns serve as direct and indirect objects, and possessive pronouns show possession or ownership. *My, your, our,* and *their* always precede nouns and thus function as possessive adjectives. *His* and *its* may or may not precede nouns.

He bought a sport shirt. (pronoun as subject)

Donald saw *them.* (pronoun as direct object)

Simon lent *her* ten dollars. (pronoun as indirect object)

That car is *theirs.* (pronoun showing ownership)

Relative Pronouns A relative pronoun relates a subordinate clause—a word group that has a subject and a predicate but does not express a complete idea—to a noun or pronoun, called an antecedent, in the main part of the sentence. The relative pronouns include the following:

who	whose	what	whoever	whichever
whom	which	that	whomever	whatever

Who in its various forms refers to people, *which* to things, and *that* to either people or things.

Mary Beth Cartwright, *who* was arrested last week for fraud, was Evansville's "Model Citizen" two years ago. (The antecedent of *who* is *Mary Beth Cartwright.*)

He took the electric razor, *which* needed a new cutting head, to the repair shop. (The antecedent of *which* is *electric razor.*)

David Bullock is someone *whom* we should definitely hire. (The antecedent of *whom* is *someone.*)

Montreal is a city *that* I've always wanted to visit. (The antecedent of *that* is *city.*)

Which typically introduces nonrestrictive clauses, that is, clauses that provide more information about whatever they modify (see pages 613–614).

The palace, *which* was in bad condition a century ago, is finally going to be restored. (Clause adds information about palace.)

That is typically used in other situations, especially to introduce restrictive clauses: those that distinguish the things they modify from others in the same class (see page 613).

The used car *that* I bought last week at Honest Bill's has already broken down twice. (Clause distinguishes writer's used car from others.)

Pages 595–596 explain the use of *who* and *whom.*

Interrogative Pronouns Interrogative pronouns introduce questions. All of the relative pronouns except *that* also function as interrogative pronouns.

who	which	whoever	whichever
whom	what	whomever	whatever
whose			

What is the matter?

Who asked you?

Whatever do you mean?

When *what, which,* and *whose* are followed by nouns, they act as adjectives, not pronouns.

Which movie should we see?

Demonstrative Pronouns As their name suggests, demonstrative pronouns point things out. There are four such pronouns.

this	these
that	those

This and its plural *these* identify recent or nearby things.

This is the play to see.

These are the times that try men's souls.

That and its plural *those* identify less recent or more distant things.

That is Mary's house across the road.

Those were very good peaches you had for sale last week.

Reflexive and Intensive Pronouns A reflexive pronoun reverses the action of a verb, making the doer and the receiver of the action the same. An intensive pronoun lends emphasis to a noun or pronoun. The two sets of pronouns are identical.

myself	herself	ourselves
yourself	itself	yourselves
himself	oneself	themselves

My father cut *himself* while shaving. (reflexive pronoun)

The Premier *himself* has asked me to undertake this mission. (intensive pronoun)

Don't substitute a reflexive pronoun for a personal pronoun.

Faulty	Jill and *myself* are going to a movie.
Revision	Jill and *I* are going to a movie.
Faulty	Give the tickets to John and *myself.*
Revision	Give the tickets to John and *me.*

Sometimes you'll hear people say things like "He made it *hisself*," "They're only fooling *theirself*," or "They bought *theirselves* sodas." Such forms are nonstandard. Say "himself" and "themselves" instead.

Indefinite Pronouns These pronouns refer to unidentified persons, places, or things. One group of indefinite pronouns consistently acts as pronouns.

anybody	everything	one
anyone	nobody	somebody
anything	no one	someone
everybody	nothing	something
everyone		

A second group may function as either pronouns or adjectives.

all	any	most	few	much
another	each	either	many	neither

Here are some examples:

Everyone is welcome. (indefinite pronoun)

Many are called, but *few* are chosen. (indefinite pronouns)

Many men but only a *few* women attend the Air Force Academy. (adjectives)

Page 588 discusses indefinite pronouns as antecedents.

Reciprocal Pronouns The two reciprocal pronouns show an interchange of action between two or more parties. *Each other* is used when two parties interact, *one another* when three or more do.

Pam and Patty accidentally gave *each other* the same thing for Christmas. (two persons)

The members of the football team joyfully embraced *one another* after their victory. (more than two persons)

Usage Considerations Many students handle pronouns carelessly, damaging the clarity of their writing. Problems include letting the same pronoun stand for different nouns or using a pronoun where detailed, vivid language would be more effective. The following passage illustrates poor pronoun usage:

My brother loves fly fishing. He thinks *it* is the only way to spend a summer weekend. In fact, whenever he's off work, he'll do *it*.

Rewritten as follows, the passage has been notably improved:

My brother loves fly fishing. He thinks that *wading a stream and casting leisurely for trout* is the only way to spend a summer weekend. In fact, whenever he's off work, he *can be found up to his hips in water, offering his hand-tied flies to the waiting rainbow trout.*

EXERCISE   *Identify each pronoun in the following sentences and indicate its type:*

1. This is the kind of movie that I like.
2. Everyone in the class came to the party she gave at term's end.
3. If you feel thirsty, pour yourself a glass of lemonade.
4. That is a terrible-looking chair. Who would buy it anyhow?
5. What do you think Sally and Bill bought each other for Christmas?
6. I myself will take the blame for anything that goes wrong with the experiment.
7. Don't ask me to change; I like myself just as I am.
8. The children splashed one another with water from the pool.

Verbs

A verb indicates action or existence: what something is, was, or will be. Verbs fall into three classes: *action verbs, linking verbs,* and *helping verbs.*

Action Verbs As their name suggests, action verbs express action. Some action verbs are transitive, others intransitive. A transitive verb has a direct object that receives or results from the action and rounds out the meaning of the sentence.

The photographer *took* the picture.

Without the direct object, this sentence would not express a complete thought. In contrast, an *intransitive* verb requires no direct object to complete the meaning of the sentence.

Lee Ann *gasped* loudly.

Little Tommy Tucker *sings* for his supper.

Many action verbs can play both transitive or intransitive roles, depending on the sentences they are used in.

Kari *rode* her bicycle into town. (transitive verb)

Karl *rode* in the front seat of the car. (intransitive verb)

Linking Verbs A linking verb shows existence—what something is, was, or will be—rather than action. Linking verbs are intransitive and tie their subjects to subject complements. Some subject complements are nouns or noun substitutes that rename their subjects. Others are adjectives that describe their subjects.

Ms. Davis *is* our new director. (Complement *director* renames subject *Ms. Davis.*)

The soup *was* lukewarm. (Complement *lukewarm* describes subject *soup.*)

The most common linking verbs are forms of the verb *to be (is, are, am, was, were, be, being, been).* Likewise, verbs such as *seem, become, appear, remain, feel, look, smell, sound,* and *taste* function as linking verbs when they do not indicate actual physical action. In such cases, they are followed by adjectives (see pages 567–569). Here is an example:

Harry looked *angry.*

When such verbs do indicate physical action, they function as action verbs and are followed by adverbs (see pages 569–571).

Harry looked *angrily* at the referee.

Helping Verbs Helping verbs accompany action or linking verbs, allowing them to express with great precision matters such as possibility, obligation, and time. Common helping verbs include the following:

has	been	had (to)
have	do	shall
had	does	will
am	did	going (to)
is	used (to)	about (to)
are	may	would
was	might	should
were	must	ought (to)
be	have (to)	can
being	has (to)	could

I *should ask* my parents. (helping verb *should* with action verb *ask*)

The driver *was being lifted* onto a stretcher. (helping verbs *was* and *being* with action verb *lifted*)

You *have been* good. (helping verb *have* with linking verb *been*)

The patient *will feel* better soon. (helping verb *will* with linking verb *feel*)

We *might go* to Calgary next weekend. (helping verb *might* with action verb *go*)

Helping verbs usually appear next to the main verbs, but they don't have to.

Ellen *will* undoubtedly *resign.*

Combinations of two or more verbs are called verb phrases.

Usage Considerations Energetic writing requires precise verbs. Don't take verbs for granted; revise them as necessary in order to strengthen a sentence. Note the improved precision of the second example sentence:

I *gave* the maître d' a ten-dollar bill.

I *slipped* the maître d' a ten-dollar bill.

EXERCISE *Identify each verb in the following sentences and indicate its type:*

1. If Butch and Jim need transportation, my car will be available.
2. Please write your name on your quiz before you give it to me.
3. Marvin has been sitting in front of the TV all morning.
4. I will be watching the Toronto Raptors play tonight.

5. The movie offered lots of action, but the plot was poor.

6. Christine's assistance on this project has been invaluable.

7. William must have finished the yard work by now.

8. Teresa will probably be elected president of the club.

Principal Parts   Verbs change in form to show time (tense) distinctions. For every action verb, tenses are built from three principal parts: *present, past,* and *past participle*. The present is the principal part you would look up in the dictionary (*win, skip, go,* and so on). If the subject of a verb is a singular pronoun (*he, she, it*) or a singular noun, add an *s* or *es* to the dictionary form (*wins, skips, goes*). Most verbs have identical past and past participles.

	Present	Past	Past Participle
I, you, we, they	talk	talked	talked
He, she, it, Henry	talks	talked	talked
I, you, we, they	stand	stood	stood
He, she, it, the decision	stands	stood	stood

Of the remaining verbs, most have different past and past participles.

	Present	Past	Past Participle
I, you, we, they	swim	swam	swum
He, she, it, the boy	swims	swam	swum
I, you, we, they	bite	bit	bitten
He, she, it, the dog	bites	bit	bitten

In a few verbs, the past and past participles are identical to the dictionary form.

	Present	Past	Past Participle
I, you, we, they	set	set	set
He, she, it	sets	set	set

If you're uncertain about the principal parts of a verb, check your dictionary.

Tense   There are six basic tenses: present, past, future, present perfect, past perfect, future perfect. They are formed from the principal parts of action and linking verbs, either alone or combined with helping verbs.

The *present tense* is formed from the present principal part of the main verb. It shows present condition and general or habitual action, indicates permanent truths, tells about past events in the historical present, and sometimes denotes action at some definite future time.

Helen *looks* beautiful in her new gown. (present condition)

John *works* on the eighteenth floor. (general action)

I *brush* my teeth each morning. (habitual action)

The earth *rotates* on its axis. (permanent truth)

On November 11, 1918, the guns *fall* silent, and World War I *comes* to an end. (historical present)

Monday, I *begin* my new job. (future action)

The *past tense* is based on the past principal part of the verb. The past tense shows that a condition existed or an action was completed in the past. The verb tense leaves the time indefinite, but surrounding words may specify it.

Paul *was* angry with his noisy neighbours. (past condition, time indefinite)

Sandy *received* a long letter yesterday. (past action, time specified by *yesterday*)

The *future tense* combines *shall* or *will* and the present principal part of the main verb. It indicates that a condition will exist or an action will take place in the future.

You *will feel* better after a good night's sleep. (future condition)

I *shall attend* the concert next week. (future action)

The *present perfect* tense is formed with *has* or *have* and the past participle of the main verb. It shows that a past condition or action, or its effect, continues until the present time.

The players *have been* irritable since they lost the championship game. (Condition continues until present.)

Jean *has driven* a United Parcel Service truck for five years. (Action continues until present.)

William *has repaired* the snow blower. (Effect of action continues until present although the action itself was completed in the past.)

The *past perfect* tense combines *had* and the past participle of the main verb. It refers to a past condition or action that was completed before another past condition or action.

He *had been* in the army two years when the war ended. (Past perfect condition occurred first.)

Vivian moved into the house that she *had built* the summer before. (Past perfect action occurred first.)

The *future perfect* tense is formed from the verbs *shall have* or *will have* plus the past participle of the main verb. It shows that a condition or an action will have been completed at some time in the future. Surrounding words specify time.

Our sales manager *will have been* with the company ten years next July. (Condition will end.)

By the end of this year, I *shall have written* the great Canadian novel. (Action will be completed.)

Each of these basic tenses has a *progressive tense* that indicates action in progress. The progressive tense always includes some form of the verb *to be* followed by a present participle, a verb that ends in *-ing*.

Present progressive	I am running.
Past progressive	I was running.

Future progressive	I will be running.
Present perfect progressive	I have been running.
Past perfect progressive	I had been running.
Future perfect progressive	I will have been running.

Page 598 discusses unwarranted shifts in tense and their correction.

Voice Transitive verbs have two voices: active and passive. A verb is in the *active voice* when the subject carries out the action named by the verb.

Barry *planned* a picnic. (Subject *Barry* performs action.)

A verb is in the *passive voice* when the subject receives the action. The performer may be identified in an accompanying phrase or go unmentioned.

A picnic *was planned* by Barry. (The phrase *by Barry* identifies the performer.)

The picnic *was cancelled.* (The performer goes unmentioned.)

A passive construction always uses a form of *to be* and the past participle of an action verb. Like other constructions, the passive may show past, present, or future time.

Amy *is paid* handsomely for her investment advice. (present tense)

I *was warned* by a sound truck that a tornado was nearby. (past tense)

I *will be sent* to Ghana soon by the Peace Corps. (future tense)

I *have been awarded* a sizable research grant. (present perfect tense)

The city *had been shelled* heavily before the infantry moved in. (past perfect tense)

By the end of this month, the site for our second factory *will have been chosen.* (future perfect tense)

To convert a sentence from the passive to the active voice, make the performer the subject, the original subject the direct object, and drop the form of *to be.*

The treaty *was signed* by the general. (passive)

The general *signed* the treaty. (active)

Technical and scientific writing commonly uses the passive voice to explain processes since its flat, impersonal tone adds an air of scientific objectivity and authority. Other kinds of writing, however, avoid the passive voice except when it is desirable to conceal the one performing the action or when the action is more significant than the actor. See pages 216–217 for more information on usage.

EXERCISE *Identify each verb in the following sentences, indicate its tense, and note any use of the passive voice:*

1. They will have arrived in Tokyo by this evening.

2. This TV program is relayed to Europe by satellite.

3. The Krause Corporation's new headquarters building will be dedicated June 30.

4. The school psychologist was asked whether she had any explanation for Tim's odd behaviour.

5. We have been told we face yet another 15 percent staff cutback.

6. Nancy bought a Garth Brooks CD.

7. The Northrups will start their vacation tomorrow.

8. Leslie works in the sales department of IBM.

Mood The mood of a verb shows whether the writer regards a statement as a:

1. fact

2. command or request

3. wish, possibility, condition contrary to fact, or the like.

English has three moods: the indicative, imperative, and subjunctive.

A sentence in the *indicative mood* states a real or supposed fact or asks a question.

Nancy *graduates* from high school tomorrow.

We *lived* in Oakville when Rachel was born.

He *had been* a sailor during the war.

Has Joe *asked* anyone to the prom yet?

Most verbs are used in the indicative mood.

A sentence in the *imperative mood* delivers a command or makes a request.

Leave the room immediately! (command)

Please *turn* the CD player down. (request)

The subject of a sentence in the imperative mood is always *you*. Although ordinarily unstated, the subject sometimes appears in the sentence.

You leave the room immediately!

The *subjunctive mood* is used

1. in *if, as if,* and *as though* clauses to express a wish, a possibility, or an action or a condition contrary to fact

2. in *that* clauses expressing orders, demands, requests, resolutions, proposals, or motions

3. with modal auxiliaries to express wishes, probability, possibility, permission, requirements, recommendations, suggestions, and conditions contrary to fact.

To express a present or future wish, possibility, condition, or action in an *if, as if,* or *as though* clause, use *were* with any personal pronoun or noun serving as the subject of the clause.

If only Stan *were* less gullible! (present wish contrary to fact)

Even if Kay *were* to explain, Mary wouldn't believe her. (future possibility)

Arthur is behaving as if he *were* a millionaire (present condition contrary to fact)

To express a wish, possibility, or condition contrary to past facts, use *had been* or *had* plus the past participle of an action verb.

If the engine *had been lubricated,* the bearing wouldn't have burned out. (past condition contrary to fact)

Alice looked as if she *had lost* her best friend. (condition expressed in clause occurs before action of verb *looked*)

When writing *that* clauses expressing orders, demands, requests, resolutions, proposals, or motions, use *be* or the present plural form of an action verb.

I move that they *be* rewarded for their bravery.

The group proposed that Margaret *go* to the scene of the accident and *inspect* it personally.

In other *that* clauses, use the appropriate indicative form of the verb.

I know that they *were* rewarded for their bravery.

The group believed that Margaret *had gone* to the scene of the accident and *inspected* it personally.

The modal auxiliaries include the helping verbs *can, could, may, might, must, shall, will, would, should,* and *ought to.* The examples below illustrate the meanings they can express.

1. Wishes *(could, would)*

   I wish I *could* shimmy like my sister Kate.

   The Reformers wish the Progressive Conservatives *would* go away and vice versa.

2. Probability *(should)*

   Because I've studied diligently, I *should* do better on my next chemistry test.

3. Possibility *(may, might, can, could)*

   Low inflation *could* cause our stock market to soar.

   I *might* stay up to watch the eclipse of the moon tonight.

4. Permission *(can, may)*

   The public *can* use these tennis courts every afternoon.

   You *may* leave as soon as you've finished filing these folders.

5. Requirements *(must)*

   The landlord has raised our rent again; we *must* find another apartment.

6. Recommendations, suggestions *(should, ought to)*

Randy *should* see a doctor about his chest pains.

All of us *ought to* exercise regularly.

7. Conditions contrary to fact *(could)*

If only I *could* live my life over!

EXERCISE   *For each of the following sentences, identify the mood as indicative (IND), imperative (IMP), or subjunctive (SUB):*

1. The next regular meeting should be postponed for a week.

2. Hot chocolate is an excellent bedtime drink.

3. Sally should learn to curb her sharp tongue.

4. Tell me all about last night's movie.

5. Someone in the crowd shrieked loudly at the sudden thunderclap.

6. If I were boss here, I'd raise everybody's wages.

7. The latest drop in interest rates should spur consumer spending.

8. Don't ever use that tone of voice to me again.

Adjectives

An adjective *modifies* a noun or pronoun by describing it, limiting it, or otherwise making its meaning more exact.

The *brass* candlestick stood next to the *fragile* vase. (*Brass* modifies *candlestick,* and *fragile* modifies *vase.*)

The cat is *long-haired* and *sleek.* (*Long-haired* and *sleek* modify *cat.*)

There are three general categories of adjectives: limiting, descriptive, and proper.

Limiting Adjectives   A limiting adjective identifies or points out the noun or pronoun it modifies. It may indicate number or quantity. Several categories of pronouns can serve as limiting adjectives, as can numbers and nouns.

Whose briefcase is on the table? (interrogative adjective)

The couple *whose* car was stolen called the police. (relative adjective)

This restaurant has the best reputation for gourmet food. (demonstrative adjective)

Some people have no social tact at all. (indefinite adjective)

Sally swerved *her* car suddenly to avoid an oncoming truck. (possessive adjective)

Three people entered the lecture hall late. (number as adjective)

The *schoolgirl* look is fashionable this year. (noun as adjective)

Descriptive Adjectives   A descriptive adjective names a quality, characteristic, or condition of a noun or pronoun. Two or more of these adjectives, members of the largest category of adjectives, may modify the same noun or pronoun.

> The *yellow* submarine belongs to the Beatles.

> He applied *clear* lacquer to the tabletop.

> The *slim, sophisticated* model glided onto the runway.

> The child was *active, happy,* and *polite.*

Proper Adjectives   A proper adjective is derived from a proper noun and is always capitalized.

> Harwell is a *Shakespearean* actor.

Articles as Adjectives   Articles appear immediately before nouns and can therefore be considered adjectives. There are three articles in English: *a, an,* and *the. The* points to a specific item; *a* and *an* do not. A precedes words beginning with consonant sounds; *an* precedes words with vowel sounds, making pronunciation easier.

> *The* right word at *the* right moment can save a friendship. (Definite articles suggest there is one right word and one right moment.)

> *A* right word can save a friendship. (Indefinite article suggests there are several right words.)

> I think I'd like *an* apple with my lunch. (No particular apple is specified.)

Sometimes the definite article refers to a class of items.

> *The* tiger is fast becoming an endangered species.

Context shows whether such a sentence refers to particular items or entire classes.

Comparison with Adjectives   Adjectives may be used to show comparison. When two things are compared, shorter adjectives usually add *-er* and longer adjectives add more. When three or more things are compared, shorter adjectives usually add *-est* and longer ones add *most.*

> John is *taller* than Pete. (short adjective comparing two things)

> Sandra seems *more cheerful* than Jill today. (long adjective comparing two things)

> John is the *tallest* of the three brothers. (short adjective comparing three things)

> Sandra is the *most cheerful* girl in the class. (longer adjective comparing more than three things)

Some adjectives, like the examples below, have irregular forms for comparisons.

> good—better—best

> bad—worse—worst

Don't use the *-est* form of the shorter adjective for comparing just two things.

> *Faulty* This is the *smallest* of the two castles.

Instead, use the *-er* form.

> *Revision* This is the *smaller* of the two castles.

Position of Adjectives Most adjectives come immediately before the words they modify. In a few set expressions (for example, heir *apparent*), the adjective immediately follows the word it modifies. Similarly, adjective pairs sometimes appear in a follow-up position for added emphasis (The rapids, *swift* and *dangerous*, soon capsized the raft). Sometimes adjectives also serve as subject complements and follow their subjects (The puppy was *friendly*).

Usage Considerations Some students overuse adjectives, especially in descriptions, but most underuse them. Review your sentences carefully to see where adding or cutting adjectives can increase the impact of your writing.

> My Buick is the talk of my friends.

> My *old, dilapidated, rusty, fenderless 1970* Buick is the talk of my friends.

> My *rusty, fenderless 1970* Buick is the talk of my friends.

The first sentence lacks adjectives that show why the car is discussed. The second sentence overcorrects this fault by including two adjectives that repeat the information provided by the others. The final sentence strikes the proper balance.

EXERCISE *Identify the adjectives in the following sentences:*

1. Tom is a very unhappy person.
2. Paul has an aunt who writes long, chatty letters to him regularly.
3. Sean ate an English muffin and drank a cup of black coffee.
4. Barton has an unusual sideboard in his dining room.
5. The tired carpenter tossed his tools into the red truck and drove home.
6. After buying a few gifts, Linda and Audrey took a slow stroll around the resort town.
7. Harvey ate three hamburgers and four helpings of salad at the picnic.
8. From the hilltop, the view was beautiful.

Adverbs

An adverb modifies a verb, an adjective, another adverb, or a whole sentence. Adverbs generally answer questions such as "How?" "When?" "Where?" "How often?" and "To what extent?"

> The floodwaters receded *very* slowly. (Adverb modifies adverb and answers the question "How?")

My sister will visit me *tomorrow.* (Adverb modifies verb and answers the question "When?")

The coach walked *away* from the bench. (Adverb modifies verb and answers the question "Where?")

The tire is *too* worn to be safe. (Adverb modifies adjective and answers the question "To what extent?")

The teller is *frequently* late for work. (Adverb modifies adjective and answers the question "How often?")

Unfortunately, the game was cancelled because of rain. (The adverb modifies the whole sentence but does not answer any question.)

Formation of Adverbs Most adverbs are formed by adding *-ly* to adjectives.

The wind is *restless.* (*Restless* is an adjective modifying *wind.*)

He walked *restlessly* around the room. (*Restlessly* is an adverb modifying *walked.*)

Many common adverbs, however (*almost, never, quite, soon, then, there,* and *too*), lack *-ly* endings.

I *soon* realized that pleasing my boss was impossible.

This movie is *too* gruesome for my taste.

Furthermore, some words such as *better, early, late, hard, little, near, only, straight,* and *wrong* do double duty as either adjectives or adverbs.

We must have taken a *wrong* turn. (*Wrong* is an adjective modifying the noun *turn.*)

Where did I go *wrong?* (*Wrong* is an adverb modifying the verb *go.*)

Comparison with Adverbs Like adjectives, adverbs can show comparison. When two things are compared, adverbs add *more.* When three or more things are compared, *most* is used.

Harold works *more* efficiently than Don. (adverb comparing two people)

Of all the people in the shop, Harold works the *most* efficiently. (adverb comparing more than two people)

Some adverbs, like some adjectives, use irregular forms for comparisons.

well—better—best

much—more—most

Position of Adverbs Adverbs are more movable than any other part of speech. Usually, adverbs that modify adjectives and other adverbs appear next to them to avoid confusion.

Her *especially* fine tact makes her a welcome guest at any party. (Adverb *especially* modifies adjective *fine*.)

The novel was *very* badly written. (Adverb *very* modifies adverb *badly*.)

Adverbs that modify verbs, however, can often be shifted around in their sentences without causing changes in meaning. *Quickly*, he slipped through the doorway.

He slipped *quickly* through the doorway.

He slipped through the doorway *quickly*.

Usage Considerations You can often sharpen the meaning of a sentence by adding a well-chosen adverb.

The student squirmed in his chair.

The student squirmed *anxiously* in his chair.

Including the adverb *anxiously* in the second sentence shows the mental state of the student.

Be careful, however, not to overuse adverbs as they can bog down your writing.

EXERCISE *Identify the adverbs in the following sentences:*

1. Harold is late more frequently than any other member of the crew.
2. After dinner, the children went outdoors and played noisily.
3. The doctor told Albert his illness, though quite serious, would respond well to treatment.
4. Lucy stepped quickly to the door and listened intently to the howling wind.
5. I often wish I could study less hard without my grades suffering.
6. The pirate ship glided swiftly and silently toward the sleeping town.
7. The tired, perspiring runner staggered wearily across the finish line.
8. You'll have to work very fast to keep up with Jody.

Prepositions

A preposition links its object—a noun or noun substitute—to some other word in the sentence and shows a relationship between them. The relationship is often one of location, time, means, or reason or purpose. The word group containing the preposition and its object makes up a prepositional phrase.

The new insulation *in* the attic keeps my house much warmer now. (Preposition *in* links object *attic* to *insulation* and shows location.)

We have postponed the meeting *until* tomorrow. (Preposition *until* links object *tomorrow* to *postponed* and shows time.)

The tourists travelled *by* automobile. (Preposition *by* links object *automobile* to *travelled* and shows means.)

Warren swims *for* exercise. (Preposition *for* links object *exercise* to *swims* and shows reason or purpose.)

The following list includes the most common prepositions, some of which consist of two or more words:

above	beside	in	out of
after	between	instead of	over
against	by	into	since
along with	by reason of	like	through
among	contrary to	near	to
at	during	next to	toward
because of	except	of	under
before	for	on	with
below	from	onto	without

Many of these combine to form additional prepositions: *except for, in front of, by way of, on top of,* and the like.

Certain prepositions sometimes occur in close association with certain verbs, forming verb units with altered meanings. When this happens, we call the prepositions verb particles. Here is an example:

The instructor let Jeff make *up* the test.

Note the great difference between the meaning of the foregoing sentence and "The instructor let Jeff make the test."

Usage Considerations   It is easy to use a small group of prepositions over and over in your writing. This habit often results in imprecise or misleading sentences. To avoid this problem, think carefully about your choice of prepositions as you revise. Read the following example:

He walked *by* the railroad tracks on his way home.

Note that two interpretations are possible.

He walked *along* the railroad tracks on his way home.

He walked *past* the railroad tracks on his way home.

Clearly you would use the preposition that conveys your intended meaning.

EXERCISE   *Identify the prepositions and their objects in the following sentences:*

1. I finally finished waxing the car just before the rainstorm.
2. Aloe lotion will give you instant relief from sunburn.
3. For reasons of security, this gate must be kept locked at all times.
4. Shortly after dark, the group arrived at the camp.
5. Across the street, George was working on his roof.
6. At the end of the concert, everyone in the hall stood and applauded.
7. Helen sprinkled the roast with a blend of herbs.
8. Because of an error, all of the information in the computer was lost.

Conjunctions

Conjunctions serve as connectors, linking parts of sentences or whole sentences. These connectors fall into three groups: coordinating conjunctions, subordinating conjunctions, and conjunctive adverbs.

Coordinating Conjunctions Coordinating conjunctions connect terms of equal grammatical importance: words, word groups, and simple sentences. These conjunctions can occur singly *(and, but, or, nor, for, yet, so)* or in pairs called correlative conjunctions *(either—or, neither—nor, both—and,* and *not only—but also)*. The elements that follow correlative conjunctions must be parallel, that is, have the same grammatical form.

Tom *and* his cousin are opening a video arcade. (Coordinating conjunction connects nouns.)

Shall I serve the tea in the living room *or* on the veranda? (Coordinating conjunction connects phrases.)

I am going to Europe this summer, *but* Marjorie is staying home. (Coordinating conjunction connects simple sentences.)

Amy *not only* teaches English *but also* writes novels. (Correlative conjunctions connect parallel predicates.)

You can study nursing *either* at the University of B.C. *or* at Kwantlen University College. (Correlative conjunctions connect parallel phrases.)

Friendship is *both* pleasure *and* pain. (Correlative conjunctions connect parallel nouns.)

Subordinating Conjunctions Like relative pronouns, subordinating conjunctions introduce subordinate clauses, relating them to independent clauses, which can stand alone as complete sentences. Examples of subordinating conjunctions include *because, as if, even though, since, so that, whereas,* and *whenever* (see pages 578–579 for a more complete list).

I enjoyed the TV program *because* it was so well acted. (Conjunction connects *it was so well acted* to rest of sentence.)

Whenever you're ready, we can begin dinner. (Conjunction connects *you're ready* to rest of sentence.)

Conjunctive Adverbs These connectors resemble both conjunctions and adverbs. Like conjunctions, they serve as linking devices between elements of equal rank. Like adverbs, they function as modifiers, showing such things as similarity, contrast, result or effect, addition, emphasis, time, and example.

The following list groups the most common conjunctive adverbs according to function:

Similarity: likewise, similarly

Contrast: however, nevertheless, on the contrary, on the other hand, otherwise

Result or effect: accordingly, as a result, consequently, hence, therefore, thus

Addition: also, furthermore, in addition, in the first place, moreover

Emphasis or clarity: in fact, in other words, indeed, that is

Time: afterward, later, meanwhile, subsequently

Example: for example, for instance, to illustrate

The job will require you to travel a great deal; however, the salary is excellent.

Sean cares nothing for clothes; *in fact,* all of his socks have holes in their toes.

Usage Considerations You can add variety to your writing by varying the conjunctions you use. If you consistently rely on the conjunction *because,* try substituting *as* or *since.* Likewise, you may periodically replace *if* with *provided that.*

When you have choppy sentences, try combining them by using a conjunction.

You can buy smoked salmon at Sally's Seafoods. You can buy it at Daane's Thriftland as well.

You can buy smoked salmon *either* at Sally's Seafoods *or* at Daane's Thriftland.

The revision is much smoother than the original sentence pair.

Interjections

An interjection is an exclamatory word used to gain attention or to express strong feeling. It has no grammatical connection to the rest of the sentence. An interjection is followed by an exclamation point or a comma.

Hey! Watch how you're driving! (strong interjection)

Oh, is the party over already? (mild interjection)

EXERCISE *Identify the coordinating conjunctions (CC), subordinating conjunctions (SC), conjunctive adverbs (CA), and interjections (I) in the following sentences:*

1. The car was not only dented but also dirty.
2. While Roger was at the movies, his brother bought a model airplane.
3. Heavens, what's all the fuss about anyhow?
4. Either the Coles or the Thurlows will drive us to the airport.
5. Although they felt under the weather, Marie and Sally attended the dance.
6. The candidate's views matched those of his audience; consequently, he received warm applause.

7. Neither William nor his brother has ever travelled out of the province.

8. Sandra is no academic slouch; indeed, she was valedictorian of her high school class.

Phrases and Clauses

Phrases

A phrase is a group of words that lacks a subject and a predicate and serves as a single part of speech. This section discusses four basic kinds of phrases: *prepositional phrases, participial phrases, gerund phrases,* and *infinitive phrases.* The last three are based on participles, gerunds, and infinitives, verb forms known as verbals. A fifth type of phrase, the verb phrase, consists of sets of two or more verbs (*has fixed, had been sick, will have been selected,* and the like).

Prepositional Phrases   A prepositional phrase consists of a preposition, one or more objects, and any associated words. These phrases serve as adjectives or adverbs.

> The picture *over the mantel* was my mother's. (prepositional phrase as adjective)

> He bought ice skates *for himself.* (prepositional phrase as adverb modifying verb)

> The toddler was afraid *of the dog.* (prepositional phrase as adverb modifying adjective)

> Our visitors arrived late *in the day.* (prepositional phrase as adverb modifying another adverb)

Frequently, prepositional phrases occur in series. Sometimes they form chains in which each phrase modifies the object of the preceding phrase. At other times some or all of the phrases may modify the verb or verb phrase.

> John works *in a clothing store / on Main Street / during the summer.*

Here the first and third phrases serve as adverbs modifying the verb *works* and answering the questions "Where?" and "When?" while the second phrase serves as an adjective modifying *store* and answering the question "Where?"

On occasion, especially in questions, a preposition may be separated from its object, making the phrase difficult to find.

> Dr. Perry is the person *whom* I've been looking *for.*

> *What* are you shouting *about?*

Participial Phrases   A participial phrase consists of a participle plus associated words. Participles are verb forms that, when used in participial phrases, function as adjectives or adverbs. A present participle ends in *-ing* and indicates an action currently being carried out. A past participle ends in *-ed, -en, -e, -n, -d,* or *-t* and indicates some past action.

> The chef *preparing dinner* trained in France. (present participial phrase as adjective)

> The background, *sketched in lightly,* accented the features of the woman in the painting. (past participial phrase as adjective)

> She left *whistling a jolly melody.* (present participial phrase as adverb)

A perfect participial phrase consists of *having* or *having been* plus a past participle and any associated words. Like a past participial phrase, it indicates a past action.

> *Having alerted the townspeople about the tornado,* the sound truck returned to the city garage. (perfect participial phrase)

> *Having been alerted to the tornado,* the townspeople sought shelter in their basements. (perfect participial phrase)

Some participial phrases that modify persons or things distinguish them from others in the same class. These phrases are written without commas. Other phrases provide more information about the persons or things they modify and are set off with commas.

> The man *fixing my car* is a master mechanic. (Phrase distinguishes man fixing car from other men.)

> Mr. Welsh, *fatigued by the tennis game,* rested in the shade. (Phrase provides more information about Mr. Welsh.)

Gerund Phrases   A gerund phrase consists of a gerund and the words associated with it. Like present participles, gerunds are verb forms that end in *-ing*. Unlike participles, though, they function as nouns rather than as adjectives or adverbs.

> Kathryn's hobby is *collecting stamps.* (gerund phrase as subject complement)

> Kathryn's hobby, *collecting stamps,* has made her many friends. (gerund phrase as appositive)

> He devoted every spare moment to *overhauling the car.* (gerund phrase as object of preposition)

Infinitive Phrases An infinitive phrase consists of the present principal part of a verb preceded by *to (to fix, to eat),* together with any accompanying words. These phrases serve as adjectives, adverbs, and nouns.

> This looks like a good place *to plant the shrub.* (infinitive phrase as adjective)

> Lenore worked *to earn money for tuition.* (infinitive phrase as adverb)

> My goal is *to have my own business some day.* (infinitive phrase as noun)

Gerunds can often be substituted for infinitives and vice versa.

> *To repair this fender* will cost two hundred dollars. (infinitive phrase as subject)

Repairing this fender will cost two hundred dollars. (gerund phrase as subject)

At times the *to* in an infinitive may be omitted following verbs such as *make, dare, let,* and *help.*

Kristin didn't dare *(to) move* a muscle.

The psychiatrist helped me *(to) overcome* my fear of flying.

Verbals Not in Phrases   Participles, gerunds, and infinitives can function as nouns, adjectives, or adverbs, even when they are not parts of phrases.

That *sunbathing* woman is a well-known model. (participle as adjective)

Dancing is fine exercise. (gerund)

The children want *to play.* (infinitive as noun)

If you're looking for a job, Sally is the person *to see.* (infinitive as adjective)

I'm prepared *to resign.* (infinitive as adverb)

Usage Considerations   Phrases can often help clarify or develop the information in a sentence.

Original	My brother is fishing.
Revision	My brother is fishing *for trout just below Barnes Dam on Sidewinder Creek.* (prepositional phrases added)
Original	The boat barely made shore.
Revision	The boat, *listing heavily and leaking badly,* barely made shore. (participial phrases added)

To avoid ponderous sentences, don't, however, weigh them down with phrases, as in the following example:

My brother is fishing for trout just below Barnes Dam on Sidewinder Creek *near Perry Pass in the Rocky Mountains.*

EXERCISE   *Identify the italicized phrases as prepositional, participial, gerund, or infinitive and tell whether each is used as a noun, an adjective, or an adverb.*

1. *Walking the dog in the rain* made me grouchy for the rest of the day.
2. *To ride the Orient Express* was Marian's fondest ambition.
3. *Opening the door a tiny crack,* Michelle stared with horror at the scene before her.
4. Sue Ellen works *in a grocery store* during the summer.
5. Tom couldn't decide which refrigerator *to buy for his mother.*
6. Old-fashioned in every way, Chester shaves himself *with a straight razor.*
7. Dave loves *flying a crop duster.*
8. *Glaring angrily at the class,* the teacher shouted for silence.

Clauses

A clause is a word group that includes a subject and a predicate. An *independent clause,* sometimes called a main clause, expresses a complete thought and can function as a simple sentence. A *subordinate clause,* or dependent clause, cannot stand by itself. Subordinate clauses may serve as nouns, adjectives, or adverbs.

Noun Clauses A noun clause can serve in any of the ways that ordinary nouns can.

What the neighbour told John proved to be incorrect. (noun clause as subject)

The woman asked *when the bus left for Sherbrooke.* (noun clause as direct object)

I'll give a reward to *whoever returns my billfold.* (noun clause as object of preposition *to*)

Noun clauses normally begin with one of the following words:

Relative Pronouns		**Subordinating Conjunctions**
who	whoever	when
whom	whomever	why
whose	that	where
what	whatever	how
which	whichever	whether

The relative pronoun *that* is sometimes omitted from the beginning of a clause that acts as a direct object.

Dr. Kant thinks *(that) he knows everything.*

If a clause is serving as a noun, you can replace it with the word *something* or *someone,* and the sentence will still make sense.

Dr. Kant thinks *something.*

If the clause is serving as an adjective or an adverb, making the substitution turns the sentence into nonsense.

The person *who wins the lottery* will receive two million dollars.

The person *someone* will receive two million dollars.

Adjective Clauses Like ordinary adjectives, adjective clauses modify nouns and noun substitutes.

Give me one reason *why you feel the way you do.* (Adjective clause modifies noun.)

I'll hire anyone *that Dr. Stone recommends.* (Adjective clause modifies pronoun.)

Generally, adjective clauses begin with one of the following words:

Relative Pronouns	Subordinating Conjunctions
who	when
whom	where
whose	why
what	after
which	before
that	

Sometimes the word that introduces the clause can be omitted.

The chair *(that) we ordered last month* has just arrived. (pronoun *that* omitted but understood)

The man *(whom) we were talking to* is a movie producer. (pronoun *whom* omitted but understood)

Sometimes, too, a preposition comes ahead of the introductory pronoun.

The grace *with which Nelson danced* made the onlookers envious.

An adjective clause may be restrictive and distinguish whatever it modifies from others in the same class, or it may be nonrestrictive and provide more information about whatever it modifies.

Flora wiped up the cereal *that the baby had spilled.* (restrictive clause)

Harriet Thomas, *who was born in Saskatchewan,* now lives in Alberta. (nonrestrictive clause)

As these examples show, restrictive clauses are not set off with commas, but nonrestrictive clauses are.

Adverb Clauses   These clauses modify verbs, adjectives, adverbs, and sentences, answering the same questions that ordinary adverbs do.

You may go *whenever you wish.* (Adverb clause modifies verb.)

Sandra looked paler *than I had ever seen her look before.* (Adverb clause modifies adjective.)

Darryl shouted loudly *so that the rescue party could hear him.* (Adverb clause modifies adverb.)

Unless everyone cooperates, this plan will never succeed. (Adverb clause modifies whole sentence.)

The word or word group that introduces an adverb clause is always a subordinating conjunction. Here are the most common of these conjunctions, grouped according to the questions they answer.

When? after, as, as soon as, before, since, until, when, whenever, while

Where? where, wherever

How? as if, as though

Why? as, because, now that, since, so that

Under what conditions? although, if, once, provided that, though, unless

To what extent? than

Occasionally in an adverb clause, the omission of one or more words won't hurt its meaning. Such a construction is called an *elliptical clause.*

While (he was) making a sandwich, Garth hummed softly. (*he was* omitted but understood)

Unlike noun and adjective clauses, adverb clauses can often be moved about in their sentences.

Garth hummed *softly while (he was) making a sandwich.*

Usage Considerations Like phrases, clauses can help develop sentences as well as smooth out choppiness.

Original	The old grandfather clock ticked loudly through the night.
Revision	The old grandfather clock *that my great-aunt gave me before she died* ticked loudly through the night. (Clause adds information.)
Original	The chemistry professor insisted on lab safety. He had been hurt in a lab explosion the previous year.
Revision	The chemistry professor, *who had been hurt in a lab explosion the previous year,* insisted on lab safety. (Clause adds smoothness.)

To avoid clumsiness, avoid overloaded sentences like the one below:

The old grandfather clock that my great-aunt gave me before she died *and that I took with me to England when my company transferred me there for two years* ticked loudly through the night.

EXERCISE   *Identify the italicized clauses as noun, adjective, or adverb.*

1. Why do Bill's parents always give him *whatever he wants?*
2. Steve pitched *as if a big-league scout were watching him.*
3. Gary is the only golfer *who putted well today.*
4. The dog barked loudly *because he was hungry.*
5. *Why anyone would want to skydive* is beyond me.
6. The secretary *Julie hired last month* has already received a raise.
7. I can't believe *that Beth has to work all weekend.*
8. Square dancing is an activity *that millions enjoy.*

Editing to Correct Sentence Errors

frag

Accepted usage improves the smoothness of your prose, makes your writing easier to understand, and demonstrates that you are a careful communicator. These assets, in turn, increase the likelihood that the reader will accept your ideas.

When you've finished revising the first draft of a piece of writing, edit it with a critic's eye to ensure that you eliminate all errors. Circle sentences or parts of them that are faulty or suspect. Then check your circled items against this section of the Handbook, which deals with the most common errors in writing.

■ Sentence Fragments

A sentence fragment is a group of words that fails to qualify as a sentence but is capitalized and punctuated as if it were a sentence. To be a sentence, a word group must (1) have a subject and a verb and (2) make sense by itself. The first of the following examples has a subject and a verb; the second does not. Neither makes sense by itself.

If you want to remain.

His answer to the question.

Methods of Revision   Eliminating a sentence fragment is not hard. Careful reading often shows that the fragment goes with the sentence that comes just before or just after it. And sometimes two successive fragments can be joined. Note how we've corrected the fragments (italicized) in the following pairs:

Faulty	*Having been warned about the storm.* We decided to stay home.
Revision	Having been warned about the storm, we decided to stay home.
Faulty	*After eating.* The dog took a nap.
Revision	After eating, the dog took a nap.

Faulty	Sally went to work. Although she felt sick.
Revision	Sally went to work *although she felt sick.*
Faulty	Dave bought a new suit. *Over at Bentley's.*
Revision	Dave bought a new suit over at Bentley's.
Faulty	*That bronze clock on the mantel. Once belonged to my grandmother.*
Revision	That bronze clock on the mantel once belonged to my grandmother.

frag

Joining a fragment to a sentence or to another fragment works only if the problem is simply one of mispunctuation. If the fragment stems from an improperly developed thought, revise the thought into correct sentence form.

Punctuating Your Corrections   When you join a fragment to the following sentence, you need not place a comma between the two unless the fragment has six or more words or if omitting a comma might cause a misreading. When joining a fragment to the preceding sentence, omit a comma unless there is a distinct pause between the two items. The preceding examples illustrate these points.

Intentional Fragments   Fragments are commonly used in conversation and the writing that reproduces it. Professional writers also use fragments to gain special emphasis or create special effects. Pages 217–219 discuss these applications.

CONNECTED DISCOURSE EXERCISE   *Identify and correct the sentence fragments in the following letter:*

Dear Phone Company:

Recently I received a phone bill for over $500. While I do use the phone fairly extensively. Most of the calls I make are local ones. In this case, many of the calls on my bill were to other countries. Including a phone call to New Delhi, India. I can hardly be held responsible for these calls. Especially since I don't know anyone who lives overseas. Since the only long-distance call I made was to Sudbury, Ontario. I have deducted the charges for all the other long-distance calls from my bill and am sending you the balance. In order to prevent this type of error from happening again. Would you please have a representative determine why these charges appeared on my bill?

Sincerely,

Desperate

EXERCISE *Twelve main clauses paired with fragments are shown below. In each case identify the sentence (S) and the fragment (F) and then eliminate the fragment.*

1. The clerk handed the package to the customer. And walked swiftly away from the counter.
2. Exhausted by his efforts to push the car out of the snowbank. Paul slumped wearily into the easy chair.
3. The dinner honoured three retirees. One of them my father.
4. After tidying up the kitchen. My parents left for the movies.
5. If Dr. Frankenstein's experiment is a success. He'll throw a monster party to celebrate.
6. Even though Ned studied very hard. He had trouble with the test.
7. The dog barked at the stranger. And chased him from the property.
8. By leaving the ballpark before the last out was made. We avoided the after-game crowd.

■ Run-on Sentences and Comma Splices

A run-on, or fused, sentence occurs when one sentence runs into another without anything to mark their junction. A comma splice occurs when only a comma marks the junction. These errors lead your readers to think that you are hasty or careless. Here are several examples:

Run-on sentence	Laura failed to set her alarm she was late for work.
Comma splice	Violets are blooming now, my lawn is covered with them.
Run-on sentence	Rick refused to attend the movie he said he hated horror shows.
Comma splice	Perry watched the road carefully, he still missed his turn.
Run-on Sentence	Janet worked on her term paper her friend studied for a calculus test.
Comma splice	Janet worked on her term paper, her friend studied for a calculus test.

Testing for Errors To check out a possible comma splice or fused sentence, read what precedes and follows the comma or suspected junction and see whether the two parts can stand alone as sentences. If *both parts* can stand alone, there is an error. Otherwise, there is not.

Darryl is a real troublemaker, someday he'll find himself in serious difficulty.

Examination of the parts preceding and following the comma shows that each is a complete sentence:

Darryl is a real troublemaker.

Someday he'll find himself in serious difficulty.

The writer has therefore8 committed a comma splice that needs correction.

Methods of Revision   You can correct run-on sentences and comma splices in several ways.

ro cs

1. Create two separate sentences.

Revision   Violets are blooming now. My lawn is covered with them.

Revision   Rick refused to attend the movie. He said he hated horror shows.

2. Join the sentences with a semicolon.

Revision   Violets are blooming now; my yard is covered with them.

Revision   Rick refused to attend the movie; he said he hated horror shows.

3. Join the sentences with a comma and a coordinating conjunction *(and, but, or, nor, for, yet, so)*.

Revision   Laura failed to set her alarm, *so* she was late for work.

Revision   Perry watched the road carefully, *but* he still missed his turn.

4. Join the sentences with a semicolon and a conjunctive adverb (see pages 573–574).

Revision   Laura failed to set her alarm; *consequently,* she was late for work.

Revision   Violets are blooming now; *in fact,* my yard is covered with them.

5. Introduce one of the sentences with a subordinating conjunction (see pages 573, 578–580).

Revision   *Because* Laura failed to set her alarm, she was late for work.

Revision   Janet worked on her term paper *while* her friend studied for a calculus test.

As our examples show, you can often correct an error in several ways.

CONNECTED DISCOURSE EXERCISE   *Identify and correct the comma splices and run-on sentences in the following letter:*

Dear Desperate:

We are sorry to hear that you are having difficulty paying your bill, it is, however, your responsibility. Unfortunately we have no way to prevent you from making overseas calls, you have to curb your own tendency to reach out and touch your friends. Following your instructions, we are sending a technician to remove your phone. Please be home this Friday morning he will arrive then. Even though we will remove your phone, you are still responsible for the unpaid portion of your bill, it is your financial obligation. We would dislike referring this matter to a collection agency, it could ruin your credit rating.

Sincerely,

Your friendly phone representative

EXERCISE   *Indicate whether each item is correct (C), is a run-on sentence (RO), or contains a comma splice (CS) and then correct the faulty items.*

1. Lee is a difficult person he becomes angry whenever he doesn't get his own way.

2. The student appeared puzzled by the instructor's answer to his question, but he said nothing more.

3. The doctor warned Allan about his high cholesterol level, he went on a high-fibre diet.

4. Sally researched her topic thoroughly and wrote her report carefully as a result she received an *A*.

5. It's nice to see you again; we should get together more often.

6. The horse stumbled and nearly fell in the backstretch, nevertheless it managed to finish second.

7. Janice thought the exercises would be easy, after finishing them she found that her whole body ached.

8. I've just started to take up chess, you can hardly expect me to play well.

■ Subject–Verb Agreement

A verb should agree in number with its subject. Singular verbs should have singular subjects, and plural verbs should have plural subjects.

Correct   My *boss is* a grouch. (singular subject and verb)

Correct   The *apartments have* two bedrooms. (plural subject and verb)

Ordinarily, matching subjects and verbs causes no problems. The following special situations, however, can create difficulties.

Subject and Verb Separated by a Word Group   Sometimes a word group that includes one or more nouns comes between the subject and the verb. When this happens, match the verb with its subject, not a noun in the word group.

Correct   Our basket of sandwiches is missing.

Correct   Several books required for my paper are not in the library.

Correct	Mr. Schmidt, along with his daughters, runs a furniture store.
Correct	The old bus, crammed with passengers, was unable to reach the top of the hill.

Two Singular Subjects Most singular subjects joined by *and* take a plural verb.

Correct	The *couch* and *chair were* upholstered in blue velvet.

Sentences like the one above almost never cause problems. With subjects like *restoring cars* and *racing motorcycles,* however, singular verbs are often mistakenly used.

Faulty	*Restoring cars* and *racing motorcycles consumes* most of Frank's time.
Revision	*Restoring cars* and *racing motorcycles consume* most of Frank's time.

When *each* or *every* precedes the subjects, use a *singular* verb in place of a plural.

Correct	Every *book* and *magazine was* badly water-stained.

Singular subjects joined by *or, either—or,* or *neither—nor* also take singular verbs.

Correct	A *pear* or an *apple is* a good afternoon snack.
Correct	Neither *rain* nor *snow slows* our letter carrier.

Finally, use a singular verb when two singular subjects joined by *and* name the same person, place, or thing.

Correct	My *cousin* and business *partner is* retiring next month.

Cousin and *partner* refer to the same person.

One Singular and One Plural Subject When one singular subject and one plural subject are joined by *or, either—or,* or *neither—nor,* match the verb with the closer of the two.

Correct	Neither *John* nor his *parents were* at home.
Correct	Neither his *parents* nor *John was* at home.

As these examples show, the sentences are usually smoother when the plural subject follows the singular.

Collective Nouns as Subjects Collective nouns (*assembly, class, committee, family, herd, majority, tribe,* and the like) are singular in form but stand for groups or collections of people or things. Ordinarily, collective nouns are considered singular and therefore take singular verbs.

Correct	The *class is* writing a test.
Correct	The *herd was* clustered around the water hole.

Sometimes, though, a collective noun refers to the separate individuals making up the grouping, and then it requires a plural verb.

Correct   The *jury are* in dispute about the verdict.

Sentences in Which the Verb Comes Ahead of the Subject Sentences that begin with words such as *here, there, how, what,* and *where* fall into this category. With such sentences, the verb must agree with the subject that follows it.

Correct   Here *is* my *house.*

Correct   Where *are* my *shoes?*

Correct   There *is* just one *way* to solve this problem.

Correct   There *go* my *chances* for a promotion.

sv agr

CONNECTED DISCOURSE EXERCISE *Identify and correct the subject–verb agreement errors in the following letter:*

Regional Accounts Manager:

One of your area phone representatives have seriously misread a letter I submitted with my bill. I refused to pay for long-distance overseas calls since neither I nor my roommate know anyone who lives overseas. Instead of deducting the calls from my bill, she sent someone to remove my phone. Now my phone, along with many of my valuable possessions, have been removed. Unfortunately the technician, whom I allowed into my apartment only after carefully checking his credentials, were a thief. He locked me in a closet and cleared out the apartment. I have called the police, but I also expect the phone company to reimburse me for my losses. There is only two choices. Either the stolen items or a cheque covering the loss need to be sent to me immediately. Otherwise I am afraid I will be forced to sue. A jury are sure to rule in my favour. In addition, I expect to find that those overseas calls has been deducted from my bill.

Sincerely,

Desperately Desperate

EXERCISE   *Choose the correct verb form from the pair in parentheses.*

1. The pictures in the drawing room of the mansion (has, have) been insured for twelve million dollars.

2. Every dish and piece of stainless that I own (is, are) dirty.

3. Look! There (is, are) Kathy and her friend Marge.

4. Reading novels and watching TV (takes, take) up most of Stanley's time.

5. Each of these proposals (represents, represent) a great amount of work.

6. Two hamburgers or a hot beef sandwich (makes, make) an ample lunch.

7. (Has, Have) either of the orchids blossomed yet?

8. The automobile with the broken headlights and dented sides (was, were) stopped by the police.

■ Pronoun–Antecedent Agreement

pa agr

The antecedent of a pronoun is the noun or pronoun to which it refers. Just as subjects should agree with their verbs, pronouns should agree with their antecedents: singular antecedents require singular pronouns, and plural antecedents require plural pronouns. Ordinarily, you will have no trouble matching antecedents and pronouns. The situations below, however, can cause problems.

Indefinite Pronouns as Antecedents Indefinite pronouns include words like *each, either, neither, any, everybody, somebody,* and *nobody.* Whenever an indefinite pronoun is used as an antecedent, the pronoun that refers to it should be singular.

> *Faulty*   *Neither* of the actors had learned *their* lines.
>
> *Revision*   *Neither* of the actors had learned *his* lines.

When the gender of the antecedent is unknown, you may follow it with *his or her,* or if this results in awkwardness, rewrite the sentence in the plural.

> *Correct*   *Anyone* who has studied *his or her* assignments properly should do well on the test.
>
> *Correct*   *Those* who have studied *their* assignments properly should do well on the test.

Occasionally, a ridiculous result occurs when a singular pronoun refers to an indefinite pronoun that is obviously plural in meaning. When this happens, rewrite the sentence to eliminate the problem.

> *Faulty*   *Everybody* complained that the graduation ceremony had lasted too long, but I didn't believe *him.*
>
> *Revision*   *Everybody* complained that the graduation ceremony had lasted too long, but I didn't agree.

Two Singular Antecedents Two or more antecedents joined by *and* ordinarily call for a plural pronoun.

> *Correct*   Her briefcase and umbrella were missing from *their* usual place on the hall table.

When *each* or *every* precedes the antecedent, use a singular pronoun.

Correct   Every college and university must do *its* best to provide adequate student counselling.

Singular antecedents joined by *or, either—or,* or *neither—nor* call for singular pronouns.

Correct   Neither Carol nor Irene had paid *her* rent for the month.

Applying this rule can sometimes yield an awkward or foolish sentence. When this happens, rewrite the sentence to avoid the problem.

Faulty   Neither James nor Sally has finished *his or her* term project.

Revision   James and Sally have not finished *their* term projects.

Singular antecedents joined by *and* that refer to the same person, place, or thing use a singular pronoun.

Correct   My *cousin* and business *partner* is retiring to *his* condo in Florida next month.

Singular and Plural Antecedents   If one singular and one plural antecedent are joined by *or, either—or,* or *neither—nor,* the pronoun agrees with the closer one.

Correct   Either Terrence James or the Parkinsons will let us use *their* lawn mower.

Correct   Either the Parkinsons or Terrence James will let us use *his* lawn mower.

Sentences of this sort are generally smoother when the plural subject follows the singular.

Collective Nouns as Antecedents   When a collective noun is considered a single unit, the pronoun that refers to it should be singular.

Correct   The *troop* of scouts made *its* way slowly through the woods.

When the collective noun refers to the separate individuals in the group, use a plural pronoun.

Correct   The *staff* lost *their* jobs when the factory closed.

CONNECTED DISCOURSE EXERCISE   *Identify and correct the pronoun–antecedent agreement errors in the following letter:*

Dear Desperately Desperate:

We were sorry to hear about the theft from your apartment.
Apparently a gang of con artists recently had their base of operations in your city. It posed as repair technicians and presented false credentials to anyone expecting their phone to be repaired.
Someone also must have intercepted your mail and written their own

pa agr

response since we have no record of any previous letter from you. Clearly neither the representative you mentioned nor the phony phone technician could have held their position with our company. Every one of our technicians must provide us with their fingerprints and take periodic lie detector tests. Further, none of our representatives will answer correspondence since it is not a part of their job description. For these reasons, we do not believe we are responsible for your losses. However, a review of our records shows that you owe $500; we have included a copy of the bill in case you have misplaced the original.

Sincerely,

Accounts Manager

EXERCISE   *Choose the right pronoun from the pair in parentheses.*

1. If everybody does *(his or her, their)* part, the pageant should go smoothly.
2. Neither Greg nor the Snows had remembered to make *(his, their)* reservations at the ski lodge.
3. The graduating class filed by the principal and received *(its, their)* diplomas.
4. Each of the performers nervously waited *(his or her, their)* turn to audition.
5. Every boot and shoe I own needs to have *(its, their)* laces replaced.
6. Either Laurie or Alicia will show *(her, their)* slides at the party.
7. Dave and Bill loudly voiced *(his, their)* complaints about the restaurant's service.
8. Pleased with the performance, the audience showed *(its, their)* pleasure by applauding loudly.

■ Avoiding Faulty Pronoun Reference

Any pronoun except an indefinite pronoun should refer to just one noun or noun substitute—its antecedent. Reference problems result when the pronoun has two or more antecedents, a hidden antecedent, or no antecedent. These errors can cause mixups in meaning as well as ridiculous sentences.

More than One Antecedent   The following sentences lack clarity because their pronouns have two possible antecedents rather than just one:

Faulty   Take the screens off the windows and wash *them.*

Faulty   Harry told Will that *he* was putting on weight.

The reader can't tell whether the screens or the windows should be washed or who is putting on weight.

Sometimes we see a sentence like this one:

Faulty   If the boys don't eat all the Popsicles, put *them* in the freezer.

In this case, we know it's the Popsicles that should be stored, but the use of *them* creates an amusing sentence.

Correct these faults by replacing the pronoun with a noun or by rephrasing the sentence.

Revision   Wash the windows after you have taken off the screens.

Revision   Take off the screens so that you can wash the windows.

Revision   Harry told Will, "I am (you are) putting on weight."

Revision   Put any uneaten Popsicles in the freezer.

pr ref

Hidden Antecedent   An antecedent is hidden if it takes the form of an adjective rather than a noun.

Faulty   The movie theatre is closed today, so we can't see *one*.

Faulty   As I passed the tiger's cage, *it* lunged at me.

To correct this fault, replace the pronoun with the noun used as an adjective or switch the positions of the pronoun and the noun and make any needed changes in their forms.

Revision   The theatre is closed today, so we can't see a movie.

Revision   As I passed its cage, the tiger lunged at me.

No Antecedent   A no-antecedent sentence lacks any noun to which the pronoun can refer. Sentences of this sort occur frequently in everyday conversation but should be avoided in formal writing. The examples below illustrate this error:

Faulty   The lecture was boring, but *they* took notes anyway.

Faulty   On the news program, *it* told about another flood in Quebec.

To set matters right, substitute a suitable noun for the pronoun or reword the sentence.

Revision   The lecture was boring, but the students took notes anyway.

Revision   The news program told about another flood in Quebec.

Sometimes a *this, that, it,* or *which* will refer to a whole idea rather than a single noun. This usage is acceptable provided the writer's meaning is obvious, as in this example:

Correct   The instructor spoke very softly, *which* meant we had difficulty hearing him.

Problems occur, however, when the reader can't figure out which of two or more ideas the pronoun refers to.

Faulty   Ginny called Sally two hours after the agreed-upon time and postponed their shopping trip one day. *This* irritated Sally very much.

What caused Sally to be irritated—the late call, the postponement of the trip, or both? Again, rewording or adding a clarifying word will correct the problem.

Revision   Ginny called Sally two hours after the agreed-upon time and postponed their shopping trip one day. This *tardiness* irritated Sally very much.

Revision   Ginny called Sally two hours after the agreed-upon time and postponed their shopping trip one day. Ginny's *change of plans* irritated Sally very much.

The first of these examples illustrates the addition of a clarifying word; the second illustrates rewriting.

CONNECTED DISCOURSE EXERCISE *Identify and correct any faulty pronoun references in the following memorandum:*

TO: Director of Food Services, Groan University

FROM: Vice-President of Services

DATE: February 19, 2003

SUBJECT: Student

Complaints about Cafeteria Complaints about food quality and cafeteria hours are common but easily resolved. They can be extended by simply installing vending machines. It might not make for a nutritious meal, but it certainly will undercut some of the dissatisfaction. Of course, no matter how good the food, they will complain. Still, you can partially defuse those complaints by having students list their major concerns and then meeting them. Of course, you can always increase student satisfaction by purchasing a soft ice cream machine and offering it for dessert.

EXERCISE *Indicate whether each sentence is correct (C) or contains a faulty pronoun reference (F) and then correct any faulty sentences.*

1. Ann told Jennifer that the boss wanted to see her.
2. Because the ring hurt her finger, Ruth took it off.
3. At the farmer's market they sell many kinds of produce.
4. I like the food in Thai restaurants because it is very spicy.
5. They tell me that the company's profits have risen 5 percent this quarter.
6. Knowing that my friends like hot dogs, I grilled them at the picnic.
7. When Jeffrey rose to make his speech, they all started laughing.
8. In the paper, it told about the province's budget surplus.

■ Avoiding Unwarranted Shifts in Person

Pronouns can be in the first person, second person, or third person. *First-person* pronouns identify people who are talking or writing about themselves, *second-person* pronouns identify people being addressed directly, and *third-person* pronouns identify persons or things that are being written or spoken about. The following table sorts pronouns according to person:

First Person	Second Person	Third Person
I	you	he
me	your	she
my	yours	it
mine	yourself	his
we	yourselves	her
us		hers
our		its
ours		one
ourselves		they
		their
		theirs
		indefinite pronouns

shft

All nouns are in the third person. As you revise, be alert for unwarranted shifts from one person to another.

Faulty	I liked *my* British vacation better than *my* vacation in France and Italy because *you* didn't have language problems.
Revision	I liked *my* British vacation better than *my* vacation in France and Italy because *I* didn't have language problems.
Faulty	Holidays are important to *everyone*. They boost *your* spirits and provide a break from *our* daily routine.
Revision	Holidays are important to *everyone*. They boost *one's* spirits and provide a break from *one's* daily routine.
Faulty	The taller the *golfer*, the more club speed *you* will have with a normally paced swing.
Revision	The taller the *golfer*, the more club speed *he* or *she* will have with a normally paced swing.

As these examples show, the shift can occur within a single sentence or when the writer moves from one sentence to another.

Some shifts in person, however, are warranted. Read the following correct sentence:

Correct	*I* want *you* to deliver these flowers to Ms. Willoughby by three o'clock. *She* needs them for a party.

Here the speaker identifies himself or herself (*I*) while speaking directly to a listener (*you*) about someone else (*she*). In this case, shifts are needed to get the message across.

case

CONNECTED DISCOURSE EXERCISE   *Identify and correct the unwarranted shifts in person in the following paragraph:*

> Good health is clearly important to you. But it is one's responsibility to ensure our own good health. You can start with simple exercises. We would like to provide you with a low-impact aerobics videotape for only $9. We guarantee that the more out of shape the customer, the quicker you will notice the benefits. The way our bodies feel affects the quality of one's lives. Let our tape help you to a better life.

EXERCISE   *Indicate whether the sentence is correct (C) or contains an unwarranted shift in person (S). Correct faulty sentences.*

1. Because many of our tour guides spoke very poor English, the tourists soon became quite frustrated.
2. We like the location of our new house very much; you are close to a couple of large shopping centres.
3. If you want me to invite Gary to the party, I'll call him right now.
4. Be sure you tell the bakery clerk that we will need the cake by tomorrow noon.
5. If you complete a degree in vocational education, anyone can expect a rewarding career.
6. Once we learn to ride a bicycle, a person never forgets how.
7. Anyone wishing to make the trip to Kelowna should make your own hotel reservations.
8. After we had finished the test, the instructor told the students she would return it on Thursday.

■ Using the Right Pronoun Case

Case means the changes in form that a personal pronoun (see page 556) undergoes to show its function in a sentence. English has three cases: the *subjective,* the *nonsubjective* (objective), and the *possessive.* The following chart shows the different forms:

Subjective Form	Nonsubjective Form	Possessive Form
I	me	my, mine
he	him	his
she	her	her, hers
we	us	our, ours
you	you	your, yours
they	them	their, theirs
who	whom	whose

The subjective case is used for subjects and subject complements, the nonsubjective for direct objects, indirect objects, and objects of prepositions. The possessive case shows ownership and is also used with gerunds.

The following pointers will help you select the proper pronoun as you revise.

We and Us Preceding Nouns

Nouns that serve as subjects take the pronoun *we*. Other nouns take the pronoun *us*.

Correct	*We* tourists will fly home tomorrow. (*We* accompanies the subject.)
Correct	The guide showed *us* tourists through the cathedral. (*Us* accompanies a nonsubject.)

If you can't decide which pronoun is right, mentally omit the noun and read the sentence to yourself, first with one pronoun and then with the other. Your ear will indicate the correct form.

My mother made *(we, us)* children vanilla pudding for dessert.

Omitting *children* shows immediately that *us* is the right choice.

Correct	My mother made *us* children vanilla pudding for dessert.

Pronouns Paired with Nouns

When such a combination serves as the subject of a sentence or accompanies the subject, use the subject form of the pronoun. When the combination plays a nonsubject role, use the nonsubject form of the pronoun.

Correct	Arlene and *I* plan to join the Peace Corps. (*I* is part of the compound subject.)
Correct	Two people, Mary and *I*, will represent our school at the meeting. (*I* is part of a compound element accompanying the subject.)
Correct	The superintendent told Kevin and *him* that they would be promoted soon. (*Him* is part of a compound nonsubject.)
Correct	The project was difficult for Jeffrey and *him* to complete. (*Him* is part of a compound nonsubject.)

Again, mentally omitting the noun from the combination will tell you which pronoun is correct.

Who and Whom in Dependent Clauses

Use *who* for the subjects of dependent clauses; otherwise use *whom*.

Correct	The Mallarys prefer friends *who are interested in the theatre.* (*Who* is the subject of the clause.)
Correct	Barton is a man *whom very few people like.* (*Whom* is not the subject of the clause.)

A simple test will help you decide between *who* and *whom*. First, mentally isolate the dependent clause. Next, block out the pronoun in question and then insert *he* (or *she*) and *him* (or *her*) at the appropriate spot in the remaining part of the clause. If *he* (or *she*) sounds better, *who* is right. If *him* (or *her*) sounds better, *whom* is right. Let's use this test on the sentence below:

> The woman *who(m) Scott is dating* works as a mechanical engineer. Scott is dating (*she, her.*)

Clearly *her* is correct; therefore, *whom* is the proper form.

> *Correct*   The woman *whom Scott is dating* works as a mechanical engineer.

case

Pronouns as Subject Complements   In formal writing, pronouns that serve as subject complements (see pages 552–553) always take the subject form.

> *Correct*   It is *I.*

> *Correct*   It was *she* who bought the old Parker mansion.

This rule, however, is often ignored in informal writing.

> It's *her.*

> That's *him* standing over by the door.

Comparisons Using *than* or *as . . . as*   Comparisons of this kind often make no direct statement about the second item of comparison. When the second naming word is a pronoun, you may have trouble choosing the right one.

> Harriet is less outgoing than *(they, them).*

> My parents' divorce saddened my sister as much as *(I, me).*

Not to worry. Expand the sentence by mentally supplying the missing material. Then try the sentence with each pronoun and see which sounds right.

> Harriet is less outgoing than *(they, them)* are.

> My parents' divorce saddened my sister as much as it did *(I, me).*

Obviously *they* is the right choice for the first sentence, and *me* is the right choice for the second one.

> *Correct*   Harriet is less outgoing than *they* are.

> *Correct*   My parents' divorce saddened my sister as much as it did *me.*

Pronouns Preceding Gerunds   Use the possessive form of a pronoun that precedes a gerund (see page 576).

> I dislike *their* leaving without saying goodbye.

> Ted can't understand *her* quitting such a good job.

This usage emphasizes the action named by the gerund instead of the person or persons performing it. Thus, in the above sentences, the possessive form of the pronoun signals that it's the *leaving* the writer dislikes and the *quitting* that Ted can't understand. The persons involved are secondary.

When the pronoun precedes a participle (see page 575), it should be in the nonsubject case. The emphasis is then on the actor rather than the action.

Jennifer caught *them* listening to records instead of studying.

In this example, Jennifer caught the listeners, not the listening.

If you have trouble deciding between the nonsubject and possessive forms of a pronoun, ask yourself whether you want to emphasize the action or the actor; then proceed accordingly.

case

CONNECTED DISCOURSE EXERCISE   *Identify and correct the pronoun case errors in the following paragraph:*

Between my brother and I, we are always able to pull at least five good-sized trout a day from the creek behind our house. Us rural trout fishermen just seem to have the knack. Of course, those city fishermen whom insist on employing artificial flies won't appreciate our methods even if they can't do as well as us. We just let our bait, usually a juicy worm, float downstream to the waiting trout. Of course, my brother won't let the fishing interfere with him sleeping. In fact, it was him that developed the idea of looping the line around his toe so that he would wake up when a trout took the bait. Others have told my brother and I that this method is dangerous, but neither of us has lost a toe yet. Of course, the people who we invite to dinner don't complain about our methods, and they seem to enjoy the fish.

EXERCISE   *Choose the right form of the pronoun for each of the following sentences:*

1. Cherie is the one student *(who, whom)* I believe has the potential to become a professional acrobat.
2. Two students, Carrie and *(I, me)*, scored 100 on the calculus test.
3. *(We, Us)* Greens pride ourselves on our beautiful lawns.
4. Ken Conwell is the only candidate *(who, whom)* I like in this election.
5. Brookfield has richer friends and a more luxurious lifestyle than *(I, me)*.
6. The friendly student told *(we, us)* visitors that we were in the wrong building.
7. As youngsters, Bill and *(I, me)* used to play tag.
8. My uncle has given Sandra and *(I, me)* tickets for tonight's Bach concert.

■ Avoiding Inconsistency in Showing Time

Inconsistencies occur when a writer shifts from the past tense to the present or vice versa without a corresponding shift in the time of the events being described. The following paragraph contains an uncalled-for shift from the present tense to the past:

time

> As *The Most Dangerous Game* opens, Sanger Rainsford, a famous hunter and author, and his old friend Whitney are standing on the deck of a yacht and discussing a mysterious island as the ship passes near it. Then, after everyone else has gone to bed, Rainsford manages to fall overboard. He swims to the island and ends up at a chateau owned by General Zaroff, a refugee from the Communist takeover in Russia. Zaroff, bored with hunting animals, has turned to hunting humans on his desert island. Inevitably, Rainsford is turned out into the jungle to be hunted down. There were [shift to past tense] actually four hunts over a three-day period, and at the end of the last one, Rainsford jumped into the sea, swam across a cove to the chateau, and killed Zaroff in the general's own bedroom. Afterward he sleeps [shift back to present tense] and decides "he had never slept in a better bed."

The sentence with the unwarranted shift in tense should read as follows:

> There are actually four hunts over a three-day period, and at the end of the last one, Rainsford jumps into the sea, swims across a cove to the chateau, and kills Zaroff in the general's own bedroom.

The time shift in the quotation part of the final sentence is justified because the sleeping has occurred before Rainsford's thoughts about it.

A second kind of inconsistency results when a writer fails to distinguish the immediate past from the less immediate past. The following sentence illustrates this error:

> *Faulty*   Mary *answered* all thirty test questions when the class ended.

This sentence indicates that Mary completed all thirty test questions during the final instant of the class, an impossibility. When you detect this type of error in your writing, determine which action occurred first and then correct the error by adding *had* to the verb. In this case, the first verb needs correcting:

> *Revision*   Mary *had answered* all thirty test questions when the class ended.

Besides adding *had*, you may sometimes need to alter the verb form.

> *Faulty*   Before he turned twenty, John *wrote* two novels.

> *Revision*   Before he turned twenty, John *had written* two novels.

CONNECTED DISCOURSE EXERCISE *Identify and correct any inconsistencies in showing time in the following passage:*

There is no better time to go swimming than at night. The summer after I had graduated from high school, I worked for a landscaping company. After a sweaty day mowing lawns and digging up gardens, all of us who worked there would jump into the back of Dick's old pickup and rattle out to Woods Lake. It is just dark as we arrive. The moon is beautiful, reflected in that black mirror set in a frame of hills. We stumble down a small, sandy hill to the beach, where we strip off our dusty jeans and sweaty shirts before plunging into the cool reflection of stars.

mis adj/adv

EXERCISE *Indicate whether each sentence is correct (C) or contains an unwarranted shift (S) in tense. Then correct the faulty sentences.*

1. Although the alarm rang, Bob continues to lie in bed.
2. When autumn arrives, we often go for long walks in the woods.
3. John is writing his dissertation but found the job tough going.
4. When the trapeze artist fell into the net, the audience gasps loudly.
5. When I baked the cake, I ate a slice.
6. Edward walks for half an hour before he ate dinner.
7. Sarah had many friends but sees them infrequently.
8. As Elaine walked toward the garden, a rabbit scampers quickly away.

■ Avoiding Misuse of Adjectives and Adverbs

Beginning writers often use adjectives when they should use adverbs and also confuse the comparative and superlative forms of these parts of speech when making comparisons.

Misusing Adjectives for Adverbs Although most adjectives can be misused as adverbs, the following seven, listed with the corresponding adverbs, cause the most difficulty.

Adjectives	**Adverbs**
awful	awfully
bad	badly
considerable	considerably
good	well
most	almost
real	really
sure	surely

The following sentences show typical errors:

Faulty   Bryan did *good* in his first golf lesson. (*good* mistakenly used to modify verb *did*)

Faulty   *Most* every graduate from our auto service program receives several job offers. (*Most* mistakenly used to modify adjective *every*)

Faulty   The speech was delivered *real* well. (*real* mistakenly used to modify adverb *well*)

Because adverbs modify verbs, adjectives, and other adverbs (see pages 569–571), and adjectives modify nouns and noun substitutes (see pages 567–569), the above sentences clearly require adverbs.

Revision   Bryan did *well* in his first golf lesson.

Revision   *Almost* every graduate from our auto service program receives several job offers.

Revision   The speech was delivered *really* well.

If you can't decide whether a sentence requires an adjective or an adverb, determine the part of speech of the word being modified and proceed accordingly.

Confusing the Comparative and Superlative Forms in Comparisons   The comparative form of adjectives and adverbs is used to compare two things, the superlative form to compare three or more things. Adjectives with fewer than three syllables generally add *-er* to make the comparative form and *-est* to make the superlative form (tall, tall*er*, tall*est*). Adjectives with three or more syllables generally add *more* to make the comparative and *most* to make the superlative (enchanting, *more* enchanting, *most* enchanting), as do most adverbs of two or more syllables (loudly, *more* loudly, *most* loudly).

When making comparisons, beginning writers sometimes mistakenly use double comparatives or double superlatives.

Faulty   Harry is *more taller* than James. (double comparative)

Faulty   The Hotel Vancouver has the *most splendidest* lobby I've ever seen. (double superlative)

The correct versions read as follows:

Revision   Harry is *taller* than James.

Revision   The Hotel Vancouver has the *most splendid* lobby I've ever seen.

In addition, writers may erroneously use the superlative form, rather than the comparative form, to compare two things.

Faulty   Barry is the *richest* of the two brothers.

Faulty   Jeremy is the *most talented* of those two singers.

Here are the sentences correctly written:

Revision   Barry is the *richer* of the two brothers.

Revision   Jeremy is the *more talented* of those two singers.

Reserve the superlative form for comparing three or more items.

Correct   Barry is the *richest* of the three brothers.

Correct   Jeremy is the *most talented* of those four singers.

*mis
adj/adv*

CONNECTED DISCOURSE EXERCISE   *Identify and correct the adjective–adverb errors
in the following paragraph:*

This year our football team is outstanding. Spike Jones, our quar-
terback, has been playing real good this past season. Stan Blunder,
the most talented of our two ends, hasn't dropped a pass all season. The team can most always count on Stan to catch the crucial
first-down pass. Of course, the team wouldn't be where it is today
without John Schoolyard's good coaching. He has made this team much
more better than it was a year ago. Only the kicking team has done
bad this season. Of course, with this most wonderfulest offence,
the defensive players haven't gotten much practice. The good news
is, then, that we can sure expect to watch some terrific university
football for years to come.

EXERCISE   *For each of the following sentences, choose the proper word from the pair in
parentheses:*

1. A person can become *(stronger, more stronger)* by lifting weights.
2. Canvasback Dunn is clearly the *(less, least)* formidable of the two main chal-
lengers for Killer McGurk's boxing crown.
3. Diane did *(good, well)* on her chemistry test.
4. *(Most, Almost)* all our salaried employees have degrees in business administration
or engineering.
5. Carol wore the *(silliest, most silliest)* hat I've ever seen to the masquerade party.
6. Don was hurt *(bad, badly)* in the auto accident.
7. Brad was the *(funniest, most funniest)* of all the performers at the comedy club.
8. Clear Lake is the *(deeper, deepest)* of the three lakes in our county.

■ Avoiding Misplaced Modifiers

A misplaced modifier is a word or word group that is improperly separated from the word it modifies. When separation of this type occurs, the sentence often sounds awkward, ridiculous, or confusing.

Usually, you can correct this error by moving the modifier next to the word it is intended to modify. Occasionally, you'll also need to alter some of the phrasing.

Faulty	There is a bicycle in the basement *with chrome fenders.* (The basement appears to have chrome fenders.)
Faulty	David received a phone call from his uncle *that infuriated him.* (The uncle appears to have infuriated David.)
Revision	There is a bicycle *with chrome fenders* in the basement.
Revision	David received an *infuriating* phone call from his uncle. (Note the change in wording.)

In shifting the modifier, don't inadvertently create another faulty sentence.

Faulty	Fritz bought a magazine with an article about Michael Jackson *at the corner newsstand.* (The article appears to tell about Jackson's visit to the corner newsstand.)
Faulty	Fritz bought a magazine *at the corner newsstand* with an article about Michael Jackson. (The corner newsstand appears to have an article about Jackson.)
Revision	*At the corner newsstand,* Fritz bought a magazine with an article about Michael Jackson.

As you revise, watch also for *squinting modifiers*—that is, modifiers positioned so that the reader doesn't know whether they are supposed to modify what comes ahead of them or what follows them.

Faulty	The man who was rowing the boat *frantically* waved toward the onlookers on the beach.

Is the man rowing frantically or waving frantically? Correct this kind of error by repositioning the modifier so that the ambiguity disappears.

Revision	The man who was *frantically* rowing the boat waved toward the onlookers on the beach.
Revision	The man who was rowing the boat waved *frantically* toward the onlookers on the beach.

EXERCISE   *Indicate whether each sentence is correct (C) or contains a misplaced modifier (MM). Correct faulty sentences.*

1. The boss asked me after lunch to type a special report.
2. Brenda returned the cottage cheese to the store that had spoiled.
3. The hikers tramped through the woods wearing heavy boots.
4. The movie was heavily advertised by the studio before sneak previews were shown.
5. Mark mailed a package to his friend sealed with masking tape.
6. The woman packing her suitcase hastily glanced out the window at the commotion in the yard.
7. We bought a dictionary that was bound in leather at the local bookstore.
8. Jerry bought an Inuit carving for his bedroom in Regina.

■ Avoiding Dangling Modifiers

A dangling modifier is a phrase or clause that lacks clear connection to the word or words it is intended to modify. As a result, sentences are inaccurate, often comical. Typically, the modifier leads off the sentence, although it can also come at the end.

Sometimes the error occurs because the sentence fails to specify who or what is modified. At other times, the separation is too great between the modifier and what it modifies.

Faulty	*Walking in the meadow,* wildflowers surrounded us. (The wildflowers appear to be walking in the meadow.)
Faulty	Dinner was served *after saying grace.* (The dinner appears to have said grace.)
Faulty	*Fatigued by the violent exercise,* the cool shower was very relaxing. (The cool shower appears to have been fatigued.)

The first of these sentences is faulty because the modifier is positioned too far away from *us.* The other two are faulty because they do not identify who said grace or found the shower relaxing.

You can correct dangling modifiers in two basic ways. First, leave the modifier unchanged and rewrite the main part of the sentence so that it begins with the term actually modified. Second, rewrite the modifier so that it has its own subject and verb, thereby eliminating the inaccuracy.

Revision	*Walking in the meadow,* we were surrounded by wildflowers. (The main part of the sentence has been rewritten.)
Revision	*As we walked in the meadow,* wildflowers surrounded us. (The modifier has been rewritten.)
Revision	Dinner was served *after we had said grace.* (The modifier has been rewritten.)

//

Revision	*Fatigued by the violent exercise,* Ted found the cool shower very relaxing. (The main part of the sentence has been rewritten.)
Revision	*Because Ted was fatigued by the violent exercise,* the cool shower was very relaxing. (The modifier has been rewritten.)

Ordinarily, either part of the sentence can be rewritten, but sometimes only one part can.

EXERCISE *Indicate whether each sentence is correct (C) or contains a dangling modifier (DM). Correct faulty sentences.*

1. Dancing at the wedding reception, my feet hurt.
2. Working in the yard, Pete was drenched by the sudden cloudburst.
3. Looking out the window, a velvety lawn ran down to the river's edge.
4. Having mangy fur, our parents wouldn't let us keep the stray cat.
5. Because of memorizing all the definitions, Pam scored 100 on the vocabulary test.
6. Reminiscing about my school days, a run-in with my principal came to mind.
7. Unaware of what had happened, the confusion puzzled Nan.
8. At the age of eight, my father wrote a best-selling novel.

■ Avoiding Nonparallelism

Nonparallelism results when equivalent ideas follow different grammatical forms. One common kind of nonparallelism occurs with words or word groups in pairs or in a series.

Faulty	Althea enjoys *jogging, to bike,* and *to swim.*
Faulty	The superintendent praised the workers *for their productivity* and *because they had an excellent safety record.*
Faulty	The banner was *old, faded,* and *it had a rip.*

Note how rewriting the sentences in parallel form improves their smoothness.

Revision	Althea enjoys *jogging, biking,* and *swimming.*
Revision	The superintendent praised the workers for *their productivity* and *their excellent safety record.*
Revision	The banner was *old, faded,* and *ripped.*

Nonparallelism also occurs when correlative conjunctions (*either—or, neither—nor, both—and,* and *not only—but also*) are followed by unlike elements.

Faulty	That sound *either* <u>was a thunderclap</u> *or* <u>an explosion.</u>
Faulty	The basement was *not only* <u>poorly lighted</u> *but also* <u>it had a foul smell.</u>

Ordinarily, repositioning one of the correlative conjunctions will solve the problem. Sometimes, however, one of the grammatical elements must be rewritten.

Revision   That sound was *either* <u>a thunderclap</u> *or* <u>an explosion.</u> (*Either* has been repositioned.)

Revision   The basement was *not only* <u>poorly lighted</u> *but also* <u>foul smelling.</u> (The element following *but also* has been rewritten.)

comp

EXERCISE   *Indicate whether each sentence is correct (C) or nonparallel (NP). Correct faulty sentences.*

1. The lemonade was cold, tangy, and refreshing.
2. Although he had practised for several days, the scout could neither tie a square knot nor a bowline.
3. This job will involve waiting on customers, and you will need to maintain our inventory.
4. My summer job at a provincial park gave me experience in repairing buildings, the operation of heavy equipment, and assisting park visitors.
5. To maintain his rose bushes properly, Sam fertilizes, sprays, prunes, and waters them according to a strict schedule.
6. Once out of high school, Barry plans either to join the navy or the air force.
7. My favourite sports are swimming, golfing, and to bowl.
8. Janice's leisure activities include collecting coins, reading, and she also watches TV.

■ Avoiding Faulty Comparisons

A faulty comparison results if you (1) mention one of the items being compared but not the other, (2) omit words needed to clarify the relationship, or (3) compare different sorts of items. Advertisers often offend in the first way.

Faulty   Irish tape has better adhesion.

With what other tape is Irish tape being compared? Scotch tape? All other transparent tape? Mentioning the second term of a comparison eliminates reader guesswork.

Revision   Irish tape has better adhesion than any other transparent tape.

Two clarifying words, *other* and *else,* are frequently omitted from comparisons, creating illogical sentences.

Faulty   Sergeant McNabb is more conscientious than any officer in his precinct.

Faulty   Stretch French is taller than anyone on his basketball team.

The first sentence is illogical because McNabb is one of the officers in his precinct and therefore cannot be more conscientious than any officer in the precinct.

Similarly, because French is a member of his basketball team, he can't be taller than anyone on his team. Adding *other* to the first sentence and *else* to the second corrects matters.

> *Revision*   Sergeant McNabb has made more arrests than any *other* officer in his precinct.

> *Revision*   Stretch French is taller than anyone *else* on his basketball team.

Comparing unlike items is perhaps the most common kind of comparison error. Here are two examples:

> *Faulty*   The cities in Ontario are larger than Nova Scotia.

> *Faulty*   The cover of this book is much more durable than the other book.

The first sentence compares the cities of Ontario with a province, while the second compares the cover of a book with a whole book. Correction consists of rewriting each sentence so that it compares like items.

> *Revision*   The cities in Ontario are larger than *those in* Nova Scotia.

> *Revision*   The cover of this book is much more durable than *that of* the other book.

CONNECTED DISCOURSE EXERCISE   *Identify and correct the misplaced modifiers, dangling modifiers, nonparallelism, and faulty comparisons in the following memorandum:*

TO: All Residency Hall Advisors in Knuckles Hall

FROM: John Knells, Residency Hall Director

DATE: March 13, 2003

SUBJECT: Noise in Residence Hall

Recently I received a report from a student that deeply disturbed me. Apparently, after quiet hours students still have visitors in their rooms, are playing their stereos loudly, and are even staging boxing matches in the halls. The student who wrote me desperately tries to study. However, he is often forced to leave his room disturbed by the noise. He was not the only one to complain. You should know that we have had more complaints about Knuckles Hall than any residence on campus. Since discussing this problem with you at the last staff meeting, things haven't seemed to get any better. The rules are not only poorly enforced but also they

are completely ignored. Your job performance is worse than the
students. If you don't improve immediately, I will be forced to
dismiss you.

EXERCISE   *Indicate whether each sentence is correct (C) or contains a faulty comparison (FC). Correct any faulty comparison.*

1. The houses on Parkdale Street are more modest than Windsor Terrace.
2. Maxine has more seniority than any other member of her department.
3. The finish on the dresser is not as smooth as the end table.
4. In contrast to your yard, I have an underground sprinkling system.
5. My mother's homemade jam has more flavour than any jam I've eaten.
6. The dresses sold at The Bay are much less expensive than the Tres Chic Shoppe.
7. Frontline reports show that during June our side lost fewer tanks.

comp

Editing to Correct Faulty Punctuation and Mechanics

Punctuation marks indicate relationships among different sentence elements. As a result, these marks help clarify the meaning of written material. Similarly, a knowledge of mechanics—capitalization, abbreviations, numbers, and italics—helps you avoid distracting inconsistencies.

This part of the Handbook covers the fundamentals of punctuation and mechanics. Review it carefully when you edit your final draft.

■ Apostrophes

Apostrophes (') show possession, mark contractions, and indicate plurals that are singled out for special attention.

Possession Possessive apostrophes usually show ownership *(Mary's cat)*. Sometimes, though, they identify the works of creative people *(Hemingway's novels)* or indicate an extent of time or distance *(one hour's time, one mile's distance)*.

Possessive apostrophes are used with nouns and with pronouns like *someone, no one, everybody, each other,* and *one another.* The possessive form is easily recognized because it can be converted to a prepositional phrase beginning with *of.*

The collar of the dog

The whistle of the wind

The intention of the corporation

The birthday of Scott

To show possession with pronouns like those above, singular nouns, and plural nouns that do not end in an *s*, add an apostrophe followed by an *s*.

Someone's car is blocking our driveway. (possessive of pronoun *someone*)

The *manager's* reorganization plan will take effect next week. (possessive of singular noun *manager*)

The *women's* lounge is being redecorated. (possessive of plural noun *women*)

With singular nouns that end in *s*, the possessive is sometimes formed by merely adding an apostrophe at the end *(James' helmet)*. The preferred usage, however, is *'s (James's helmet)* unless the addition of the *s* would make it awkward to pronounce the word.

Moses's followers entered the Promised Land. (awkward pronunciation of *Moses's*)

Moses' followers entered the Promised Land. (nonawkward pronunciation of *Moses'*)

Plural nouns ending in *s* form the possessive by adding only an apostrophe at the end.

All the *ladies'* coats are on sale today. (possessive of plural noun *ladies*)

The *workers'* lockers were moved. (possessive of plural noun *workers*)

To show joint ownership by two or more persons, use the possessive form for the last-named person only. To show individual ownership, use the possessive form for each person's name.

Ronald and *Joan's* boat badly needed overhauling. (joint ownership)

Laura's and *Alice's* term projects are almost completed. (individual ownership)

Hyphenated nouns form the possessive by adding *'s* to the last word.

My *mother-in-law's* house is next to mine.

Never use an apostrophe with the possessive pronouns *his, hers, whose, its, ours, yours, theirs.*

This desk is *his;* the other one is *hers.* (no apostrophes needed)

Contractions Contractions of words or numbers omit one or more letters or numerals. An apostrophe shows exactly where the omission occurs.

Wasn't that a disappointing concert? (contraction of *was not*)

Around here, people still talk about the blizzard of *'79.* (contraction of *1979*)

Don't confuse the contraction *it's,* meaning *it is* or *it has,* with the possessive pronoun *its,* which should never have an apostrophe. If you're puzzled by an *its* that you've written, try this test. Expand the *its* to *it is* or *it has* and see whether the sentence still makes sense. If it does, the *its* is a contraction and needs the apostrophe. If the result is nonsense, the *its* is a possessive pronoun and does not get an apostrophe. Here are some examples:

> *Its* awfully muggy today.

> *Its* been an exciting trip.

> Every dog has *its* day.

The first example makes sense when the *its* is expanded to *it is.*

> *It is* awfully muggy today.

The second makes sense when the *its* is expanded to *it has.*

> *It has* been an exciting trip.

Both of these sentences therefore require apostrophes.

> *It's* awfully muggy today.

> *It's* been an exciting trip.

The last sentence, however, turns into nonsense when the *its* is expanded.

> Every dog has *it is* day.

> Every dog has *it has* day.

In this case, the *its* is a possessive pronoun and requires no apostrophe.

> Every dog has *its* day.

Plurals   To improve clarity, the plurals of letters, numbers, symbols, and words being singled out for special attention are written with apostrophes.

> Mind your *p*'s and *q*'s. (plurals of letters)

> Your *5*'s and *6*'s are hard to tell apart. (plurals of numbers)

> The formula was sprinkled with *¶*'s and *β*'s. (plurals of symbols)

> Don't use so many *however*'s and *therefore*'s in your writing. (plurals of words)

Apostrophes are sometimes used to form the plurals of abbreviations.

> How many *CD*'s (or *CDs*) do you own? (plurals of abbreviation for *compact discs*)

When no danger of confusion exists, an *s* alone will suffice.

> During the late *1960s,* many university students demanded changes in academic life.

CONNECTED DISCOURSE EXERCISE   *Supply, delete, or relocate apostrophes as necessary in the following memorandum:*

TO: The Records Office Staff
FROM: The Assistant Registrar
DATE: January 27, 2003
SUBJECT: Faulty Student Transcripts

Recently, we have had too many student complaints' about handwritten transcripts. Apparently its hard to tell the Bs and Ds apart. One staff members' handwriting is totally illegible. This staffs carelessness is unacceptable. Someones even gone so far as to write grade change's in pencil, which allows students to make changes. This cant continue. In a short time, John and Marys student assistants will be typing the past transcripts into our new computer system. Once grades are entered, the computers ability to generate grade reports will solve this problem. Until that time, lets make an effort to produce clear and professional-looking transcripts.

EXERCISE   *Supply apostrophes where necessary to correct the following sentences:*

1. The bosss speech reviewed the companys safety record.
2. Lets find out whats wrong with Melanys bicycle.
3. Daves and Marvins fiancées are identical twins.
4. Its highly unlikely that this movie will ever earn back its production costs when its released.
5. Sues test score was higher than all her friends test scores.
6. There are two *ls* and two *es* in the name Colleen.
7. When everyones ready, well start the slide show.
8. Alice overloads her sentences with *consequentlys* and *accordinglys*.

■ Commas

Since commas (,) occur more frequently than any other mark of punctuation, it's vital that you learn to use them correctly. When you do, your sentence structure is clearer, and your reader grasps your meaning without having to reread.

Commas separate or set off independent clauses, items in a series, coordinate adjectives, introductory elements, places and dates, nonrestrictive expressions, and parenthetical expressions.

Independent Clauses   When you link two independent clauses with a coordinating conjunction (*and, but, or, nor, for, yet,* or *so*), put a comma in front of the conjunction.

> Arthur is majoring in engineering, *but* he has decided to work for a clothing store following graduation.

> The water looked inviting, *so* Darlene decided to go for a swim.

Don't confuse a sentence that has a compound predicate (see page 551–552) with a sentence that consists of two independent clauses.

> Tom watered the garden and mowed the lawn. (single sentence with compound predicate)

> Tom watered the garden, *and* Betty mowed the lawn. (sentence with two independent clauses)

Here's a simple test. Read what follows the comma. Unless that part can stand alone as a sentence, don't use a comma.

Items in a Series   A series consists of three or more words, phrases, or clauses following on one another's heels. Whenever you write a series, separate its items with commas.

> *Sarah, Paul,* and *Mary* are earning *A*'s in advanced algebra. (words in a series)

> Nancy strode *across the parking lot, through the revolving door,* and *into the elevator.* (phrases in a series)

> The stockholders' report said *that the company had enjoyed record profits during the last year, that it had expanded its work force by 20 percent,* and *that it would soon start marketing several new products.* (clauses in a series)

Coordinate Adjectives   Use commas to separate coordinate adjectives—those that modify the same noun or noun substitute and can be reversed without altering the meaning of the sentence.

> Andrea proved to be an *efficient, cooperative* employee.

> Andrea proved to be a *cooperative, efficient* employee.

When reversing the word order wrecks the meaning of the sentence, the adjectives are not coordinate and should be written without a comma.

> Many new brands of videocassette recorders have come on the market lately.

Reversing the adjectives *many* and *new* would turn this sentence into nonsense. Therefore, no comma should be used.

Introductory Elements   Use commas to separate introductory elements—words, phrases, and clauses—from the rest of the sentence. When an introductory element is short and the sentence will not be misread, you can omit the comma.

Correct   After bathing, Jack felt refreshed.

Correct   Soon I will be changing jobs.

Correct   Soon, I will be changing jobs.

Correct   When Sarah smiles her ears wiggle.

Correct   When Sarah smiles, her ears wiggle.

The first example needs a comma; otherwise, the reader might become temporarily confused.

After bathing Jack . . .

Always use commas after introductory elements of six or more words.

Correct   Whenever I hear the opening measure of Beethoven's *Fifth Symphony,* I get goose bumps.

Places and Dates   Places include mailing addresses and geographical locations. The following sentences show where commas are used:

Sherry Delaney lives at 651 Daniel Street, Westmount, Quebec H4Z 6W5.

I will go to Calais, France, next week.

Chicoutimi, Quebec, is my birthplace.

Note that commas appear after the street designation and the names of cities, countries, and provinces, except when the name of the province is followed by a postal code.

Dates are punctuated as shown in the following example:

On Sunday, June 9, 1991, Elaine received a degree in environmental science.

Here, commas follow the day of the week, the day of the month, and the year. With dates that include only the month and the year, commas are optional.

Correct   In July 1989 James played chess for the first time.

Correct   In July, 1989, James played chess for the first time.

Nonrestrictive Expressions   A nonrestrictive expression supplies added information about whatever it modifies. This information, however, is *nonessential* and does not affect the basic meaning of the sentence. The two sentences below include nonrestrictive expressions:

Premier Clark, *the leader of the British Columbia New Democratic Party,* faces a tough campaign for re-election.

My dog, *frightened by the thunder,* hid under my bed while the storm raged.

If we delete the phrase *the leader of the British Columbia New Democratic Party* from the first sentence, we still know that Premier Clark faces a tough re-election battle.

Likewise, if we delete *frightened by the thunder* from the second sentence, we still know that the dog hid during the storm.

Restrictive expressions, which are written *without commas,* distinguish whatever they modify from other persons, places, or things in the same category. Unlike nonrestrictive expressions, they are almost always *essential* sentence elements. Omitting a restrictive expression alters the meaning of the sentence, and the result is often nonsense.

Any person *caught stealing from this store* will be prosecuted.

Dropping the italicized part of this sentence leaves us with the absurd statement that any person, not just those caught stealing, faces prosecution.

Parenthetical Expressions   A parenthetical expression is a word or a word group that links one sentence to another or adds information or emphasis to the sentence in which it appears. Parenthetical expressions include the following:

Clarifying phrases
Names and titles of people being addressed directly
Abbreviations of degree titles
Echo questions
"Not" phrases
Adjectives that come after, rather than before, the words they modify

The examples that follow show the uses of commas:

All of Joe's spare time seems to centre around reading. Kevin, *on the other hand,* enjoys a variety of activities. (phrase linking two sentences together)

Myra Hobbes, *our representative in Calgary,* is being transferred to Kamloops next month. (clarifying phrase)

I think, *Jill,* that you'd make a wonderful teacher. (name of person addressed directly)

Tell me, *Captain,* when the cruise ship is scheduled to sail. (title of person addressed directly)

Harley Kendall, *Ph.D.,* will be this year's commencement speaker. (degree title following name)

Alvin realizes, *doesn't he,* that he stands almost no chance of being accepted at McGill? (echo question)

Mathematics, *not home economics,* was Tammy's favourite high school subject. ("not" phrase)

The road, *muddy and rutted,* proved impassable. (adjectives following word they modify)

CONNECTED DISCOURSE EXERCISE   *Add or delete commas as necessary in the following letter:*

Dear Loy Norrix Knight:

While we know you will be busy this summer we hope you will take time to join us for the twenty-five-year reunion of the graduating class of 1973. The reunion will include a cocktail hour a buffet dinner and a dance. For your entertainment we are going to bring in a professional band and a band starring some of your good, old high school chums. John Mcleary who is now a well-known professional nightclub performer will serve as the emcee. Do you remember him hosting our senior-year assemblies?

Yes many of your former, hardworking teachers will be at the reunion. You can thank them for the difference they made in your life or you can tell them what you've thought of them all these years. This reunion will also be your opportunity to catch up on the lives of your former friends find out what that old flame now looks like and brag a little about your own successes. And if you are really lucky you might even be able to sneak a dance with your high school prom partner.

We hope you will make plans, to join us here at the Penticton Hilton on July 28, 2003 at 7 P.M. Wear your best 1970s-style clothes. Remember revisiting the past, can be fun.

                                Sincerely,
                                The Reunion Committee

EXERCISE   *Supply commas as necessary to correct the following sentences:*

1. Before leaving Jim stopped to say goodbye to Lisa.
2. Although our prices continue to go up people will probably keep buying our video games.
3. This store's burglar alarm system which is very outdated should be replaced immediately.
4. Stepping into the cool pleasant bake shop Annette bought a large cinnamon doughnut for a snack.
5. Mr. Kowalski was born in Warsaw Poland and became a Canadian citizen on February 15 1975.
6. The brakes on our car aren't working so we'll have to take the bus.
7. The moviegoing couple bought popcorn candy bars and large Cokes at the lobby concession stand.
8. For more information about the Scotland tour write Doreen Campbell 218 Riverdale Street Windsor Ontario M6T 3Y7.

■ Semicolons

The main use of the semicolon (;) is to separate independent clauses, which may or may not be connected with a conjunctive adverb (see pages 573–574). Other uses include separating

> two or more of a series of items
>
> items containing commas in a single series
>
> independent clauses that contain commas and are connected with a coordinating conjunction.

Independent Clauses   The examples that follow show the use of semicolons to separate independent clauses.

> The fabric in this dress is terrible; its designer must have been asleep at the swatch. (no conjunctive adverb)
>
> Steve refused to write a term paper; *therefore,* he failed the course. (conjunctive adverb *therefore* joining independent clauses)

Conjunctive adverbs can occur within, rather than between, independent clauses. When they do, set them off with commas.

> Marsha felt very confident. Jane, *on the other hand,* was nervous and uncertain. (conjunctive adverb within independent clause)

To determine whether a pair of commas or a semicolon and comma are required, read what comes before and after the conjunctive adverb. Unless both sets of words can stand alone as sentences, use commas.

Two or More Series of Items   With sentences that have two or more series of items, writers often separate the series with semicolons in order to reduce the chances of misreading.

> My duties as secretary include typing letters, memos, and purchase orders; sorting, opening, and delivering mail; and making plane and hotel reservations for travelling executives.

The semicolons provide greater clarity than commas would.

Comma-Containing Items Within a Series   When commas accompany one or more of the items in a series, it's often better to separate the items with semicolons instead of commas.

> The meal included veal, which was cooked to perfection; asparagus, my favourite vegetable; and brown rice, prepared with a touch of curry.

Once again, semicolons provide greater clarity than additional commas.

Independent Clauses with Commas and a Coordinating Conjunction   Ordinarily, a comma is used to separate independent clauses joined by a coordinating conjunction.

When one or more of the clauses have commas, however, a semicolon provides clearer separation.

> The long black limousine pulled up to the curb; and Jerry, shaking with excitement, watched the Prime Minister alight from it.

The semicolon makes it easier to see the two main clauses.

CONNECTED DISCOURSE EXERCISE *Add and delete semicolons as appropriate in the following letter. You may have to substitute semicolons for commas.*

```
Dear Student:

Our university, as you are well aware, has been going through a
number of changes, and these developments, both in the registration
system and the curriculum, will continue next year. In the end
these improvements will only benefit you; but we know that many of
you have been anxious about the exact nature of the changes. To an-
swer your questions, we have arranged an open forum with Linda
Peters, president of the university, Drake Stevens, the registrar,
and Jerry Mash, vice-president of academic affairs. The meeting
will be held in Johnston Hall; 2 P.M.; March 23. Please come with
your questions, this is your opportunity to put your fears to rest.

                              Sincerely,
                              John X. Pelle
                              Dean of Students
```

EXERCISE *Supply semicolons wherever they are necessary or desirable in the following sentences. You may have to substitute semicolons for commas. If a sentence is correct, write C.*

1. The garage sale included women's coats, hats, and purses, men's shoes, shirts, and ties, and children's scarves, mittens, and boots.
2. James couldn't stand his sarcastic boss, therefore, he quit his job.
3. Our house is far too small, we should start looking for a larger one.
4. Morris wanted to work for a company that was small, environmentally responsible, and located in a midsize city, and finally, after a dozen job interviews, he went to work for Greenland, Inc.
5. This has been a good year for raspberries, I've gotten over thirty quarts from my small patch of bushes.
6. The road ahead has been washed out by a flood; you'll have to make a detour.
7. After touring the company's facilities, we had lunch with Giles Seymour, its president, Cheryl James, its sales manager, and Daryl Brewer, its research director.
8. Penny is a real cat lover; in fact, she has six.

■ Periods, Question Marks, and Exclamation Points

Since periods, question marks, and exclamation points signal the ends of sentences, they are sometimes called *end marks*. In addition, periods and question marks function in several other ways.

Periods Periods (.) end sentences that state facts or opinions, give instructions, make requests that are not in the form of questions, and ask indirect questions—those that have been rephrased in the form of a statement.

> Linda works as a hotel manager. (Sentence states fact.)

> Dean Harris is a competent administrator. (Sentence states opinion.)

> Clean off your lab bench before you leave. (Sentence gives instruction.)

> Please move away from the door. (Sentence makes request.)

> I wonder whether Ruthie will be at the theatre tonight. (Sentence asks indirect question.)

Periods also follow common abbreviations, as well as a person's initials.

.?!

Mr.	Sr.	P.M.
Mrs.	B.C.	a.s.a.p.
Jr.	A.D.	St.
Dr.	A.M.	Corp.

> Mark J. Valentini, Ph.D., has consented to head the new commission on traffic safety.

Writers today often omit periods after abbreviations for the names of organizations or government agencies, as the following examples show:

CBC	GST	RCAF	TD
PST	IBM	UPS	WTO

An up-to-date dictionary will indicate whether a certain abbreviation should be written without periods.

Periods also precede decimal fractions and separate numerals standing for dollars and cents.

0.81 percent	$5.29
3.79 percent	$0.88

Question Marks A question mark (?) ends a whole or a partial sentence that asks a direct question (one that repeats the exact words of the person who asked it).

> Do you know how to operate this movie projector? (whole sentence asking a direct question)

> Has Cinderella scrubbed the floor? Swept the hearth? Washed the dishes? (sentence and sentence parts asking direct questions)

Dr. Baker—wasn't she your boss once?—has just received a promotion to sales manager. (interrupting element asking a direct question)

The minister inquired, "Don't you take this woman to be your lawful wedded wife?" (quotation asking a direct question)

A question mark may be used to indicate uncertainty.

Jane Seymour (1509?–1537), third wife of Henry VIII, was a lady in waiting to his first two wives.

Exclamation Points Exclamation points (!) are used to express strong emotion or especially forceful commands.

Darcy! I never expected to see you again!

Sam! Turn that radio down immediately!

Help! Save me!

Use exclamation points sparingly; otherwise, they will quickly lose their force.

CONNECTED DISCOURSE EXERCISE *Add, change, or remove end marks as necessary. You may want to do some slight rewording.*

It was horrifying, the mob of screaming fans grabbed Jack Slitherhips as he left the concert hall. Soon all I could see were his arms reaching for help. But it never came. Why do fans act this way. I am left wondering whether they love or hate their idols? They tore the clothes off Slitherhips, they tore out patches of his hair, someone even snatched his false teeth. Is this any way to treat a fading rock star. Jack is now in the hospital in a complete body cast; when I finally got to see him, he mumbled that he was giving up show business, he plans to settle down on a small farm. Who can blame him?

EXERCISE *Supply periods, question marks, or exclamation points wherever they are necessary. You may have to change existing punctuation marks. If a sentence is correct, write C.*

1. The instructor asked Margie why she hadn't finished her process paper.
2. The videotape of the movie *Casablanca* retails for $2995.
3. Good lord, quit popping that gum before you drive me nuts.
4. Lock the front door before you go to bed.
5. Where do you plan to spend your vacation this year.
6. While you were in Vancouver, did you go to GM Place and see a Canucks game.
7. Would you be interested in having dinner with me tonight.
8. When it's 5 pm in British Columbia, it's 8 pm in Ontario.

■ Colons, Dashes, Parentheses, and Brackets

Colons, dashes, parentheses, and brackets separate and enclose, thereby clarifying relationships among the various parts of a sentence.

Colon   Colons (:) introduce explanations and anticipated lists following words that could stand alone as a complete sentence.

> His aim in life is grandiose: to corner the market in wheat. (explanation)

> Three students have been selected to attend the conference: Lucille Perkins, Dan Blakely, and Frank Napolis. (list)

> Three factors can cause financial problems for farmers: (1) high interest rates, (2) falling land values, and (3) a strong dollar, which makes it difficult to sell crops abroad. (numbered list)

The first of the following sentences is incorrect because the words preceding the colon can't stand alone as a sentence:

> *Faulty*   The tools needed for this job include: a hacksaw, a file, and a drill.

> *Revision*   The tools needed for this job include a hacksaw, a file, and a drill.

Colons also frequently introduce formal quotations that extend beyond a single sentence.

> The speaker stepped to the lectern and said: "I am here to ask for your assistance. Today several African nations face a food crisis because drought has ruined their harvests. Unless we provide help quickly, thousands of people will die of starvation."

In such situations, the material preceding the quotation need not be a complete sentence.

Colons also separate hours from minutes (8:20 a.m.), salutations of business letters from the body of the letters (Dear Ms. Stanley:), titles of publications from subtitles (*The Careful Writer: A Guide to English Usage*), numbers indicating ratios (a 3:2:2 ratio), and chapter from verse in biblical references (Luke 6:20–49).

Dashes   Like colons, dashes (—) set off appositives, lists, and explanations, but are used in less formal writing. A dash emphasizes the material it sets off.

> Only one candidate showed up at the political rally—Jerry Manders. (appositive)

> The closet held only three garments—an out-at-the-elbows sports coat, a pair of blue jeans, and a tattered shirt. (list)

> I know what little Billy's problem is—a soiled diaper. (explanation)

Dashes set off material that interrupts the flow of thought within a sentence.

Her new car—didn't she get it just three months ago?— has broken down twice.

Similarly, dashes are used to mark an interrupted segment of dialogue.

"I'd like to live in England when I retire."

"In England? But what will your wife—?"

"My wife likes the idea and can hardly wait for us to make the move."

Dashes set off parenthetical elements containing commas, and a dash can set off comments that follow a list.

The comedian—short, fat, and squeaky-voiced—soon had everyone roaring with laughter. (parenthetical element with commas)

A brag, a blow, a tank of air—that's what the Director is. (comment following a list)

Type a dash as two unspaced hyphens and leave no space between it and the words on either side of it.

Parentheses Parentheses () are used to enclose numbers or letters that designate the items in a formal list and to set off incidental material within sentences. Except in the kind of list shown in the first example below, a comma does not usually precede a parenthesis.

Each paper should contain (1) an introduction, (2) several paragraphs developing the thesis statement, and (3) a conclusion.

Some occupations (computer programming, for example) may be overcrowded in ten years.

If the material in parentheses appears within a sentence, don't use a capital letter or period, even if the material is itself a complete sentence.

The use of industrial robots (one cannot foresee their consequences) worries some people today.

If the material in parentheses is written as a separate sentence, however, then punctuate it as you would a separate sentence.

Paula's angry outburst surprised everyone. (She had seemed such a placid person.)

If the material in parentheses comes at the end of a sentence, put the final punctuation after the closing parenthesis.

This company was founded by Willard Manley (1876–1951).

In contrast to dashes, parentheses de-emphasize the material they enclose.

Brackets In quoted material, brackets [ ] enclose words or phrases that have been added to make the message clearer. They are also used with the word *sic* (Latin for "thus") to point out errors in quoted material.

()[]

"This particular company [Zorn Enterprises, Inc.] pioneered in the safe disposal of toxic wastes," the report noted. (The bracketed name is added to the original.)

"[John Chafin's] expertise in science has made him a popular figure on the lecture circuit," his friend stated. (The bracketed name replaces *his* in the original.)

"The principle [sic] cause of lung cancer is cigarette smoking," the article declared. (the word *principal* is misspelled "principle" in the original.)

To call attention to an error, follow it immediately with the bracketed *sic*. The reader will then know that the blame rests with the original writer, not with you.

CONNECTED DISCOURSE EXERCISE   *Supply any necessary or appropriate colons, dashes, parentheses, and brackets in the following letter:*

```
Wayout Auto Company

We at Oldfield Sales a subsidiary of Jip, Inc., have had a serious
problem with the cars we ordered from your company for leasing to
our customers who will probably never return to us again. Two major
parts fell off while the cars were sitting in the customers' drive-
ways the exhaust system and the transmission. If this had happened
while they were driving thank goodness it didn't, our customers
could have been killed. Just imagine what that especially once it
got into the newspapers would have done to our business. We must
hold you to your claim that "while our cars are the cheepest sic on
the market, we garnishee sic every car we sell." We expect immedi-
ate reimbursement for all the cars we purchased from you plus one
million dollars to cover the damage to our reputation. A menace, a
rip-off, a bad business deal, that's what your cars are. If you
don't issue a formal recall for all your vehicles by 530 P.M.,
Friday, July 23, we will be forced to forward this matter to the
federal government.

                              Sincerely,

                              Ken Swindelle

                              Service Manager
```

EXERCISE   *Supply colons, dashes, parentheses, and brackets wherever they are necessary.*

1. Worthington's new house mansion would be a better term has twenty-eight rooms.
2. This resort offers unsurpassed facilities for three winter sports ice skating, skiing, and tobogganing.
3. Two long meetings, a shopping trip, a dinner engagement I've had a busy day!

4. The main parts of the pressure tester include 1 an indicator dial, 2 a hose connection, 3 a damper valve, and 4 a sensing unit.

5. At the tone, the time will be 330 p.m. exactly.

6. The headline stated, "Students Voice They're sic Disapproval of Tuition Hike."

7. "His Charles Darwin's book *On the Origin of Species* touched off a controversy that still continues," the lecturer declared.

8. One major social problem will remain with us for several decades the population explosion.

Quotation Marks

Quotation marks (" ") set off direct quotations, titles of short written or broadcast works, subdivisions of books, and expressions singled out for special attention.

Direct Quotations A direct quotation repeats a speaker's or writer's exact words.

"Tell me about the movie," said Debbie. "If you liked it, I may go myself."

The placement director said, "The recruiter for Procter and Gamble will be on campus next Thursday to interview students for marketing jobs." (spoken comment)

"The trade deficit is expected to reach record levels this year," the *Wall Street Journal* noted. (written comment)

Jackie said the party was "a total flop."

As these sentences show, a comma or period that follows a direct quotation goes inside the quotation marks. When a quotation is a sentence fragment, the comma preceding it is omitted.

When an expression like "he said" interrupts a quoted sentence, use commas to set off the expression. When the expression comes between two complete quoted sentences, use a period after the expression and capitalize the first word of the second sentence.

"Hop in," said Jim. "Let me give you a ride to school."

"Thank you," replied Kelly, opening the car door and sliding into the front seat.

"I can't remember," said Jim, "when we've had a worse winter."

Titles of Short Works and Subdivisions of Books These short works include magazine articles, essays, short stories, chapters of books, one-act plays, short poems, songs, and television and radio episodes.

The article was titled "The Real Conservatism." (article)

Last night I read John Cheever's "The Enormous Radio," "Torch Song," and "The Swimmer." (short stories)

Many Stompin' Tom Connors fans consider "Sudbury Saturday Night" to be his greatest piece of music. (song)

The unsuccessful TV show *Pursued* ended its brief run with a segment titled "Checkmate." (TV episode)

Here, as with direct quotations, a comma or period that follows a title goes inside the quotation marks.

Expressions Singled Out for Special Attention Writers who wish to call the reader's attention to a word or symbol sometimes put it inside quotation marks.

The algebraic formula included a "p," a "Q," and a "D."

"Bonnets" and "lifts" are British terms for car hoods and elevators.

More frequently, however, these expressions are printed in italics (page 633).

Again, any commas and periods that follow expressions set off by quotation marks go inside the marks.

Quotation Marks Within Quotation Marks When a direct quotation or the title of a shorter work appears within a direct quotation, use single quotation marks (' ').

"I heard the boss telling the foreman, 'Everyone will receive a Christmas bonus,'" John said.

The instructor told the class, "For tomorrow, read Jack Hodgin's 'Separating.'"

Note that the period goes inside both the single and double quotation marks.

Positioning of Semicolons, Colons, and Question Marks Position semicolons and colons that come at the end of quoted material after, not before, the quotation marks.

Marcia calls Francine "that greasy grind"; however, I think Marcia is simply jealous of Francine's abilities.

There are two reasons that I like "Babylon Revisited": the characters are interesting and the writing is excellent.

When a question mark accompanies a quotation, put it outside the quotation marks if the whole sentence rather than the quotation asks the question.

Why did Cedric suddenly shout, "This party is a big bore"?

Put the question mark inside the quotation marks if the quotation, but not the whole sentence, asks a question or if the quotation asks one question and the whole sentence asks another.

Marie asked, "What college is your brother planning to attend?" (The quoted material, not the whole sentence, asks the question.)

Whatever possessed him to ask, "What is the most shameful thing you ever did?" (The whole sentence and the quoted material ask separate questions.)

CONNECTED DISCOURSE EXERCISE *Use quotation marks correctly in the following paragraph.*

Mr. Silver recently lectured our class on Stephen Crane's The Bride Comes to Yellow Sky. One thing we shouldn't forget, Mr. Silver insisted, is that the town is deliberately named Yellow Sky. What is the significance of Crane's choice of the words Yellow Sky? Mr. Silver pointed out a number of possible associations, including cowardice, the setting sun, the open expanse of the West, freedom, the sand in the concluding passage. The story, Mr. Silver stated, is drenched in colour words. For example, he pointed out, in the first three paragraphs alone Crane mentions vast flats of green grass, brick-coloured hands, new black clothes, and a dress of blue cashmere.

EXERCISE *Supply properly positioned quotation marks wherever they are necessary.*

1. Jeffrey called the novel's plot a hopeless mishmash.
2. I think, said Tom, that I'll go to Niagara Falls for the weekend.
3. What poem has the lines Home is the sailor, home from the sea, / And the hunter home from the hills?
4. Denise tells everyone, I prefer classical music; however, her CD collection includes only hard rock and country music.
5. Nearly every educated person now knows that the Russian word *glasnost* means openness.
6. At last my paper is finished, John said happily. Now I can start typing it.
7. Does anyone here know that the word dilatory means tardy?
8. Why did Neil's wife ask him, How would you like me to dispose of your remains?

■ Hyphens

Hyphens (-) are used to join compound adjectives and nouns, compound numbers and word-number combinations, and certain prefixes and suffixes to the words with which they appear. In addition, hyphens help prevent misreadings and awkward combinations of letters or syllables and are used to split words between two lines.

Compound Adjectives and Nouns Hyphens are often used to join separate words that function as single adjectives and come before nouns. Typical examples follow:

Howard is a very *self-contained* person.

The *greenish-yellow* cloud of chlorine gas drifted toward the village.

Betty's *devil-may-care* attitude will land her in trouble someday.

When the first word of the compound is an adverb ending in *-ly* or when the compound adjective follows the noun it modifies, no hyphen is used.

The *badly* burned crash victim was rushed to the hospital.

The colour of the chlorine gas was *greenish yellow.*

When two or more compound adjectives modify the same last term, the sentence will flow more smoothly if that term appears just once, after the last item in the series. The hyphens accompanying the earlier terms in the series are kept, however.

Many seventeenth-, eighteenth-, and nineteenth-century costumes are on display in this museum.

Hyphenated nouns include such expressions as the following:

secretary-treasurer	good-for-nothing
sister-in-law	man-about-town

Here is a sentence with hyphenated nouns:

Denton is *editor-in-chief* of the largest newspaper in this province.

Compound Numbers and Word–Number Combinations   Hyphens are used to separate two-word numbers from twenty-one to ninety-nine and fractions that have been written out.

Marcy has worked *twenty-one* years for this company.

One-fourth of my income goes for rent.

Similarly, hyphens are used to separate numerals from units of measurement that follow them.

This chemical is shipped in *50-gallon* drums.

Prefixes and Suffixes   A prefix is a word or set of letters that precedes a word and alters its meaning. A suffix is similar but comes at the end of the word. Although most prefixes are not hyphenated, the prefixes *self-* and *all-* do get hyphens, as does the suffix *-elect*. Also the prefix *ex-* is hyphenated when it accompanies a noun.

This stove has a *self-cleaning* oven.

Let Claire Voyant, the *all-knowing* soothsayer, read your future in her crystal ball.

Ethel is the *chairperson-elect* of the club.

Several *ex-teachers* work in this department.

A prefix used before a capitalized term is always hyphenated.

The *ex-RCMP* officer gave an interesting talk on the operations of that organization.

Preventing Misreadings and Awkward Combinations of Letters and Syllables Hyphens help prevent misreadings of certain words and also break up awkward combinations of letters and syllables between certain prefixes and suffixes and their core words.

> The doctor *re-treated* the wound with a new antibiotic. (The hyphen prevents the misreading *retreated.*)

> The company plans to *de-emphasize* sales of agricultural chemicals. (The hyphen prevents the awkward repetition of the letter *e* in *deemphasize.*)

Between Syllables Whenever you have to split a word between two lines, place a hyphen at the end of the first line to show the division. The word is always broken, and the hyphen inserted, between syllables. (Any good dictionary shows the syllable divisions of each word it includes.) Never divide a one-syllable word or leave two letters to be placed on the second line, even if those two letters constitute a syllable.

EXERCISE *Supply hyphens wherever they are necessary. If the sentence is correct, write C.*

1. The task of residing the house will take three days.
2. Margaret is the most selfsufficient person that I've ever met.
3. Judge Grimm gave the convicted arsonist a ten to twenty year prison sentence.
4. Nearly three fourths of our chemistry majors go on to graduate school.
5. When I was thirty five years old, I quit my job and opened my own small business.
6. Most of my exsoldier friends belong to veterans' organizations.
7. Jeremiah's antigovernment tirades have caused most of his friends to avoid him.
8. The orange red flowers growing next to the house contrasted strongly with the dark grey of its walls.

cap

■ Capitalization

Capitalize the first word in any sentence, the pronoun *I,* proper nouns and adjectives, titles used with—or in place of—names, and the significant words in literary and artistic titles.

Proper Nouns A proper noun names one particular person, group of persons, place, or thing. Such nouns include the following:

Persons
Organizations
Racial, political, and religious groups
Countries, provinces and states, cities, and streets
Companies and buildings
Geographical locations and features
Days, months, and holidays
Trademarks
Languages
Ships and aircraft

Abbreviations for academic degrees
Sacred writings and pronouns standing for God and Jesus
Titles used in place of names

The sentences below show the capitalization of proper nouns:

Sigmund works for the *National Psychoanalytical Institute,* an organization that has done much to advance the science of psychiatry.

How much does this roll of *Saran Wrap* cost?

Gwen Greene moved to *Paris, France,* when her father became the consul there.

On *Friday, December* 10, 1993, *Celine Dion* visited our city.

Larry has a master of arts degree, and his sister has a *Ph.D.*

My father works for the *Ford Motor Company,* but I work for *Chrysler.*

Do not capitalize words like *institute, college, company,* or *avenue* unless they form part of a proper name. Likewise, do not capitalize the names of courses unless they start a sentence, are accompanied by a course number, or designate a language.

I have a 95 average in *Economics* 112 but only a 73 average in sociology.

Harry plans to take intermediate *German* in his junior year.

Do you plan to attend *Queen's University* or some other university?

Proper Adjectives   Adjectives created from proper nouns are called proper adjectives. Like the nouns themselves, they should be capitalized.

Lolita Martinez, our class valedictorian, is of *Spanish* ancestry. (*Spanish* is derived from the proper noun *Spain.*)

Abbreviations   As a general rule, capitalize abbreviations only if the words they stand for are capitalized.

Milton DeWitt works for the *NDP.* (*NDP* is capitalized because *New Democratic Party* would be.)

The flask holds 1500 *ml* of liquid. (The abbreviation *ml* is not capitalized because *millilitres* would not be.)

A few abbreviations are capitalized even though all or some of the words they stand for aren't. Examples include TV (television) and VCR (videocassette recorder). Others are shown on page 629.

Personal Titles   Capitalize a personal title if it precedes a name or is used in place of a name. Otherwise, do not capitalize.

The division is under the command of *General* Arnold Schafer.

Tell me, *Doctor,* do I need an operation?

The *dean* of our engineering division is Dr. Alma Haskins.

cap

Many writers capitalize titles of high rank when they are used in place of names.

The *Prime Minister* will sign this bill tomorrow.

The *prime minister* will sign this bill tomorrow.

Either usage is acceptable.

Titles of Literary and Artistic Works   When citing the titles of publications, pieces of writing, movies, television programs, paintings, sculptures, and the like, capitalize the first and last words and all other words except *a, an, the,* coordinating conjunctions, and one-syllable prepositions.

Last week I played *Gone with the Wind* on my VCR and read Christopher Isherwood's *Goodbye to Berlin.* (the preposition *with,* the article *the,* and the preposition *to* are not capitalized.)

John is reading a book called *The Movies of Abbott and Costello.* (The preposition *of* and the coordinating conjunction *and* are not capitalized.)

Although I'm no TV addict, I used to watch every episode of *Murder, She Wrote.* (All of the words in the title are capitalized.)

Note that the titles of literary and artistic works are italicized. If you don't have access to italic print on your computer program, underline the titles.

ab

EXERCISE   *Identify any word or abbreviation that should be capitalized in the following sentences:*

1. The recipe for this stew comes from *the canadian family cookbook.*
2. My cousin has accepted a job with the federal national mortgage association and will move to ottawa, ont., in july.
3. The announcement said that sergeant brockway had received a second lieutenant's commission.
4. The aclu has asked midville to scrap its ordinance prohibiting christmas religious displays on private property.
5. The newest municipal judge in boyle city is judge martha berkowicz.
6. Unless sales increase markedly in the next quarter, the delta corporation will be forced into bankruptcy.
7. We need to buy some wheaties, mother.
8. What are your postretirement plans, professor?

■ Abbreviations

Items that are abbreviated include certain personal titles, names of organizations and agencies, Latin terms, and specific and technical terms.

Personal Titles   Abbreviate *Mister, Doctor,* and similar titles when they come just ahead of a name, and *Junior, Senior,* and degree titles when they follow names.

Will *Mr.* Harry Babbitt please come to the front desk?

Arthur Compton, *Sr.,* is a well-known historian; his son, Arthur Compton, *Jr.,* is a television producer.

This article on marital discord was written by Irma Quarles, Ph.D.

Names of Organizations and Agencies Many organizations and agencies are known primarily by their initials rather than their full names. Several examples follow:

CAA	CTV	NATO	WHO
CARE	IMF	SPCA	WTO
CMA	IRA	UNESCO	CRTC

Latin Terms Certain Latin terms are always abbreviated; others are abbreviated when used with dates or times.

e.g. (*exempli gratia:* for example)
i.e. (*id est:* that is)
etc. (*et cetera:* and [the] others)
vs. or v. (*versus:* against)
A.D. (*anno Domini:* in the year of our Lord)
a.m. or A.M. (*ante meridiem:* before noon)
p.m. or P.M. (*post meridiem:* after noon)

The play starts at 8 P.M.

Many writers (*e.g.,* Dylan Thomas and Truman Capote) have had serious problems with alcohol.

For consistency with A.D., the term "before Christ" is abbreviated as B.C.

Scientific and Technical Terms For brevity's sake, scientists and technicians abbreviate terms of measurement that repeatedly occur. Terms that the reader would not know are written out the first time they are used, and they are accompanied by their abbreviation in parentheses. Unfamiliar organizations and agencies that are mentioned repeatedly are handled in like manner.

The viscosity of the fluid measured 15 centistokes (cs) at room temperature.

Common practice calls for writing such abbreviations without periods unless they duplicate the spelling of some word.

Standard dictionaries list common abbreviations. When you don't recognize one, look it up. Use abbreviations sparingly in essays. If you're unsure about what is appropriate, don't abbreviate.

EXERCISE *Supply abbreviations wherever they are necessary or are customarily used.*

1. The conference on poverty in the 1990s will be chaired by Donald Frump, Doctor of Philosophy.

2. When writing, don't use Latin terms like *id est* and *exempli gratia* except as comments in parentheses and footnotes.

3. The United Nations Educational, Scientific, and Cultural Organization sponsors programs in primary education throughout the Third World.

ab

4. My physics instructor, Doctor Seth Greenfield, Junior, has just completed a textbook on optics.

5. The thermometer on my front porch says that the temperature is 25° Celsius.

6. At 10:20 *ante meridiem,* the local TV station announced that a tornado had been sighted near Leesville.

7. This fall, the Columbia Broadcasting System will air nine new sitcoms.

8. Which would you prefer, Mister Bartleby, tea or coffee?

■ Numbers

Some instructors ask their students to use figures for numbers larger than ninety-nine and to spell out smaller numbers.

Banff is *100* kilometres from here.

Banff is *ninety-nine* kilometres from here.

Other instructors prefer that students switch to figures beginning with the number ten.

My son will be *nine* years old on his next birthday.

My son will be *10* years old on his next birthday.

With either practice, the following exceptions apply.

Numbers in a Series Write all numbers in a series the same way regardless of their size.

Gatsby has *64* suits, *110* shirts, and *214* ties.

In just one hour the emergency room personnel handled *two* stabbings, *five* shootings, and *sixteen* fractures.

We have *150* salespeople, *51* engineers, and *7* laboratory technicians.

Dates Use figures for dates that include the year.

February *14, 1985* (not February 14th, 1985)

When the date includes the day but not the year, you may use figures or spell out the number.

June 9

June ninth

the ninth of June

Page Numbers and Addresses Use figures for page numbers and street numbers in addresses.

Check the graph on page *415*.

I live at *111* Cornelia Street, and my office is at *620* Victoria Avenue.

num

Numbers Beginning Sentences   Spell out any number that begins a sentence. If this requires three or more words, rephrase the sentence so that the number comes after the opening and numerals can be used.

The year *1989* was a good year for this wine.

Sixty thousand fans jammed the stadium.

An army of *265 000* troops assaulted the city. (If this number began the sentence, five words—an excessive number—would be needed to write it out.)

Decimals, Percentages, Times   Use figures for decimals and percentages as well as for expressions of time that are accompanied by A.M. or P.M.

The shaft has a *0.37*-inch diameter.

Last year the value of my house jumped *25* percent.

The plane leaves here at *9:50* a.m. and reaches Winnipeg at *2:30* P.M.

One Number Following Another   When a number-containing term that denotes a unit of weight or measurement comes immediately after another number, spell out the first number, if smaller than 100, and use numerals for the second one. If the first number is larger than 100, use numerals for it and spell out the second one.

We ordered *six 30*-gallon drums of solvent for the project.

The supplier shipped us *600 thirty*-gallon drums by mistake.

> **EXERCISE**   *Identify any miswriting of numbers in the following sentences and rewrite these numbers correctly:*
>
> 1. 50 000 people ride this city's buses each day.
> 2. The article on page fifty-nine of this week's issue of *Maclean's* discusses Alanis Morissette's latest video.
> 3. Next Saturday at one-thirty p.m., the city will test its emergency warning sirens.
> 4. My grandparents' golden wedding anniversary was July seventeen, nineteen ninety-one.
> 5. Mildred has 500 books, two hundred CDs, and fifty-five videocassettes.
> 6. It is not uncommon for credit-card holders to pay interest rates of eighteen percent or more.
> 7. Laura's plane will leave for Halifax at two-thirty p.m. on May the sixteenth.
> 8. The thickness of this piece needs to be increased by fifteen hundredths of an inch.

■ Italics

Italics are used for the titles of longer publications, the names of vehicles and vessels, foreign words and phrases, and expressions singled out for special attention. Unless your computer program allows you access to italic print, use underlining to represent italics when writing or typing papers.

ital

Titles of Longer Publications and Artistic Works These items may include the following:

books	record albums	long musical works and poems
magazines	paintings	plays
newspapers	movies	sculptures

As noted on pages 623–624, quotation marks are used for the titles of articles, short stories, short poems, one-act plays, and other brief pieces of writing.

> Last night I finished Michael Ondaatje's *The English Patient* and read two articles in *Geist*. (book, magazine)

> Michelangelo's *David* is surely one of the world's greatest sculptures. (sculpture)

> *The Globe and Mail* had praise for the revival of Tomson Highway's *The Rez Sisters*. (newspaper, play)

> Stephen Vincent Benét's poem *John Brown's Body* won a Pulitzer Prize in 1929. (book-length poem)

Do not use italics when naming the Bible and its parts or other religious works such as the Torah and Koran.

> Joanna's favourite book of the Bible is the Book of Ecclesiastes, part of the Old Testament.

ital

Names of Vehicles and Vessels Names of particular airplanes, ships, trains, and spacecraft are italicized.

> The plane in which Charles Lindbergh flew over the Atlantic Ocean was named *The Spirit of St. Louis*.

Foreign Expressions Use italics to identify foreign words and phrases that have not yet made their way into the English language.

> The writer has a terribly pessimistic *weltanschauung*. (philosophy of life)

> This season, long skirts are the *dernier cri*. (the latest thing)

When such expressions become completely assimilated, the italics are dropped. Most dictionaries use an asterisk (*), a dagger (†), or other symbol to identify expressions that need italicizing.

Expressions Singled Out for Special Attention These include words, letters, numerals, and symbols.

> The Greek letter *pi* is written P.

> I can't tell whether this letter is meant to be an *a* or an *o* or this number a *7* or a *9*.

> In England, the word *lorry* means truck.

As noted on page 624, quotation marks sometimes replace italics for this purpose.

CONNECTED DISCOURSE EXERCISE   *Use hyphens, capitalization, abbreviations, numbers, and italics properly in the following passage.*

Because I can speak Russian fluently, I was recruited by the central intelligence agency while still at Boston college. I suspected that it was professor Hogsbottom, a Political Science teacher, who had suggested that they consider me. After all, he had been a General during World War II and still had connections with the intelligence community. It turned out that my brother in law was responsible; he was an ex FBI agent. Soon I was an american spy located, of all places, in England. Who would suspect that we had to spy on the english? For 3 years I posed as a british aristocrat who was a general bon vivant and man about town. I went by the alias of Mister Henry Higgins, Junior. Everyone, of course, wanted to know if I had seen My Fair Lady. Personally I thought the whole thing was a monty python type of joke until I found a position in the british secret service. Who could have believed the british kept so many secrets from their american allies? For twenty one years I spied on the british without anyone suspecting that I was an all american boy. I did find out recently, however, that because of my fluent russian they had suspected me of being a russian spy and had been feeding me false information all along.

EXERCISE   *Supply italics wherever they are necessary.*

1. To keep abreast of the business news, I read both Investor's Daily and Forbes.
2. Next week, Boris is taking the Siberian Express to Irkutsk, Siberia.
3. Of all my art prints, I like Erte's Fishbowl best.
4. According to fashion forecasts, miniskirts will be de rigueur next summer.
5. My uncle served on the cruiser Indianapolis during World War II.
6. Because Pam lost her brother's copy of Moby Dick, she bought him a new one.
7. Sometimes when I try to print a b I make a d instead.
8. In Scotland, the term lum refers to a chimney.

Spelling

"Why the big deal about accurate spelling?"
"Does it really make that much difference if I have an *i* and an *e* turned around or if I omit a letter when spelling a word?"

sp

Students frequently question the importance of proper spelling. Perhaps the answer is suggested by the following sentence, taken from a student essay:

I spent over seven hours *studing* one day last week.

The omission of a *y* in *studing* changes the person from one who is studious to one who is a dreamer. Not only does inaccurate spelling smack of carelessness, but also it sometimes drastically alters meaning.

Although there is no sure-fire way of becoming a good speller, you can minimize the difficulties by learning basic spelling rules, applying helpful spelling tips, and memorizing the proper spelling of troublesome words.

Spelling Rules

The following four rules should ease spelling pains.

Rule 1 If a word has the double vowels* *ie* or *ei* and the combination has a long *e* sound (as in *me*), use *ie* except after *c*. If the combination has an *a* sound, use *ei*.

ie (as long *e*)	*ei* after *c*	*ei* (as *a*)
relieve	deceive	freight
belief	receive	neighbour
grieve	receipt	reign
piece	perceive	weigh

The main exceptions to this rule include *either, financier, leisure, neither, seize, species,* and *weird*.

---

*The vowels are *a, e, i, o,* and *u.* The consonants are the remaining letters of the alphabet.

Rule 2 If a one-syllable word (example: *sin*) ends in a single consonant preceded by a single vowel, double the consonant before adding a suffix that starts with a vowel. Apply the same rule with a word of two or more syllables (example: *admit*) if the final syllable is accented and ends with a single consonant preceded by a vowel, or if the final consonant is *l, p, s,* or *t* (example: *travel*).

Words with Single Syllables	**Words with Two or More Syllables**
rig—rigged	admit—admittance
sin—sinned	control—controller
stop—stopping	equip—equipped
counsel—counsellor	

If the accent does not fall on the last syllable, do not double the final consonant.

audit—audited   chatter—chattered   simmer—simmering

Rule 3 If a word ends in *y* preceded by a single consonant, change the *y* to an *i* unless you are adding the suffix *-ing*.

y* changed to *i	***y* retained**
beauty—beautiful	copy—copying
fury—furious	defy—defying
easy—easily	dry—drying
vary—various	vary—varying

Rule 4 If a word ends in a silent *e,* the *e* is usually dropped when a suffix starting with a vowel is added.

blue—bluish   fame—famous
dense—density   grieve—grievous

In a few cases, the *e* is retained to avoid pronunciation difficulties or confusion with other words.

dye—dyeing (not dying)   singe—singeing (not singing)
shoe—shoeing (not shoing)

The *e* is also retained when it is preceded by a soft *c* sound (pronounced like the letter *s*) or a soft *g* sound (pronounced like the letter *j*) and the suffix being added starts with an *a* or an *o*.

peace—peaceable   courage—courageous
change—changeable   manage—manageable

■ Helpful Spelling Tips

Here are some tips that can further improve your spelling:

1. Examine each problem word carefully, especially prefixes (*au*dience, *au*dible), suffixes (superintend*ent,* descend*ant*), and double consonants (sate*ll*ite, roo*mm*ate, and co*ll*apsible).

2. Sound out each syllable carefully, noting its pronunciation. Words like *height, governor,* and *candidate* are often misspelled because of improper pronunciation.

3. Make a list of your problem words and review them periodically. Concentrate on each syllable and any unusual features (ar*c*tic, ambig*uous*).

4. Use any crutches that will help: there is *gain* in *bargain;* to *breakfast* is to *break a fast;* a disease causes *dis-ease.*

5. When you copy anything from the blackboard or a textbook, copy it carefully. Writing a word correctly helps you to spell it correctly the next time.

6. Buy a good dictionary and look up the words you don't know how to spell (See pages 225–227 for more information on dictionaries.)

7. If you have a word processor that has a spell checker, use it.

List of Troublesome Words

Students frequently misspell the words in the following list. Study these words carefully until the correct spelling becomes automatic. Then have a friend read them to you while you write them down. Tag the ones you misspell and whenever you revise a paper, check especially for these words.

sp

abandoned	acquitted	among	attendance
abbreviate	address	analysis (analyses)	average
absence	advice	analyze	bachelor
absorb	advise	anonymous	balance
absorption	aerial	anxiety	balloon
absurd	aggravate	apartment	barbarous
academy	aggravated	apparent	barbiturate
accelerate	aggression	appearance	beautiful
accept	aggressive	appreciate	beggar
access	aging	appropriate	believe
accessible	alcohol	architecture	beneficial
accident	allege	arctic	benefit
accidentally	alleviate	argue	benefited
accommodate	alley(s)	arguing	biscuit
accomplish	allot	argument	boundary
accumulate	allotted	arithmetic	bourgeois
accustom	allowed	ascent	breathe
achieve	all right	assassin	Britain
achievement	already	assent	bulletin
acknowledge	although	assistance	bureau
acknowledgment	altogether	assistant	bureaucracy
acquaintance	always	athlete	business
acquire	amateur	athletics	cafeteria
acquit	ambiguous	attempt	calendar

sp

camouflage	convenient	drunkenness	gases
campaign	coolly	echoes	gauge
candidate	cooperate	ecstasy	genius
carburetor	corollary	efficiency	genuine
carriage	corps	efficient	government
carrying	corpse	eighth	grammar
casual	correlate	eligible	guarantee
category	counterfeit	eliminate	guard
causal	courteous	embarrass	handkerchief
ceiling	criticism	emphasis	harass
cellar	criticize	employee	height
cemetery	cruelty	engineer	heroes
changeable	curiosity	enthusiastic	hindrance
changing	curriculum	environment	hygiene
characteristic	dealt	equal	hypocrisy
chauffeur	deceit	equip	hysterical
chief	deceive	equipment	illiterate
colloquial	decent	equipped	illogical
colonel	decision	equivalent	illusion
column	defence	especially	immediate
commission	defendant	exaggerate	implement
commit	definite	exceed	impromptu
commitment	definitely	excellent	inadequate
committed	dependent	except	incident
committee	descendant	excerpt	incidentally
committing	descent	excess	independent
comparatively	describe	excitement	indict
competent	description	exercise	indispensable
competition	desert	existence	individual
concede	desirable	experience	inevitable
conceive	despair	extraordinary	infinitely
condemn	desperate	extremely	ingenious
condescend	dessert	fallacy	ingenuous
confident	develop	familiar	innocent
congratulations	development	fascinate	intelligent
connoisseur	difference	fascist	interest
conqueror	dilemma	February	interfere
conscience	disappear	fiery	irresistible
conscientious	disastrous	finally	irresponsible
conscious	discernible	financier	jeopardy
consistency	disciple	foreign	judgment
consistent	discipline	foreword	judicial
conspicuous	discussion	forfeit	knowledge
contemptible	disease	forward	knowledgeable
continuous	dissatisfied	friend	laboratory
controversy	dissipate	fulfill	legitimate
convenience	dominant	gaiety	leisure

library
licence
lightning
loneliness
loose
lose
magnificent
maintain
maintenance
manoeuvre
manual
marriage
mathematics
mattress
meant
medicine
medieval
mediocre
melancholy
miniature
minute
miscellaneous
mischievous
misspell
modifies
modify
modifying
moral
morale
mortgage
mosquitoes
muscle
mysterious
necessary
neither
nevertheless
niece
noticeable
obedience
occasion
occasionally
occur
occurred
occurrence
occurring
official
omission

omit
omitted
omitting
opinion
opponent
opportunity
optimistic
original
outrageous
pamphlet
parallel
paralysis
parliament
particularly
pastime
patent
peaceable
perceive
perfectible
perform
permanent
permissible
perseverance
persuade
physical
physician
picnic
picnicked
playwright
pleasant
pleasurable
politician
possess
possession
possible
potatoes
practice
practise
precede
precedent
precious
predominant
preference
preferred
prejudice
preparation
privilege

probably
procedure
proceed
professor
prominent
pronounce
pronunciation
propaganda
propagate
propeller
prophecy
prophesy
prostate
prostrate
protein
psychiatry
psychology
pursue
pursuit
quantity
questionnaire
quiet
quite
quiz
quizzes
realize
receipt
receive
recipe
recognizable
recommend
refer
reference
referring
reign
relevant
relieve
religious
remembrance
reminisce
reminiscence
reminiscent
rendezvous
repellent
repentance
repetition
representative

resemblance
resistance
restaurant
rhetoric
rhyme
rhythm
roommate
sacrifice
sacrilege
sacrilegious
safety
salary
sandwich
scarcely
scene
scenic
schedule
science
secretary
seize
sensible
separate
sergeant
severely
siege
similar
simultaneous
sincerely
skeptical
skiing
skillful
skis
society
sophomore
source
specifically
specimen
sponsor
spontaneous
statistics
steely
strategy
studying
subtle
subtlety
subtly
succeed

sp

success	tenant	unconscious	villain
successful	tendency	undoubtedly	waive
succinct	thorough	unmistakable	warrant
suffrage	thought	unnecessary	warring
superintendent	through	until	weather
supersede	traffic	unwieldy	Wednesday
suppose	trafficking	urban	weird
suppress	tragedy	urbane	whether
surprise	tranquillity	usage	whole
syllable	transcendent	useful	wholly
symmetry	transcendental	using	wield
sympathize	transfer	usual	wintry
synonym	transferred	usually	wiry
synonymous	transferring	vacancy	worshiped
tangible	translate	vacillate	(or worshipped)
tariff	tries	vacuum	wreak
technical	truly	valuable	wreck
technique	twelfth	vegetable	writing
temperament	tyrannical	vengeance	written
temperature	tyranny	victorious	yield
temporary	unanimous	village	

Glossary of Word Usage

The English language has many words and expressions that confuse writers and thereby lessen the precision and effectiveness of their writing. These troublesome items include the following:

Word pairs that sound alike or almost alike but are spelled differently and have different meanings

Word pairs that do not sound alike but still are often confused

Words or phrases that are unacceptable in formal writing

The following glossary identifies the most common of these troublemakers. Familiarize yourself with its contents. Then consult it as you revise your writing if you have even the slightest doubt about the proper use of a word, phrase, or expression.

a, an   Use *a* with words beginning with a consonant sound (even if the first written letter is a vowel); use *an* with words beginning with a vowel or a vowel sound.

a brush, *a* student, *a* wheel, *a* risky situation, *a* once-in-a-lifetime opportunity

an architect, *an* apple, *an* unworthy participant, *an* interesting proposal, *an* honest politician

accept, except   *Accept* is a verb meaning "to receive" or "to approve." *Except* is used as a verb or a preposition. As a verb, except means "to take out, exclude, or omit." As a preposition, it means "excluding," "other than," or "but not."

She *accepted* the bouquet of flowers.

Linda *excepted* Sally from the list of guests. (verb)

All of Linda's friends *except* Sally came to the party. (preposition)

access, excess   *Access* is a noun meaning "means or right to enter, approach, or use." In the computer field it is a verb meaning "gain entrance to." *Excess* is an adjective meaning "too much; more than needed; lack of moderation."

I have *access* to a summer cottage this weekend.

The code permits users to *access* the computer.

The airline booked an *excess* number of passengers on that flight.

adapt, adopt   To adapt is "to adjust," often by modification. To *adopt* is "to take as one's own."

He *adapted* to the higher elevations of the Rocky Mountains.

She *adopted* the new doctrine expounded by the prophet.

adverse, averse   *Adverse* is an adjective meaning "unfavourable." *Averse* is an adjective meaning "disinclined" or "feeling distaste for."

Adverse circumstances caused the ceremony to be postponed.

Martha was *averse* to naming all the guilty children.

advice, advise   *Advice* is a noun meaning "a recommendation about how to deal with a situation or problem." *Advise* is a verb meaning "to recommend or warn."

The young man followed his sister's *advice*.

Mr. Smith *advised* John to buy 10 000 shares of the stock.

affect, effect   Although both words may function as nouns and verbs, usually *affect* is a verb and *effect* is a noun. The verb *affect* means "to influence, cause a change in, or arouse the emotions of." The noun *affect* is a technical term in psychology and refers to feeling. The noun *effect* means "result or outcome." The verb *effect* means "to bring about or achieve."

His speech *affected* me greatly. (verb)

The *effect* of the announcement was felt immediately. (noun)

The doctor was soon able to *effect* a cure. (verb)

aggravate   *Aggravate* is a verb meaning "to intensify or make worse" an existing situation. The use of *aggravate* to mean "annoy" or "anger" is colloquial.

Colloquial	Susan's behaviour at the dance really *aggravated* me.
Standard	Marcy's interference only *aggravated* the conflict between Bill and Nadine.

ain't   This nonstandard term for *isn't, aren't, hasn't,* or *haven't* is unacceptable in formal writing.

all ready, already   *All ready* means "completely prepared" or "everyone is ready." *Already* means "previously, even now, even then."

The scouts are *all ready* for the camp out.

When we arrived we found he had *already* gone.

The report is *already* a week overdue.

all right, alright   *Alright* is a nonstandard spelling of *all right* and is not acceptable in formal writing.

all together, altogether   *All together* means "all in one place" or "in unison." *Altogether* is an adverb meaning "completely, entirely."

> The family was *all together* at the wedding.

> *All together,* men, push!

> Mr. Doe is *altogether* at fault for writing the letter.

allusion, delusion, illusion   An *allusion* is an indirect reference. A *delusion* is a mistaken belief, often part of a psychological condition. An *illusion* is a deceptive appearance presented to the sight or created by the imagination.

> In his sermon, the minister made many *allusions* to the New Testament.

> He suffers from the *delusion* that he is a millionaire.

> They wore makeup to give the *illusion* of beauty.

a lot, alot   *Alot* is an erroneous spelling of the two words a lot. The phrase *a lot* is usually colloquial; in formal writing replace it with "many."

already   See *all ready, already.*

alright   See *all right, alright.*

alternately, alternatively   *Alternately* means "occurring by turns, one after the other." *Alternatively* means "providing a choice between two items."

> The American flag has seven red and six white stripes, arranged *alternately.*

> Highway 44 offers the most direct route to Junction City. *Alternatively,* Highway 88 is much more scenic.

altogether   See *all together, altogether.*

among, between   Use *between* when referring to two things and *among* when referring to more than two.

> He divided the candy *between* Allan and Stephanie.

> He divided the candy *among* the five children.

amoral, immoral   *Amoral* means "neither moral nor immoral; morally neutral." *Immoral* means "contrary to the moral code."

> The movie, which takes no clear position on the behaviour it depicts, seems curiously *amoral.*

> Murder is an *immoral* act.

usage

amount, number   *Amount* refers to total quantities, things in bulk, or weight. *Number* refers to countable things. Never use amount when referring to people.

Cassandra inherited a large *amount* of money.

Cassandra now has a large *number* of friends.

an, a   See *a, an.*

and/or   Although often used in commercial and legal documents, this combination should be avoided in other writing.

angry, mad   *Mad* means "insane," although it is often used colloquially to mean "annoyed" or "angry." To be precise, use *mad* only to mean insane.

Colloquial   I was *mad* at Debbie.

Standard   I was *angry* with Debbie.

any, any other   Do not use *any* when you mean *any other.* Using *any* in the following example would mean that Theresa is more qualified than herself:

Theresa is more qualified than *any other* candidate.

anyone, any one   *Anyone* means "any person." *Any one* means "any single person or thing."

I can whip *anyone* in this room.

I saw three movies last week but didn't like *any one* of them.

appraise, apprise   *Appraise* means "to determine the value of something." *Apprise* means "to notify" or "to tell."

The jeweller *appraised* the gold brooch at $1500.

Having been *apprised* of the situation, the family priest was able to reconcile the parents and the children.

apt, liable, likely   Both *apt* and *liable* express a tendency or inclination. *Liable* suggests something unpleasant or likely to result in legal action. It should be used only when the event may have unpleasant consequences.

We are *liable* to miss the train.

My lawyer said that I was *liable* for the damage my car had caused.

If the probable consequences are not unpleasant, *apt* is the better word.

I am *apt* to buy books if we go to the shopping centre.

Likely merely implies strong probability.

Sandra is *likely* to pass this course without any difficulty.

usage

around   *Around* is colloquial use for "approximately" or "about."

Colloquial	She arrived *around* 10:00 p.m.
	The blouse cost *around* $15.
Standard	She arrived at *approximately* 10:00 p.m.
	The blouse cost *about* $15.

as   *As* is frequently used as a weak substitute for *because, since, when,* and *while.*

Weak	She ran out of the house *as* it was on fire.
Better	She ran out of the house *because* it was on fire.

As should not be used in place of *whether* or *that.*

Nonstandard	I don't know *as* I like her.
Standard	I don't know *that* I like her.
	I don't know *whether* I like her.

as, like   *As* may be used as a conjunction that introduces an adverb clause, but *like* should not be used this way.

Unacceptable	*Like* my father always said, "You can fool some of the people all of the time."
Standard	*As* my father always said, "You can fool some of the people all of the time."

Like may, however, be used as a preposition.

In times *like* this, it's hard not to despair.

Any woman *like* Sally can expect a successful career in business.

assure, ensure, insure   To *assure* is "to make safe from risk, to guarantee" or "to convince." *Ensure* and *insure* can be variant spellings meaning "to make certain." *Insure,* however, is now generally associated with the business of insurance.

The counsellor tried to *assure* the students that they had made a wise choice.

The captain *assured* them that they would be rescued.

The father, wanting to *ensure* his son's higher education, applied for a federally *insured* loan.

averse   See *adverse, averse.*

awful, awfully   In everyday speech, *awful* is used to describe things disagreeable or objectionable: "an *awful* movie," "an *awful* character." *Awfully* is used colloquially as an intensifier: "*awfully* nice," "*awfully* bad." Unless they are used to mean "solemnly impressive," however, both words should be avoided in formal writing.

The *awful* majesty of the cathedral silenced the chattering tourists.

usage

awhile, a while   *A while*, consisting of the noun *while* and the article *a*, means "a period of time." *Awhile* is an adverb meaning "for a short time."

Dinner will be served in *a while*.

Sit *awhile* and tell me the latest gossip.

bad, badly   *Bad* is an adjective. *Badly* is an adverb. *Badly* is colloquial when used to mean "very much."

Unacceptable	She feels *badly* about her mistake.
	Tom behaved *bad* at the circus.
Colloquial	I want a new car *badly*.
Standard	She feels *bad* about her mistake. (adjective as subject complement)
	Tom behaved *badly* at the circus. (adverb)
	I want a new car *very much*.

being as, being that   When used as substitutes for *because* or *since*, these expressions are nonstandard.

Nonstandard	*Being that* I was the first in line, I was able to purchase choice tickets.
Standard	*Because* I was first in line, I was able to purchase choice tickets.

beside, besides   Both words are prepositions, but they have different meanings. *Beside* means "at the side of," and *besides* means "in addition to."

Sheila and Bill sat *beside* the trailer to eat their lunch.

Besides Harvey, Seymour is coming to dinner.

between   See *among, between*.

breath, breathe   *Breath* is a noun and *breathe* is its verb counterpart.

Nicole stepped outside the stuffy cabin for a *breath* of fresh air.

The cabin was so stuffy that Nicole could hardly *breathe*.

broke   *Broke*, when used to mean "without money," is colloquial.

Colloquial	Because Shelley was *broke,* she had to miss the movie.
Standard	Because Shelley *had no money,* she had to miss the movie.

can, may   *Can* refers both to permission and to the ability to do something, while *may* refers to permission only.

I think I *can* pass the exam on Friday. (ability)

My mother says I *can* go to the movies. (permission)

When used to denote permission, *can* lends a less formal air to writing than does *may*.

cannot, can not   The use of *cannot* is preferred unless the writer wishes to italicize the *not* for emphasis.

You *cannot* expect a raise this year.

No, you can *not* expect a raise this year.

can't hardly   This nonstandard form for *cannot, can't,* or *can hardly* is unacceptable in formal writing.

can't help but   In formal writing, this colloquial phrase should be revised to the simpler I *can't help* or I *cannot help.*

Colloquial   I *can't help but* wish that I were going to the concert.

Standard   I *can't help* wishing that I were going to the concert.

capital, capitol   *Capital* means "a city that serves as a seat of government." *Capitol* means "a building in which a legislature meets" in the U.S. or "the building in which Congress meets."

Dover is the *capital* of Delaware.

The *capitol* in Dover is popular with visitors.

Capital can also refer to wealth or assets, to an offence punishable by death, or to something excellent or first-rate.

My *capital* consists entirely of stocks and bonds.

Murder is a *capital* crime in this country.

That's a *capital* suggestion!

censor, censure   To *censor* is "to judge"—literature, movies, letters, and the like—and to decide what material is unfit to be read or seen. To *censure* is "to judge harshly" or "find fault with."

The warden *censored* all the prisoners' mail.

The judge *censured* Clyde's criminal behaviour.

childish, childlike   Both of these terms mean "like a child." *Childish,* however, has a negative connotation.

He is fifty-two years old, but he behaves in a *childish* manner.

Jon's face has a *childlike* quality that everyone likes immediately.

cite, sight, site   *Cite* means "to mention or quote as an example," *sight* means "to see" or "a view," and *site* means "a location."

Cheryl *cited* E. J. Pratt's *Towards the Last Spike* in her talk.

He was able to *sight* the enemy destroyers through the periscope.

The building *site* is a woody area south of town.

climactic, climatic　*Climactic* is an adjective that means "of, being, or relating to a climax." *Climatic* is an adjective meaning "of or relating to a climate."

Riding the roller coaster was the *climactic* event of Alice's day.

The *climatic* features of Victoria are desirable to many people.

complement, compliment　Both words can act as nouns or verbs. As a noun, *complement* means "something that completes or makes up the whole." As a verb, it means "to complete or perfect." As a noun, *compliment* means "a flattering or praising remark." As a verb, it means "to flatter or praise."

A *complement* of navy personnel boarded the foreign freighter. (noun)

This fruit will *complement* the meal nicely. (verb)

Scott paid Sara Jane a lovely *compliment* at the time of her graduation. (noun)

Mother *complimented* me for cleaning my room. (verb)

conscience, conscious　*Conscience* refers to the sense of moral right or wrong. *Conscious* refers to the awareness of one's feelings or thoughts.

Edgar's *conscience* forced him to return the money.

Basil was not *conscious* of his angry feelings.

Do not confuse *conscious* with *aware;* although these words are similar in meaning, one is *conscious* of feelings or actions but *aware* of events.

contemptible, contemptuous　*Contemptible* means "deserving of contempt." *Contemptuous* means "displaying contempt."

Peter's drunkenness is *contemptible.*

Mary is *contemptuous* of Peter's drunkenness.

continual, continuous　*Continual* means "frequently or regularly repeated." *Continuous* means "uninterrupted."

The telephone's *continual* ringing made the morning a nightmare.

His wound caused him *continuous* pain for a week.

could have, could of　*Could of* is an unacceptable substitute for *could have* because a preposition cannot substitute for a verb.

| *Nonstandard* | I *could of* gone with my parents to Portugal. |
| *Standard* | I *could have* gone with my parents to Portugal. |

council, counsel　A *council* is a group of people that governs or advises. *Counsel* can be used as both a noun and a verb. The noun means "advice," and the verb means "to advise."

The city *council* meets on the second Tuesday of every month.

The lawyer's *counsel* was sound. (noun)

The psychologist *counsels* many abused children. (verb)

couple   *Couple* denotes two things and should not be used to refer to more than that number.

criteria, criterion   *Criterion* is always singular, *criteria* always plural.

The primary *criterion* for performing this job is manual dexterity.

Manual dexterity is but one of many *criteria* on which you will be judged.

cute   *Cute,* an overused colloquialism, should be avoided; it has too many connotations to be used precisely in writing.

data   *Data* is the plural of *datum.* Although *data* is sometimes used with a singular verb, this use is considered incorrect.

Standard	These *data* are incorrect.
Unacceptable	This *data* is incorrect.

definite, very definite   Since *definite* means "precise" or "unmistakable," *very definite* is repetitive. One really cannot be more definite than *definite.*

delusion   See *allusion, delusion, illusion.*

desert, deserts, dessert   *Desert* is land that is arid. With the accent on the last syllable, it is a verb meaning "to abandon." *Deserts* means "that which is deserved." *Dessert* is food served after dinner.

The Sonoran *desert* is full of plant life.

You'll get your just *deserts* if you *desert* me now.

They had cheesecake for *dessert* every Thursday night.

device, devise   *Device* is a noun meaning "a mechanical contrivance, gadget, or tool." *Devise* is a verb meaning "to plan or invent."

This new *device* gives us better gas mileage.

We must *devise* a new approach to our problem.

different from, different than   *Different from* is preferred over *different than.*

His ideas on marriage were *different from* those of his wife.

Different than is accepted, however, when a clause follows and the *from* construction would be wordy.

Acceptable	Susan looks *different than* she did last summer.
Wordy	Susan looks *different from* the way she looked last summer.

usage

discreet, discrete   To be *discreet* means to be "prudent, tactful, or careful of one's actions." *Discrete* means "distinct or separate."

> Jack was always *discreet* when he talked to his grandparents.

> When two atoms of hydrogen combine with one atom of oxygen, they are no longer *discrete* entities.

disinterested, uninterested   A person who is *disinterested* is impartial or unbiased. A person who is *uninterested* is indifferent or not interested.

> We need a *disinterested* judge to settle the dispute.

> Joe is completely *uninterested* in sports.

don't   This contraction for *do not* should never be used with singular subjects such as *he, she,* or *it*. Instead, use *doesn't*, the contraction for *does not*, with singular subjects.

Nonstandard	*Don't* he know how to spell?
	She *don't* think of anyone except herself.
	That mistake *don't* help your image.
Standard	*Doesn't* he know how to spell?
	She *doesn't* think of anyone except herself.
	That mistake *doesn't* help your image.

due to   *Due to* has always been acceptable following a linking verb.

> Her success was *due to* hard work.

Purists, however, object to *due to* when it is used in other situations, especially in introductory phrases.

> *Due to* the many requests we have had, not everyone who wishes tickets will receive them.

In such cases, you may wish to recast the sentence.

> *Because* we have had so many requests, not everyone who wishes tickets will receive them.

effect   See *affect, effect.*

e.g.   This abbreviation, from the Latin *exempli gratia,* means "for example." Avoid using it except in comments in parentheses and in footnotes.

elicit, illicit   *Elicit* is a verb that means "to draw forth." *Illicit* is an adjective meaning "not permitted."

> A good professor can always *elicit* responses from students.

> He was engaged in many types of *illicit* activities.

usage

emigrate, immigrate   When people *emigrate,* they move out of a country. When people *immigrate,* they move into a country.

> The family *emigrated* from Poland.

> Many Russians *immigrated* to Canada.

eminent, imminent   *Eminent* means "prominent," whereas *imminent* means "about to happen."

> Niels Bohr was an *eminent* physicist.

> Our instruments show that an earthquake is *imminent.*

ensure   See *assure, ensure, insure.*

enthused, enthusiastic   *Enthused* is a colloquial word and should not be used in place of *enthusiastic.*

> Colloquial   John was *enthused* about the prospects for jobs in his hometown.

> Standard   John was *enthusiastic* about the prospects for jobs in his hometown.

especially, specially   The term *especially* means "particularly, notably." *Specially* means "for a specific purpose."

> He is an *especially* talented pianist.

> He was *specially* chosen to represent his group.

et al.   This expression, from the Latin *et alia,* means "and others," referring to people. Ordinarily, the abbreviation should be used only in footnotes and bibliographic entries.

etc.   This abbreviation, from the Latin *et cetera,* means "and other things" and is used in reference to objects rather than people. It should be avoided except in comments in parentheses or in footnotes. It should never be preceded by *and.*

everyone, every one   *Everyone* means "every person." *Every one* means "every particular person or thing."

> *Everyone* who wants to go to the ball game should let me know today.

> If you carefully check *every one* of your paragraphs, you can improve your writing.

except   See *accept, except.*

excess   See *access, excess.*

explicit, implicit   *Explicit* means "clearly expressed" or "straightforward." *Implicit* means "implied" or "understood without direct statement."

> You must state your needs *explicitly* if you want them fulfilled.

usage

When I took on the project, I made an *implicit* commitment to see it through.

extant, extent   *Extant* is an adjective meaning "still existing." *Extent* is a noun meaning "scope, size, range, limit."

The dodo bird is no longer *extant*.

From Nova Scotia to Prince Edward Island is the *extent* of my travels.

farther, further   The traditional distinction is that *farther* refers to physical distance and *further* to distance in time. Only *further* should be used to mean "additional" or "additionally."

In the race for the Muscular Dystrophy Association, Janet ran *farther* than Cindy.

If you think *further* on the matter, I am certain we can reach an agreement.

Let me make one *further* point.

fewer, less   *Fewer* refers to countable items. *Less* refers to quantity or degree.

Mrs. Smith has *fewer* dogs than cats.

There is *less* money in Joan's chequing account than in Stanley's.

Jack was *less* ambitious in his later years.

Never use *less* to refer to people.

> *Nonstandard*   *Less* people were there than I expected.

> *Standard*   *Fewer* people were there than I expected.

flaunt, flout   To *flaunt* is "to display in a showy way." To *flout* is "to express contempt" or "to show scorn."

Jay *flaunted* his handsome physique before all his friends.

Jerrold *flouted* the convention of dressing for dinner by arriving in tennis shoes.

formally, formerly   *Formally* means "according to established forms, conventions, and rules; ceremoniously." *Formerly* means "in the past."

The ambassador *formally* greeted his dinner guests.

Formerly, smallpox was one of our most serious diseases.

funny   *Funny* refers to something that is amusing. In formal writing it should not be used to mean "odd" or "unusual."

> *Colloquial*   I felt *funny* visiting my old fourth-grade classroom.

> *Standard*   I felt *odd* visiting my old fourth-grade classroom.

further   See *farther, further.*

get   *Get*, in any of its many colloquial senses, should not be used in writing.

    Colloquial   Her way of looking at a man really *gets* me.
                     I'll *get* him if it's the last thing I do.

    Standard   Beth will *get* at least a *B* in this course.

good and   Replace this colloquial phrase with *very*.

    Colloquial   She is *good and* tired of the cafeteria food.

    Standard   She is *very* tired of the cafeteria food.

good, well   Do not mistakenly use *good* as an adverb when an adjective is required.

    Unacceptable   John did *good* on his first test.

    Standard   John is making *good* progress on his report.
                   John is a *good* student.

Well can be used as an adjective meaning "in good health." Otherwise it should always be used as an adverb.

    Last week I had a bad cold, but now I am *well*. (adjective)

    John did *well* on his first test. (adverb)

got, gotten   Both are acceptable past-participle forms of the verb *to get*.

had ought, hadn't ought   Both are incorrect in formal writing. The correct forms are *ought* and *ought not*.

    I *ought* to start studying.

    You *ought not* to cut class again.

hanged, hung   People may be *hanged*. Objects may be *hung*.

    The prisoner was *hanged* at noon.

    Mavis *hung* the picture in the dining room.

hisself, theirself, theirselves   These are nonstandard forms of *himself* and *themselves*.

hopefully   *Hopefully* means "in a hopeful manner." In informal speaking, it is used to mean "it is hoped" or "I hope," but this usage is not correct in formal writing. (Compare this with *carefully*, which means "in a careful manner"; no one uses *carefully* to mean "it is cared.")

    Colloquial   *Hopefully*, it will not rain during the class picnic.

    Standard   Sally walked *hopefully* into the boss's office to ask for a raise.

hung   See *hanged, hung*.

usage

i.e.   This abbreviation, meaning "that is," comes from the Latin *id est*. Avoid using it except in comments in parentheses or footnotes.

if, whether   *If* is used to introduce adverb clauses, where it means "assuming that."

> *If* I finish my report on time, I'll attend the concert with you.

If and *whether* are often used interchangeably to introduce noun clauses that follow verbs such as *ask, say, doubt, know,* and *wonder.* In formal writing, however, *whether* is preferred.

> *Less Desirable*   I don't know *if* we'll be able to see the North Star tonight.
>
> *More Desirable*   I don't know *whether* we'll be able to see the North Star tonight.

illicit   See *elicit, illicit.*

illusion   See *allusion, delusion, illusion.*

immigrate   See *emigrate, immigrate.*

imminent   See *eminent, imminent.*

immoral   See *amoral, immoral.*

impact   Although *impact* is sometimes used in colloquial speech as a verb meaning "affect," this use is unacceptable in formal writing.

> *Colloquial*   This new law will greatly *impact* political campaigning.
>
> *Standard*   This new law will greatly *affect* political campaigning.

implicit   See *explicit, implicit.*

imply, infer   To *imply* is "to indicate indirectly or give implication." To *infer* is "to conclude from facts, evidence, or indirect suggestions."

> Jack *implied* that he wanted a divorce.

> Doris *inferred* that Jack wanted a divorce.

As these examples indicate, speakers and writers imply; listeners and readers infer.

incidence, incidents   *Incidents* are separate, countable experiences. *Incidence* refers to the rate at which something occurs.

> Two *incidents* during childhood led to her reclusiveness.

> The *incidence* of cancer in Japan is less than that in Canada.

incredible, incredulous   *Incredible* means "fantastic, unbelievable." *Incredulous* means "skeptical, disbelieving."

> That she could run so fast seemed *incredible.*

> Why is Bill wearing that *incredulous* look?

infer   See *imply, infer.*

ingenious, ingenuous   *Ingenious* means "clever and inventive." *Ingenuous* means "unsophisticated and innocent."

>   Sue presented an *ingenious* solution to our problem.

>   Mary's *ingenuous* comments amused everyone in the room.

in regards to   This is an incorrect use of *in regard to.*

insure   See *assure, ensure, insure.*

inter-, intra-   *Inter-* means "between or among." *Intra-* means "within."

>   From Calgary to Saskatoon is an *interprovince* drive of approximately 700 kilometres.

>   From Osoyoos to Vancouver is an *intraprovince* drive of about 500 kilometres.

in terms of   Avoid this vague, overused expression.

>   *Vague*   *In terms of* the price he is asking, I would not recommend purchasing Tom's car.

>   *Preferred*   *Because* of the price he is asking, I would not recommend purchasing Tom's car.

irregardless   This nonstandard form of *regardless* includes the repetitive elements of *ir* and *less,* both of which mean "without."

is when, is where   *Is when* properly refers only to time.

>   April *is when* our lilac bush blooms.

Is where properly refers only to place.

>   Athens *is where* I met him.

The following sentences are *faulty* because of poorly phrased predicates which indicate that muckraking is a place and an abscess is a time:

>   Muckraking *is where* someone investigates corporate or governmental abuses of power.

>   An abscess *is when* some spot in body tissue fills with pus.

These sentences should be rephrased to eliminate the faulty assertion.

>   Muckraking is the investigation of corporate or governmental abuses of power.

>   An abscess occurs when some spot in body tissue fills with pus.

its, it's, its'   *Its* is a possessive pronoun. *It's* is a contraction of *it is* or *it has.*

>   The gold chair was ruined, for someone had torn *its* seat.

>   *It's* all I have to offer. (It is all I have to offer.)

>   *It's* been a difficult day. (It has been a difficult day.)

There is no correct use for *its'*.

usage

kind of, sort of In formal writing, these are unacceptable substitutes for *somewhat, rather,* or *slightly.*

Colloquial	She is *sort of* angry. I am *kind of* glad she went away.
Standard	She is *somewhat* angry. I am *rather* glad she went away.

When *kind* and *sort* refer to a type, use them with singular nouns and verbs. With their plural forms, *kinds* and *sorts,* use plural nouns and verbs.

Unacceptable	These *kind* of exams are difficult.
Standard	This *kind* of exam is difficult. These *kinds* of exams are difficult.

In such constructions, be certain that *kind of* or *sort of* is essential to your meaning. Otherwise, these phrases are unnecessary.

later, latter *Later* refers to time; *latter* points out the second of two items. If more than two items are listed, use last to refer to the final one.

He arrived at the party *later* than he was expected.

Although Professors Stein and Patterson both lectured during the course, only the *latter* graded the final exam.

Of my three cats, Sheba, Tiger, and Spot, only the *last* still needs the vaccination.

lay, lie *Lie* means "to recline" or "to remain in a particular position." It never takes a direct object. *Lay* means "to place" and always takes a direct object. These verbs are often confused, in part because the past tense of *lie* is *lay.* (The past tense of *lay* is *laid.*)

If I *lie* here a minute, I shall feel better.

As I *lay* asleep, a robber entered by apartment and stole my stereo.

Lay the book on the table, please.

He *laid* a hand on her shoulder.

leave, let *Leave* means "to depart," and *let* means "to allow." Never use *leave* when *let* is meant.

Nonstandard	*Leave* him figure it out alone.
Standard	*Let* him figure it out alone.

lend, loan Traditionally, *loan* has been classed as a noun and *lend* as a verb. Today, the use of *loan* as a verb is so commonplace that it is accepted as colloquial English.

Standard	I have applied for a *loan* so that I can buy a car. (noun) Please *lend* me your class notes. (verb)
Colloquial	Please *loan* me your class notes. (verb)

less See *fewer, less.*

liable See *apt, liable, likely.*

like See *as, like.*

likely See *apt, liable, likely.*

literally The word *literally* means "restricted to the exact, stated meaning." In formal writing, use *literally* only to designate factual statements.

Colloquial	It was 15°, but I was *literally* freezing.
Standard	Our dog was *literally* foaming at the mouth.
	It was 15°, but I was *very* cold.

loan See *lend, loan.*

loose, loosen, lose *Loose* can be used as both a verb and an adjective. As a verb, it means "untie or unfasten"; as an adjective, it means "unattached, unrestrained, not confined." *Loosen* is a verb meaning "undo or ease." *Lose* can be used only as a verb meaning "mislay, fail to win, fail to maintain."

He *loosed* the restraints on the tiger. (verb)

One should wear *loose* clothing when bowling. (adjective)

When will Mrs. Brady *loosen* her control over young Tom?

You would *lose* your nose if it were not attached to your face.

lots, lots of *Lots* and *lots of* colloquially mean "many, much, a large amount, or a great amount." Avoid these expressions in formal writing.

Colloquial	I've spent *lots of* money in my life.
Standard	I have spent *much* money in my life.

mad See *angry, mad.*

many, much *Many* is used when referring to countable items; *much* is used when referring to an indefinite amount or to abstract concepts.

There are *many* students in the biology class.

How did Betty learn so *much* in so little time?

may See *can, may.*

may be, maybe *May be* is always used as a verb phrase. *Maybe* is an adverb meaning "perhaps."

I *may be* chairman of the board by next June.

Maybe we will see Jim at home.

medium, media *Medium* is the singular form of this word; *media* is the plural.

Television is the *medium* I use most to get the news.

The *media* have given extensive coverage to the brain transplant story.

usage

much   See *many, much.*

myself   *Myself* is an intensive and a reflexive pronoun; it cannot substitute for a personal pronoun such as *I* or *me.*

Unacceptable	Four other students and *myself* founded the club.
Standard	Four other students and *I* founded the club.

nice   *Nice* is an adjective suggesting delicacy, precision, subtlety, accuracy, the ability to discriminate, or the need for great care.

These two seemingly identical proposals actually have several *nice* differences.

This author's short stories have a *nice* touch.

Nice as a term of approval meaning "pleasing, enjoyable, attractive" is too generalized for use in formal writing.

not hardly   This is a nonstandard variation of *hardly* and is inappropriate in formal writing.

number   See *amount, number.*

of between, of from, off of   Eliminate the unnecessary *of* from these colloquial phrases.

Colloquial	There was a crowd *of between* three and four thousand people at the contest. Get *off of* my property!
Standard	The crowd at the contest numbered *between* three and four thousand people. Get *off* my property!

on account of   When used to begin an adverb clause (see page 579), this is a nonstandard substitute for *because.*

Nonstandard	The team was unable to practise *on account of* everyone was still upset over Tuesday's loss.
Standard	The team was unable to practise *because* everyone was still upset over Tuesday's loss.

When *on account of* precedes a single word or a phrase, it is considered colloquial.

Colloquial	The game was called *on account of* rain.

passed, past   *Passed* is a verb designating activity that has taken place. *Past* is a noun or an adjective designating a former time.

The parade *passed* the reviewing stand at 10:30 a.m.

In the *past*, few people were concerned about the environmental effects of pesticides.

This *past* summer, I visited France.

patience, patients   *Patience* means "the ability to wait or endure without complaining." *Patients* are "people being treated by health-care professionals."

Thad's *patience* was exhausted by the slow service in the restaurant.

Following the tornado, doctors in the emergency room treated over sixty *patients.*

persecute, prosecute   *Persecute* means "to harass persistently because of race, religion, or belief." *Prosecute* means "to bring legal suit against."

Ethnic groups are often *persecuted.*

The company will *prosecute* anyone caught stealing.

personal, personnel   *Personal* is an adjective meaning "private, individual." *Personnel* are the people working in an organization.

Religious preference is a *personal* matter that you do not have to reveal during a job interview.

The *personnel* of the sanitation department will not be involved in the city workers' strike.

plenty   When used as an adverb, *plenty* should be replaced by *very.*

Colloquial   That geology exam was *plenty* hard.

Standard   That geology exam was *very* hard.

precede, proceed   *Precede* means "to go before or ahead of." *Proceed* means "to go on" or "to go forward."

The ritual of sharpening his pencils always *preceded* doing his homework.

The guide then said, "If you will *proceed,* I will show you the paintings by da Vinci."

predominant, predominate   *Predominant* is an adjective meaning "chief, main, most frequent." *Predominate* is a verb meaning "to have authority over others."

The *predominant* European influence on South American culture was Spanish.

In Canada, the will of the people should *predominate.*

presently   *Presently* means "soon" rather than "at the present time." *Currently* is correct for the second meaning.

I will be there *presently.*

Currently, I am otherwise engaged.

principal, principle   *Principal,* which means "chief," "most important," or "the amount of money on which interest is computed," is used as both a noun and an adjective. *Principle* is used only as a noun and means "truths, beliefs, or rules generally dealing with moral conduct."

The *principal* suspect in the case was arrested last Friday by the police.

usage

The *principal* of Lewiston High School is Alison Cooperstein.

At this interest rate, your *principal* will double in ten years.

His *principles* are unconventional.

proceed   See *precede, proceed.*

prosecute   See *persecute, prosecute.*

quiet, quite   *Quiet* is an adjective meaning "silent, motionless, calm." *Quite* is an adverb meaning "entirely" or "to a considerable extent or degree."

The class grew *quiet* when the teacher walked in.

He is *quite* wrong.

The movie was *quite* good.

raise, rise   *Raise* is a transitive verb and therefore requires a direct object. *Rise,* its intransitive counterpart, takes no direct object.

We plan to *raise* horses on our new farm.

The temperature is expected to *rise* to 30°C tomorrow.

Raise can also be a noun meaning "an increase in pay."

Tammy received a 25 percent *raise* last week.

real, really   *Real* is an adjective; *really* is an adverb.

He had *real* plants decorating the bedroom.

When used as an adverb, *real* is a colloquialism and should be replaced with *really.*

Colloquial   We had a *real* good time at the party.

Standard   We had a *really* good time at the party.

reason is because, reason is that   The *reason is because* is colloquial and unacceptable in formal writing; the *reason is that* is the correct usage.

Colloquial   The *reason is because* I love her.

Standard   The *reason is that* I love her.

respectfully, respectively   *Respectfully* means "with respect." *Respectively* indicates that the items in one series are related to those in a second series in the order given.

Joseph should treat his parents *respectfully.*

Tom, Anna, and Susan were assigned *Bleak House, Great Expectations,* and *Dombey and Son, respectively,* for their reports.

rise   See *raise, rise.*

sensual, sensuous   *Sensual* refers to bodily or sexual sensations. *Sensuous* refers to impressions experienced through the five senses.

Singles bars offered *sensual* pleasures without emotional commitments.

The Tivoli Garden provides many *sensuous* delights for visitors.

set, sit   Generally, *set* means "to place" and takes a direct object. *Sit* means "to be seated" and does not take a direct object.

Alice *set* her glass on the mantel.

May I *sit* in this chair?

When it refers to the sun, however, *set* is used without a direct object.

As the sun *set,* we turned homeward.

shall, will   *Shall* is used in first-person (see page 593) questions and in specialized forms of writing such as military orders and laws. Otherwise, *will* is generally used.

Shall we go to the movies tonight?

The company *shall* fall into formation at precisely twelve noon.

No family home *shall* be assessed at more than 50 percent of its actual value.

should have, should of   *Should of* is an unacceptable substitute for *should have* because a preposition cannot substitute for a verb.

Nonstandard	I *should of* gone to the lake.
Standard	I *should have* gone to the lake.

[sic]   This Latin word, always enclosed in brackets, follows quoted errors in grammar, spelling, or information. Inclusion of [sic] indicates that the error appeared in the original, which is being quoted exactly.

sight   See *cite, sight, site.*

sit   See *set, sit.*

site   See *cite, sight, site.*

so   *So* is an acceptable coordinating conjunction but tends to add an informal effect to writing and should therefore be used sparingly. For example, "Tom said he was divorcing me, *so* I began to cry" would be more effective if restated as follows: "When Tom said he was divorcing me, I began to cry." Do not use *so* as a substitute for *extremely* or *very* except with adverb clauses beginning with *that.*

Colloquial	You are *so* careless in what you say.
	The discussion was *so* informative that I took many notes.
Standard	You are *very* careless in what you say.
	The discussion was *extremely* informative.

usage

some   *Some* is colloquial and unacceptable in writing when used as an intensifier (We had *some* time of it!) or an adverb (He'll probably pout *some* after you leave).

sometime, some time, sometimes   *Sometime* means "at a future unspecified time," *some time* means "a span of time," and *sometimes* means "occasionally."

We should get together *sometime* and play bridge.

The weather has been hot for *some time.*

Sometimes I go to dinner with Ethel.

sort of   See *kind of, sort of.*

specially   See *especially, specially.*

stationary, stationery   *Stationary* means "not moving" or "fixed." *Stationery* means "paper for writing letters."

The circular part in the centre must remain *stationary,* or the machine will not function.

Sue always writes on scented *stationery.*

such, such . . . that   The use of *such* when it means "very" or "extremely" is unacceptable unless it is followed by a *that* clause completing the thought.

Colloquial	They were *such* good cookies.
Standard	They were *such* good cookies *that* I asked Steve for his recipe.

suppose to, supposed to   *Suppose* to is the nonstandard form of *supposed to.* In speech, it is difficult to hear the final *d* on *supposed,* and one may say *suppose to* without being detected; however, the correct written form is always *supposed to.*

sure, surely   *Sure* is colloquial for the adverb *surely.*

Colloquial	You *sure* know how to make good coffee, Mrs. Olsen.
Standard	You *surely* know how to make good coffee, Mrs. Olsen.

Although *surely* is correct, it may sound too formal and insincere. Therefore, *certainly* is often a better word to use.

take and, try and   Avoid these expressions. Simply eliminate them from the sentence or substitute *try to* for *try and.*

Unacceptable	If you *take and* cover the tomato plants, they probably won't freeze. I think you should *try and* settle your differences.
Standard	If you cover the tomato plants, they probably won't freeze. I think you should *try to* settle your differences.

than, then   *Than* is used to make comparisons; *then* means "at that time, in that case," or "after that."

Jill is taller *than* her brother.

First we will eat, and *then* we will discuss business.

that, which   These two words have the same meaning. *That* may refer both to things and groups of people; *which,* only to things. When referring to things, *that* is generally used with clauses that distinguish the things they modify from others in the same class (restrictive clauses). *Which* is generally used with clauses that add information about the things they modify (nonrestrictive clauses).

> Any book *that* she likes is certain to be trashy. (restrictive clause)

> The Winthrop Building, *which* cost two million dollars to construct, could not now be duplicated for ten times that much. (nonrestrictive clause)

See pages 613–614 of the Handbook for a more complete explanation of restrictive and nonrestrictive expressions.

their, there, they're   These three separate words are often confused because they sound alike. *Their* is the possessive form of *they. There* is an expletive that appears at the beginning of a sentence and introduces the real subject, or it is an adverb meaning "in or at that place, at that point." *They're* is a contraction of *they are.*

> It is *their* basketball.

> *There* are many reasons why I cannot come.

> Put the sofa down *there.*

> *They're* going to be here soon.

theirself, theirselves   See *hisself, theirself, theirselves.*

then   See *than, then.*

there   See *their, there, they're.*

thorough, through   *Thorough* means "careful, complete, exact, painstaking." *Through* means "in one side and out the other, from end to end, from start to finish, over the whole extent of, finished."

> Brenda has done a *thorough* job.

> Let's run *through* the plan again.

thusly   *Thusly* is a nonstandard form of *thus.*

to, too, two   *To* is a preposition meaning "as far as, toward, until, onto." *Too* is an adverb meaning "excessively" or "also." *Two* is a number.

> I'm going *to* the store.

> Are you going *too?*

> This car is *too* expensive for me.

> There are *two* characters in the play.

toward, towards   Both forms are correct. *Toward* generally is used in North America and *towards* in England.

try and   See *take and, try and.*

usage

two   See *to, too, two.*

uninterested   See *disinterested, uninterested.*

unique   *Unique* means "without an equal" or "extremely unusual" and thus should not be modified by an adverb such as *very.*

use to, used to   *Use* to is the nonstandard form of *used to.* In speech it is difficult to hear the *d* on *used,* and one may say use to without being detected; however, the correct written form is always *used to.*

used to could   This phrase is nonstandard for *used to be able to.*

> *Nonstandard*   I *used to could* run twenty kilometres.

> *Standard*   I *used to be able to* run twenty kilometres.

very definite   See *definite, very definite.*

wander, wonder   *Wander* is a verb meaning "to move about without a plan or set destination." *Wonder* is a noun meaning "something causing surprise, admiration, or awe" or a verb meaning "to be curious about."

> Some people like to *wander* through shopping malls for recreation.

> That child is a *wonder* at mathematics.

> I *wonder* whether I have received an *A* on that test.

way, ways   *Ways* may be used to refer to two or more means or methods but not to time or distance.

> *Unacceptable*   Puerto Vallarta is a long *ways* from Canada.

> *Standard*   There are two *ways* of thinking about that issue.
> Puerto Vallarta is a long *way* from Canada.

usage

well   See *good, well.*

were, where   *Were* is the past form of the verb *to be. Where* is an adverb or a pronoun meaning "in, at, to, from a particular place or situation" or "which or what place."

> I'm sorry that you *were* ill yesterday.

> Mr. Morris will show you *where* to register.

where . . . at, to   *At* and *to* are unnecessary after *where.*

> *Wordy*   *Where* are you taking the car *to?*
> *Where* does she live *at?*

> *Standard*   *Where* are you taking the car?
> *Where* does she live?

whether   See *if, whether.*

which   See *that, which.*

who, whom In formal writing, *who* should be used only as a subject in clauses and sentences and *whom* only as an object.

Unacceptable	*Who* are you taking to dinner on Friday?
	I know *who* the boss will promote.
	John is the candidate *whom* I think will be elected.
Standard	*Whom* are you taking to dinner on Friday?
	I know *whom* the boss will promote.
	John is the candidate *who* I think will be elected.

See pages 595–596 of the Handbook for a more detailed discussion of *who* and *whom*.

who's, whose *Who's* is a contraction of *who is* or *who has*, and *whose* is the possessive form of *who*.

Who's coming to see us tonight?

I would like to know *who's* been dumping trash in my yard.

Whose book is that?

will See *shall, will*.

wise Do not randomly add *wise* to the ends of nouns. Such word coinings are ineffective.

Ineffective	Personality*wise*, Sheila is ideal for the job.
Standard	Sheila has an *ideal personality* for the job.

wonder See *wander, wonder*.

would have, would of *Would of* is an unacceptable substitute for *would have*. A preposition cannot substitute for a verb.

Nonstandard	I *would of* enjoyed seeing the Picasso exhibit.
Standard	I *would have* enjoyed seeing the Picasso exhibit.

would have been, had been When *would* occurs in the main part of a sentence, use *had been* (not *would have been*) in an "if" clause.

Nonstandard	If the engine *would have been* lubricated, the bearing *would not have* burned out.
Standard	If the engine *had been* lubricated, the bearing *would not have* burned out.

your, you're *Your* is a possessive form of *you; you're* is a contraction of *you are*.

Where is *your* history book?

Tell me when *you're* ready to leave.

usage

Acknowledgments

Allen Abel, "Sweet Nothings," *Saturday Night*, Oct. 1997:13-14.

R. T. Allen, "The Porcupine," from *Children, Wives, and Other Wildlife* by Robert Thomas Allen. Copyright © 1970 by Robert Thomas Allen (New York: Doubleday, 1970).

"Antigen," *Encyclopaedia Britannica*, 1974, I, 417.

Margaret Atwood, *Alias Grace*. Copyright © 1996 by O.W. Toad Ltd. (Toronto: McClelland & Stewart, Inc. The Canadian Publishers, 1996.)

Patricia A. Baird, "Should Cloning Be Permitted?" *Annals of The Royal College of Physicians and Surgeons of Canada*, Volume 33, Number 4, June 2000, pp. 235–237. © The Royal College of Physicians and Surgeons of Canada.

Kerry Banks, "As a Dad, Will I Do Right by My Daughter?" *Chatelaine*, June 1993.

Brian Bergman, "When Children Are Vicious," *Maclean's*, Aug. 12, 1996:12.

Bruno Bettelheim, "Joey: A 'Mechanical Boy,'" *Scientific American*, March 1959, p. 122.

Andrew Beyak, "The Sweet Bird of Youth Is Showing Signs of Age," *Georgia Straight*, Jan. 1-8, 1998:11.

Neil Bissoondath, "No Place Like Home," *New Internationalist*, Sept. 1998: 20+.

Alan Borovoy, "Security's Serpentine Coils," *The Globe and Mail*, 1 Aug. 2002: A19. Reprinted with permission of the author.

Dionne Brand, "Blossom: Priestess of Oya, Goddess of Winds, Storms and Waterfalls" from *Other Solitudes: Canadian Multicultural Fictions*, (Don Mills, Ont: Oxford University Press, 1990.)

"The Brink of a Disaster," *America*, March 31, 1979, p. 247.

Claude Brown, *Manchild in the Promised Land* (New York: Macmillan, 1965), p. 304.

Bill Bryson, "Idiosyncrasies, Anyone?" from *European Travel and Life*, September 1989. Reprinted by permission of Bill Bryson.

James L. Buckley, "Three Cheers for the Snail Darter," *National Review, September 14*, 1979, pp. 1144–45.

Canadian Government, Canadian Multiculturalism: An Inclusive Citizenship. 10 Jul 2002, p. 8, http://www.pch.gc/progs/multi/inclusive_e.cfm.

Emily Carr, "D'Sonoqua" from *Klee Wyck*. Copyright © Gage Educational Publishing Limited, 1941.

Gladys Hasty Carroll, *Sing Out the Glory* (Boston: Little Brown, and Co., 1958).

Rachel Carson, *Silent Spring* (Boston: Houghton Mifflin, 1962).

Stephen L. Carter, "The Insufficiency of Honesty." Copyright © 1996. Reprinted by author's permission.

John Ciardi, "What Is Happiness?" in Manner of Speaking (New Brunswick, NJ: Rutgers University Press, 1972).

Robert Claiborne, "Future Schlock," *The Nation*, January 25, 1971, p. 117.

Cecil Clutton and John Stanford, *The Vintage Motor-car* (New York: Charles Scribner's Sons, 1955), p. 135.

Chris Cobb, "Conspiracy Theories Spin out of Control on the Web," *Ottawa Citizen*, Nov. 16, 1996:B2.

Joseph Conrad, *Lord Jim* (New York: Holt, Rinehart and Winston, 1957), p. 13.

"Controlling Phobias Through Behavior Modification," *USA Today*, August 1978.

Robertson Davies, "Living in a Country Without a Mythology," *The Merry Heart: Reflections on Reading, Writing, and the World of Books*, Toronto: Viking Penguin, 1997, p. 50.

Vine Deloria, Jr. "Custer Died for Your Sins," *Playboy*, Aug. 1969.

Lester del Ray, *The Mysterious Sky* (New York: Chilton Book Company, 1964).

Magda Denes, *In Necessity and Sorrow: Life and Death in an Abortion Hospital* (New York: Basic Books, 1976), p. xiv.

Christopher Dewdney, "After Deep Blue," from *Last Flesh: Life in the Transhuman Era*, published by HarperCollins Publishers Ltd. Copyright 1998 by Christopher Dewdney.

Robert Dick-Read, *Sanamu: Adventures in Search of African Art* (New York: E.P. Dutton, 1964), pp. 228–29.

Joan Didion, "On Self-Respect," in *Slouching Toward Bethlehem* (New York: Farrar, Straus and Giroux, 1968), pp. 143–44.

"Distorted Picture," Canada & the World Backgrounder, Dec. 1996.

Ian Dunbar, "Fast Track to Perfection," *Dog Fancy*, April 1999, reprinted by permission of the author.

Leo Durocher, *Nice Guys Finish Last* (New York: Simon & Schuster, 1975), p. 54.

Wayne Dyer, *What Do You Really Want for Your Children?* (New York: William Morrow, Inc., 1985).

Loren Eiseley, *The Unexpected Universe* (New York: Harcourt Brace Jovanovich, 1969) p. 88.

Loren Eiseley, "The Judgment of the Birds," in *The Immense Journey* (New York: Random House, 1956), pp. 174–75.

Marian Engle, review of The Goddess and Other Women, by Joyce Carol Oates, *New York Times* Book Review, Nov. 24, 1974, p. 7.

Howard Ensign Evans, *Life on a Little-Known Planet* (New York: E.P. Dutton, 1968), pp. 107–8.

Brad Evenson, "Native Postmodern," *Saturday Night*, Oct. 1998:17.

Henry Fairlie, "A Victim Fights Back," *The Washington Post*, April 30, 1978.

Candace Fertile, "The Oldest Profession: Shopping," from *POP CAN: Popular Culture in Canada*, Toronto: Prentice Hall, 1999: 77–81. Reprinted with permission by Pearson Education Canada Inc.

David Finkelstein, "When the Snow Thaws," *The New Yorker*, Sept. 10, 1979, p. 127.

"Formlessness" from *Roget's International Thesaurus*, 5th edition by Peter Mark Roget, Copyright © 1992 by HarperCollins Publishers, Inc. Reprinted by permission of HarperCollins Publishers, Inc.

Daniel Francis, "My Life with Riley," *Geist 23*, Fall 1996.

Adam Frank, excerpts from "Winds of Change," in *Discover*, June 1994, pp. 100–4.

Bruce Jay Friedman, "Eating Alone in Restaurants." From *The Lonely Guy's Book to Life*, copyright © 1978 by McGraw-Hill, Inc. Reprinted by permission of the McGraw-Hill Companies.

Otto Friedrich, "There are 00 Trees in Russia," *Harper's Magazine*, Oct. 1964.

Chief Dan George, "I Am a Native of North America" *My Heart Soars*. Clarke Irwin, 1974.

Eve Golden, "Dangerous Curves." Reprinted by permission of *Men's Health Magazine*. Copyright 1994 Rodale Press, Inc. All rights reserved.

Ellen Goodman, "The Company Man." Reprinted with the permission of Simon & Schuster from *At Large* by Ellen Goodman. Copyright © 1981 by The Washington Post Company.

Charles Gordon, "A Guided Tour of the Bottom Line," from *Reader's Choice: Essays for Thinking, Reading, and Writing*, Second Canadian Ed., Michael Flachmann, et al., Scarborough: Prentice Hall, 1997, pp. 439–440.

Amy Gross, "The Appeal of the Androgynous Man." *Mademoiselle*. Copyright © 1976 by The Condé Nast Publications, Inc. Reprinted by permission of Amy Gross.

L.D. Hamilton, "Antibodies and Antigens," *The New Book of Knowledge* 1967, I, 317.

Trevor Harriot, "Generation unto Regeneration," *The Globe and Mail*, 25 May 2002: A15. Reprinted with permission by the author.

Bob Harvey, "Loyalty: A Last Virtue," *Ottawa Citizen*, Mar. 2, 1996:C5.

Lesley Hazleton, "Assembly Line Adventure," reprinted with the permission of *The Free Press*, a division of Simon & Schuster, Inc., from Driving to Detroit: An Automotive Odyssey by Lesley Hazleton. © 1998 by Lesley Hazleton.

David Helwig, "The Quiet of the Backstretch," *Canadian Geographic*, Sept./Oct. 1998:106.

John Hersey, Hiroshima (New York: Modern Library, 1946), p. 4.

Mark Higgins, "Shrimp Appeal," *Nature Canada*, Spring 1998:27.

Nancy K. Hill, "Scaling the Heights: The Teacher as Mountaineer," *The Chronicle of Higher Education*, June 16, 1980, p. 48.

Jack Hodgins, Spit Delaney's Island. Copyright © Jack Hodgins 1976. (Toronto: The Macmillan Company of Canada Limited, 1976)

Thomas Henry Huxley, "A Liberal Education and Where to Find It," *Macmillan's Magazine*, March 17, 1868.

Dina Ingber, "Computer Addicts," *Science Digest*, July 1981.

Washington Irving, "The Spectre Bridegroom," in *Selected Writings of Washington Irving*, ed. Saxe Commins (New York: Modern Library, 1945), p. 53.

Bruce Jackson, "Who Goes to Prison: Caste and Careerism in Crime," *Atlantic Monthly*, Jan. 1966, p. 52.

Robert Jastrow, *Until the Sun Dies* (New York: Norton, 1977).

P.T. Jensen, "Lament for the Short and Stubby," *The Globe and Mail*, May 29, 1998:A22.

Helen Keller, "Three Days to See," *Atlantic Monthly*, Jan. 1933, p. 35.

Martin Luther King, Jr., "I Have a Dream." Reprinted by arrangement with the heirs to the Estate of Martin Luther King, Jr., c/o Joan Daves Agency as agent for the proprietor. Copyright 1963 by Martin Luther King, Jr., copyright renewed 1991 by Coretta Scott King.

Martin Luther King, Jr., "Pilgrimage to Nonviolence," in *Stride Toward Freedom* (New York: Harper & Row, 1958), p. 84.

Kalle Lasn, "Media Carta," from *Culture Jam: The Uncooling of America*, New York: Eagle Brook, 1999: 185–199. Reprinted with permission by the author.

Evelyn Lau, "An Insatiable Emptiness," *The Georgia Straight*, 1995.

John Lovesey, "A Myth is as Good as a Mile," *Sports Illustrated*, Nov. 9, 1964.

Chris MacDonald, "Yes, Human Cloning Should Be Permitted," *Annals of The Royal College of Physicians and Surgeons of Canada*, Volume 33, Number 7, October 2000, pp. 437–438. © The Royal College of Physicians and Surgeons of Canada.

Marilyn Machlowitz, "Workaholism: What's Wrong with Being Married to Your Work?" *Working Woman*, May 1978, p. 51.

James MacKinnon and Jeremy Nelson, "The True Cost of Groceries," *Adbusters*, Nov/Dec 2002, 24 Oct 2002, http://www.adbusters.org/magazine/44/articles/true_cost_groceries/ch.

Alistair MacLeod, "The Boat." From *The Lost Salt Gift of Blood*. McClelland and Stewart, 1976.

Rod McQueen, "Millionaire Questionnaire," *Financial Post*, Feb. 26, 1998:25.

Marshall Mandell, "Are You Allergic to Your House?" *Prevention*, Sept. 1979, p. 101.

Marya Mannes, "Wasteland," in *More in Anger* (Philadelphia: J. B. Lippincott, 1958), p. 40.

Margaret Mead, "New Superstitions for Old," from *A Way of Seeing by Margaret Mead and Rhoda Metraux*. Copyright © 1966 by Margaret Mead and Rhoda Metraux.

L. David Mech, "Where Can the Wolves Survive?" *National Geographic*, Oct. 1977, p. 536.

Thomas H. Middleton, "The Magic Power of Words," *Saturday Review*, Dec. 11, 1976, p. 90.

Don Ethan Miller, "A State of Grace: Understanding the Martial Arts," *Atlantic Monthly*, Sept. 1980. Copyright © 1980 by Don Ethan Miller.

Celia Milne, "Pressures to Conform," *Maclean's*, Jan. 12, 1998:60.

Moses Milstein, "Memories of Montreal—and Richness," *The Globe and Mail*, April 28, 1998: A16.

Rohinton Mistry, "Lend Me Your Light," from *Tales from Firozsha Baag*. (Toronto: McClelland & Stewart, Inc. The Canadian Publishers, 1997.) Used by permission of the publisher.

Susanna Moodie, *Roughing It in the Bush*. London: Richard Bentley, 1852.

Alice Munro, "An Ounce of Cure," from *Dance of the Happy Shades and Other Stories*. (Toronto: McGraw-Hill Ryerson, 1968).

Kristine Nyhout, "Send in the Clowns," *Chatelaine*, April 1998: 165–166.

Michael Ondaatje, *In the Skin of a Lion*, Copyright © Michael Ondaatje, 1987. (Toronto: Penguin Books Canada Ltd., 1988)

George Orwell, excerpt from "Shooting an Elephant," in *Shooting an Elephant and Other Essays*, copyright 1950 by Sonia Brownell Orwell; renewed 1978 by Sonia Pitt-Rivers. Reprinted by permission of Harcourt Brace Jovanovich, Inc., and Martin Secker & Warburg Ltd.

Jo Goodwin Parker, "What Is Poverty?" in *George Henderson, America's Other Children:Public Schools Outside Suburbia* (University of Oklahoma Press, 1971).

Stephen Perrine, "The Crystal Healer Will See You Now." Reprinted by permission of *Men's Health Magazine*. Copyright 1993 Rodale Press, Inc. All rights reserved.

Geoff Pevere and Greig Dymond, "Introduction" from *Mondo Canuck*. (Scarborough, Ont: Prentice Hall Canada, 1996.)

Lord Richie-Calder, "The Doctor's Dilemma," *The Center Magazine*, Sept./Oct. 1971.

Philip Ross, "The Boy and the Bank Officer." From *New York*, March 13, 1979. Reprinted by permission of Roberta Pryor, Inc. Copyright © 1979 by Philip Ross.

Kathy Roth, "How to Adopt a Stray." Reprinted from *The Cat Catalog: The Ultimate Cat Book*, ed. by Judy Fireman. © 1976 Workman Publishing Company. New York. Reprinted by permission of the publisher.

Bertrand Russell, *The ABC of Relativity* (London: Allen and Unwin, 1965), pp. 46–47.

Bertrand Russell, "Respect for Law," *San Francisco Review*, Winter, 1958, pp. 63–65. Reprinted by permission of June Oppen Degnan.

Nancy Masterson Sakamoto, "Conversational Ballgames," from *Kinsiedo*, Ltd., 1982. Reprinted by permission of Nancy Masterson Sakamoto. All rights reserved.

Mark Schapiro, "Children of a Lesser God," *Harper's Bazaar*, April, 1996: 205–18.

Laurence Shames, "The Sweet Smell of Success Isn't All That Sweet." Copyright © 1986 by The New York Times Company. Reprinted by permission.

Carol Shields, *Larry's Party*, Random House of Canada, 1997, pp. 242–243.

Gideon Sjöberg, "The Origin and Development of Cities," *Scientific American*, Sept. 1965, p. 55.

Elliott L. Smith and Andrew W. Hart, *The Short Story: A Contemporary Looking Glass* (New York: Random House, 1981).

Russell Smith, "Battered by Blandness," *The Globe and Mail*, 24 Oct 2002: R7.

Andrew Struthers, "How Spell-Check Is Destroying English: With No Governing Body, Our Language Lies Prone to Market Forces," *Vancouver Sun*, 17 Aug. 2002: H8. Reprinted with the permission by Vancouver Sun.

Joyce Susskind, "Surprises in a Woman's Life," *Vogue*, Feb. 1979, p. 252.

David Suzuki, " How Much Stuff Is Enough," *Science Matters*, 19 July 2002, 24 Oct 2002, www.davidsuzuki.org/Dr David Suzuki Archives/weekly07190201.asp.

David Suzuki, "Protesters' Message Lost on the Media," *Science Matters*, 5 Jul 2002, 23 Oct 2002, www.davidsuzuki.org/Dr David Suzuki Archives/weekly07190201.asp.

Deborah Tannen, "Gender Gap in Cyberspace," from *Newsweek*, 16 Apr 1994. Newsweek, Inc. All rights reserved. Reprinted by permission.

Deems Taylor, "The Monster" in *Of Mice and Music* (New York: Simon & Schuster, 1965).

James Alexander Thom, "The Perfect Picture." Reprinted with permission from the August 1976 *Reader's Digest*. Copyright (1976) by The Reader's Digest Ass'n., Inc.

Lewis Thomas, "The Technology of Medicine, pp. 31–36," copyright © 1971 by The Massachusetts Medical Society, from *The Lives of a Cell by Lewis Thomas*. Used by permission of Viking Penguin, a division of Penguin Books U.S.A., Inc.

Douglas Todd, "In a Girl's World It Can Be Tough Being a Boy," *Vancouver Sun*, Feb. 10, 1998:G3. Reprinted with the permission by Vancouver Sun.

Beth Wald, "Let's Get Vertical!" from *Listen: Journal of Better Living*. June 1989. Reprinted by permission.

Paul Wells, "A Justifiable Power Grab," Time Canada, 17 Dec. 2001: 51. Copyright 2001 TIME Inc. Reprinted with permission.

Marion Winik, "What Are Friends For?" from *Telling* by Marion Winik, © 1994 by Marion Winik. Used by permission of Villard Books, a division of Random House, Inc.

Tom Wolfe, *The Pump House Gang* (New York: World Journal Tribune, 1966), p. 293.

Orvill Wyss and Curtis Eklund, *Microorganisms and Man* (New York: John Wiley and Sons, 1971), pp. 232–33.

Rafael Yglesias, excerpt from *Fearless*, New York, Warner Books, 1993.

David Zimmerman, "Are Test-Tube Babies the Answer for the Childless?" *Woman's Day*, May 1979, p. 26.

Index